D1112714

THE
DANIEL J. BOORSTIN
READER

THE
DANIEL J. BOORSTIN
READER

EDITED BY RUTH F. BOORSTIN

THE MODERN LIBRARY

NEW YORK

Portions of this work were originally published in *The Americans: The Colonial
Experience, The Americans: The National Experience, The Americans: The Democratic
Experience, Democracy and Its Discontents, The Discoverers, The Creators, Cleopatra's Nose,*
(Random House, Inc.); *The Genius of American Politics* and *The Lost World of Thomas
Jefferson* (The University of Chicago Press); *Hidden History* and *The Republic of
Technology* (HarperCollins Publishers, Inc.); *America and the Image of Europe* (Peter
Smith); *The Image* (Atheneum); and, *The Republic of Letters* (Library of Congress).

Jacket photograph by © Jerry Bauer

Printed on recycled, acid-free paper.

Library of Congress Cataloging-in-Publication Data is available.

ISBN 0-679-60165-1

Manufactured in the United States of America

2 4 6 8 9 7 5 3 1

INTRODUCTION

D
ANIEL J. BOORSTIN tells us that, as an historian, he is an amateur in the true sense of that word—one who loves his calling for itself. In the case of Boorstin, the rewards of this love extend to his readers. He has followed his own interests in choosing subjects rather than searching through the catalog of a particular academic discipline. The result, thus far, has been a body of work—books, essays, reviews, and edited series—that is as remarkable for its brilliance and variety as for its sheer volume.

Boorstin's writings include both history and critiques of contemporary society. They range from a collection of essays about the life, times, and thought of the third president, *The Lost World of Thomas Jefferson* (1948) to the magisterial sweep of *The Discoverers* (1983)—a chronicle of man's quest to know the world—and *The Creators* (1992), which Boorstin calls "a saga of Heroes of the Imagination." *The Image* (first published in 1961) is a study of "pseudo-events"—Boorstin's own phrase—largely perpetrated by the modern media and gratefully embraced by a public hungry for heroes and mind-boggled by extravagant expectations.

This diversity of subject matter (and there are many more examples in the collective opus of Daniel J. Boorstin) is the result of his freedom as an amateur. His historic ambition was first stirred by reading Gibbon's *The Decline and Fall of the Roman Empire* while an undergraduate at Harvard. But, except for a year-long digression into premedical studies inspired by the passing of his much-loved grandfather ("I wanted to see if I could find a way to prevent death"), Boorstin studied law at Oxford and later at Yale.

If he has focused on one subject more than any other it is American history . . . not only as a chronicler but also as a perceptive and original analyst. In his 1953 book *The Genius of American Politics* Boorstin postulates a society singularly free of dogma and/or ideology. "The Puritans," he wrote, "were the first and perhaps the last sizable community in American history to import from Europe a fully developed and explicit social dogma, and to try to live by it on this continent." Later in the same volume he desimplifies our basic assumption about the American revolution—that thirteen colonies went to war against Britain and when it was over—voilà!—America, unique unto itself, stood upon the plains of history. Instead, writes Boorstin, "The American Revolution was in a very special way conceived as both a vindication of the British past and an affirmation of the American future. The British past was contained in ancient and living institutions rather than in doctrines, and the American future was never to be contained in a theory."

Boorstin's three-volume history *The Americans*, divided into *The Colonial Experience*, *The National Experience*, and *The Democratic Experience* is composed of the great themes of the country's progress from its colonial infancy to the Kennedy administration; it is also a unique work in that it ponders the details and fads of daily life that more conventional historians would consider unimportant. Boorstin chronicles the history of early hotels, the career of Davy Crockett, the invention and development of packaging, the establishment and growth of black churches in the South, the evolution of the supermarket—to mention only a few examples in a vast array of our society's artifacts and institutions—and he devotes several chapters to American speech and grammar.

The Americans is both widely admired and controversial for its author's views of the national character. "A great resource of America is vagueness," he writes in *The National Experience*. "American uncertainties, products of ignorance and progress, were producers of optimism and energy. Although few acknowledged it, in the era between the Revolution and the Civil War this vagueness was a source of American strength. Americans were already distinguished less by what they clearly knew or definitely believed than by their grand and fluid hopes."

Such assumptions do not rest well with conventional thinkers about the American character, who tend to boil its immense complexity down to a few prototypes. Boorstin is sensitive to the myriad influences, evolutions, and, above all, experiences that shape all character. "My subject," he has said, "is the human race."

* * *

Daniel J. Boorstin was born in Atlanta, Georgia, on October 1, 1914, and grew up in Tulsa, Oklahoma. His father, Sam Boorstin, was a lawyer (this slightly eccentric, didactic, and irrepressibly optimistic man is the subject of one of this book's most fascinating essays). Daniel J. Boorstin attended Harvard, where he majored in English history and literature. He studied Roman and English law at Balliol College, Oxford, and was admitted as a barrister at the Inner Temple in London. Returning to the United States in 1937 he entered Yale University's law school, where he took a doctorate in judicial science and was admitted to the Massachusetts bar. He taught briefly at Harvard and Radcliffe and then for twenty-five years at the University of Chicago.

His first book, *The Mysterious Science of the Law*, was published in 1941 while Boorstin was teaching at Harvard. That same year he married Ruth Frankel, who has been his constant companion and editor ever since. "Without her," he told an interviewer, "I think my works would have been twice as long and half as readable."

In 1969 Boorstin moved to Washington, D.C., to become director of the Smithsonian Institution's National Museum of American History. After a stint as senior historian of the Smithsonian he was nominated as Librarian of Congress by President Gerald Ford and confirmed by the Senate in 1975. Although he had been turning out books, articles, and essays during his teaching and administrative careers, he finally retired from the library in 1987 to devote himself full-time to writing.

He has been the recipient of the Bancroft, the Parkman, and the Pulitzer prizes as well as a National Book Award for Lifetime Contribution to American letters. He is the first Librarian of Congress Emeritus. Daniel J. Boorstin has received decorations from the French, Japanese, Belgian, and Portuguese governments, and his books have been translated into more than twenty-five languages. He has served as visiting professor at the universities of Rome, Geneva, Puerto Rico, and Kyoto, and at the Sorbonne; he was Pitt Professor of American History and Institutions at Cambridge University.

* * *

In writing history, Daniel J. Boorstin says that he is guided by three principles:

First, the amateur spirit. He hasn't been trained in what he calls "history's ruts." He is not afraid of the large simplicities.

Second, Boorstin believes in what he calls a fluid world, in human mystery. "Gibbon," he says, "believed in history surrounded by the wonder of people."

Third, he insists that great history must be great literature. The surviving works of Herodotus, Thucydides, Gibbon, Parkman, and Prescott—among others—are all literary masterpieces.

Boorstin regards literature as his vocation. "I happen to have fallen into writing history," he says. "History is a mosaic. You have no fixed objective as in chemistry or medicine. History is a search for history, for the mystery of the human race."

True to his third principle of writing history, Daniel J. Boorstin is, what Clifton Fadiman once called him, "The most readable of our eminent historians." Some of his books—most notably *The Discoverers* and *The Creators*—have spent months on the bestseller lists. This is not the result of some literary contrivance to win popular approval. As a man who regards himself first and foremost a writer, Boorstin creates in the manner of any sensible author of nonfiction. He devotes as much effort to outlines as to the actual writing of the text. "I spend a lot of time revising," he says. "I'm not afraid of throwing things away."

Boorstin resembles the description of his hero, Edward Gibbon, that he wrote in his 1987 collection of essays, *Hidden History:* "Gibbon remained uncommitted to any but his own opinions."

The congenial, engrossing style of Boorstin's prose is supported by his prodigious learning. From Aristotle to Georges-Louis Leclerc, comte de Buffon, from Galen to Josh Billings, Boorstin has read over the vast acreage of the world's conjecture and learning that stretches from the early Greeks to our own time. One of his friends recently said, "The problem is to figure out what Dan *hasn't* read. My guess would be some thirteenth century Chinese treatise on trigonometry."

Yet for all he knows, Boorstin does not strut his erudition. He includes in his books and essays only that which needs inclusion to illustrate, narrate, or make points. In *The Discoverers* he wrote, "the great obstacle to progress is not ignorance but the illusion of knowledge."

Prepare, then, to be enthralled and made wiser as you begin *The Daniel J. Boorstin Reader.* Those of us who have read his works can only envy those who are about to embark on their first voyage with this extraordinary man.

RODERICK MACLEISH

CONTENTS

FROM THE AMERICANS: THE DEMOCRATIC EXPERIENCE

FROM THE DISCOVERERS

FROM THE CREATORS

ESSAYS

I. SEARCH FOR COMMUNITY

II. MODERN TIMES AND PSEUDO-EVENTS

III. PREPARING FOR THE UNEXPECTED

AUTHOR'S NOTE

My own way of writing history has been a product of lucky opportunities. I have written for the love of it, on subjects that piqued my curiosity. Growing up in Tulsa, Oklahoma, I experienced the latter-day American frontier. Reading Edward Gibbon's *Decline and Fall of the Roman Empire* as a student at Harvard College persuaded me that history could be great literature. Three years of studying English and Roman law at Oxford whetted my appetite for the refreshing American experience. Without having gone through professional training as a historian, but with the enthusiasm and freedom of the amateur, I inducted myself into history. Teaching American history to graduate students at the University of Chicago, I was allowed to define the subject according to my interests. Coming to Washington as the director of the Smithsonian's National Museum of American History, then serving for twelve years as the Librarian of Congress, I had the opportunity for a closer view of American democracy at work. Meanwhile, over thirty years I enjoyed writing about the American experience, which became the three volumes of *The Americans*. Feeling the need to deprovincialize myself and reach out to the world on a wider canvas in space and time, I continued to be interested not in wars and empires but in human fulfilment. Out of this came *The Discoverers* and *The Creators*, a history of the search to know (the sciences) and to make the new (the arts), products of the last twenty years. Looking about America and the world in my time, I have been tempted to explore in essays the never-ending search for community, the proliferating wilderness of modern technology, the changing fashions of discovery, and unimagined vistas of the unexpected. Wary of dogmas, ideologies, and other skeleton keys to human experience, I have focused on people and their mysteries, not forgetting that the historian himself is part of the story.

Essential to my life and work as a writer was my marriage in 1941 to Ruth Frankel who ever since has been my companion and editor for all my books.

This Modern Library reader is a selection of chapters from my books.

FROM

THE
AMERICANS
The Colonial Experience

"It may be said that in a
Sort they began the World a New."
JARED ELIOT

America began as a sobering experience. The
colonies were a disproving ground for utopias.
We will see how dreams made in Europe—the
dreams of the zionist, the perfectionist, the philanthropist, and the transplanter—were dis-
sipated or transformed by the American reality.
Ways of thinking, of speaking, of teaching and
learning, of reading and writing, of law and medicine, all changed in ways which could not have
been predicted. They were revised and refreshed
by the unfamiliar. Science took on a new cast, language acquired a new accent, culture and the
printed word took on a new life. War and diplomacy had a new look. A new civilization was being
born less out of plans and purposes than out of
the unsettlement which the New World brought
to the ways of the Old.

WANTED:

A Philosophy of the Unexpected

CHAPTER 24

B Y THE EARLY 17th century, Europe had accumulated a rich but cumbersome cultural baggage. Systems of thought, established institutions, professional traditions, dogmatically defined bodies of knowledge regarded as all that was worth knowing—these cluttered the landscape of England and of Europe. The bare earth was almost nowhere visible.

Systems always breed more systems; when new liberating movements arose in England and on the continent during the 17th and 18th centuries, they took the familiar European form of anti-systems. Thus, "the Enlightenment," which claimed to free men from superstition and from the dogma of old authority and petrified thought, itself acquired much of the rigidity and authoritarianism of what it set out to combat. The European Enlightenment was in fact little more than the confinement of the mind in a prison of 17th- and 18th-century design. The new "rationalism"—which Europeans boasted was their new freedom—was the old human dogmatic servitude. What Carl Becker described as "The Heavenly City of the 18th-Century Philosophers" was a mirage of freedom. The best European minds of that age labored to build the new-model walls in which they were to be confined. Liberation could not be conceived in any other way in Europe.

Life in America was to give new meaning to the very idea of liberation. For Americans, cultural novelty and intellectual freedom were not to mean merely the exchange of one set of idols for another; they meant removal into the open air.

The most fertile novelty of the New World was not its climate, its plants, its animals, or its minerals, but its new concept of knowledge. The wealth of the new-found land could enable men to live well by Old World standards, but the realization that knowledge itself might be different from what men had before believed—this opened up realms never before dreamed of. Men in the New World found unsuspected possibilities in life everywhere. No American invention has influenced the world so powerfully as the concept of knowledge which sprang from the American experience. To understand that discovery we must look to the earliest colonial days.

When has a culture owed so little to its few "great" minds or its few hereditarily fortunate men and women? One of the contrasts between the culture of Europe and that of the United States is that the older culture traditionally depended on the monumental accomplishments of the few, while the newer culture—diffused, elusive, process-oriented—depended more on the novel, accreting ways of the many.

In most past societies—certainly in the aristocratic societies of western Europe—rulers and priests had been the "explaining" classes. They were the acknowledged possessors of the ways of knowing, the secret keys to the ancestral treasurehouse of mystery and of knowledge. The Protestant Reformation, with its dogma of the universal priesthood of all believers, did, of course, discourage reverence toward a special class of "knowers," but there soon arose a "protestant" priesthood (in the Geneva of Calvin or the London of Archbishop Laud) which, in its turn, denied freedom of discovery to the laity or to heretics. The common people could show their good sense only by acting according to ways approved by their "betters."

American life quickly proved uncongenial to any special class of "knowers." Men here were more interested in the elaboration of experience than in the elaboration of "truth"; the novelties of a New World led them to suspect that elaborate verification might itself mislead. As William James explained at the close of the 19th century, technically completed verifications are seldom needed in experience. In America, he said, "the possession of truth, so far from being . . . an end in itself, is only a preliminary means toward other vital satisfactions." Sometimes consciously, sometimes through the force of circumstance, Americans listened to the dictates of "self-evidence." Before long this appeal to self-evidence became a distinctive popular epistemology—a substitute for philosophy or a philosophy for nonacademic thinkers.

The more encumbered a society is with ancient culture and institutions, the more likely is its most profound and well-organized thought to diverge from its way of acting. One of the ways in which American experience liberated the New World was by freeing men from the notion that every grand institution needed a grand foundation of systematic thought: that successful government had to be supported by profound political theory, that moving religion had to be supported by subtle theology—in a word, that the best living had to have behind it the most sophisticated thinking. This mood was to explain the superficially contradictory strains of the practical and the traditional in the American mind—the openness to novel ways that worked and the readiness to accept ancient and traditional laws—for both common sense and common law were time-proven and unreflective ways of settling problems.

In America what seemed to be needed was not so much a new variant of European "schools" of philosophy as a philosophy of the unexpected. Too much of the best-elaborated thinking of the European mind added up to proof that America and its novelties were impossible. A less aristocratic and more mobile New World required a way of interpreting experience that would be ready for the outlandish and would be equally available to everyone everywhere.

"Common sense" was, of course, an old and thoroughly respectable notion in western European civilization. Some Scottish thinkers in the 18th century—they were not without their influence in America and one actually had become the favorite philosopher of George III—elaborated a special "philosophy" of common sense. In America, however, the more influential appeal to self-evidence did not take any such academic form; it was a philosophy which had no philosophers. It had to be so, for it was a way of thinking pervaded by doubt that the professional thinker could think better than others.

The appeal to self-evidence did not displace more academic and more dogmatic modes of thinking among all Americans, but American life nourished it until it became a prevailing mode. It was not the system of a few great American Thinkers, but the mood of Americans thinking. It rested on two sentiments. The first was a belief that the reasons men give for their actions are much less important than the actions themselves, that it is better to act well for wrong or unknown reasons than to treasure a systematized "truth" with ambiguous conclusions, that deep reflection does not necessarily produce the most effective action. The second was a belief that the novelties of experience must be freely admitted into men's thought. Why strain the New World through the philosophical sieves of the Old? If philosophy denied the innuendoes of experience, the philosophy—not the experience—must be rejected. Therefore, a man's mind was wholesome not when it possessed the most refined implements for dissecting and ordering all knowledge, but when it was most sensitive to the unpredicted whisperings of environment. It was less important that the mind be elegantly furnished than that it be open and unencumbered.

HOW ORTHODOXY MADE THE
PURITANS PRACTICAL

N EVER was a people more sure that it was on the right track. "That which is our greatest comfort, and meanes of defence above all others," Francis Higginson wrote in the earliest days, in *New-Englands Plantation*, "is, that we have here the true Religion and holy Ordinances of Almightie God taught amongst us . . . thus we doubt not but God will be with us, and if God be with us, who can be against us?"

But their orthodoxy had a peculiar character. Compared with Americans of the 18th or the 19th century, the Puritans surely were theology-minded. The doctrines of the Fall of Man, of Sin, of Salvation, Predestination, Election, and Conversion were their meat and drink. Yet what really distinguished them in their day was that they were less interested in theology itself, than in the application of theology to everyday life, and especially to society. From the 17th-century point of view their interest in theology was practical. They were less concerned with perfecting their formulation of the Truth than with making their society in America embody the Truth they already knew. Puritan New England was a noble experiment in applied theology.

The Puritans in the Wilderness—away from Old World centers of learning, far from great university libraries, threatened daily by the thousand and one hardships and perils of a savage America—

were poorly situated for elaborating a theology and disputing its fine points. For such an enterprise John Calvin in Switzerland or William Ames in Holland was much better located. But for testing a theology, for seeing whether Zion could be rebuilt if men abandoned the false foundations of the centuries since Jesus—for this New England offered a rare opportunity.

So it was that although the Puritans in the New World made the Calvinist theology their point of departure, they made it precisely that and nothing else. From it they departed at once into the practical life. Down to the middle of the 18th century, there was hardly an important work of speculative theology produced in New England.

It was not that the writing of books was impossible in the New World. Rather, it was that theological speculation was not what interested the new Americans. Instead, there came from the New England presses and from the pens of New England authors who sent their works to England an abundance of sermons, textual commentaries, collections of "providences," statutes, and remarkable works of history. With the possible exception of Roger Williams, who was out of the stream of New England orthodoxy anyway, Massachusetts Bay did not produce a major figure in theology until the days of Jonathan Edwards in the mid-18th century. And by then Puritanism was all but dead.

During the great days of New England Puritanism there was not a single important dispute which was primarily theological. There were, to be sure, crises over who should rule New England, whether John Winthrop or Thomas Dudley or Harry Vane should be governor, whether the power or representation of different classes in the community should be changed, whether the Child Petition should be accepted, whether penalties for crime should be fixed by statute, whether the assistants should have a veto, whether outlying towns should have more representatives in the General Court. Even the disputes with Anne Hutchinson and Roger Williams primarily concerned the qualifications, power, and prestige of the rulers. If, indeed, the Puritans were theology-minded, what they argued about was institutions.

One gets the same impression in looking for evidences of political speculation, for philosophical inquiry into the nature of community and the function of government. Nothing in Puritanism itself was uncongenial to such speculation; Puritans in England at the time were discussing the fine points of their theory: What was the true nature of liberty? When should a true Puritan resist a corrupt civil government? When should diversity be tolerated? And we need not look only to giants like John Milton. The debates among the officers in Cromwell's Puritan Army between 1647 and 1649 reveal how different their intellectual atmosphere was from that of New England. They were not professional intellectuals, but soldiers and men of action; yet even they stopped to argue the theory of revolution and the philosophy of sovereignty.

In England, of course, "Puritanism" was much more complex than it was in Massachusetts Bay Colony. It included representatives of a wide range of doctrines, from presbyterians, independents, and separatists, through levelers and millenarians. Which of these was at the center of English Puritanism was itself a matter of dispute. Within the English Puritan ranks, therefore, there was much lively debate. It was not only criticism from fellow-Puritans that Cromwell and his men had to face. They well knew that any community they built in England would have to find some place for the dozens of sects—from Quakers through Papists—who had made England their home. English Puritan literature in the 17th century sparkled with polemics.

Seventeenth-century America had none of the speculative vigor of English Puritanism. For Massachusetts Bay possessed an orthodoxy. During the classic age of the first generation, at least, it was a community of self-selected conformists. In 1637 the General Court passed an order prohibiting anyone from settling within the colony without first having his orthodoxy approved by the magistrates. Perhaps never again, until the McCarran Act, were our immigrants required to be so aseptic. John Winthrop was bold and clear in defense of the order. Here was a community formed by free consent of its members. Why should they not exclude dangerous men, or men with dangerous thoughts? What right had supporters of a subversive Mr. Wheelwright to claim entrance to the colony? "If we conceive and finde by sadd experience that his opinions are such, as by his own profession cannot stand with externall peace, may we not provide for our peace, by keeping off such as would strengthen him and infect others with such dangerous tenets?"

In the eyes of Puritans this was the peculiar opportunity of New England. Why not for once see what true orthodoxy could accomplish? Why not in one unspoiled corner of the world declare a truce on doubts, on theological bickering? Here at last men could devote their full energy to *applying* Christianity—not to clarifying doctrine but to building Zion. Nathaniel Ward was speaking for Puritan New England when, in his *Simple Cobler of Aggawam* (1647) he declared, "I dare take upon me, to be the Herauld of New-England so farre, as to proclaime to the world, in the name of our Colony, that all Familists, Antinomians, Anabaptists, and other Enthusiasts, shall have free Liberty to keep away from us, and such as will come to be gone as fast as they can, the sooner the better."

The Puritans in New England were surprisingly successful for some years at keeping their community orthodox. In doing so, they also made it sterile of speculative thought. Their principal theological treatises were works by William Ames (who never saw New England) and John Norton's *Orthodox Evangelist*, a rudimentary summary of the works of English divines. In England the presbyterians and independents and levelers within Puritanism were daring each other to extend and clarify their doctrines; but we see little of this in America.

A dissension which in England would have created a new sect within Puritanism simply produced another colony in New England. The boundless physical space, the surrounding wilderness, deprived the New England ministry of the need to develop within its own theology that spaciousness, that room for variation, which came to characterize Puritanism in England. When Anne Hutchinson and her followers caused trouble by their heterodox views and unauthorized evening meetings, she was tried and "excommunicated." The result, as described by Winthrop, was that in March 1638, "she . . . went by land to Providence, and so to the island in the Naragansett Bay, which her husband and the rest of that sect had purchased of the Indians, and prepared with all speed to remove unto." The dissi-

dence of Roger Williams—the only movement within Massachusetts Bay in the 17th century which promised a solid enrichment of
theory—led to his banishment in October, 1635. It was only after
Williams' return to England and his developing friendship with
John Milton that he wrote his controversial books.

In New England the critics, doubters, and dissenters were expelled from the community; in England the Puritans had to find
ways of living with them. It was in England, therefore, that a modern
theory of toleration began to develop. Milton and his less famous
and less reflective contemporaries were willing to debate, as if it were
an open question, "whether the magistrate have, or ought to have,
any compulsive and restrictive power in matters of religion." Such
was the current of European liberal thought in which Roger Williams found himself. But Williams was banished from Massachusetts
Bay Colony and became a by-word of heterodoxy and rebellion. He
died in poverty, an outcast from that colony. If his little Providence
eventually prospered, it was never to be more than a satellite of the
powerful orthodox mother-colony.

What actually distinguished that mother-colony in the great age
of New England Puritanism was its refusal, for reasons of its own, to
develop a theory of toleration. In mid–17th century England we
note a growing fear that attempts to suppress error would inevitably
suppress truth, a fear that magistrates' power over religion might
give them tyranny over conscience. "I know there is but one truth,"
wrote the author of one of the many English pamphlets on liberty of
conscience in 1645, "But this truth cannot be so easily brought forth
without this liberty; and a general restraint, though intended but for
errors, yet through the unskilfulness of men, may fall upon the truth.
And better many errors of some kind suffered than one useful truth
be obstructed or destroyed." In contrast, the impregnable view of
New England Puritanism was expressed in the words of John Cotton:

> The Apostle directeth, Tit. 3.10 and giveth the Reason, that
> in fundamentall and principall points of Doctrine or Wor-
> ship, the Word of God in such things is so cleare, that hee
> cannot but bee convinced in Conscience of the dangerous

Errour of his way, after once or twice Admonition, wisely and faithfully dispensed. And then if any one persist, it is not out of Conscience, but against his Conscience, as the Apostle saith, vers. 11. He is subverted and sinneth, being condemned of Himselfe, that is, of his owne Conscience. So that if such a Man after such Admonition shall still persist in the Errour of his way, and be therefore punished; He is not persecuted for Cause of Conscience, but for sinning against his Owne Conscience.

The leaders of Massachusetts Bay Colony enjoyed the luxury, no longer feasible in 17th century England, of a pure and simple orthodoxy.

The failure of New England Puritans to develop a theory of toleration, or even freely to examine the question, was not in all ways a weakness. It made their literature less rich and gave much of their writing a quaint and crabbed sound, but for a time at least, it was a source of strength. Theirs was not a philosophic enterprise; they were, first and foremost, community-builders. The energies which their English contemporaries gave to sharpening the distinctions between "compulsive" and "restrictive" powers in religion, between "matters essential" and "matters indifferent" and to a host of other questions which have never ceased to bother reflective students of political theory, the American Puritans were giving to marking off the boundaries of their new towns, to enforcing their criminal laws, and to fighting the Indian menace. Their very orthodoxy strengthened their practical bent.

American Puritans were hardly more distracted from their practical tasks by theology and metaphysics than we are today. They transcended theological preoccupation precisely because they had no doubts and allowed no dissent. Had they spent as much of their energy in debating with each other as did their English contemporaries, they might have lacked the singlemindedness needed to overcome the dark, unpredictable perils of a wilderness. They might have merited praise as precursors of modern liberalism, but they might never have helped found a nation.

HOW PURITANS RESISTED THE TEMPTATION OF UTOPIA

I F there was ever a people whose intellectual baggage equipped them for a journey into Utopia it was the New England Puritans. In their Bible they had a blueprint for the Good Society; their costly expedition to America gave them a vested interest in believing it possible to build Zion on this earth. In view of these facts it is remarkable that there was so little of the Utopian in their thinking about society. There are a number of explanations for this. The English law was a powerful and sobering influence: colonists were persuaded by practical interests such as the retention of their charter and the preservation of their land-titles, as well as by their sentimental attachment to the English basis of their legal system. The pessimism, the vivid sense of evil, which was so intimate a part of Calvinism, discouraged daydreams. Finally, there was the overwhelming novelty and insecurity of life in the wilderness which made the people more anxious to cling to familiar institutions, and led them to discover a new coincidence between the laws of God and the laws of England (and hence of New England).

The peculiar character of their Biblical orthodoxy nourished a practical and non-Utopian frame of mind. Their political thought did not turn toward delineating the Good Society, precisely because the Bible had already offered the anatomy of Zion. Moreover, the Bible was a narrative and not a speculative work; theirs was at most

15

a common-law utopianism, a utopianism of analogies in situation rather than of dogmas, principles, and abstractions.

Perhaps because their basic theoretical questions had been settled, the Puritans were able to concentrate on human and practical problems. And strangely enough, those problems were a preview of the ones which would continue to trouble American political thought. They were concerned less with the ends of society than with its organization and less with making the community good than with making it effective, with insuring the integrity and self-restraint of its leaders, and with preventing its government from being oppressive.

The problems which worried the Puritans in New England were three. The first was how to select leaders and representatives. From the beginning what had distinguished the Puritans (and had laid them open to attack by Lechford and others) was their strict criterion of church-membership, their fear that if the unconverted could be members of the church they might become its rulers. Their concept of a church was, in its own very limited way, of a kind of ecclesiastical self-government: there were to be no bishops because the "members" of each church were fit to rule themselves. Many of the major disputes of early New England were essentially debates over who were fit rulers and how they should be selected. The early political history of Massachusetts Bay could almost be written as a history of disagreements over this problem. What were to be the relations between the magistrates and the deputies? How many deputies from each town? Many of their sermons and even their "speculative" writings were on this subject.

Their second concern was with the proper limits of political power. This question was never better stated than by John Cotton. "It is therefore most wholsome for Magistrates and Officers in Church and Common-wealth, never to affect more liberty and authority then will do them good, and the People good; for what ever transcendant power is given, will certainly over-run those that give it, and those that receive it: There is a straine in a mans heart that will sometime or other runne out to excesse, unlesse the Lord restraine it, but it is not good to venture it: It is necessary therefore, that all power that is on earth be limited. . . ." The form of the early compilations of their laws shows this preoccupation. The first compilation of Massachusetts law (1641) was known, significantly, as "The Body of Liberties" and managed to state the whole of the legal system in terms of the "liberties" of different members of the community. It began with a paraphrase of Magna Charta, followed by the limitations on judicial proceedings, went on to the "liberties" of freemen, women, children, foreigners, and included those "of the brute creature." Even the law of capital crimes was stated in the form of "liberties," and the church organization was described as "the Liberties the Lord Jesus hath given to the Churches." The preamble to this first Body of Liberties would have been impressive, even had it not come out of the American wilderness:

> The free fruition of such liberties Immunities and priviledges as humanitie, Civilitie, and Christianitie call for as due to every man in his place and proportion without impeachment and Infringement hath ever bene and ever will be the tranquillitie and Stabilitie of Churches and Commonwealths. And the deniall or deprivall thereof, the disturbance if not the ruine of both.

The Puritan's third major problem was, what made for a feasible federal organization? How should power be distributed between local and central organs? Congregationalism itself was an attempt to answer this question with specific institutions, to find a means by which churches could extend "the free hand of fellowship" to one another without binding individual churches or individual church-members to particular dogmas or holding them in advance to the decisions of a central body. The practical issues which did not fall under either of the two earlier questions came within this class. What power, if any, had the General Court of the colony over the town of Hingham in its selection of its captain of militia? This was the occasion when one of the townspeople "professeth he will die at sword's point, if he might not have the choice of his own officers." Or, what was the power of the central government to call a church synod? The deputies of the towns (in a dispute over the character of their union which foreshadowed the issues of the Revolution and the Civil War) were willing to consider an invitation to send delegates, but objected to a command.

All the circumstances of New England life—tradition, theology, and the problems of the new world—combined to nourish concern with such practical problems. It is easy to agree with Lechford's grudging compliment that "wiser men then they, going into a wildernesse to set up another strange government differing from the setled government here, might have falne into greater errors then they have done."

THE QUEST FOR MARTYRDOM

CHAPTER 6

To the pilgrims, the Puritans, and the Quakers, America seemed an opportunity to create a society according to plan. Their escape from persecution was perhaps less significant to them than their ascent to rule. America was not merely a way out of prison; it offered a throne in the wilderness. Such swift changes of fortune have always strained the characters of men, and never were changes more dizzying than those which occurred on American soil in the earliest colonial years.

The Puritans, by building institutions in New England, had nourished a worldly human pride which diluted their sense of providence and their faith in the omnipotence of God. The Puritan success was accompanied, if not actually made possible, by the decline of American Puritanism as an uncompromising theology. Quaker success offers a dramatic contrast, for when the opportunities of governing came to them, they preferred to conserve a pure Quaker sect rather than build a great community with a flavor of compromised Quakerism.

English Quakerism had begun as a protest movement. The Quakers believed, in George Fox's classic phrase, "that every man was enlightened by the divine Light of Christ" but that theology, like most other human knowledge, simply obscured men's vision. Fox, the founder of English Quakerism, said in his *Journal*:

These three,—the physicians, the priests, and the lawyers,—
ruled the world out of the wisdom, out of the faith, and out
of the equity and law of God; one pretending the cure of the
body, another the cure of the soul, and the third the protection of the property of the people. But I saw they were all
out of the wisdom, out of the faith, out of the equity and
perfect law of God.

In England Quakers remained a minority, raising an accusing and
critical voice. In America the earliest Quaker voices had much the
same sound. While others saw an opportunity here to pursue their
orthodoxy unmolested, the Quakers engaged in a relentless quest for
martyrdom. Their spirit was expressed by William Dewsbury, a
leading English Quaker who helped ship immigrants to America,
when he said that he "as joyfully entered prisons as palaces, and in
the prison-house, I sang praises to my God and esteemed the bolts
and locks upon me as jewels." From this point of view the earliest
Quaker immigrants to the American colonies sought, and found,
adornment aplenty. In colonial Rhode Island, where the rulers refused to persecute them, Quakers were unwilling to stay. "We finde
that in those places where these people aforesaid, in this coloney, are
most of all suffered to declare themselves freely, and are only opposed by arguments in discourse," observed the Rhode Island Court
of Trial, "there they least of all desire to come."

The story of earliest Quaker activities in America is puzzling to
anyone unacquainted with the mystic spirit and the character of the
martyr. It is not merely that these men and women preferred "to die
for the whole truth rather than live with a half-truth." One after another of them seemed to lust after hardships, trudging thousands of
wilderness miles, risking Indians and wild animals, to find a crown of
martyrdom. Never before perhaps have people gone to such trouble
or traveled so far for the joys of suffering for their Lord. The courage and persistence shown by 17th-century American Quakers in
seeking out the whipping-post or the gallows is equaled only in
Cortes' quest for the treasure of the Aztecs or Ponce de León's
search for the Fountain of Youth. Never was a reward sought more
eagerly than the Quakers sought out their crown of thorns.

The English "Friends" (as the Quakers called themselves) were proud of the abuse willingly suffered by American Quakers at the hands of the New England Puritans. As early as 1659, Humphrey Norton's *New England's Ensigne* made a byword of their suffering. And George Bishop, also in England, prepared a *Book of Martyrs*, first published in 1661, and later several times reprinted, under the title *New England Judged by the Spirit of the Lord*. In this thick volume he collected harrowing tales of the punishment of Quaker visitors to Massachusetts Bay.

A few examples will give a hint of the Friends' bizarre and dauntless spirit. In 1658, Sarah Gibbons and Dorothy Waugh left Rhode Island, where they were not being molested, and traveled mostly on foot from Newport to Salem in Massachusetts. Groping through March blizzards and sleeping in the woods, they eventually reached their destination, and they preached undisturbed for about two weeks. Then they "felt moved" to go to Boston, where they received the expected barbaric whipping before being sent packing back to Rhode Island. In the summer of the same year Josiah Coale and Thomas Thurston traveled even farther to suffer for the Truth. They walked from Virginia to New England "through Uncouth Passages, Vast Wildernesses, Uninhabited Countries." The Susquehanna Indians took pity on them, guiding them to New Amsterdam and nursing Thurston when he was critically ill. Like so many others, these two men felt what the Quakers called "the fire and the hammer" in their souls. Finally reaching New England, they preached, first to the Indians and then to the white colonists, until they were committed to prison and driven at last from the colony.

One of the most persistent of the martyrs was Christopher Holder, "valiant apostle of New England Quakerism," who had arrived in 1656 from England to preach the gospel of his sect. In Salem, one Sunday morning in September 1657, he was bold enough to speak a few words after the minister had done. He did not get very far before someone seized him by the hair, and "His Mouth violently stopp'd with a Glove and Handkerchief thrust thereinto with much Fury, by one of your Church-Members and Commissioners." Although he had already been at least once expelled, he and his companion had continued their preaching. They were conveyed to

Boston, where the exasperated Governor and Deputy-Governor of the colony inflicted on them a brutal punishment which went even beyond all existing laws. Merely reading the account is strong medicine, but it contributes to our understanding of the price the Quakers sought to pay for their Truth. First the two Quakers were given thirty stripes apiece with a three-cord knotted whip, during which one of the spectators fainted. Then they were confined to a bare cell, without bedding, for three days and nights without food or drink. After that they were imprisoned during nine weeks of the New England winter without any fire. By special order the prisoners were whipped twice each week, the first time with fifteen lashes and each succeeding time by three additional. Having miraculously survived this ordeal, Holder took ship for Barbados, where he spent the remainder of the winter before returning to Rhode Island to preach his gospel without molestation. But this did not satisfy him. In August 1658 he was arrested in Dedham, Massachusetts, and again taken to Boston, where one of his ears was cut off.

The New England Puritan leaders were not sadists. But they too were single-minded men; they had risked everything and traveled three thousand miles for their own opportunity. They wanted to be let alone to pursue their orthodoxy and to build Zion according to their model. What right had the Quakers (or anyone else) to interfere? The Puritans had not sought out the Quakers in order to punish them; the Quakers had come in quest of punishment. Why could not these zealots stay in Rhode Island where they were tolerated, and allow the Puritans to go about their business? Or, as a Puritan minister said in defending the 117 blows with a tarred rope which had brought the Quaker William Brend near to death, he "indeavoured to beat the Gospel ordinances black and blew," and it seemed but just to beat *him* black and blue.

In trying to keep the Quakers away, the governors of Massachusetts Bay were at their wit's end. They showed how little they understood the problem by increasing the legal penalties against intruders. Had they known the Quakers better they might have foreseen that this could only make their colony more attractive to seekers of martyrdom. There was very little popular enthusiasm in Massachusetts

Bay for the death penalty against Quakers, but it was enacted in 1658, having passed the House of Deputies by a majority of only one vote.

It was not long before another group of Quakers, inspired by what their own historian called an unquenchable fire, departed from the safety of Rhode Island and arrived in Boston. They were "commissioned" by God; they came to "look your Bloody Laws in the Face." Unflinching before the threat of death, they came prepared. Alice Cowland even brought linen for wrapping the dead bodies of those who were expected to be martyred. One of these unwelcome visitors, William Robinson, wrote in the Boston jail late in 1659:

> In Travelling betwixt Newport in Rhode Island, and Daniel Gold's House, with my dear Brother, Christopher Holder, the Word of the Lord came expressly to me which did fill me immediately with Life and Power, and heavenly love, by which he constrained me and commanded me to pass to the Town of Boston, my life to lay down in His will, for the Accomplishing of his Service, that he had there to perform at the Day appointed. To which heavenly Voice I presently yielded Obedience, not questioning the Lord how He would bring the Thing to pass . . . and willingly was I given up from that time, to this Day, the Will of the Lord to do and perform, what-ever became of my Body. . . . I being a Child, and durst not question the Lord in the least, but rather willing to lay down my Life, than to bring Dishonour to the Lord.

The story of Mary Dyer, who left her husband in Newport to court danger and defy evil in Boston, demonstrates both the uneasiness of the Puritans in crowning the Quaker martyrs and the persistence of the Quakers in earning that crown. Her story, one of the most impressive in all the annals of martyrdom, is worth recounting. Shortly after arriving in Boston in the early fall of 1659, she and her companions (including an eleven-year-old girl, Patience Scott) were banished on pain of death. After only a brief stay in Newport, she returned to Boston. "Your end shall be frustrated, that think to restrain them, you call Cursed Quakers, from coming among you, by any Thing you can do to them," she explained, "Yea, verily, he hath a Seed here among you, for whom we have suffered all this while, and yet Suffer." She was tried on October 19, 1659, along with William Robinson and Marmaduke Stephenson, who had shared her mission. The next day, after a sermon cursing them, Governor Endicott pronounced their death sentence. "The Will of the Lord be done," Mary Dyer replied, and as the marshal took her away, she stolidly remarked, "Yea, joyfully shall I go."

A week later the three Quakers were to be executed. Mary Dyer marched to the gallows between the two young men condemned with her, while drums beat loudly to prevent any words they might preach on the way from being heard by the watching crowd. When an official asked Mrs. Dyer if she did not feel shame at walking publicly between two young men, she answered, "It is an Hour of the greatest Joy I can enjoy in this World. No Eye can see, No Ear can hear, No Tongue can speak, No Heart can understand the sweet incomes and refreshings of the Spirit of the Lord which I now enjoy." Still the Puritan officials tried to deprive her of the martyr's ecstasy. The two men were executed, and Mary Dyer was mounted on the gallows, her arms and legs bound and her face covered with a handkerchief as the final preparation for hanging. Then, as if by a sudden decision, she was reprieved from the gallows.

This barbarous proceeding, as we now know, had been planned in advance. During Mary Dyer's trial, the Massachusetts General Court had secretly recorded their judgment that she be banished; but they had also provided that she be present at the execution of the others and be prepared as if for her own hanging. Her reprieve was surely due, in part, to the uneasiness of citizens who still recalled their own sufferings in England.

Mary Dyer's response to this act of grace was thoroughly in character. She refused to accept the reprieve unless the law itself was repealed. But the determined judges sent her off on horseback in the direction of Rhode Island. If they thought they could so easily be rid of Mary Dyer, they were mistaken. "She said," records John Taylor, one of her fellow Quaker missionaries, "that she must go and desire the repeal of that wicked law against God's people and offer up her life there." On May 21, 1660, less than a year after her banishment from the colony, the irrepressible Mary Dyer returned to Boston and once more heard her sentence of death. But now, insisted Governor Endicott, it was to be executed. Again there were pleas for her life. And again, as she stood on the ladder of the gallows, she was offered her life if she would just leave the colony. But this time she was not to be thwarted. "Nay," she declared, "I cannot. . . . In obedience to the will of the Lord God I came and in his will I abide faithful to death." And she was hanged.

However hard we may find it to understand the motives of the Quakers in their American quest for martyrdom, we must admire their courage. As William Brend wrote:

> I further Testify, in the Fear of the Lord, and witness God, with a Pen of Trembling, That the Noise of the whip on my Back, all the Imprisonments, and Banishing upon pain of Death . . . did no more affright me, through the Strength and Power of God in me, than if they had threatened to have bound a Spider's Web to my Finger.

Even the sympathetic Quaker historian Rufus Jones describes as an "almost excessive Quaker frankness" the spirit which moved Josiah Southwick after his successive whippings to tell his persecutors that "it was no more terrifying unto him, than if ye had taken a Feather and blown it up in the Air, and had said, Take heed it hurteth him not."

HOW QUAKERS MISJUDGED
THE INDIANS

T HE POLITICAL SUCCESS, even the very survival of an American colony, often depended on a realistic estimate of the Indian. But the Quakers' view of the Indian was of a piece with their attitude toward war: it was unrealistic, inflexible, and based on false premises about human nature. The problem was never better summarized than in the speech by Teedyuscung, Chief of the Delawares, at a conference with Pennsylvania leaders in July 1756. In his hand he held a belt of wampum, which had lately been given him by the Iroquois: a large square represented the land of the Indians; on one side stood an Englishman and on the other a Frenchman—both ready to seize the land. Chief Teedyuscung pleaded that the Pennsylvanians show their friendship by guaranteeing that no more land would be taken from the Indians. While the Chief's description was an oversimplification he had surely stated the heart of the matter. The increasing, westward-flowing population of the Province was passing like a tidal wave over Indian lands. The troubles of the Indians could no longer be reduced to niceties of protocol, to maxims of fair play, or to clichés of self-reproach. Here was one of those great conflicts in history when a mighty force was meeting a long-unmoved body; either the force had to be stopped or the body had to move.

But the Quakers chose not to see it that way. Their policy in this

crisis of the affairs of Pennsylvania showed a spectacular, if not altogether surprising, failure of practical vision. They seemed as blind to
the long-term problems and interests of the Indians as to the character of these unfamiliar people with whom they were dealing. In 1748,
for example, the Quaker Assembly had refused to vote money for the
defense of Philadelphia, but appropriated £500 for the Indians, accompanying it by the pious wish that the money be used to "supply
them with necessities towards acquiring a livelihood and cultivate
the friendship between us and not to encourage their entering into a
war." How could Quaker men of the world have failed to guess that
Indian lead and powder would not be used solely to shoot bear and
deer? For that failure of practical judgment Irish and German settlers on the western border would have to pay dearly. Some years
later, in the fall of 1756, when the Quaker Assembly in Philadelphia
heard of the bloodbath in the west, they at once began to investigate
the source of Indian grievances. Instead of providing for military defense, the Assembly produced a bill for the better regulation of trade
with the Indians, authorizing commissioners who would see that the
Indians were fairly treated and enacting such guarantees as maximum prices on goods sold to them. Such admirable measures were
small comfort to backwoodsmen who saw their homes in flames,
their crops ruined, their wives and children scalped or captured.

The political conflict between the non-Quaker Deputy-
Governor Robert Hunter Morris and the Quaker Assembly came to
the fore. The Deputy-Governor, in defense of the Proprietors, declared that Indian grievances against the Proprietors had nothing to
do with the massacres and that the real trouble lay in Quaker pacifism which had left the province defenseless. On the other side, the
Quakers traced all ills to the wicked policies of the Proprietors. In
the middle stood Franklin, who now had a considerable following
among the less orthodox Quakers; he did not oppose a more just
Indian policy, but he demanded immediate measures for military defense. Still the minority of die-hard Quakers which controlled the
Assembly would not budge from its traditional pacifism, though the
whole border might burn for it.

The massacres continued; panic gripped western Pennsylvania.

Murder was rampant; whole townships were broken up, their populations driven from their homes. George Stevenson wrote from
York, on November 5, 1755, that the real question there was
"whether we shall stand or run? Most are willing to stand, but have
no Arms nor Ammunition." The government gave no answer to appeals. "People from Cumberland are going thro this Town hourly in
Droves and the Neighbouring Inhabits are flocking into this Town
Defenseless as it is." While settlers on the border suffered the murderous blows of the tomahawk, those further east had the burden of
supporting growing numbers of refugees.

It is hardly surprising that the patience of the people of Pennsylvania had worn thin. Toward the end of November 1755, about
three hundred desperate Germans from the west arrived in Philadelphia to demand action of the Assembly. They succeeded in frightening the Assembly into a show of compliance and, through the
Provincial Agent, petitioned the English Privy Council to remedy
their defenseless condition. These months saw a growing and unprecedented division of sentiment within the Quaker community itself. The Philadelphia Yearly Meeting in September still evaded the
issue by refusing to take a position on the large military appropriation needed for defense. Many would have agreed with Israel Pemberton that the events of the summer and fall of 1755 had "produc'd
a greater & more fatal change both with respect to the state of our
affairs in general & among us as a Society than seventy preceding
years."

By July 1756, the French commandant at Fort Duquesne reported with satisfaction that he had "succeeded in ruining the three
adjacent provinces, Pennsylvania, Maryland, and Virginia, driving
off the inhabitants, and totally destroying the settlements over a tract
of country thirty leagues wide reckoning from the line of Fort Cumberland. . . . The Indian villages are full of prisoners of every age and
sex. The enemy has lost far more since the battle than on the day of
his defeat."

But still the Quakers had not been shocked into discovering the
weaknesses of their idealized Indians. They seemed indifferent to
the fact that the Indian leaders with whom they dealt were some-

times half-demented with drink. For example, the wildly contradictory demands of their good friend Teedyuscung, while the Quakers
were purporting to represent him in late July 1756, were made while
he was under the influence of liquor. But somehow, whether from
optimism, pity, or blindness, the Quakers were not prepared to take
this fact into account.

The needs of the London Government and the policies of Virginia and Maryland identified Pennsylvanians in the eyes of the Indians with British expansion, and with land-grabbing enterprises like
the Ohio Company, however much the people of Pennsylvania
might deplore it. Indian politics were no simple matter: a gesture of
friendship to one tribe might be taken as a declaration of war by that
tribe's enemies. By choosing an alliance in 1742 with the Iroquois,
for example, Pennsylvania had willy-nilly become involved in the
troubles between the Iroquois and the Delawares and thus sowed
seeds of trouble to be reaped thirteen years later. When, in 1756, the
Quakers were present at negotiations with Teedyuscung, Chief of
the Delawares, they pressed their non-Quaker Governor to conclude a peace treaty, but Governor Morris had the good sense to see
that such a separate peace would probably incense the powerful Iroquois. This was all an intricate and delicate business not to be settled
by moral slogans or abstract principles.

Some initiative by the Quakers was urgent if they were not to
lose all popular support at a time when the colony was panicked by
Indian violence. They chose to take this initiative entirely outside
the government, even in competition with it, when, in July of 1756,
they formed the "Friendly Association for Regaining and Preserving
Peace with the Indians by Pacific Measures." Through this non-
governmental association the Quakers intended to deal with the Indians and to pacify them without sacrifice of principles. Despite their
noble intentions, the Quakers' activities among the Indians in those
desperate times can hardly be called anything but meddling. The
Governors of Pennsylvania, however tactless or ineffective, did at
least see quite accurately the character of the Indian problem. The
Friendly Association succeeded only in further confusing matters, in
leading the Indians to distrust those rulers of Pennsylvania with

whom they would finally have to deal, and in postponing any arrangement satisfactory to the new settlers of Pennsylvania.

On one occasion during the slippery negotiations of 1756, the Quakers persuaded the Delaware Indians to designate Israel Pemberton, a Quaker leader, as the representative with whom the Governor of Pennsylvania would have to deal in all Indian affairs. This ambiguous confidence pleased the Quakers, but they had only the vaguest notion of whom or what they were representing. Actually they were in no position to serve either the Indians or the people of Pennsylvania. They simply complicated the Governor's problem and led him to threaten that he would treat them as enemies of the King if they did not cease their tampering.

The Quaker preoccupation with their principles blinded them to the most obvious facts. In April 1751, for example, the Quaker Assembly, refusing the offer of the Proprietors of the Province to help build a fort, showed their usual complacency. "As we have always found that sincere, upright Dealing with the Indians, a friendly Treatment of them on all Occasions, and particularly in relieving their Necessities at proper Times by suitable Presents, have been the best Means of securing their Friendship, we could wish our Proprietaries had rather thought fit to join with us in the Expence of those presents, the Effects of which have at all Times so manifestly advanced their Interests with the Security of our Frontier Settlements." Even after the storm broke on the frontier and after the western inhabitants of Pennsylvania had begun to reap the fiery harvest of a half-century of Quaker generosity and non-resistance to the Indians, many Quakers remained blind to the practical moral of it all. One of the most fantastic examples of this blindness is found in the journal of Daniel Stanton, one of the numerous itinerant Quaker zealots who carried the messages of the Philadelphia Yearly Meeting to remote parts of America. To him the relatively small number of Quakers massacred by the Indians during the frontier attacks of 1755–56 was a testimony of God's approval of the Quaker policy. He could not deny that the Indians had been "an heavy rod of chastisement on this land; yet remarkable it was, that through the protection of Almighty, which was as the shadow of a mighty rock in a wearied land, few called by our name were ill used during all this calamity." A more valid explanation of Quaker luck, though less flattering to their self-righteousness, was that almost all the Quakers were then living in the eastern portion of the province, separated by two hundred miles of mountainous and river-traced terrain from the "barbarous and cruel enemy."

Franklin was not impressed by the fact that the Quakers on the eastern seaboard had, by good luck or God's grace or whatever other means, still escaped the fury of the Indians. He was more concerned, in August 1756, to see "our frontier people continually butchered," and he lamented the delays in fighting back. "In short," Franklin concluded with characteristic directness, "I do not believe we shall ever have a firm peace with the Indians, till we have well drubbed them."

FROM COUNTRY SQUIRE TO
PLANTER CAPITALIST

Chapter 18

I

N ENGLAND people had long believed in the mystique of the gentleman. "A gentleman I could never make him," King James I had replied to his nurse who requested that he make her son a gentleman, "though I could make him a lord." In Virginia, as we have seen, an aura also surrounded the gentleman, but an aristocratic family could more easily be manufactured with money. Colonial Virginia thus foreshadowed the wholesome crudity of the American attitude toward aristocracy. Whenever coats of arms can be bought for ready cash, people are bound to be skeptical of all charters of nobility. The obvious salability of social position in America has helped dissipate the mystique of the European hereditary aristocracy. If the poor see their "betters" pay cash for their titles, how can they believe the myth of a charter sealed by God?

The spirit of business enterprise was kept alive in Virginia even among the congealing aristocracy. Leading Virginia families like the Ludwells, Spencers, Steggs, Byrds, Carys, and Chews, to mention only a few, were but recently descended from merchants. For several reasons a successful planter was likely to remain something of a merchant, constantly seeking new investments for his capital. First, there were the characteristics of Virginia's tobacco-agriculture. Since Virginians did not replenish the nitrogen and potash which growing tobacco sucked from the soil, it was only on virgin land that tobacco could flourish; the second crop was usually the best. After the fourth season land was customarily abandoned to corn and wheat, before finally being turned back to wild pine, sorrel, and sedge. Under this system a prudent planter dared not put more than a small portion— say, ten per cent—of his acreage in tobacco at any one time. Fore-sight required that he continually add to his landholdings since every year he was, in the Virginia phrase, "using it up." Soon the term "tobacco land" became synonymous with "new land." The "sour land" or "old fields" which had presumably yielded all their profit provided the sites for schools and churches in tidewater Virginia. A prudent planter thus had to be a land speculator, alert to opportu-nity, ready to make new purchases. The landholdings of the princi-pal families were constantly increasing and often shifting location. The most ancient plantation houses—like those of the Carters, Ran-dolphs, and Byrds—remained fixed and became wellsprings of fam-ily tradition, but the lands from which these families drew their wealth were capital equipment to be discarded or exchanged when they no longer yielded a fair return. Under these circumstances, large planters discovered special advantages in an enslaved labor-force which could be moved about the countryside as one or another piece of land promised greater profit. This wasteful system was not an unmixed evil, at least from the point of view of the civic institu-tions of Virginia, for it subjected the wealthy planter class—who were also the political leaders—to an unrelenting test of alertness and enterprise.

The second factor which stimulated a mercantile and enterpris-ing spirit among the planters and which had shaped the character of the plantation system itself was the lack of large towns. "The inhabi-tants do not live close together," noted the French traveler Francis L. Michel in 1702, "and the country is not settled in villages, because every twenty or thirty years new ground must be broken." This was not the only reason. The simple facts of geography were equally im-portant. Tidewater Virginia, extending southeastward toward the Chesapeake Bay, was a rich lowland which was cut into fingers by several deep and navigable rivers: the Potomac, the Rappahannock, the York, and the James. Each finger was in turn reticulated by a veinwork of smaller rivers, many of which were large enough to carry traffic toward the ocean. These were the circulatory channels of economic life. Up came ships carrying Negro slaves from Africa and the West Indies, clothing and household furnishings from London; down went ships laden with hogsheads of tobacco from the vast plantations of the Lees, the Carters, and the Byrds.

From a commercial point of view, then, cities were superfluous. Each of the larger planters had his private dock. The tobacco grower could load his hogsheads directly from his own dockside onto the ship which went to his agent in London; his imports could be landed at his private port-of-entry. For this reason Virginia had no commercial capital, no Boston or Philadelphia, during the colonial period; her commerce dwelt in these scores of private depots scattered along the riversides. "No Country in the World can be more curiously watered," observed John Clayton in his Letter to the Royal Society in 1688. "But this Conveniency, that in future Times may make her like the Netherlands, the richest Place in all America, at the present I look on the greatest Impediment to the Advance of the Country, as it is the greatest Obstacle to Trade and Commerce. For the great Number of Rivers, and the Thinness of the Inhabitants, distract and disperse a Trade. So that all Ships in general gather each their Loading up and down an hundred Miles distant; and the best of Trade that can be driven is only a sort of Scotch Peddling; for they must carry all Sorts of Truck that trade thither, having one Commodity to pass off another. This (i.e.) the Number of Rivers, is one of the chief Reasons why they have no Towns." Why, asked the authors of *The Present State of Virginia* a few years later, should the planter-merchant, comfortably seated in the country with his customers all about him, wish to change his life or invite the competition of town merchants?

In an age when land transportation was rudimentary, in a new country where roads barely existed, the Virginia planters and those who bought at their docks seemed favored by nature. "Most Houses are built near some Landing-Place," the Rev. Hugh Jones noted in 1724, "any Thing may be delivered to a Gentleman there from London, Bristol, &c. with less Trouble and Cost, than to one living five

Miles in the Country in England; for you pay no Freight for Goods from London, and but little from Bristol; only the Party to whom the Goods belong, is in Gratitude engaged to freight Tobacco upon the Ship consigned to her Owners in England."

The critics of Virginia frequently complained that the low state of culture, religion, and commerce was due to this lack of towns. Because the work of English furniture-makers was so cheaply carried to Virginia plantations in the holds of ships coming for bulky hogsheads of tobacco, native craftsmen were discouraged. The very ease of river transportation actually provincialized the thinking of many planters. "At the first settlement of the Country," Governor Spotswood reported in 1710, "people seated themselves along the banks of the great Rivers and knew very little of the inland parts beyond the bounds of their own private plantations, being kept in awe by the Indians from vent'ring farther; neither had they any correspondence than only by Water." To promote "cohabitation" in towns would, critics said, produce the higher forms of civilization. Some proposed legislation, tax-benefits for town-dwellers, and other enticements, but all these failed and geography had its way. Until late in the 18th century, the commercial life of Virginia—and, with it, the commercial virtues—remained diffused among the larger planters. Because there were no towns, the Virginia country gentleman, more than his English counterpart, had to acquire the town talents: a spirit of enterprise, a capacity for sharp-dealing, and a townsman's eye for profit and loss.

Tobacco, unlike the crops of many English country gentlemen, was not part of a traditional subsistence economy; it was a commercial crop, raised for profit. The planters' investments in slaves, land, and equipment were supported by large cash loans. The account-books of George Washington and many others tell this story with discouraging vividness. Virginia was, as some complained, "a colony founded on smoke," and Jefferson, like others before him, pleaded for a more diversified economy. But the plantation system, exemplified in the West Indies and Virginia, was, according to some historians, the first great experiment in large-scale commercial agriculture since the Roman Empire.

The English country gentleman was traditionally interested in the details of his farm. Even so great a lord as the eighth Duke of Devonshire (several decades later) experienced "the proudest moment of his life" when his pig won first prize at Skipton Fair. The large Virginia planter could not be satisfied by prizes at a local fair. His tobacco had entered the exacting competition of the world market, and he had to keep a sharp eye on the cost of a hundred different tasks. When M. Durand de Dauphiné visited Rosegill, the magnificent Wormeley estate in 1686, he thought he was entering "a rather large village." Life on a large plantation was far from that in a simple agrarian economy. There were hundreds of slaves, white craftsmen, overseers, stewards, and traders who were producing tobacco as a money-crop, raising food, and manufacturing tools, farm instruments, and clothing for their own use and for sale in local and foreign markets to which they were sometimes carried in the planter's own ships. A Virginia plantation was an 18th-century version of a modern "company town" rather than a romantic rural village. The plantation owner needed both business acumen and a large store of practical knowledge to run his little world of agriculture, trade, and manufacturing. Breadth and versatility, so impressive in men like William Byrd and Thomas Jefferson, were common to the larger and more successful Virginia planters of the 18th century: they were interested in natural history, had a respectable knowledge of medical remedies and mechanics, were at home in meteorology, and felt obliged to know the law. How devious it is to explain these plantation necessities as if they were inspired by the distant example and abstract teachings of the European Enlightenment! They were nothing more than an index to the problems of a Virginia planter.

If all these influences produced a breed of men with some characteristic New World virtues, the product was none the less aristocratic. While the Virginia gentleman felt more incentive to enterprise, was less fearful of soiling his hands in trade, was more capitalistic in his frame of mind, had a sharper eye for the cash-balance sheet, and was more versatile in his intellectual interests, he was still a member of a small privileged class. Foundations of this class had been solidly laid before the opening of the 18th century.

Col. Robert Quarry reported back to the Lords of Trade in 1704 that on each of Virginia's four great rivers there lived between ten and thirty men "who by trade and industry had gotten very competent estates." By mid-century the number of such men had increased, and there were some upstarts, like the Jeffersons and Washingtons among them. But the very process which had multiplied the larger planters had decimated the smaller ones. The social gulf between a substantial gentleman planter and everybody else was probably never wider in Virginia than around the year 1750.

That heyday of the tobacco aristocracy in Virginia—the middle decades of the 18th century—was the youth of nearly all the leaders of Revolutionary Virginia and of those who were to become the "Virginia Dynasty" in the young Federal government. Washington was born in 1732; Monroe, the last of the group, in 1758. The biographies and letters of these men reveal a closely intermarried social "four-hundred." When Governor Alexander Spotswood reported to the Secretary of State on March 9, 1713 that he had finally filled three vacancies in the Governor's Council with three suitable men "of good parts, loyal and honest principles, and of plentiful Estates," he complained that but for these three he could find none qualified. All others already held places of profit under the government "or else. . . . are related to one particular Family [the Burwells] to which the greatest part of the present Council are already nearly allyed." In the list of ninety-one men appointed to the Governor's Council from 1680 till the American Revolution, there appear only fifty-seven different family names, nine names providing nearly a third, and fourteen others about another third. Five Councilors were called Page; three each went by the name of Burwell, Byrd, Carter, Custis, Harrison, Lee, Ludwell, or Wormeley. A member of the Council would be likely to hold more than one office. "The Multitude of Places held by the Council," some complained, "occasions great Confusion, especially in such things wherein the Places are incompatible: As when their Collectors Office obliges them to inform their Judges Office against an unfree Bottom: Or when their Honours, as Counsellors, sit upon and pass their own Accounts, as Collectors." This monopoly of offices was not confined to the

Governor's Council; in local communities, the same substantial planter was likely to be vestryman, justice of the peace, commander of the militia, and delegate to the House of Burgesses.

The few surviving letters of Thomas Jefferson's youth (written between 1760 and 1764), which tell us nearly all we know about him firsthand before the age of twenty-one, read much like the Society Page: the names in his social pageant are almost without exception those of the "best" Virginia families. The Rebecca Burwell who was his first romantic love came of that very family which ruled the Governor's Council fifty years before. "Dear Will," he wrote to young Fleming, "I have thought of the cleverest plan of life that can be imagined. You exchange your land for Edgehill, or I mine for Fairfields, you marry S[ucke]y P[otte]r, I marry R[ebecc]a B[urwel]l, [join] and get a pole chair and a pair of keen horses, practise the law in the same courts, and drive about to all the dances in the country together. How do you like it?" Through the letters of this young socialite run the names of Page, Mann, Carter, Nelson, Lee, Bland, and Yates, none of which could have been excluded from a Virginia Social Register.

No wall separates this world of the 1760's and 50's and 40's from 1776. No mutation of ideas distinguishes the thinking of the late years from those of the middle years of the century. On the contrary, the more we learn of Virginia life the more continuity we see between the ways of the Revolutionary generations and those of their fathers and grandfathers. The more we begin to see the local lineage of their ideas, the less we need seek a cosmopolitan philosophic ancestry or try to explain them as ideas which lack a local habitation but are supposed to have been "in the air" all over the world. The motives of the Revolution will dissolve into the commonplace. The philosophers of the European Enlightenment who have been hauled into the court of historians as putative fathers of the Revolution may then seem as irrelevant as the guilty cousin who suddenly appears in the last scene of a bad mystery play. The motives and patterns of action which were to reach a climax in the Revolution were already taking form a century before in the daily life of Virginia.

"PRACTICAL GODLINESS":

Toleration Without a Theory

T HE VAST EXTENT of the Virginia parishes naturally affected the quality of their religious experience. By 1740 a small parish measured about twenty miles in length and possessed a scattered population of about seven or eight hundred white persons gathered in about a hundred and fifty families. A larger parish might be sixty miles long, or even more if it extended southwestward toward the dim border between Virginia and North Carolina. Churches were ten or more miles apart. "Their large extent," the Rev. Alexander Forbes (whose own parish was sixty miles long and eleven miles wide) complained in 1724, "is not only the cause of the omission of Holy days; but very often I have found that labor to be fruitless, which I have imployed in room of their observation; for sometimes after I have travell'd Fifty Miles to Preach at a Private House, the Weather happening to prove bad, on the day of our meeting, so that very few or none have met; or else being hindred by Rivers & Swamps rendered impassable with much rain, I have returned with doing of nothing to their benefit or mine own satisfaction." As a quantitative measure of religious zeal, he added that while parishioners were faithful enough to go five or six miles to church, ten or fifteen miles were simply too much for them. The large numbers of recently arrived Africans or unassimilated white indentured servants made cautious planters reluctant to leave their plantations unattended by an adult male of the family.

The lack of any central church authority to enforce uniformity of ritual, and the scarcity of church "ornaments," bred an informality alien to the spirit of the English Church. "After the minister had made an end," a Sunday visitor to a tidewater church noted in 1715, "every one of the men pulled out his pipe, and smoked a pipe of tobacco." We do not know for sure how many, like those later parishioners of neighboring Carolina who so annoyed the Rev. Charles Woodmason, actually brought their dogs to church. But we do know that in some places there was no font for baptizing; in others no surplice for the minister; elsewhere it became common for people to take communion in their seats instead of kneeling before the altar. "Every Minister," the Rev. Hugh Jones wrote, "is a kind of Independent in his own Parish, in Respect of some little particular Circumstances and Customs." Many rituals of the church came to be performed at home.

> The Parishes being of great Extent . . . many dead Corpses cannot be conveyed to the Church to be buried: So that it is customary to bury in Gardens or Orchards, where whole Families lye interred together, in a Spot generally handsomely enclosed, planted with Evergreens, and the Graves kept decently: Hence likewise arises the Occasion of preaching Funeral Sermons in Houses, where at Funerals are assembled a great Congregation of Neighbours and Friends; and if you insist upon having the Sermon and Ceremony at Church, they'll say they will be without it, unless performed after their usual Custom. In Houses also there is Occasion, from Humour, Custom sometimes, from Necessity most frequently, to baptize Children and church Women, otherwise some would go without it. In Houses also they most commonly marry, without Regard to the Time of the Day or Season of the Year.

The vast American spaces were accomplishing in Virginia what in England had required decades of theological controversy. In their own peculiar way, and even without intending it, Virginians were "purifying" the English church of its atmosphere of hierarchy and of excessive reliance on ritual. And were not these the very defects which Massachusetts Puritans had strenuously and stridently attacked?

While space "purified," it also diffused the religious spirit. The more we learn of the spirit of the Church of Virginia, the more natural it seems that Virginia should have become a haven of toleration in the 18th century, and even that Virginia should have been among the first of the colonies with established churches to disestablish them. In Virginia this process began in 1776; while in Connecticut, Church and State remained united until 1818 and in Massachusetts until 1833. We need not look abroad to violent winds of doctrine to explain the moderation of Virginians.

The key to toleration in Virginia was the practical compromising spirit which built the Church of England in its English home and gave it new vitality when transplanted. It was Edmund Pendleton, devoted supporter of the Established Church, and others like him who organized the government and held Virginia together during the anarchic days of the Revolution. Pendleton, as Philip Mazzei, the traveling Florentine, recorded, was popularly known by the nickname of "Moderation." Virginians were not passionate about religious dogma, for the simple reason that they often knew nothing about it. George Washington, though an active vestryman, probably could not have told the difference between the Church of Virginia and any other, except that the Established Church stood for moderation in all things and was the bulwark of decency in his community.

Virginians had founded their community, not as religious refugees held together by a common fanaticism, but as admirers of the English way of life who hoped to preserve its virtues on this side of the water. Their desire to increase their population and their lack of interest in theology made them generally lax in enforcing laws against dissenters. They were tolerant even of Papists and Quakers so long as they kept the peace. William Fitzhugh, himself a devoted Anglican, lived happily beside George Brent, a Catholic; he even developed a scheme for importing Catholics to a settlement of their own. Yet he also sought to attract French Huguenots. Many other leading Virginia Anglicans tried to make their colony a haven for all decent Christians. A Quaker, John Pleasants, despite the letter of the law, was elected to the House of Burgesses, and only because he refused to take the oath of office did he vacate his seat. When King James II in 1687 issued his edict suspending the laws against nonconformists (both Protestant and Roman Catholic), the news was received with such enthusiasm in Virginia that it occasioned the beating of drums and the firing of guns! The Council prepared an address of thanks. The Burgesses approved, and a Roman Catholic was duly elected a member from Stafford County. Against the Quakers, who had shown their usual unwillingness to help defend the community, and whose itinerant ways made them a source of information for the colony's French and Indian enemies, Virginians remained ready to use force. But they distinguished even among Quakers; when Thomas Story early in the 18th century won their confidence, they permitted him to wander at will preaching heterodoxy.

Men who wished to strengthen their colony with a solid citizenry—of English non-conformists, of Scots, Irish, Huguenots, Germans, and Dutch—could not split theological hairs. "With regard to the affair of Mr. Davis the Presbyterian," the English Board of Trade wisely advised the Council of Virginia in 1750, "A Toleration and a free exercise of Religion is so valuable a branch of true Liberty, and so essential to the improving and enriching of a Trading Nation, it should ever be held Sacred to his Majesty's Colonies." From time to time, of course, they had to restrain religious troublemakers who menaced the peace or security of the colony. Virginians forbade the coming of Puritans in 1640 and the assembly of Quakers in 1662; a hundred years later (1770) they imprisoned wild Baptist preachers. But these were emergency measures which expressed no general spirit of persecution.

Before the middle of the 18th century, dissenting sects—Presbyterians, Baptists, and even Quakers—had acquired a recognized place in the life of the colony. "If there are among you any dissenters from this Church with consciences truly scrupulous," Gooch declared in his inaugural address as Lieutenant-Governor in 1728, "I shall think an indulgence to them to be so consistent with the genius of the Christian Religion that it can never be inconsistent with the interest of the Church of England." The laws against Quakers seem to have been enforced not to insure religious orthodoxy but rather to prevent violence or to guard against their helping the colony's military enemies under their guise of itinerant preaching. In 1721, the court of King George County dismissed charges against persons presented for not going to the Anglican parish church, because the defendants called themselves Presbyterians. In 1724, Hanover parish in that same county actually erected a chapel for a group of dissenters and provided a salary for their minister, instead of requiring them to attend the parish chapel. By 1744, the colony embodied its attitude in law: the Act of that year, while still requiring all to attend church regularly, permitted any Virginian to satisfy the law by attending the church of his choice.

When the militant, sometimes called "New Light," Presbyterians invaded Virginia in the 1740's, the Rev. Patrick Henry (uncle of the famous Patrick, and Anglican minister of the parish of St. Paul's Hanover) described their ways:

> They thunder out in awful words, and new coin'd phrases, what they call the terrors of the law, cursing & scolding, calling the old people, Greyheaded Devils, and all promiscuously, Damn'd double damn'd, whose [souls] are in hell though they are alive on earth, Lumps of hell-fire, incarnate Devils, 1000 times worse than Devils &c and all the while the Preacher exalts his voice puts himself into a violent agitation, stamping and beating his Desk unmercifully until the weaker sort of his hearers being scar'd, cry out, fall down & work like people in convulsion fits, to the amazement of spectators, and if a few only are thus brought down, the Preacher gets into a violent passion again, Calling out Will no more of you come to Christ? thundering out as before, till he has brought a quantum sufficit of his congregation to this condition, and these things are extoll'd by the Preachers as the mighty power of God's grace in their hearts, and . . .

they who don't are often condemn'd by the lump as hard-
ened wretches.

Ministers like these, he warned, would stop at nothing. "Enthusias-
tick Preachers," who said that they were "as sure of going to Heaven
at last, as if they were there already," could inspire criminals with the
confidence that no crime prevented salvation. Despite this threat to
public order, the Rev. Henry did not give up hope of domesticating
the New Lights. He even allowed one of their leaders, George
Whitefield, to preach from his pulpit—on condition that the Book
of Common Prayer be read before the sermon!

The Virginians can hardly be blamed if they trembled at revival-
ist antics. Was it tyrannical simply to require erratic preachers to
register the places of their preaching? Many refused even to do this.
The *cause célèbre* during this wild evangelical campaign was the
"case" of the Rev. Samuel Davies, whom the authorities had willingly licensed as the minister of seven meeting-houses in five different counties in 1748. But they refused to license him as minister of
any more congregations. Did he, they wondered, envisage a new
kind of itinerant absenteeism, or a network of religious agitators presided over by some super-pastor to keep them stirred up?

The so-called Separate Baptists invaded Virginia around 1767.
The Regular Baptists had lived in peace in Virginia for a decade and
were undisturbed by the law; in fact there was no record in Virginia
of a Baptist suffering any punishment for his religion until the later
Baptist itinerants came into the colony. In this new group, many
were lay preachers who were ineligible for licensing: the others, who
were ordained by their denomination, refused to obey the simple requirement that they register for licenses as ministers, and that they
list their "preaching-points" and meeting-houses. The nearly fifty
Separate Baptist preachers who were sent to jail between 1768 and
1776 were imprisoned not on ecclesiastical charges, but for "disturbing the peace" or refusing to give bond to keep the peace in the future.

"I apprehend the Gospel of Christ will justify no other than mild
and gentle arguments," Col. William Green, Culpeper County jus-

tice of the peace and a vestryman, wrote on February 7, 1767, to the Baptist minister who was preaching in his parish. "And whoever proceeds further, however fond he may be of his own Opinions, and whether he be Churchman or Anabaptist, or by whatever Name or title he may be called has not, I humbly conceive a True Christian Spirit in him." His explanation might well have been the manifesto of Virginia's "Practical godliness":

For my part, I think I Could Live in Love & Peace, with a good Man of any of the various Sects Christians; Nor do I perceive any necessity for differing or quarreling with a Man, because he may not Think exactly as I do. I might as well quarrel with him for not being of the same Size or Complexion with myself. For the different Operations of the Mind are not to be accounted for. . . . God is no Respector of persons; therefore it is a high Presumption and Folly, for us to pretend to confine God's Mercies to any particular Nation, or Sect.

Only a few months later, Col. John Blair of Williamsburg, a member of the Governor's Council, urged forbearance on his fellow Anglicans because, he said, these very Baptists had done some good: they had reformed some sinners, had brought some to repentance, and, by censuring idlers, had made them provide for their families.

In Quaker Pennsylvania, Franklin also rejoiced in the happy diversity of doctrine by which different gods led men in diverse ways to decent and productive lives. But Virginians had become accustomed to another way of thinking. Their first thought was to include all within their church: to transform the Church of Englishmen into the Church of Virginians. Their church was not a fellowship of visible saints, nor a society of the pure of conscience, nor even a communion of possessors of the True Dogma. It was a loose practical affiliation of those whose Christianity, in different and inarticulate ways, helped them to be good Englishmen and decent Virginians. It was a convenient umbrella for all men of good will.

The drama of the Rev. Patrick Henry lending his Anglican pulpit to the heterodox George Whitefield was reënacted in a thousand different ways. When confronted by the movers and ranters of the so-called Great Awakening, the Virginians' first instinct was to draw them into the Church of Virginia, to learn from them whatever was good, and to infect them with a contagious respectability and decorum. From neighboring Maryland, whose established Church was substantially indistinguishable from that of Virginia, the Rev. Hugh Jones reported in 1741 that within the Church he found "enthusiasm, deism, and libertism."

In a country without a bishop, or without even a church assembly, who would enforce orthodoxy? The religious doctrine of many of the leading Virginians, including George Washington, Thomas Jefferson, Patrick Henry, and James Madison, was nondescript. This did not mean that they were unorthodox Anglicans; no one knew for sure what one had to believe to be a good member of the Church of Virginia. They were members of a catholic church: "catholic" not in the sense that it possessed a dogma for all men (for its dogma was vague and inarticulate), but in the sense that all, excepting only fanatics and agitators, could live within it while holding their own private dogmas. This was, indeed, a foreshadowing of the interdenominationalism of 20th-century American religious life.

In England the higher clergy of the 18th century wrote books of great intellectual distinction. One of the most impoverished eras in the spiritual life of the church was one of the richest in philosophic works by churchmen; Bishop Berkeley, Bishop Butler, and Bishop Hoadley modernized theology for the battles of a new age. But as each defined his ideas and clarified his distinctions he separated himself from his neighbors. Virginia was barren of such products, not only because it had no bishops, but also because such distinctions did not interest its leaders. The very "weaknesses" of intellectual life in Virginia thus helped save the community from theological division.

The College of William & Mary was established by charter in 1693 "for the breeding of good Ministers," and its first president was Commissary James Blair, technical head of the Church of Virginia. The orthodox Anglican clergy came to think of the college as "an advantageous and laudable Nursery and strong Bulwark against the

contagious dissentions in Virginia," but it never acquired that clerical or theological orientation which some of its English founders
looked for. Instead it became a bulwark of the moderate, catholic,
and secular culture which was the life of Virginia in the 18th century.
Thirty years after the founding of the College, the Rev. Hugh Jones
prescribed the ingredients of successful clergymen in Virginia:

> They likewise should be Persons that have read and seen
> something more of the World, than what is requisite for an
> English Parish; they must be such as can converse and know
> more than bare Philosophy and speculative Ethicks, and
> have studied Men and Business in some measure as well as
> Books; they may act like Gentlemen, and be facetious and
> good-humour'd, without too much Freedom and Licen-
> tiousness; they may be good Scholars without becoming
> Cynicks, as they may be good Christians without appearing
> Stoicks. They should be such as will give up a small Matter
> rather than create Disturbance and Mischief. . . .

But from the fact that Virginia was barren of religious acrimony
we must not conclude that she was barren of religious sentiment.
Among the leaders of Virginia, religion itself nourished tolerance
and an unwillingness to contend over the dots on theological *i*'s. The
catholic and compromising spirit of their Anglican church had made
toleration a religious institution in Virginia long before its Act for
Religious Freedom. Luckily, Virginia—appropriately called "The
Old Dominion"—had become a community before the hundred-
and-one dissenting sects had separated from the Church of England,
before the 17th century had made England a jungle of religious
monstrosities. And even in the 17th century she remained happily
remote from the cut-throat enthusiasms and fanatic fervor of the
Age of the Puritans. In Virginia, moreover, there was ample time to
consolidate this catholic spirit of the Established Church.

"Persecution, religious pride, the love of contradiction," Crèvecoeur observed in late 18th-century America, "are the food of what
the world commonly calls religion. These motives have ceased here;

zeal in Europe is confined; here it evaporates in the great distance it has to travel; there it is a grain of powder inclosed, here it burns away in the open air, and consumes without effect." Moderation has too often been confused with lukewarmness. Since it is easier to measure the *odium theologicum* than the love of God, the ages and nations in which men are readiest to kill for religion acquire the reputation of being the most religious.

That liberal spirit in religion which we properly honor, and whose American patron saints were the great Virginians, need not be explained by any desire to displace tradition by something new and "enlightened." Without clericalism there cannot be anti-clericalism. The identification of the great Virginians with French "atheism" and "rationalism" was mostly accomplished long after the fact, by theological enthusiasts like Timothy Dwight who could not imagine a decent society surviving doctrinal diversity. But the life of Virginia had given the lie to library distinctions. Just as the faith of many Virginians in republican government stemmed from their happy experience with gentlemen freeholders in a planting aristocracy, so men raised under the broad Virginia Church could not be horrified by diversity of religious belief. They had seen diversity in their own well-ordered community.

THE FLUIDITY OF PROFESSIONS

CHAPTER 31

T HE AMERICAN PROVINCIAL AGE, we have already seen, was not an age of genius so much as an age of liberation. Its legacy was not great individual thinkers but refreshed community thinking. Old categories were shaken up, and new situations revealed unsuspected uses for old knowledge.

Colonial America was not the first age or place where such breaking of old molds had occurred. The Protestant Reformation in Europe had opposed the distinction between priest and layman, between the holders of the Keys to Heaven and the multitude who sought admission. But what the Reformers could accomplish was limited by their institutional inheritance. In England, for example, the ancient Universities of Oxford and Cambridge, which were to exercise such a pervasive influence on English high culture, were a legacy of the Universal Church of the middle ages, when clergymen were a different species from laymen. The mere persistence of those great Universities perpetuated many of the old distinctions, especially those between the custodians of the sacred learning and the community at large. Provincial America was free from all this; it was therefore freer to allow a new fluidity to life and thought. The universal priesthood of all believers attained a fuller expression in American ways of daily living.

By the 18th century in Europe the departments of thought had

49

been frozen into professional categories, into the private domains of different guilds, city companies, and associations of masters; and the professions separated the areas of thought. Every professional field of learning bore a "No Trespassing" sign duly erected by legal or customary authority. In the newer culture of America few such signs had been erected; from the sheer lack of organized monopolists, old monopolies could not be perpetuated. America broke down distinctions: where life was full of surprises, of unexplored wildernesses, and of unpredictable problems, its tasks could not be neatly divided for legal distribution. Any man who preferred the even tenor of his way, who wished to pursue his licensed trade without the competition of amateurs, intruders, or vagrants, or who was unwilling to do jobs for which he had not been legally certified was better off in England.

At least four decisive facts about colonial America promoted this new fluidity in man's thinking about himself and about the departments of his knowledge. These were the product of no man's foresight but of the circumstances of a New World.

Regression. When a man finds himself plunged back into the conditions of an earlier age, he inevitably discovers many things. He rediscovers forgotten uses of his tools, and learns to think about them in the cruder categories of a primitive age. The sharp stone which early man used for killing was hardly different from the one he used for cutting, but in more developed cultures there arose a distinction between "weapon" and "tool" as each of them became a more specialized implement. Thus, in 18th-century Europe, the firearm became primarily a weapon; but for the colonial American backwoodsman, who had to protect himself and his family from marauding savages and who often shot meat for his table, the distinction between *weapon* and *tool* once again had little meaning. What was true of implements was also true of institutions and occupations. Under primitive conditions, there seem to have been few distinctions among those who practiced the different modes of healing and curing—between the man who muttered the incantation, the man who inserted the knife, and the man who mixed the potion. But in 18th-century England all these tasks were distinguished: each had become the private preserve of a different group—the barber-surgeons, the doctors of physick, and the apothecaries. In America such distinctions would have been difficult to preserve; the healer (sometimes a lawyer or a governor or a clergyman) once again performed all these different tasks.

Versatility required by the unexpected. Where the round of daily life has been worn into a groove by many generations living in the same place, men can prepare simply for the tasks which their ancestors have faced before them. But not in a New World. Here the unexpected was usual, and men had to be ready for it. The layman had to be prepared to act the lawyer, the architect, and the physician, and to practice crafts which others (only to be found across the ocean) knew much better. Versatility was no longer merely a virtue; it was a necessity. The man who could not be a little bit of everything was not qualified to be an American.

The scarcity of institutions. Where institutions were scarce, they could not be sharply distinguished from each other. Even the priests of different religions gradually tended to become assimilated. Puritanism gradually became less puritanical; Episcopalianism became less bishoply and more congregational; and religions like Quakerism which would not compromise with the New World could not long govern in it. "Thus all sects are mixed as well as all nations," remarked Crèvecoeur in 1782, "thus religious indifference is imperceptibly disseminated from one end of the continent to the other; which is at present one of the strongest characteristics of the Americans. Where this will reach no one can tell. . . ."

The last serious colonial effort to set up a guild in the medieval mold took place in Philadelphia in 1718. Next to the occupational guilds, the most important agencies for monopolizing knowledge in the Old World had been the ancient educational institutions. But those too were lacking in America, and the New World thawed the categories of thought.

Labor-scarcity and land-plenty. Labor and skills were scarce in colonial America; men had to do many things for themselves simply because they could not hire others to do them. Inevitably they came to set a lower standard, for otherwise a task could not have been done at all. The carpenter had to be cooper, cabinetmaker, and cobbler. The printer became writer, paper-manufacturer, binder, ink-maker, postmaster, and public figure. Land-plenty meant that even as a farmer the American generally needed to be much less efficient in order to make a living. Where men could "use up" their land, where they took for granted large tracts in reserve for the future, they lacked an incentive which prodded 18th-century English agriculture to reforms. Where everything, including the old homestead, was for sale, men were less attached to any particular piece of land. Once it ceased to support them, they would move on. Land itself lost many of its ancient legal and social peculiarities. The making of a living here required less specialization. At least for free white colonials, there were many different ways of earning a living and it was easy to change one's trade or the place where one practiced it.

"Strangers are welcome," Franklin explained in his *Information to those who would remove to America* (1782), "because there is room enough for them all, and therefore the old Inhabitants are not jealous of them." Since land was cheap, any diligent young man could rise. "Hence there is a continual Demand for more Artisans of all the necessary and useful kinds, to supply those Cultivators of the Earth with Houses, and with Furniture and Utensils of the grosser sorts, which cannot so well be brought from Europe. Tolerably good Workmen in any of those mechanic Arts are sure to find Employ, and to be well paid for their Work, there being no Restraints preventing Strangers from exercising any Art they understand, nor any Permission necessary." In America, he observed, everyone might hope and expect to become a Master, for any industrious young man could secure an apprenticeship which might have been too expensive for him in Europe. "In America, the rapid Increase of Inhabitants takes away that Fear of Rivalship, and Artisans willingly receive Apprentices from the hope of Profit by their Labour, during the Remainder of the Time stipulated, after they shall be instructed. Hence it is easy for poor Families to get their Children instructed; for the Artisans are so desirous of Apprentices, that many of them will even give Money to the Parent, to have Boys from Ten to Fifteen Years of Age bound Apprentices to them till the Age of Twenty-one; and many poor Parents have, by the means, on their Arrival in the Country, raised Money enough to buy Land sufficient to establish themselves, and to subsist the rest of their Family by Agriculture."

* * *

A new and fruitful social vagueness thus came into being in America. The ancient, familiar, and respectable idea of a "calling" had been displaced by the idea of opportunity. Historians in recent years have written a great deal about the change which supposedly occurred in Europe at the time of the Protestant Reformation. In contrast to the medieval Catholic view, according to Max Weber, all Protestant denominations took a novel view of men's occupations. This new view, says R. H. Tawney, required a man to give thought to his "choice" of a calling. But, in fact, European life offered very little choice to most men; they had no freedom but to perform the tasks to which their own family station assigned them. In Europe to hallow a man's "calling" was simply to sanctify his efficiency in his traditional job.

Few American men dared look to their inherited stations to define their callings. They had to look to their opportunities, to the unforeseen openings of the American situation. Where a rapid-flowing life informed a man of his tasks, he would be lost if he anchored himself to any fixed role. No prudent man dared be too certain of exactly who he was or what he was about; everyone had to be prepared to become someone else. To be ready for such perilous transmigrations was to become an American.

CULTURE BY THE BOOK:

The Spelling Fetish

CHAPTER 43

THE MOST INFLUENTIAL American writer on language was Noah Webster, Spelling-Master to America. The colossal popularity of his spellers—they had sold over sixty millions before the end of the 19th century—was both a symptom and a symbol of the mobility of American society. Webster's *American Spelling Book*, "containing an easy Standard of Pronunciation," appeared in 1789, but the demand it met, as Webster himself noted, had long been there.

In America there flourished a ritual or game which popularized the effort to make "proper" speech accessible to all. This was the spelling-bee; and the word "bee" in this sense was appropriately an Americanism. In this public ceremony contestants and audience bore witness that there was no secret about how to speak or write the most "correct" language of the community and hence that the linguistic upper class was open to all. The spelling-bee was already familiar, especially in New England, in the time of the Revolution. As early as 1750, Franklin had proposed a public competitive game of spelling; by the latter half of the 18th century spelling matches had become well-established in the schools. In rural communities and on the western frontier, where spelling was especially valued as a symbol of culture, the institution took on a new life in the 19th century, described, for example, in Bret Harte's "Spelling Bee at Angels." There we learn from Truthful James:

Thar's a new game down in Frisco, that ez far ez I can see
Beats euchre, poker, and van-toon, they calls the "Spellin' Bee."

At the particular bee which Bret Harte describes, all went peacefully—even through the spelling of *separate, parallel,* and *rhythm*—but the miners finally found it necessary to settle the spelling of *gneiss* by a fight with bowie knives.

Emphasis on "rules" of proper speaking and writing profoundly influenced the whole American attitude toward pronunciation. It explains what is still perhaps the most important distinction between English and American pronunciation, the American tendency toward "spelling-pronunciation." Very early, Americans began trying to discover how a word "ought" to be pronounced by seeing how it was spelled. This seemed to provide a ready standard of pronunciation in a land without a cultural capital or a ruling intellectual aristocracy.

We have become so accustomed to our own equation of spelling and pronunciation that we find it hard to imagine that a tendency to pronounce by custom rather than by spelling may have been an older and more "literary" tradition. Yet that seems to have been the case. The casual way of pronouncing which followed caste and custom and not the spelling-book had long prevailed in the English of England.

Our insistent spelling-pronunciation shows itself in our habit of preserving the full value of syllables. In long words like *secretary, explanatory, laboratory,* and *cemetery,* we preserve the full value of all, including the next-to-last syllable, while the English almost drop that syllable and say "secret'ry," "explanat'ry, "laborat'ry," and "cemet'ry." These are only a few examples of the American insistence on giving every spelled syllable its fully pronounced due. Some of these cases turn out to be historically complicated by the fact that the secondary accent we have preserved in the next-to-last syllable of a word like *secretary* seems also to have been characteristic of 17th- and 18th-century spoken English. But while in England these syllables have tended to become lost, in America they have been studiously preserved. This would not alter the argument but would simply show that American spelling-pronunciation, like much else in our speech, is conservative. Our deference to spelling as a guide to pronunciation has been so strong that we have kept alive here ways of speech which soon died in England. The ritual of the spelling-bee also tended to preserve the full pronounced values of syllables, and to promote literalness in pronunciation. In the early days, spelling was taught by reading a word aloud from the Speller letter by letter and syllable by syllable: "o, r—or; d, i—di; n, a—na; r, y—ry; ordinary." Students who had been taught the language in this fashion (often under the incentive of team competition) would be apt to remain careful, deliberate, and literal in pronunciation for the rest of their lives. Our weakness for spelling-pronunciation affected the pronunciation of proper names, and especially the names of places. In England these had a purely traditional and casual pronunciation, but Americans who hear *Worcester* pronounced *Wooster* are apt to spell it that way; and *Birmingham* is fully and carefully pronounced, never in the elided English manner.

The "Dictatorship of the Schoolmarm," often attacked by sophisticated students, has dampened our ebullience and ingenuity. But the Schoolmarm, like her predecessor the Schoolmaster, by declaring teachable rules of language has helped dissolve class distinctions and has kept one more avenue open in a mobile society. Who could have predicted that a free and equalitarian society would be promoted by a pedantically precise standard of language?

H. L. Mencken has summed up the wider meaning of the special precision of American speech:

> It may be described briefly as the influence of a class but lately risen in the social scale and hence a bit unsure of itself—a class intensely eager to avoid giving away its vulgar origin by its speech habits. . . . Precision in speech thus became the hall-mark of those who had but recently arrived. Obviously, the number of those who have but recently arrived has always been greater in the United States than in England, not only among the aristocracy of wealth and fashion but also among the *intelligentsia*. The average American schoolmarm, the chief guardian of linguistic niceness in the Republic, does not come from the class that has a tradition

of culture behind it, but from the class of small farmers and city clerks and workmen. This is true, I believe, even of the average American college teacher. Such persons do not advocate and practise precision in speech on logical grounds alone; they are also moved, plainly enough, by the fact that it tends to conceal their own cultural insecurity. From them come most of the gratuitous rules and regulations that afflict schoolboys and harass the writers of the country. They are the chief discoverers and denouncers of 'bad English' in the books of such men as Whitman, Mark Twain and Howells. But it would be a mistake to think of their influence as wholly, or even as predominantly evil. They have thrown themselves valiantly against the rise of dialects among us, and with such success that nothing so grossly unpleasant to the ear as the cockney whine or so lunatic as the cockney manhandling of the *h* is now prevalent anywhere in the United States. And they have policed the general speech to such effect that even on its most pretentious levels it is virtually free from the silly affectations which still mark Standard English.

In this particular way, the American language has expressed both the *literate* and the *non-literary* character of American culture. A printed standard presupposes widespread literacy; the Dictatorship of the Schoolmarm would never have been possible unless everybody in the country had come under her jurisdiction through universal public education. Moreover, if America had had a powerful centralized literary aristocracy able to set up its casual practice as the criterion for the speech of all cultivated men, textbook standards of precision would have been superfluous and impossible. Literacy displaces aristocracy. Students of language note that the tendency to make the spoken conform with the written form of a word "in general grows as the printed and written aspects of language become more prominent in the language consciousness of a people." While there has been some such tendency in England, it has been much stronger in America. "Each new group of American citizens," Krapp observes, "has entered into possession of the language not as a natural inheritance, not as a privilege, but as an acquisition, as something to be gained through intelligent application and study." Through learning to read, write, and speak the common language many peoples were amalgamated into a single nation.

The early New England settlers, middle-class and literate, champions of the common school, had a good deal to do with establishing uniformity in the first place. The Yankee schoolmaster, like the Yankee peddler, traveled widely, and both carried the spelling-book, the yardstick of linguistic respectability. In the early 19th century, a New England storekeeper could list for sale "Everything: whiskey, molasses, calicoes, spelling-books, and patent gridirons." Noah Webster profited handsomely from the fact that the uniformity of the American language depended on schooling and universal literacy. "Nothing but the establishment of schools and some uniformity in the use of books [preferably Webster's Speller!]," he argued in his *Dissertations on the English Language* (1789), "can annihilate differences in speaking and preserve the purity of the American tongue." But this would not have been possible without a high standard of living and of literacy:

> Let Englishmen take notice that when I speak of the American yeomanry, the latter are not to be compared to the illiterate peasantry of their own country. The yeomanry of this country consist of substantial independent freeholders, masters of their own persons and lords of their own soil. These men have considerable education. They not only learn to read, write and keep accounts; but a vast proportion of them read newspapers every week, and besides the Bible, which is found in all families, they read the best English sermons and treatises upon religion, ethics, geography and history; such as the works of Watts, Addison, Atterbury, Salmon, &c. In the eastern states, there are public schools sufficient to instruct every man's children, and most of the children are actually benefited by these institutions.

Webster obviously had great faith in a printed, external standard for language. Having made his fortune out of a spelling-book, he could hardly have been expected to believe otherwise. "To reform the abuses and corruption which, to an unhappy degree, tincture the conversation of the polite part of the Americans . . . and especially to render the pronunciation . . . accurate and uniform by demolishing those obvious distinctions of provincial dialects which are the subject of reciprocal ridicule in different states"—so read Webster's petition for copyright for his textbooks, and the introduction to his spellers.

At the same time that Webster legislated on language, he disclaimed the purpose of a legislator. All such legislation was superfluous, he said, because the real authority in matters of language was the American people. This was doubtless one of the things Webster meant when in the preface to his Dictionary he quoted Franklin: "Those people spell best who do not know how to spell." The trouble with most earlier (and especially English) writers on language, according to Webster, was that they tried to dictate, and "instead of examining to find what the English language *is*, they endeavor to show what it *ought to be* according to their rules." In contrast to this, Webster declared for himself, "The *general practice* of a nation is the rule of propriety, and this practice should at least be consulted in so important a matter, as that of making laws for speaking." His standards he found in "the rules of the language itself": or, in a phrase which he could not repeat often enough, in "the general practice of the nation."

A democratic respect for folkways was possible, Webster observed in his *Dissertations,* only in a country of social equality. In England, he explained, the appeal to general usage (the only true purifier and enlivener of language) was impossible for the simple reason that there a small isolated aristocracy, arrogant of its privileges, had elevated its own peculiarities.

While all men are upon a footing and no singularities are accounted vulgar or ridiculous, every man enjoys perfect liberty. But when a particular set of men, in exalted situations, undertake to say, "we are the standards of propriety and elegance, and if all men do not conform to our practice, they shall be accounted vulgar and ignorant," they take a very great liberty with the rules of the language and the rights of civility.

But an attempt to fix a standard on the practice of any particular class of people is highly absurd: As a friend of mine once observed, it is like fixing a light house on a floating island. It is an attempt to fix that which is in itself variable; at least it must be variable so long as it is supposed that a local practice has no standard but a local practice; that is, no standard but itself. . . .

But this is not all. If the practice of a few men in the capital is to be the standard, a knowledge of this must be communicated to the whole nation. Who shall do this? An able compiler perhaps attempts to give this practice in a dictionary; but it is probable that the pronunciation, even at court, or on the stage, is not uniform. The compiler therefore must follow his particular friends and patrons; in which case he is sure to be opposed and the authority of his standard called in question; or he must give two pronunciations as the standard, which leaves the student in the same uncertainty as it found him. Both these events have actually taken place in England, with respect to the most approved standards; and of course no one is universally followed.

The appeal to an aristocratic standard in language was thus only one example of the general error of elevating local practice into a general rule.

Variations in pronunciation over the American continent seemed to him no objection at all to making the "universal practice" of Americans the standard for the country. In his Speller he purported simply to give voice to this universal practice. "I have no system of my own to offer," he insisted. "General custom must be the rule of speaking, and every deviation from this must be wrong. The dialect of one State is as ridiculous as that of another; each is authorized by local custom; and neither is supported by any superior excellence." The standard for an American language would be distilled somehow from the very air of America.

Even before the Revolution, as the English editor of David Ramsay's *History of the American Revolution* (1791) noted, the American language had acquired a standard of its own. This dialectless language of the New World was to become more uniform and more universal than any yet known to Western man. Time would prove that Webster had spoken with the cryptic voice of prophecy when he urged that "we should adhere to our own practice and general customs." From these we would develop a standard American language, a language which, as Krapp says, "has grown, and is growing, in a thousand different places, by mixture, by compromise, by imitation, by adaptation, by all the devices by which a changing people in changing circumstances adapt themselves to each other and to their new conditions." Americans would show enthusiasm both for linguistic legislation and for linguistic folkways. Just as in their attitude to all other laws, Americans would combine a naïve faith in legislation with a profound reverence for ancient customs and the common law. This alchemy of opposites which gave vitality to our written Federal Constitution also gave vitality to our language.

Precisely because no part of our culture is more plainly borrowed, no other part could so well reveal the peculiarities of American life. James Fenimore Cooper summed up the development in his *Notions of the Americans* in 1828:

> That the better company of London must set the fashion for the pronunciation of words in England, and indeed for the whole English empire, is quite plain; for, as this very company, comprises all those whose manners, birth, fortune, and political distinction, make them the objects of admiration, it becomes necessary to imitate their affectations, whether of speech or air, in order to create the impression that one belongs to their society. . . .
>
> There exists a very different state of things in America. If we had a great capital, like London, where men of leisure, and fortune, and education periodically assembled to amuse

themselves, I think we should establish a fashionable aristocracy, too, which should give the mode to the forms of speech
as well as to that of dress and deportment. . . . we have no
such capital, nor are we likely, for a long time to come, to
have one of sufficient magnitude to produce any great effect
on the language. . . . The habits of polite life, and even the
pronunciation of Boston, of New York, of Baltimore, and of
Philadelphia, vary in many things, and a practised ear may
tell a native of either of these places, from a native of any one
of the others, by some little peculiarity of speech. There is
yet no predominating influence to induce the fashionables
of these towns to wish to imitate the fashionables of any
other. . . .
If the people of this country were like the people of any
other country on earth, we should be speaking at this moment a great variety of nearly unintelligible patois; but, in
point of fact, the people of the United States, with the exception of a few of German and French descent, speak, as a
body, an incomparably better English than the people of the
mother country. . . . In fine, we speak our language, as a nation, better than any other people speak their language.
When one reflects on the immense surface of country that
we occupy, the general accuracy, in pronunciation and in the
use of words, is quite astonishing. This resemblance in
speech can only be ascribed to the great diffusion of intelligence, and to the inexhaustible activity of the population,
which, in a manner, destroys space.

Here, in place of the "King's English," there had developed a "People's English," peculiarly suited to a country without a capital, where
everybody was privileged to speak like an aristocrat.

THE RISE OF THE NEWSPAPER

T HE AMERICAN PRINTER was the servant of literacy rather than of literature. While he produced few literary books, his presses turned out countless other items more urgently needed for business and government. In these he was at least the equal of his English contemporaries. His job was not the same as that which tradition and aristocracy had cut out for his fellow-craftsmen on the other side of the ocean.

The colonists, as we have seen, possessed a ready-made body of belles-lettres which they simply imported from the mother-country, and the leading books of English literature were probably just as available in the principal colonial cities as in the English provincial towns. If a printer could import and sell a book from London, why should he strain to produce an inferior and more expensive colonial edition? Colonial printers did not produce a complete Bible in English until 1782, but by 1663 they had already issued over a thousand copies of John Eliot's famous translation of the Bible "into the Indian tongue." Bibles in English could easily enough be procured from England, but the Indian translation essential to New England's mission could be had nowhere else. The American printer was left free to serve the special needs of his community. Jefferson, with some exaggeration, boasted that, while Americans were saved from the "swarm of nonsense" which issued from the European presses, they were far ahead of Europe in the production of useful scientific matter.

As we shall see, it was the needs of the colonial governments that supported printers in the beginning. Also, the dispersion of government into several colonial capitals very early diffused agencies of literacy and of public information. The printing press did not spread generally into English provincial towns until after 1693, when the last restriction acts finally expired; there were still no presses in such English towns as Liverpool, Birmingham, and Leeds. But, by the end of that year in the American colonies, presses had already appeared in Cambridge, Boston, St. Mary's City (in Maryland), Philadelphia, and New York. If each colony had had to wait for presses until the demand for books or for commercial printing produced an adequate income, many decades would have passed, but American presses were flourishing by the mid-18th century. Everywhere they owed their first establishment to government subsidy. In 1762 when Georgia, the last of the thirteen colonies to acquire a press, attracted James Johnston to Savannah as government printer, there were already about forty presses operating throughout the colonies.

In the earliest years the bulk of what issued from the presses was government work: statutes and the votes and proceedings of colonial assemblies. The first item printed in English America was not a poem or a sermon; it was a printed legal form, the Freeman's Oath of 1639. Legal and commercial forms were a staple commodity, for their demand did not fluctuate with the tides of literary taste. When Franklin opened his stationer's shop in about 1730, his first stock included many such blanks, which his *Autobiography* modestly describes as "the correctest that ever appear'd among us." The numerous colonial governments, each with its own regulations and its own system of courts and records, multiplied the number of forms required.

Poor Richard's fame has overshadowed the myriad other almanacs which served daily needs; every ambitious colonial printer issued his own. Almanacs offered an 18th-century American farmer the services now performed by agricultural extension, urban newspapers, magazines, radio, and television. The hours of the rising and setting of the sun, the cycles of the moon and the tide, and the prospects of weather were the time-table of his life—as necessary to him as the railroad schedule to a modern commuter. For many a farmer, the almanac was the most important printed matter he possessed other than the Bible. It told him the dates of court-sessions and the schedules of post-riders, coaches, and packet-boats. It combined features of *Better Homes and Gardens*, *Popular Mechanics*, and *The Reader's Digest*. It contained practical hints, like the recipe offered in Jonas Green's *Almanack for the Year 1760* "by which Meat, ever so stinking, may be made as sweet and wholesome, in a few Minutes, as any Meat at all." Few printers failed to offer sage, if shopworn, advice, and special thoughts for "the solitary dwellings of the poor and illiterate, where the studied ingenuity of the learned writer never comes." Old issues were preserved, to pass the long winter days, to amuse the overnight guest, or to use for notebooks and accounts. A thumbed-over accumulation of a dozen or more back numbers, with their ever-relevant snippets of advice, information, and literary gems, became the staple of remote readers. Almanacs spread up-to-date political information, opinion, and arguments in the years just before the Revolution.

While no printer could make his mark without publishing an almanac, the larger income and future lay with the newspaper. The account-books of Franklin's printing partnership (1748–65) with David Hall show that income from the *Pennsylvania Gazette* in this period was much the largest single item (over sixty per cent) of their business; the remainder was about equally divided between public and job printing and miscellaneous publishing, including *Poor Richard's Almanack*. While the size of Franklin's business was unusual, its proportions were probably typical—a heavy emphasis on contemporary and topical works, a meager list of "literature." Before the end of the 18th century, an English observer who had made a survey of American printed matter could report:

The newspapers of Massachusetts, Connecticut, Rhode Island, Pennsylvania, and Maryland, are unequalled, whether considered with respect to wit and humour, entertainment or instruction. Every capital town on the continent prints a weekly paper, and several of them have one or more daily papers.

In the early decades of the 18th century, when the first English provincial newspapers were being printed, newspapers had already become a familiar institution in the American colonial capitals. By 1730 seven newspapers were being published regularly in four colonies; by 1800 there were over 180. The *New York Gazette or Weekly Post Boy* boasted (April 16, 1770):

> 'Tis truth (with deference to the college)
> News-papers are the spring of knowledge,
> The general source throughout the nation,
> Of every modern conversation.
> What would this mighty people do,
> If there, alas! were nothing new?
> A news-paper is like a feast,
> Some dish there is for every guest;
> Some large, some small, some strong, some tender,
> For every stomach, stout or slender.

At the end of the 18th century, the Rev. Samuel Miller noted that although the population of the United States was but half that of Britain, the number of newspapers circulating here annually, estimated at over twelve million, was more than two-thirds the number circulated in the mother country. "The Reading Time of most People," Franklin wrote from Philadelphia in 1786, "is of late so taken up with News Papers and little periodical Pamphlets, that few now-a-days venture to attempt reading a Quarto Volume."

This precocious development of the American newspaper was in some ways merely a colonial expression of what was also taking place in England, but it was further stimulated by many local circumstances: the spread of literacy, the extent of the country, the existence of several capitals each with its own political news, and the competition among a number of seaboard cities. Much that Americans said about their reading habits was patriotic exaggeration, but there were plenty of facts to confirm the Rev. Samuel Miller's portrait of America about 1785:

> A spectacle never before displayed among man, and even yet without a parallel on earth. It is the spectacle, not of the learned and the wealthy only, but of the great body of the people; even a large portion of that class of the community which is destined to daily labor, having free and constant access to public prints, receiving regular information of every occurrence, attending to the course of political affairs, discussing public measures, and having thus presented to them constant excitements to the acquisition of knowledge, and continual means of obtaining it. Never, it may be safely asserted, was the number of political journals so great in proportion to the population of a country as at present in ours. Never were they, all things considered, so cheap, so universally diffused, and so easy of access.

The most appropriate literary expression of an American life so shifting, so full of novelty, motion, and variety was the kaleidoscopic, ephemeral, miscellaneous newspaper. A newspaper has to be useful and relevant, but it cannot require long study or concentration; it must be literate, but it cannot separate the artistic and expressive from the commercial and productive areas of living. It must mix public and private; it must take the community into account, but with a view to action and the specific event rather than to the universal principle. The newspapers were a symbol of how America broke down all distinctions. "They have become the means of conveying, to every class in society," a contemporary printer observed, "innumerable scraps of knowledge, which have at once increased the public intelligence, and extended the taste for perusing periodical publications."

In saving newspapers from becoming too "literary" nothing was more important than the advertisement, which tied it to daily commercial concerns. "The advertisements, moreover, which they daily contain, respecting new books, projects, inventions, discoveries and improvements," Isaiah Thomas, the colonial printer-historian explained, "are well calculated to enlarge and enlighten the public mind, and are worthy of being enumerated among the many methods of awakening and maintaining the popular attention, with which more modern times, beyond all preceding example, abound." Very early the American newspaper had to justify itself as a commodity rather than as a purveyor of orthodoxy. While in France Robespierre and Mirabeau each owned his own newspaper to address his constituents, this was not the American style. Jefferson indignantly denied any control over the press that defended his point of view. Only for an interlude of about a half-century after 1790 was the American press dominated by a bitterly partisan spirit. For most of the history of American journalism, the independence and high quality of the American press have been tied instead to the commercial spirit and the need to offer his money's worth to a purchaser in the open market.

While the earliest American magazines bore some mark of their locality, they were far less essential than the newspaper to the round of daily life. And so they were slower to flourish on the American scene. The magazine, like the book, is a "mixed" literary form, containing miscellaneous entertainment and instruction; it approaches the book in format, in permanence of interest, and in demands made on the printer. Its unprecedented success in America did not come for another century and a half, when it became a sign of the pervasively literate though emphatically non-literary character of our culture. In 18th-century England the magazine still bore the flavor of that small circle of literati for whom it was designed.

Not until 1741 did the first American magazine with a continuous history begin to appear. Until the era of the Revolution, American magazines were few, short-lived (the longest had lasted three years), and pallid. It was almost the end of the 18th century before a viable, widely distributed, distinctively American magazine made its appearance. Most early American magazines frankly imitated the English *Gentleman's Magazine* and *London Magazine;* they were, as Frank Luther Mott says, little more than "British magazines published in the Colonies." Their lack of literary invention was impressive; they seem to have been composed primarily with the scissors rather than with the pen. American periodicals were in the habit of copying at least three-fourths of their content from other (mostly English) books, pamphlets, newspapers, and magazines—a means of composition easier in the days before copyright made plagiarism disrespectable.

WHY COLONIAL PRINTED MATTER WAS CONSERVATIVE

CHAPTER 51

W HEN PRINTING PRESSES, type-fonts, paper, and ink had to be imported, when land transportation was crude and cities were few, no man could own or operate a printing press without the knowledge and assent of the government. Never was the press more effectively controlled than during the earliest years of the American colonies. One did not find in this vast unsettled country those "secret presses" which in England tantalized and enraged the authorities during the 17th century.

In none of the colonies was there anything that would today be recognized as "freedom of the press." By 1686 the English government was including in its regular instructions to provincial governors the following paragraph:

And forasmuch as great inconvenience may arise by the liberty of printing within our said territory under your government you are to provide by all necessary orders that no person keep any printing-press for printing, nor that any book pamphlet or other matters whatsoever be printed without your especial leave and license first obtained.

This control remained among the legal duties of royal governors as long as there were royal governors in the thirteen colonies. Although difficult or imprudent to enforce, the power was in the background and must have deterred colonial printers.

Authorities were still impressed by the great power for irresponsible attack which a press could put in any man's hands. The European governing classes would no more have thought of leaving the manufacture of explosive printed matter unregulated than they would have permitted the unlicensed manufacture of gunpowder or the raising of private armies. In America control was exercised, sometimes in one way, sometimes in another, and the need to censor varied with the flow of events. But one fact is clear: the traditional European idea of monopolizing the press to cement the social order was successfully transplanted to American shores. American circumstances made that control even more effective than it had been in England.

Between 1639 and 1763, more than half the imprints of American presses came from New England, and all but a small number of these were printed in and around Boston. The Massachusetts press restrictions were therefore one of the largest single influences of the early age. For two decades after the establishment of the first printing-press in Massachusetts in 1638, there was no official board of censorship, but the meager output of the Cambridge press included not a single item that could have displeased the magistrates. Disputes within the community—such as the Anne Hutchinson affair or the demand for legal reform led by Dr. Robert Child—produced no printed matter in Massachusetts to support the discontented. The Cambridge press was supervised by the president of Harvard College. In 1662 the Massachusetts legislature, worried by "incendiaries of commonwealths," passed an Act "for prevention of irregularities & abuse to the authority of this country by the printing presse," and the law set up a board to censor all copy before it went to press. The story of printing in colonial Massachusetts, then, is simply a tale of different forms and degrees of control. Censorship was strictly enforced until about 1685, somewhat more laxly for the next forty years. After 1723, the colonial government did not exercise its control by censoring manuscripts before they went to press but by frequent threats of prosecution (and occasional actual prosecutions) under the extensive law of libel.

In England during these years, the increase of population, the multiplication of presses, and the rise of liberal ideas had made government control of the press harder to enforce. But government control of the press remained effective in Massachusetts. Because Massachusetts was a colonial government acting under its own laws, the lapses in the English law of censorship (as for a period after 1679) and even the expiration of all English censorship laws in 1695 did not have the same permissive effect on the American side. Censorship (that is, control *before* publication), though somewhat relaxed, continued in Massachusetts Bay for another quarter-century. Thus, when the *News-Letter*, the first regular newspaper in America, appeared in Boston on April 24, 1705, it carried the insignia of censorship already obsolete in England: the tell-tale phrase "published by authority." The Governor's Council continued to maintain an unquestioned right to suppress offensive printed matter.

Effective press control continued into the era of the Revolution. In 1770, during the early stages of the Revolutionary agitation in Massachusetts, the English Lords of the Council for Plantation Affairs complained that the colonial government had failed to punish "seditious and libellous publications." The Massachusetts Governor's Council replied that, within the constitutional limits, it had actually been more successful than the House of Lords had been in England. "Why is there not a charge against the House of Lords . . . that they do not suppress those seditious and libellous publications at home? If we have any amongst us, there are fifty in England to one here." Nevertheless, the Council tried to vindicate itself by starting libel prosecutions against offensive printers. By the time of the Revolution, suppression of opposition presses was an established practice; freedom of printing had acquired no general support, nor had it become fixed in the habits of the community. Therefore, as the Revolutionary spirit rose in Boston, the radical party used mob terror against writers and printers who dared defend King and Parliament. When Massachusetts drew up its new consittution in 1778, it included a declaration in favor of freedom of the press, but the declaration was rhetorical and ambiguous, probably because of widespread doubts of the wisdom of such a novel institution. During the

War, when all publications unfavorable to the Revolutionary movement were suppressed, there was no effective freedom of the press.
After peace came, political leaders in Massachusetts demanded, not a
"free press," but return to a "well-regulated" press.

John Adams, for example, had long argued that "license of the
press is no proof of liberty." As early as 1774, when a defender of the
British cause argued that the Revolutionary accusations of tyranny
were unfounded because the most diverse opinions were allowed to
be published in Massachusetts, Adams complained of "the scandalous license of the tory presses." "There is nothing in the world so
excellent that it may not be abused. . . . When a people are corrupted, the press may be made an engine to complete their ruin; and
it is now notorious, that the ministry are daily employing it, to increase and establish corruption, and to pluck up virtue by the roots. . . .
and the freedom of the press, instead of promoting the cause of liberty, will but hasten its destruction." It is not surprising that John
Adams and his fellow Federalist leaders in Massachusetts favored the
Alien and Sedition Acts of 1798; they were worried only that the laws
might not be effective. "If there is ever to be an amelioration of the
condition of mankind," Adams was still warning two decades later,
"philosophers, theologians, legislators, politicians and moralists will
find that the regulation of the press is the most difficult, dangerous,
and important problem they have to resolve. Mankind cannot now
be governed without it, nor at present with it."

In colonial Massachusetts, ruling clergymen, like the Mathers in
their heyday, had found ways outside the law to enforce their standards. When Increase Mather wrote a book in 1700 attacking the
practices of a church newly established in the colony by the Rev.
Benjamin Colman and his friends, the accused minister prepared a
reply, but to secure its publication he had to send his manuscript to
New York. "The Reader is desired to take Notice," Colman's
pamphlet explained, "that the Press in Boston is so much under the
aw of the Reverend Author, whom we answer, and his Friends, that
we could not obtain of the Printer there to print the following
Sheets, which is the only true Reason why we have sent the Copy so
far for its Impression and where it [is] printed with some Difficulty."

Bartholomew Green, the Boston printer, explained the good commercial reason behind his refusal: the last time he had done a printing job without advance government approval, he had been required to revise and reprint it before publication to meet official criticism.

Printing began under government sponsorship in all the colonies. The press was supposed to be a prop for existing institutions; where there was danger that it might serve another purpose, authorities preferred no press at all. "I thank God, we have not free schools nor printing," Sir William Berkeley, governor of Virginia for thirty-eight years, boasted in 1671, "and I hope we shall not have these hundred years. For learning has brought disobedience and heresy and sects into the world; and printing has divulged them and libels against the government. God keep us from both." Some Virginia leaders of the next century did not share Berkeley's enthusiasm for illiteracy, but for many years his modest ambitions for Virginia were fulfilled at least with regard to the press. In 1682, the government received its first scare from a press and printer imported by John Buckner, rich landowner and merchant of Gloucester County, whose offense was to print some of the colony's laws without authority. Buckner was called before the Governor and Council, was ordered to cease his subversive activities, and "for prevention of all troubles and inconveniences, that may be occasioned thorow the liberty of a presse" was required to post bond for his good behavior. In 1683 the King of England ordered that to prevent any such "troubles and inconvenience" in the future, the Governor of Virginia should "provide by all necessary orders and Directions that no person be permitted to use any press for printing upon any occasion whatsoever." Until 1730, when William Parks set up shop in Williamsburg, there was no printing press in Virginia. From then until 1766 Virginia had only a single press and that was the official organ of the government. "I do not know that the publication of newspapers was ever prohibited in Virginia," Jefferson recalled many years later. "Until the beginning of our revolutionary disputes, we had but one press, and that having the whole business of the government, and no competitor for public favor, nothing disagreeable to the governor could be got into it."

Outside of Boston, the two leading colonial printing centers were Philadelphia and New York City. In both places, the right of the authorities to control printed matter—if not by censorship, then by libel prosecutions and by legislative censure—continued to be recognized at least until the Revolution. In Philadelphia, William Bradford, who was Pennsylvania's first printer (first imprint: 1686), was in continual trouble with the government and the Society of Friends, usually for the most trivial indiscretions. Finally, in 1693, when he was prosecuted for publishing a tract on one side of an internal Quaker dispute, he left the colony in disgust and became the royal printer in New York. For the next half-dozen years, there was no press at all in Philadelphia. William Bradford's son, Andrew, who returned to Philadelphia and became the official "Printer to the Province" in 1719, was only slightly more successful than his father in satisfying the authorities. Libel trials and suppression of the opposition press were common there until the eve of the Revolution.

Much the same story is told of New York, which did not begin to rival Boston or Philadelphia as a source of printed matter until after 1760. The famous case of John Peter Zenger (1734–35), which affirmed the power of juries in libel cases to decide the law as well as the fact, is important in retrospect and as a landmark of legal doctrine. But it was not a turning point in the practices of the community; even after the Zenger case, the question in New York was not whether the press should be "well-regulated" but who should have the power of regulation. Zenger's reward for his vindication in the trial which made him a hero in later histories of freedom of the press, was his appointment to the monopoly of "Publick Printer" in 1737. Twenty years later another printer, Hugh Gaine, was brought to the bar of the Assembly and reprimanded; he "humbly asked their Pardon" but still was required to pay costs—all for the offense of printing part of the public proceedings of the representative body! James Parker, Printer to the General Assembly of New York, obeyed Governor Clinton's ban in 1747 on publishing the Assembly's remonstrance against the Governor; although the next year he dared to print it among the Assembly's votes. But within a decade, in 1756, the Assembly itself declared Parker "guilty of a high Misdemeanor and a Contempt of the Authority of this House" for printing an article critical of them in his newspaper. And so it went.

It was not only by government control, by censorship, and by threat of libel prosecution that the American colonial press was confined. The earliest American presses owed their very existence to the colonial governments, a fact which inevitably affected the character of printers and the output of their shops: government support meant government control. In these scattered colonial communities—where what little passion there was for literature could be satisfied with books imported from the mother country—the introduction of printing presses might have been delayed for decades if it had depended on the market for polite literature. But soon after the first settlements, each government needed a printing press to circulate proclamations and laws, to provide copies of debates, proceedings, decisions, and votes to the members of the governors' councils and representative assemblies, and to supply the legal forms needed every day. Even in the earliest years of each colony, when the market for commercial printing was small, the demand for locally printed books non-existent, and the market for newspapers and periodicals still undeveloped, the government could offer an annual contract with an assured income to anyone who promised to meet its needs.

The story of the introduction of printing into the American colonies is, in short, an account of how the thirteen different governments subsidized a public service. In Massachusetts the earliest press was, as might be expected, under the close surveillance of the leading clergymen and of Harvard College; it served church and state at the same time. Its scope and limits were symbolized in its first three products: the recently revised Freeman's Oath (1639); an almanac calculated for New England (1639); and the famous Bay Psalm Book (1640), a new and supposedly more literal translation of the Psalms by three New England divines. The staples of this earliest press in the English colonies were the enactments of the General Court.

Benjamin Franklin, being an enterprising businessman, valued his appointment as clerk of the Pennsylvania Assembly mainly as a way to secure the government printing business for his presses. Within less than a dozen years (1739–50) Franklin received as clerk's fees and for printing statutes and paper currency the sum of £2,762 of Pennsylvania money. Franklin's *Modest Enquiry into the Nature and Necessity of a Paper Currency* (1729), which he had both written and printed, urged the printing of more provincial paper money secured by Pennsylvania's plentiful supply of land. "My friends there (in the House,) who conceiv'd I had been of some service, thought fit to reward me by employing me in printing the money; a very profitable jobb and a great help to me. This was another advantage gain'd by my being able to write." On another occasion, Franklin was even paid for destroying the colony's currency when it had become worn through use. About this time, too, the neighboring colony of Delaware gave Franklin its contract to print money, laws, and government proceedings.

William Parks, who in 1730 brought Virginia its first press in a half-century, had only a few years before set up shop in Annapolis as official printer to the province of Maryland, which had attracted him by a guaranteed annual fee for printing the debates, votes, and laws of its Assembly. Parks set up his press in Williamsburg only after the Virginia legislature had offered him their official printing and an increasing yearly sum which began at £120 and reached £280 before his death. Not all the colonies were so fortunate; some had to send their work to neighboring colonies or even abroad. Although the Assembly of South Carolina began offering a bounty as early as 1722 in order to attract a printer, it was nine years before one could be persuaded to settle there.

Under these circumstances, the colonial press could hardly be a nursery of novel, startling, or radical ideas. The printer had to be a "government man," acceptable to the ruling group in his colony. Only the government business made it at all possible for a man to live by his press in the colonies; therefore, government printing held the first claim on a prudent printer's time, as was evidenced by the many apologetic prefaces to privately supported books that had been delayed or had to appear in abridged form. As the commerce and population of each colony grew, however, government printing gradually became a smaller proportion of the total printing business. Only then did it become financially possible for a dissident or unconventional printer to make his way.

DEFENSIVE WARFARE AND NAÏVE DIPLOMACY

CHAPTER 53

T HE PERIOD during which the American colonies were founded is generally described as the Age of Limited Warfare in Europe. From about the time in the early 17th century when the Puritans settled Massachusetts Bay until the French Revolutionary Wars near the end of the 18th century, Europe showed notable restraint. After the bloodbath of the religious wars, the "Enlightened Age" offered Europe a relief, less from the fighting itself than from its worst horrors. War was moderated less through efforts to abolish it than through the growth of formal rules of warfare and by the specialization of the military function. Since the restraints which made wars less destructive also made them less decisive, European history during the colonial period was a story of continual indecisive warfare. "Now it is frequent," Daniel Defoe remarked in 1697, as the War of the Dutch Alliance dribbled out, "to have armies of fifty thousand men of a side stand at bay within view of one another, and spend a whole campaign in dodging, or, as it is genteelly called, observing one another, and then march off into winter quarters. The difference is in the maxims of war, which now differ as much from what they were formerly as long perukes do from piqued beards, or as the habits of the people do now from what they then were. The present maxims of war are—

> Never fight without a manifest advantage,
> And always encamp so as not to be forced to it.

And if two opposite generals nicely observe both these rules, it is impossible they should ever come to fight."

Battles tended to take place on large open fields, where the customary rules and formations could be obeyed. At the opening of a battle, the opposing forces were set up like men on a chessboard; each side usually knew what forces the other possessed, and each part of an army was expected to perform only specific maneuvers. Sneak attacks, irregular warfare, and unexpected and unheralded tactics were generally frowned on as violations of the rules. "This way of making war," Defoe succinctly put it, "spends generally more money and less blood than former wars did." Though armies increased, casualties declined. In the year 1704, which witnessed decisive battles of the War of the Spanish Succession, only 2000 British soldiers and sailors died in action and no more than 3000 died of wounds, disease, or other causes connected with the war.

Such moderation would have been impossible if the waging of wars had not become a specialized occupation from which the mass of the people felt removed. War had become the task of warriors, whose functions were as separated from those of the common man as were the tasks of the learned barrister, the doctor of physick, or the cleric. Officers of opposing sides enjoyed the fraternity of all professionals and of the international European aristocracy: between engagements they wined and entertained one another with balls, concerts, and dinner parties. Usually aristocratic professionals, they were drawn from the nobility and the upper classes, for whom the duty of military service to their prince remained a relic of feudal days. Private soldiers, who had not yet acquired the kudos of "fighting for their country," were few by modern standards and tended more and more to be the dregs of society. Driven to recruit from the jails and taverns, the sovereign preferred, if he could afford it, to fill his ranks with such mercenary professionals as the Swiss or the Hessians.

War, then, was not an encounter fought by two fully mobilized communities and hallowed by patriotism. Military engagements occurred not in the rubble of factories and cities, but usually on a military playing field, a plain at some distance from the populace. There the "rules of warfare" were neatly and scrupulously followed, with the least possible interference to the peaceful round of household, farm, and fair. Commanders would no more have undertaken a battle in thick underbrush or woods, at night, or in bad weather, than a modern professional baseball team would consent to play in dense woods on a wet day. There were exceptions, but surprisingly few.

From the middle of the 17th until near the end of the 18th century, European war was merely an instrument of policy. It was not waged to exterminate another people or to change their ways of life or their political or economic institutions. Usually it was the effort of one ruling prince to extend his territory, to vindicate his honor, or to secure a commercial advantage from an opposing sovereign, who was likely to be his cousin. Objectives were much more limited than they had been during the religious wars of the 16th and early 17th centuries.

The pan-European character of the aristocratic literary culture provided the common ideas out of which grew a specialized literature defining the just occasions and proper limits of warfare. During most of this period, the leading handbook was Grotius' *De jure belli ac pacis* (On the Law of War and Peace), 1625–31, which set up authoritative "rules" for civilized nations; it was displaced in the later 18th century by Vattel's *Le droit des gens* (The Law of Nations), 1758, which made some changes but still assumed that civilized nations were bound in peace or war by certain natural regulations.

The American Indian who lay in wait for the earliest colonists had, unfortunately, not read Grotius or Vattel. He had no international aristocracy, nor was he persuaded of the advantages of limited warfare that was waged only during clear weather in open fields. He had his own weapons and his own ways, the ways of the forest. He was not accustomed to pitched battles nor to the trumpet-heralded attack. The Indian bow, unlike the matchlock, was silent, accurate, and capable of rapid fire even in wet weather; the tomahawk was a more versatile weapon than the fifteen-foot pike. When the Indian captured an enemy he did not obey Grotius' laws of war by taking prisoners and seeking to exchange them. On the contrary, massacre and torture were his rule; he thought nothing of flaying his enemy or bleeding him to death with jabs of pointed sticks. The Rev. Joseph Doddridge observed the savage attacks in Western Virginia in the later 18th century:

> The Indian kills indiscriminately. His object is the total extermination of his enemies. Children are victims of his vengeance, because, if males, they may hereafter become warriors, or if females, they may become mothers. Even the fetal state is criminal in his view. It is not enough that the fetus should perish with the murdered mother, it is torn from her pregnant womb, and elevated on a stick or pole, as a trophy of victory and an object of horror to the survivors of the slain. If the Indian takes prisoners, mercy has but little concern in the transaction. He spares the lives of those who fall into his hands, for the purpose of feasting the feelings of ferocious vengeance of himself and his comrades, by the torture of his captive.

This American scene created a new type of adventure literature— stories of Indian captivities—which recounted the suffering and heroism of ordinary settlers, their wives, and children.

The Indian was omnipresent; he struck without warning and was a nightly terror in the remote silence of backwoods cabins. The New England settlers, Cotton Mather recalled, felt themselves "assaulted by unknown numbers of devils in flesh on every side"; to them the Indians were "so many 'unkennell'd wolves.' " Every section of the seacoast colonies suffered massacres. The bloody toll of the Virginia settlements in 1622, and again in 1644, was never forgotten in the colony. In Virginia in 1676, Nathaniel Bacon's Rebellion expressed the demand of western settlers for more aid against the Indians. We have already seen how the Indian massacres of the mid-18th century sharpened the crisis of the Quaker government of Pennsylvania. Such nightmares shaped the military policy of settlers until nearly the end of the 18th century. The Indian menace, which haunted the fringes of settlement through the whole colonial era, remained a terror to the receding West well into the 19th century. Not until ten years after the massacre of Custer's force in 1876, when the few remaining Indians had been removed to Indian Territory or to reservations, did the Indian threat disappear.

The Indian was not the only menace. Parts of the English colonies suffered intermittent threats of invasion by European powers— the French, the Dutch, or the Spanish. While England remained relatively safe from foreign invasion from the time of the Armada (1588) at least until the time of Napoleon, the earliest settlers of Virginia were often in terror that the Spanish massacre of the Huguenots at Fort Caroline in Florida might be repeated in their own province. More than once the pioneer settlers of Jamestown raised the alarm that Spanish ships were coming up their rivers; they anxiously watched every approaching sail in fear that it might bring invaders. Boston was alarmed by the approach of La Tour in a French ship of 140 tons in 1643, and on numerous later occasions had reason to fear attack from some European force. Even the pacifism of Pennsylvania Quakers was strained by the appearance of Spanish ships in the very harbor of the city.

Such threats forced whole communities to huddle together in time of danger. The garrison house, built as a common dwelling and refuge during Indian raids, became a symbol of the unlimited nature of warfare in America. At the first alarm of Indian attack, neighboring inhabitants would collect their most valuable belongings and gather in the garrison. In New England, such garrisons increased during the alarms of King Philip's War in 1676, and a number continued to be maintained during the French and Indian Wars well into the 18th century. The same general scheme was followed up and down the colonies. Sometimes a particular private dwelling— suitably constructed with thick walls perforated by loopholes, with an overhanging second story, and possibly with flankers at the corners for lookout—was agreed upon as the customary refuge. Or, some towns—like Hadley, Northampton, and Hatfield in the Connecticut Valley—imitated the Indians by surrounding the town with a defensive stockade.

The crowded life of the garrison houses, as the Rev. Doddridge reminds us, was no picnic; it made settlers dread what they called the "Indian summer."

> A backwoodsman seldom hears this expression without feeling a chill of horror. . . . during the long continued Indian wars sustained by the first settlers of the west, they enjoyed no peace excepting in the winter season, when, owing to the severity of the weather, the Indians were unable to make their excursions into the settlements. The onset of winter was therefore hailed as a jubilee by the early inhabitants of the country, who, throughout the spring and the early part of the fall, had been cooped up in . . . uncomfortable forts, and subjected to all the distresses of the Indian war. At the approach of winter, therefore, all the farmers, excepting the owner of the fort, removed to their cabins on their farms, with the joyful feelings of a tenant of a prison recovering his release from confinement. All was bustle and hilarity in preparing for winter, by gathering in the corn, digging potatoes, fattening hogs, and repairing the cabins. To our forefathers the gloomy months of winter were more pleasant than the zephyrs and the flowers of May. It however sometimes happened, after the apparent onset of winter, the weather became warm; the smoky time commenced, and lasted for a considerable number of days. This was the Indian summer, because it afforded the Indians another opportunity of visiting the settlements with their destructive warfare. The melting of the snow saddened every countenance, and the genial warmth of the sun chilled every heart with horror. The apprehension of another visit from the Indians, and of being driven back to the detested fort, was painful in the highest degree, and the distressing apprehension was frequently realized.

In such colonial warfare all were soldiers because all lived on the battlefield. The bravery of women became a byword. In 1766 in Shenandoah county in the Valley of Virginia, two men were taking their wives and children in a wagon toward the safety of a fort when they were attacked by five Indians and both men were killed. "The women," Kercheval reported, "instead of swooning at the sight of their bleeding, expiring husbands, seized their axes, and with Amazonian firmness, and strength almost superhuman, defended themselves and children. One of the Indians had succeeded in getting hold of one of Mrs. Sheetz's children, and attempted to drag it out of the wagon; but with the quickness of lightning she caught her child in one hand, and with the other made a blow at the head of the fellow, which caused him to quit his hold to save his life. Several of the Indians received pretty sore wounds in this desperate conflict, and all at last ran off, leaving the two women with their children to pursue their way to the fort." Only a few years later, Mrs. Experience Bozarth, in whose house a number of neighbors had taken refuge, defended them all after their two men were severely injured, by skillfully handling an axe with which she brained two Indians and disembowelled a third. The backwoods was no place for the squeamish; anyone who waited for the arrival of "troops" did not last long.

The boys' pastimes early prepared them for defense. Shooting small game with a bow or a gun and throwing a tomahawk became life-saving skills when Indians attacked. By the time a boy reached the age for service in the militia he was already at home in the forest and knew the ways of the Indian. "A well grown boy," Doddridge noted of the Valley of Virginia in the 1760's, "at the age of twelve or thirteen years, was furnished with a small rifle and shot-pouch. He then became a fort soldier, and had his port-hole assigned him. Hunting squirrels, turkeys and raccoons, soon made him expert in the use of his gun."

Hunting, Indian-fighting, and skirmishes in the backwoods encouraged numerous American improvements in the rifle. By the mid-18th century, the "Pennsylvania" rifle, later to achieve fame as the "Kentucky" rifle, was already noticeably different from its Alpine prototype. It was longer and more slender; had a smaller bore (a calibre of about .50), used a ball weighing only about half an ounce, and was more accurate. In contrast, even as late as the American Revolution, the German rifle was still clumsy, heavy, and short-barrelled; it used a ball about twice the weight, was slower to fire, was heavier in recoil, and offered much less range and accuracy. Slow loading—with short iron rod, mallet, and ramrod—had not disqualified the rifle for backwoods use, but the American developed a quicker and less strenuous means of loading: the "patch," a small greased cloth encasing a lead ball (slightly smaller than the bore), which could be pushed smoothly down the barrel. By insuring a tight fit in the rifling, the patch also prevented waste of fire-power. The resulting weapon had unprecedented convenience, economy, and accuracy.

By the Revolution this weapon, still practically unknown in England and found only among hunters in the mountain fastnesses of Europe, had become common in the American backwoods. "Rifles, infinitely better than those imported, are daily made in many places in Pennsylvania," an Anglican minister wrote from Maryland in 1775, "and all the gunsmiths everywhere constantly employed. In this country, my lord, the boys, as soon as they can discharge a gun, frequently exercise themselves therewith, some a fowling and others a hunting. The great quantities of game, the many kinds, and the great privileges of killing making the Americans the best marksmen in the world, and thousands support their families by the same, particularly riflemen on the frontiers, whose objects are deer and turkeys. In marching through woods one thousand of these riflemen would cut to pieces ten thousand of your best troops." Such reports as these made the English regulars expect every American to be a sharpshooter.

The myth of the omnipresent American marksman, clothed not in a military uniform but in a hunting shirt, became potent in psychological warfare. Dixon & Hunter's *Virginia Gazette* (Sept. 9, 1775) reported an exhibition by riflemen bound for Boston: while one man held between his knees a small board with a bull's-eye the size of a dollar, a rifleman at sixty yards put eight successive bullets through the bull's eye. Washington arranged a similar exhibition on Cambridge Common in August 1775, hoping that spies would carry the frightening word back to the British troops. At this very time the British musket was so crude that the official army manual did not even contain the command "aim" for its musketeers. Early in the Revolution, General George Washington issued an order in which he "earnestly" encouraged "the use of Hunting Shirts, with long Breeches made of the same Cloth. . . . it is a dress justly supposed to carry no small terror to the enemy, who think every such person a complete Marksman." But the rifle, unlike the European musket, was not equipped with a bayonet and was a slower, more fragile weapon of special skill. Ill-suited to the European formal battle-array, it remained a highly individualistic weapon, admirable for skirmishing or for picking off an individual enemy. Such tactics unnerved a rigidly trained professional army; they would help convince British officers that subduing the American populace was a hopeless task.

In America war had become an institution for the citizenry as well as the warriors. The colonials were in the habit of defending themselves on neighboring ground instead of employing professionals on a distant battlefield. Just as everybody in America was somewhat literate but none was greatly literary, everybody here was a bit of a soldier, none completely so. War was conducted without a professional army, without generals, and even without "soldiers" in the strict European sense. The Second Amendment to the Federal Constitution would provide: "A well regulated Militia, being necessary to the security of a free State, the right of the people to keep and bear Arms, shall not be infringed."

The distinctive American experience would, of course, make difficulties whenever Americans would be arrayed in war or diplomacy against Europeans, for in Europe the professional army with its aristocratic officer class had made war a sophisticated, attenuated activity. To that sophistication there were two aspects. On the one hand, specialization of the soldier's function had made possible the limitation of warfare. On the other hand, it made possible a sophisticated diplomacy by which sovereigns used professional armies to serve their trivial or devious purposes and under which an uninterested populace lightly allowed their "nation" (i.e., the professional soldiery) to be committed to battle. A professional army was casually sent wherever the sovereign wished for imperial, dynastic, or commercial strategy. European war by the 18th century was far removed from the naïve defense of the hearth: specialized fighters were trained to kill for reasons they did not understand and in distant lands for which they had no love. As the 18th century wore on, such wars of policy commanded more and more of the blood and treasure of Europe. But these wars were barely intelligible, much less defensible, among colonial Americans, to whom war was the urgent defense of the hearth by everybody against an omnipresent and merciless enemy. Americans would long find it hard to understand the military games played by kings, ministers, and generals who used uniformed pawns on distant battlefields, or the diplomatic games in which such wars were only interludes.

FROM

THE
AMERICANS
The National Experience

"There is nothing like the elbow room of a new country."

JOHN TYLER

America grew in the quest for community. Between the Revolution and the Civil War the young nation flourished not in discovery but in search. It prospered not from the perfection of its ways but from their fluidity. It lived with the constant belief that something else or something better might turn up. A by-product of looking for ways of living together was a new civilization, whose strength was less an idealism than a willingness to be satisfied with less than the ideal. Americans were glad enough to keep things growing and moving. When before had men put so much faith in the unexpected?

INVENTING RESOURCES:

Ice for the Indies

NEW ENGLAND DID NOT raise pepper or coffee or sugar or cotton, or any other staple crop to sell the world. The greatest resource of New England was resourcefulness. Using the sea, New England versatility made the very menaces of the landscape into articles of commerce. "New England," went the common taunt, "produces nothing but granite and ice." The supreme proof of New England ingenuity was her ability to turn her rocky soil and heavy winters to profit.

Until almost the middle of the 19th century, ice for summer cooling had been a rare luxury. The ancient Romans had brought snow down from the mountains as a curiosity. But from the beginning of history, diet had been limited by the seasons. Generally speaking, fresh fruit and vegetables were available only when just ripe, meat only as it was slaughtered, milk only as it came fresh from the cow. A recipe for a syllabub about 1800 instructed the housewife: "Sweeten a quart of cyder with double refined sugar, grate nutmeg into it, then milk your cow into your liquor." Before the days of refrigeration, milk could be preserved only in the form of butter or cheese, and meat had to be dried or salted. Everything was spiced to lend variety or to conceal the staleness.

In the 18th century, ice cream was found in Paris, in London, or in the colonies only on aristocratic tables. Occasionally on the sideboard of a great English country house one might see a water cooler which used ice. An icehouse was part of the luxurious equipment of the palace of the royal governors of Virginia at Williamsburg, of Washington's Mount Vernon, of Jefferson's Monticello, and of Monroe's Ash Lawn. Before the end of the 18th century, a few Philadelphia families had got together to maintain an icehouse and at least one rich Cambridge estate had an icehouse of its own. But there had been almost no progress in the general use of refrigeration since that winter day in 1626 when Sir Francis Bacon caught a fatal chill while experimentally burying a chicken in the snow.

Since North American summers in the same latitude were hotter than those of Europe, food spoiled here even more quickly. Putrid meat, tainted poultry, rancid cream, and sour milk were items which unfriendly European tourists in the 18th and 19th centuries especially noted in the American cuisine.

Then, quite suddenly, in the half century before the Civil War, there was a greater increase in the consumption of ice than in the whole millennium before. By 1860 the household icebox (the word had lately been invented in America) was a commonplace in growing American cities; cookbooks took it for granted. Ice cream had become a common dish, described by *Godey's Lady Book* (August 1850) as one of the necessities of life; a party without ice cream was said to be like a breakfast without bread or a dinner without a roast. Some New York families even had ice water all summer.

The rapid growth of cities put more and more people farther from sources of fresh milk, meat, and vegetables, while the increasing number of household refrigerators enlarged the demand for ice. New Orleans, which in the late 1820's consumed less than 400 tons of ice a year, in one decade increased its consumption tenfold, in another decade twentyfold, and before the Civil War seventyfold. Within the same period ice consumption in such northern cities as New York and Boston increased almost as spectacularly. By the late 1830's, when New England merchants suffered from high tariffs and when Boston's carrying trade between Calcutta and Europe had fallen disastrously, the new ice industry provided a staple New England export which helped save the port of Boston and incidentally revived Boston's commerce to the East and West Indies.

The "Ice Age" of American diet—with its emphasis on sanitation, nutrition, and refreshment, on the health of the body rather than the pleasures of the palate—had begun. By mid-20th century, the word "ice" in various combinations had provided more new compounds than perhaps any other word in the American language.

The man who did more than anyone else to make ice an American institution was Frederic Tudor of Boston, who came to be known as the "Ice King." An enterprising businessman cast in a New England mold, he was no Horatio Alger hero. He succeeded not by the prosaic, abstemious virtues but by a flamboyant, defiant, energetic, and sometimes reckless spirit. He was not considerate and gentle, generous and frugal, but, on the contrary, he was imperious, vain, contemptuous of competitors, and implacable to enemies. While energetic in competition, he preferred legalized monopoly. He had not risen from poverty but, like many another substantial Massachusetts merchant, amassed wealth by exploiting all opportunities, including his family connections and his social position.

Tudor came of a prominent Boston family. His father, a Harvard graduate, had studied law in the office of John Adams, had served George Washington as judge-advocate-general and then built a prosperous law practice. His three brothers graduated from Harvard, but Frederick instead began in business at thirteen. It was he who gave his brothers employment and eventually recouped the family fortunes. Despite his omnivorous mind and insatiable curiosity, he idealized work and the life of action. He distrusted the idle "academic" life and worried when, visiting his brother John's room at Harvard one day, he found it littered with the paint brushes and canvasses of John's roommate, the romantic painter Washington Allston.

In the winter of 1805, when Tudor was barely twenty-one, his brother William at a gay Boston party whimsically asked why the ice on nearby ponds was not harvested and then sold at ports in the Caribbean. Frederick took up the suggestion, as if to prove that no enterprise was too outlandish, no commodity too commonplace, for New England commerce. He purchased a notebook, calling it his "ice house diary," and made his first entry on August 1, 1805 in what was to be a classic record of New England business enterprise. On the leather cover he printed the motto: "He who gives back at the first repulse and without striking the second blow despairs of success[,] has never been, is not, and never will be a hero in war, love or business."

All Boston derided him as a madman when, within the year, he invested ten thousand dollars in shipping 130 tons of ice to the sweltering island of Martinique. He then went to Martinique to promote sales by personally showing prospective customers how to preserve and use ice. From St. Pierre's he wrote back on March 10, 1806:

> The man who keeps the Tivoli garden insisted ice creams could not be made in this country and that the ice itself would all thaw before he could get it home! I told him I had made them here; . . . I wrote an order for 40 lbs. of ice, and in a pretty warm tone directed the man to have his cream ready and that I would come to freeze it for him in the morning, which I did accordingly, being determined to spare no pains to convince these people that they can not only have ice but all the luxuries arising as well here as elsewhere. The Tivoli man recd. for these creams the first night $300; after this he was humble as a mushroom. . . .

But the Martinique venture lost nearly four thousand dollars when the whole cargo melted within six weeks.

It was fifteen years before Tudor established the ice trade as a paying business. During all this time he struggled: to secure legal monopolies of the trade, and exclusive rights to build icehouses in Charleston, Havana, and in the British and French West Indies; to dominate the New England ponds which were the source of ice; to create a demand for ice, iced drinks, ice cream, and ice-preserved fruit, meat, and milk in every part of the world his ships could reach. For a while, Tudor sold chilled beverages at the same price as unchilled beverages, hoping to encourage a taste for cold drinks. He demonstrated the use of ice in hospitals. Wherever he managed to build an efficient storage depot, he had a great advantage against competitors: he would sell his ice at a penny a pound till his competitor's stock had all melted at the dock and then he would raise his price to recoup his profit. "Drink, Spaniards, and be cool," he exhorted the perspiring patrons of the West Indian coffee houses, "that I, who have suffered so much in the cause, may be able to go home and keep myself warm."

Had he not conquered the technical problems, none of this would have been possible. And he doggedly devoted himself to the task of designing an efficient icehouse. Deliberately risking yellow fever in Havana to experiment on the spot, he tried every conceivable kind of insulating material—straw, wood shavings, blankets. Watch in hand, he stood outside his Havana icehouse and measured the melting water hour by hour. He recorded the effects of changes in design and of opening the icehouse doors on the rate of melting. Finally he produced an economical and efficient design for an ice depot in tropical climates. The seasonal loss from melting in icehouses of the old underground type was over sixty per cent, but in Tudor's houses it was less than eight per cent.

To secure large quantities of ice for tropical areas, Tudor had to perfect a way of harvesting ice from New England ponds so that it could be conveniently transported and preserved. The early 19th-century ice harvests had been laboriously cut by hand into pieces of miscellaneous size. When a warm winter, like that of 1818, shortened the supply from New England ponds, the captain of a Boston brig would risk ship and crew to pry fragments off a Labrador iceberg with picks and crowbars. These irregularly shaped pieces were troublesome to ship and uneconomical to store. Ship captains were ordinarily willing enough to ballast ice instead of rocks on their voyages southward, but shipowners objected because these pieces could not be tightly packed, they shifted in the hold, and their melting spoiled other cargo. It was necessary, therefore, to find a way to mass-produce uniform blocks from natural ice.

By a lucky collaboration, Tudor solved this problem. He enlisted the ingenuity of another well-born Cambridge man, Nathaniel Jarvis Wyeth, who had inherited a part of the shore of Fresh Pond, one of the best sources of ice around Cambridge. Although his father had been a Harvard graduate, Wyeth, like Tudor, passed up Harvard to go into business. Before he was thirty he was successfully running the Fresh Pond Hotel which, with its rowboats, tenpin alley, and other concessions, was an attractive summer resort for nearby cities. In 1824, Wyeth became manager of Tudor's ice company, which reaped the winter crop from Fresh Pond. Before long he invented a machine that revolutionized the harvesting of ice and without which the great New England ice industry might not have been possible.

Wyeth's solution was simple, probably suggested by the marks left by sleigh-runners on the surface of Fresh Pond in winter. His ice cutter consisted of two parallel iron runners about twenty inches apart drawn by a horse. Each runner was notched with saw teeth, making a device which cut two parallel grooves as it was pulled along. These grooves were deepened by repeating the operation; additional parallel grooves were cut by using one of the grooves as a guide. By pulling the device at right angles to the original grooves, one formed a checkerboard of squares in the ice. A few men with iron bars then pried off the cubes and floated them into a channel, quickly producing a great number of blocks of uniform dimension. At the end of the channel Wyeth provided a novel horse-drawn hoist which lifted the blocks out of the water up to a chute, which then deposited them in the icehouse on the shore of the pond.

These devices, which Wyeth had in workable form by 1825, reduced the cost of harvesting ice from thirty cents to ten cents a ton. Under the arrangement with Wyeth, Tudor controlled the use of all these devices. But these were not Wyeth's only inventions for the ice industry; he went on elaborating until, by the time of his death in 1856, its technology was almost entirely of his making. He designed a new type of ice-scraper to clean the surface of the ice before harvesting, in this way producing a still more uniform product. He discovered that sawdust could be used to prevent blocks from melting together in transit, thus keeping them neat for sale—and incidentally creating a demand for the until then useless by-product of the Maine lumber mills.

But Wyeth was no mere mechanic. During a five years leave from the ice business, after 1832, he led an overland expedition to Oregon and organized a company to exploit the Columbia River region for salmon, fur, timber, and tobacco. He thus became one of "the pioneers of the pioneers" of the Pacific Northwest. Despite a series of dramatic misadventures—lightning striking his company's ship at Valparaiso, struggles with the Rocky Mountain Fur Trading Company and the Hudson's Bay Company over the fur trade—he founded Fort Hall, a well known trading station on the Oregon and California trails. Lacking resources to establish a permanent fur-trading company of his own, he returned to Boston and re-entered the ice business for himself. He improved techniques still further. His versatile new type of ice cutter was melodramatically tested in 1844, when the Cunard steamship *Britannia* was frozen in Boston harbor; within three days he had cut a two-hundred-foot channel seven miles long to the open sea.

Despite competition from Wyeth and others, Tudor remained the Ice King. But his adventuring energies were never confined. In his early years he had traded in pimento, nutmeg, flour, sugar, tea, candles, cotton, silk, and claret. Later he dug for coal on Martha's Vineyard; he invented a siphon for pumping water from the holds of vessels; he made a new design for the hull of a ship *(The Black Swan)* and for a "double dory," supposedly an improvement over earlier fishing vessels; he operated a graphite mine; he made paper from white pine; and he experimented with the raising of cotton and tobacco at Nahant. He brought to New England the first steam locomotive, an engine of one-half horsepower which ran on the sidewalk at four miles an hour pulling a car for one passenger. He set up what was probably the first amusement park in America. And he even tried raising salt-water fish in Fresh Pond.

Tudor's miscellaneous speculations from time to time plunged him deeply into debt, even after he had put the ice trade on a profitable basis. For example, his speculations in coffee involved him to the extent of $200,000 before the end of 1834, but this drove him to redouble his efforts in the ice trade, out of which he managed to repay the coffee debt in the next fifteen years.

Tudor had now decided to ship his ice halfway around the world—to the East Indies. In May 1833, in the most spectacular experiment of his career, Tudor sent his ship *Tuscany* with 180 tons of ice to Calcutta. To reach India from Boston the *Tuscany* had to cross the equator twice, preserving its cargo unmelted for four months. Tudor reminded his captain that ice had never been carried so far south; this was a "discovery ship." The *Tuscany* reached its destination, bringing the combined delights of a new toy and a new candy. The first shipment sold profitably, Tudor's reputation soared, and before long the ice trade flourished between Boston and the Far East. Using experience gained in the Caribbean, Tudor built a large Calcutta ice depot and encouraged Anglo-Indians to buy household refrigerators and water coolers; he tried to change their eating habits by his well-preserved shipments of apples, butter, and cheese.

Soon ice was being shipped from Boston to all parts. By 1846, sixty-five thousand tons were shipped; only ten years later more than twice that amount went in nearly four hundred different shipments to over fifty different destinations in the United States, the Caribbean, South America, the East Indies, China, the Philippines, and Australia. Ice had become a major commodity, a New England staple for the world market.

One brochure proposing a railroad to connect Fresh Pond with the docks at Charlestown asked whether ice did not contribute "as much to refreshment in the South as coal does to comfort in the North?" Others urged the importance of ice in promoting good morals. "How often do men in health drink ardent spirits as a beverage because they cannot procure good or only tepid water that ice would render palatable?" Edward Everett, American minister to England, reported receiving the thanks of a Persian prince for the New England ice which was saving the lives of patients in Persia, whose fevers were reduced by applying ice to their foreheads.

Tudor's ice industry reached not only to Persia but even to the fastnesses of nearby Walden Pond, where it disturbed a would-be recluse named Thoreau who reported in the winter of 1846–47:

> A hundred Irishmen, with Yankee overseers, came from Cambridge every day to get out the ice. They divided it into cakes by [Wyeth's] methods too well known to require description, and these, being sledded to the shore, were rapidly

hauled off on to an ice platform, and raised by grappling irons and block and tackle, worked by horses, on to a stack, as surely as so many barrels of flour, and there placed evenly side by side, and row upon row, as if they formed the solid base of an obelisk designed to pierce the clouds. They told me that in a good day they could get out a thousand tons, which was the yield of about one acre. . . . They told me that they had some in the ice-houses at Fresh Pond five years old which was as good as ever. . . . the sweltering inhabitants of Charleston and New Orleans, of Madras and Bombay and Calcutta, drink at my well. . . . The pure Walden water is mingled with the sacred water of the Ganges.

INVENTING RESOURCES:

Granite for a New Stone Age

E ARLY NEW ENGLAND FARMERS cursed the rocks that broke their ploughs, the rocks they laboriously collected along their boundaries to make fences as they cleared. The first settlers of Boston occasionally built with boulders they found strewn loose on the land, but stone in this form was not plentiful enough to become a common construction material. When houses were not built of wood, the usual materials were clay, brick, slate, cement, or red Connecticut sandstone. The great rough granite boulders made foundations and doorsteps but, even for this purpose, they soon became so scarce that the town meeting of Braintree, for example, in 1715 penalized anyone who carried a boulder away from the commons. To build King's Chapel in Boston, boulders were dug up, heated by a fire built directly on the stone, and then split by the dropping of heavy iron balls. This, the usual technique, was haphazard and expensive, and it could only be applied to boulders having a free side. In mid-18th century, German immigrants in Braintree began using gunpowder to split off large chunks of granite (hoping for the best shapes) which they then cut into smaller pieces by laboriously making a groove with a hammer having a cutting edge like that of an axe.

At the end of the 18th century an energetic governor of Massachusetts, while traveling about the state to find cheap stone for a new

State Prison to be built at Charlestown, came upon a workman near Salem who used the novel method of drilling holes several inches apart and then splitting the stone in a straight line along the holes. When this improved technique for cutting granite came into general use, it halved the price of hewn granite, which now for the first time began to be in wide demand as a building material. The new Middlesex Canal, the longest in the country, from Chelmsford to Boston (employing granite for its sixteen locks), opened a convenient water passage from granite-source to port-city.

The great "Stone Age" of New England architecture, sometimes called the Greek Revival, followed. Not since the Mayans and Aztecs had North America seen so many buildings of monumental stone. In 1818, $25,000 worth of hewn granite was shipped for a church in Savannah, Georgia. And before long New England's best architects (Charles Bulfinch, Alexander Parris, Solomon Willard, Ammi Burnham Young, Gridley Bryant, and H. H. Richardson) used New England granite for homes, churches, markets, and public buildings all over the eastern and southern United States. Their work was possible only because New Englanders—by opening quarries, by inventing new ways of shaping, handling, and transporting granite, and by using their old ally, the sea—had now made stone a profitable export.

The American Revolution, in a strange and unforeseen way, was also indirectly responsible for the exploitation of Quincy granite. William (brother of Frederic) Tudor, who had first casually suggested the sale of ice in the Caribbean, is also credited with the first proposal in 1822 that a monument ("the noblest column in the world") be built on Bunker Hill to commemorate the first battlefield defense of the Republic. The design and engineering of the Bunker Hill Monument were the work of Solomon Willard, a talented jack-of-many-trades. Though coming from an old New England family, and a descendant of the famous minister, Samuel Willard, he was of the class of "self-made men" (his contemporary biographer explained) "peculiar to our own country, born with its birth—existing even before its birth as a nation—and growing with its growth, with a vigor which proves its congeniality, if not its indigenousness to the soil." As the son of a carpenter, Solomon Willard had only a common-school education and himself became a carpenter. By teaching himself the rudiments of architecture, by working hard, and by seizing his opportunities, he became a prosperous and prominent citizen. Under the direction of Charles Bulfinch, in 1818 he made the architect's model of the national capitol. In the 1820's, when American sources of coal were beginning to be exploited, he developed a hot-air system with a basement furnace and pipes leading to different rooms, which became the first widely used American system of central heating.

In 1825, Willard was chosen architect and superintendent of construction of the Bunker Hill Monument, for which he bore responsibility during nearly twenty troublesome years. The actual cost of the monument, Willard calculated, was over one hundred thousand dollars; including uncompensated services, it must have cost several times that. It had been entirely financed by voluntary contributions, but the citizens of Boston had taken twice as long to build the monument as they had to win the Revolution. At the dedication in 1843 in the presence of President John Tyler and his cabinet, Daniel Webster, who had delivered one of his most famous orations at the laying of the cornerstone 18 years before, gave the principal address. This monument, Webster commented, bore no inscription—"and it needs none, since the lessons of patriotism it is designed to commemorate, can only be inscribed upon the hearts of those who behold it."

An unexpected by-product of the building of Bunker Hill Monument was the great New England granite industry. Seeking a suitable material for the Monument, Willard had walked three hundred miles to examine different quarries until he finally discovered the granite quarry in Quincy. This was purchased in June 1825 by Gridley Bryant, who sold it to the Bunker Hill Monument Association for $350 (still giving Bryant what was then called a "handsome profit"). From the so-called "Bunker Hill Ledge" in the Quincy quarry came the stone for the Monument. In securing this stone, Solomon Willard invented nearly every piece of machinery later used in the granite industry: lifting-jack, pulling-jack, hoist, and other devices for moving and placing large blocks of granite. Part of the construction scheme was the famous Granite Railway, planned and built by Gridley Bryant and sometimes called the first railroad in the United States. Over a primitive wooden track six inches high, covered with iron plates and resting on stone sleepers, granite blocks were hauled by horses from quarry to tidewater. It was while building this road, too, that Bryant developed his famous eight-wheel car and such other fundamental railroad devices as the switch, portable derrick, movable truck, turntable, and snowplow.

The Bunker Hill Quarry soon became a full-scale experiment in granite production. By selling granite at prime cost—only the cost of labor and materials directly used in procuring it—which was about one fourth of the going commercial price, Willard antagonized his competitors but he did widen the market. After completion of the Bunker Hill Monument, Willard could boast that the widespread use of granite as a building material was largely a result of improvements developed during its construction. "A business has grown . . . since the work commenced, and in a space of a few miles, amounting . . . to $3,000,000, which would not otherwise have been done at these quarries, and of which the work on the obelisk is but about one-thirtieth part."

In cities all along the eastern and southern seaboard, the most prominent public structures—customs houses, courthouses, markets, banks, and merchants' exchanges—were now built of granite. Willard's improved techniques of moving and placing the stone actually produced a new architectural style. Until then granite had been used mostly in small pieces for cellar walls, underpinnings, and lintels. Willard was now able to use it in large blocks, creating a monumental effect, the first example of which was, of course, the Bunker Hill Monument itself. Willard noted with satisfaction the improved construction of the granite drydocks in Charlestown and Norfolk, built soon after the commencement of the Monument. He observed a consequent improvement in "architectural taste and mechanical execution" in many buildings: in the Astor House and the Merchants' Exchange in New York, in the Tremont House, the Exchange and the Customs House in Boston, and in numerous public buildings and store-blocks elsewhere. In an age of gingerbread and gewgaws, the very intractability of granite encouraged a happy simplicity of design.

A coincidental interest in public health and landscape architecture fed a movement to replace the fetid charnel houses and the haphazard, crowded burial grounds of the colonial period with new "garden cemeteries." The leader of this movement was the versatile Boston botanist-physician Jacob Bigelow who founded Mount Auburn Cemetery in Cambridge in 1831. Its grandiose Egyptian portal, its markers and monuments for the wealthy and the famous buried there, and its neat granite curbing for its winding drives, consumed large quantities of stone from the Bunker Hill quarries. As garden cemeteries became popular, they created a large new market for Quincy granite.

With the growth of cities, the demand for a hard paving stone increased. Solomon Willard laid the first such blocks of Quincy granite in front of the Tremont House in 1840. Before the end of the century, New England was producing over sixty million granite paving blocks each year.

The influence of granite reached out—to the edge of the sea, across the sea, and among people working on the sea. When Harriet Martineau visited Massachusetts in the fall of 1835–36, she found the remote New Englanders of Cape Ann using the sea to help them harvest the granite of the land. She found them employing ox teams and sleds to embark stone for foreign parts. "Blocks of granite lay by the road-side, marked . . . prepared to order for some great building in New York, or Mobile, or New Orleans. . . . We went into a quarry, and saw an untold wealth of fissured stone. The workmen contrive to pursue their business even in the winter. When the snow is on the ground, and the process of drilling is stopped, they remove ordinary pieces out of the way, and make clear for their spring labours. They 'turn out' 250,000 dollars'-worth a-year; and the demand is perpetually on the increase."

A *tour de force* in granite was Minot's Ledge Lighthouse in Boston Harbor, completed only after eight years of planning and construction. Because of the peculiar location of the site, stones could be placed only when there was a perfectly smooth sea, a dead calm, and low spring tide. Even then nothing larger than a small sailboat could be used to carry the two-ton stones to the only point at which a boat could be brought up to the ledge. When Minot's Ledge Lighthouse first shone on November 15, 1860, it was celebrated as a prodigy of architecture and marine engineering. It was, in fact, a demonstration not only of the wonderful qualities of granite, but of the ability of New Englanders to meet the challenge of the sea. And it was not long before New England's most respectable orators had reversed the proverbial taunt. No one now could deny their boast, uttered by Charles Francis Adams, Jr., that "the three great staples of New England are ice and rocks and men."

THE BUSINESSMAN AS AN AMERICAN INSTITUTION

Chapter 16

THE AMERICAN BUSINESSMAN—a product (and a maker) of the upstart cities of the American West between the Revolution and the Civil War—was not an American version of the enterprising European city banker or merchant or manufacturer. Not an American Fugger or Medici or Rothschild or Arkwright, he was something quite different. His career and his ideals are an allegory of an American idea of community, for he was born and bred in the dynamic American urbanism in the period of our greatest growth.

The changing meaning of his very name, "businessman," gives us a clue. In 18th-century England to say someone was a "man of business" was primarily to say he engaged in public affairs. Thus David Hume in 1752 described Pericles as "a man of business." Before the end of the 18th century the expression had begun to lose this, its once primary meaning, and instead to describe a person engaged in mercantile transactions; it became a loose synonym for "merchant." But our now common word "businessman" seems to have been American in origin. It came into use around 1830 in the very period when the new Western cities were founded and were growing most rapidly. Even a casual look at this early American businessman, who he was, what he was doing, and how he thought of his work, will show how inaccurate it would be to describe him as simply a man engaged in mercantile transactions. We might better characterize him as a peculiarly American type of community maker and community leader. His starting belief was in the interfusing of public and private prosperity. Born of a social vagueness unknown in the Old World, he was a distinctive product of the New.

The new fast-growing city, where nothing had been before, a city with no history and unbounded hopes, was the American businessman's first natural habitat. In the period when he first appeared, his primary commodity was land and his secondary commodity transportation. This transformation of land rights and transport rights from political symbols and heirlooms into mere commodities was also an American phenomenon.

The businessman's characteristics would appear in the story of any one of the thousands who made their fortunes in the early 19th century. "I was born close by a saw-mill," boasted William B. Ogden (1805–77), "was early left an orphan, was cradled in a sugar-trough, christened in a mill-pond, graduated at a log-school-house, and at fourteen fancied I could do any thing I turned my hand to, and that nothing was impossible, and ever since, madame, I have been trying to prove it, and with some success." He was destined to be an upstart businessman on a heroic scale. Born into a leading local family in a small town in the Catskills in New York, he was actively dealing in real estate before he was fifteen. Before thirty he was elected to the New York Legislature on a program to construct the New York & Erie Railroad with State aid. He was a great booster for his State, to whose growth he called the new railroad essential. "Otherwise," he argued "the sceptre will depart from Judah. The Empire State will no longer be New York. . . . Philadelphia is your great rival, and, if New York is idle, will gather in the trade of the great west."

But Ogden's enthusiasm for New York was not immovable. In 1835, the very year when the money was appropriated for the New York & Erie Railroad, he met some Eastern investors who had formed the American Land Company. They had already shown the foresight to invest heavily in Chicago real estate. One of these was Charles Butler, a politically and philanthropically minded lawyer of Albany, who married Ogden's sister. Butler himself (once a clerk in the law office of Martin Van Buren) was an energetic promoter of real estate and railroads. A man of wide public interests, he was a founder of Hobart College and of Union Theological Seminary, and an early supporter of New York University, among his other community works. He asked Ogden to go to Chicago to manage his interests. Ogden then joined in the purchase of considerable tracts there.

William B. Ogden arrived in Chicago in June 1835. The town census showed a population of 3265, almost all of whom had come since 1832 (when the settlement had numbered under a hundred). Quickly Ogden transferred his extravagant hopes from the Empire State to the City of Chicago. In 1837, when Chicago was incorporated, Ogden was elected its first mayor, and the city census counted 4170—an increase of almost thirty per cent in two years.

"He could not forget," one of Ogden's fellow businessmen observed, "that everything which benefitted Chicago, or built up the great West, benefitted him. Why should he?" His commodity was land, whose value rose with the population. And Chicago now grew as few cities had ever grown before. The population approximately trebled, decade after decade: from 29,963 in 1850, to 109,260 in 1860, and to 298,977 in 1870. Chicago held over half a million people in 1880 and over a million by 1890, when it was already the second city on the continent. Meanwhile, real-estate values, especially in choice locations such as those Ogden was shrewd enough to buy, rose even more spectacularly. Men like Ogden proudly recorded their business success as the best evidence of their faith in their city. "In 1844," Ogden recalled, "I purchased for $8000, what 8 years thereafter, sold for 3 millions of dollars, and these cases could be extended almost indefinitely." Property he had bought in 1845 for $15,000 only twenty years later was worth ten million dollars. Successes were so common and so sudden, it was hard to know where fact ended and where fable began. Some of this purchasing was, of course, sheer speculative mania. The Chicago *American* (April 23, 1836) boasted of a piece of city property sold for $96,700 which, in romanticized arithmetic, they said had "risen in value at the rate of *one hundred per cent per* DAY, on the original cost ever since [1830], embracing a period of *five years* and a half."

Not to boost your city showed both a lack of community spirit and a lack of business sense. "Perhaps, the most striking trait of his character," a contemporary remembered of Ogden, "was his absolute faith in Chicago. He saw in 1836, not only the Chicago of today, but in the future the great City of the continent. From that early day, his faith never wavered. Come good times—come bad times—come prosperity or adversity—Chicago booming, or Chicago in ashes, its great future was to him a fixed fact." Quite naturally Ogden became a leader in community affairs, and within a few years Chicagoans called him their "representative man."

There was hardly a public improvement in which he did not play a leading role. He built the first drawbridge across the Chicago river, laid out and opened many miles of streets in the north and west parts of the city, promoted the Illinois and Michigan Canal and advocated laws for its construction and enlargement, projected and built thousands of miles of railroads serving Chicago, and did a great deal to develop Chicago's water supply, sewage system, and parks. More than a hundred miles of streets and hundreds of bridges were built at the private expense of Ogden and his real-estate clients. He helped introduce the McCormick reaping and mowing machines into the West, and helped build the first large factory for their manufacture. He was the first president of Rush Medical College (the first institution of its kind in Chicago), a charter member of the Chicago Historical Society, president of the Board of Trustees of the first "University of Chicago," and one of the first directors of the Merchants Loan and Trust Company (1857). He was elected to the Illinois Senate by the Republicans in 1860. He supported the Theological Seminary of the Northwest, the Academy of Sciences, and the Astronomical Society. The French historian Guizot only slightly exaggerated when he said Ogden had built and owned Chicago.

Characteristic also was Ogden's interest in improving transportation. An upstart community, a community of boosters measuring itself by its rate of growth, depended on transportation in a new way. Settled communities of the Old World—Bordeaux, Lyon, Manchester, or Birmingham—especially when, as in the early 19th century, they were fast becoming industrial towns, needed transportation to feed raw materials and labor to their factories and to take away finished products. But Chicago and the other upstart cities of the American West needed it for their very lifeblood. In the Old World a city might grow or decline, prosper or languish, depending on its transportation, among other facilities. But here, without transportation there was no city at all.

An American city had to "attract" people. The primary community service was to make it easier, cheaper, and pleasanter for people to join your community. In all this, too, William B. Ogden was a paragon, for he pioneered the railroads. One of the first to run out of Chicago was the Galena & Chicago Union Railroad, built to connect Chicago with the great Mississippi River traffic. Chicago businessmen bought a controlling interest in 1846, and tried to raise money from local citizens to complete the railroad. Ogden worked hard to obtain numerous individual subscriptions in small amounts. This, its first railroad, opened a new era in the life and expansion of Chicago. Citizens subscribed its stock "as a public duty, and not as an investment." "Railroads," one of Ogden's collaborators later boasted, "were built as public enterprises, and not as money-making speculations. They were regarded as great highways constructed by the people, either at the expense of the government or by means of private capital, to accommodate the public, and not for the especial benefit of the stockholders." In April 1849 the first locomotive started west from Chicago on the Galena line.

Ogden took the lead in promoting many more railroads for Chicago. In 1853 he was a director of the Pittsburg, Ft. Wayne & Chicago Railroad; in 1857, president of the Chicago, St. Paul & Fond-du-Lac Railroad which later became part of the Chicago & Northwestern Railroad, of which he was also president (1859–68). A transcontinental railroad with Chicago as the great junction was, of course, his dream. In 1850 he presided over the National Railway Convention and, on the organization of the Union Pacific Company in 1862, its first president was William B. Ogden.

The Ogden story was re-enacted a thousand times all over America—wherever there were upstart cities. Scenes were different, stakes smaller, and dimensions less heroic, but the plot everywhere was much the same. Here was a new breed: the community builder in a mushrooming city where personal and public growth, personal and public prosperity intermingled.

Another example was Dr. Daniel Drake (1785–1852), born in New Jersey, and raised in Kentucky, whose family sent him when he was only fifteen to study in the offices of a leading physician of the small town of Ft. Washington (later called Cincinnati). Within a few years he himself became the town's most prominent practitioner. He opened a drug store where, in 1816, he pioneered in the sale of artificial mineral water; soon he was also running a general store. His *Picture of Cincinnati in 1815*, with its full statistics, and its vivid account of the archaeology, topography, climate, and promise of the city, was translated and circulated widely abroad. Drake, in his own way, was as much a booster as Ogden; using subtler techniques of precise and calculated understatement, he produced the first detailed account of an upstart city. Many believed him when he concluded that small towns like Cincinnati were "destined, before the termination of the present century, to attain the rank of populous and magnificent cities." Drake had established himself in the high noon of Cincinnati prosperity, before the Panic of 1819.

Drake's boosterism was as energetic as Ogden's. Hoping to make Cincinnati a great medical center in 1819, he founded the Ohio Medical College (later the Medical College of the University of Cincinnati). He did a great deal to promote all kinds of community enterprises: the Commercial Hospital and Lunatic Asylum, the eye infirmary, the circulating library, the teacher's college. He helped plan and develop canals and he promoted railroads leading toward the South, which included the successful municipal line, the Cincinnati Southern Railway.

Still another example with a more western habitat was General William Larimer (1809–75). Born and raised in Pennsylvania, he tried many different businesses around Pittsburgh: a general store, a freight service, horse trading, a coal company, a wholesale grocery, his father's hotel, railroads, and banking. When he lost everything in the depression of 1854, Larimer, quickly resolving to start afresh far-

ther west, was in Nebraska the very next spring. There he too became the instantaneous booster of a town which did not yet exist.
We have an intimate record in letters he sent east. On May 23, 1855:

> I have taken two claims at La Platte, Nebraska Territory
> . . . and we are laying out a town. I am elected President of
> the Company, and secured ⅓ of the town. . . . I like this
> country very much indeed. . . . I think I can make a big raise
> here in a few years.

Already he claimed a good chance of being elected to Congress from
Nebraska. Within a week his optimism had risen still higher: he
planned to pay off his creditors with town lots, for he owned a thousand acres within the proposed city.

> Now my plan is this: I intend to live in La Platte City. I
> intend to open up a large farm. I can raise hemp, corn or
> anything. . . . I will go on with the farm and if the land is ever
> wanted for a town it is ready. . . . I intend not only to farm
> simply but I will open a Commission House. I expect to sup
> ply the Territory with iron nails, lumber, etc., this will not
> only be profitable in itself but will be the great means of
> building up the city. If I go there I can build the city if I do
> not go only to sell lots as the city may never rise.

Larimer expected the transcontinental railroad to go through La
Platte, but this proved a miscalculation. Then, after a heavy winter,
the town suffered deep spring floods. "We were not long in coming
to the conclusion that La Platte was doomed as a town site." The
pattern of western hope was all-or-nothing.

From La Platte, Larimer moved on to Omaha. There he lived in
a prefabricated house that had actually been framed in Pittsburgh,
knocked down, and shipped out in 1856. When Omaha, too, looked
unpromising (as it did within less than two years) he moved to Leavenworth, Kansas. This was in 1858, just in time for him to learn of
the discovery of gold at Cherry Creek by Pike's Peak. Unwilling to

wait for the better traveling conditions of the following spring, Larimer and his son immediately made up a party and left that fall. After a forty-seven-day trip, the Larimers were among the first to arrive at the mouth of Cherry Creek, where they found two dozen cabins under construction.

This, the first settlement in Colorado, was named Auraria. Larimer's son recorded the events of November 17, 1858:

> On our very first night here, my father, without consulting anyone outside of our own Leavenworth Party, packed his blankets and some provisions, left camp and crossed the Creek to pick out a new site. He left instructions for us to get up the oxen and join him, as he believed the east side of the Creek was much the best location for a town and no one in the country laid claim to it, or if so had abandoned it and left the country. . . . When we finally reached the eastern side of Cherry Creek, we found him near the bank with a camp fire awaiting us. He had 4 cottonwood poles crossed, which he called the foundation of his settlement and claimed the site for a town,—for *the* town which has now grown into the one of which Colorado is the proudest.

This time Larimer chose well. He had located on the site of Denver.

At first there was competition between the sites on either side of Cherry Creek. Then the stockholders combined and became a single city named Denver (in honor of the Virginian who had become Governor of the Kansas Territory) in 1860. "I am Denver City," Larimer wrote in a letter in February 1859. And his whole later career proved the extraordinary ability of the American businessmen of these upstart cities to fuse themselves and their destiny with that of their community—at least so long as the community remained prosperous or promising.

At the beginning Larimer had been put in charge of the town and made "Donating Agent," which authorized him to give two city lots to anyone who would build a cabin there measuring at least 16 by 16 feet. He promoted a good hotel and gave valuable shares to men "who were already or could be induced to become interested in the welfare of the city and might be influential in bringing a stage line into the country with Denver as its objective point." He encouraged the founding of drugstores, general stores, sawmills, and newspapers. Complaining that the town lacked the ultimate convenience, he finally helped organize a cemetery.

Examples could be multiplied. But even these three—Ogden, Drake, and Larimer—suggest the variety of opportunities, motives, and attitudes which created the new species *Businessman Americanus*. None of the characteristics of his American habitat was quite unique but their extreme American form and their American combination were.

Cities with no history. The upstart western cities were the rare examples of a dynamic urban environment where almost nothing had been pre-empted by history. Cities were proverbially the centers of institutions, where records were kept and the past was chronicled, hallowed, and enshrined. They were sites of palaces, cathedrals, libraries, archives, and great monuments of all kinds. The American upstart city, by contrast, had no past. At its beginning, it was free of vested interests, monopolies, guilds, skills, and "No Trespassing" signs. Here was the fluidity of the city—the spatial dimension of cosmopolitanism, movement, diversity, and change—but without the historical dimension. There were no ancient walls between classes, occupations, neighborhoods, and nationalities. The American upstart cities began without inherited neighborhood loyalties, without ghettos. "Everything," recalled Larimer, "was open to us."

Quick growth and high hopes. The pace of growth of the upstart cities fired imaginations. A town where nobody was ten years ago, but which today numbered thousands, might be expected to number tens or hundreds of thousands in a few decades. Mankind had required at least a million years to produce its first urban community of a million people; Chicagoans accomplished this feat in less than a century. Within a few days' wagon ride of Drake's Cincinnati, hundreds of towns were laid out, all guaranteed to have unrivalled advantages. Precisely one week after Larimer cut his four cottonwood poles on the future site of Denver, he wrote his wife back east that "we expect a second Sacramento City, at least." In 1834, H. M. Brackenridge noted, his Pittsburgh was changing so fast that anyone returning after ten years felt himself a stranger. He confidently foresaw that the settlement which had grown from village to big city in a quarter-century would very soon reach half a million. He could not be surprised that Cincinnati had grown from a forest to a city in thirteen years. He himself had hopes "of attaining, on the Ohio or Mississippi, distinction and wealth, with the same rapidity, and on the same scale, that those vast regions were expanding into greatness." The centennial history of St. Louis in 1876 called the city's site superior to that of any other in the world, and predicted that, when its railroad network was completed, it would outstrip Chicago and the eastern metropolises. "And yet, when this has been said, we have but commenced to tell of the wonders of a city destined in the future to equal London in its population, Athens in its philosophy, art and culture, Rome in its hotels, cathedrals, churches and grandeur, and to be the central commercial metropolis of a continent."

Community before government. On this landscape too it was normal to find communities before governments. Men in sudden urban proximity, bound together by specific, concrete purposes, first felt their common needs. Afterwards they called governments into being. From force of circumstance, then, government became functional. Early Chicagoans, and their upstart counterparts elsewhere, were not confronted with the problem of evading obsolete regulations or of transmuting time-honored tyrannies. They simply combined to provide their own water, their own sewage system, their own sidewalks, streets, bridges, and parks. They founded medical schools and universities and museums. Eager for these and other services, they created municipal governments and enlisted state and federal government aid. An upstart government had neither the odor of sanctity nor the odium of tyranny. It was a tool serving personal and community prosperity at the same time.

Intense and transferable loyalties. In upstart cities the loyalties of people were in inverse ratio to the antiquity of their communities, even to the point of absurdity. Older towns could point only to the facts of limited actual accomplishment, while the uncertain future was, of course, ever more promising. Ogden removed his enthusiasm from New York to Chicago; Larimer removed his from La Platte to Omaha to Leavenworth to Auraria to Denver. Men could do this in the twinkling of an eye, and without so much as a glance over the shoulder. Promise, not achievement, commanded loyalty and stirred the booster spirit. One was untrue to oneself and to the spirit of expanding America if one remained enslaved to a vision which had lost its promise. The ghost town and the booster spirit were opposite sides of the same coin.

Competition among communities. The circumstances of American life in the upstart cities of the West produced a lively competitive spirit. But the characteristic and most fertile competition was a competition among communities. We have been misled by slogans of individualism. Just as the competition among colonial seaboard cities helped diffuse American culture and kept it from becoming concentrated in a European-style metropolis, so the competition among western upstart cities helped create the booster spirit. Where there had been no cities before, where all were growing fast, there was no traditional rank among urban centers. If Lexington, Kentucky, could quickly arise by 1800 to be the most populous city of the West, if St. Louis and Cincinnati and Chicago had so suddenly arisen, might not some new Lexington displace them all? Many of each community's institutions had been founded to give it a competitive advantage. Dr. Drake's medical college helped Cincinnati keep ahead of Lexington, just as Ogden's streets and bridges and parks helped Chicago lead Cincinnati. Where individual and community prosperity were so intermingled, competition among individuals was also a competition among communities.

*   *   *

The emerging businessman of the upstart cities had much in common with the energetic American of an earlier generation. He was the Franklin of the West. He was the undifferentiated man of the colonial period, but in a more expansive setting. The new language of that day called him a "businessman"; the retrospective language of our century calls him the booster. He thrived on growth and expansion. His loyalties were intense, naïve, optimistic, and quickly transferable.

Versatility was his hallmark. He usually had neither the advantages nor the disadvantages of specialized skills or monopolistic protection. In Dr. Drake's Cincinnati, physicians became merchants, clergymen became bankers, lawyers became manufacturers. "The young lawyer," H. M. Brackenridge shrewdly advised the Western seeker after fortune (in one of the first recorded uses of the word "businessman") "should think more of picking up his crumbs, than of flying like a balloon. He must be content to become a *business man*, and leave the rest to fortune." For success in this environment, the specialized skills—of lawyer, doctor, financier, or engineer—had a new unimportance. Rewards went to the organizer, the persuader, the discoverer of opportunities, the projector, the risk-taker, and the man able to attach himself quickly and profitably to some group until its promise was tested.

"PALACES OF THE PUBLIC"

CHAPTER 18

"T HE HOTEL," a Briton visiting the United States in the mid-1850's reported, "is quite a 'peculiar institution' of this country." Even the words describing travelers' accommodations had acquired a new meaning. In England a "tavern" had been a place of refreshment where one could buy food and drink, while a place of lodging was called an "inn." In America (as Noah Webster recorded), this distinction like many others disappeared. Here food and lodging were found in either an "inn" or a "tavern." By the era of the American Revolution, a new American word, "hotel," had become common for the public houses accommodating travelers and strangers. This was destined to be the name for a new institution. Borrowed from the French, in which "hotel" meant a noble house or (in the expression "hotel de ville") a city hall, here it named a new kind of community enterprise.

One conspicuous clue to this distinctiveness was architecture. When Alexander Mackay, an English barrister, traveled about this country in 1846–47, he observed that government buildings were often quite unimpressive. In New Orleans, for example, he found the public offices "neither elegant nor imposing." But the St. Charles Hotel, "with its large and elegant Corinthian portico, and the lofty swelling dome which surmounts it," was impressive. "With us [in England] hotels are regarded as purely private property, and it is sel-

118

dom that, in their appearance, they stand out from the mass of private houses around them. In America they are looked upon much more in the light of public concerns, and generally assume in their exterior the character of public buildings." The American hotel was a far cry from the English inn, and not only in appearance. For here it played a much larger and more important public role.

The splendor of these "first-class" modern hotels, as the *National Intelligencer* explained (June 19, 1827), had fully earned them the name, "Palaces of the Public." Some called them "People's Palaces." Lacking a royal palace as the center of "Society," Americans created their counterpart in the community hotel. The People's Palace was a building constructed with extravagant optimism expressly to serve all who could pay the price. Even into the 20th century, hotels typically remained among the grandest buildings of all large American cities; in medium-sized and smaller cities, they often overshadowed all other structures. This has become so obvious a feature of American culture, and has been so widely transplanted to cities elsewhere in the world, that Americans have largely ignored its meaning.

From the early days of the 19th century, hotels were social centers. What more appropriate "palaces" for a migratory people? In the period of most rapid urban growth, it was not by churches or government buildings but by hotels that cities judged themselves and expected others to judge them. Hotels were usually the centers of lavish private entertainment (which, being held there, acquired a public significance) and of the most important public celebrations. The hotel lobby, like the outer rooms of a royal palace, became a loitering place, a headquarters of gossip, a vantage point for a glimpse of the great, the rich, and the powerful.

A distinctive architectural and engineering style soon developed, the first and most influential example of which was the Tremont House, opened in 1829 in Boston. David Barnum's lavish six-story City Hotel in Baltimore, completed three years earlier, already showed features of the modern American hotel: the size ("200 apartments"), the public aspect, and the expert management. But the design which for decades remained the standard for the American first-class hotel came out of New England. It was the work primarily of Isaiah Rogers (1800–1869), a self-educated architecture prodigy. The son of a shipbuilder in Massachusetts, he had the good luck to work in the architectural office of Solomon Willard—the same Willard who had developed the Quincy granite quarries, had built the Bunker Hill Monument, and (more important for present purposes) had developed the first widely used American system of central heating. At twenty-six, Rogers opened his own office and within two years had the commission for the Tremont House.

Building this new hotel for Boston had become a civic enterprise when the Boston Exchange Coffee House burned down in 1818. The lamented "Exchange Hotel," as the older building was commonly called, had been financed and operated by a group of local merchants. With about 300 rooms, banquet halls, dining rooms, and many other public facilities, it had often been called the largest building and the best hotel in the country. There David Barnum, "the Metternich of all hosts" and "the emperor of American landlords," first made his national reputation as a hotelkeeper. Its destruction by fire was a civic calamity, but the Panic of 1819 prevented immediate rebuilding. In 1825, a committee of merchants headed by William Havard Eliot obtained a charter for a hotel company and commissioned young Isaiah Rogers as architect.

This was a stroke of good luck for Rogers, for Boston, and, in the long run, for every American community destined to thrive with (and partly through) its hotels. Rogers, although he had almost no models to follow, succeeded in designing the Tremont House to give an unmistakable impression of elegance and public purpose, for which the Greek-revival orders, stylish in that day, were, of course, admirably suited. Its four-story façade of Quincy granite was dominated by a colonnaded portico and pilasters at the corners. The central, richly trimmed rotunda office, the numerous large public rooms, a lavish formal dining hall with a deeply coffered ceiling and a screen of Ionic columns at either end, all confirmed a feeling as different as possible from that of the 18th-century inn.

Rogers' elegant and convenient plan quickly became the prototype for the new-style American first-class hotel, and Rogers himself

soon became the leading hotel architect in the nation. His work included many of the largest and best known hotels constructed in his
lifetime: the Bangor House (1834) in Bangor, Maine; the Astor
House (1836) in New York City; the Charleston Hotel (1839) in
Charleston, South Carolina; the Exchange Hotel (1841) in Richmond, Virginia; the Burnet House (1850) in Cincinnati; the famous
second St. Charles Hotel (1851) in New Orleans; the Battle House
(1852) in Mobile; the second Galt House (c. 1865) in Louisville; and
the six-hundred-room Maxwell House (begun 1859; completed
1869) in Nashville. The American "Palace of the Public" was, in
large part, the creation of Isaiah Rogers.

The American hotel pioneered the incorporation of mechanical
equipment, comforts, and gadgets into architectural design. The future importance of plumbing, heating, ventilating, air-conditioning,
and scores of other real or supposed conveniences in American
building was already foreshadowed. Some architectural historians
call the Tremont House the first modern building. It was the first
hotel—perhaps the first large building of any kind in modern
times—with extensive plumbing. Its most famous feature was a bat-
tery of eight water-closets. Since plumbing above the ground floor
was still virtually unknown, these were all on the ground floor at the
rear of the central court and were connected by glazed corridors to
the bedroom wings, dining room, and rotunda. They were probably
the first in America, outside of a few in mansions. Bathrooms in the
basement were fitted with cold running water, which also went to
the kitchen and laundry. In Rogers' next large hotel, the Astor
House in New York, one of the most astonishing features was
plumbing on the upper floors. Each floor had its own water-closets
and its own bathrooms (seventeen in all, plus two showers), fed from
a roof tank to which water had been raised by a steam pump.

From that early day, American hotels remained testing places for
the most advanced domestic conveniences. The great amount of
capital employed in hotel construction and the desire to outshine
competitors for both business and civic reasons made them laboratories and showcases of progress in the technology of everyday life.
The large transient population of hotels provided a rare opportunity

to whet public appetite for machines, conveniences, and gadgets of all kinds. And this opportunity for large-scale experiment and display eventually played a part in developing an American standard of living.

One domestic convenience after another was first tried, and then first widely used, in American hotels. For example, the first public building in America heated by steam was the Eastern Exchange Hotel in Boston (1846). Soon after, several leading hotels boasted steam-heat on all floors. But central heating was generally confined to the public rooms and the hallways of the bedroom floors, while the guest rooms themselves were still heated by parlor stoves and fireplaces. The passenger elevator (originally called the "vertical railway") had its earliest trials and its first general use in hotels. Holt's Hotel in New York had a steam-powered lift, used mainly for baggage, as early as 1833. The first practical passenger elevators, installed in the old Fifth Avenue Hotel in New York in 1859, produced solid commercial benefits. Until then, rooms on the top floors had been cheaper, but with the aid of the elevator, as one writer facetiously suggested, a guest atop a hotel could "look down on surrounding buildings in the same manner as our most gracious English nobility look down upon the peasants beneath them."

New techniques of lighting also had their first extensive trial in hotels. A novelty of the Tremont House was gaslight in its public rooms (whale-oil lamps still lighted the guest chambers). Six years later, when the American House opened in Boston in 1835, it was gaslit throughout. The widely admired gaslighting of the public rooms of the Astor House in New York was facilitated by its own gas plant. Very soon after Thomas A. Edison announced the commercial feasibility of his incandescent lamp (on October 21, 1879), it was tried in hotels. Early in 1882 the Hotel Everett on Park Row in New York, the first hotel lit by electricity, was burning 101 incandescent lamps in its main dining room, lobby, reading room, and parlors. A few months later, the Palmer House in Chicago employed its own electrical plant for ninety-six incandescent lamps in two dining rooms.

Hotels were also among the first buildings to use electricity for communication. The "electro-magnetic annunciator" in Boston's Tremont House provided a system (as one wag put it) of "One ring for ice-water, two for bell-boy, three for porter, four for chambermaid,—and not a darned one of them will come." These push buttons, reputedly the first in America, buzzed the office, where they dropped metal disks showing room numbers. These were pleasantly silent compared to the hand bells which guests had used before. Hotels also pioneered the telephone. When New York's first telephone exchange opened in 1879, several hotels were among the few original subscribers. The first installation of room phones and a private switchboard for them (in New York's Hotel Netherland) came in 1894. Many minor comforts of American life also had their first trial in hotels. The spring bed, still unknown when the Tremont House opened in Boston, was patented in 1831 and within a dozen years it was used in the best hotels, although it was almost forty years before the invention of a machine for producing bedsprings would make the spring bed generally available.

The splendor and elegance of American hotels became a byword. Foreign visitors were quick to discover why these should be called the "Palaces" of a democratic people. "The American hotel," an overwhelmed London journalist wrote in 1861, "is to an English hotel what an elephant is to a periwinkle. . . . An American hotel is (in the chief cities) as roomy as Buckingham Palace, and is not much inferior to a palace in its internal fittings. It has ranges of drawing rooms, suites of private rooms, vast staircases and interminable layers of bedchambers. An English comedian staying at New York's lavish St. Nicholas—an Arabian Nights hodgepodge of window curtains costing $700 apiece, gold embroidered draperies costing $1000, mahogany panelling, rosewood carved furniture, sofas upholstered in Flemish tapestry, figured Turkish rugs, and deep Brussels carpets—refused to leave his shoes outside his door to be shined, for fear someone would gild them.

Appropriately enough, some of the first efforts to make the American hotel something new began with fanfare as part of the effort to create a suitable new national capital at Washington, D. C. The site chosen by President Washington in 1790 was not occupied by the Federal government until 1800, but, as early as 1793, before the city actually existed, there were plans to assure the capital city of its hotel. The Commissioners of the Federal City engaged an enterprising New Englander, Samuel Blodget, who had already invested in Washington real estate, to promote the undertaking. They emphasized the public significance of the building when they appointed the same architect, James Hoban, whom they had commissioned to design the President's House. The cornerstone was laid by Freemasons at a public ceremony on July 4, 1793. Blodget then tried to raise the construction money by a federal lottery (authorized by the Commissioners), the first prize to be ownership of the hotel itself (supposedly worth $50,000). It was to be called the Union Public Hotel (probably the first building to announce itself as a "public hotel"), but although widely touted as an important community undertaking, it never opened as a hotel. When the building was finally completed in 1810, it housed a Post Office and the Patent Office. The capital city did not have a first-class hotel until Gadsby's National Hotel was ceremoniously opened with a Washington's Birthday Ball in 1827.

In New York City, too, as early as the 1790's, leading merchants used an ingenious scheme to finance the building: in their "Tontine" Association, the interest of each subscriber increased as the number of subscribers was diminished by death, until finally the last survivor inherited the whole property. At least two New York hotels, including the famous City Hotel which dominated the scene between 1800 and 1830, were successfully constructed under schemes of this kind. In other places, Tontine Associations or still more complex arrangements were tried, allowing numerous small investors to help build an impressive hotel for the community.

Laying the cornerstone of a hotel was a public ceremony, commonly held on the Fourth of July. That was the date chosen for Boston's Tremont House in 1828, for New York's Astor House in 1834, and for many less famous hotels elsewhere. At the inaugural dinner of the Tremont House on October 16, 1829, Daniel Webster, Edward Everett, and a hundred other leading citizens honored the new institution with their toasts.

In the older cities of the eastern seaboard—in Boston, New York, Baltimore, or Charleston—hotels had public functions not yet acquired in Europe. The first American merchants' exchanges were informal meetings in hotels; many hotels, for example the Boston Exchange Hotel, were actually called "exchanges"; some secured banking privileges and issued paper currency. As late as the 1860's, the Burnet House in Cincinnati was issuing five-dollar bills authenticated by the hotel cashier and an engraved likeness of the building. In New Orleans, for example, the lobby of the St. Charles Hotel was the site of public slave auctions. In upstart cities, partly from the lack of other public buildings, hotels were the usual meeting places of civic committees, of associations of businessmen, and even, in the early days, of the city council and other government agencies.

Here, too, was the public information center, where new arrivals brought the latest word from distant places. The old-fashioned hotel register (in this country, contrary to common belief, not a legal requirement but only a business custom) provided reading matter for the general public. In the 1820's an English farmer stopping at a hotel in Zanesville, Ohio, noted the "folio register, in which travelers write their names, from whence they come, and whither they are bound, with any news which they bring with them." The place left for "remarks" gave an opportunity to write a few lines recommending one's wares, commenting on business conditions or on the state of the world. "G. Squires, wife and two babies," wrote a guest at Trenton Falls, New York, and added "No servant, owing to the hardness of the times." The next guest, who inscribed himself "G. W. Douglas and Servant" retorted, "No wife and babies, owing to the hardness of the times."

In Presidential election years, the citizens who recorded their political preferences in the hotel register made it one of the first opinion polls. "Each person entered the name of the Presidential candidate for whom he intended to vote," the English traveler J. S. Buckingham noted of the register at Ball's Hotel in Brownsville, Pennsylvania, in 1840. "Thus the column contained the entries of— Harrison against the world—Van Buren for ever—Henry Clay, the Pride of Kentucky—Little Van, the Magician—Old Tippecanoe, and no Sub-Treasury—the Farmer of North Bend—Hurrah for Jackson—Van Buren again—Log Cabin and Hard Cider—and so on, page after page. In this way some attempt is made to ascertain the strength of the parties; the best is most imperfect." Later the hotel became the headquarters of the first local telegraph office.

The "reading-room," too, was a leading attraction before the day of the public library. Boston's Tremont House, for example, collected newspapers from all over, offering their use free to hotel guests and for a small annual fee to local citizens.

Throughout the 19th century, after a city fire, the community hotel was usually among the first buildings reconstructed. When Boston's Exchange Coffee House Hotel burned in 1818, an editor demanded its rebuilding "for the honor of the town." So it was after the St. Louis fire of 1867. The Great Chicago Fire of October 8, 1871, destroyed nearly all the city's hotels, including the Palmer House, which had been open only a year and had been advertised as "the only fireproof hotel in the world"—but within six years Chicago had sixteen new first-class hotels (each containing from 200 to 800 rooms) and about 140 others. It is not surprising that when Barnum's hotel in Baltimore was involved in litigation in 1860, a Baltimore judge ruled it had to be kept open because, as a first-class hotel, it was a "public institution and a public necessity."

* * *

In early 19th-century America, then, the hotel had become something recognizably new. Even before the Civil War, it was being widely imitated in Europe and elsewhere. But in the upstart cities of the West, the hotel, like the newspaper, played a role that could not be imitated in the Old World. Here were booster hotels to match the booster press. In England the railroad hotels were the pioneers, but in America first-class hotels appeared even before the railroad. They were, in fact, often built for the purpose of attracting railroads, along with settlers, newspapers, merchants, customers, lawyers, doctors, salesmen, and all the other paraphernalia of metropolitan greatness. No wonder the age of upstart towns was the spawning season of hotels.

Anthony Trollope's lively chapter on "American Hotels" in his book on North America in the early 1860's went to the heart of the matter:

> The American inn differs . . . is altogether an institution apart, and a thing of itself. Hotels in America are very much larger and more numerous than in other countries. They are to be found in all towns, and I may almost say in all villages. In England and on the Continent we find them on the recognized routes of travel and in towns of commercial or social importance. On unfrequented roads and in villages there is usually some small house of public entertainment in which the unexpected traveller may obtain food and shelter, and in which the expected boon companions of the neighborhood smoke their nightly pipes, and drink their nightly tipple. But in the States of America the first sign of an incipient settlement is an hotel five stories high, with an office, a bar, a cloak-room, three gentlemen's parlours, two ladies' parlours, a ladies' entrance, and two hundred bedrooms. . . . Whence are to come the sleepers in those two hundred bedrooms, and who is to pay for the gaudy sofas and numerous lounging chairs of the ladies' parlours? In all other countries the expectations would extend itself simply to travellers;—to travellers or to strangers sojourning in the land. But this is by no means the case as to these speculations in America. When the new hotel rises up in the wilderness, it is presumed that people will come there with the express object of inhabiting it. The hotel itself will create a population,—as the railways do. With us railways run to the towns; but in the States the towns run to the railways. It is the same thing with the hotels.

In some places in the West, the sudden gathering of people created a need for sleeping accommodations before there were even any solid buildings. At Lawrence, Kansas, for example, in the 1850's the first "hotel" was a large tent, divided by a row of boxes into two apartments (one for men, the other for women) with straw on the ground for beds. In the booming Dakota Territory, about twenty-five years later, an enterprising citizen of Aberdeen offered sleeping space in a circus tent, until he could build a sod structure to take its place. This was not what people meant when they talked about an American hotel mania.

What they did mean was hotel buildings ridiculously disproportionate to their surroundings—hotels built not to serve cities but to create them. Just as newspapers in the upstart West often began publication before the cities existed to support them and their editors wrote copy under elm trees and issued papers from log-cabins, so hotels sprang up in lonely woods or cornfields. They, too, attested somebody's hope of a metropolis. Facing the river at Memphis, Tennessee, for example, the imposing white-columned façade of the Gayoso House, advertised as a "spacious and elegant hotel" (completed in 1846, three years before Memphis was incorporated as a city, a decade before it had a railroad), stood surrounded by forest. By a kind of homeopathic magic, such a hotel was supposed to make a city grow. Somehow Memphis would become a cotton capital because it already had a public palace worthy of one.

About 1823 a group including Nicholas Biddle, President of the Bank of the United States, and Saunders Coates, editor of the Mobile *Register*, planned a city in the Northwest Territory to outstrip Detroit and St. Louis. They set about constructing Port Sheldon (a now abandoned site about twelve miles northeast of Holland, Michigan) at the mouth of Pigeon River. The first big item on their agenda was a "Large and Commodious Hotel." Ottawa House, which cost about $200,000, was completed just before the Panic of 1837. This grand structure, two stories high and 80 by 150 feet, fronted by a Grecian colonnade of six grooved pillars, was erected in what they hoped would be the heart of the imagined city. When built, it was in the heart of a black pine forest. Inside furnishings alone, "in a style not surpassed by any House in the country . . . entirely new, selected in Eastern Cities," were said to have cost $60,000. The last notation on the register of Ottawa House was March 1, 1842, barely five years after its opening. When the city failed, the hotel was dismantled. Four of its pillars were dragged away by ox-team for a mansion in Grand Rapids.

Corydon, the territorial capital of Indiana, which hoped to become a city, in 1816 (when it was hardly more than a hypothesis) already possessed a new stone hotel, with walls eighteen inches thick and great ceiling timbers. When Ignatius Donnelly set out to develop Nininger City, Minnesota, in 1856 he naturally included plans for a hotel, toward which each share-owner would subscribe one thousand dollars. "It is literally a cornfield, so I cannot have it surveyed," explained Charles Elliot Perkins, superintendent for the Burlington Railroad, who was exploring the land west of Ottumwa, Iowa, in 1866, "but yesterday a man came to arrange to put a hotel here. This is a great country for hotels."

"We shall have a good hotel here by spring," William Larimer wrote his wife in November 1858 from the almost vacant site that was to become Denver. The building, he said, was already under construction, and a good hotelkeeper was on his way from Omaha. As early as 1835, Chicago (which just two years before had had a population of only 350) acquired its first brick hotel. The Lake House was on the north side of the river at Michigan and North Water Streets, then a fashionable residential area. This establishment, so elegant that its restaurant actually supplied napkins, offered the first printed menus in Chicago. Said to be "equal to the City Hotel of New York," it was "the pride of the city and the admiration of strangers." By the mid-1850's Chicago, which then had some sixty thousand inhabitants, was said to possess one hundred and fifty hotels.

Hotels were among the earliest transient facilities that bound the nation together. They were both creatures and creators of communities, as well as symptoms of the frenetic quest for community. Americans were already forming their habit of gathering from all corners of the nation for mixed public-private, business-pleasure purposes. Conventions were the new occasions, and hotels were distinctively American facilities making conventions possible. Within a century, the United States would be the most conventioning nation in the world. The first national nominating convention of a major party (that of the National Republican Party, which met on December 12, 1831 and named Henry Clay for President) was held in Baltimore, whose hotel was then reputed to be the best in the country. The presence in Baltimore of Barnum's City Hotel, a six-story building with two hundred apartments, helps explain why many other early national political conventions were held there.

In the longer run, too, the American hotels made other national conventions not only possible but pleasant and convivial. The growing custom of regularly assembling from afar the representatives of all kinds of groups—political, commercial, professional, learned, and avocational—then in turn supported the multiplying hotels. By mid-20th century, conventions accounted for over a third of the yearly room occupancy of all hotels in the nation; about eighteen thousand different conventions were held annually with a total attendance of about ten million persons.

In America the hotelkeeper, who was no longer the genial, deferential "host" of the 18th-century European inn, became a leading citizen. Holding a large stake in his community, he exercised power to make it prosper. As owner or manager of the local Palace of the Public, he was maker and shaper of a principal community "attraction." Travelers from abroad were surprised and mildly shocked by his high social position. Things were really topsy-turvy in a country where the innkeeper honored the guest by his company.

Foreign observers in the mid-19th century attributed the country's flourishing hotels "to the manner in which the population has been scattered over the surface of the Union in the natural course of its industrial development." They guessed that not one American in ten was residing in the town of his birth. The census of 1850 showed "outsiders" (the foreign-born and those residing outside the state where they were born) to be about one-third of the whole population. "It can be easily conceived what a network of relationship this makes all over the Union, and how much travelling to and fro this must give rise to, especially among a people in whom the domestic affections are so strong as the Americans."

Old World distinctions between "private" and "public" aspects of life tended to lose meaning. "Home," in England an intimate and emotion-laden word, in America became almost interchangeable with "house." Here was both less privacy and more publicity. Americans lived in a new realm of uncertain boundaries, in an affable, communal world which, strictly speaking, was neither public nor private: a world of first names, open doors, front porches, and front lawns, and naturally, too, of lunch counters, restaurants, and hotel lobbies.

In this new limbo, family life lost much of its old privacy. Casual acquaintances soon seemed "members of the family." The classic locale for this new American vagueness, for this dissolving of old distinctions, was the hotel. And a clue to its personal meaning was the new scheme, originated in American hotels, which from the beginning was called the "American Plan." The fee paid by hotel guests included meals and they ate together in a common dining room. This practice became established in the 1830's and '40's when Americans were churning around the West, and the upstart cities were springing up. At first British travelers called this the *table d'hôte* from the manner of serving (supposedly resembling the French). All the food was put on the table for guests to serve themselves. There was no need for a menu until later, when the system of service changed, allowing guests to choose among items to be brought them individually. "It is the invariable custom in the United States," the English traveler Thomas Hamilton complained as early as 1833, "to charge by the day or week; and travellers are thus obliged to pay for meals whether they eat them or not." The "American Plan" had become so standard here that Boston's Parker House (opened in 1855) became widely known as the first hotel in this country operated on what by contrast was called "European Plan," meaning that meals were not included in the price of the room. By the end of the 19th century, Baedeker's *United States* carefully distinguished hotels by whether they offered American or European plan.

From the outset, the new American custom indicated that Americans regarded hotels not merely as places for a night en route but as dwelling-places: "a home away from home." Travelers from abroad, impressed by the number, size, and conveniences of American hotels, were shocked by how many Americans lived in them permanently. There was no denying that, by contrast with those in Europe,

American hotels contained a large number of permanent residents. "The chance travellers," Anthony Trollope remarked, "are but chance additions to these, and are not generally the main stay of the house." With his tourist's license to exaggerate, Trollope described hotel-living in the American middle classes:

> Housekeeping is not popular with young married people in America, and there are various reasons why this should be so. Men there are not fixed in their employment as they are with us. If a young Benedict cannot get along as a lawyer at Salem, perhaps he may thrive as a shoemaker at Thermopylae. Jefferson B. Johnson fails in the lumber line at Eleutheria, but hearing of an opening for a Baptist preacher at Big Mud Creek moves himself off with his wife and three children at a week's notice. Aminadab Wiggs takes an engagement as a clerk at a steam-boat office on the Pongowonga river, but he goes to his employment with an inward conviction that six months will see him earning his bread elsewhere. Under such circumstances even a large wardrobe is a nuisance, and a collection of furniture would be as appropriate as a drove of elephants. Then, again, young men and women marry without any means already collected on which to commence their life. They are content to look forward and to hope that such means will come. In so doing they are guilty of no imprudence. It is the way of the country; and, if the man be useful for anything, employment will certainly come to him. But he must live on the fruits of that employment, and can only pay his way from week to week and from day to day. And as a third reason I think I may allege that the mode of life found in these hotels is liked by the people who frequent them. It is to their taste.

Our imperfect statistics suggest that, in the first half of the 19th century, many urban Americans were living in hotels or boarding houses. This was especially true in the Western upstart cities, and more especially, too, among the middle classes, the leading citizens who set the tone of life. The English feminist, Mrs. Bodichon, remarked in the late 1850's that every large town in the United States had five or six, and in some places twenty or more, large hotels or boarding houses containing several hundred inhabitants. Most of this population, she said, consisted of families living there permanently. For example, in Chicago in 1844, of persons listed in the city directory, about one in six was living in a hotel, and about one in four was living in a boarding house or with his employer. Another obvious explanation, besides the migratory habits of young married Americans, was the preponderance of men in the population of these new-settled places and the scarcity of women to make households.

Still another peculiarly American circumstance encouraged hotel-living by the middle classes. This, a by-product of American equality and American opportunity, was the scarcity and high price of domestic servants. An Irish cook or housemaid, a British traveler of the mid-1850's observed, in America was an expensive luxury. "She insists on being mistress of the house. Native-born Americans are a degree more expensive and more domineering. Under these circumstances, it is natural that the American matron of seventeen or eighteen should seek refuge from this domestic terrorism in the gilded saloons of the St. Nicholas or St. Charles, or whatever other Saint may offer his protection for two and a half dollars a day." But, Mrs. Bodichon observed, the female character deteriorated in the idleness of hotel life. She compared the American hotel "ladies" to women she had seen in the Eastern seraglios. "The ladies of the East spend their days in adorning themselves to please one lord and master—the ladies of the West to please all the lords of creation."

Anyone who frequented hotels soon discovered how many Old World distinctions were dissolved in America. The European middle classes counted the right to be by oneself or alone with one's family or chosen friends among the amenities, a sign of civilized respectability. But a western traveler who found himself sharing his dinner table, and called upon to chat familiarly, with a miscellaneous company of common soldiers, farmers, laborers, teamsters, lawyers, doctors, ministers, bankers, judges, or generals, soon discovered that Americans considered the desire for privacy a vice akin to pride. To want to be left alone was "a species of neglect, if not offense, which is decidedly felt, though it may not be expressed. You may sin and be wicked in many ways, and in the tolerant circle of American Society receive a full and generous pardon. But this one sin can never be pardoned." Captain Basil Hall, traveling the country in 1827–28, complained that a "sitting-parlour" where one could be alone was almost unobtainable, even in the largest hotels and that to have a meal alone was a rare luxury, never secured without an extra fee, and usually not available at any price. Anthony Trollope, thirty-five years later, wistfully recalled the wonderfully private luxury of an English inn—one's tea, one's fire, and one's book. "One is in a free country . . . and yet in an American inn one can never do as one likes. A terrific gong sounds early in the morning, breaking one's sweet slumbers, and then a second gong sounding some thirty minutes later, makes you understand that you must proceed to breakfast, whether you be dressed or no. You certainly can go on with your toilet and obtain your meal after half an hour's delay. Nobody actually scolds you for so doing, but the breakfast is, as they say in this country, 'through.' . . . They begrudge you no amount that you can eat or drink; but they begrudge you a single moment that you sit there neither eating nor drinking. This is your fate if you're too late, and therefore as a rule you are not late. In that case you form one of a long row of eaters who proceed through their work with a solid energy that is past all praise."

American hotels were a microcosm of American life. People in transient and upstart communities had to become accustomed to live and eat and talk in the presence of those they knew only casually. This was living "American Plan" in every sense of the word. "The tangible republic—the only thing palpable and agreeable that we have to show in common life, as republican"—this is what the American style of hotel-living seemed in 1844 to the popular wit N. P. Willis. "There are some republican advantages in our present system of hotels which the country is not yet ready to forgo. Tell a country lady in these times that when she comes to New York she must eat and pass the evening in a room by herself, and she would rather stay at home. The going to the Astor and dining with two hundred well dressed people, and sitting in full dress in a splendid drawing room with plenty of company—is the charm of going to the city! The theaters are nothing to that! Broadway, the shopping and the sights, are all subordinate—poor accessories to the main object of the visit." What good was a hotel, or a republic, if it was not a place where citizens "tolerably well dressed and well behaved" could rub elbows at a public table?

As hotel life became a symbol of the fluidity of dynamic America, Southerners boasted their immunity "from the bane of hotel life and the curse of boarding-houses." A hotel suited transients, of whom the Old South (luckily, they said) had few. Where men stayed put, then every citizen was a landholder with strong "home feeling." His fixed residence on the land rooted his feeling for the permanency of his country's institutions.

But if "American Plan," a way of life for migratory, enterprising people in upstart cities, was not without its vices, it also had its virtues. If it loosened family ties, at the same time it broke down caste walls. If intimacy and individuality were stifled, a sense of fellowship was invigorated. In America perhaps men were becoming affiliated in a new way.

THE BALLOON-FRAME HOUSE

CHAPTER 19

I N UPSTART TOWNS citizens could lounge in the fancy salons and bars of a public palace, yet might not find a bed of their own or shelter against the rain. Some "community" facilities were grand enough for a great metropolis, yet many private facilities were unworthy of a village. There were accomplished newspapermen and hotelkeepers in surprising numbers, but ordinary carpenters were hardly found at all.

Under pressure to build houses quickly and in large numbers when they had few or no skilled carpenters, the upstarts invented a new way of building which would set a pattern for decades to come. This story is another American parable of the unpredictable advantages of American crudities and American scarcities. Just as the lack of skilled gunsmiths had stirred Eli Whitney and other versatile New Englanders to find ways of making guns without gunsmiths, the lack of skilled builders in the upstart West also produced unexpected dividends. The "balloon-frame" house, which is everywhere in the 20th century, remains an unacknowledged monument to the Americans of these upstart towns. It was at bottom very simple: a common-sense way to meet the urgent housing needs of impatient migratory people.

For centuries Englishmen and others in temperate climates of Western Europe had been building their wooden houses (or houses

136

with wooden frames) in a certain traditional manner. To insure strength and durability, the house was built on a sturdy frame of heavy timbers about a foot thick. These were held together by cutting down the end of one beam into a tongue ("tenon"), which was then fitted into a hole ("mortise") in the adjoining beam. Where there was a pull on the joint, the pieces were held by a wooden peg fitted into an auger hole through the joined timbers. This kind of construction was generally supposed to be the only proper way to build a house. It also required a great deal of skill: shaping tongues and grooves, boring auger holes, making wooden pegs, and finally fitting all these neatly together required the tools and the training of a carpenter. Even to suggest other methods was to question a whole guild.

The very rigidity of this belief led to the making of the first modern prefabricated houses. At first it seems surprising that, in the 17th century, prefabricated houses were shipped across the ocean to an America of virgin forests. But the need to prefabricate, then as now, came in large part from the scarcity of skills where the building was to be erected. As late as 1820, when pious Bostonians wanted to ease the life of missionaries in far-off Hawaii, they shipped a prefabricated house, the essential parts of which were a massive hewn frame, knocked down and ready to be reassembled with mortise, tenon, and wooden pegs. The old Mission House, carried eighteen thousand miles round the Horn, is the oldest wooden building in the islands, and still stands in downtown Honolulu.

This way of exporting houses was feasible in places reached directly by sea but, in the days before railroads, moving them overland was quite another matter. The needs of the upstart cities of the American West required an entirely different approach to the problem. And these cities saw a revolutionary change in the way of building houses. In the manner of other American innovations, this too was a way of making better products with fewer traditional skills.

It is appropriate that this great innovation should still be known by the derisive name, at first used to contrast its flimsiness with the crafthewn heaviness of the traditional house. "Balloon-frame" is what respectable builders first called it because it was ridiculously light. The first strong wind, they said, would surely blow it away. But the construction they were ridiculing would, within decades, become conventional. Into the 20th century, this was the style that made possible the vast American housing developments; without it the quick-grown American city, the high standard of American housing, and the extensive American suburbs would be hard to imagine.

We do not know for sure who invented the balloon-frame. We do know that it appeared in Chicago in 1833 and that within twenty years it had prevailed in the American urban West. The first balloon-frame building was probably St. Mary's Church, erected under the direction of Father John M. I. St. Cyr, first priest appointed for the city. It was thirty-six feet long, twenty-four feet wide, a single story twelve feet high, covered by a low-pitched gable roof. The builder (perhaps also an inventor of this construction) was Augustine Deodat Taylor, a carpenter from Hartford who had arrived in Chicago only a month before. The church cost about $400 and was put up in about three months with the labor of three men. This was approximately half the expenditure of time and money then required for a similar building of conventional design. Early visitors to Chicago were astonished at the speed with which balloon-frame houses were built. In one week in April 1834, seven new buildings appeared; by mid-June, there were seventy-five more. In early October 1834, a writer noted that, although a year before there had been only fifty frame houses in the city, "now I counted them last Sunday and there was 600 and 28 and there is from 1 to 4 or 5 a day and about two hundred and 12 of them stores and groceries." The normal time between commissioning and completing a house was now one week!

What was the "balloon-frame"? The basic new idea was so simple, and today is so universally employed, that it is hard to realize it ever had to be invented. It was nothing more than the substitution of a light frame of two-by-fours held together by nails in place of the old foot-square beams joined by mortise, tenon, and pegs. The wall plates (horizontals) and studs (uprights), the floor joists, and roof rafters were all made of thin sawed timbers (2 × 4 inches, 4 × 4, 2 × 6, 2 × 8), nailed together in such a way that every strain went in the direction of the fibre of the wood (i.e., against the grain). "Basket-frame" was the name sometimes given it, because the light timbers formed a simple basketlike cage to which any desired material could be applied inside and out. Usually, light boards or clapboards covered the outside. Nothing could be simpler. Today about three-quarters of the houses in the United States are built this way.

This remarkable invention would not have been possible without the revolutionary advances in nail manufacturing which had been accomplished, mostly in New England, before 1830. The old craft of making and heading each nail by hand had been replaced by an American system of manufacturing which, by mechanizing the process, produced nails quickly and cheaply.

In more ways than one, the scarcity of skilled labor was crucial. For in Chicago (the balloon-frame until the 1870's was widely known as "Chicago construction") laborers of all kinds, and especially skilled carpenters, were scarce. If the flood of people who poured into the new city were to be housed quickly, houses had to be built in a new way.

The balloon-frame building, then, arose as a solution to peculiar problems of the American upstart city. In older settled communities, even in the United States, there was likely to be more balance between the demand and the supply. In older communities, too, those who needed housing could make shift—with friends or neighbors, in boarding houses, taverns, or barns—until their needs could be met. In the backwoods, a lean-to (like the one Lincoln's father made when he moved to Southern Indiana in 1816) could be put up in short order; with a little more time and a little help, a man could build a log house. But city people could not live in lean-tos, sod huts, or half-face camps; they had no time to build log-cabins, even if enough logs had been handy. Carpenters were not numerous enough nor well enough organized to persuade people that every house required their skills. People urgently needing shelter were slow to believe there was only one way to build; nor were they easily convinced that a simpler way was dangerously flimsy. Anyway a speed-minded and economy-minded people were willing to be satisfied with "lower" standards.

At first some Chicagoans, nostalgic for "handsome houses" of heavy timber and solid brick, lamented that so much of their new city was of the novel light construction, but gradually most of them discovered that balloon houses, which some sneeringly still called "shanties," actually were stronger and more durable than their sturdier-looking predecessors. For moisture tended to accumulate in the mortise-and-tenon joints and cause the timbers to rot. "A Balloon Frame looks light," recalled the architect-authors of *Woodward's Country Homes,* a widely used construction handbook, in 1865, "and its name was given in contempt by those old fogy mechanics who had been brought up to rob a stick of timber of all its strength and durability, by cutting it full of mortices, tenons and auger holes, and then supposing it to be stronger than a far lighter stick differently applied, and with all its capabilities unimpaired." The balloon-frame of thin pieces held together by nails, pointed out Solon Robinson, agricultural editor of the New York *Tribune,* was not only easier to put up, but actually "incalculably stronger when finished, than though it was composed of timbers ten inches square, with a thousand auger holes and a hundred days' work with the chisel and adze, making holes and pins to fit them."

Even before the invention of the balloon-frame, foreign visitors had been amazed at how Americans moved their buildings about. New England frame houses were sometimes picked up whole and transported to more convenient places, but to survive such treatment they had to be especially well joined together. Migratory Americans found the new balloon-frame much easier to take apart and put back together. A house simply nailed together was quickly taken down; its light parts could be piled compactly and conveniently transported, and the whole put together again by anyone who could handle a hammer. Three times within ten years of its erection in 1833, St. Mary's Church in Chicago, which was originally constructed on the canal near the southwest corner of State and Lake Streets, was taken down, moved away, and erected on a new site.

Americans on the move often wanted to take their houses along or ship them ahead. In Omaha, General William Larimer in 1856 lived in a balloon house that had been framed in Pittsburgh, then knocked down and shipped out by steamboat; when Omaha grew, he moved the house to another site. Making standardized, prefabricated houses, churches, and even hotels which could be ordered by mail for shipment to farmsites or cities in the West had become a thriving business by mid-century. By 1850, in New York alone some 5000 such prefabs had been made or were under contract to relieve the housing shortage in California. One concern there shipped 100 portable wooden houses to be carried on pack mules across the Isthmus of Panama, and another 175 went all the way by sea around the Horn. The San Francisco Astor House, a three-and-a-half story hotel 180 feet long, containing ten shops and 100 rooms, was sent out that year in prefabricated parts by the same New York firm.

Within twenty years of the building of the first balloon-frame in Chicago, influential writers like Solon Robinson preached its virtues. "To lay out and frame a building [of traditional design] so that all its parts will come together," he said in 1855, "requires the skill of a master mechanic, and a host of men and a deal of hard work to lift the great sticks of timber into position. To erect a balloon-building requires about as much mechanical skill as it does to build a board fence."

A HALF-KNOWN COUNTRY:

Settlement Before Discovery

"D ISCOVERY" OF AMERICA had only begun. One of the decisive American anachronisms, one of the odd, lucky, shaping facts about this nation, was that it had begun to flourish even before it was explored—and partly even because it had not yet been explored. This explained much of its precocity and vitality. In the New World, a nation could grow while it discovered itself.

For Americans, then, discovery and growth were synonymous from the very beginning. Old World nations knew—or thought they knew—their extent, their boundaries, their topography, and their resources. Americans expected their nation to grow as they discovered where they were and what they had to work with. If America had not remained a "dark continent" throughout nearly the whole first century of its national existence, it is doubtful whether Americans could have been so vital and so excited.

America was so fertile a repository of hopes because it was so attractive a locale for illusions. The map of America was full of blank spaces that had to be filled. Where solid facts were scarce, places were filled by myths—largely European in origin. A mere rumor that Coronado had somewhere reached the sea became the cartographic certainty that he had touched the great Western Ocean. Coronado's places wandered all over the map, dragging with them names offered by Niza and other early bewildered explorers.

Quivira, in origin probably a little village of Wichita Indians in central Kansas, became the great mysterious Empire of Quivira. Mapmakers with nothing new to report were grateful for mythical place names—Quivira and Tiguex and Cibola and Tontoneac—which they moved fancifully about. "They could be used wherever a white space would otherwise evidence geographic ignorance, and since their customers would certainly never go to Quivira to ascertain the truth, they were quite safe." The wanderings of these and other mythic places are depicted in Carl I. Wheat's magnificent volumes, unparalleled Odysseys of fabled cities tossed about on the turbulent sea of imagination.

To illustrate this fertile ignorance, I will only briefly tell the story of a single cluster of these illusions. The tale of the mythical River of the American West—the "San Buenaventura"—is rich in symbolism and irony. The antiquity and grandeur of this particular illusion, and its vivid survival into mid-19th century, give it special interest. European encounters with America in the late 15th century had been, of course, largely a result of European interest in the Orient. Hope for a westward water passage to Asia dominated all else. When the North American continent was found to be an obstruction, the waterway through the continent was only more eagerly sought. As the outlines of the New World were gradually defined, the hardening lines of knowledge excluded a westward sea passage at one place after another. But the hope for a waterway did not die; it simply moved to some still blank spot on the map. This cartographic migration is one of the most pathetic stories in the history of man's wishful thinking. It was to be capped by an irony worthy of some malicious god.

Search for the seaway across the continent proceeded in both directions. In the Pacific between the 16th and the 18th century, Spanish explorers who were seeking the transcontinental passage actually reconnoitered the coast of North America to above sixty degrees north latitude. The Dominguez-Escalante Expedition of 1776, hoping to find a route from Santa Fe to the Spanish settlement at Monterey on the California coast, explored and first mapped the great Colorado Plateau. Their map hopefully depicted a single great

Lake Timpanogos (a combination of the Great Salt Lake and Utah Lake) with a large, supposedly navigable river flowing westward, presumably to the Pacific Ocean. Optimistic Spanish fathers in California meanwhile elaborated the fiction of a waterway to the interior, imagining that the streams descending from the Sierras had originated in the Rockies. These rivers, they said, were probably navigable, and hence promised the long sought commercial routes between Spain and China.

All these notions were incorporated in a 1784 map of Spanish North America which, despite its faults, was the best yet. Its streams on the Pacific Coast showed how the waters from the western slopes of the Rockies north of the Colorado River flowed westward into the Pacific. Up to 1793, Spaniards in the Pacific continued probing for the western water entrance across the continent. At the same time, Spanish explorers from Louisiana came up the valley of the Missouri reaching for the ocean. Explorers eager to magnify their discoveries, travel-writers eager to please their readers, and cartographers eager to ornament the blank places on their maps, collaborated to perpetuate the ancient respectable belief in a waterway through the continent.

Disagreement centered not on *whether*, but on *where*, the transcontinental sea passage would be found. The Scottish explorer Alexander Mackenzie, in his journal (1802), suggested the Columbia (which he mistook for the Fraser River, which actually ran far north in British Columbia) as the probable future route between Atlantic and Pacific. Thomas Jefferson himself mistakenly identified the Columbia River with the Oregon (or "River of the West," a vestige of the mythical "Sea of the West," whose reputation reached back to the time of Verrazano). He believed the passage to India would be by way of the Missouri and the Columbia. And so he hopefully instructed Meriwether Lewis in 1803: "The object of your mission is single, the direct communication from sea to sea formed by the bed of the Missouri, and perhaps the Oregon. . . ." Of course, Lewis and Clark did establish *land* communication between the Missouri and the Columbia rivers, but the Rocky Mountain passes they found were steep and they certainly found no navigable water route. As traffic increased and knowledge grew in that area, it appeared ever more plain that the longed-for sea passage must be found elsewhere.

Once again the inextinguishable hopes had to be relocated. By now there remained only two areas where geographic darkness offered attractive locales. One, of course, was the Arctic. When the ice barrier east of Greenland melted between 1815 and 1817, the English, who had not sought the passage to India there for two centuries, energetically revived their quest. The other likely area, the last large repository of geographic ignorance in the present area of the United States, was what we now call the Great Basin. This was the territory between the forty-second parallel and the Mojave River. A great deal of "evidence" suddenly seemed to point to the actual existence of the long sought transcontinental water passage in that last resort.

The first half of the 19th century thus saw what Gloria G. Cline has aptly called a "cartographic extravaganza," in which, again and again, myth nearly conquered reality. The influential maps of Alexander Von Humboldt, Zebulon Pike, and Lewis and Clark between 1810 and 1814, all documented the myth which was to last still another three decades. This is not surprising since Pike and Lewis and Clark had copied Humboldt's map; Humboldt himself had never seen the region, but had copied a still earlier map that dated back nearly forty years. Lewis and Clark showed the coveted river starting in the Rockies and running straight through the mountains westward to the Ocean. Other enterprising mapmakers, assuming that if there was one such river passage, there must be others, drew half a dozen Rocky-Mountain-fed rivers into the Pacific. The broadest, most appealing, and longest-lived of these, first sketched by the cartographer for the Spanish expedition of 1776, was the river known as the "San Buenaventura." The prosaic daily experiences of fur traders like Ashley, Smith, Walker, and Peter Skene Ogden did little to dry up that river. Nor did the maps of Gallatin, Bonneville, and Burr, which began to fill the blank spot with an interior basin lacking any drainage to the sea. These maps were all published before 1840, but they either did not circulate or were too disheartening to be believed. "Some of the maps consulted, supposed of course to be correct," John Bidwell wrote of his preparations for his epochal 1841 overland trip to California, "showed a lake in the vicinity of where Salt Lake now is; it was represented as a long lake, three or four hundred miles in extent, narrow and with two outlets, both running into the Pacific Ocean, either apparently longer than the Mississippi River." The salty waters of the Great Salt Lake were, of course, a diabolical coincidence which made it harder than ever to doubt that this might be an inreaching arm of the great Western Ocean.

Belief that there must somewhere exist a westward waterway was widespread and respectable. Senator Thomas Hart Benton, of Missouri, argued long and loud for a sea passage to India. First he was inclined to follow Jefferson's route up the Missouri River, but he was optimist enough to send his son-in-law John C. Frémont in quest of still others. There was, of course, a wonderfully appealing symmetry to a majestic San Buenaventura River. The continent had been largely explored by water, at first along the Atlantic coast and later down the rivers of the Mississippi basin. What more providential or more appropriate than that there be similar passageways all through the West?

The last resting place of the fabled westward passage to the Orient was magnificently ironic, for now finally explorers and cartographers and visionary statesmen had desperately located their heart's desire—their San Buenaventura—in the one great area of the North American Continent that not only had no grand rivers, but actually had no outlet at all to the sea! They had put it, of all places, in the Great Basin! This place was actually a geographic monstrosity: in the heart of a well-watered continent a vast area dispersed its waters not to any of the oceans, but in some mysterious way into the very earth itself. What more suitably unpredictable ending for one of the most indomitable of American illusions?

In 1844, and not before, Frémont concluded that this supposed locale of the transatlantic waterway was not only no habitat of rivers flowing oceanward, but was actually without any exterior drainage at all. On May 23, 1844, almost precisely a year after having left Kansas, Frémont, encamped on the shores of Utah Lake, finally described the great area between the Wasatch and the Sierra Mountains (including much of Oregon, virtually all of Nevada, western Utah, and California north of the Mojave River) as a land of interior drainage, a "Great Basin" without outlets to the sea. This was not simply the removal of another blank space on the map, but a great geographic discovery in the long unveiling of North America, for it laid waste the last imaginary habitat of the mythic San Buenaventura. It was a sobering and disillusioning experience.

* * *

The tale of the San Buenaventura is only one episode in the American Decameron of men's love affairs with their illusions. In the early 19th century, North America, especially the part contiguous to the new United States, was ideally qualified to seduce explorers, cartographers, botanists, geologists, illustrators, anthropologists, and scores of other devotees of still new sciences. The New World dwelt in an enticing penumbra, neither so well lit as to stultify imagination nor so darkly unknown as to intimidate the half-courageous.

Many circumstances in the American West worked to preserve the general ignorance of the nation's geography. Colonial rivalries had not fostered publicity of such information as there was. The early Spanish explorers of North America were not eager to share their meager knowledge, which was a precious instrument of empire, as closely guarded as a nation's skilled workers or gold bullion.

The chronicles of Western exploration are therefore full of unknown first discoveries. Lives were wasted simply because the earliest discovery was not publicized. The famous South Pass in Wyoming through which California immigrants poured in mid-century had probably been discovered in 1812 by Robert Stuart in John Jacob Astor's employ, but the information had not got around. No one was sure precisely where Stuart had been. Knowledge of the Pass was not general until after Jedediah Smith's rediscovery of it in 1824, when it began to come into use by fur traders. Similarly, the honor of discovering the Great Salt Lake is much disputed. Did it belong to Jim Bridger? Early in 1825 while exploring the mouth of the Bear River on one of Ashley's fur-trapping parties (possibly headed by Bill

Sublette), Bridger followed the river through its canyon, and reached the edge of the salty lake, believing it an arm of the sea. Had the trapper Étienne Provost possibly seen the Lake in the fall of 1824? If neither of these actually saw the Lake, the honor may go to Peter Skene Ogden's Snake Country Expedition of 1824–25. In that expedition's journal for May 5, 1825, Ogden recorded "a fine Plain covered with Buffaloes and thousands of Small Gulls the latter was a Strange Sight to us I presume some large body of Water near at hand at present unknown to us all." If any of this group saw the Lake, it was probably not Ogden, but one of his men. Ogden himself very likely did not see the Lake till December 26, 1828. What is remarkable is how little each of these knew of what the others had done or were doing.

One advantage of these failures of communication was that the joys of first discovery were spread among many people. In September 1843, fifteen years after Ogden first glimpsed the Great Salt Lake, Frémont saw "the object of our anxious search—the waters of the inland sea, stretching in still and solitary grandeur far beyond the limits of our vision." "We felt pleasure also in remembering that we were the first who, in the traditional annals of the country, had visited the islands and broken with the sound of human voices, the long solitude of the place." Frémont did not know that almost twenty years before, in 1826, Jim Bridger's party of trappers had paddled around most of the lake in improvised boats of buffalo or elk hide. Perhaps this was just as well, for it left him free to enjoy his "discovery."

On his next expedition, in 1845, when Frémont and his party moved westward from the southern edge of the Great Salt Lake again they enjoyed a "first" encounter with one of the grand features of the continent. He was told no one had ever crossed the vast plains in that direction. The Indians on the spot reassured him of this; there was no water out that way. The guides on his staff, knowledgeable mountain men like Kit Carson and Robert Walker, knew nothing of that country. Again, in retrospect, we see how ill-informed they were, for nearly twenty years earlier Jedediah Smith had actually crossed the Great Salt Desert.

The reasons for such costly failures to pool information were not far to seek. As William H. Goetzmann has explained, the fur trapper who knew rich streams and easy ways to reach them was like the man who knows a good fishing hole. He was not eager to share what he knew. Successful trappers knew their way to the most rewarding beaver streams by the easiest passes and through the greenest natural pasture; they knew the safest way to cross the desert. Their business was furs, not maps. For example, Jedediah Smith, who probably knew as much as anyone in his day about the West, sketched very few maps, and they were all lost. Jim Bridger, who guided the Stansbury expedition to the Great Salt Lake in 1850 and Captain William F. Raynolds' Yellowstone expedition of 1859, could, when requested, supply nothing better than a crude chart extemporaneously drawn with charcoal on a piece of buffalo hide.

The rendezvous system, which, as we have seen, demanded an extraordinary organizing talent, also required an intimate knowledge of the landscape. Year after year several hundred men, dispersed to remote corners of the fur trappers' West, managed to reassemble on schedule. "They did not resemble Achilles," Bernard De Voto explains, "but they were prepared to meet several hundred others on the day appointed and at the place assigned, and did not care if the geographers had moved it a full ten degrees. They went about the blank spaces of the map like men going to the barn. The Great American Desert was their back yard." They themselves had little need of maps; they carried their information in their heads. This made them personally indispensable and kept the American West long a mystery to the outside world.

Had geographers known more, or had they known less, the unfilled continent might not have been so inviting. This providential half-knownness of the American scene helps explain the energy and the passion, the obsessive singlemindedness and the fickle shiftiness, with which Americans so quickly moved their hopes from one San Buenaventura to another.

With little to go on, hopes and fears often ran to wild extremes. The mind embroidered what it had; reluctant to fill blank spaces in maps with anything so commonplace as arid plains or temperate grasslands, people seized evidence of more interesting, more color-ful, more dangerous, or more rewarding landscapes.

"I saw in my route in various places," Zebulon Pike had reported of his trip west of the ninety-fifth meridian in 1806, "tracts of many leagues where the wind had thrown up the sand in all the fanciful forms of the ocean's rolling waves and on which not a speck of vege-table matter existed." In 1819–20, Stephen H. Long of the United States Topographical Engineers traveled from an encampment at the junction of the Platte and the Missouri Rivers (now the border between Nebraska and Iowa), along the Platte to the front range of the Rockies, then south and east through Oklahoma to Fort Smith in Arkansas. "In regard to this extensive section of country," he incau-tiously reported, "I do not hesitate in giving the opinion, that it is almost wholly unfit for cultivation, and of course, uninhabitable by a people depending upon agriculture for their subsistence. Although tracts of fertile land considerably extensive are occasionally to be met with, yet the scarcity of wood and water, almost uniformly prevalent, will prove an insuperable obstacle in the way of settling the coun-try." The vast neighboring areas east of the Rockies, he said, might be well suited for buffaloes, wild goats, and other wild game but for nothing else. On his map, published in 1823, he here inscribed in large letters "Great American Desert." He thus helped create a new geographic myth, destined to be one of the most vivid and most po-tent myths of the first half of the 19th century.

Numerous ambiguities surrounding the meaning of "desert" compounded the uncertainties of the landscape. As that word gained currency to describe parts of the West, to some it meant a kind of American Sahara, to others an unpleasant place fit only for Indians, and to still others it carried a variety of other forbidding connota-tions. It became almost as indefinite in its meaning as in its location.

The widespread scarcity of wood and water were of course real facts which Walter Prescott Webb and others in the 20th century showed to be shaping influences of this West. But the waterless, treeless, uninhabitable desert east of the Rockies—the desert born in Long's imagination and confirmed by scores of other mapmakers, travelers, writers, and fireside taletellers—was pure myth, no more substantial than the majestic San Buenaventura. But just as the un-founded hope for a great Mississippi of the West had enticed explor-ers to risk their lives, incidentally discovering the unexpected but very solid facts, so did belief in this Great American Desert move thousands of Americans until after the Civil War. Haunted by vi-sions of broiling sands and blinding sun, Americans hastened west-ward. Imaginary perils of geography were added to the real threats from nature and the Indians, and the scarcities of wood, water, and other resources. They thus left behind the hospitable plains of the midwest on their unknowing way to more arid regions. The Great Plains became a barrier to be crossed with all possible speed, perhaps delaying settlement of the fertile midwest by several decades.

The frightening visions had other effects. Was not such a Great American Desert admirably suited to contain the Indians? In 1823, Secretary of War John C. Calhoun proposed to President Monroe that the approximately fourteen thousand Indians then in the Old Northwest (the region around the Great Lakes and between the Ohio and the Mississippi rivers) be removed to the northern part of the Desert, and that the seventy-nine thousand Indians compris-ing the southern tribes be removed to its southern part. Among the resulting advantages listed by Calhoun were the opening of valuable eastern lands to white settlement, the prevention of future conflict between the races, and the removal of Indians from further conta-gion by white men's sins and diseases. The thirty thousand dollars required to persuade the Indians, Calhoun explained, was a small price for this "permanent" solution of the Indian problem. While some professional geographers and government officials, as Francis Paul Prucha has recently shown, would not have agreed that the In-dians were being removed to a "desert," such was the popular view. Calhoun's plan for a "Permanent Indian Frontier," enacted in 1825, proved less permanent than he had supposed, for the myth of the Great American Desert did not live forever. As it was gradually dis-pelled, white men began to wonder whether this land west of the ninety-fifth meridian might not, after all, be better than the Indians deserved.

The people who, despite everything, in the 1830's and '40's and

'50's settled in large numbers west of the Mississippi in the very heart of the "Great Desert," rebelled against this slander of their chosen land. The executive committee of the Kansas Historical Society in 1860 reported how well they remembered that in their school days "the books taught us that this central plain we now occupy was a portion of the great American desert." They built a counter-myth of their own. Not merely disavowing their region's barrenness, they fabricated a new legend of its rare fertility. But the older myth gave ground only slowly. The Pacific Railway Surveys in the 1850's still drew a forbidding picture. The Union Pacific Railway Charter in 1862 was meant less to provide a link to the plains than to assure a speedy bridge across them. It was a cut through the mid-continental barrier, connecting settlers in the Mississippi Valley with those on the Pacific Coast.

The new myth, no less than the old, testified to man's indomitable will to believe. Now the settlers who moved up the valleys of the Platte and the Kansas rivers, as Henry Nash Smith eloquently recounts, replaced the myth of the Desert with the myth of the Garden. From earliest colonial times, Europeans had seen the land of the Atlantic settlements as a New World garden long kept virgin to redress the overcultivation of the Old. It was easy to extend this myth beyond the Mississippi.

The magic by which the imagined desolation would be transmuted into an imagined Eden was hinted by Josiah Gregg in his *Commerce of the Prairies* as early as 1844. Might not the arrival of settlers itself do the job?

> Why may we not suppose that the genial influences of civilization—that extensive cultivation of the earth—might contribute to the multiplication of showers, as it certainly does of fountains? Or that the shady groves, as they advance upon the prairies, may have some effect upon the seasons? At least, many old settlers maintain that the droughts are becoming less oppressive in the West. The people of New Mexico also assure us that the rains have much increased of latter years, a phenomenon which the vulgar superstitiously

attribute to the arrival of the Missouri traders. Then may we not hope that these sterile regions might yet be thus revived and fertilized, and their surface covered one day by flourishing settlements to the Rocky Mountains?

Gregg himself suggested that this great climatic change was accomplished by the very process of irrigation.

A still more appealing version of the myth was spread by newspapermen reporting the construction of the Union Pacific amid the growing populations of Kansas and Nebraska in 1866 and 1867. As more people arrived out there, they said, somehow rainfall increased. Welcome "scientific" foundation for the new mythic hopes was supplied by the widely publicized Geological and Geographical Survey of the Territories, which began work under federal auspices and under the direction of Ferdinand V. Hayden, in Nebraska in 1867. Its technical reports were remarkably popular in the West. "It is believed," Hayden publicly informed the Secretary of the Interior (1867), ". . . that the planting of ten or fifteen acres of forest-trees on each quarter-section will have a most important effect on the climate, equalizing and increasing the moisture and adding greatly to the fertility of the soil. The settlement of the country and the increase of the timber has already changed for the better the climate of that portion of Nebraska lying along the Missouri, so that within the last twelve or fourteen years the rain has gradually increased in quantity and is more equally distributed through the year. I am confident that this change will continue to extend across the dry belt to the foot of the Rocky Mountains as the settlements extend and the forest-trees are planted in proper quantities."

This appealing theory was supported by the monograph on "Agriculture in Colorado" by Hayden's entomologist and botanist, Cyrus Thomas, which recorded the scientist's "firm conviction" that increasing rainfall somehow came from settlement of the country "and that, as the population increases, the amount of moisture will increase." Respectable agronomists like Samuel Aughey, Professor of Natural Sciences at the new University of Nebraska, espoused the optimistic theory. Their collaborative efforts were happily assisted by a series of abnormally wet years after the Civil War. A slogan was coined and repeated for decades: "Rain Follows the Plough."

It is not hard to understand the booster appeal of this doctrine. The notion may originally have been borrowed from French or English scientists. But in the booming West, to deny it, even to doubt it, was to betray the community. Cattlemen who refused to believe were accused of selfishly wanting to discourage immigration so they might keep for range what might have become valuable cultivated land. Irrigation projects were opposed, not only because a large enough number of new arrivals would make irrigation superfluous, but also because talk about irrigation reduced land values by advertising the insufficiency of natural rainfall.

Soon the extravagance of this booster answer to the myth of a Great American Desert far exceeded the extravagance of the myth it was answering. Especially attractive to city-developers was the doctrine of the flamboyant William Gilpin (1813–92). A versatile soldier-explorer-editor who had accompanied Frémont on his expedition of 1843, he joined Thomas Hart Benton in promoting a central route for the transcontinental railroad and became the first territorial governor of Colorado. In three books, *The Central Gold Region* (1860), *Mission of the North American People* (1873), and *The Cosmopolitan Railway* (1890), Gilpin elaborated an appealingly simple theory of his own which he had been widely advocating in speeches and essays since about 1846.

Drawing on the German philosopher-naturalist Alexander Von Humboldt, he developed a theory of geographic determinism designed to please the most enthusiastic midwestern booster. Following Humboldt, Gilpin found the key to his prophecies in the "Isothermal Zodiac." This was an undulating belt of approximately thirty degrees (about 2300 miles wide; from about the twenty-fifth to the fifty-fifth degree) encircling the earth across the Northern Hemisphere. Through the middle of this belt ran the "axis of intensity," roughly along the fortieth degree of north latitude, where the mean annual temperature was 52° Fahrenheit. "Within this isothermal belt, and restricted to it, the column of the human family, with whom abides the sacred and inspired fire of civilization, accompanying the sun, has marched from east to west, since the birth of time. Upon this axis of intensity have been constructed the great primary cities, which have been from age to age the foci from which have radiated intellectual activity and power. . . . the Chinese, the Indian, the Persian, the Grecian, the Roman, the Spanish, the British, finally, the republican empire of the people of North America. . . . this zone belts the globe around where the continents expand and the oceans contract: it undulates with the axis of warm temperature (52 degrees of mean heat): it contains ninety-five one-hundredths of the white people of the globe, and all its civilization!"

What more obvious then, than the need for a world railroad encircling the globe along the Axis of Intensity? Hydrographic maps in Gilpin's *Central Gold Region* showed that the Great Basin of the Mississippi was "the ampitheatre of the world . . . the most magnificent dwelling marked out by God for man's abode." Compare the continents: Europe culminates in its center into the icy masses of the Alps; Asia similarly rises into the Himalayas; Africa and South America, so far as they were known at all, were "perplexed into dislocated fragments."

> In contrast, the interior of North America presents towards heaven an expanded bowl, to receive and fuse into harmony whatsoever enters within its rim. So, each of the other continents presenting a bowl reversed, scatter everything from a central apex into radiant distraction. . . . In geography the antithesis of the old world, in society we are and will be the reverse.

Each of Gilpin's cosmic generalizations resounded with booster overtones for the projects in the midwest in which Gilpin himself happened to be interested. For example, the central route (along the thirty-ninth parallel) for the transcontinental railroad. In the 1840's, Gilpin had bought land on the edge of Independence along the Missouri River. Then he had persuaded the city council to extend the town limits to include his property, which he subdivided into town lots. This land, as it happened, was at the center of Gilpin's hydro-graphic circles on the continent. The map which Gilpin prepared and circulated of "Centropolis" showed that the national capital by a higher geographic necessity should be moved to the very heart of Gilpintown. While promoting this particular property, he discovered another geographic law: the great emporiums of the world were located on the great rivers, and in North America these cities had to be about one hundred leagues (350 miles) apart. Luckily this was just the distance Independence and Gilpintown stood from St. Louis.

When his ambitious project for Gilpintown collapsed, Gilpin discovered happily that he had put his great central city ten miles too far east. In 1858, then, his new map of "Centropolis" located the capital at the present site of Greater Kansas City, to which Gilpin had shifted his booster loyalties. When, a dozen years later, Gilpin had moved these loyalties still farther westward to Denver, his science kept pace with his investments. Gilpin's *Notes on Colorado* (1870) announced his discovery that, because population had begun to condense itself farther west along the Axis of Intensity, Denver was now the "focal point of impregnable power in the topographical configuration of the continent." At this last locus of Gilpin's personal fortunes he found the true gateway for all transcontinental movement.

*   *   *

In the geographic darkness of the West, some like Gilpin managed to convince themselves and others that they had found what they wanted. That same darkness concealed many a swindler, who lured his quarry to a blank place on the map, there to find whatever he chose to plant. The hoax became a minor western institution, and figured prominently in western folklore. Mythic mines were legion; they multiplied in vast regions of half-knowledge, where weariness, desperation, and optimism prepared travelers to believe they had found Golconda. A beautiful example was the Great Diamond Hoax of 1872, commonly called the biggest western mining swindle of the 19th century.

One foggy morning early in 1872, two dishevelled prospectors, looking as if they had just returned from distant diggings, entered a bank in San Francisco and asked a bank officer to see them privately. With elaborate furtiveness, they instructed him to keep safely for them a small bag whose contents they reluctantly revealed to be diamonds. They swore him to secrecy, then disappeared. The clerk, of course, immediately communicated the secret information to the other bank officers, who in turn passed it on confidentially to a select group of the richest men in San Francisco, who at once began a search for the two mysterious prospectors. By a happy coincidence, within a few weeks Philip Arnold and John Slack reappeared. After considerable persuasion (which included payment to them of about $600,000) they allowed themselves to be included in a new mining company, whose sole purpose was to exploit the mythic but still un-located diamond mines. Arnold went East with some backers so that the diamonds could be examined for genuineness by Tiffany & Company of New York. Tiffany reported the diamonds to be real and an additional group of New York backers was then organized. To reassure themselves and other potential investors, they hired an impeccably honest mining-consultant to prepare an on-the-spot report of the mines. Henry Janin (who had made his reputation by condemning nearly every scheme he had been called to report on) agreed to visit and assess the diamond fields. Arnold and Slack then took Janin to the fields, the location of which by elaborate subter-fuges was still kept secret. Janin returned to announce that the diamond fields were real. Before long, at least one investor had put in $660,000 and others had "invested" to the tune of $10,000,000.

Arnold and Slack, far from being the bumpkins they seemed, proved to be two of the most sophisticated swindlers of modern times. On remote mesas in northwestern Colorado, they had actu-ally staked out a claim, and had spared no trouble or expense in salt-ing it with small diamonds and rubies. Their protection, of course, was the vastness of the country, the remoteness of their find, and the general geographic ignorance. If they could keep the location of their diamond fields secret from the general public, allowing only a few credulous colleagues to be guided to the spot, they might pyra-mid their investment into a substantial fortune before they could be exposed.

The diamond fever rose from May to November of 1872. Other

swindlers—or promoters—appeared all over the West, not only in San Francisco, but in Denver, Salt Lake City, and elsewhere. Exposure of the hoax might have been indefinitely delayed had not the hoaxers thoughtlessly located their diamond field in the neighborhood of the fortieth parallel. In 1867 the Congress had authorized its famous Fortieth Parallel Survey: "a geological and topographical exploration of the territory between the Rocky Mountains and the Sierra Nevada mountains, including the route or routes of the Pacific railroad." In charge was the indomitable Clarence King, whom Henry Adams idolized as "the ideal American they all wanted to be." In the summer of 1872, King and his men were still at work on their survey. When King heard about the diamond fields (of which he had so far found no trace), he was troubled. An assigned purpose of his survey was to advise Congress and the nation of the natural resources of the area; if he had actually missed something as valuable as a diamond field, his own professional reputation, and the reputation of the whole Fortieth Parallel Survey (as well as of future surveys), would be put in doubt.

By uncannily clever detective work, King and three of his fellow-surveyors pieced together the fragmentary clues incautiously dropped by the diamond promoters. These clues led to the Yampa-Green River country of northern Colorado and Utah and southern Wyoming. In the end, King's party had nothing to follow but a hint that Janin had accidentally let slip: the diamond hunters had camped at the foot of a pine-covered mountain, which in June was still covered by some snow, and to the northeast side of which no high mountains could be seen. Finally, in early November, King found the desolate place where claim notices had been posted. (It is still called Diamond Peak in Colorado.) Tracks from the notices converged on a sandstone ledge. There, near the surface, they found numerous small diamonds and rubies. King, already puzzled that gems should be found in this kind of geologic formation, noticed that the diamonds and rubies appeared only near the windswept table rock that was the heart of the claim. He also noted the curious fact that for every twelve rubies there was one diamond. His party then took out their sieves and tried the surrounding area. They found gems only in those places where the earth was already disturbed. A few were discovered inside anthills, but only where a telltale footprint had been left nearby. As a final test, King and his party dug a deep hole and sifted all the earth; they found no gems.

King was now convinced that the diamond mine was a hoax, and that he could prove it. He raced across country to the railroad for San Francisco, anxious to reach Janin and other innocent backers before rumors might give the hoaxers a chance to escape or to capitalize further on their swindle. King succeeded in persuading the investors of their deception. The hoaxers were never brought to justice but King became a hero for his courage, his scientific sleuthing, and his command of Western geography. It was ironic that, while the seven large volumes of the Fortieth Parallel Survey (1870–78) set a new scientific standard for government publications, became an international geographic classic, and led to establishment of the United States Geological Survey (1878) with King at its head, it was his lucky exposure of the Diamond Hoax that brought King public notice. The San Francisco *Chronicle* thanked "God and Clarence King" for escape from "a great financial calamity." Other newspapers, too, said that this one act had more than paid for the survey of the fortieth parallel, and proved that further surveys were desirable. Unwittingly, the hoaxers of Diamond Gulch thus promoted exploration of the continent.

* * *

The vagueness that inspired the extravagances of mapmakers and the wild promises of hoaxers also made Americans eager for pictures of their exotic continent. The scarcity of precise knowledge gave such knowledge as there was a peculiar appeal. In the colonial period the ungathered novelties of this new world had fostered a natural-history emphasis. The wealth of new sights in the early 19th century continued to stir naturalists to name and classify and depict what they saw. John James Audubon (1785–1851), who had spent much of his youth in Kentucky before becoming a taxidermist in Cincinnati, had early begun to draw and paint the birds of the New World in their natural setting. In 1826 he went to Britain, and with the help of a London engraver produced his elephant folios (*The Birds of America*, 1827–38) which offered over a thousand life-sized illustrations of five hundred species, in color. But such works as Audubon's were for the naturalist or the rich collector. A widespread demand for pictures of the West, and for vivid representations of the outer fringes of settlement, enabled landscape painters to flourish as never before.

Enormous panoramic paintings of the Mississippi River were among the most spectacular efforts to capture the continent's varied grandeur. The most famous of the panorama-painters was John Banvard, who was born in New York City in 1815, and who, at the age of fifteen, wandered out West where he taught himself how to paint. About 1841 he conceived his plan "to paint a picture of the beautiful scenery of the Mississippi, which should be as superior to all others, in point of *size*, as that prodigious river is superior to the streamlets of Europe—a gigantic idea!—which seems truly kindred to the illimitable forests and vast extents of his native land." "The idea of gain never entered his mind when he commenced the undertaking," wrote his anonymous biographer (probably Banvard himself), "but he was actuated by a patriotic and honorable ambition, that he should produce the largest painting in the world." To secure the sketches for his masterpiece, he spent over a year riding up and down the River in a skiff, suffering every hardship.

Banvard's completed canvas, when first exhibited at Louisville, in October 1846, was an immediate success. The Louisville *Courier* hailed it as "the greatest and proudest work of art in the world." The "program notes" (which included a version of the Mike Fink legend, "The Last of the Boatmen . . .") were entitled: *Description of Banvard's Panorama of the Mississippi River, Painted on Three Miles of Canvas, exhibiting a View of Country 1200 Miles in Length, extending from the Mouth of the Missouri River to the City of New Orleans, being by far the Largest Picture ever executed by Man.* When Banvard took his painting on tour, he was everywhere acclaimed. "I see a panorama of the Mississippi advertised," Longfellow, who had just completed the first part of *Evangeline*, wrote in Boston in his journal. "This comes very *a propos*. The river comes to me instead of my going to the river; and as it is to flow through the pages of the poem, I look upon this as a special benediction." And after attending the artist's performance he noted: "Went to see Banvard's moving diorama of the Mississippi. One seems to be sailing down the great stream, and sees the boats and the sand-banks created with cottonwood, and the bayous by moonlight. Three miles of canvas, and a great deal of merit." After successes in New Orleans, New York, and Washington (where the Senate and House passed resolutions declaring the Panorama "a truly wonderful and magnificent production"), Banvard, armed with a letter of commendation from Edward Everett, late minister to England, to the president of the Royal Geographical Society, went on to greater triumphs abroad, where he was honored by Queen Victoria's summons to a command performance at Windsor Castle.

His method of displaying his ten-foot-high canvas was ingenious but simple. Rolled on upright revolving cylinders about twenty feet apart, the picture passed gradually before the spectators as the artist commented on his work. "Upon a platform is seated Mr. Banvard," reported the *Illustrated London News*, "who explains the localities as the picture moves, and relieves his narrative with Jonathanisms and jokes, poetry and patter, which delight his audience mightily; and a pianoforte is incidentally invoked, to relieve the narrative monotony." Since the painting was in motion and had to be viewed from a distance, it was more like stage-scenery than studio art. A press notice explained:

> You pass by, as in a rapid voyage, "temple, tower, and town"; and in an hour and a half's sitting, there is brought vividly before you all the chief incidents of savage and of civilized life, from the wigwams of the Indian and the log hut of the settler, to the lofty domes and graceful spires of the gay and crowded city. You flit by a rice swamp, catch a glimpse of a jungle, dwell for an instant on a prairie, and are lost in admiration at the varied, but ever glorious dress, in which, in the Western world, Nature delights to attire herself.

Banvard was not without competition. At least four other painters offered their own versions of "The Greatest Painting in the World," depicting the greatest river in the world. Each claimed to be the "true originator" of the idea, and boasted that his canvas was bigger, and therefore better, than the others. John Rawson Smith, Banvard's earliest rival, described his own work as "one-third longer than any other pictorial work in evidence; Four miles in Length" and "beyond all comparison, better than the smaller painting called Banvard's." The supposed measurements of all the panoramas had the truth—and the appeal—of other tall tales. The prize for actual size should probably have gone to Henry Lewis, whose "Great National Work" did measure twelve feet high and nearly 4000 feet (about three-quarters of a mile) long, and had to be seen in two evenings.

The interest of these works was more geographical than artistic: both painters and promoters advertised them as an educational and scientific experience. "In America," John Rawson Smith explained, "the country itself is ever on the change, and in another half century those who view this portrait of the Mississippi will not be able to recognize one twentieth part of its details. Where the forest now overshadows the earth, and affords shelter to the wild beasts, corn fields, orchards, towns, and villages, will give a new face to the scene, and tell of industry and enterprise, which will stimulate to new and untiring efforts." "Alligators and other creatures of the deep, of which Europeans only hear and read, are seen sporting in several places: and thus the beholder is constantly reminded that it is of no familiar scene he is the beholder." The desire of Americans for such information about the West was attested by the fact that in six weeks at Saratoga, New York, Smith's panorama earned twenty thousand dollars.

It was not only these folk painters of geographic newsreels who prospered. The mid-century was the heyday of an important and aesthetically more respectable group whom James Thomas Flexner has christened the American "Native School." As Flexner explains, they expressed widespread "communal experiences and ideals" by portraying the grandeur, the mystery, the variety, and the color of the American landscape. In the later 18th century, the great American painters—Gilbert Stuart, Benjamin West, John Trumbull, and others—produced portraits or historical or allegorical scenes, very much in the academic European tradition. But portrait-painting, somehow, was more congenial to an aristocratic society, like that of 18th-century England, or to a commercial society like that of 17th-century Holland, than to America. By the mid-19th century, some of the best American painters were still sometimes serving their apprenticeship and earning their bread and butter by doing jobs that would later fall to the photographer, but the important and distinctive work of the age was of another sort. William Cullen Bryant pointed the peculiar American challenge when he warned a painter who was about to depart for Europe:

> Fair scenes shall greet thee where thou goest—fair
> But different—everywhere the trace of men.
> Paths, homes, graves, ruins, from the lowest glen
> To where life shrinks from the fierce Alpine air.
> Gaze on them, till the tears shall dim thy sight,
> But keep that earlier, wilder image bright.

Works by living American painters—many of whom depicted "that wilder image"—had a popular appeal which was probably never exceeded. New York exhibits of such works, between 1839 and 1851, attracted an average annual attendance equal to over half the population of the city; this was, proportionately, three times as many as those who attended the Metropolitan Museum of the city a century later.

The vigor of these portrayers of the American landscape was impressive. There was the pioneering of Thomas Cole and Asher B. Durand, founders of the so-called Hudson River School, who went into the Catskill Mountains and painted precise, if romanticized, images of wild scenery direct from nature. There were the great illustrators of the West of the American Indians. Lewis and Clark had not taken an artist with them, but when Major S. H. Long crossed the Great Plains to the Rockies in 1819–20, he was accompanied by Samuel Seymour, an illustrator, whose drawings of Indian life soon excited wide interest. The greatest and most self-conscious of the recorders of the Indian was George Catlin (1796–1872), who had been raised in the Wyoming Valley of Pennsylvania among memories of some of the bloodiest Indian raids of the Revolutionary era. After attending the famous law school in Litchfield, Connecticut, and after an abortive career in law, Catlin turned to painting and made a living briefly as a portraitist; then, in Philadelphia about 1824, when he saw a delegation of Indians from the West—"in all their classic beauty with shield and helmet, tunic and manteau—tinted and tasseled off exactly for the painters' palette"—he determined (on the analogy of Charles Willson Peale's portrait gallery of Revolutionary notables) to make his own "Indian Gallery."

During the next years Catlin traveled over the West with his wife, painting and sketching "to use my art and so much of the labors of my future life as might be required in rescuing from oblivion the looks and customs of the vanishing races of native man in America." His problems were very different from those of the fashionable portrait artist who posed an aristocratic clientele, for many Indians feared they would die if he possessed their painted image. In his drawings and paintings, and in his *Letters and Notes on the Manners, Customs, and Condition of the North American Indians* (1841), he left a brilliant record of exotic features of the American landscape. Even art, however, did not escape the politics of Westward expansion, and the problems arising out of the uncertainties of the western border. In 1852, when Daniel Webster led Northern Senators to support the purchase of Catlin's "Indian Gallery" for the nation, the Southern majority voted the bill down. Southerners wanted the West for the expansion of their Peculiar Institution, and they feared Catlin's paintings would arouse sympathy for the Indians whom the Southerners and their slaves would displace.

Catlin was only one of a galaxy of painters of the Indian West; Karl Bodmer, Alfred Jacob Miller, and Charles Deas, and others who flourished before the Civil War, added vividness to the nation's uncertain western boundaries. Their work was supplemented by that of other artists who sought scenery far wilder and more forbidding than that which had enticed the Hudson River School. Albert Bierstadt, founder of a Rocky Mountain School, and Thomas Moran who did huge canvases of the Grand Canyon of the Yellowstone and the Chasm of the Colorado (bought by the Congress for ten thousand dollars apiece), and still others whose names became attached to remote western lakes and mountains and rivers, reminded Americans of how much in the land they had settled still remained to be conquered and discovered.

* * *

America was one of the last places where settlers would come in large numbers before the explorers, the geographers, the painters, and the professional naturalists. Already in the colonial period, this curious fact had brightened American thinking as physical and intellectual expansion became synonymous. Knowledge came naturally, and this shaped the very definition of knowledge. This was crucial too for the spirit of the new nation.

It was hard to be confined by knowledge still ungathered. On a half-known continent, it was difficult to disprove even the most extravagant visions—of sea passages to India, of a mythic garden destined for great cities, of a new Golconda. All this made the booster spirit possible and kept it alive. It also kept alive the competition between communities. What could not be disproved of a Nininger could not be disproved of a Hastings. Ignorance itself was an unacknowledged source of imagination and energy. What they didn't know couldn't stop them. Of course the actual settlers in the West were occasionally haunted by Great American Deserts which did not exist. But, more important, they were also often enticed by extravagant visions of a future which did exist, which the very extravagance of their vision helped call into existence. Discouraging facts could be discounted, or mistaken for their opposites, while booster extravagances could not be disproved. If the ignorance at the very scene was vast, it was even vaster on the eastern seaboard where many crucial decisions had to be taken.

GOVERNMENT AS A SERVICE INSTITUTION

CHAPTER 30

A MERICA, THEN, OFFERED a novel opportunity to "create" property owners, and no governmental power was more important than the power to give title to pieces of the New World. Power of governments over the land shaped distinctive American attitudes to government. Those who came to think that their birthright included a piece of the continent, came also to think it a task of governments to make the land accessible, to increase its value and its usefulness. And there were enough different forms and shapes and sizes of government to provide citizens continually with some political agency or other from whom they could expect such services.

"Plenty of good land," Adam Smith explained in his *Wealth of Nations* (1776), "and liberty to manage their own affairs their own way, seem to be the two great causes of prosperity of all new colonies." Smith boasted that Britain had come closer than other countries to making colonial lands widely available for cultivation and improvement. In British colonies, he said, far less than elsewhere, was land monopolized by a few large holders. But Americans still did not find British land policy free enough for their taste. The Declaration of Independence accused the King of having "endeavored to prevent the population of these States; for that purpose obstructing the Laws of Naturalization of Foreigners; refusing to pass others to encourage their migration hither, and raising the conditions of new

Appropriations of Lands." By its Proclamation of 1763, which declared the Appalachians the western boundary between their settlements and a permanent Indian reservation, the British had hemmed in the colonists. Then, by the Quebec Act of 1774, Parliament had extended the boundaries of Canada down behind the colonies to the Ohio River, including vast tracts long claimed by several colonies. But for many other reasons, too, including the wasteful ways of colonial agriculture, Americans wanted more and more land.

During and after the Revolution, lands remained the main stumbling block to a new American nation. Of the original thirteen colonies, seven claimed extensive and often overlapping western lands (several running to the Western Ocean); the rest were confined in clearly marked narrow boundaries along the seacoast. The small or hemmed-in states, led by Maryland, delayed entering a new government to persuade the others to put their unsettled western lands into a common treasury, from which they could later be parcelled out by the new central government. Maryland refused the Articles of Confederation until such concessions were made. When Virginia (1781) and Massachusetts (1785) yielded their lands, the new nation became a substantial reality. Not until 1802 did the last of the great landowning states give in. For this great "public domain," there was no close analogue in the modern history of Europe. The weak new nation, still unsure of its powers to tax or to legislate, had at its disposal a landed territory greater than all the states together and larger than any established Western European nation.

In the decades after Independence, this posed a unique challenge to government in the United States: first to the federal government and then indirectly to other units of government. How to occupy and exploit the continent itself? How to disperse landed property among the people? How to make these lands valuable and productive, and their new communities prosperous? Governments in America, from force of circumstance, then, were agencies for creating and protecting new property. Americans, from the beginning, expected their governments to help them make the most of their unprecedented opportunities. Governments here had thrust on them new tasks and new expectations of service.

The notion rooted in American patriotic pseudo-folklore that "free" land left the American a self-dependent individual hardly accords with the facts. In more settled societies like England, where the landed wealth had been appropriated by individuals long centuries before, a man received his land through the generosity of his lord, his landlord, his father, his grandfather, or his brother. The American contrast was striking. Here, though the scope for individual initiative in securing land was greater than ever before, the direct help of government was also newly important. Only a government could convert possession into ownership. No wonder, then, that in America—where everybody, or nearly everybody, hoped to become a landowner, and where government was the great landowner—everyone looked to governments for some personal benefaction. Americans expected their governments to give them clearly bounded parcels of land, to confirm their ownership, and to protect their possession against French, Spanish, or other European intruders, and against Indian marauders. They expected the government, in addition, to help make and keep their land accessible and to help increase its value. The whole American situation led them to expect more from large organized political units, the states and the federal government, than did their contemporaries in the Old World.

Take, for example, the American mode of building railroads. In England railroads, as well as most canals, were built by private funds, unaided by government. In the United States, by contrast, every form of government—federal, state, county, and municipal—gave substantial help. Why the difference? In England the large capital required for railroad-building was available in private hands, but in the United States capital was still scarce and the corporation was only beginning to be developed. Furthermore, in England and often too on the European continent, a railroad ran along established and flourishing avenues of trade. A line between London and Manchester, for example, could count on heavy traffic as soon as it was in operation. But an American railroad (as the London *Times* once observed) might run from "Nowhere-in-Particular to Nowhere-at-All." The American railroad, like the booster hotel and the community newspaper of the upstart city, was often built in the hope that the railroad itself would help call into being the population by serving which it would prosper.

"No new people can afford to construct their own railroads." So ran the refrain in Henry Varnum Poor's *American Railroad Journal*, which repeatedly distinguished between long-settled regions, which had accumulated capital in private hands, and the American West, which still needed government aid. "A great and extensive country like this," William H. Seward of New York told the Senate in 1850, "has need of roads and canals earlier than there is an accumulation of private capital within the state to construct them." To American railroad promoters this seemed a plain fact, which justified or even required the aid of all governments. The enterprising men who secured government subsidies, grants, and loans for building canals and railroads out into risky unsettled territory should rank high among pioneer builders of the American West. They, like the fur trappers, the river boatmen, the organizers of westward-moving wagon trains, and the boosters of upstart cities had seized peculiarly American opportunities.

Among these opportunities we must count the numerousness of government units (federal, state, and local) and the lucky fact that a great public domain of unprecedented wealth and proportions was at the disposal of governments. The newness of these governments—and their lack of established traditions and of time-honored dogmas—made them readier to experiment with their wealth and their power to lend and to borrow toward any promising public purpose. Without a simple traditional concept of "national interest" or a rigid doctrine of the boundaries of public enterprise, they listened more sympathetically to all requests for aid.

During the pioneer age of railroad building, in the decades before the Civil War, Americans showed great ingenuity in devising ways for governments to help them construct their long and expensive new lines. The muckraking bias of the late 19th century has put these activities in a false perspective. Hardly a textbook of American history fails to reprint the map of "Federal Land Grants for the Construction of Railroads and Wagon Roads, 1823–71," which shows vast stretches, a sizable proportion of the area of western states, granted to railroad builders. The common innuendo is that there was something peculiarly corrupt about these proceedings, otherwise why would so much land have been given away? But railroad companies were only one class of beneficiaries of the nearly universal government assistance.

The government promotion of railroads, and of the canals before them, which Carter Goodrich has documented, is a parable of the distinctive roles of governments in America. Communities grew and population expanded as government-aided canals and railroads were built ahead of the traffic. The railroads themselves brought into being the population that used them. Whether this could have happened without the substantial government assistance is debatable, but the historical facts are clear. The westward expanders were pushing out to places they hoped to make into thriving communities. Their booster railroads universally expected help from public agencies; they were not disappointed.

Aid came from all units of government. States, counties, and cities, in varying proportions, continually helped during the 19th century. Federal aid came in great lumps when expansion met a large natural obstacle, where settlement was too sparse, or where local governments were too weak to give the needed help. First, in the great push across the Appalachians, the federal government acknowledged its responsibilities when, in 1806, Congress authorized surveys for a National Road or Turnpike (later commonly known as the Cumberland Road), eventually to run from Cumberland, Maryland, across the mountain barrier to Wheeling on the Ohio River and beyond (roughly along what later became U.S. Highway 40). This road was constructed directly by the federal government.

Then, in 1808, Albert Gallatin, Jefferson's imaginative Secretary of the Treasury, gave the Senate his remarkable Report on Roads and Canals, a comprehensive scheme he had worked out with Jefferson for a federally aided transportation system to cover the nation, connecting the eastern rivers with the Mississippi basin. The impending war with Great Britain delayed Gallatin's projects, but nearly every one was finally accomplished over the next sixty years— by varying combinations of private, local, state, and federal resources. The second great federal push began when the empty prairies had to be crossed, and reached its climax with the conquest of the Rocky Mountains and the Sierra Nevadas. Here was no avenue along safe and settled lines of trade, but an eighteen-hundred-mile leap from the remote Missouri River to the Pacific Ocean across lands nearly unsettled. The result was the largest federal grants to railroads.

Forms of aid varied as promoters devised requests suited to their peculiar needs and to the prejudices and temptations of legislators and commissioners. Most familiar, and most important for the longer routes, was the gift of public lands by both the federal government and the states. Texas, for example, which had retained its public lands when it entered the Union in 1845, eventually made gifts to railroads amounting to over thirty-two million acres, over one-sixth of the area of the state. The land grants for railroads, like those for wagon-roads before them, were not merely for the right-of-way, but included (in the usual federal grants) alternate sections (640 acres) within a specified number of miles on either side of the road. In grants to railroad companies the minimum width of this strip was ten miles, the maximum eighty miles, ranging then from five to forty sections on either side.

Every other conceivable form of aid was given. Direct grants of money came sometimes from treasury surpluses, sometimes from public borrowing. The state of North Carolina, having exhausted its borrowing capacity in 1873, authorized counties along the line of a railroad to levy a special tax payable either in cash or in country produce. Remission of taxes and exemption from state and local taxes were another form of aid. For example, the federal government from time to time remitted duties on iron imported for rails. As early as 1787, the state of South Carolina had offered credits against duties on the importation of slaves as encouragement of improvements of the Catawba and Wateree rivers. The ingenuity of promoters and their legislative friends was inexhaustible.

By 1860, state and local governments had given for improvements in transportation (in addition to lands, materials, and special privileges) direct financial grants with a face value of over four hun-

dred million dollars. About sixty per cent of this, Goodrich estimates, came from the seven states directly facing the Appalachian
barrier. New York State spent nearly seventy million, Virginia over
fifty million. Western states like Missouri and Tennessee spent
amounts equally large in proportion to their population. Although
local governments as a whole spent only a quarter of the total, Baltimore's expenditure was greater than that of many state governments. Portland, Louisville, and Mobile each spent more for such
improvements than did their respective states.

After the failure of numerous projects in the depression years
following 1837 and 1839, some states adopted legal prohibitions
against state aid to internal improvements. Despite the many discouraging experiences, some programs of state aid were actually at
their height during the 1850's. But by 1861 clauses against state aid
were common in state constitutions. One important effect of these
was to pass more responsibility for aid down to the local governments. And during the '50's the federal government, too, had returned with large-scale aid to the railroads in the form of land grants.
While the particular source of government aid was frequently shifting, expectations of some form of public assistance never died.

Such a large and varied assortment of governmental units made
possible a nearly unbroken pattern of government aid. When President Monroe withdrew federal support from the Cumberland Road
because of a supposed lack of constitutional authority, the states
stepped into the breach. When the states became cautious of financial involvement in the early 1840's the prosperous and optimistic
upstart cities were ready to help. Meanwhile, by the 1850's, the federal government once again was ready to give its strong support. An
alert American railroad-promoter or land-developer could nearly always find some public agency or other ready to contribute capital
and share the risk of exploiting and improving the continent. In the
half-century before the Civil War, American governments, despite
(or perhaps because of) their overlapping, vaguely defined, and ill-
organized responsibilities, delivered the expected services.

Just as the boundaries between one governmental unit and another were vague, so too were the boundaries between "public" and

"private" responsibilities. The basic importance of real estate as a resource and a commodity in a newly developing country made the distinctions between one man's interest and another's hard to define. Everybody seemed to profit from growing populations and expanding, prospering communities. Another American peculiarity, as Goodrich has pointed out, was that public and private activities in promoting internal improvements were generally not considered competitive. Nor were they thought to be exclusive alternatives. Jared Sparks, a strong supporter of all such improvements, voiced a general opinion in the *North American Review* (1821) when he appealed for support "equally to individuals, corporate bodies and state legislatures." The same meetings held to urge government aid also roused enthusiasm for private contributions. Promoters of the Western Railroad went house to house in Boston "to urge upon each one, as a matter of duty, as well as of interest, to do their share to advance this great work." When an Iowa court forbade Marshalltown from giving municipal funds to a railroad, the city fathers declared a holiday, while the local band helped raise the funds by voluntary gifts. A flourishing community spirit in the upstart towns made people eager to get the job done. If not by one arm of government, then by another; if not by the government, then directly by the people.

But the booster spirit was also a competitive spirit. The rivalry that inspired the county-seat wars or the struggle for a state prison or a university, inspired an equally bitter fight for the advantages of a turnpike, canal, or railroad. As early as December 1806, the Commissioners to lay out the National Road noted the special difficulties they faced from "the solicitude and importunities of the inhabitants of every part of the district, who severally considered their grounds entitled to preference." The Erie Canal (constructed 1817–25), by connecting Albany on the Hudson River with Buffalo on Lake Erie opened a waterway eastward from Ohio, Indiana, Michigan, Wisconsin, and Illinois, and gave a great competitive advantage to both Buffalo and New York City. "They have built the longest canal in the world," boasted a speaker at its opening, "in the least time, with the least experience, for the least money, and to the greatest public

benefit." Governor De Witt Clinton had been the principal promoter, the state of New York had been the organizer and financier,
and subscriptions had come almost entirely from citizens of the
state, in modest amounts. Other regions and metropolises would not
be left behind. Maryland and Baltimore met the challenge by two
great enterprises reaching across the mountains to the Monongahela
and the Ohio. On July 4, 1828, the first earth was turned for the
Chesapeake and Ohio Canal and for the Baltimore and Ohio Railroad, both competing for the opportunity to help the community
grow. The canal was supported mainly by the state of Maryland and
the railroad by the city of Baltimore. Meanwhile complaints were
heard in Virginia that too much of that state's wealth had been allowed to "pass out of her hands to enrich the coffers of her neighbors." South Carolina, urged on by its energetic Governor George
McDuffie, hoped by its own project (1836) for crossing the Appalachians to make Charleston into "the New York of the South."

Each successful project spawned others supposed to benefit from
its predecessor. For example, the prospering Erie Canal intensified
the rivalry between Troy and Albany to be the main Hudson River
junction for traffic from the West. Troy spent nearly three-quarters
of a million dollars on a municipally owned railroad; Albany coun-
tered with a quarter-million grant to the Mohawk and Hudson line.

Upstart western cities battled furiously for advantages. In Ohio
nearly every railroad built between 1836 and 1850 received financial
support from counties or cities. Cincinnati lavished its efforts to attract metropolitan connections both eastward (through the Little
Miami) and westward to St. Louis. When the census of 1860 showed
the city slipping from its first rank west of the Appalachians, Cincinnati's *Daily Times* declared it was "a matter of life or death" to secure
a railroad southward to meet the competition of Louisville. The provision in the Ohio state constitution against a city becoming "a
stockholder" in railroads was evaded when Cincinnati built the railroad *entirely* on its own account. St. Louis, fired by the booster spirit,
before 1861 had subscribed over six million dollars for railroads to
make the city and county great. The county distributed its shares of
railroad stock to property owners, "thus giving every taxpayer an in-

terest in the road in proportion to the amount of his taxes" and "a voice in the election of directors and location of the road." A similar practice was followed in Iowa and elsewhere.

The railroad promoters, asking communities to bid against one another, profited by deflecting their route this way or that. Citizens of North Liberty, Iowa, in public meeting adopted a resolution (December 13, 1865), "That Johnson County donate half a million dollars rather than this Rail Road should be made twenty miles east or west of us." In 1869 Indiana railroad-builders were openly offering to run their line through Covington in return for a donation of eighty thousand dollars; otherwise, they threatened to move it in the direction of Perryville. Sometimes this competition produced bizarre results. The New York and Oswego Midland railroad, completed in 1873, had gone zigzagging across the state in search of municipal bonds. When larger cities like Syracuse refused to subscribe, the line actually secured some six million dollars in municipal aid from nearly fifty towns, mostly small. To pick up these sums it ended up crossing the breadth of the state without passing through a single major city.

It is no wonder that the transcontinental line, the greatest of American railroad projects, was long delayed by local competition for places along the route. Not until secession removed from Congress the advocates of a southern route was it possible to begin to approach a decision on federal aid. But a bitter struggle still continued between the advocates of a central and those of a northern route. The route of the proposed transcontinental line, a New Mexico representative complained, would not be acceptable "unless it starts in the corner of every man's farm and runs through all his neighbors' plantations." The Pacific Railway Acts (1862; 1864) would have fixed the eastern terminus at Omaha and would have been a victory for the "Iowa-Chicago interest" (supported by New York) over the "Kansas-St. Louis interest" (supported by Cincinnati, Baltimore, and Philadelphia). The competing pressures were too great. Federal aid finally made the Omaha route only one out of five. What might have been a great artery, as one critic objected, now became nothing but a sprinkler.

THE MYTHOLOGIZING OF
GEORGE WASHINGTON

CHAPTER 39

NEVER DID A MORE incongruous pair than Davy Crockett and George Washington live together in a national Valhalla. Idolized by the new nation, the legendary Washington was a kind of anti-Crockett. The bluster, the crudity, the vulgarity, the monstrous boosterism of Crockett and his fellow supermen of the subliterature were all qualities which Washington most conspicuously lacked. At the same time, the dignity, the reverence for God, the sober judgment, the sense of destiny, and the vision of the distant future, for all of which Washington was proverbial, were unknown to the Ring-tailed Roarers of the West. Yet both Crockett and Washington were popular heroes, and both emerged into legendary fame during the first half of the 19th century.

The legendary Washington, no less than the legendary Crockett, was a product of the anachronism and abridgment of American history. Crockett and his kind, however, had first been spawned by spontaneous generation. They began as by-products of American life rather than as artifices of an American literature. The legends of the comic supermen, which had originated in oral anecdote, never entirely lost the sound and accent of the raconteur's voice, even when frozen into their crude literary form.

There were elements of spontaneity, of course, in the Washington legend, too, but it was, for the most part, a self-conscious product. The Crockett and Fink legends caught the spoken echoes of campfire and saloon, captured and diffused them in crudely printed almanacs, in sporting magazines, and anonymous wheezes. The Demigod Washington was to be a cumbersome figure of literary contrivance. The contrast between the Crockett subliterature (flimsy, ephemeral scraps which seldom could be dignified as "books") and the Washington literature (heavy, elegantly printed works, copiously illustrated by maps and engravings, the proud personal product of eminent statesmen and famous writers) was as striking as that between the legendary characters of the two men themselves.

Although both were peculiar products of America, only Washington became part of the national protocol. How this happened showed how different was the Washington legend from its superficially similar counterparts in the Old World. There, names like Romulus and Remus, Aeneas, Charlemagne, Boadicea, King Alfred, St. Louis, St. Joan, and the Cid, glorified the founding of their nations. Some were more mythical than others, but when the modern nations of Italy, France, England, and Spain became self-conscious, the challenge to national historians was to give these hazy figures some historical reality, to make them more plausible by clothing them in historical fact. These nations, which had attained their nationality gradually over the centuries, already possessed legendary founding heroes when they became nations. The challenging task was to historicize them.

Not so in the United States. Here a new nation sprang into being almost before it had time to acquire a history. At the outbreak of the Civil War, there were men alive who could remember the death of Washington; he was still an emphatically real historical person. The national problem was not how to make Washington historical; quite the contrary: how could he be made into a myth? The very brevity of American history made special demands, but Americans of the age proved equal to them.

A measure of their success is how much has been popularly forgotten of the true story of George Washington, especially of his later years. Few Americans remember that Washington had more than his share of enemies, that for all his life he was a controversial figure, and that during his presidency he was personally libelled with a venom aimed at few of his successors. We cannot understand how powerful were the marmorealizing forces of the early 19th century unless we recall the acrimony, the bitter partisanship, the malicious rumor, and the unscrupulous lies which stormed about Washington during the last decade or so of his life. He had already become the arch-villain for all those who opposed the Federalists, including Jefferson and his followers, but the climax of Washington's unpopularity came with Jay's Treaty. This had been negotiated with Britain by John Jay, Washington's emissary, to resolve differences left unsettled at the end of the Revolution, or which had newly arisen since then. When the terms of the treaty were published in March 1795, furor shook the country. Southerners objected to its provisions for payment of pre-Revolutionary debts (in large part owed by Virginians); New Englanders objected to its restrictions on United States shipping to the West Indies. Attacks on Washington, who was held responsible for the treaty, were collected by Benjamin Bache, Franklin's grandson, who printed many of them in his *Aurora* in Philadelphia, to be widely copied by such Republican papers as the New York *Argus*, the Boston *Chronicle*, the *Kentucky Herald*, and the *Carolina Gazette*.

"The American People, Sir," the *Aurora* warned, "will look to death the man who assumes the character of a usurper." "If ever a nation was debauched by a man," it added in December 1796, "the American nation has been by Washington." "If ever there was a period for rejoicing, it is this moment," Bache announced on March 6, 1797, when Washington left office to be replaced by John Adams. "Every heart, in unison with the freedom and happiness of the people, ought to beat high in exultation, that the name of Washington ceases from this day to give a currency to political iniquity and to legalize corruption." Washington was accused of every kind of crime, including stealing from the public treasury. When the circulation of some of these papers fell off, Jefferson himself urged Republicans to support them by soliciting subscriptions; he called them the last bulwark of free speech and representative institutions.

Federalists aimed their notorious Alien and Sedition Acts of 1798 (many of the leading anti-Federalist writers were European refugees) at these publications. Then Washington himself, smarting under the venomous attacks, approved the prosecutions which, on dubious evidence, he called necessary to prevent "a disunion of the States."

When Washington died on December 14, 1799, he was anything but a noncontroversial figure. Not only his judgment but his integrity had been publicly impugned. He had been taunted into condoning means of dubious constitutionality to punish his enemies and to silence their presses. But he was destined to a stature in death which he had never attained in life.

What is most remarkable is not that Washington eventually became a demigod, Father of his Country, but that the transfiguration happened so quickly. There is no better evidence of the desperate need Americans felt for a dignified and worshipful national hero than their passionate haste in elevating Washington to sainthood. Never was there a better example of the special potency of the Will to Believe in this New World. A deification which in European history might have required centuries, was accomplished here in decades.

Between Washington's death in the last month of the last year of the 18th century and the outbreak of the Civil War, his worship had acquired a full cultic apparatus. To this end many people had collaborated, but the cult could not have grown so quickly or so vigorously without the peculiar American needs and vacuums.

The Sacred Life. It was appropriate to the cultic character of the Washington legend that its first high priest and one of its leading inventors was a charlatan—an amiable and energetic charlatan, but nevertheless a charlatan. And it was appropriate to the American character of the cult that this high priest should have been a salesman, in fact a supersalesman who had thoroughly mixed religion with salesmanship. The notorious Mason Locke Weems, better known as "Parson Weems," even before Washington's death had been collecting biographical materials. Born in Maryland in 1759, the youngest of nineteen children, he was in Britain studying medicine at the time of the Revolution. In 1784 he became one of the first Americans after the War fully ordained by the Archbishop of Canterbury for the Anglican ministry in the United States. After a brief and desultory clerical career, he turned to bookselling, for which he had both passion and genius. Although he had no permanent pulpit after about 1793, he continued to exercise his ministry with gusto through the printing, writing, and especially the selling of edifying books. Weems, during the last thirty years of his life (1795–1825), traveled the country between New York and Georgia as an itinerant salesman of salvation and printed matter. Besides selling his own books, he was agent for Matthew Carey and C. P. Wayne of Philadelphia. Traveling about in a wagon which carried his wares, he was ready, depending on the circumstances, to deliver a sermon or a political oration, or play his fiddle. After he had gathered his crowd and warmed them to good humor, he would sell the books from his wagon—patent medicine for all the ills of the spirit. "Part Whitefield, part Villon," Albert J. Beveridge accurately characterized him, "a delightful mingling of evangelist and vagabond, lecturer and politician, writer and musician."

Wandering over the countryside, he became a one-man market-research enterprise. Never was a cult devised for an audience better pretested, nor a national hero more calculatedly concocted to satisfy the demand. As early as 1797, Weems pointed out to Carey a rich untapped market. "Experience has taught me that small, i.e. quarter of dollar books, on subjects calculated to *strike* the Popular Curiosity, printed in very large numbers and properly *distributed*, w^d prove an immense revenue to the prudent and industrious Undertakers. If you could get the life of Genl. Wayne, Putnam, Green &c., Men whose courage and Abilities, whose patriotism and Exploits have won the love and admiration of the American people, printed in small volumes and with very interesting frontespieces, you w^d, without doubt, sell an immense number of them. People here think nothing of giving ⅙ (their quarter of a dollar) for anything that pleases their fancy. Let us give them something worth their money." Weems turned to the work himself, and on June 24, 1799, he wrote Carey from his home at Dumfries, Virginia, where he was to raise a family of ten children.

I have nearly ready for the press a piece christen^d, or to be christen^d, "The Beauties of Washington." tis artfully drawn up, enliven^d with anecdotes, and in my humble opinion, marvellously fitted, "ad captandum—gustum populi Americani!!!!["] What say you to printing it for me and ordering a copper plate Frontispiece of that HERO, something in this way. George Washington Esqr. The Guardian Angel of his Country "Go thy way old George. Die when thou wilt we shall never look upon thy like again" M. Carey inver.&^{c}. NB. The whole will make but four sheets and will sell like flax seed at quarter of a dollar. I cou'd make you a world of pence and popularity by it.

In October he again wrote Carey that he now had "on the Anvil and pretty well hammer'd out a piece that will sell to admiration.

THE TRUE PATRIOT
or
BEAUTIES OF WASHINGTON
Abundantly Biographical & Anecdotical
Curious & Marvellous"

Weems, therefore, was ready and waiting with his commodity when the great demand was created by the death of Washington. Less than a month after Washington's death, Weems effervesced to Carey:

I've something to whisper in your lug. Washington, you know is gone! Millions are gaping to read something about him. I am very nearly prim^d and cock^d for 'em. 6 months ago I set myself to collect anecdotes of him. You know I live conveniently for that work. My plan! I give his history, sufficiently minute—I accompany him from his start, thro the French & Indian & British or Revolutionary wars, to the Presidents chair, to the throne in the hearts of 5,000,000 of People. I then go on to show that his unparrelled rise & elevation were owing to his Great Virtues. 1 His Veneration for the Diety, or Religious Principles. 2 His Patriotism. 3 [d] his Magninmity. 4 his Industry. 5 his Temperance & Sobriety. 6 his Justice, & [c]. & [c]. Thus I hold up his great Virtues (as Gov [r] McKean prays) to the imitation of Our Youth. All this I have lin [d] and enliven [d] with *Anecdotes apropos interesting and Entertaining*. I have read it to several Gentlemen whom I thought judges, such as Presbyterian Clergymen, Classical Scholars & [c]. & [c]. and they all commend it much. it will not exceed 3 royal sheets on long primer. We may sell it with great rapidity for 25 or 37 Cents and it w [d] not cost 10. I read a part of it to one of my Parishioners, a first rate lady, and she wish [d] I w [d] print it, promising to take one for each of her children (a bakers dozen). I am thinking you could vend it admirably: as it will be the first. I can send it on, half of it, *immediately*.

Carey was too slow for Weems, who within three weeks had found other means. Four printings of this eighty-page booklet arranged by Weems himself appeared in 1800, but Weems still kept after Carey "to make this thing profitable and beneficial—Everybody will read about Washington. . . . I know you desire to do *Good* . . . We may preach through the Example and Virtues of Washington—Adams & Jefferson both will approve of our little piece.—I am in expectation of good things shortly for you. You know what I mean—Money." This happy marriage of philanthropy and avarice produced Weems's life of Washington, destined to be perhaps the most widely read, most influential book ever written about American history.

Soon after Washington's death, his nephew Bushrod Washington persuaded Chief Justice John Marshall to undertake the official life. This enterprise too was to have a shaping influence on American thinking about American history, not through its success but through its resounding failure. Weems had been employed by the publisher C. P. Wayne of Philadelphia to sell subscriptions to Marshall's monumental five volumes at $3 a volume. When the first instalment of Marshall's work finally reached subscribers in 1804, it quickly established the book as the publishing catastrophe of the age.

The whole Volume One, called "Introduction," was consumed by a pedantic account of colonial history beginning with Columbus; toward the end were two casual mentions of Washington. Dull, laborious, rambling, and secondhand, the work lumbered into its third, fourth, and fifth volumes. According to John Adams, Marshall's life was not really a book at all, but rather "a Mausoleum, 100 feet square at the base and 200 feet high."

Weems, seeing a public hungry for a readable story about the National Hero, was frantic with disgust and disappointment. He repeatedly begged Carey to dispose of the Marshall venture and provide something more salable. Even before the Marshall fiasco was fully disposed of, Weems returned in earnest to do the job himself. Profiting from Marshall's mistakes, in 1806 he revised his little pamphlet to give it everything Marshall's work had lacked. Though still only eighty pages, it now had more form, more facts (invented when necessary), and contained a number of appealing new anecdotes. After Marshall's final volume appeared in 1807 and Weems was disburdened of the whole profitless business, he turned his spare energies to enlarging his pamphlet to a book of some two hundred pages ("6th edition," 1808). On the title page Weems styled himself "Formerly Rector of Mount-Vernon Parish," which added authenticity for all readers who did not know that such a parish never existed. After 1808 only minor changes and additions were made.

In substantially this form, Weems's *Life of George Washington: With Curious Anecdotes, Equally Honourable to Himself and Exemplary to His Young Countrymen* went through twenty more "editions" before Weems's death in 1825. Within a decade of its first publication, this work probably sold well over 50,000 copies (Marshall's had sold closer to 5000!), making it a best seller for its time. Still Weems, who had made the mistake of selling the copyright of his book to Carey in 1808 for a mere $1000, failed to persuade Carey to let him enlarge the work further or to issue an "elegant edition" at three or four dollars. "You have a great deal of money lying in the bones of old George," Weems wrote Carey in January 1809, on a theme he repeated again and again, "if you will but exert yourself to extract it."

While Weems aimed to produce a book primarily for "the admiring eyes of our *children*," his book should be classified neither as juvenile nor as nonfiction but as booster literature. Others applied their booster enthusiasm and booster optimism to the future; he applied his to the past. While others were boosters for this or that part of the country, he was one of the first national boosters. Weems, like other boosters, asserted facts for which there was little or no foundation, but we must not forget that, in the contagious vagueness of American life, distinctions which elsewhere seemed sharp—between fact and wish, between history and prophecy—were hard to draw. Thus Weems began his chapter on the birth and education of his Hero:

> To this day numbers of good Christians can hardly find faith to believe that Washington was, bona fide, a *Virginian!* "*What! a buckskin!*" say they with a smile, "*George Washington a buckskin! pshaw! impossible! he was certainly an European: So great a man could never have been born in America.*"
>
> *So great a man could never have been born in America!*— Why that's the very *prince of reasons* why he should have been born here! Nature, we know, is fond of *harmonies;* and *paria paribus*, that is, *great things to great*, is the rule she delights to work by. Where, for example, do we look for the *whale* "the biggest born of nature?" not, I trow, in a *millpond*, but in the main ocean; "*there go the great ships*," and there are the spoutings of whales amidst their boiling foam.
>
> By the same rule, where shall we look for Washington, the greatest among men, but in *America?* That greatest Continent, which, rising from beneath the frozen pole, stretches far and wide to the south, running almost "*whole the length of this vast terrene*," and sustaining on her ample sides the roaring shock of half the watery globe. And equal to its size, is the furniture of this vast continent, where the Almighty has reared his cloud-capt mountains, and spread his sea-like lakes, and poured his mighty rivers, and hurled down his

thundering cataracts in a style of the *sublime*, so far superior to any thing of the kind in the other continents, that we may fairly conclude that great men and great deeds are designed for America.

This seems to be the verdict of honest analogy; and accordingly we find America the honoured cradle of Washington, who was born on Pope's creek, in Westmoreland county, Virginia, the 22d of February, 1732.

As the work begins, so it ends. The three final chapters, on the character of Washington, describe his religion, his benevolence, his industry, and his patriotism—all as the natural response of the greatest of all men to the greatest of all challenges, America.

George's father, we are told by Weems, took every chance to implant virtues in his son. When the boy was only five, his father and a cousin took him walking one fall in the apple-orchard. "Now, George, said his father, look here, my son! don't you remember when this good cousin of yours brought you that fine large apple last spring, how hardly I could prevail on you to divide with your brothers and sisters; though I promised you that if you would but do it, God Almighty would give you plenty of apples this fall. Poor George could not say a word; but hanging down his head, looked quite confused, while with his little naked toes he scratched in the soft ground. . . . George looked in silence on the wide wilderness of fruit; he marked the busy humming bees, and heard the gay notes of birds, then lifting his eyes filled with shining moisture, to his father, he softly said, 'Well, Pa, only forgive me this time; see if I ever be so stingy any more.' "

And, of course, there is the famous story of the cherry tree:

> "*I can't tell a lie, Pa; you know I can't tell a lie. I did cut it with my hatchet.*"—*Run to my arms, you dearest boy,* cried his father in transports, *run to my arms; glad am I, George, that you killed my tree; for you have paid me for it a thousand fold. Such an act of heroism in my son, is more worth than a thousand trees, though blossomed with silver, and their fruits of purest gold.*

And then the story of how George's schoolmates wept when George left them. How George hated to fight, yet performed feats of strength. How, after Braddock's defeat, a "famous Indian warrior" swore that "Washington was not born to be killed by a bullet! For, I had seventeen fair fires at him with my rifle, and after all could not bring him to the ground." How, during her pregnancy with George, his mother dreamed a dream which foretold his greatness and the history of the Revolution.

The great gap in our documentary knowledge of Washington, especially in his early life, Weems filled with materials borrowed, stolen, or invented, describing events which, from their very nature, were virtually impossible to disprove. Who could confidently assert that the cherry-tree episode had *not* occurred in the privacy of the elder Washington's household? Or that Mary Washington had *not* experienced such and such a dream? Perhaps, as Marcus Cunliffe ventures, these apocryphal anecdotes survived precisely because they did express, however crudely and inexactly, some sort of general truth about the Hero. Certainly what Weems said was what many people wanted to believe. And by these tales Weems sold his book, and through his book he sold another commodity, the Hero. Was this or wasn't this a hoax? Who could say?

Weems was only one of scores of acolytes of the Washington cult. Before Washington's death, although there were brief biographical sketches in magazines or in general works like Jedidiah Morse's *American Geography* (1789), there seems to have appeared no book-length treatment of his life. Soon after Weems's revised version of 1806, several other more or less readable lives appeared, but most of these were serious works, not directed to the juvenile audience or the unliterary public. For some years Weems had a virtual monopoly of the popular market. Then in 1829 appeared Anna C. Reed's life, written for the Sunday Schools (a newly flourishing American institution), and in the centennial year, 1832, Samuel G. Goodrich, whose literary factory produced over a hundred children's books under the pseudonym of "Peter Parley," offered a successful juvenile biography. The life of the Hero was being celebrated in many other forms—in long poems, plays, and even in *A Life of George Washington in Latin Prose* (1835) by an Ohio schoolteacher.

Meanwhile, the story of Washington's life was being retold in heavy tomes by scholars and men of letters. Perhaps there is no better evidence of the piety which the name of Washington excited than that, in the centennial year of Washington's birth (1832), there appeared a revised edition of Marshall's *Life*, only slightly condensed. It was followed by a one-volume school edition (1838). Others too turned out works that were less readable than monumental. Of these ambitious tomes, the least heavy was the two-volume life (1835) by the novelist James Kirke Paulding. Then came Jared Sparks's pious and ponderous life, which appeared as Volume One (1837) of his edition of the *Writings*. The best of these works was Washington Irving's five volumes, but he too was afflicted by the contagion of dullness. Judging from the sets of Irving which survive into the 20th century with virgin pages, these volumes also were more widely bought than read. But Washington's posthumous life had only begun.

The Sacred Writings. The Washington cult, it is important to note, flourished long before there existed any printed collection of the writings of the Hero. Nowhere could the scholar, much less the citizen, read the authentic words of Washington himself. The more widely Washington was adored, the more superfluous—and in many ways the less interesting—his own writings became.

In this cultic spirit, a third of a century after his death, the first edition of Washington's writings appeared. At an early age Jared Sparks (1789–1866) had begun to think about a collection of the Hero's writings. Sparks was a New Englander of humble birth who, after working his way through Harvard College, had by his social grace established himself among the Boston élite. He studied divinity and then filled a Unitarian pulpit in Baltimore for a few years. Returning to Boston, he took over the *North American Review*, which he built into the leading critical journal of national circulation. He was a man of many talents, with a sense for the tastes and book-buying interests of the intellectual community. It was the edition of Washington's writings that established Sparks's national reputation and led to his appointment in 1838 as McLean Professor of Ancient and Modern History at Harvard—the first professor of history (other than ecclesiastical) in a university in the United States—and then to his presidency of Harvard (1849–53).

Securing permission of the Washington family to publish the writings of their ancestor was no easy matter. George Washington's literary executor and the inheritor of Mount Vernon was his nephew, the rigid and unimaginative Bushrod Washington (Associate Justice of the Supreme Court, 1798–1829), who, in refusing Sparks (March 13, 1826) explained that he and Marshall were planning three volumes of selected letters from the Revolutionary period, to be followed later by a pre-Revolutionary selection. Six months later, Sparks, undiscouraged, tried again to persuade Bushrod Washington to give him access to the papers, adding that he would go ahead anyway, gathering copies of the papers wherever he could find them, and that, since the papers would eventually reach the public eye, Bushrod might better choose to supervise the work. Sparks would allow him to withhold whatever he thought unsuitable for publication. "If the entire works of Washington were presented to the public in a form suited to the dignity of the subject, a national interest and a national feeling would be excited, and a wide and honorable patronage might be expected." Sparks then added an argument more substantial: an offer to give Bushrod Washington half the profits of publication. In January 1827 (after urging by John Marshall, who had been prodded by Sparks), Bushrod Washington accepted the proposal. Under the final terms, half the profits were to go to Sparks, the other half to be equally divided between Bushrod Washington and John Marshall.

Over the next several years Sparks collected manuscripts, copied official documents, and showed an energy in gathering materials which was unprecedented in American historical scholarship. He soon decided that the number of volumes should be determined by "the probable demand in the market, as well as the nature of the work." Sparks's twelve-volume edition (1834–37) included eleven volumes of selected writings and Sparks's biography of Washington (1837). Despite the large editorial expenses ($15,357.37) which had to be deducted, the net returns were sizable. In 1837, when Sparks sent the first share of profits to the heirs of Bushrod Washington and John Marshall, the total sum to be divided was $15,384.63. For twenty years Sparks was sending additional shares of the profits to the Washington and the Marshall families.

Sparks's *Life and Writings of George Washington* was greeted by loud and indiscriminate applause. Surviving members of the Washington family found it perfect and sent Sparks a cedar cane cut from the tree which shaded Washington's tomb. Sixty-three pages by Edward Everett in the *North American Review* exhausted superlatives: "Not a single trait of indiscretion is disclosed in his work." George Bancroft, still near the beginning of his career, found the work "beyond my praise for its calmness, accuracy, and intense interest of authenticity."

"You are a lucky fellow," Bancroft had written Sparks as early as 1827, "selected by a favoring Providence to conduct a good ship into the haven of immortality, and to have your own name recorded as the careful pilot." And Sparks was less the historian than the acolyte, less the discoverer of the true than the adorer of the good. Appropriately, the founder of historical scholarship in the United States was a high priest of the Washington cult. Sparks again and again went through the motions of strenuous historical research. Before his publication of the diplomatic correspondence of the Revolution (12 vols., 1829–30), of the writings of Washington, and of Franklin (10 vols., 1836–40), no substantial printed sources were available on the crucial era of American history. But for the study of modern history in American universities this was, as Samuel Eliot Morison observes, a "false dawn." Sparks, the first professor of his subject, left no disciples, and it would be nearly a half-century before American history would begin to flourish as a profession. One reason must be found in how Sparks and his contemporaries conceived the subject. The vice of Sparks's historical work was not that it was conceived in sin, but rather that it was conceived in virtue.

Sparks followed the style of his day. His biography, which prefaced the writings, was pious, pallid, and reverential. The Hero was of commanding figure, symmetrical features, indomitable courage, pure character, and perfect judgment; "his moral qualities were in perfect harmony with those of his intellect." Sparks's appendix, "Religious Opinions and Habits," was an ingenious whitewash in which Washington's failure to attend communion became an argument for his religiosity. "He may have believed it improper publicly to partake of an ordinance, which, according to the ideas he entertained of it, imposed severe restrictions on outward conduct, and a sacred pledge to perform duties impracticable in his situation. Such an impression would be natural to a serious mind . . . a man of a delicate conscience and habitual reverence for religion." There was no passage in Washington's writings, Sparks noted, which expressed doubt of the Christian revelation. In a man of such Christian demeanor, what more conclusive proof that he was a true and tolerant Christian?

The writings were edited in a similar spirit. In selecting a mere eleven from what might have filled four times that many volumes, Sparks had ample freedom to ennoble his subject. While Sparks did not actually add passages of his own, he omitted passages at will without warning the reader and he improved the language when it seemed unworthy of the Hero. He explained all this in his introduction: "It would be an act of unpardonable injustice to any author, after his death, to bring forth compositions, and particularly letters, written with no design to their publication, and commit them to the press without previously subjecting them to a careful revision." Challenged later on his editorial methods, Sparks argued with charming naiveté that he was really being true to his subject because Washington himself in his old age had revised his early letters. Wherever Sparks had the choice he preferred Washington's own later revisions (again without warning the reader) in place of what had actually been written in the heat of the events. And Sparks made changes on his own. Where, for example, Washington had written of the "rascally crews" of New England privateersmen, Sparks emended the text to read simply "the crews." Washington's reference to the "dirty mercenary spirit" of the Connecticut troops became "the mercenary spirit," and their "scandalous conduct" was softened to their "conduct." "Old Put." became the more dignified

"General Putnam." When Washington referred contemptuously to a small sum of money as "but a fleabite at present," Sparks improved it to read "totally inadequate to our demands at this time." Sparks again and again and again changed the words to make them worthy of his Hero.

Nearly fifteen years passed before any respectable public voice objected to Sparks's unobtrusive embellishments of Washington. In 1833, when Sparks sent Justice Joseph Story a specimen volume, Story privately expressed his enthusiastic approval: Sparks had "done exactly what Washington would have desired you to do, if he were living." But Story indicated concern lest a "cynical critic" should sometime in the future cavil over these improvements. Not until 1851 was there so much as a peep from any such "cynical critic," when two letters by an unidentified writer to the New York *Post* compared Sparks's version with another recently published version of certain letters from Washington to Joseph Reed, his military secretary during the Revolution.

The opening gun in a major (though finally unsuccessful) attack on Sparks's editorial integrity was fired by an Englishman, who was a noble lord and an accomplished scholar. The cultic sacredness of Washington's writings was revealed in the indignation against this attack and in the solid support of the American scholarly world for Sparks's way of elevating the American Hero. In December 1851, Lord Mahon (later Lord Stanhope), a well-known English man of letters, who had been active in the Historical Manuscripts Commission, published the sixth volume of his seven-volume *History of England from the Peace of Utrecht to the Peace of Versailles.* "Mr. Sparks," he observed in the appendix, "has printed no part of the correspondence precisely as Washington wrote it; but has greatly altered, and, as he thinks, corrected and embellished it." He accused Sparks of "tampering with the truth of history." This remark, so inconspicuously placed, might have been little noticed had it not touched so sacred a figure. The immediate reply was an eighty-page counterattack by John Gorham Palfrey, the well-known Unitarian clergyman and historian who had followed Sparks as editor of the *North American Review,* in the form of a review of Mahon's work. In a pamphlet-war that lasted nearly three years, Sparks (then President of Harvard College) defended himself and his Hero; hostilities ended in a personal truce between Lord Mahon and Sparks.

The great significance of this controversy was to reveal an orthodoxy among American scholars who competed with one another in expressions of cultic reverence. Among Sparks's supporters were Francis Parkman, William H. Prescott, Senator Charles Sumner (who hailed Sparks "triumphant"), James S. Mackee (Librarian of the State Department and official custodian of the Washington Papers, which were now owned by the government) and, most appropriately, the eminent Professor Andrews Norton, who had attained fame as a pioneer in the use of new "critical" techniques to establish the genuineness of the New Testament. The best evidence of the general satisfaction with Sparks's way of editing was that, during the half-century after the appearance of Sparks's edition, there was no other edition of the Writings.

The Sacred Remains. The struggle over the possession and proper location of the bodily remains of the Hero, if not equaling that over the Holy Grail, expressed a not dissimilar cultic spirit.

At the death of Washington, Congress unanimously adopted a joint resolution directing "That a marble monument be erected by the United States at the Capitol of the city of Washington, and that the family of General Washington be requested to permit his body to be deposited under it, and that the monument be so designed as to commemorate the great events of his military and political life." Mrs. Washington approved the plan and a year later, in December, 1800, the House passed a bill appropriating $200,000 to construct a marble mausoleum, pyramidal in shape, with a base one hundred feet square, to receive Washington's body. At that time the Capitol building still consisted of only one wing; the present rotunda and crypt below it were not yet built. There seems to have been a notion of somehow including the tomb of Washington in the Capitol complex itself. Some Southerners opposed the project, arguing that the sacred remains properly belonged where they already were, at Mount Vernon. Partly because of the division of opinion, nothing was done. A new House committee in 1830 recommended that "the remains of George Washington and Martha Washington be entombed in the same national sepulchre, that immediately over the centre of his tomb and in the grand floor of the Capitol shall be placed a marble cenotaph in the form of a well-proportioned sarcophagus. . . . Immediately above this, in the centre of the Rotunda, a full length marble equestrian statue of Washington, wrought by the best artist of the present time. . . . These memorials, little costly and ostentatious as they may appear, will better accord with the feelings of this Nation and more appropriately commemorate the pure and elevated character of our Washington than could any the most expensive or splendid monument or mausoleum." Meanwhile, as 1832, the centenary of Washington's birth, approached, sectional passions (sharpened by the South Carolina nullification movement) ran high.

After the British, who occupied the city in 1814, had burned the interior of the Capitol building, Charles Bulfinch had rebuilt the central portion (1818–29) with a crypt designed to receive Washington's body. The plan of the joint Congressional committee for the Washington centennial celebration centered around the transfer of Washington's body from Mount Vernon to the Capitol crypt. In a bitter Congressional debate during January and February of 1832, Southerners, reluctant to part with the National Relic, concocted all sorts of reasons against allowing the removal. A representative from Maine charged that the whole debate was a contest between the State of Virginia and the great United States. Henry Clay of Kentucky urged the removal because "he would himself discriminate between Washington and any man who had lived, from Adam down."

Southern representatives, foreseeing civil war and their separation from the Union, imagined the resulting indignities. "Remove the remains of our venerated Washington," warned Wiley Thompson of Georgia, "from their association with the remains of his consort and his ancestors, from Mount Vernon and from his native State, and deposit them in this capitol, and then let a severance of the Union occur, and behold! the remains of Washington on a shore foreign to his native soil." Others objected that, with the westward movement of the population, the capitol would doubtless also be moved: "Shall the remains of our Washington be left amidst the ruins of this capitol, surrounded by the desolation of this city?" "If our population is to reach to the Western Ocean," replied Joel B. Sutherland of Pennsylvania, "and the seat of Government is to be removed, when we carry away the ensigns of power from this place, we will carry with us the sacred bones of Washington." Others argued that the very presence of Washington's remains would somehow mollify and sanctify the deliberations of Congress. "No act can be done by the Government," pleaded Jonathan Hunt of Vermont, "that would have so deep and permanent a moral influence in uniting the people and cementing the Union of this confederacy, as the burial of Washington in the capitol."

The debate came to an abrupt end on February 16, when, less than a week before the proposed ceremony, John Augustine Washington, then the occupant of Mount Vernon, flatly refused to allow removal of the Hero's body. After a mysterious attempt to steal Washington's body from his tomb at Mount Vernon in the 1830's, a new tomb was completed there; it was locked, and the key was thrown into the Potomac.

The Annual Rites and a Declamatory Liturgy. In the mid-20th century, the only birthday anniversary (other than December 25) celebrated as a legal holiday by every state of the Union is February 22, the birthday of Washington. In the early 19th century, when the new nation still had almost no history, the birthday of Washington shared with the Fourth of July—the birthday of the Republic itself—the annual patriotic rites. On both these occasions, the center of interest, the usual ritual, was an oration. Repetitious, florid, pompous, bombastic, and interminable, the oration followed a pattern that was as set as if it had been prescribed by a liturgical authority. One example will do almost as well as another. Daniel Webster declared at the centennial of Washington's birth on February 22, 1832:

> Washington stands at the commencement of a new era, as well as at the head of the New World. A century from the birth of Washington has changed the world. The country of Washington has been the theatre on which a great part of the change has been wrought; and Washington himself a principal agent by which it has been accomplished. His age

and his country are equally full of wonders; and of both he is the chief.

Orators said the brevity of American history was more than off-set by the grandeur of a Washington. John Tyler (later President) declared at Yorktown in 1837 that the Hero was greater than Leonidas or Moses, for, conspicuously unlike Washington, the one died with his men and the other never entered the Promised Land. John Quincy Adams found combined in Washington, more than in Aeneas or King David, "the spirit of command and the spirit of meekness." "To add brightness to the sun or glory to the name of Washington," Abraham Lincoln said at Springfield on February 22, 1842, "is alike impossible. Let none attempt it. In solemn awe pronounce the name, and in its naked deathless splendor leave it shining on."

Most popular and most repeated was Edward Everett's oration, which he delivered on circuit for the Mount Vernon Association to raise funds to purchase Washington's residence as a public shrine. From 1856 to 1860, Everett traveled over the country, and by delivering the same two-hour oration some 129 times, he raised about $90,000. His oration, "The Character of Washington," immediately became a classic in the national liturgy. Starting with the young Washington—"twenty-four years of age, a model of manly strength and beauty, perfect in all the qualities and accomplishments of the gentleman and the soldier, but wise and thoughtful beyond his years, inspiring at the outset of his career that love and confidence which are usually earned only by a life of service"—Everett sketched the heroic career. In an age "first in the annals of our race for great names, great events, great reforms, and the general progress of intelligence," Washington was greatest of all. Shining above the tawdry tyrannies of Peter the Great of Russia, Frederick the Great of Prussia, and Napoleon the Great of France, was the star of Washington.

A great and venerated character like that of Washington, which commands the respect of an entire population, however divided on other questions, is not an isolated fact in

History to be regarded with barren admiration,—it is a dispensation of Providence for good. It was well said by Mr. Jefferson in 1792, writing to Washington to dissuade him from declining a renomination: "North and South will hang together while they have you to hang to." Washington in the flesh is taken from us; we shall never behold him as our fathers did; but his memory remains, and I say, let us hang to his memory. Let us make a national festival and holiday of his birthday; and ever, as the 22d of February returns, let us remember, that while with these solemn and joyous rites of observance we celebrate the great anniversary, our fellow-citizens on the Hudson, on the Potomac, from the Southern plains to the Western lakes, are engaged in the same offices of gratitude and love. Nor we, nor they alone,—beyond the Ohio, beyond the Mississippi, along that stupendous trail of immigration from East to West, which, bursting into States as it moves westward, is already threading the Western prairies, swarming through the portals of the Rocky Mountains and winding down their slopes, the name and the memory of Washington on that gracious night will travel with the silver queen of heaven through sixty degrees of longitude, nor part company with her till she walks in her brightness through the golden gate of California, and passes serenely on to hold midnight court with her Australian stars. There and there only, in barbarous archipelagos, as yet untrodden by civilized man, the name of Washington is unknown; and there, too, when they swarm with enlightened millions, new honors shall be paid with ours to his memory.

As sectional antagonisms sharpened, Washington's light was made to illuminate more brightly one side or the other. For Calhoun, he became the patron saint of Independence; for Webster and Lincoln, the patron saint of Union.

Washington had become the Savior as well as the Father of his Country. "From the first ages of the world," Representative Benjamin C. Howard of Maryland observed in Congress (February 13,

1832), "the records of all time furnished only two instances of birthdays being commemorated after the death of the individual: those two were the 22d of February and the 25th of December." "To 'Mary the Mother of Washington,' whose incomplete monument at Fredericksburg lies shamefully neglected," said the Rev. J. N. Danforth in Virginia on July 4, 1847, "we owe all the mighty debt due from mankind to her immortal son."

The Icon. Nothing better reveals the cultic, sacred character of Washington than the conventional appearance of his familiar portrait. Seldom has a historic figure been cast so universally in a single mold: the stereotype of Washington was cast by Gilbert Stuart. Many contemporary portraits of Washington were painted or sculpted between 1772 and 1799 by the best artists of the age: the Peales (Charles Wilson, James, and Rembrandt), John Trumbull, William Dunlap, Edward Savage, Du Simitière, Houdon, Ceracchi, and others. Every known medium was employed, not only oils and marble, but wood, ivory, wax-reliefs, life-masks, shadow-pictures, and profile-drawings with the aid of a mechanical pantograph called the "physionotrace." Washington became inured to long and repeated sittings. What became the classic portrait was highly idealized. Lasting popular devotion significantly fixed on Gilbert Stuart's unfinished portrait (the "Atheneum") that was suffused with an unworldly haze.

Gilbert Stuart, who had been born in Rhode Island, decided at the age of twenty that the American colonies were no place for a painter. In 1775 he went to England, where he spent five years in the studio of another expatriate American, Benjamin West. Quickly acquiring a rich and fashionable portrait clientele, he competed successfully with Ramsay, Reynolds, Romney, and Gainsborough. When he returned to the United States in about 1793, possibly to escape imprisonment for debt, his avowed object was to recoup his fortunes by painting Washington; Stuart hoped eventually to make "a plurality of his portraits" with which to repay English and Irish creditors. His first painting of Washington, done from life in 1795, brought him orders from thirty-one subscribers for thirty-nine "copies." This was only a beginning, for no one knows precisely how many copies of his portraits were made by Stuart or his disciples or imitators.

The peculiar appeal of the Stuart portraits may be their very stiffness, which seems a kind of idealization. In human vividness they are much inferior to the portraits by Rembrandt Peale, which never had the vogue or appeal of Stuart's. The explanation, as Rembrandt Peale himself recounts it, is quite irreverently commonplace.

> Judge Washington informed me . . . . that the day his Uncle first sat to Stuart, he had placed in his mouth a new sett of teeth, made by the elder Gardette: they were clumsily formed of Sea-horse Ivory, to imitate both teeth & Gums, and filled his mouth very uncomfortably, so as to prevent his speaking, but with difficulty; giving to his mouth the appearance of *being rinced with Water*—(these were Judge Washington's Words). At a subsequent period, Mr. Stuart himself told me that he never had painted a Man so difficult to engage in conversation, as was his custom, in order to elicit the natural expression, which can only be selected and caught in varied discourse. The teeth were at fault; and, unfortunately for Mr. Stuart, they were always again put in at each sitting, with the expectation that eventually they would become easy—but they were finally rejected. It was fortunate for me that my Study was begun *before* the new teeth were finished, and that my Sitter each time came to me with the old Sett furnished him in New York many years before.

These dental circumstances, combined with Stuart's genius for idealizing his subject, produced a portrait perfectly suited to the American's ideal of his Hero.

Not oil, but marble, seemed the most appropriate material for the character and the image of Washington. A catalogue of the sculptured icons itself fills a volume. There was the famous life-size bust by the French sculptor, Houdon, of which countless replicas were made and which has become standard. There was the bust made from life by the Italian adventurer Ceracchi, which he then repeated in colossal size. There was the statue by the celebrated Canova.

Most impressive (and controversial) of all was the work of Horatio Greenough, the New England sculptor who had been given a government commission in 1832 to make a statue of Washington for the Capitol rotunda, at a fee of $5000. After eight years' labor in his studio in Florence, Italy, Greenough produced the statue; it was ten and a half feet high and weighed twenty tons. The freight bill across the Atlantic was $7700 and the cost of removal from the Navy Yard to the Capitol rotunda was another $5000. The Capitol entrance had to be widened to admit the colossus, but, when in place, its weight was too much for the floor; it was removed outdoors to the east front. The bill to this point was $21,000. By now it had become a public scandal, not only because of its cost, but because, ironically, Greenough's very effort to deify the Hero had outraged public decency and seemed itself a kind of blasphemy.

Greenough's statue, modelled after Phidias' colossal ivory and gold Zeus for the temple at Olympia, showed Washington seated on a carved throne, naked to the waist, with drapery over his legs and sandals on his feet. Patriotic Americans were shocked that Washington, of all people, should be displayed without clothing. "Washington was too prudent, and careful of his health," wrote the New York socialite Philip Hone, "to expose himself thus in a climate so uncertain as ours, to say nothing of the indecency of such an exposure, a subject on which he was known to be exceedingly fastidious." The same public whose committee of clergymen had approved Hiram Powers' totally naked female *Greek Slave* and had approved the nakedness of Greenough's earlier *Chanting Cherubs* "awoke," as Greenough said, "with a roar at the colossal nakedness of Washington's manly breast." The statue remained controversial until, a half-century later, it was removed to the decent obscurity of an alcove in the Smithsonian Institution where it remains. "Did anybody ever see Washington nude?" Nathaniel Hawthorne asked in 1858. "It is inconceivable. He had no nakedness, but I imagine he was born with his clothes on, and his hair powdered, and made a stately bow on his first appearance in the world."

The public shock at this fleshly version of the Hero made it easier for the Washington Monument Association to complete its fund-raising ($87,000 by the end of 1847). This Monument appropriately enough, commemorated the Hero not in any human form, however godlike, but in a geometric obelisk of abstract perfection.

The Sacred Name. In the United States the very name of Washington has been honored uniquely. In 1791, while the Hero himself was still alive, the Commissioners for the proposed capital, although they had no legal authority to name the city, christened it the City of Washington. Despite the prevailing partisan bitterness, their choice was not effectively disputed. Washington, too, was the only person after the colonial period whose name was given to a state. "There has been but one Washington upon earth," observed a member of Congress in 1853, during the debate on the organization of Washington Territory (later to become the State of Washington), "and there is not likely to be another, and, as Providence has sent but one, for all time, let us have one State named after that one man." In mid-20th century Washington, leading all others, appeared in the name of at least 121 post offices. He was far ahead, too, in the number of counties named after him; thirty-two states have Washington counties. Of the states which have no such counties, as George Stewart remarks, six were among the smaller of the thirteen original colonies and thus already had their counties named before 1775; and most of the rest were states in the far west which were not organized until after the Civil War, when the Washington cult had declined.

* * *

A cult confers immortality on its acolytes as well as on its object. Davy Crockett shared his earthy American world of comic supermen not with the Hero, but with the Salesman of the Hero. In the third part of the "Autobiography" of Davy Crockett, which describes Davy's journey to Texas from his home in Weakley County, Tennessee, he recounts how in that year of 1835 (when actually the body of Parson Weems was already ten years in its grave) Weems's spirit and his evangelical salesmanship went marching on. At Little Rock, Arkansas, Crockett found a traveling puppeteer about to be attacked by a crowd because he was too drunk to put on the show they awaited. There was no one to play the fiddle, and the puppeteer's "sick wife and five hungry children" were going to suffer. The salesman-parson who had just arrived with his ramshackle wagon full of books and pamphlets for sale promptly came to the rescue. After reading from "God's Revenge against Drunkenness," a pamphlet he offered for sale from his wagon, the ghost of Weems played his fiddle, saved the show, and took up a collection for the friendless showman and his family. The immortal Parson "placed his trunk of pamphlets before him, and proceeded on his pilgrimage, the little children following him through the village with bursts of gratitude."

FROM

THE
AMERICANS
The Democratic Experience

"American life is a powerful solvent."
GEORGE SANTAYANA

The century after the Civil War was to be an Age of Revolution—of countless, little-noticed revolutions, which occurred not in the halls of legislatures or on battlefields or on the barricades but in homes and farms, in factories and schools and stores, across the landscape and in the air—so little noticed because they came so swiftly, because they touched Americans everywhere and every day. Not merely the continent but human experience itself, the very meaning of community, of time and space, of present and future, was being revised again and again; a new democratic world was being invented and was being discovered by Americans wherever they lived.

LAWLESS SHERIFFS AND HONEST DESPERADOES

CHAPTER 4

G O-GETTER MORALITY BROUGHT an age of Good Bad Men and Bad Good Men. While sheriffs and marshals were in the pay of rustlers and cattle barons, outlaws and vigilantes were taking oaths "to enforce the law." A Go-Getter's loyalty was his willingness to stick by his guns to avenge a friend, to defend his cattle, or to secure a fortune. It was a time of boon companions, of pals and "pardners," and of quick and mortal enemies. It was far easier to recognize a friend or an enemy, to tell a good proposition when you saw one, than to know whether or not the "law" was on your side.

*   *   *

The prevalence of firearms and the high value placed on the quick draw made a sure shot the test of manliness. From earliest colonial times, the needs of the wilderness and the threat of Indians had put firearms in the American household. The right to bear arms had been hallowed in the Constitution.

The six-shooter, a stepchild of the West, would for the first time provide a portable, rapid-shooting repeater which put "law enforcement" in the reach of any trained arm. The perfection of the six-shooter was a response to the special needs of Texan cattlemen in the treeless Great Plains. Menaced by the Comanche Indians, the settlers who went to Texas from the United States in the early nineteenth century, found themselves at a dangerous disadvantage. Their encounters with the Indians were commonly on horseback. But the skillful Comanche could ride three hundred yards and shoot twenty arrows in the time it took the Texan to reload his firearm once. Even if a Texan went the limit and actually carried two heavy single-shot pistols in addition to his rifle, he still had no more than three shots before he was forced to stop and reload. Anyway, the rifle could not be used effectively from horseback.

When Samuel Colt, a sixteen-year-old Connecticut sailor, whittled his first wooden model of a revolver on the long voyage to Singapore in 1830, he could hardly have been thinking of the needs of Texas pioneers. Two years later Colt sent a description of his revolver to the Patent Office in Washington. Employing the new techniques of interchangeable parts, Colt's company manufactured his revolvers, but the United States government refused to take these revolvers, nor were they extensively bought by private citizens in the East.

The new six-shooter did have great appeal out in the new Republic of Texas. In fact, so much of the demand came from there that Colt himself christened his first popular model "the Texas." The Captain of the Texas Rangers, Samuel H. Walker, went to New York to confer with Colt on improvements. Colt's new model, heavy enough to use as a club in close combat, and easier to reload, was then named "the Walker." The name "six-shooter" itself seems to have been introduced by the Texas Rangers. "They are the only weapon," Ranger officers insisted, "which enabled the experienced frontiersman to defeat the *mounted* Indian in his own peculiar mode of warfare . . . your six-shooter is the arm which has rendered the name of Texas Ranger a check and terror to the bands of our frontier Indians." Probably the first use of the six-shooter in a mounted battle against Indians was at the Pedernales in 1840 when some fifteen Texas Rangers defeated about seventy Comanches.

But in the East the demand was so small that the Colt factory went bankrupt in 1842. The United States Army still could not see the value of the weapon. When war with Mexico broke out in 1845, the Texas Rangers at first used their own six-shooters, and then urgently demanded that the United States government provide a supply. Colt, who at the time did not possess even one six-shooter to use as a model, resumed production. "He had made a better gun," explains Walter Prescott Webb, eloquent historian of the Great Plains, "it had blazed a pathway from his door to the Texas Rangers and the Plains, and the world was now to pave that pathway with gold." The Mexican War established the six-shooter as the characteristic American weapon of the West and Southwest.

* * *

To many of the cattlemen and cowboys who gathered in the West in the late 1860's and '70's, the Civil War had given a new familiarity with all kinds of firearms. That bloodiest war of the century had accustomed them to the face of death and the smell of carnage. How all these experiences and opportunities came to focus among Western Go-Getters was illustrated in the remarkable career of Wild Bill Hickok.

As a boy James Butler Hickok loved to hunt, and he had a reputation for being the best shot in northern Illinois. In 1855, when he was only eighteen, he joined the Free State forces in Bleeding, Kansas. Serving briefly as a town constable, he then found a job driving a stage across the Santa Fe Trail, which gave him further opportunity to test his fighting prowess. On one occasion he used his bowie knife to kill a bear. When driving on the Oregon Trail in 1861, he shot it out with the infamous McCanles Gang. His service as scout and spy for the Union in the Civil War was full of dangerous adventure and narrow escapes, which kept his shooting arm well practiced. In the public square in Springfield, Missouri, he killed a former friend of his, a fellow Union scout who had joined the Confederates. Then, after the war, as deputy U.S. marshal for a vast area around Fort Riley, Kansas, he became famous as a recoverer of stolen property and a killer of outlaws. As marshal of several rough Kansas cow towns, including Abilene, he proved faster on the draw than some of the most notorious desperadoes, until the number of men he had killed in single combat was reputed to be greater than that killed by any of his contemporaries. He became a public performer, touring the country with Buffalo Bill in 1872–73. Three years later when he returned to one of his old haunts, Deadwood, Dakota Territory, he was shot in the back of the head by a local citizen from whom he had won some money at cards earlier in the day. He was only thirty-nine years old. His murderer was tried and acquitted by the local court.

After Wild Bill's burial in Deadwood, the monument and railing around his grave were dismantled piece by piece by people who wanted a memento of so great a killer. Nobody knows exactly how many he actually shot down in open personal combat; some put the figure as high as eighty-five, but it was surely not less than thirty. He managed all these killings without once being brought into court even for a charge of manslaughter. During much of his active life Wild Bill Hickok wore the badge of the law. Still, a tantalizing ambiguity surrounded many of his killings, for his rule in doubtful cases seemed to be to shoot first and investigate afterwards. Admirers of Western ways have called Wild Bill "the greatest bad man ever in likelihood seen upon the earth." According to General Custer, "on foot or on horseback he was one of the most perfect types of physical manhood I ever saw. His manner was entirely free from all bluster and bravado. He never spoke of himself unless requested to do so. His influence among the frontiersmen was unbounded; his word was law. Wild Bill was anything but a quarrelsome man, yet none but himself could enumerate the many conflicts in which he had been engaged." If a willingness to take another's life on slight or half-proven cause was the sign of a *bad* man, Wild Bill was surely one. Yet if a willingness to risk one's life to defend the law and the right was the sign of a *good* man, Wild Bill was surely one of those, too.

"Desperado" was the name commonly used for the Western bad man whose services often were not covered by the badge of the law. But in the world of the cattlemen, there were few if any notorious "bad men" who had not at some time or other worn the badge of the law, and risked their lives for what some men in their neighborhood called law and order. Beneath the widespread admiration for the "manhood" of the quick-on-the-trigger desperado was a gnawing suspicion that the desperado himself was often (perhaps even more often than his opponents) on the side of the right. "The 'bad men,' or professional fighters and man-killers," wrote Theodore Roosevelt in 1888 after one of his trips out West, "are of a different stamp [from the common criminal, horse thief or highway robber], quite a number of them being, according to their light, perfectly honest. These are the men who do most of the killing in frontier communities; yet it is a noteworthy fact that the men who are killed generally deserve their fate." Some described desperadoes as simply engaged in a modern American version of the ancient trial by combat. "It was the undelegated right of one individual against that of another. The law was not invoked," observed Emerson Hough, who himself was a witness, "—the law would not serve. Even as the quickest set of nerves flashed into action, the arm shot forward, and there smote the point of flame as did once the point of steel. The victim fell, his own weapon clutched in his hand, a fraction too late. The law cleared the killer. It was 'self-defense.' 'It was an even break,' his fellowmen said; although thereafter they were more reticent with him and sought him out less frequently."

Was this perhaps another example of Americans' giving the law and the right to the man who "got there first"? Unwritten Law, so rigid and unbending in the static society of the older South, in another form thus came to rule the free-ranging West. But while in the South men could look to the traditional practices of the "best" people, and few dared doubt who those were, in the West there were no such people. Out there, the Unwritten Law showed all the vagueness and unpredictableness of a law each man chose for himself. It was in the lands of new property—of gold and silver and of cattle—that the peculiarly ambiguous American bad man flourished. Although the "ideal desperado" of course did not kill for money alone, in the early days most desperadoes were involved in or at least somehow were accused of "unlawfully" acquiring property.

* * *

Unexpected subtleties, the classic confusions of Go-Getter Morality, appear in the careers of nearly all the eminent cattle-country desperadoes. We can examine them conveniently in the life of the most notorious of them all—Billy the Kid. William H. Bonney (his real name) was born in New York City in 1859 and as a boy was taken West by his family. His father died when they were living in Kansas, and his mother moved to Colorado and then on to New Mexico. His character as a young man was described by his some-time friend and co-worker, later his assassin and biographer, Sheriff Pat Garrett:

> Bold, daring, and reckless, he was open-handed, generous-hearted, frank and manly. He was a favorite with all classes and ages, especially was he loved and admired by the old and decrepit, and the young and helpless. To such he was a champion, a defender, a benefactor, a right arm. He was never seen to accost a lady, especially an elderly one, but with his hat in his hand, and did her attire or appearance evidence poverty, it was a poem to see the eager, sympathetic, deprecating look in Billy's sunny face, as he proffered assistance or afforded information. A little child never lacked a lift across a gutter, or the assistance of a strong arm to carry a heavy burden when Billy was in sight. . . . Billy loved his mother. He loved and honored her more than anything else on earth.

At the age of twelve, Billy was reputed to have stabbed a man to death for insulting his mother.

Billy's first serious job was at the age of sixteen when he and a companion tried to persuade three peaceable Apache Indians on the reservation to supply them with horses. This is how Billy himself (reported by Garrett) described the venture:

> It was a ground hog case. Here were twelve good ponies, four or five saddles, a good supply of blankets, and five pony loads of pelts. Here were three blood-thirsty savages, revelling in all this luxury and refusing succor to two free-born, white American citizens, foot sore and hungry. The plunder had to change hands—there was no alternative—and as one live Indian could place a hundred United States troops on

our trail in two hours, and as a dead Indian would be likely to take some other route, our resolves were taken. In three minutes there were three "good Injuns" lying around there careless like, and, with ponies and plunder, we skipped. There was no fight. It was about the softest thing I ever struck.

In the course of various adventures in Old and New Mexico, Billy was soon credited with a dozen more killings. All of which seemed qualifications for the job he found in 1877 when he arrived at the Pecos Valley.

At that time there was brewing in southern New Mexico a struggle, the Lincoln County War, destined to become the bloodiest of all the cattlemen's wars. This was not unlike the later Johnson County War in Wyoming in the readiness of both sides to hire gunmen and use the powers of "law-enforcement" officers. Here, however, the issue was not between the big and the small cattlemen. Rather, it was between two nearly equal factions of rich owners of large herds, both of whom were using all available means to secure contracts to supply the government posts and Indian agencies. Each faction accused the other of foul play and of stealing its cattle. From this distance it seems that they were both right. Soon nearly every cattleman in those parts was involved on one side or the other. In the late winter of 1877 when Billy the Kid started working for J. H. Tunstall on his ranch in Lincoln County on the Felix River, the feud had climaxed in a complicated lawsuit as a result of which the opposing faction, headed by Lawrence G. Murphy, sent a deputy sheriff and a posse of their own men to Tunstall's ranch to seize his cattle. Murphy controlled the wagon trains and dominated the finances of the region. On February 18, 1878, Murphy's men killed Tunstall in the presence of his foreman and Billy the Kid. The long-brewing Lincoln County feud now became open warfare.

This gave Billy the Kid a purpose from which he never relented—to punish the murderers of his friend Tunstall. Tunstall's foreman was sworn in as a "special deputy" by McSween, the leader of the anti-Murphy faction, and he gathered Billy the Kid along with a dozen others to wreak their revenge. Billy led several of the fights which followed. He and six cohorts ambushed and killed the sheriff of Lincoln County and his deputy, both of whom were partisans of the Murphy crowd. Then Billy and the other McSween men went on a law-enforcement spree of their own. Carrying a warrant issued by a justice of the peace authorizing them to recover stolen horses, they killed another of the Murphy men. The climax came in July 1878 when federal troops, summoned by a new sheriff of Lincoln County, who was a tool of the Murphy faction, brought up a company of cavalry to arrest McSween and his men. When they refused to surrender, the Murphy men set fire to McSween's house, but all except two of the party escaped in the night. The Lincoln County War did not begin to come to an end until General Lew Wallace (the Civil War hero who later wrote *Ben Hur*), carrying "extraordinary powers" from President Harrison, arrived as governor of New Mexico in August. He brought a truce to southern New Mexico, but he could not bring to justice the crimes of the past year. Someone suggested that the only way to give everyone his due was to hang the whole population of Lincoln County. But after many indictments, the cases were gradually dismissed, showing the inability of the official law to meet the needs of a society that lived by Go-Getter Morality.

Although more than sixty men had been killed, the only man actually brought to trial for a killing in the Lincoln County War was Billy the Kid. Governor Wallace summoned him to a meeting where, in the presence of witnesses, he asked Billy to lay down his arms and stand trial, promising that if Billy was convicted, the governor would give him a pardon. Some doubted the general's word and suspected that Billy was to be made a scapegoat. "There is no justice for me in the courts of this country now," Billy is reported to have replied as he refused to stand trial. "I've gone too far."

Billy the Kid now began a new chapter of desperate adventures. He had become too accustomed to the excitement of a professional gunman to settle for the cowboy routine of fence riding and round-ups. With a dozen old associates he roamed the countryside stealing cattle, killing old enemies, and seeking out new enemies whom he suspected of wanting to avenge his earlier killings. The courageous

Pat Garrett, newly elected sheriff of Lincoln County, captured Billy the Kid, and managed to secure his conviction for his long-past murder of Sheriff Brady. But before the Kid could be hanged, he killed his guards and made another bold escape. It was two months before Garrett again found Billy the Kid, and as the Kid walked into the house of a friend, killed him under cover of darkness.

Theodore Roosevelt was so impressed by Garrett that he named him Collector of Customs at El Paso, but the President later withdrew his favors when he caught Garrett lying. Garrett himself was finally shot by one of his own tenants. The killer pleaded self-defense and the jury brought in a verdict of not guilty despite the fact that Garrett had been shot in the back of his head and had died with a glove on his trigger-finger hand. Ranchers in the neighborhood long remembered the barbecue offered by a prosperous local cattleman to celebrate the acquittal of Garrett's killer.

The gallery of Good Bad Men and Bad Good Men—of lawless sheriffs and honest desperadoes—could be lengthened indefinitely. It would include every shape and mix of good and evil. It would have to include mining-town Go-Getters like Henry Plummer, sometimes called "the gentleman desperado," who actually served as officer of the law while he led his band of road agents, then in disguise boldly joined the band of vigilantes organized to hunt him down. His commission as a U.S. marshal arrived while he was standing ready to be executed on the gallows. Of course, in those towns, too, there were a few, like Boone Helm, who seemed entirely without conscience (on one occasion when starving in the woods, he actually ate the flesh of a companion) and who never sought the cover of the law.

Alongside the authentic man of mixed motives and confusions, whose inner uncertainties reflected the uncertain possibilities of the American landscape, there arose a man of simpler stamp, the creation in large part of the telegraph, of the newly prospering, sensation-hungry daily press. He was the "Imitation Desperado—the Cheap 'Long Hair'" as the cowboy historian Emerson Hough labels him, "the counterfeit bad man . . . produced by Western consumptives for Eastern consumption. . . . There always existed in the real, sober, level-headed West a contempt for the West-struck man who was not really bad, but who wanted to seem 'bad.' " He was the twentieth-century "Drugstore Cowboy." But the man really guided by Go-Getter Morality was a man who felt newly free, a man in the open air who still could not quite forget that society made discomfiting demands of him. The imitation bad man of the West, on the contrary, simply carried out West the criminal ways of a settled society.

Cowboy, cattle rustler, and cattle baron—Western sheriff and Western desperado—were all creatures of free land and the open range. They were all enticed by strange new opportunities and temptations. Men who had once made their living on free buffalo saw nothing odd about free cattle. The disappearance of the open range, the rise of the barbed-wire fences, and the selling and leasing of the West would put an end to many of the opportunities and temptations, and to the cast of characters of the cattleman's heyday. While counterparts might survive in the mountains, in a world of new flowing minerals, and later in the cities, the lawless sheriff and honest desperado would no longer roam the world of the stockman. These men, with their moral-legal ambiguities, would pass, but the Go-Getter Morality would survive.

EXPLOITING THE FEDERAL COMMODITY:

Divorce and Gambling

I N THE WOMB of the federal system itself there lay hidden some remarkable money-making opportunities. As novel as the cattle trade which prospered on the public domain, or the oil business which drilled rocks for a flowing black mineral to light the lamps of China and bring fortunes to businessmen in Cleveland and New York, was a new competitive American business of lawmaking.

The most spectacular scene of these unpredicted opportunities was Nevada. One of the largest states in the Union (2,500 square miles larger than the combined areas of Maine, New Jersey, Vermont, Connecticut, Massachusetts, Maryland, Delaware, West Virginia, New Hampshire, and Rhode Island), for most of its history Nevada had had the smallest population of any state. As late as 1940 the United States Census gave Nevada only 110,247, and in 1970 it still had the least population density of any state but Alaska. Except for the Colorado River, which runs a hundred miles along the extreme southeastern corner, and twenty-mile-long Lake Tahoe at the southwestern corner, Nevada was marked off by no natural boundaries. It was a vast and arbitrary geometric chunk for which there appeared no reason in geography.

* * *

The real explanation for the extent and dimensions of Nevada lay hidden underground. The area later to become Nevada had been

215

acquired from Mexico in 1848, and two years later became part of the new Mormon-controlled Territory of Utah. When, in 1859, the rich Comstock Silver Lode was discovered at Virginia City at the extreme western end of Utah Territory, newly arrived miners, distrusting the Mormon government, petitioned Congress, and a separate Nevada Territory was created in 1861. Many residents of the territory did not want statehood, for they assumed it would bring increased taxes. But President Abraham Lincoln needed the support of a new state, which would add two votes in the Senate and one in the House. Anxious for the congressional votes to pass the Thirteenth Amendment, Lincoln said bluntly that it was "a question of three votes or new armies." Also in the upcoming presidential election of 1864 a new state of Nevada would add three votes (almost certainly for Lincoln) in the Electoral College. The bill making Nevada a state was signed by Lincoln on October 31, 1864, one week before Election Day. With their usual talent for euphemism, Nevadans in the latter nineteenth century christened themselves the "Battle-Born State."

In fact, Nevada had been the creature not of freedom's battle, nor of tradition, nor of nature, but of politics and silver. For about twenty years, while the Comstock Lode held out, the state somehow prospered. But it was not a democratic prosperity. In California, the people who arrived to seek their fortunes found gold, if they were lucky, in the streams, where a pan and some hard work gave a man his chance. In Nevada, by contrast, the silver was sequestered deep inside a mountain in the heart of a desert. Large sums of capital and expensive heavy equipment were required to extract the ore from the rock and then to transport it to where it could be refined. From the very beginning you needed giant hoisting machines, pumps, stamps, and drills.

The great drama of the Comstock Lode was not a story of mining-camp justice, of unshaven fortune seekers or reckless claim-jumpers. Nevada silver was not the hard-won reward of penniless prospectors but the loot which wealthy bankers and businessmen, mostly from San Francisco, systematically drained from Nevada mines. In the twenty years after 1859, about $500 million in silver and gold was extracted. From the time of its discovery until the mid-1880's, the Lode was producing annually about half the silver being mined in the United States.

Then the Comstock, which had appeared like a comet, disappeared with hardly a trace. Other gold and silver deposits were found at Tonopah and elsewhere in the state, but they were nothing to compare to the Comstock. San Francisco bankers and businessmen went back to California with their Nevada profits. Between 1880 and 1903, when other mountain states were increasing their population threefold, the population of Nevada declined from 65,000 to 45,000. Nevada came to be described as a place you had to go through to get from Ogden, Utah, to California. There were some efforts to promote farming and cattle raising. The Southern Pacific Railroad, anxious to attract settlers, published cheery pamphlets ("The New Nevada: The Era of Irrigation and Opportunity"), but they persuaded very few. Eastern journalists began to call Nevada the nation's "rotten borough." And they asked whether a region once admitted to the Union ought not to be deprived of statehood when it ceased to have any considerable population.

But here they simply showed how little they understood of the West. The end of Nevada's Silver Age was the beginning of a New Nevada. The fewer the people, the greater the share for each in the benefits of "sovereignty." Nevada politics at the opening of the twentieth century, as Gilman Ostrander observes, had a kind of "town-meeting" air about it. Exploiting this advantage, Nevadans showed how enterprise and ingenuity could make a new resource out of statehood itself.

Under the federal system there was, of course, nothing new about a state that was "small" in area or in population using its "sovereignty" to exert a disproportionate power. Maryland, by staying out of the American confederation until 1781, had forced Virginia to yield to the whole nation her state's claims to the vast northwest. And Rhode Island had stayed away from the Constitutional Convention of 1787, hoping that her hold-out position would increase her power to bargain. But in the twentieth century, being a small state yielded a different kind of advantage. Not simply a disproportionately potent voice in the councils of the nation. This new advantage required a mobile population and depended on speedy, inexpensive transportation.

* * *

The Nevada legislature's first effort to outdo the other sovereign states came in 1903 with its passage of a new law of business corporations. Businessmen were to be enticed to set up their companies in Nevada because under Nevada's lax new rules there would be no annual tax on corporations, no troublesome supervision over the issuance of stock or the conduct of business. But other states quickly matched these advantages, and some states, such as California, tried to outlaw their competitors by making it illegal for any corporation to sell its stock within their borders unless the corporation had met their own strict requirements.

Nevada's first real opportunity for profitable legislative competition was found in a less prosaic branch of the law—divorce. Here was an area of ancient controversy where Nevada's other peculiar advantages would make it possible for her legislative ingenuity and enterprise to pay off.

Marriage, divorce, and celibacy had of course (long before Henry VIII!) been a battleground for competing jurisdictions. "Wherefore they are no more twain, but one flesh," Jesus had said, "What therefore God hath joined together, let not man put asunder" (Matthew, xix, 6). The Roman Catholic Church included marriage among the seven sacraments. Like the perpetual mystic union between Christ and his Church, a valid marriage of man and wife would never be dissolved. The Church therefore did not really recognize divorce at all. What was called divorce (*divortium a vinculo*) was really annulment, and in theory could be granted only for disabling causes (such as impotence or a legally existing prior marriage) which had prevented the supposed marriage from taking place at all. What the canon lawyers called *divortium a mensa et thoro* (divorce from bed and board) was only judicial separation, and carried no privilege of remarriage. Abuses in the Church's handling of matters of marriage had been among the arguments for the Protestant Reformation. Marriage, according to Martin Luther, was not a sacrament, but "a secular and outward thing, having to do with wife and children, house and home, and with other matters that belong to the realm of the government, all of which have been completely subjected to reason." Therefore the rules of marriage and divorce "should be left to the lawyers and made subject to the secular government."

The New England Puritans took Luther's distinction so seriously that they not only required marriages to be solemnized by a civil magistrate but in 1647 actually forbade the preaching of a wedding sermon. They feared the popish tendency to make marriage a sacrament. Before the end of the seventeenth century, the General Court of Massachusetts felt secure enough on this matter to allow ministers as well as justices of the peace to perform the marriage ceremony. During the colonial period, the New England colonies made their own laws of divorce. The Southern colonies followed English law, but this really left them without remedies, since they had no ecclesiastical courts. In the middle colonies, royal officials cracked down on attempts to pass divorce laws. While the grounds for divorce remained strict by modern American standards, they were generally much wider than those allowed in England. In the late eighteenth century, and especially in the 1770's as part of an effort to tighten control over the colonies, the British government (for example, in their instructions to royal governors, November 24, 1773) disallowed colonial laws "for the divorce of persons joined together in Holy Marriage." This must be counted among the minor irritations that stirred aggrieved American husbands and wives to fight for independence.

The winning of independence, then, confirmed the freedom of each state to go its own way in the law of divorce. The spirit of the times, the enthusiasm for freedom, and the hatred of tyranny of all kinds which awakened in some quarters the movement to abolish Negro slavery, encouraged others to try to abolish domestic tyranny, to bring relief to those (in the phrase of one pamphleteer in 1788) "who are frequently united together in the worst of bondage to each other . . . relief to the miserable, hen-pecked husband, or the abused, and insulted, despised wife. . . . They are not only confined like a criminal to their punishment, but their confinement must last till death."

Between the Revolution and the Civil War, most states liberalized their laws of divorce. Generally speaking, the new states formed from the Old Northwest were more liberal, and the seaboard states more strict. New York and South Carolina being strictest of all. In nearly every state the movement was to regularize and standardize divorce procedure. By 1867, thirty-three of the then thirty-seven states had outlawed legislative divorce. This was an important step toward democratizing divorce, since the "Private Act" of the state legislature had been a device by which persons of wealth and influence obtained special treatment. But there remained a wide variety of rules because under the federal system, marriage and divorce remained the province of the states.

A result of the federal system, then, from the very beginning, was the practice of "migratory" divorce. A married person who found the laws of his own state inconvenient would go temporarily to another state to secure his divorce. Before the Civil War, unhappily married Easterners were going west to Ohio, Indiana, and Illinois in search of marital freedom. "We are overrun by a flock of ill-used, and ill-using, petulant, libidinous, extravagant, ill-fitting husbands and wives," the *Indiana Daily Journal* reported in 1858, "as a sink is overrun with the foul water of a whole house." Horace Greeley objected that a well-known New Yorker had gone to Indiana, secured his divorce by dinnertime "and, in the course of the evening was married to his new inamorata, who had come on for the purpose, and was staying at the same hotel with him. They soon started for home, having no more use for the State of Indiana; and, on arriving, he introduced his new wife to her astonished predecessor, whom he notified that she must pack up and go, as there was no room for her in that house any longer. So she went." In 1873 the Indiana legislature enacted a strict new law which destroyed the state's migratory divorce business. But Chicago remained a notoriously popular divorce center, and this business, like others, moved West with the population. Stories were told of how specially convened miners' meetings in Idaho would oblige one of their number by ceremoniously dissolving his marriage.

Among the enticements which Western states offered were their loose definitions of the admissible grounds for divorce. Some states actually enacted an "omnibus" clause allowing any cause the court might find proper. Equally important in the competition for the migratory divorce business were their vague, almost nonexistent, residence requirements. In Western states, where nearly everybody had arrived only recently, if there were to be any voters at all recent arrivals had to be considered legal residents. Boosters for upstart cities, anxious to attract a population, made newcomers into full-fledged "residents" in short order. Territories and states that required only brief residence for the right to vote found that requirement suitable for other purposes as well.

Dakota Territory, with a three-month residence requirement, was attracting divorce seekers from the East before 1880. North Dakota and South Dakota, both admitted as states in 1889, preserved this hospitable residence requirement, and so laid the foundation for a thriving divorce business. Hotel owners, saloon keepers and merchants, and of course lawyers, all prospered from the free-spending visitors who had come for the quickest route from misery to bliss. "The notoriety South Dakota has got," a local lawyer boasted, "is doing us no harm. It advertises us abroad, brings thousands of dollars here, not only to pay expenses of divorce suits, but, for investment as well." For this promising new business, there arose a lively civic competition between Sioux Falls and Yankton. Sioux Falls, which already had two colleges, had the advantage also of a thirty-three-year-old judge, of "just that ardent and susceptible age when woman's distress appeals to man most strongly. In all the cases that Judge Aikens has heard where the fair sex has appeared in complaint, his course has been marked by the tenderest sympathy and the most delicate solicitude for their interests." But Yankton, although it still had only one college, had the compensating advantage of a new hotel which was advertised in an elegant brochure "sent by the hundreds to society in New York, Boston, and Philadelphia."

The two Dakotas themselves were also in competition for the

divorce business. When the Episcopal bishop of Sioux Falls in his New Year's sermon on January 1, 1893, delivered a jeremiad against the "consecutive polygamy" of quick remarriage after divorce and began lobbying in the state capital for stricter divorce laws in South Dakota, a hotel owner from Fargo, North Dakota, reportedly joined his campaign, in the hope that if South Dakota laws were stricter, the North Dakota divorce business would profit. But within a few years both Dakotas raised their residence requirements to one year, and so put themselves out of the competition.

This pattern—an early period of liberal divorce laws, followed by scandals, a conservative campaign for reform, and the tightening of laws, thereby spoiling the divorce business—was repeated all over the West. In the early years of the twentieth century, in addition to the Dakotas, several other Western territories and states (including Oklahoma, Wyoming, Texas, Nebraska, Idaho, and Nevada) counted the manufacture of divorce among their first local industries.

Their loose divorce laws were only the natural federal complement to the strict divorce laws of New York and South Carolina. The Nevada divorce mills thrived on the "morality" of New York. It was easier, too, for New York to retain its hypocritical chastity (and hence more difficult to change the laws of New York) because well-to-do New Yorkers always had the Reno alternative.

*   *   *

In the state of Nevada, divorce actually became a major force in the economy. And if there, more than elsewhere, the chronicle of divorce was spiced with scandal and romance, there too it bore vivid witness to the enterprising competitive spirit of the communities who built the West.

Until the beginning of the twentieth century, there were relatively few divorces granted in Nevada. For there were relatively few women residents in the state, and Nevada had not yet established its competitive advantage for migratory divorce. The first notorious Nevada divorce occurred in 1900 when Earl Russell, an English nobleman, after establishing the required six-month residence, secured his Nevada divorce, and promptly married another woman whom he took back with him to England. There his first wife, alleging that the Nevada divorce was invalid, sued for an English divorce on grounds of adultery. Earl Russell was indicted for bigamy, tried by his peers in the House of Lords, convicted, and eventually confined in the Tower of London. If this advertisement for Nevada divorces was somewhat ambiguous, it did at least publicize the brevity of the Nevada residence requirement and the laxity of its divorce laws.

The first "favorable" publicity in building this Nevada business came in 1906 when newspapers headlined the story of the unhappy Laura Corey, who secured release from her adulterous husband by a Nevada divorce. William E. Corey was a self-made steel manufacturer who had risen from being a laborer in the Braddock, Pennsylvania, mills to become, at thirty-seven, president of the United States Steel Corporation. His colleagues described him as an "icicle in business." But outside the office he showed considerably more warmth, and in fact unceremoniously deserted his wife and family for the attractive musical-comedy singer Mabelle Gilman. Then his wife, a poor miner's daughter whom he had married early in life, went to Reno for a divorce. Within nine months after the divorce, Corey married Miss Gilman. The press fumed with righteous indignation against Corey, but praised the laws of Nevada as the shield of the injured innocent.

The Nevada divorce business boomed, though not always for the benefit of violated innocence. Nevada lawyers advertised in Eastern newspapers that their state's six-month residence requirement was the shortest in the country. They described Nevada's numerous, easy-to-prove grounds for divorce, explained the state's convenient lack of requirement for corroborative proof of facts, and reminded readers that there was no Nevada bar to immediate remarriage. At least one lawyer was suspended briefly by the Nevada Supreme Court for such advertising. But the divorce practice grew, providing widespread financial benefits in the state. In 1910 (when Nevada divorces numbered three hundred per year), the familiar reform cycle began. Under pressure from clergymen and then from the Progressives, the state legislature in 1913 increased the residence requirement from six months to a year. But the lawyers, merchants, bar-tenders, hotelkeepers, and others quickly registered their protest. The Republican governor who had signed the divorce reform bill was defeated for reelection in 1914, along with some of the legislators who had supported the bill. At the very next biennial session of the state legislature in 1915, the bill was repealed and the six-month residence restored. The divorce business quickly revived, with the lucky assistance of a much-publicized visit from the movie queen Mary Pickford, who came for a Nevada divorce from her first husband so she would be free to marry Douglas Fairbanks.

Nevada still had competitors, and the legislature remained alert. In 1927, in the face of a growing threat from France and Mexico, and a rumor that Wyoming might reduce her residence requirement to three months, the Nevada legislature enacted a law requiring only three months' residence. Then again in 1931, when there were rumors that Idaho and Arkansas were about to enact the three-month residence, the Nevada legislature hastily reduced their residence requirement to six weeks.

"REVIVAL OF GOLD RUSH DAYS PREDICTED. BEAT THIS ONE, IF YOU CAN" read the headline in the *Nevada State Journal*. The divorce business, as the historian Nelson Blake has pointed out, became increasingly confused with the tourist business. Instead of divorce seekers coming to establish residence to secure the desired legal result, and incidentally spending their money on entertainment, people came for fun, and incidentally found it convenient to get their divorce. It became hard to distinguish between fun-hungry vacationers and disconsolate divorce seekers. They all spent money in Nevada. In the early 1920's, when the six-month requirement was still in effect, Nevada had granted about 1,000 divorces each year; with the residence reduced to three months, the annual figure in 1928 reached 2,500; and the new six-week law in 1931 skyrocketed the number that year to 5,260. During the depths of the Depression the market for Nevada divorces, like that for other luxuries, declined. But the prosperity years of World War II brought new highs: 11,000 Nevada divorces in 1943, and three years later, 20,500. In the 1950's the number declined to an annual 10,000.

Nevada had also loosened its laws of marriage. In 1940, after California required a blood test and a three-day waiting period, Nevada was still offering (in Gilman Ostrander's phrase) "instant marriage, around the clock." This brought in a new crop of hasty honeymooners.

Tourism, too, stirred a lively new competitive spirit. Reno, which had been specially developed to accommodate divorce seekers, for several decades had almost all the divorce business. Of the 5,260 Nevada divorces in 1931, 4,745 were granted in Reno. But the day of the upstart town had not passed. Las Vegas, which was not even incorporated as a city until 1911, within twenty years had numerous neon-gleaming night clubs with a dazzling array of "chorus girls," comedians, and high-priced celebrities of stage and screen. "Getting it is half the fun." Divorce seekers from Los Angeles and elsewhere were soon persuaded that it was more fun to get unhitched in Las Vegas. By the late 1950's Las Vegas was granting nearly half the state's divorces. The divorce business and the entertainment business stimulated each other. In Nevada, in the two decades after 1950, the annual number of divorces per 1,000 of resident population was about ten times the national average, and the number of marriages about twentyfold. Nevada's divorce rate was five times that of any of the closest competitors (Florida, Oklahoma, Texas, Arizona, Idaho, Wyoming, and Alaska); and its marriage figure was ten times that of its closest competitor (South Carolina).

* * *

Divorce was not the only business by-product of the federal system. Another was gambling. Here, again, an unpopulous state like Nevada was peculiarly well qualified to profit. Some historians have observed that Nevada's whole history was nothing but one long gamble. A less metaphorical explanation lies in the working of the federal system and in the legislated prudery of Nevada's sister states. Horse racing, for reasons of tradition, tended to be excepted from those common-law prohibitions brought over from England which made the keeping of a common gambling house indictable as a public nuisance. In 1887 New York, for example, allowed betting under special legal regulation at the race tracks. But in the early twentieth century, in some states, because of the rise of "bookies" (the first recorded use of this Americanism is 1909) and other abuses, race tracks were closed. Then, in the late '20's and early '30's, the legalized parimutuel system (facilitated by the completely electrical "totalizer" introduced in 1933), which used automatic vending machines to sell betting tickets, gave horse-race betting a new popularity. Still, legalized betting was tightly restricted: off-track betting was generally not allowed, and public gambling houses remained illegal. The states commonly outlawed gambling devices, and either regulated or prohibited pool halls, slot machines, and punch boards. The opportunities for gambling which were offered by boxing led some states to outlaw that sport, and led others to regulate it strictly under a public commission.

When the Depression hit Nevada in 1931, the divorce market lagged and there was widespread fear that other states might liberalize their divorce laws. Nevadans felt that merely reducing the divorce-residence requirement to six weeks might not be enough to insure economic recovery. The Nevada legislature in 1931, then, partly as a recovery measure, legalized gambling. But the tradition of clandestine gambling, from the days when it was illegal, was hard to overcome. Since gambling, when illegal, had been a discreetly private activity, there was no established pattern of promotion or advertising to widen the reach of the newly legalized gambling houses. Nevada's new laws opened the door for a new brand of Go-Getter.

Raymond Smith was the pioneer. With no experience as a professional gambler, Smith, bringing his two sons, came to Reno from California during the Great Depression in search of a living. Drawing on his earlier experience as a carnival barker, he used his native flair for organization to make gambling into a popular public entertainment. While illegal gamblers had survived by keeping their operations quiet, Smith saw that the success of legalized gambling would depend on advertising. From the day when he opened his first small casino on Virginia Street in Reno, he began an advertising campaign which culminated in thousands of billboards along the highways of the country. And he made "Harolds Club" (named after

Raymond Smith's son Harold; the omitted apostrophe was part of the trademark) into a national brand. He persuaded timid and suspicious middle-class Americans all over the country that they could put the same confidence in Harolds Club that they put in other nationally advertised products and services.

In short order Raymond Smith (whose career is delightfully chronicled by Gilman Ostrander) succeeded in democratizing gambling, "as Henry Ford had democratized the automobile." Before Smith, gambling casinos had thrived on the "high rollers" (the flamboyant sports of Mississippi river boats and of American folklore), the professional male gamblers who played for big stakes. A casino's profit or loss might depend on the draw of a card or a throw of the dice. Raymond Smith changed all this. By lowering the stakes and so enlarging his clientele, he aimed to produce a Woolworth's of the gambling business. Harolds Club was as different from the old gambling casino as the five-and-ten-cent store was different from the élite specialty shop.

To attract his Depression-stricken customers, Smith offered penny roulette and other stunts such as mouse roulette, in which a live mouse picked the winning number. And he set up rows of slot machines which enticed nickels, dimes, and quarters from people who did not even know the rules of poker or dice. (It was twenty years later that the slot machine acquired the American nickname of "one-armed bandit.") To make women feel at home and attract them to the gambling tables, he employed women dealers and women shills drawn from the past or prospective customers of the quickie divorce courts. These friendly feminine dealers were instructed to play according to fixed rules set by the house so that they never matched wits against the players. Part of their job was to advise inexperienced customers how to play. Smith even provided babysitters so that mothers would not have to leave their children unattended in motel rooms while they enjoyed Harolds Club.

True to the booster pattern, Raymond Smith became a notable local philanthropist. He built a museum of Western Americana for his customers, and offered scholarships to needy students at the University of Nevada. To customers of Harolds Club who had not heeded Smith's warning that they gamble no more than they could afford to lose, Smith actually lent small sums to help them get back home.

Harolds Club set the pace, and others followed. The Nevada Club prospered, and then came Harrah's Club (named after its proprietor William Harrah, who profited from the convenient confusion of names), and many others.

*   *   *

Nevada gambling flourished as a border industry—just over the border from illegality and from other states. None of the Nevada gambling resorts was located near the center of the state. Reno in the west was a scant dozen miles from the California boundary. Las Vegas in the southeastern tip was close to California, Arizona, and Utah; and Lake Tahoe actually marked the state's southwestern border with California. The Las Vegas town site, bought by the railroad back in 1903, had been headquarters for construction of the nearby Hoover Dam and was ready for the gambling boom created by the new Nevada laws in 1931. It had the advantage over Reno of being within easier driving distance from Los Angeles, San Diego, and other fast-growing centers in Southern California. After World War II, Las Vegas set a new pattern. If Reno was offering a five-and-ten for gambling customers, Las Vegas would provide grand new department stores of gambling. Just outside Las Vegas a new luxury gambling-and-entertainment development sprang up on "the Strip," a street in a new unincorporated area which called itself by the booster name of Paradise. Within a decade there appeared a galaxy of de luxe chromium-plated hotel-motel-night-club-casinos boasting extravagantly romantic names: the Desert Inn, Sahara, Showboat, Royal Nevada, Riviera, Moulin Rouge, Stardust, Martinique, Tropicana, Vegas Plaza, Casa Blanca, San Souci. Even the more modest of these cost $5 million. Drawing on Hollywood only two hundred and fifty miles away, they competed in Big Names to draw the Big Spenders. By 1955 it was estimated that $20 million was being spent annually around Las Vegas for entertainment offered free to patrons of the gambling tables.

Then in the 1950's came Lake Tahoe, pioneered by William Harrah from Reno, who had bought the especially desirable Nevada acreage just adjoining the California border. Casinos located there would be most inviting to Northern California gamblers. Finding that the five-hour car drive from San Francisco to his casinos was keeping customers from coming for the day, Harrah planned his own bus line. For advice he turned to the Stanford Research Institute, which, for a fee of $16,000, provided "An Investigation of Factors Influencing Bus Scheduling," along with valuable insights into Harrah's potential clientele. His most likely customer, the Institute predicted, was "elderly, in low occupational status, unmarried, a renter rather than a home owner, and without a car. . . . an unusual segment of the total population." Harrah then aimed his advertising at these customers in the smaller cities around San Francisco. He did everything to make their trip to his casino easy, to keep them happy there, and to keep them spending. When others followed Harrah's lead, Lake Tahoe grew into a potent competitor to Reno and Las Vegas.

After World War II, Nevada became a refuge not only for the activities, but also for the people outlawed in other states. In 1946, at a cost of $7 million, a racketeer, "Bugsy" Siegel, who controlled the local use of Al Capone's racing wire service, built the Flamingo Hotel on the Las Vegas Strip. Within a year Siegel was murdered by gangster rivals, and the battles of the gangs for control of Nevada gambling had begun. Senator Estes Kefauver's hearings on organized crime exposed a network of criminal control over the state's profitable new industry. The state tightened its laws for licensing casino owners, but Nevada laws could not keep out the gangsters.

While ex-convicts, refugees from the law and from unsavory reputations, seeped into Nevada as another by-product of the federal system, the state's growing population created a host of new problems. At Stateline on Lake Tahoe, two of the new casinos every day produced an estimated half-million additional gallons of effluvium. At first the Nevadans tried to dispose of this surplus sewage by treating it and then spraying it on the trees, but the runoff into the lake began to turn the pure waters of Tahoe a dirty green and bred algae that spoiled the swimming. It was then found more convenient and more economical to pipe the treated effluvia directly into Tahoe. As the polluted waters of the lake flowed across state lines, the neighboring Californians were warned not to "drink, fish, swim, or wade in this water." Californians were paying for Nevada's federal opportunities.

* * *

In far-off Washington, D.C., unpopulous Nevada reaped still another, more predictable, advantage of the federal system. Senators from Nevada came to play a disproportionately large role in the legislative councils of the nation, for the Senate had organized itself in a fashion which gave states like Nevada a good deal more than equality. "Small"-state senators could be more certain of reelection back home and so they became more effective in securing what they wanted in the Senate. Since they represented fewer major economic interests, they were in a better position to trade votes to secure what their constituents really wanted. And in proportion to the population of their states, they usually had at their disposal a larger federal patronage than other senators. In Nevada after 1889, few elected senatorial incumbents were defeated for reelection. As a result of the senatorial seniority system, then, Nevada senators had a leading, and often a decisive, voice in powerful committees. Senator Pat McCarran of Nevada became, by seniority, the chairman of the Senate Judiciary Committee; Senator Key Pittman of Nevada became chairman of the Foreign Relations Committee. These elected representatives from the least populous state were quietly altering the balance of forces in the representative system. The American people might rush to the cities, but the Constitution continued to provide new resources of wealth and power, and powerful voices, for the interests of a new West.

A DEMOCRACY OF CLOTHING

I N THE MIDDLE of the nineteenth century, European travelers to the United States were struck by a new American peculiarity. Just as travelers before them in the eighteenth century had noted the difficulty of distinguishing between American social classes by the habits of speech, and had noted that master and servant, even in the South, spoke in accents far more similar than did their English counterparts, they now noted the strange similarities of clothing.

In America it was far more difficult than in England to tell a man's social class by what he wore. The British consul in Boston in the early 1840's, Thomas College Grattan, complained of American equality; he found servant girls "strongly infected with the national bad taste for being over-dressed, they are, when walking the streets, scarcely to be distinguished from their employers." The Hungarian politician Francis Pulszky, traveling the country in 1852, missed the colorful Old World distinctions. In Europe there was "the peasant girl with the gaudy ribbons interlaced in her long tresses, her bright corset, and her richly-folded petticoat; there the Hungarian peasant with his white linen shirt, and his stately sheepskin; the Slovak in the closely fitting jacket and the bright yellow buttons; the farmer with the high boots and the Hungarian coat; the old women with the black lace cap in the ancient national style, and none but the young ladies appareled in French bonnets and modern dresses." He lamented that in New York, "no characteristical costumes mark here the different grades of society, which, in Eastern Europe, impress the foreigner at once with the varied occupations and habits of an old country." No wonder that the snobbish British merchant W. E. Baxter was irritated in 1853–54 to find common workmen so over-dressed by English standards. "You meet men in railroad-cars, and on the decks of steamboats, rigged out in super-fine broadcloth and white waistcoats, as if they were on their way to a ball-room, and common workmen you find attired in glossy black clothes while performing work of the dirtiest description. . . . The farmers are the only class who wear rough garments. . . . The people have yet to learn that apparel should be chosen for use not show, that shabby broadcloth is the most pitiful of all costume, and that it is no mark of gentility to wear a dress unsuitable to one's means and employment."

Before the end of the nineteenth century, the American democracy of clothing would become still more astonishing to foreign eyes, for by then the mere wearing of clothes would be an instrument of community, a way of drawing immigrants into a new life. Men whose ancestors had been accustomed to the peasant's tatters or the craftsman's leather apron could show by a democratic costume that they were as good as, or not very different from, the next man. If, as the Old World proverb went, "Clothes make the man," the New World's new way of clothing would help make new men.

*   *   *

In the twentieth century Americans would be the best-clothed and perhaps the most homogeneously dressed, industrial nation. It is hard to imagine how it could have happened without the sewing machine.

The sewing machine, however, like the system of interchangeable parts, was not first conceived in America. In England, in 1770, Thomas Saint had been granted a patent for a machine to sew leather. By 1830 Barthélemy Thimonnier, a French tailor who had long been obsessed with the idea, had patented and perfected an effective sewing machine. When eighty of his machines were making uniforms for the French army, Paris tailors, alarmed at the threat to their jobs, smashed the machines and drove Thimonnier out of the city.

Perhaps the first of many American sewing-machine inventors was Walter Hunt. He was pure inventor, so obsessed by inventing and so bored by the prosaic tasks of exploiting his novelties that his very genius was destined to deny him a place in the history books. His inventions included a flax-spinning machine, a knife sharpener, a yarn twister, a stove (some say the first) to burn hard coal, a nail-making machine, ice plows, velocipedes, a revolver, a repeating rifle, metallic cartridges, conical bullets, paraffin candles, a street-sweeping machine, a student lamp, and paper collars. According to his draftsman friend who had been making drawings to accompany Hunt's numerous patent applications, Hunt designed a patentable safety pin quickly in order to get the money to pay him a debt of $15. Within three hours Hunt worked out the idea, made a model from an old piece of wire, and sold the patent rights for $400.

By the early 1830's in his workshop on Amos Street in New York City, Hunt had made several machines that actually sewed. Although they were rudimentary, sewing only a straight seam and requiring readjustment of the cloth every few inches, they did include the basic features that later would make a fortune for others. Hunt's revolutionary new idea was an eye-pointed needle moved by a vibrating arm and a shuttle which carried a second thread to make an interlocking stitch. This was the great stroke of imagination that liberated sewing-machine inventors from the temptation to imitate the seamstress' hand. But Hunt had neither the capital nor the organizing talent to make money out of his idea.

Others did. And there was enough money in the sewing machine to enrich scores of inventors, would-be inventors, lawyers, promoters, salesmen, and businessmen. The two giants in the War of the Sewing Machine, which climaxed about 1850, were Elias Howe, Jr., and Isaac Merrit Singer. They battled not merely for money but for the honor of having been "the principal inventor" of the sewing machine.

Elias Howe, born in 1819, was the son of a Massachusetts

farmer. At the age of twenty, when he was working as a journeyman machinist for a Boston scientific-instrument maker, his interest was awakened by a customer's effort to perfect a knitting machine. Some years later, under pressure to support a wife and three children and desperately casting about for some way to add to his salary of $9 a week, he decided to try to make his fortune from a sewing machine. After many false starts, in 1844 he too was inspired by the idea of an eye-pointed needle, using a second thread on a shuttle, on the analogy of the loom. By April 1845 he was actually sewing a seam on his machine. In 1846 he received a patent.

To persuade the public that his machine would really work, Howe took it to the Quincy Hall Clothing Manufactory in Boston, seated himself before it and offered to sew up any seam that anyone would bring. For two weeks he astonished all comers by doing 250 stitches a minute, about seven times the speed by hand. He then challenged five of the speediest seamstresses to race his machine. The experienced tailor whom he had called in as umpire announced Howe's victory and declared that "the work done on the machine was the neatest and strongest."

Even these demonstrations did not persuade people to buy Howe's machines. Some objected that it was still imperfect, because it did not make a whole garment; others feared it would put tailors and seamstresses out of work. All were discouraged by the cost of a machine, at the time about $300. Howe determined to try the English market. When his brother, Amasa, took the machine to London, he awakened the interest of a shrewd corset manufacturer who bought the English rights for a song, and then persuaded Elias Howe to come to London to adapt the machine to the needs of corset making. By working hard for eight months, Howe accomplished the difficult assignment, whereupon his employer (who proved to be a Dickensian villain) fired him. Suffering from the tragedy of his wife's death (he had to borrow a suit to attend her funeral!) and the loss of all his household goods in a shipwreck off Cape Cod, in 1849 Howe returned penniless to New York.

In Howe's absence, the sewing machine had become a popular curiosity. A machine was actually being carried about western New

York and exhibited as "A Great Curiosity!! The Yankee Sewing-Machine," for an admission fee of twelve and a half cents. Ladies carried home specimens of machine sewing to show their friends. Machines were now being made and sold in considerable numbers by persons Howe had never known, many of these using features that Howe had patented. Determined to protect his legal rights, Howe sent to England to recover his original machine and the Patent Office papers he had pawned.

Howe then warned the infringers, offering to sell them licenses for a royalty fee. All but one agreed, but that one organized the rest, and Howe had to fight his case in court. For this purpose Howe needed money, which he finally secured from a Massachusetts lawyer who financed the infringement suits, but was secured against loss by a mortgage on Howe's father's farm.

The stage was set for one of the decisive industrial battles of the century. It might have been planned as an allegory, for there were the figures who would reappear with monotonous regularity: the competing "first inventors" and the Go-Getting lawyers. The dramatic struggle produced a mass product and eventually created a new consumption community. Incidentally, the prolonged and sensationalized courtroom struggle helped fill the new mass-circulating newspapers, and awakened consumer interest in the sewing machine by the public debates over its remarkable new features.

Isaac Merrit Singer, Howe's antagonist, also had inventive talent, but his flair for salesmanship made him a man of quite another stamp. Raised in upstate New York as the son of a millwright, he had, while still a young man, secured a patent for a rock driller and a carving machine. But he had also been an actor and a theater manager. In 1850, when he happened to see a sewing machine, he determined to improve the machine so it could do a greater variety of work. According to Singer's own account, after eleven days and nights of intense work during which he slept and ate only irregularly, he produced his improved model. Immediately he began manufacturing, selling—and, above all, promoting—this machine. In one way at least Singer's machine was superior to Howe's, for it could do continuous stitching. But what explained Singer's success was his genius as advertiser and organizer, and his determination to sell sewing machines to the millions.

Singer refused to pay Howe a royalty. For, he claimed, Howe had not in fact been the inventor of the sewing machine. Singer tried to prove in court that fourteen years before Howe's 1846 patent, Walter Hunt had actually made a working sewing machine; that Howe's machine was nothing but a copy of Hunt's. After a long search, Singer and his lawyers located Walter Hunt, and some fragments of Hunt's early machine were finally discovered in a garret. In 1854, after a costly three-year trial, the court held in favor of Howe. Though Hunt had been on a right track, the court said, Hunt had never patented his invention, nor had he made a practical, salable machine. "For all the benefit conferred upon the public by the introduction of a sewing-machine, the public are indebted to Mr. Howe." Howe's fortunes abruptly changed. He obtained $15,000 from Singer, and soon was receiving a $25 royalty on every sewing machine made in the country.

This bonanza did not last long. Other sewing-machine inventions forced Howe to compromise. To keep his own machines salable in a competitive market, he had to incorporate improvements patented by others. Soon three other large manufacturers, each controlling some essential patent, were suing one another.

The upshot of these and other widening disputes, which now involved another half-dozen large manufacturers, was the great Sewing Machine Combination in 1856. The patent owners pooled all their patents on the essential features of the sewing machine into a single franchise for a single fee, and the owners of the different patents shared the franchising fees. Before signing, Howe insisted that at least twenty-four manufacturers be franchised. Howe himself received $5 for each machine licensed to sell in the United States and $1 for each machine exported, which eventually brought him about $2 million. Numerous manufacturers, willing to pay the costly licensing fees, now entered the race for sales.

By 1871 the sewing machine, which only twenty years before had been a curiosity to be exhibited at fairs for twelve and a half cents' admission, was being manufactured at the rate of 700,000 a year. The machine was constantly being improved; before the end of the century nearly eight thousand patents had been issued on the sewing machine and its accessories. American manufacturers sent their machines all over. Competing in their claims for creating a new worldwide consumption community, the I. M. Singer Company asserted that by 1879 three quarters of the machines being sold were Singers. An 1880 Singer brochure, immodestly entitled *Genius Rewarded; or, the Story of the Sewing Machine*, proclaimed:

> On every sea are floating the Singer Machines; along every road pressed by the foot of civilized man this tireless ally of the world's great sisterhood is going upon its errand of helpfulness. Its cheering tune is understood no less by the sturdy German matron than by the slender Japanese maiden; it sings as intelligibly to the flaxen-haired Russian peasant-girl as to the dark-eyed Mexican Senorita. It needs no interpreter, whether it sings amid the snows of Canada or upon the pampas of Paraguay; the Hindoo Mother and the Chicago maiden are to-night making the self-same stitch; the untiring feet of Ireland's fair-skinned Nora are driving the same treadle with the tiny understandings of China's tawny daughter; and thus American machines, American brains, and American money are bringing the women of the whole world into one universal kinship and sisterhood.

The new machine was supposed to relieve drudgery. "Now," *Godey's Lady's Book* rejoiced in 1860, ". . . what philanthropy failed to accomplish, what religion, poetry, eloquence and reason sought in vain, has been produced by—The Sewing Machine." But there is little evidence that the sewing machine much eased the lives of seamstresses, or that the housewife actually spent less time on sewing. "Where is the woman," James Parton asked in the *Atlantic Monthly* in 1867, "who can say that her sewing is less a tax upon her time and strength than it was before the sewing machine came in? . . . As soon as lovely woman discovers that she can set ten stitches in the time that one used to require, a fury seizes her to put ten times as many stitches in every garment as she formerly did."

In the 1860's, styles changed. Just as the improvement of wood-carving machinery produced ever more ornate furniture, now the sewing machine produced elaborately draped overskirts, a new opportunity to display fancy sewing and intricate trimmings. In this way, too, a use was found for the numerous sewing-machine attachments: hemmers, fellers, binders, tuckers, rufflers, shirrers, puffers, braiders, quilters, hemstitchers, and even an etcher adept at "beautiful machine embroidery in imitation of the Kensington hand stitch."

The consequences of the sewing machine were not merely aesthetic or humanitarian. In America the sewing machine helped change the social meaning of clothing: a larger proportion of people than ever before could wear clothes that fit them, and could look like the best-off men and women. "The sewing-machine," observed Parton, "is one of the means by which the industrious laborer is as well clad as any millionaire need be, and by which working-girls are enabled safely to gratify their woman's instinct of decoration."

* * *

In the latter half of the nineteenth century the United States experienced a Clothing Revolution—more far-reaching, perhaps, than any that had occurred since the birth of modern textile technology. Alexander Hamilton had noted in his *Report on Manufactures* (1791) that four fifths of the American people's clothing were made in their own households for themselves. Only the rich could afford to employ tailors. At first these tailors traveled the countryside working on material supplied by customers, and eventually they settled down in the cities.

A ready-made-clothing industry did not begin to develop until the early decades of the nineteenth century. At first only the cheapest grades of clothes could be bought in stores. Shops in New Bedford, Massachusetts, for example, supplied sailors with the clothing they needed quickly when they had just returned from a long voyage or when they were hastily preparing to sail again. Sailors put these store-boughten clothes in their sea chests, generally known as "slop chests" (after the Old Norse word for the loose smock or the baggy breeches of the kind sailors wore). The clothes they bought were therefore called "sailors slops," and the places where these were sold were called "slopshops." "Slop clothes" or "slops" became a synonym for ready-made clothes. Cheap ready-made clothing was also in demand in the South for Negro slaves, and in upstart Western towns for newly arrived miners who had no household to make clothes for them.

All over Europe in the eighteenth century there were depots for renovating and distributing castoff clothes. Until well into the nineteenth century almost the only kind of ready-made clothing for sale was secondhand. Before the rise of a clothing industry, before machine manufacture had made textiles cheap, the clothing which had originally been tailor-made for the rich was the main source of ready-made clothing for the poor. "In this Country," the English economist Nassau Senior wrote in 1836, "the poor are, to a great extent, clothed with garments originally provided for their superiors." Around this fact Senior actually built a whole theory of expenditure.

In those days neither the buying nor the selling of secondhand clothes was disreputable; and even today in poorer nations castoff clothing is a staple of country fairs and cheap city shops. In the United States, too, before the Civil War, there was a sizable trade in castoff clothing, much of it destined for the South and West. Metropolitan newspapers like the New York *Herald* printed scores of advertisements for secondhand clothing.

Work clothes for Negroes and for sailors long remained the only clothing manufactured in quantity. A few ready-made garments were turned out as a sideline by the custom tailor. The demand for ready-made clothing grew fastest in the South and West, and establishments grew on the eastern seaboard to satisfy these needs.

The American revolution in clothing, which was well under way before 1900, was a double revolution: in the making of clothing (from the homemade and the custom-made to the ready-made or factory-made) and in the wearing of clothing (from the clothing of class display, by which a man wore his social class and his occupation on his sleeve, to the clothing of democracy, by which, more than ever before, men dressed alike). In Western mining camps, on wagon-train journeys west, on long sea voyages, men could not carry elaborate wardrobes. Specialized skills were few, and qualified custom tailors scarce. At the same time that wealthy Americans found it hard to dress as elegantly as wealthy Europeans, the new technology of the garment industry was making it easier for Americans in moderate circumstances to dress well.

By mid-century, the sewing machine was being used in the factory production of clothing. When the chain stitch, which unraveled if the thread was broken at any point, was displaced by the lock stitch, machine sewing was as strong as that by hand. Improvements and attachments, like the buttonholer, made the machine versatile enough for most sewing tasks. And new cutting machines which could slice through eighteen thicknesses of cloth made it easy to prepare numerous garments of the same size.

Then the Civil War brought an unprecedented demand for large quantities of men's wear. In mid-1861 the need was for uniforms to outfit an army of hundreds of thousands; in the fall of 1865, for civilian clothing to outfit the demobilized hundreds of thousands. The clothing business suddenly became attractive and profitable. The demand for uniforms had encouraged standardization. When the government supplied measurements for the uniforms it required, it had given manufacturers the most commonly recurring human proportions. With this information, manufacturers developed a new science of sizing and began to make garments in regular sizes. Between 1880 and 1890 the total value of the products of manufacturing industries that used the sewing machine increased by 75 percent, to well over $1 billion. This was due largely to the sudden growth of the ready-made-clothing industry, including shoes, which accounted for 90 percent of sewing machine products.

The wearers of all sorts of factory-made clothing increased by the ten of thousands. As early as 1832 there had been an American shirt factory; the manufacturing of men's detachable collars grew about the same time, and within a few years there was a thriving business in shirts and collars. The value of manufactured men's garments nearly doubled between 1860 and 1870. In the next two decades the business was still one for pioneers. As late as 1880 less than half of men's clothing was purchased ready-to-wear. But by the beginning of the twentieth century it had become rare for a man or boy not to be clothed in ready-made garments. Now even the wealthy, who had once employed tailors, were buying clothes in the better shops. By 1890 the value of clothing sold in shops amounted to about $1.5 billion; about three quarters of the woolen cloth made in the United States were being consumed in the manufacture of ready-made clothing.

Alexander Hamilton's statistics had been reversed. Now, according to the best estimates at the time, nine tenths of the men and boys in the United States were wearing clothing made ready to put on. "Little by little," William C. Browning, a pioneer in the business, boasted in 1895, "the early prejudice, founded upon the character of 'slop' clothes first introduced, was overcome. Men who had fancied that they would never wear 'hand-me-downs,' as they were vulgarly called, soon found that neither in respect of style nor materials was the best ready-made clothing inferior to the handiwork of the merchant tailor. . . . there was a wonderful advance in the quality of goods manufactured." The Americanism "hand-me-down" (in England it was "reach-me-down" to signify clothing that was simply reached down from a rack) had come into general use to signify shabby clothing. New expressions were needed for the good-quality new clothing now sold in shops. "Ready-to-wear" in the early twentieth century began to supplant "ready-made" with a significant new emphasis not on the maker but on the wearer.

Not only suits and coats, but everything else that people wore—hats, caps, shirts, undergarments, stockings, and shoes—were now for the first time generally beginning to be bought ready-made. Until the mid-nineteenth century, the shoes that could be bought ready-made in shops were "straights"—that is, there was no difference between rights and lefts. Then American manufacturers began to turn out "crooked shoes," specially cut to fit the right or the left foot, and the increase in the mass production of shoes in the decade before 1860 brought (in the language of the Census Report of that year) a "silent revolution" in footwear. By 1862 Gordon McKay, a Massachusetts industrialist, had perfected a machine that sewed the soles to the uppers, just in time to help supply the Union demand for army shoes by the thousands. After the war the working class was buying factory-made shoes, but it was several decades before the middle classes and well-to-do were provided with factory shoes to their taste.

It happened, too, that the character of immigrants who came in the last twenty-five years of the nineteenth century stimulated the clothing industry. Many from Germany, Russia, Poland, and Italy were tailors. Among the four hundred thousand Jewish immigrants in the first decade of the twentieth century, more than half were in the needle trades. At the same time the new sewing machine, requiring very little skill, attracted into the work many wives and sons and daughters of the immigrants in the Eastern cities.

An infamous by-product of the sewing machine was the "sweat-shop" (an Americanism first noted about 1892), where women and children worked long hours at piecework for low wages. But in the clothing industry, too, where the business unit was small and the machinery inexpensive, it was less difficult than elsewhere to move up from wageworker to employer. In many predicted ways, then, the nation's new clothing industry could be an agent of democracy. "The multitude is clothed by the clothier, not by the tailor," a pioneer American merchant-clothier boasted at the turn of the century. "And if . . . the condition of a people is indicated by its clothing, America's place in the scale of civilized lands is a high one. We have provided not alone abundant clothing at a moderate cost for all classes of citizens, but we have given them at the same time that style and character in dress that is essential to the self-respect of a free democratic people."

Ready-made clothing instantly Americanized the immigrant. When David Levinsky, the hero of Abraham Cahan's Yiddish novel, arrived in New York from Russia in 1885, his benefactor, eager to make him at once into an American, took him to store after store, buying him a suit of clothes, a hat, underclothes, handkerchiefs (the first white handkerchiefs he ever possessed), collars, shoes, and a necktie. "He spent a considerable sum on me. As we passed from block to block he kept saying, 'Now you won't look green,' or 'That will make you look American.' " Nothing else could so rapidly and painlessly transform the foreigner into one who belonged.

CONSUMERS' PALACES

CHAPTER 10

Between the civil war and the beginning of the new century there appeared grand and impressive edifices—Palaces of Consumption—in the principal cities of the nation and in the upstart cities that hoped to become great metropolises. A. T. Stewart's, Lord & Taylor, Arnold Constable, R. H. Macy's in New York City; John Wanamaker in Philadelphia; Jordan Marsh in Boston; Field, Leiter & Co. (later Marshall Field & Co.) and the Fair in Chicago. And even smaller cities had their impressive consumers' palaces—Lazarus in Columbus, Ohio, and Hudson's in Detroit, among others.

The distinctive institution which came to be called the department store was a large retail shop, centrally located in a city, doing a big volume of business, and offering a wide range of merchandise, including clothing for women and children, small household wares, and usually dry goods and home furnishings. While the stock was departmentalized, many of the operations and the general management were centralized. If the department store was not an American invention, it flourished here as nowhere else. "Department store" was an Americanism in general use before the opening of the twentieth century.

The grand new consumers' palaces were to the old small and intimate shops what the grand new American hotels were to the Old World inns. Like the hotels, the department stores were symbols of faith in the future of growing communities. For citizens of the sprouting towns the new department-store grandeur gave dignity, importance, and publicity to the acts of shopping and buying—new communal acts in a new America.

* * *

Alexander Turney Stewart, at the age of seventeen, came to New York City from Northern Ireland and began his business with a stock of Irish laces. Only fifteen years later, in 1846, he built an impressive structure at Broadway and Chambers streets, known as the Marble Dry-Goods Palace. Like many another earlier palace, it expanded with addition after addition until it extended along a two-hundred-foot frontage on City Hall Park and covered the whole block on Broadway. In 1862, when Stewart's outgrew these premises, it moved into another palace—this time eight stories high and no longer of marble. This building, which became famous as Stewart's Cast Iron Palace, was reputed to be the largest retail store in the world.

The new department stores, unlike the elegant exclusive shops of Old World capitals, were palatial, public, and inviting. Cast iron made it easier than ever to make buildings impressive on the outside, and on the inside to offer high ceilings, and wide, unbroken expanses for appealing display. In the five-story E. V. Haughwout Department Store, built in 1857 at Broadway and Broome Street in New York City, Daniel Badger, pioneer in manufacturing iron for buildings, offered his most impressive work. The intricate façades of the Venetian *palazzos* were easily reproduced in cast iron. Their elegant patterns of columns, spandrels, and windows could be endlessly extended around a building, and the architectural orders could be piled one above another indefinitely.

When James Bogardus (the prolific inventor whose works included a metal-cased pencil with a lead "forever pointed," improvements in the striking parts of clocks, a new machine for making postage stamps, and an improved mill for making lead paint) turned his genius to finding new uses for cast iron, the needs of the department store excited his imagination. These new iron structures, he exulted, could be raised to a height of ten miles. Bogardus would exploit qualities in the cast-iron frame—lightness, openness, adaptability, and speed of construction—similar to those which three decades before had given the balloon frame its special American appeal.

The climax of this new Iron Age was the Cast Iron Palace which Bogardus built on Broadway between Ninth and Tenth streets for A. T. Stewart. It was the largest iron building of its day, one of the largest of any kind. On the exterior, the molded iron panels were painted to resemble stone; the repeating column-and-beam design added dignity and expansiveness. Each floor took the weight of its own outer walls, in the structural scheme which would make possible the skyscraper. The thin walls at the ground floor produced a spacious, open lobby, and the slender iron columns kept vistas open on every floor, vistas of appealing merchandise of all shapes, color, and description, objects one had never thought of seeing, much less of buying. And one could see out there among the merchandise the enticing crowds and clusters of buyers, shoppers, and just lookers. The palatial ground floor was dominated by a grand stairway and a great rotunda brightened by daylight which streamed through an overarching glass dome. Up and down these stairs, frequenting the high-ceilinged grandeur of these consumers' palaces, came the lords and ladies of these domains by the thousands and tens and hundreds of thousands.

The traditional elegance of the grand stairway was complemented by the modern charm of the elevator, which made the upper floors more easily accessible. Incidentally, the elevator car pushed together in sudden intimacy random members of the public who had the same destination. Elevators had been tried before for freight, and there had been experiments in using them for passengers in hotels. But the department store gave everybody a chance to enjoy them.

The essential problem was to combine speed and safety. The old freight elevators, in which the cage was counterweighted by a plunger that descended into the ground to a depth equal to the height of the building, was relatively safe but slow. To obtain faster movement it was necessary to use a system of pulleys, which increased the wear on the ropes holding up the cage. This increased the danger of a plummeting cage. Then, to insure against such accidents, Elisha Graves Otis, an ingenious New Englander who had been born and raised on his father's Vermont farm, invented a safety device. He set up ratchets along each side of the shaft and attached teeth to the sides of the cage. These teeth were held clear of the ratchets by the rope which held up the cage, but when the rope ceased to be in tension, the teeth were released against the sides of the shaft and gripped the cage safely in place. Otis himself sold the public on his device at the Crystal Palace Exposition in New York City in 1854. He had his elevator drawn up, then he melodramatically cut the supporting rope and displayed himself in the cage safely held in place.

It was in the Haughwout Department Store in 1857 that Otis first put his safety elevators into permanent use. Experiments with the elevator had been made in hotels as early as 1833, and the old Fifth Avenue Hotel in 1859 installed a practical passenger elevator. When Strawbridge & Clothier in Philadelphia carried its customers up and down in an elevator in 1865, anybody could enjoy free of charge this novel sensation. Otis patented a steam-powered elevator in 1861. By the time the Eiffel Tower was built for the Paris Exposition of 1889, three hydraulic elevators (one made by Otis) arranged in stages carried a visitor to the top in seven minutes. Even faster were the new electric elevators, which first appeared that year and which soon were carrying the public in Macy's and Wanamaker's.

Glass would play an important new role in this new consumer's world. Before the introduction of electric lighting, large windows were needed to bring daylight into the extensive buildings. But at least until the mid-nineteenth century, large sheets of glass were costly and difficult to make. "Plate glass" (the word came into English about 1727), a flat sheet smooth and regular enough for mirrors or large windows, was made from a rough sheet of glass which was then laboriously ground and polished. At first the rough sheets were produced by blowing (which could make a plate no bigger than about 50 inches by 30 inches); then, in the early eighteenth century, the French perfected a system of casting glass in sheets. In 1839 an

Englishman simplified the process for removing irregularities. Further improvements pointed the way to the continuous plate-glass process using rollers, which could make sheets of any length with the transparency of the old plate.

The larger sheets of glass, combined with the light cast-iron frame of the building, transformed the ground floor of department stores. The windows at street level were no longer merely openings to admit light and sun, but vivid advertisements—literally "show windows," an Americanism which came into use about the mid-nineteenth century for a shopwindow in which goods were displayed. The shop itself, the stock, and the goods themselves had become a powerful new form of advertising. Now for the first time the society's full range of material treasure would be laid out for all to see. "Window-shopping" was the name for a new and democratic popular pastime. The effectiveness of a building, the desirability of a retailing location, were now measured by the numbers in the passing crowds.

* * *

These urban crowds were brought to the city center by two important devices, neither of them quite new, but both newly flourishing in the United States after the Civil War. One made it easier for people to come to the department store; the other stirred them with the latest merchandising news, arousing their desire to come.

Public transportation did not appear in American cities until the second half of the nineteenth century; until then the ordinary citizen commonly shopped within walking distance, that is to say, within a radius of about two miles. Except for wealthy customers who could afford their own carriages, or for visitors from afar, a city merchant drew his customers from those who could walk to his shop from their house. This helped explain the importance of the neighborhood community. Almost all a man's activities, including his buying and selling, were with people who lived nearby and who as neighbors were very likely known to him personally. A neighborhood community was a walking community: of passers-by, of casual streetcorner encounters, of sidewalk greetings and doorway conversations.

Streetcars in the cities helped change all this. The early alternatives to walking were the omnibus (a kind of city stagecoach which held few passengers, was expensive, appeared infrequently, and lumbered slowly over the streets of cobblestone or mud) or the steam-driven railroad. Although the railroad was speedy, the noise, smoke, and embers from the locomotive made it a menace on the streets, and it was not suited to a line with frequent stops. The first effective public transportation within cities was the horse railroad, whose level tracks made the ride more comfortable, and which was well adapted to stop at any corner. We have become so accustomed to public transportation in our cities that we forget what a revolution in city life came with the first cheap public transportation.

The revolution occurred in many places at about the same time. As good an example as any other is the story of Boston, which has been admirably told by Sam B. Warner, Jr. In 1850, congested urban Boston extended out only about two miles from City Hall. By 1872 the horse railroads had pushed the radius out another half-mile. By 1887 the horsecar had pushed on for still another mile and a half, doubling the 1850 radius, and incidentally, of course, quadrupling the area of dense settlement. When by the 1890's the horsecar was displaced by the electrified trolley, which moved twice as fast and could carry three times the number of passengers, public transportation reached out for at least another two miles, now making a greater Boston that reached six miles from City Hall.

The profits and enthusiasms of suburban investors and streetcar builders accelerated the process. The first street railway in Greater Boston, a single car in 1852 running between Harvard Square, Cambridge, and Union Square, Somerville, was so profitable that it invited imitation by other investors. It seemed simple enough to lay tracks on the roadbeds already provided by the city, to mount a coach on the rails, and buy a horse or two to provide the power. Booster real estate men who had bought tracts on the edge of the city had as much interest in linking their lots to the city centers as the earlier boosters of upstart towns had in bringing the railroad their way. Optimistic businessmen like Henry M. Whitney, the steamship magnate who consolidated the Boston lines in 1887, tried to attract more passengers by a standard five-cent fare and free transfers.

Meanwhile the boosters for streetcar monopolies urged the great "moral influence" of street railways. At long last, they said, the workingman who had been crowded into a multifamily tenement in the congested center of the city could buy his own lot, build his own house, and enjoy the wholesome delights of the rural suburb. The rapid expansion of street railways brought a scramble for franchises and entangled urban politics in the quest for monopolies, what Lincoln Steffens called *The Shame of the Cities* (1904). But regardless of the motives, the result was to draw more customers into the orbit of the city.

Streetcar tracks were rigid channels. A man in a streetcar had to go where it took him. And the streetcar, in almost any city, was likely to take him into the center; there were the great consumers' palaces.

* * *

Along with the centralizing influence of the streetcar, which brought city dwellers to department stores, came a new indrawing power over customers' minds and desires: the daily newspapers with large circulation concentrated in the cities. The department store, through its heavy newspaper advertising, contributed substantially to the success of these papers, and so helped keep them independent of subsidy by political parties. In this way the department store, like other large advertisers, indirectly contributed toward the political impartiality of American news reporting that would contrast sharply with the partisan-dominated press of France, Italy, and some other countries. The urban dailies also did much to help the great consumers' palaces to attract their vast constituencies. Just as the rise of the suburbs in the late nineteenth century was inseparable from the story of the streetcar, so the rise of the department store was one with the rise of newspaper advertising. The department-store pioneers were pioneers in the art and science of advertising.

R. H. Macy, like the mail-order pioneer Richard Warren Sears, was a bold and ingenious advertiser in the days before merchants had made advertising a part of their regular operations. Macy used repetition, composed bad verse, and combined hundreds of tiny agate-sized letters (the only kind which newspaper editors tolerated at the time) to make the Macy star or to produce larger letters. Beginning in 1858, he dared to leave large white spaces in the expensive columns; he advertised frequently, and put his ads in four or five different papers at the same time, to overshadow his more conservative competitors. John Wanamaker of Philadelphia was another vigorous leader. He pioneered in 1879 with his first full-page newspaper advertisement; within ten years Wanamaker's full-page advertisements were appearing regularly. Other department stores followed, and big-city dailies all over the country profited. In 1909, when Wanamaker's in New York City began putting full-page advertisements in the evening newspapers daily, this gave the lead to the evening over the morning newspapers in advertising linage. In Chicago, too, Marshall Field had become a big newspaper advertiser. Mandel Brothers made news when it contracted with the Chicago *Tribune* to run its full-page advertisement six days a week throughout 1902, for an annual fee of $100,000.

By the beginning of the twentieth century, the department store had become a mainstay of the big-city daily newspaper throughout the country. And as the circulation of dailies increased, the dailies became the mainstay of department stores, the increasingly powerful enticers of their hundreds of thousands of customers. City newspapers had become streetcars of the mind. They were putting the thoughts and desires of tens of thousands of people in the new cities on tracks, drawing them to centers where they joined the hasty fellowship of new consumption communities.

* * *

The department store, as Émile Zola observed in France, "democratized luxury." We have forgotten how revolutionary was the new principle of free admission for the whole public. In the old fairs and bazaars, the stall keepers had of course shown off their goods to the passing crowds. But the goods displayed to the common view were of the familiar sorts, to satisfy familiar wants. Any passer-by could look at the fruits and vegetables, at the sides of beef or the slabs of pork, at pots and kitchen utensils, at a basket or a length of cheap cloth. The costlier textiles or home furnishings were kept in an inner room, to be brought out only for serious customers who could afford such goods. In the great cities of the world, the better shops hung their symbols over the door, but they boasted their exclusiveness, displayed the coat of arms of the noble family who had appointed them to be their supplier, and exhibited little or none of the merchandise to the casual passer-by. The less expensive shops, too, were specialized, and their stocks of ready-made goods were small. In the latter part of the eighteenth century "shop" became a verb: then people began to "go shopping"—that is, go to the shops to see what they might buy. But still, common citizens might spend their lives without ever seeing a wide array of the fancy goods that they could not afford.

The department store helped change all this. Now a flowing, indiscriminate public wandered freely among attractive, open displays of goods of all kinds and qualities. One needed no longer be a "person of quality" to view goods of quality. Anyone could enter a department store, see and handle the most elegant furnishings. In this new democracy of consumers it was assumed that any man might be a buyer. Just as standard of living, by contrast with wealth, was a public and communal fact, so, too, buying and "shopping" became public. In the department store, as in the hotel, the distinction between private and public activities became blurred.

An urban shopper now could stroll through the world of actual goods as casually as a farmer soon would be leafing through the mail-order catalogue. Architects now aimed to make goods into their own advertisement: a permanent exposition for consumers and would-be consumers. Formerly merchandise had remained mostly dispersed into its raw forms, awaiting a customer's command or design. But this world of the ready-made was now a world of "consumers." Goods that had been assembled in advance into shoes, suits, or furniture were offered enticingly to the whole milling passing public. In these palaces of awakening desire, the new merchandisers hoped to offer something near enough to what the customer might already have wanted, and to stir him to wants he had never imagined.

In other, subtler ways, the market was homogenized and democratized. One of the most interesting, and least noticed, was the fixed-price, one-price policy of the great new department stores. The old practice, still a spice of life in the world's bazaars, was for the seller to bargain individually with each buyer, asking a price determined by that particular buyer's social position, his need, and his desire for that particular item. Some merchants marked each item with its cost (in private symbols), and then sought to secure from the customer the highest price above that which he could manage to extract. The refusal to bargain was considered churlish or unsociable, and it surely made life less interesting. The price actually paid for an item varied with the bargaining ability of each customer.

It is not surprising, then, that doctrinaire egalitarians had objected to this way of pricing. George Fox, founder of English Quakerism, as early as 1653 urged his followers to refuse to haggle, and advised merchants to fix the one fair price for every item and for all customers. Like some other Quaker principles, this was considered odd, but it had its business compensations. Customers who distrusted their own bargaining ability, Fox himself explained, would be reassured by the thought that "they might sende any childe and be as well used as themselves at any of these [Quaker] shopps."

The progress of the fixed-price policy had been slow, but department stores were quickly committed to it. The pioneering Paris department store Bon Marché had a fixed-price policy as early as 1852. For the large American department stores the policy was inevitable. In 1862, when Stewart's already had a staff of about two thousand, most of them on meager salaries and personally unknown to the store owner, it was not feasible to entrust bargaining to the individual salesman. A consequence, then, was the democratization, or at least the equalization, of prices. One price for everybody! Regardless of age, sex, wealth, poverty, or bargaining power. The price was marked for all to see. As the merchandise itself had become public and the intimate shop had been transformed into a palatial lobby where the best merchandise was open to vulgar eyes, so, too, the price was no secret.

Goods were priced for mass appeal, and department-store services were offered to the general public: free delivery, freedom to return or exchange goods, and charge accounts. These services, like "satisfaction guaranteed or your money back" (an early department-store slogan), were not a product of private promises between shop-keeper and customer, but were part of a "policy," publicly proclaimed and advertised, from the firm to all consumers.

In a new sense now every sale and every purchase became a public act. The consumer was accepting an offer made, not only to him, but to anyone, usually in advertising. And advertising developed into the characteristic commercial relationship of the new age. Now it was no longer buyer and seller, the custom maker and the customer. It was advertiser and consumer: much of the advertiser's appeal was in his bigness; the consumer was a numerous horde whose strength was in numbers. The consumer now was being persuaded not merely to become a customer but to join a consumption community. He was being offered something that was not just for him but for everybody like him, and as both advertiser and consumer knew, there were millions.

CHRISTMAS AND OTHER
FESTIVALS OF CONSUMPTION

CHAPTER 18

IN 1939, WHILE the nation's business still suffered from the Depression, the month of November happened to have five Thursdays and Thanksgiving Day was scheduled to fall on November 30. But celebration of the holiday on the traditional last Thursday would have been unfortunate for the nation's merchants. With business lagging, they needed every fillip they could find, and by tradition the Christmas shopping season did not begin until the day after Thanksgiving. In New York City, Detroit, and elsewhere, the opening of the season was customarily marked by a Christmas-oriented Thanksgiving Day parade. It is not surprising, then, that under the circumstances an enterprising Ohio department-store owner, Fred Lazarus, Jr., proposed that the nation move the celebration of Thanksgiving to the earlier Thursday, November 23, which would add a whole week to the "Christmas shopping" season. The Ohio State Council of Retail Merchants and the Cincinnati *Enquirer* endorsed the idea. In Washington, President Franklin D. Roosevelt greeted the suggestion with enthusiasm, and proclaimed that in 1939 Thanksgiving should come on November 23.

President Roosevelt's "tampering with the calendar" (like the establishing of Standard Time a half-century before) was labeled by some as an interference with the divine order, but within a few years, all the states had fallen in line by enacting Thanksgiving as the fourth Thursday. Only a few continued to declare their independence from federal fiat by authorizing a Thanksgiving holiday on both the fourth and the last Thursday.

It was a little-known oddity of American life that the United States, unlike other nations, actually had no "national" holidays established by law. Under the federal system the legalizing of holidays had been left to the states. The President's only power over holidays was to issue proclamations focusing national attention and to give a day off to federal employees in the District of Columbia and elsewhere. Thanksgiving had grown up simply as a national custom. President Lincoln in 1863 was the first to issue a presidential Thanksgiving proclamation, and then the legal holiday was created by separate laws in each of the states. This trivial shift in the date of President Roosevelt's proclamation of a national Thanksgiving was significant mainly for what it revealed of the American Christmas; and for what it told of the transformation of this ancient festival into an American Festival of Consumption.

* * *

In the eyes of the early New England Puritans, Christmas was a menace to the pure Christian spirit. Fearing "popish" idolatry, the General Court of Massachusetts in 1659 passed an act punishing with a fine of five shillings for each offense "anybody who is found observing, by abstinence from labor, feasting, or any other way, any such days as Christmas day." By 1681 they felt secure enough against "popery" to repeal the law, but they still feared giving the day any ritualistic significance. In his diary for 1685, Judge Samuel Sewall, for example, expressed his satisfaction that on Christmas day he saw everybody conducting business as usual. During the next two centuries, while Christmas was somehow Americanized, it still remained a simple folk holiday marked by no grand religious observance and with little commercial significance. The season is hardly recognizable, for example, in the pages of the New York *Tribune* for the month of December 1841, which are barren of flashy Christmas advertising and simply repeat the unchanging copy which merchants had run for months. In a few instances when gifts are mentioned, they are referred to as "Christmas and New Year's" presents; Santa Claus had not yet entered the Christmas scene.

By the era of the Civil War the old festival, characterized by folksy conviviality, was beginning to be transformed. There were signs that the holiday was on its way to becoming a spectacular nationwide Festival of Consumption. On December 24, 1867, the first Christmas Eve when R. H. Macy's remained open until midnight, the store set a record with one-day receipts of $6,000. In 1874 Macy's offered its first promotional window displays to have an exclusively Christmas motif, featuring the Macy collection of dolls, and from then on the Christmas windows became an annual institution. During the next years, those Macy departments whose volume depended heavily on the Christmas trade increased their share of the store's total sales. Other department stores, too, began the practice of staying open late during the last two weeks before Christmas. December began to become the big month for retailers, and by 1870, December sales were already double those of May, the next best month.

Still, in 1880 Christmas was so undeveloped that a manufacturer of Christmas-tree ornaments had difficulty persuading F. W. Woolworth to take $25 worth of his product. Within a few years Woolworth's annual order of Christmas-tree ornaments from this supplier alone came to $800,000. In the next half-century, he drew on numerous suppliers and his orders totaled $25 million. "This is our harvest time," Woolworth instructed his store managers in December 1891. "Make it pay."

> Give your store a holiday appearance. Hang up Christmas ornaments. Perhaps have a tree in the window. Make the store look different. . . . This is also a good time to work off "stickers" or unsalable goods, for they will sell during the excitement when you could not give them away other times. Mend all broken toys and dolls every day.

By 1899 Woolworth's Christmas trade was reaching a half-million dollars. In order to avert a strike at that crucial time of year, Woolworth introduced a system of Christmas bonuses ($5 for each year of service, with a limit of $25).

The mail-order houses began to issue special Christmas catalogues. At the 1939 Christmas season Montgomery Ward and Company gave away 2.4 million copies of "Rudolph the Red-Nosed Reindeer," a versified story written by an employee in their advertising department. Gene Autry's singing version became a runaway best-selling record.

Display type was used for Christmas advertising even before it became common for other purposes. Newspaper advertising peaked in December, and then fell off sharply after Christmas. By 1910 more than one third of the nation's annual output of books was being delivered in the six weeks before Christmas. Before mid-century, one quarter of the whole year's jewelry purchases were being made in December.

The Christmas Club, which first appeared in 1910, was an arrangement by which a person deposited a specified amount every week during the year, to be accumulated in a special savings account for withdrawal at Christmas time. By 1950 there were more than 10 million members of such clubs in 6,200 banks, in all states of the Union; and their deposits for the year exceeded $950 million.

With the passing decades of the twentieth century, Christmas became overwhelmingly a season of shopping. Gifts which first had the force of good manners actually acquired the force of law. The Christmas bonus (soon "expected but not appreciated") became a part of the anticipated compensation of employees. In 1951, when a firm reduced its Christmas bonus and the union appealed to the National Labor Relations Board, the board ruled the "Christmas" bonus to be not in fact a gift at all. The employer, they said, was not free to discontinue this practice. Christmas gifts to policemen, mailmen, janitors, and others tended to become a kind of insurance against poor service during the coming year. And the "executive gift" sometimes became a convenient device for evading the laws of bribery.

* * *

One of the most distinctive features of the American Christmas was Santa Claus, who was speedily transformed out of all recognition from his Old World character. There had been a real St. Nicholas, a fourth-century bishop of Myra in Asia Minor, who became the patron saint of Russia, and of mariners, thieves, virgins, and children. According to legend, St. Nicholas had saved three poor virgins from being forced to sell their virtue, by throwing a purse of gold through their windows on three successive nights.

In the United States, St. Nicholas early became a familiar figure of folklore and pseudo-folklore. His earliest conspicuous appearance in American literature was in Washington Irving's *Knickerbocker's History of New York* (1809), where St. Nicholas traveled through the skies in a wagon, and began to acquire some of his other features. The American Santa Claus's rotund figure, jolly mien, and white beard were conferred on him by Thomas Nast in his series of Christmas drawings for *Harper's Weekly* beginning in 1863. By the late nineteenth century, "belief" in Nast's Santa Claus had become a symbol of childhood innocence and adult warm-heartedness.

No sooner had Santa become the patron saint of a Saturnalia for children, "bringing treasures for the little rogues," than he was elevated to patron of a nationwide Saturnalia of consumption. The department store was the proper habitat of *Santa Claus Americanus*. And he above all others was responsible for moving the primary scene of the festival from the church to the department store. By 1914 a well-organized Santa Claus Association, with headquarters in New York City, had as its object "to preserve Children's faith in Santa Claus." The association aimed to secure from the post office the letters addressed to Santa Claus and then reply to them in the name of Santa with letters or gifts. When there was public objection, postal authorities intervened. "All I ask," the founder of the association urged, "is that these people don't sock it to us at this time of the year and spoil the faith of little children."

Widespread demand led to the founding of "schools" for "real" Santa Clauses. The curriculum of the first such school (in Albion, New York) included indoctrination in the history of Santa Claus, dressing for the role, wearing beards, handling children, and other special techniques. A firm called Santa's Helpers rented out trained Santas for special occasions. In 1948 the City Council of Boston, acting on the complaint of a council member that "there is a Santa on every corner and children are beginning to wonder," formally requested the mayor to "permit only one Santa in the city in 1949 and to station him on the historic Boston Common." A bill in the California Senate in 1939 (required, a senator explained, by the sight of Santas "selling everything from bottled beer to automobiles") aimed legally to restrict the use of Santa's image.

"Belief" in Santa Claus was widely defended. A sentimental editorial, "Yes, Virginia, There Is a Santa Claus!," became the classic declaration of faith for agnostic Americans. When a savings bank in Muskegon, Michigan, displayed a sign in 1949 declaring "There Is No Santa Claus—Work—Earn—Save," local parents protested. And when the sign was removed, the bank president wryly commented, "The myth of Santa Claus is far-reaching and implies a nation of people who seem to accept a Santa Claus with headquarters at Washington." Judges issued facetious opinions from the bench *(ex parte Santa Claus)* to defend Santa, and held in contempt of court those who impugned him.

A few dared to put Santa Claus in the tradition of the great American hoaxes. But psychiatrists, the new authorities on national myths, could not take him so lightly. One solemnly declared that "any child who believes in Santa Claus has had his ability to think permanently injured." Others diagnosed the Santa myth as a symptom of parental insecurity, although some, including the influential Dr. Arnold Gesell, were not unduly alarmed.

*   *   *

The Christmas tree, too, acquired a special American character, and with its numerous accessories it became a significant seasonal industry. One story is that trimmed trees were first introduced to the United States during the Revolution by Hessian soldiers trying to recreate here the holiday of their homeland. In the nineteenth century the Christmas-tree custom was widespread in northern Europe. But the elaboration and electrification, and finally the syntheticizing of the Christmas tree, were reserved for the United States. By 1948 about 28 million Christmas trees were being distributed annually in the United States. The 100,000 acres devoted to Christmas trees were producing a crop valued at $50 million annually. At least after Woolworth began featuring Christmas-tree decorations in the 1880's, the business of decorations, ornaments, and accessories flourished. The Christmas tree was officially recognized in 1923 when the President began the practice of lighting a tree on the White House lawn. Raising trees became more profitable with the development of the ingenious technique of "stump-culture" (by which the tree was severed above live-branch whorls, leaving a pruned number of these to grow, in turn, into trees for the next season). But the rising prices of trees, together with fire hazards and a growing interest in forest conservation, combined to create a new market for synthetic, plastic reusable Christmas trees.

Another thriving American industry—greeting cards—was a byproduct of the American Christmas. Louis Prang, a sixteen-year-old refugee from the German revolutions, came to New York in 1850, acquired a reputation as a lithographer, and pioneered in making colored lithographs of famous works of art (he christened them "chromos" and the name stuck) which he sold for $6 apiece. In 1875 he applied his techniques to producing colorful cards for Christmas, and these came to be esteemed as works of art. Prang's elegant eight-color chromos of the Nativity, of children, young women, flowers, birds, and butterflies (a few, too, of Santa Claus) gave a certain tone to the practice of sending greeting cards at Christmas and dominated the market until about 1890. When the Christmas card was democratized by the import of cheaper cards from Germany, Prang retired from the business, but even less expensive cards of American make recaptured the market within another twenty years. By the early twentieth century the practice of sending Christmas cards, and then other greeting cards, had become widespread. By mid-century, about 1.5 billion Christmas greeting cards were being sold each season.

As the custom became more widespread, cards tended to become less and less religious in motif. The message, even in Prang's first deluxe items, had never been predominantly religious. The friendly secularized texts became acceptable to Jews and others who did not subscribe to such theological messages as still remained in the American Christmas.

Americans found other ingenious ways to elide religious issues in order to share in the national Festival of Consumption. While the Rabbinical Assembly of America in 1946 protested the school practice of singing Christmas carols as an infringement of freedom of religion, the Jews themselves helped "solve" the problem. They promoted Chanukah, historically only a minor Jewish festival, into a kind of Jewish Christmas, with *eight* gift-giving days. More than one Jewish child probably asked, "Mother, dear, are we having Chanukah for Christmas this year?"

*   *   *

In a nation of consumption communities, there was a tendency for all festivals somehow to become Festivals of Consumption. Mother's Day was an example.

Something like a Mother's Day—the fourth Sunday before Easter, a day to honor Mary, the mother of Jesus—had been observed in European countries. "Mothering Sunday" was when servants and apprentices were given a day off to "go a-mothering," to go visit their mothers. Sometimes the eldest son would bring his mother a "mothering cake," which was then shared by the family. There appears to be no evidence that Mother's Day was an American holiday before 1907. In that year an enterprising young lady from West Virginia, Anna Jarvis, much attached to her mother who had died two years before, consulted the Philadelphia merchant John Wanamaker about a suitable way to honor the nation's mothers. He advised her to campaign for a national observance. Helped by evangelists, newspaper editors, and politicians, the campaign for a nationwide Mother's Day quickly succeeded. The governor of West Virginia issued the first Mother's Day proclamation in 1912, and the Mother's Day International Association was founded. On May 9, 1914, pursuant to a Congressional Resolution, President Wilson issued the first presidential Mother's Day proclamation urging that the flag be flown on that day.

The simple old "mothering cake" was transmuted into a whole range of Mother's Day gift merchandise. The practice of noting the day by going to church (wearing a red carnation for a living mother or a white carnation for one deceased) blossomed into a bonanza for telegraph and telephone companies, candy shops, florists, jewelers, and cosmetic manufacturers. Like other American festivals which had originated in church, Mother's Day too ended in the department store.

In 1934, when retailers needed every possible stimulus to business, Postmaster General James A. Farley ordered a Mother's Day stamp showing Whistler's "Mother." The stamp, said to have been personally designed by President Roosevelt, actually offered a cropped and barely recognizable version of Whistler's well-known painting, which had been improved for the purpose by a vase of carnations prominently added in the lower left-hand corner. While the American Artists' Professional League objected to this "mutilation" of Whistler's painting, Anna Jarvis, the mother of Mother's Day, went personally to the Postmaster General to protest the transformation of her holiday into an advertisement for the florists' trade. She finally secured an apology. On the occasion of Mother's Day 1961 (according to a retail association estimate), more than 55 million families bought Mother's Day gifts for a total of some $875 million.

It is not surprising, then, that there was also to be a Father's Day, and the authorship of this idea was claimed by many. In 1910 a lady in Spokane, Washington, supported by William Jennings Bryan, began to campaign for a Father's Day; in 1916 President Wilson pressed a button in Washington to open the Spokane celebration. In June 1921 the governor of Virginia was persuaded to proclaim a Father's Day by a young lady who in 1932 registered the name "National Father's Day Association" with the United States Patent Office. Then, in 1935, a National Father's Day Committee was established "dedicated to building a democratic world through wholesome child upbringing." The prime mover for this holiday, Mrs.

John Bruce Dodd, unlike the founder of Mother's Day, was not troubled by the danger of commercialization or the practice of making the day a time for gifts. "After all," she observed, "why should the greatest giver of gifts not be on the receiving end at least once a year?" The gift idea, she explained, was "a sacred part of the holiday, as the giver is spiritually enriched in the tribute paid his father."

CONDENSE!

Making Food Portable Through Time

CHAPTER 35

I N NOVEMBER 1846 the Donner Party of eighty-seven emigrants on their way from Sangamon County, Illinois, to California were trapped in deep snow while camping at Truckee Lake in the Sierra Nevada mountains. According to the familiar story, they would all have starved to death had not the survivors sustained themselves by eating the flesh of those who had died. The rescue parties from California managed to bring out forty-seven survivors. For practical-minded Americans of the day this was not only an episode in the history of morals; it also dramatized the peculiar needs of Americans on the move.

* * *

When Gail Borden, a surveyor and land agent at Galveston in the recently annexed state of Texas, heard of the starvation of the Donner Party and the hunger of the others who were trying to cross the continent, he was stirred to invent a way of making food more portable. Born on a farm in central New York, he had meandered west with his parents, first to Ohio, and then on to Kentucky and Indiana. He personally knew the problems of westward travel. He taught himself surveying, then earned his living as a schoolteacher on the borderlands of Mississippi before joining his family at Stephen A. Austin's colony in Texas in 1829. There Austin put him in charge of the official land surveys, which gave him the power to make and break fortunes. In 1835, when the colony needed a newspaper, the versatile Borden and a friend founded the weekly *Telegraph and Texas Register*. The tenth newspaper started in Texas, Borden's *Telegraph* was the first to last longer than two years. He knew the usual troubles of the backwoods booster press—scarce materials, scarce news, subscribers who could not be found or who would not pay when they were found. To make ends meet, he became the official printer to the new Republic of Texas, and the Texas Declaration of Independence was published by his press in March 1836. When the site of Houston was chosen for the capital, Borden was named official surveyor. Then he moved on again to Galveston Island, where he served as Collector of the Port, helped lay out streets, planned a water supply, sold city lots, and became a passionate booster for "The New York of Texas."

But Borden was no ordinary public servant. "He has dozens of inventions," a Galveston neighbor observed, "and he is the most wonderful of them all himself." His "Locomotive Bath House," for example, could be carried out into the Galveston surf so that ladies could bathe in modest privacy. His wedding present to his wife was his homemade revolving dining table, with a fixed rim the width of a dining plate, and a revolving center on which the dishes to be served could be rotated to each person. Noting that yellow fever was conquered by the first frost, he devised his own public-health program; by using ether, "to freeze you down to, say, 30° or 40°—I mean, to keep you for a week as if under a white frost. . . . lock up every soul in a temporary winter." Then there was his own design for a steamboat propelled not by a screw or a paddle wheel, but by a moving belt the full length of the keel mounted with paddle boards. More remarkable still was his "Terraqueous Machine"—a sail-driven prairie schooner for land and sea. When he demonstrated the machine to a crowd of his fellow townsmen at the beach, his passengers sailed into the Gulf, and so proved that his boat was really amphibious; but unfortunately the boat capsized and dumped the passengers into the water.

"I never drop an idea," boasted Borden, "except for a better

one." The "better idea" to which he turned from his Terraqueous
Machine would lead him to fame and fortune. When he tried to con-
coct a new kind of portable food for his friends who were traveling to
California in July 1849, he made an "important discovery . . . an
improved process of preserving the nutritious properties of meat, or
animal flesh, of any kind, by obtaining the concentrated extract of it,
and combining it with flour or vegetable meal, and drying or baking
the mixture in an oven, in the form of a biscuit or cracker."

This was Borden's first application of the creed which would
guide him in business for a lifetime. "Condense your sermons," he
advised the minister of his Galveston church. "You can do almost
any thing with every thing. If you plan and think, and, as fast as you
drop one thing, seize upon another. . . . The world is changing. In
the direction of condensing. . . . Even lovers write no poetry, nor any
other stuff and nonsense, now. They condense all they have to say, I
suppose, into a kiss . . . Time was when people would. . . . spend
hours at a meal. Napoleon never took over twenty minutes. . . . *I* am
through in fifteen. People have almost lost the faculty of fooling
away their time."

Borden spent six years developing his Meat Biscuit. And in his
own brochure in 1850 he listed some of those whom his biscuit
would benefit: the Navy and all men at sea; travelers "on long journeys, through destitute regions" where, he pointed out, "the fire for
cooking is one of the greatest dangers in Indian country, as it betrays
the situation of the camp to the hostile Indians"; geologists and sur-
veyors; explorers "in making geological and mineralogical surveys of
our newly acquired territories, as well as those running the boundary"; hospitals, where "a patient can, at the shortest notice, have it
prepared to any degree of nutrition, from a weak broth to the most
nutritious soup"; and all families, "especially in warm weather." Elisha Kent Kane's first Arctic expedition carried several canisters of
Borden's meat biscuits. Hoping to secure acceptance of the meat biscuit by physicians and by the United States Army, Borden made a
partner of Dr. Ashbel Smith, a Yale graduate and surgeon-general to
the Texas Republic. Smith, whose main use was in public relations,
wrote an article for *De Bow's Review* explaining how the manufacture

of meat biscuits would help diversify Southern industry. At the Crystal Palace Exhibition in London, in May 1851, Smith exhibited the Meat Biscuit alongside other ingenious American products, including Herring's Patent Salamander Safe (£500 to anybody who could pick the lock), Colt's revolver, and McCormick's Virginia Reaper. When it happened that Dr. Ashbel Smith was the American appointed to the international jury a consequence was that the highest award for contribution to the food industry went to Gail Borden of Texas.

"It appears to be a part of the mission of America," Dr. Smith boasted, ". . . not merely to furnish a home to refugees from the oppressions and crowded population of the old world, but also, to feed in part the poor of those countries who never taste good meat: and to whom, even a miserable flesh is a great rarity." Borden spent six years and $60,000 in promoting his meat biscuit. But the powerful suppliers of fresh meat to the Army made it difficult for Borden's biscuit to get a fair trial. There were other problems, too. When people complained that Borden's biscuit was "unsightly" and unpalatable, Borden himself confessed that he alone really knew how to prepare his biscuit. Frederick Law Olmsted on his travels through Texas finally fed his meat biscuit to the birds, declaring that he would "decidedly undergo a very near approach to the traveler's last bourne, before having recourse to it." But even before the meat biscuit had plainly failed, Borden had turned to an even better idea which before the end of the century would make the name of Borden a synonym for milk.

* * *

On the rough ocean voyage back from the London exhibition in the fall of 1851, one story goes, Borden learned that the cows in the ship's hold became so seasick that they could not be milked. When he heard the hungry cries of the immigrant babies, he began to wonder whether he could not somehow use his condensing technique to provide milk for such emergencies. This was a difficult assignment, for milk was the most fragile of foods, which people all over the world had vainly tried to find ways to preserve in fresh and tasty form. To make cheese was, of course, a kind of answer to the problem. But Borden determined to find some way to condense whole milk.

Luckily, Borden did not know enough to be confused by the theories of the day, all of which had proved that it couldn't be done. So Borden simply tried his own hand with a panful of milk. In Europe there had been some success in evaporating milk for preservation, but none of the products had been marketable. And Borden probably did not know of them.

Preserving milk in some form was not too difficult. But preserving quality and taste were quite another matter. First Borden boiled milk in an open pan on a sand bath heated by charcoal, and then he added brown sugar. When the resulting liquid was sealed in glass, it would keep for months, but it had a dark color and smelled like molasses. At the Shaker Colony in New Lebanon, New York, where Borden first saw a vacuum pan, he obtained one, and with it tried condensing milk. But as the milk was heated it stuck to the side of the pan, then foamed and boiled over. Experts advised him to give up, but Borden merely greased the pan, and in that remarkably simple way perfected his technology of condensing milk. Borden's innovation was in fact so simple that he had trouble convincing the patent commissioners in Washington that he had done anything really new. But with a testimonial from the editor of the *Scientific American* and with a pile of charts and affidavits, he finally persuaded the patent officials that he had invented an essential new item: evaporating milk *in a vacuum*.

Borden's intuitive explanation, though not designed to satisfy a modern organic chemist, showed his talent for going to the heart of the matter. Milk, like blood, he said, was a "living fluid" and "as soon as drawn from the cow begins to die, change, and decompose." The vacuum would keep the milk from "dying" until it had been sealed. In 1856, Borden received both English and American patents.

Even before his condensed milk had found a market, Borden was trying to condense coffee, tea, and "other useful dietary matters." Condensing became his obsession. "I mean to put a potato into a pillbox, a pumpkin into a tablespoon, the biggest sort of watermelon into a saucer ... The Turks made acres of roses into attar of roses. ... I intend to make attar of everything!"

Condensed milk quickly proved to be a commercial success. Enlisting the financial support of a wealthy New York wholesale grocer whom he happened to meet on a train, Borden founded the New York Condensed Milk Company, and in 1858, in a village about a hundred miles north of the city, established his first large-scale milk-condensing plant. Neighboring farmers brought their milk to his factory, where it was condensed before being taken into the city. And in *Leslie's Illustrated Newspaper* for May 22, 1858, an advertisement, probably written by Borden himself, announced:

> BORDEN'S CONDENSED MILK, Prepared in Litchfield County, Conn., is the only Milk ever concentrated without the admixture of sugar or some other substance, and remaining easily soluble in water. It is simply Fresh Country Milk, from which the water is nearly all evaporated, and nothing added. The Committee of the Academy of Medicine recommended it as "an article that, for purity, durability and economy, is hitherto unequaled in the annals of the Milk Trade."
>
> One quart, by the addition of water, makes 2½ quarts, equal to cream—5 quarts rich milk, and 7 quarts good milk.
>
> For sale at 173 Canal Street, or delivered at dwellings in New York and Brooklyn, at 25 CENTS per quart.

It was a strategic moment to bring a superior milk product into the New York market. For at the time the city was shaken by scandals of "milk murder." The same newspaper which carried Borden's advertisement had been rousing New Yorkers by its exposure of the needlessly high infant mortality rate, caused, it said, by filthy milk. The milk then commonly distributed in the city was called "swill-milk" because it came from city cows fed on distillers' "swill" or "still-slops," the residue from the distilleries. Such milk contained almost no butterfat, and to cover up its unsavory blue, it had to be artificially colored. Manure and milk were hauled in the same wagons, and *Leslie's* told tales of how sick cows were propped up for a last milking before they expired. The city swill-dairies were a kind of "Vesuvius which belched forth intolerable and stinking stench." Swill-milk, the leading dairy authority reported, had an effect "on the system of young children . . . very destructive, causing diseases of various kinds, and, if continued, certain death."

With Borden's dairy-fresh sanitary product, the sales of the New York milk routes increased, and more routes were added. Borden set a new standard of cleanliness and quality, sending his inspectors out into the countryside where they instructed the dairy farmers. He took no milk from cows that had calved within twelve days, and he required that udders be washed in warm water before milking, that barns be clean, and that manure be kept away from the milking stalls. He demanded that the wire-cloth strainers be scalded and dried morning and night. Inspectors at the factory rejected milk that arrived with a temperature above 58 degrees. In many ways this complicated the lives of farmers, but it simplified their lives, too. For Borden had turned the dairy farmer into a milk wholesaler, who no longer had to peddle his milk around the countryside, nor did he have to churn butter or mold cheese. The farmer who had made a contract with Borden and continued to meet the Borden standards could deliver his milk to the factory dock and receive a regular check from the company.

When the Civil War broke out, then, Borden was ready to supply the Army. One of his sons, John Gail, was fighting for the Union, while his other son, Lee, had joined the Texas Cavalry on the side of the Confederacy. But the Union Army bought Borden's condensed milk as a field ration and Borden himself was committed to the Union. Even after his New York plant was turning out sixteen thousand quarts a day, he still could not keep up with the government orders, so he licensed plants in other parts of the country. By the end of 1866 the Elgin, Illinois, plant alone was purchasing from farmers nearly a third of a million gallons of milk each year.

In 1875, a year after Gail Borden's death, the Borden Company began selling fluid fresh whole milk. Although his company now was stricter than ever in its standards for dairy farmers, there were limits to what it could do. Bacterial count as a test for milk was still unknown, and the only standard of sanitation was how the milk was produced and handled. Milk was still delivered by ladling it out of large cans into the buyer's container. Until milk was bottled at the dairy and distributed in smaller units in closed containers, it was impossible to insure sanitary fresh milk in the home. By 1885 the Borden Company, under Gail's elder son, was beginning to sell milk in bottles. But it was another decade before Louis Pasteur's work made bacterial count a standard for market milk and "pasteurization" became widespread; and still another twenty years before the tuberculin testing of cattle was protecting children against tuberculosis. In one state after another, medical commissions were set up to "certify" milk.

* * *

While Borden was finding ways to condense milk and put it into a can to be kept indefinitely, scores of other enterprising Americans were finding ways to bring everything to everybody year-round. The basic process of canning had been invented by a French wine maker and food supplier, Nicholas Appert, who won a prize from Napoleon in 1809 for finding a new way of supplying fresh provisions for the French navy. Appert had invented the cooking and sealing process which produced a flourishing canning industry in nineteenth-century Europe, and with a few basic improvements, continued in use into the twentieth century.

In the 1840's the American canning industry gained momentum. Corn, tomatoes, peas, and fish were canned for travelers journeying to California. Baltimore, on Chesapeake Bay, where the oysters, crabs, and fish were plentiful, became the first great American canning center. But canning techniques were still rudimentary, and when they went awry, a whole season's pack could be spoiled. Since the processing with boiling water took up to six hours for each batch, even the most efficient canners could produce no more than two or three thousand cans a day.

The outbreak of the Civil War gave the great impetus. The Union commandeered Borden's output of canned milk for the Army, but if the Army's needs were to be supplied, there would have to be a faster way to process canned goods. The maximum temperature of water boiling in an open container was 212 degrees Fahrenheit. Earlier in the century the English chemist Sir Humphry Davy had found that adding calcium chloride increased the temperature of boiling water to 240 degrees or above. In 1861, when a Baltimore canner, Isaac Solomon, made use of this discovery, he at once cut the average processing time from six hours to a half-hour. During the war many men had their first taste of canned foods, in army camps, on gunboats and in hospitals; and when the armed forces dispersed, they carried the word all over the country. While the demand for canned goods was still small, the canners had remained near the ocean, where they could put up oysters, lobsters, and other seafood for part of the year, and keep their plants at work processing small quantities of fruits and vegetables at other times. Now, with a widespread demand for all sorts of foods in cans, large-scale canneries appeared inland, in Cincinnati, Indianapolis, and elsewhere. In the decade after 1860 the number of cans of food put up annually rose from five million to thirty million.

Large-scale canning required containers by the thousands. Appert's original process for "canning" was actually a scheme for preserving food in glass containers. About the same time an Englishman had patented a technique for preserving food in tin. But cans were still fashioned by hand, and a tinsmith could make only sixty in a whole day. Then during the early nineteenth century, Americans improved tin cans and made machinery to turn them out by the thousands—machines for stamping out the tops and bottoms, for soldering the joint on the side, and for crimping and sealing the top. By 1880 a single machine worked by two men with two boys helping could turn out fifteen hundred cans in one day. Tinsmiths, who saw themselves being displaced, defended their jobs by arguing that machine-made cans were a menace to health. The solder used on the can-manufacturing machines, they said, was poisonous; and for a while some people would not eat food from a machine-made can. But by the 1920's more than a billion and a half pounds of tin plate was annually being made into cans. The tin can had begun to play its new leading role helping the American housewife—and cluttering the American landscape.

WALLS BECOME WINDOWS

T HE NEW WORLD dissolving of distinctions touched the intimacies of daily life. Of this, there is no more vivid or more neglected example than the story of glass. For glass gave a new, uncertain meaning to the wall, which now became something it had never been before; this in turn made something quite new of glass. The consequence for everyday experience was to give a new ambiguity to where people were and to confuse the boundaries of place.

The century after the Civil War vastly expanded the uses of iron and steel, and found widespread new uses for a fluid masonry, at least as old as the Romans, called concrete. These opaque materials made possible new forms that soared and reached, and so the shapes of buildings were extended and freed. But because glass was transparent it transformed the very meaning of indoors and outdoors, and the relations between them. Glass was a miracle material, which made it possible to be outdoors when you were indoors, to enjoy the flood of sun and daylight while you were sheltered. It would allow Americans to protect themselves against wind and weather, against heat and cold, while it liberated their vision.

The story of glass in the United States is all the more dramatic because glass was so ancient a material, whose meaning was so recently and so quickly transformed. In the history of technology the oldest arts are those which change most slowly. The ancient Egyptians used glass for the glazing of soapstone beads and to make imitation precious stones; glass-blown vessels were widely known in the Mediterranean before the birth of Jesus. During the Middle Ages, techniques were elaborated to make fancy containers, chandeliers, and small mirrors. By the thirteenth century, when Venice was the glassmaking center of Europe, the glassmaker's secrets were counted among the city's treasures. Venetians found a way to make a pure, colorless, and transparent glass, which was then fashioned into fragile objects to be prized in palaces. Glass, a raw material of filigreed luxury, was treated as a kind of transparent silver.

Only gradually did glass come to be used for windows. In buildings of the early Middle Ages, windows were few and small, for glass was expensive and flat glass could be made only with difficulty and in small sizes. The vivid stained-glass windows of the medieval Gothic cathedrals of France and England displayed the limitations as well as the powers of the glassmakers. It was easy to make colored glass (the color came from the quantity of different "impurities"), but hard to make perfectly clear glass. These small pieces of colored flat glass offered the architects an opportunity to use lead and to arrange them into elegant compositions. Around the sun-drenched Mediterranean, where stained-glass windows first flourished, stained glass appealed for its ability to keep out the hot sunshine while it transformed sunlight into ornamental images. Leaded windows of small panes, imitated in the twentieth century by neoromantic architects, were originally made that way not for ornamental reasons, but because larger panes were not available. Even into the nineteenth century, tax laws in the Old World found it convenient to tax household property not by square footage or the total construction cost, but by the number of its windows. The English window tax (1696 to 1851) became a model for the French door and window tax (1798 to 1917). And the connection between the number of your windows and your ability to pay was not entirely fanciful. Glass windows were not for the common people.

* * *

In modern America, just as ice was changed from an item of personal luxury consumption into a commodity for everybody, so too was glass. Democratizing glass in the United States meant making it another way of removing spatial distinctions, and a means for conquering the seasons. From being the precious substance of the decorative arts, prized for its colorful, reflective brilliance, glass became a basic building material and a universal medium of vision. Again, the great theoretical discoveries and many of the basic new techniques came from abroad, mostly from Europe. But by the twentieth century the American genius for organization and diffusion had made glass into an unprecedented necessity for unprecedented numbers of people and for unprecedented purposes. Before this could happen, more economical techniques of glassmaking were required.

The commonest way of making sheet glass throughout the eighteenth century was the "crown" window-glass process, so called because the product bore a "crown," or bull's eye. This was an elaborate process commonly requiring a team of ten men and boys. The globe of glass already blown by the pipe was rolled on an iron table until it had a conical shape. Then a solid iron rod was attached to the flat base of the cone (opposite the blowpipe) and the blowpipe was removed, leaving the hot glass cone open at the small end. The most skilled member of the team then spun the cone rapidly in a reheating furnace until centrifugal force caused it to flash out into a flat disk, still adhering to the iron rod at the center (or "crown"). At that instant the glassmaker removed the disk from the furnace, and to retain its flat shape, kept whirling it until it became cooler and stiffer. An assistant then cut the glass disk free from the rod so it could be taken to a kiln for annealing. The circular sheets that could be made by this process were relatively small and became still smaller if they were cut square. And of course they always bore the tell-tale bull's-eye or "crown" in the middle. Because the glass was blown, it was uneven in thickness and thin at the edges.

Until about 1830 the bull's-eye process was the usual way to make glass for windows. It was occasionally supplemented by another, equally complicated and difficult technique, the hand-cylinder process. By this method, globes of hot glass, which had been produced by the glass blowers, were elongated into cylinders by being swung in a deep trench (sometimes reaching a depth of ten feet). The cylinder was then slit lengthwise, flattened out, and allowed to cool. This required special skill in the blower, who had to make a cylinder of uniform thickness.

Until the mid-nineteenth century, too, the glassmaker, like the alchemist or the physician, possessed a prestige and mystique. Glassmaking was a world of traditional formulae and secret processes, and unlike other men who worked with their hands, the glassmaker held the status of "gentleman." While the noble and the wealthy remained the customers for glassware, glassmaking itself remained a monopoly, and was perhaps the most aristocratic of the crafts.

The American situation from the beginning offered opportunities for the glassmaker. A whole glass plant could be built on the personal knowledge of a single glassmaker. And the main raw materials required—sand, and wood for the furnace—were abundant on the eastern seaboard. As a result, glassmaking was probably the first industry established in British America. Polish and German glassmakers were brought to Virginia in 1608, followed by Italian glassmakers a few years later, and before the mid-seventeenth century, Massachusetts Bay was offering land to attract its own glassmakers. These craftsmen made bottles, lamps, tableware, a few pieces of window glass, and incidentally provided some glass beads for the Indian trade. By 1740 a German immigrant, Caspar Wistar, was operating a glassworks with four experienced Belgian glass blowers, to whom he soon added glass blowers from Germany and Portugal. His son Richard carried on the works, and in the tax-troubled year 1769 advertised in Franklin's *Pennsylvania Gazette* that "our glass is of American manufacture—and it is of interest to America to encourage her own manufactures, more especially those upon which duties have been imposed solely to raise revenue." Richard Wistar actually used the slogan "Buy American Manufactured Goods."

About the same time another German immigrant, the flamboyant Henry William Stiegel, who had imported English and German glassmakers, was producing his own elegant glassware. Drinking glasses, lenses, measures, perfume bottles, and other luxury items came from his large glass factory in Lancaster County, Pennsylvania. His grand manner of living earned him the apocryphal title of "Baron von Stiegel," and the beauty of his product made Stiegel glassware precious collector's items in later centuries. But since his glassware was still made to satisfy the expensive tastes of an Old World aristocracy, Stiegel had trouble marketing his product here. He went bankrupt, languished in a debtors' prison, and finally died in poverty. In the age of the American Revolution, a new society on the edge of a continental wilderness had needs more urgent than for the rich blues and purples of Stiegelware. When a prosperous American glass industry came into being, it was for a much wider and more characteristically American market.

*   *   *

So long as the making of sheets of glass was tied to the ancient, skilled arts of the glass blower, so long as the preparation of flat glass depended on human lung power, the reshaping of the material from a luxury-treasure into a democratic medium for transforming space was impossible. By the mid-nineteenth century some new mechanical methods of making flat glass had been developed in Europe, and these were beginning to displace the glass blower. In the twentieth century, American techniques and machines would open a new age for one of the world's most ancient crafts.

As early as the seventeenth century, a revolutionary new way of making flat glass was in use in France. A lump of molten glass was poured onto a "casting table," and while still molten, was pressed out by a roller which forced it between guides, fixed so as to insure an even surface and uniform thickness. The glass was left to anneal or cool for about ten days, then both surfaces were ground down by a smaller plate of glass, and finally polished with felt-covered boards and rollers. This technique had been imported to England before the end of the eighteenth century, but did not displace the hand-cylinder process. As a result of improvements in the hand-cylinder process, by the mid-nineteenth century it had become possible to make sheets of glass eight times the size of those known before. But the processes remained tricky and laborious, partly because of the difficulty of making durable casting tables that would not crack under extreme heat. It was still hard to conceive that glass could ever become a universal building material.

But in 1851 for the international exhibition in London, Joseph Paxton, a gardener and horticulturist, designed a structure like a greenhouse. As an observer noted at the time, it was "the first great building which was not of solid masonry construction." Paxton had become famous in 1849 when he succeeded in bringing the exotic equatorial South American water lily to bloom indoors. In the exhibition building, which he had designed following the example of earlier greenhouses in France and his own conservatories in England, Paxton gave a new prominence to glass. The whole construction was planned around the largest standard sheet of glass, then four feet long. This "Crystal Palace," as it came to be called, housed the first great international exhibit to show, in the words of Prince Albert, how modern industry was leading toward "the union of the human race." The exhibition structure itself, enclosing a ground area about four times that of St. Peter's in Rome, was by far the most extensive single building the world had seen. It foreshadowed how technology would remove the barriers of space. The whole vast building, a dazzled spectator exclaimed, "dissolves into a distant background where all materiality is blended into the atmosphere. . . . I call the spectacle incomparable and fairylike. It is a Midsummer Night's Dream seen in the clear light of midday."

Glass was now revealed on a grand scale as a medium that could erase old barriers. But before glass could shape the experience of the bulk of the American people, there had to be new mechanized techniques for making glass cheaply and in large quantities. Even before the Crystal Palace was up, Sir Henry Bessemer, later of steelmaking fame, had experimented with a revolutionary process for producing sheets of glass by passing the molten glass through rollers. The purpose was to find a continuous process, a flow technology for glass, which would avoid the need to make glass batch by batch and sheet by sheet. New tank furnaces were designed to produce a steady flow of molten glass which could be somehow flattened into long broad ribbons of uniform thickness. Sir William Siemens, the German-born inventor who emigrated to England, devised new regenerative gas-fired furnaces which reused the gases emitted by the heated glass to provide a continuous flow of large quantities of molten glass. Such gas-fired furnaces came only slowly to the United States, partly because wood was cheaper here and the glassworks had been smaller. By the 1880's, Chance Brothers, the pioneer British glass manufacturers, were passing molten glass between pairs of rollers to produce sheets, which were then ground and polished.

About the same time an ingenious method was devised to draw a flat sheet of glass direct from the furnace. A "bait," or sheet of metal, was dipped into the molten glass, and as the glass adhered to the bait, the bait was drawn upward to pull the glass out into a sheet. But as the molten glass was drawn upward the sheet tended to narrow and thicken into a thread, which made it hard to keep the withdrawing sheet of glass uniform in width or thickness. An elaborate cooling system was required to solidify the glass into the proper shape. The French were producing glass commercially in this way before World War I.

By the end of the nineteenth century, Americans were beginning to take the lead in organizing glass production and in developing new machinery. The rise of canning had increased the demand for jars, and there were numerous American improvements—for example, Mason's screw-top jar, which was patented in 1858. But the first important American contribution was in devising semi-automatic machines for making bottles. These were the most important new machines since the ancient invention of the glass-blowing iron for the making of glass containers. At the age of ten Michael J. Owens, son of a poor West Virginia miner, was shoveling coal into the furnace of a Wheeling glass factory. At the age of fifteen he was a skilled glass blower. Then, while working as manager of Edward Drummond Libbey's glass factory in Toledo, Ohio, Owens developed his pioneer bottle-blowing machine. Owens' essential idea was beautifully simple. From the surface of a pot of molten glass, a piston pump sucked a heated lump into a mold, and then the pump was reversed to blow the glass into the shape of a bottle. Owens patented this process by 1895, and within a decade had devised a completely automatic machine. On the perfected Owens machine (which was made of more than nine thousand parts), two men could produce twenty-five hundred bottles an hour. It was this machine, too, that would help light up the nation by making possible the quantity production of electric light bulbs.

Owens, who had no business experience, had the good luck to acquire his boss as collaborator. For Libbey, a New Englander who had inherited a glassworks from his father, was a businessman of energy, imagination, and organizing ability. In 1888 he had set up a new factory in Toledo, where he was attracted both by the large quantities of natural gas for firing the furnaces, and by the good glass sand found in the neighborhood. Libbey, though no inventor, knew a revolutionary invention when he saw one. He financed Owens' efforts to perfect his machine and actually put it to work in his factories. He then made Owens his partner and organized a firm to manufacture Owens' bottle-making machines for a world market. Libbey organized the Toledo Museum of Art in 1901, used his fortune to erect its first building in 1912, and helped make it a model for the dynamic role of museums in American education.

In contrast to bottle making, the machine making of flat glass, surprisingly enough, proved to be more complicated. The earnings of Owens' new bottle machine financed a new plate-glass industry when, in 1912, Libbey bought the patents of Irving Wightman Colburn for manufacturing sheet glass and then supported him while he perfected his processes. Colburn, also a New Englander, came from a Fitchburg, Massachusetts, textile-manufacturing family and very early turned the inventive bent of his family toward the new world of electricity. At the age of twenty-two he had started the town's first agency for the sale of electrical equipment, he installed its first electric-lighting and telephone systems, and then organized his own company for manufacturing electrical equipment. Moving west to Toledo, Colburn somehow became engrossed in glass manufacture, and gave the last nineteen years of his life to solving its problems.

The Colburn Window-Glass Machine was hailed by the *Scientific American* in 1908 as "the first machine for drawing window-glass continuously in any width." Colburn had devised a way, while drawing upward a sheet of molten glass from a glass furnace, to control the width of the sheet as it was pulled. The obvious problem was still that molten glass, like all viscous substances, tended to narrow to a thread as it was elongated upward. Colburn's clever device, which he spent years perfecting, was simply a set of rotating fire-clay cylinders on the surface of the molten-glass tank, one on each side of the emerging sheet. By rotating these in opposite directions and away from the middle of the emerging sheet, Colburn could keep the glass ribbon stretched as it emerged, and at the same time produce a glass free from wavy lines and blemishes. After the sheet was drawn vertically for a few feet it was reheated enough to be bent over a horizontal roller, and then it was pulled in a continuous process through an annealing oven. "The process is remarkable," the *Scientific American* observed, "for the quality of its product. The surface of the glass has a beautiful mirror-like fire polish far superior to the blown window-glass which we see every day. Even plate glass has a surface no better. . . . the spheres in the working chamber can be adjusted to produce glass of any thickness. We have seen specimens of glass made by this machine almost as thin as fine porcelain and other specimens almost as thick as plate glass." In 1916 Colburn's machines in the vast new factory of the Libbey-Owens Sheet Glass Company at Charleston, West Virginia, were turning out hundreds of square yards of plate glass in a continuous flow. A new era had arrived for one of man's oldest materials: a new means for opening windows to the world, for giving Americans a new kind of indoor-outdoor experience.

The next stages simply improved the technology of flow. The Corning ribbon machine, for example, used the same rollers which drew out the molten glass to impress on the ribbon the shape of glass bulbs, into which puffs of compressed air were injected. Then techniques were devised for drawing the plate horizontally between water-cooled rollers. When the assembly-line production of automobiles required vast, fast quantities of glass in a continuous stream, Henry Ford built a glass-making machine at River Rouge from which a 51-inch-wide ribbon of glass for automobiles emerged uninterruptedly at the rate of three and a half miles per day for two years, to a total length of nearly two thousand miles; and the Libbey-

Owens Glass Company became Libbey-Owens-Ford. The needs of the automobile for anti-glare glass, and especially for safety glass of various curved shapes, stirred glassmakers to a new range of products. The needs to soundproof and interline the automobile, and the search for simpler ways of making automobile bodies, produced fiberglass. Some even imagined that one day glass might displace steel as the basic material for cars. Meanwhile, glass did allow motorists to enjoy parlor comforts and indoor security as the landscape raced past.

* * *

But even before glass was bringing the outdoors indoors, and changing the architecture of life on the move, it was transforming the walls of buildings. The first great school of American skyscraper construction, the "Chicago School," was marked not only by its new uses of steel, but just as much by its pioneer use of glass. Steel framing, in place of heavy masonry, provided a new open framework for windows, of which Daniel Burnham, John Root, Louis Sullivan, and others took advantage. Even while Chicago architects like William Le Baron Jenney were still using cast iron, they began to put plate glass to dramatic new uses; for example, by designing wide panels to be filled with plate-glass windows. Contemporaries hailed Jenney's Leiter Building (1889) as "a giant structure . . . healthy to look at, lightsome and airy while substantial . . . a commercial pile in a style undreamed of when Buonarroti erected the greatest temple of Christianity." Daniel Burnham's Reliance Building (1894) was described as "a glass tower fifteen stories high." Louis Sullivan's classic Carson, Pirie, Scott Building (1899–1904) was distinguished by its "Chicago windows," as regular in width as the columned exterior of a Venetian *palazzo*, in which the dominant wall feature now was flat, transparent glass.

Glass became the basis of a new international style. In Germany, Walter Gropius and Mies van der Rohe (who were both later to come to America) and Le Corbusier in France played with glass in new ways. They used it for curtain walls, they exploited its brilliance and reflectiveness. By the mid-twentieth century the rhythmic, geometrical glass wall had become the most prominent feature of the American skyscraper, and it was the basic material for "enclosing" man now that he had begun living and working in the high air.

With the mass production of large sheets of transparent glass, unimagined new possibilities were found in the ancient material. For glass is nonyielding under pressure, it can be bent many times without showing the "fatigue" common in metals, it resists corrosion, and the raw materials of which glass is made are practically limitless in supply. By the mid-twentieth century the new technology had produced a vast and unprecedented array: variable transmission glass, electroluminescent glass, electrically conducting glass, microporous glass with variable resistance to air flow, solar-energy-collecting glass, malleable glass of steel-like strength, and countless other varieties. Glass was even used to produce white "blackboards" to brighten schoolrooms. There were "variable transmittance" windows which automatically became lighter or darker as the intensity of the sun's rays varied, and "limited vision" glass especially designed for acoustical and visual privacy "without total visual isolation."

Glass became a commonplace and a key to modern home design. A symbol of the modern American spirit was this removal of the sharp visual division between indoors and outdoors, with its new peril of walking through a glass door by mistake. "Sliding glass doors," one glass manufacturer advertised, "add new dimension to living by uniting the indoor-outdoor environment. . . . Glass makes smaller homes look bigger. On exterior walls it creates the dramatic indoor-outdoor flow looked for by homemakers. As room dividers, glass creates walls that close off and yet allows an open feeling."

In America, in the twentieth century, a window was almost as much to look into as to look out of or to receive light from. Glass became a symbol of the American ambivalence about all kinds of walls. By mid-century, "picture window" meant "a large window in a house usually dominating the room or wall in which it is located, and often designed or decorated to present an attractive view as seen from inside or outside the house."

Glass, which brought together indoors and outdoors and leveled the environment, became a medium of display, to excite and titillate everybody's desires for all the objects which one's fellow citizens possessed and which comprised the American Standard of Living. As we have seen, the light cast-iron frames of the early department stores used large sheets of glass to offer ground-floor windows, making the merchandise its own vivid advertisement, and by the mid-nineteenth century "show window" had entered the language. The ambiguous expression "window dressing," the concern of specialized artists and technicians, was on its way, and "window-shopping" became a new form of consumer onanism.

In these and countless other ways, glass expressed the magic of the new technology, the democratization of things. The fragile luxury material of the Older World became a sturdy medium for erasing the distinctions between places, between indoors and outdoors, and so, too, for blurring the distinctions among people.

MAKING EXPERIENCE REPEATABLE

"**H**ERE THEY ARE," Decca Records advertised in December 1934, "your favorite stars of radio, screen, and stage—in their greatest performances of instrument and voice! . . . Hear them *when* you want—as *often* as you want—right in your own home." Before the mid-twentieth century, Americans had perfected many new techniques for repeating sights and sounds at their own convenience. Uniqueness had once been the hallmark of experience. Each moment of life was supposed to be unrepeatable; the visible body and gestures, and the voice of a man, lasted during the brief span of his life and then dissolved with his death. Images of the past required the artistry of painter or sculptor; bygone actions could be recaptured only by the mimicry of the actor. The most vivid accounts of the dead were the work of men of letters.

Now without anyone having so intended it, a host of inventions and innovations, large and small, were beginning to add up to a whole new grasp on past experience. The terminus of human life was, of course, still there, but the content of the years of life was transformed. And the range of sights and sounds that any man could enjoy in a single lifetime was vastly widened.

* * *

The decisive innovation was photography. The story of the rise and perfection and simplification of photography has often been told, but photography as a transformer of experience has not been given its due. Such repeatable experience as was possible in Old World cultures had been mainly through the aristocratic arts of literature, painting, sculpture, and music, or through the popular but limited arts of minstrelsy, folklore, folk art, and folk music. Only language itself, or the ritual and liturgy of church and state, had tied people to the past by repetitions of word and gesture.

Photography took the first giant step toward democratizing the repeatable experience. This it did by transcending language and literature so that anybody, without even needing to be literate, could preserve at will the moments of experience for future repetition. Again the basic theoretical discoveries that would make this possible came from the Old World, and once again Americans were ingenious and resourceful in finding ways to apply these discoveries, in organizing, democratizing, and diffusing their uses.

For a full half-century after the Frenchman L. J. M. Daguerre made public his daguerreotype process in 1839, and even after the Englishman W. H. Fox Talbot had devised a way to make many positives from a single negative, photography remained an esoteric technique. On seeing Daguerre's photographs, the French artist Paul Delaroche exclaimed, "From today painting is dead!" Photography was already beginning to take over and transform some of the traditional roles of the artist, but photography in America would reach out far beyond the former domain of the artist.

By the time of the Civil War, many Americans had begun to feel the impact of photography. Even before the war, Mathew Brady's photographic portrait studios in New York and Washington were doing a thriving business. Then, during the Civil War, and soon thereafter, photographs by Brady and Alexander Gardner and others were exhibited in galleries, sold in books, and reproduced in newspapers. They brought to Americans a more vivid and more realistic view of that war than of any that had happened before. While action photography was not yet possible, photographs with startling and novel authenticity did portray the war's architectural and human debris.

But photography was still cumbersome and complicated. Traveling across the battlefields, Brady needed a special wagon to carry his equipment. Until about 1880, the photographer's equipment included (in addition to the camera, several lenses, and a tripod) bottles of different solutions for coating, sensitizing, developing, and fixing his negatives, besides glass plates, dishes, measures, funnels, a pail to carry rinsing water, and sometimes even a supply of water, and (so that he could perform the essential chemical operations on the spot) a portable dark-tent. The equipment even for a single day commonly weighed more than a hundred pounds, which the photographer who did not have a photographic wagon had to push around in a special wheelbarrow, or "photographic perambulator."

"Wet plates" made all this necessary. As long as the complicated wet-plate collodion process was the best and fastest way of making photographs, the photographer had to make his own photographic plates on the spot, and had to develop them instantly after they were exposed. The key to this system was a solution of collodion (guncotton dissolved in ether) containing potassium iodide, which, just before the picture taking, was poured onto a glass plate that was tilted back and forth until the solution formed an even, sticky coat. The sticky glass plate was then made sensitive to light by immersion in a silver nitrate solution. The picture had to be taken while the plate was still wet, because as the collodion dried its light-sensitivity was progressively lost; for this reason, too, the picture actually had to be developed before the glass plate had dried. This meant, of course, that the photographer had to carry his whole laboratory with him. And also that you could not be a photographer unless you were something of a photographic chemist adept at preparing as well as developing your photographic plates. Since the papers for making prints were not very sensitive, photographs were seldom enlarged, and therefore serious photographers had to use large plates (12 by 16 inches was not unusual), which were heavy to carry and required a bulky camera. Despite ingenious devices, no way was found for the photographer to manage without his dark-tent.

Photography could not become universal until there was some simpler method of taking a picture. By about 1880, English chemists had found a way to coat a glass plate with light-sensitive chemicals that would not lose their sensitivity when dry. Soon commercially produced glass plates were on the market. These "dry plates" could be used in a camera without any special chemical preparation on the spot by the photographer. But the glass plates still required were heavy, fragile, and hard to ship.

*   *   *

Centuries of chemical progress in the Old World had been required to make photography possible at all, but the transformation of photography into a popular, universal medium had to await one extremely practical, and apparently trivial, improvement. The missing link in the chain of progress toward democratizing photography was the invention of a new artificial substance, to be called "celluloid."

John Wesley Hyatt, an unsung American hero, was the son of a blacksmith in rural New York. In 1853, at the age of sixteen, he went west to Illinois, where he started life as a printer, and at twenty-four he had begun his inventing career with a new way of making solid emery wheels to sharpen kitchen knives. Then he heard of a $10,000 prize offered by a New York manufacturer for some new material which would be a satisfactory substitute for ivory in the making of billiard balls. Hyatt spent his nights and Sundays trying to solve the problem, and he finally succeeded by combining paper flock, shellac, and collodion, and won the prize. When he noticed that a removable "artificial skin" was left when the collodion dried, he began to look for still other new materials. Since he was not a chemist, he did not realize that he might easily have blown himself up by heating guncotton (nitrocellulose) under pressure, and he had not been discouraged by the earlier failures of English plastics chemists, because he did not even know of them. Another incentive for his experiments was the interest of dentists (plagued by the high price charged by the "rubber monopoly") in finding a cheaper substitute for rubber in molding dentures.

In 1873 Hyatt invented and registered the name "celluloid." What he had invented was actually not a new combination of chemicals but a new way of molding the plastic and making it stay hard. For some years Hyatt used celluloid only for making solid objects.

Hyatt went on to a versatile career of invention. By 1882 he and his brother had perfected a new system of water filtration. The previous systems had brought the water to a tank where coagulants were added to remove the impurities, which after twelve hours would settle to the bottom. Hyatt's ingenious scheme added the coagulants to the water while it was on the way to the filter, and thus removed the need for the large tanks and the long settling time. He invented a new kind of sugar-cane mill, which was cheaper to run and which produced a cane dry enough to serve as fuel. Besides an improved sewing machine which could make fifty lock stitches at once, a new way of making school slates, and a method of solidifying wood for bowling balls and golf-club heads, he devised a roller bearing which General Motors eventually made the basis for many of its improvements in the automobile.

The opportunity for Hyatt's celluloid to help transform the American consciousness came from the collaborating talents of another upstate New Yorker who combined a bent for invention with a talent for organization and for marketing. George Eastman, the son of a penmanship teacher who started the first commercial college in Rochester, began clerking in a bank and became so interested in photography that in 1877, when he was making only $1,500 a year, he spent $94 on a photographic outfit. Seeing that the new "dry plates" would make possible a whole new market for photographic equipment, within two years Eastman had invented and patented a new machine for coating the glass plates. He saw, too, that the perfection of dry-plate photography would be more than merely a convenience for professional photographers, because now, for the first time, the taking of a picture could be separated from the making and the developing of the plate. But he also saw that a popular market for photography would have to await a substitute for the heavy, breakable, hard-to-ship glass plates. Until the 1880's, of course (because photographs were commonly made on emulsion-coated glass), photography was not especially associated with the word "film." What Eastman needed was some flexible, light, and unbreakable substance that could be coated with the photographic emulsion. In 1884 Eastman patented a way of coating strips of paper so that they would work in a camera, and from this starting point he initiated the popular revolution in photography.

To dramatize the novelty of his kind of camera, he decided to make up a word that would be short, distinctive, and (looking toward a world market) pronounceable in any language. It is said that he started with "K," the first letter of his mother's maiden name, and finally came up with "Kodak." Eastman registered the trademark "Kodak" in 1888 and put his new camera on the market. A marvel of compactness and simplicity, his little black box was about the size of the later familiar "Brownie" box camera. "The Kodak," Eastman's first advertisement read, "is the smallest, lightest and simplest of all Detective Cameras—for the ten operations necessary with most Cameras to make one exposure, we have only *3 simple* movements. No focusing. No finder required. Size 3½ by 3¾ by 6½ in. Makes 100 Exposures. Weight 35 oz."

The camera had no focusing apparatus and only a single speed on the shutter. Of course, since the camera also had no finder, the photographer might not be able to include precisely what he wanted in the picture, but on the other hand, he did not have to worry about adjusting or focusing his apparatus. Eastman had made everybody into a photographer. And his Kodak flourished on the slogan "You press the button—we do the rest."

Eastman shrewdly had made an additional selling point of the smallness of his Kodak by calling it a "detective camera." Other manufacturers had already put on the market an assortment of smaller cameras camouflaged in the shape of opera glasses, paper parcels, luggage, books, and watches; some were made to be hidden in hats or behind neckties. These were called "detective" cameras because, in contrast to the old large boxes, they were supposed to be able to take a picture surreptitiously, as a detective would. There was something intriguing about this idea, but actually these other products were little more than toys.

Eastman's was a "detective camera," too. But unlike the others, his was inexpensive for its day, and it really worked! What he offered Americans was a photographic system as remarkable in its own way as the organizing achievements of nineteenth-century fur traders or of twentieth-century assembly-line builders. The $25 which East-man charged for one of his simple black boxes included the first roll of film, together with the processing of all its one hundred pictures. When the owner had used up the roll, he sent the whole camera to the factory. Then the factory sent back his camera (loaded with a new roll of film, for $10) and the mounted prints of all his successful pictures. George Eastman's system, like Eli Whitney's interchange-able system, was a substitute for skill. To any American with $25 (however ignorant of chemistry or photography) Eastman now of-fered the power to make pictures.

The weak link in Eastman's system was the film itself. At the Kodak factory, the emulsion bearing the image had to be stripped from the paper, then pressed into a sheet of clear gelatin, and dried. To avoid this delicate operation there was need for a better film ma-terial, preferably one that was both flexible and transparent. Cellu-loid, which had been on the market for fifteen years, would prove to be the solution to the problem. While Eastman was one of the first to discover this fact, others too grasped the possibility and entered the race for a practical film. Until this time Hyatt's celluloid had been used only for solid objects. Then, in 1888 a Philadelphia photographer-plate manufacturer asked Hyatt to produce sheets of clear celluloid with a uniform thickness of 1/100 inch, which he then coated with the photographic emulsion. This celluloid was still too thick and inflexible for roll film.

The first application for a patent on transparent roll film made of celluloid came from the Reverend Hannibal W. Goodwin, a sixty-five-year-old Episcopal minister of Newark, New Jersey, who had been trying to find some material that was better than glass for the photographic illustrations of Scriptural stories he was making for Sunday Schools. After ten years' labor, on May 2, 1887, he applied for a patent for a "Photographic Pellicule." Meanwhile Eastman had set one of his researchers to work, and two years later Eastman re-ceived his own patent for the "manufacture of flexible photographic films." There followed the familiar lengthy litigation over patent rights. And it was fifteen years (just before Goodwin's death) before Goodwin actually received his patent. During this time the energetic

Eastman had been manufacturing celluloid film on a vast scale. He was now producing nearly 90 percent of all roll film, and he had monopolized the world market.

With his new celluloid roll film, easily loaded and easily developed (no need any more for the delicate stripping operation), Eastman opened up the world of amateur photography. The novel features of the Kodak, as an English historian observed, "enabled the camera, like the bicycle, to enrich the leisure hours of the many." Soon millions of Americans were snapping pictures, and camera clubs sprang up all over the world. While the earlier photography had flourished on the making of studio portraits and the occasional outdoor photographing of significant scenes by professionals, the new popular photography found new subjects. What had once been advertised as the "Royal Road to Drawing" now became the democratic highway to art. Everyman could be his own artist. Years before, when Oliver Wendell Holmes saw Brady's realistic "stereographs" of Civil War battlefields, he had called the camera "the mirror with a memory." Now anyone could provide himself with such a mirror, so that his everyday experience could be captured for visual repetition at any time in the future. Now, instead of merely photographing persons or scenes that were especially memorable or historic, Americans would photograph at random and then remember the scenes *because* they had been photographed. Photography became a device for making experience worth remembering.

* * *

On October 8, 1888, a statement was filed with the Patent Office by Thomas A. Edison:

> I am experimenting upon an instrument which does for the eye what the phonograph does for the ear, which is the recording and reproduction of things in motion, and in such a form as to be both cheap, practical and convenient. This apparatus I call a Kinetoscope, "moving view." . . . The invention consists in photographing continuously a series of pictures occurring at intervals . . . and photographing these

series of pictures in a continuous spiral on a cylinder or plate
in the same manner as sound is recorded on a phonograph.

Soon after beginning work on his Kinetoscope, Edison made
certain basic discoveries. He found, for example, that while his recording phonograph had to run continuously to provide a record of
continuous sound, a camera record of pictures of motion would have
to run intermittently so that the phenomenon of persistence of vision would give the viewer the illusion of motion. It had to be possible, therefore, to take pictures at rapid intervals, and then show them
successively without a blur. But at first Edison had been dominated
by the analogy with his rudimentary phonograph, which then
worked by recording sound on a cylinder. Tiny pictures arranged in
series on a cylinder were viewed directly through a magnifying lens.
Edison very early sensed the importance of celluloid. The perfection of a feasible camera and projector that would show moving
pictures of considerable duration depended on finding a suitably
flexible substance for the film. It is hard to imagine how Edison
could have made his movie camera without celluloid, or something
like it. When he first saw the emulsion-coated sheets of celluloid,
which were still too rigid to be handled in rolls, he wrapped some
sheets around the big cylinder of his Kinetoscope machine. But with
celluloid of suitable characteristics he hoped to be able to abandon
his cylinder design and (as had been impossible with glass plates)
somehow run continuous strips of film directly through his machine.
Edison was no longer working on a "phonograph arrangement"
(as Eastman had called Edison's earlier efforts, because they were so
closely modeled on the phonograph), but on an entirely new type of
camera for taking and projecting moving pictures. When he heard of
Eastman's improved roll film, he urged Eastman to help him make a
motion-picture camera by producing the flexible film in long strips.
And when Edison's assistant, in late 1889, brought him the first fifty-
foot strip, Edison, with a "seraphic smile," shouted, "That's it—
we've got it—now work like hell!"
With the new strip film Edison made his first working Kinetoscope, which was the grandfather of all later motion-picture ma-

chines. Positive prints on strip film were rolled from one spool to another inside a cabinet while the spectator looked directly at the illuminated film through a magnifying lens in a fixed eyepiece in a hole in the cabinet. This was a peep show for only one person at a time. The screen was yet to come, but the basic ideas were there. When Edison applied for a patent on an "Apparatus for Exhibiting Photographs of Moving Objects" in August 1891, he still made no mention of a projecting apparatus or a white screen. In any case, the photographs he had been using were so crude that they would not bear magnifying and projecting. Edison still assumed that the whole entertainment future of moving pictures would be like that of the phonograph, which was then used by individuals who inserted a coin in a machine to hear their favorite tune. Edison, "The Man of a Thousand Ideas," was still so casual about this peep-show toy that when his lawyers advised him to take out European patents at a cost of $150, he refused because, he said, "It isn't worth it."

While Edison sometimes misjudged the commercial promise of his ideas, he did have the inventor's genius for recognizing the essence of a problem and so seeing the simple solution. He showed this in his approach to moving pictures by intuitively avoiding the blind alleys which had already brought modest fame to others. English and French inventors, whose work Edison knew, had tried to record motion by placing numerous cameras along the line of movement, each photographing a successive scene. Eadweard Muybridge, an English-born photographer working in California, had created a world-wide sensation in 1878 with his series of pictures published as "The Horse in Motion." He had first taken these in order to satisfy a whim of former Governor Leland Stanford of California, who wanted to advertise his prize trotter, Occident, and he incidentally answered an old question by proving that a galloping horse actually had all his feet off the ground at certain moments. Muybridge's work had stimulated a French professor of physiology who was interested in animal locomotion to invent a camera which would take a series of exposures on a single glass plate and so photograph the motion from a single point of view. Edison made his crucial simplifying decision when he determined not to follow the path of Muybridge. Instead of making a series of motion photographs from different points of view, he decided, following the French professor's hint, to devise a machine that would photograph motion from a single point of view.

Edison's other elementary insight (which now seems so obvious as hardly to be an insight at all) was to imagine a simple unified system; that is, an arrangement which would somehow make use of the very same film on which the moving pictures were recorded as the moving pictures to be viewed. Could a series of photographs that had been taken on a single film somehow provide the pictures to be viewed in motion? For a feasible motion-picture system this idea was as crucial as Eastman's idea of separating picture taking from picture developing had been in popularizing still photography. In Edison's scheme, then, what a single camera saw and recorded was precisely what the spectator would see.

Edison boldly adopted celluloid film in a standard width for both cameras and projectors. Then he added another marvelously simple idea, never before used on photographic film: he perforated the edge of the film. The two tiny rectangular perforations which he punched on each side of each picture solved many problems at once. By using two toothed wheels, one on each side of the film to be exposed or to be projected, Edison could now produce the controlled intermittent motion of the film which his predecessors had been unable to provide and which was required to give the viewer the illusion of motion. The Edison-designed film became the standard. While railroad gauges varied throughout the world, while some nations used Fahrenheit and others Centigrade, while mankind could not all agree on a system of measuring land or of weighing potatoes, Edison's 35-millimeter film would rule the world. In this there was a poetic appropriateness; for movies were the American invention which, more than any other before, focused the vision of the world. And motion pictures became the great democratic art, which, naturally enough, was the characteristically American art.

*   *   *

The technology of repeatable experience was self-propagating. Each step taken toward capturing, recording, and making replayable another aspect of experience opened the way and created a demand for still another improvement and still newer techniques. Edison's own interest in motion pictures had been awakened by his determination to use photography, along with the phonograph, to make talking pictures. And the phonograph, even more than the camera, would be a product of American energy and ingenuity. Perhaps this was because sound was a simpler phenomenon than sight. The problem of recording sound was essentially mechanical. It required very little new theory, and very little chemistry.

There are few modern inventions of comparable importance which in their first making owed as much to a single man as did the phonograph. Others abroad were conceiving the possibility of a machine to record and replay sounds, but it was Edison who made the first practical talking machine. He had been led toward the phonograph by his work on an instrument to record and repeat telegraph dots and dashes. Then, in 1877, after he had invented a transmitter for Alexander Graham Bell's telephone, Edison became worried that the high cost of telephones might limit their use. He thought that many more people would benefit from the telephone if there could be what he called a "telephone repeater." Edison's notion was that if somehow a person could record his spoken message, then the record could be taken to a central station where it could be replayed and transmitted to the addressee over a telephone. In this way even a person who could not afford a telephone might still send a message in his own voice. When Edison had his inspiration for the shape of the machine, he made a model. It was a rotating, grooved metal cylinder around which a piece of tin foil was wrapped to record the sounds. Into the machine Edison shouted the verses of "Mary Had a Little Lamb"; then the machine played back Edison's voice to Edison and his assistants. "I was never so taken aback in all my life," he recalled. "Everybody was astonished. I was always afraid of things that worked the first time." Edison applied for his patent in December 1877, and received it within two months—an unusually brief time, because the patent officials could find in their files nothing remotely resembling this device.

The news of this latest example of Edison's wizardry created a sensation. Around the country in public halls the machine was demonstrated as a novelty. A single "exhibition" phonograph brought in more than $1,800 in one week in Boston, where people gladly paid admission to hear a machine that could talk in any language, that could bark like a dog, crow like a cock, and cough "so believably that physicians in the audience could instinctively begin to write prescriptions." In the *North American Review* for June 1878, Edison forecast ten uses for his phonograph:

1. Letter writing, and all kinds of dictation without the aid of a stenographer.
2. Phonographic books, which will speak to blind people without effort on their part.
3. The teaching of elocution.
4. Music.—The phonograph will undoubtedly be liberally devoted to music.
5. The family record; preserving the sayings, the voices, and the last words of the dying members of the family, as of great men.
6. Music boxes, toys, etc.—A doll which may speak, sing, cry or laugh may be promised our children for the Christmas holidays ensuing.
7. Clocks, that should announce in speech the hour of the day, call you to lunch, send your lover home at ten, etc.
8. The preservation of language by reproduction of our Washingtons, our Lincolns, our Gladstones.
9. Educational purposes; such as preserving the instructions of a teacher so that the pupil can refer to them at any moment; or learn spelling lessons.
10. The perfection or advancement of the telephone's art by the phonograph, making that instrument an auxiliary in the transmission of permanent records.

For more than fifteen years Edison insisted that his Number 1 use— for dictating letters—was the only one likely to find a wide market. With scant musical knowledge or sensitivity himself (Edison was partially deaf), at first he found it hard to believe it would be profitable to mass-produce the recordings of musical performances. Nevertheless, by 1894 Edison had decided to try to promote the phonograph for entertainment, and he had begun designing an inexpensive machine to sell to everybody. In 1897 he made a machine that sold for $20. But for some time, the most popular use of the phonograph was in public places for machines that played a record for a nickel.

Edison's phonograph cylinders were inconvenient and expensive to reproduce. They were to the phonograph what the glass plate was to the camera. The popularizing of the phonograph and a mass market for recordings would await the invention of a new design and new materials.

This problem was not solved by Edison himself, but by Emile Berliner, the music-loving son of a Talmudic scholar in Hanover, Germany, who emigrated to the United States at the age of eighteen. Although he had only a grade-school education, he found work in a scientific laboratory where he began studying acoustics and electricity. Before Berliner was twenty-six he had invented a telephone transmitter which was superior to the one that Alexander Graham Bell had exhibited at the Philadelphia Centennial Exhibition in 1876, based on a new principle that later made possible the microphone. In 1878 Berliner sold his telephone invention to the Bell Company for a large sum; then, turning his attention to the phonograph, he developed a new way of recording.

Edison's original phonograph operated on the "hill-and-dale" method. The sound caused the recording needle to vibrate up and down and made vertical grooves of varying depths; these were the movements which, when replayed, reproduced the sound for the listener. As the wax phonograph cylinder was rotated, the needle followed this groove. In order to keep the needle and sound box moving along the length of the cylinder to follow the groove of Edison's rotating wax cylinder, a special screw mechanism was required.

Berliner simplified both the recording and the reproducing machines, and incidentally made easier the mass production of records. Instead of a cylinder, Berliner used a flat disk. And instead of the up-and-down movement of the needle in Edison's "hill-and-dale" system, Berliner recorded his sound with a needle's sideways zigzag. This scheme, which Berliner had working successfully by 1888, proved to have many advantages. The need for a special screw mechanism was removed, since the spiral groove on the revolving platter automatically kept the needle moving along at the proper speed. Disks, compared with cylinders, were simpler and easier to reproduce, and more convenient to store.

None of these advances could have democratized the phonograph without some inexpensive way of duplicating the disks. And Berliner soon supplied this, too. Instead of making the master record on an all-wax plate, he used a disk of zinc covered with wax. After the music was recorded on this wax surface, acid was applied to etch the characteristic zigzags into the zinc. And this provided the "master" from which duplicates could be made. A metal casting (or negative matrix) was made of the original record, and then stamped into a suitable material, leaving the impression of the original. In this way thousands of duplicates could be made from a single original recording. It was still necessary to find a suitable material for the duplicates, but after six years of experiment, Berliner succeeded in that too. He used hard rubber, and then made a new durable material from shellac. At first these were called "plates," but by 1896 they were known by the new name of "record." On Berliner's inventions, and on his simplification of the phonograph and its records, the vast American record industry would be founded. This was not the end of Berliner's ingenuity or imagination. In 1919 when he was nearly seventy, this remarkable man helped design a helicopter that actually flew.

Berliner's "Gramophone" (the trademark for his invention) awakened the imagination of the twenty-nine-year-old owner of a small machine shop in Camden, New Jersey, to whom Berliner had taken his primitive machine to improve its motor. "It sounded like a partially educated parrot with a sore throat and a cold in the head," Eldridge Johnson recalled, "but the little wheezy instrument caught my attention and held it fast and hard." It was Johnson's craftsmanship and production know-how which, by 1897, had transformed the expensive "partially educated parrot" into the mass-produced "Improved Gramophone." Before long "His Master's voice" made the irrelevant image of a black-and-white fox terrier listening to Johnson's machine one of the leading images in American iconography. Johnson founded the Victor Talking Machine Company, which helped create, and then for a while dominated, this new market. An unpredicted advantage of the disk appeared in 1904, when an enterprising New Yorker started a German company with the novel idea of stamping a record with grooves on *both* sides.

*   *   *

"The Menace of Mechanical Music," in *Appleton's Magazine* for September 1906, was a blast against the newly repeatable experience by one of the nation's most popular composers. John Philip Sousa, son of a Portuguese immigrant, had composed the International Fantasy for Offenbach's orchestra at the Philadelphia Centennial Exhibition in 1876, and as conductor of the United States Marine Band from 1880 to 1892 was to the march (some said) what Johann Strauss was to the waltz. Financed by a musical impresario, he formed Sousa's Band, performed at the Chicago Columbian Exposition of 1893, and became rich and famous by regular tours around the United States. Sales of the sheet music for his most famous composition, "Stars and Stripes Forever" (composed in 1897), brought him about $300,000. "I foresee a marked deterioration in American music and musical taste," Sousa warned, "an interruption in the musical development of the country, and a host of other injuries to music in its artistic manifestation, by virtue—or rather by vice—of the multiplication of the various music-reproducing machines."

Exercising his considerable imagination, Sousa conjured up the future horrors of "musical automatics." Going on from the menace of the player piano, he heard "the exclamation of the little boy who rushed into his mother's room with the appeal: 'O mamma, come into the drawing-room; there is a man in there playing the piano with his hands!' "

There was a time when the pine woods of the north were sacred to summer simplicity. . . . But even now the invasion of the north has begun, and the ingenious purveyor of canned music is urging the sportsman, on his way to the silent places with gun and rod, tent and canoe, to take with him some disks, cranks, and cogs to sing to him as he sits by the firelight, a thought as unhappy and incongruous as canned salmon by a trout brook.

In the prospective scheme of mechanical music, we shall see man and maiden in a light canoe under the summer moon upon an Adirondack lake with a gramophone caroling love songs from amidships. The Spanish cavalier must abandon his guitar and serenade his beloved with a phonograph under his arm. . . . Never again will the soldier hear the defiant call of the bugle to battle, and the historical lines must be changed to:

"Gentlemen of the French guards, turn on your phonographs first."

And the future d'Auteroches will reply:

"Sir, we will never turn on our phonographs first; please to turn yours first."

Sousa was outraged by the prospect that the authentic, spontaneous voice of man's soul should be hampered by "a machine that tells the story day by day, without variation, without soul, barren of the joy, the passion, the ardor that is the inheritance of man alone." And he asked, "When a mother can turn on the phonograph with the same ease that she applies to the electric light, will she croon her baby to slumber with sweet lullabys, or will the infant be put to sleep by machinery? Children are naturally imitative, and if, in their infancy, they hear only phonographs, will they not sing, if they sing at all, in imitation and finally become simply human phonographs—without soul or expression?" Sousa finally observed that, in 1906, the copyright laws appeared to give no protection to the composer when his work was sold on records. And if these new machines should deprive composers of their reward, would musicians still go on composing?

The 1909 copyright law provided protection for composers, and pressure by the American Society of Composers, Authors, and Publishers (founded in 1914) succeeded in procuring royalties. Before the third decade of the twentieth century, the nation was flooded with "musical automatics." By 1914 more than 500,000 phonographs were being produced each year, and five years later the figure reached 2¼ million. In 1921 the annual production of records exceeded 100 million; in the post–World War II year of 1947, over 400 million records were sold. Improvements in the technique of recording (with an electrical in place of a mechanical or "acoustic" method, by 1925) and reproducing, and improvements in the fidelity of the sound, increased the demand and before long produced an exacting and sophisticated new audience for *recorded* sound.

The new techniques which the British Coastal Command had required in World War II for the training records they made to illustrate the difference between the sounds of German and of British submarines eventually produced "full frequency range reproduction" (ffrr), and set a new standard of fidelity for reproduced music. Then in 1948 came the long-playing microgroove disk, which slowed down the speed from 78 to 33⅓ revolutions per minute and increased the playing time from four to twenty-three minutes.

Just as the Kodak made every man his own artist, now with the phonograph every man became his own musician. And so the vaudeville joke: "Do you play on the piano?" "No, but I do play on the phonograph." The phonograph was used, of course, to spread the pleasures of the classical-music repertoire. But it gave a new incentive to the makers of popular music. Formerly the famed music makers had been those who composed or performed ceremonial or symphonic or operatic or chamber-music works under the patronage of wealthy aristocrats. Now the great American public could become the patron. Music was being democratized, not only because the nation's millions could now enjoy music once reserved for a few, but also because the millions now commanded the most profitable musical market, had a new power to shape musical taste, a way of making it worth a composer's or performer's while to give the millions what *they* wanted.

Without the phonograph, it is difficult to imagine how American popular music, before the era of radio, could have sent its sounds around the world. In May 1917 Victor turned out its first "jass" record—"the latest thing in the development of music"—a blues and a one-step played by the Original Dixieland Jazz Band. The fat profits of the record companies in the early 1920's, as we have seen, were explained mainly by the annual sales of millions of jazz records. Never before had a form of music so permeated a vast nation, or become so universal an influence in the daily life of a whole society. "Does Jazz Put the Sin in Syncopation?" was being asked by an August 1921 article in the *Ladies' Home Journal*. And the National Music Chairman of the General Federation of Women's Clubs denounced jazz—

> that expression of protest against law and order, that bolshevik element of license striving for expression in music. . . . Dancing to Mozart minuets, Strauss waltzes and Sousa two-steps certainly never led to the corset check-room, which holds sway in hotels, clubs, and dance halls. Nor would the girl who wore corsets in those days have been dubbed "old ironsides" and left a disconsolate wallflower in a corner of the ballroom. . . . Such music has become an influence for evil.

The phonograph now made popular fashions in music possible on a new scale. By the mid-1950's the test of a musical celebrity was how many "golden records" of at least one-million circulation he had turned out. The phonograph was making a commonplace of musical classics. While the fortunes of the "top ten" popular records themselves became news as the ratings changed every week, it was now finally possible in everybody's living room to revive the best music of earlier centuries. "This mechanical civilization of ours," Jacques Barzun observed in 1954, "has performed a miracle . . . it has, by mechanical means, brought back to life the whole repertory of Western music. . . . Formerly, a fashion would bury the whole musical past except a few dozen works arbitrarily selected. . . . the whole literature of one of the arts has sprung into being—it is like the Renaissance rediscovering the ancient classics and holding them fast by means of the printing press."

The paradoxes of repeatable experience were nowhere more dramatic. A record that was in the top ten one week might become unsalable a few weeks later. Yet in 1954 Americans could find in their record stores five unabridged versions of Bach's *St. Matthew Passion*, ten of Mozart's *D Minor Piano Concerto*, twenty-one versions of Tchaikovsky's *Romeo and Juliet* or of Beethoven's *Eroica*. The machines that brought a vast new stock of repeatable experience into everyone's living room or automobile had the power both to enrich musical experience and to trivialize it.

Which force was running stronger? In scores of new ways, the record makers enlivened the common experience with new categories of musical experience and actually brought novel forms of music into being. In 1956 the Broadway production of *My Fair Lady* was entirely financed by the Columbia Broadcasting System with a view to the exclusive rights to sell the records. Their investment proved fully justified by the unprecedented sales of five million of the original-cast albums. After that it was common for Broadway musicals to be financed by record companies which hoped to recoup their investment by selling the repeated experience on records.

When music became only another, universally accessible form of repeatable experience, it lost much of its distinctiveness as an experience. Music then was only another element in the atmosphere and the environment, like the temperature, the humidity, or the illumination. By 1960 the new techniques were being used to make music of any and every kind ubiquitous. "We don't sell music," a spokesman for Muzak, the most prosperous seller of piped-in sound, declared, "we sell programing. We believe that the best results are attained when you consider the factors of time, environment and activity." Before the 1950's were out, Muzak sound conditioning could be heard in (among other places) the Yankee Stadium, Fenway Park, Slenderella Reducing Salons, cemeteries in Los Angeles and San Angelo, Texas, a Kansas City puppet factory, a Chicago sausage plant, pet hospitals, the vaults of the Federal Reserve banks, an olive-stuffing plant in Cincinnati, a uranium company in Denver, and under water in the swimming pool at Eaton's Motel in Hamilton, Ohio. When "music" was everywhere, was it music any more? Were listeners really listening? Did Americans really know whether or not they were listening?

* * *

The capacity of the camera and the phonograph to make experience repeatable was still limited by the time required to develop the film or to manufacture the record that could be replayed. The coming of "instant replay"—techniques for recording experience in a form that was immediately replayable—was another decisive step in dissolving the uniqueness of an experience.

The crucial new idea was magnetic recording. If sound could be transformed into magnetic impulses and a wire could be magnetized a little piece at a time, then the wire would record the sound, which could immediately be played back simply by transforming the magnetic impulses into sound again. A device to accomplish this was the invention of Valdemar Poulsen, a young Danish engineer who patented it first in Denmark in 1898, then in the United States two years later. The whole idea seemed to contradict the current experience with magnets. For example, it was common knowledge that when a bar magnet was broken into little magnets, all the little magnets would be equally magnetized, each with its two poles; and if they were stuck back together again, the result would be only one magnet. Could it be possible, then, to magnetize not a whole bar, but just one spot on a wire? perhaps this could be done by drawing the wire rapidly past the electromagnet so that different spots would be magnetized to a different degree. If this could somehow be managed there would be obvious advantages over all the other known kinds of recording: a magnetic recording could be used countless times without a loss in acoustical quality, and the recording material could be used again and again simply by demagnetizing. Poulsen called his device the "telegraphone," and with it won the Grand Prix at the Paris Exposition of 1900, where it was as sensational as the telephone had been in Philadelphia in 1876.

When the American Telegraphone Company proved a financial

failure, the idea of magnetic recording seemed to be dead, and it was not resurrected for two decades. In Poulsen's original design the recording wire had to travel so fast that enormous quantities of wire were required, and rewinding it took so long that it caused a delay in playback; and also the playback level was too low for practical use. But the United States Naval Research Laboratory continued its researches with the result that tape began to replace wire in the 1930's. During World War II, magnetic recording was revived and exploited for its obvious advantages under extremes of heat, cold, and vibration when disk recording was not feasible. Wire-recording devices were soon compacted into pocket size. By the end of the war, magnetic recording had been proven superior to disk recording for many purposes. A steel tape, it was found, could be replayed a hundred thousand times without measurable deterioration; improvements in amplification and in recording materials such as homogeneous paper and plastic tape with magnetic coating promised a new versatility.

The magnetic recording of visual images was more complicated, but it came soon enough, hastened by the rise of television. Immediate video playback would not only provide the viewer with instant images of what had just happened; it meant that the producer of a program could monitor pictures while he was taking them. But the earliest video-tape recorders posed problems similar to those of sound tape: they ran at excessive speeds and used too much tape. By 1956 a video recorder was developed that ran at the same speed as sound recorders. The next year the first practical video-tape recorder was manufactured by RCA and Ampex, and came into general use; although it gave a sharp image, the recording apparatus was cumbersome. By the mid-1960's the improved "helical scan recorder" offered a less sharp image, but used a light and portable recording machine that could be taken anywhere.

By the 1960's, "instant replay" had become commonplace. Americans watching a boxing match, a horse race, or a baseball or football game could, at the pleasure of the producer, see any moment replayed any number of times. But tragedy and melodrama could also be replayed. On November 24, 1963, video tape showing Jack

Ruby shooting Lee Harvey Oswald, the assassin of President Kennedy, was reshown within hours across the nation.

Ever since the advent of radio, Americans had listened in on the excitement at Times Square as the old year ebbed. The American's new sense of time was symbolized on New Year's Eve, December 31, 1971, and reported nostalgically in *The New Yorker*'s Talk of the Town:

> The holy moment came: Lombardo counted backward "Nine, eight, seven, six, five . . . ," the glowing ball atop the Allied Chemical Building fell, the faithful little miracle had occurred. Horns, shouting, television patterns and spirals, "Auld Lang Syne." Then, incredibly, the whole half-minute was replayed in instant replay. "Seven, six, five, four . . ." and the same horns silently blew and the same spirals wildly flickered, and we seemed to be being asked to inspect some nuance in the event. Had it been a quarterback sneak? A double reverse? Had something replayable indeed occurred? If not, was the second time less real than the first? Were we insane? Or was the replayer? Pondering such bottomless questions, we curled up in our small fever and fell numbly into 1972.

Home tape recorders soon gave the American consumer his opportunity to relive at will any of his personally experienced moments. Families gathering at birthdays, Thanksgiving, or Christmas were no longer driven to reminisce in order to compare impressions of earlier occasions. On went the tape recorder to make reminiscence superfluous.

One of the charms of photography was the suspense as to whether and, if so, how your picture "came out." And of course this led to the taking of repeated photographs just to be sure that there would be one satisfactory result. In 1947 an ingenious, Go-Getting New Englander, Edwin H. Land, invented what he described as a "camera that delivers a finished photograph immediately after exposure is made." Photographic historians and critics, and Land himself, first hailed the new achievement as important mainly for the *art* of photography. In the early days, they recalled, the man who made a daguerreotype or a tintype could see a finished positive within a few minutes after he had taken the picture. But the later negative-positive system postponed the opportunity for such comparisons by dividing the process of *taking* from the process of *making* a photograph.

Land's Polaroid camera provided a new version of the one-step technique. Now the Polaroid photographer, like any other artist, could observe the subject and see his likeness of it at the same time. As Land himself explained:

> By making it possible for the photographer to observe his work and his subject matter simultaneously, and by removing most of the manipulative barriers between the photographer and the photograph, it is hoped that many of the satisfactions of working in the early arts can be brought to a new group of photographers. . . . The process must be concealed from—non-existent for—the photographer, who by definition need think of the art in the *taking* and not in *making* photographs. . . . In short, all that should be necessary to get a good picture is to *take* a good picture, and our task is to make that possible.

The ordinary citizen, impatient for a replica of the moment, found in Polaroid the convenience of seeing a copy of his experience (a "double take") only a minute after. In May 1972 Polaroid announced a camera that produced a positive print instantaneously, just as it came out of the camera, within two seconds after exposure.

*   *   *

In their beginning the new techniques of repeatable experience had added a dimension to life, making experience richer and subtler. "You cannot say you have thoroughly seen anything," the French novelist Émile Zola observed in 1900, "until you have got a photograph of it, revealing a lot of points which otherwise would be unnoticed, and which in most cases could not be distinguished." Everybody's new power to take pictures and, after the tape recorder, to make sound recordings, was more than another source of sparetime pleasure. This new technology was reshaping human consciousness.

In the democratic booster-enthusiasm for life enrichment through art and hobby-fun, the wider meaning of these techniques was easily overlooked. It was easy to see that the camera and the phonograph instantly increased knowledge or widened experience. But it was hard to foresee that in the longer run, these and other machines that made experience repeatable could actually dilute experience, dull consciousness, and flatten sensations. Originally, many of the charms of the photograph and of the phonograph record came from their novelty—and from the very difficulty of securing a good photograph or a good recording. But within a few decades, when these techniques had become instamatic, cheap and easy and universal, what was their meaning in the American's experience?

Did the very perfection of techniques for widening experience, and especially those for creating and diffusing the repeatable experience—did all this, somehow, impoverish experience in the very process of democratizing it? Was it inevitable that a democratized experience, however rich and technologically sophisticated, should be impoverished? Was there an inherent contradiction between the aim of democracy—to enrich the citizen's everyday life—and its modern means? Did the very instruments of life enrichment, once available to all, somehow make life blander and less poignant? Could it possibly be true that while *democratizing* (the process) enriched, *democracy* (the product) diluted? These were some novel, tantalizing questions which would haunt American democracy in the twentieth century.

All this suggested still another question, a clue perhaps to the hidden rationale of the American booster spirit. Was the brighter, richer, more open life that America promised a product, then, not of a *high* standard of living, but only of an always *rising* standard of living? Did the human richness of American democracy come not from the attainment of wealth, but from the reaching for it? Perhaps, then, the mission and the doom of American technology were the continual discovery of new techniques. Perhaps the best things in democracy came not from having but from seeking, not from being well off but from becoming better off. Would a high standard of living, no matter how high, always open vistas that would become flat and stale? And was it necessary to keep the standard of living ever rising if the vistas were to remain wide and open and fresh?

EXTENDING EXPERIENCE:

The New Segregation

ÉMILE ZOLA'S OBSERVATION that "you cannot say you have thoroughly seen anything until you have got a photograph of it," now applied a hundredfold in the world of television. By the late twentieth century the man on the spot, the viewer of the experience where it actually happened, began to feel confined and limited. The full flavor of the experience seemed to come only to the "viewer," the man in the television audience. Suddenly, from feeling remote and away the televiewer was painlessly and instantaneously transported *into* the experience. Television cameras made him a ubiquitous viewer. The man there in person was spacebound, crowd-confined, while the TV viewer was free to see from all points of view, above the heads of others, and behind the scenes. Was it he who was *really* there?

Making copies of experience, sights and sounds, for *later* use was one thing. Conquering space and time for instantaneous viewing was quite another, and even more revolutionary.

*   *   *

Before the Civil War, Morse's telegraph had hastened the pace of business and was speeding news to the papers within a day after it happened. When Bell's telephone was displayed at the Philadelphia Centennial Exposition in 1876, in the very year that Alexander Graham Bell had received his first telephone patent, it was still a great curiosity. Only two years later the first telephone appeared in the White House, under President Rutherford B. Hayes. Scores of inventors, including Thomas A. Edison and Emile Berliner, improved the telephone. By the early twentieth century the telephone had become an everyday convenience, and Bell's company, overtaking U.S. Steel, had grown to be the largest corporation in the United States. On remote farms and ranches, medical care by telephone saved the life of many a child—and incidentally saved the doctor a long ride, in the days when doctors still commonly made house calls. New businesses were started by Go-Getters who sold their goods exclusively by telephone, having discovered that customers who had formed the habit of throwing away their "junk mail" would still answer every ring. The telephone (like the typewriter, which was perfected at about the same time) provided a whole new category of jobs for women.

By the time the fifty-millionth American telephone was ceremoniously placed on President Dwight D. Eisenhower's desk, it was unusual for any American family to be out of reach of the telephone. The business of government was conducted by phone. The United States possessed more than half the telephones in the world, and by 1972 nearly a half-billion separate phone conversations were being carried on in the United States each day. Still, the telephone was only a convenience, permitting Americans to do more casually and with less effort what they had already been doing before. People found it easier to get their message to other individuals whom they wanted to reach.

Television was a revolution, or more precisely, a cataclysm. For nobody "wanted" television, and it would create its own market as it transformed everyday life. It extended simultaneous experience, created anonymous audiences even vaster and more universal than those of radio, and incidentally created a new segregation.

Back in the 1920's, as we have seen, young David Sarnoff had had difficulty persuading his RCA colleagues that radio had an all-American future. Earlier commercial forms of communication had routed a message to a specific addressee. He believed that this novelty could prove to be radio's special virtue. And Sarnoff imagined a democratized world of anonymous addressees. His own experience must have impressed on him the advantages of this way of communicating. In April 1912, when Sarnoff was manning the wireless station which Wanamaker's in New York had installed as a publicity stunt to keep in touch with their store in Philadelphia, by chance he had caught the wireless message: "S.S. *Titanic* ran into iceberg. Sinking fast." He quickly established communication with another steamer, which reported that the *Titanic* had sunk and that some survivors had been picked up. While President William Howard Taft ordered all other stations to remain silent, the twenty-year-old Sarnoff stayed at his post for seventy-two hours, taking the names of survivors which, along with the name of Sarnoff, became front-page news.

Five years later, when working for the American Marconi Company, Sarnoff urged the marketing of "a simple 'Radio Music Box.' " His plan, he noted, "would make radio a 'household utility' in the same sense as the piano or phonograph." In 1920 he proposed a plan for manufacturing these radio music boxes for $75 apiece, and prophesied that at least one million families would buy them within three years. He proposed that money would be made from selling advertising in *Wireless Age* (a magazine that RCA had bought), which would carry an advance monthly schedule of the programs to be broadcast. Sarnoff's optimistic production schedule for the one million sets proved conservative. Radio was launched on a career that transformed the American entertainment world, as well as the world of advertising and news reporting.

By 1930, advertisers were spending $60 million annually on the radio, a figure that was to be multiplied tenfold in the next ten years. Thirty years after the granting of the first commercial broadcasting license to KDKA (Pittsburgh) in 1920, there were more than two thousand stations and more than 75 million receiving sets. Before World War II, the annual production of radio sets numbered 10 million. By 1960 the national average showed three radio sets per household.

Radio had remained primarily an "entertainment" and "news"

medium, allowing people to enjoy the melodrama of "soap serials," the jokes of Jack Benny, Fred Allen, and Bob Hope, the songs of Bing Crosby, the breathless sportscasting of Grantland Rice. The newscaster himself—H. V. Kaltenborn or Lowell Thomas—was a kind of "performer" who told the radio listener in solemn or lively tones what it was really like to be there.

*   *   *

Television opened another world. It did not simply multiply the sources of news and entertainment, it actually multiplied experience. At the TV set the viewer could see and hear what was going on with a rounded immediacy. Simultaneity was of the essence. When you took a picture you had to wait to have it developed; when you bought a phonograph record you knew in advance how it would sound. But now on TV you could share the suspense of the event itself. This new category of experience-at-a-distance would transform American life more radically than any other modern invention except the automobile.

On the surface, television seemed simply to combine the techniques of the motion picture and the phonograph with those of the radio, but it added up to something more. Here was a new way of mass-producing the moment for instant consumption by a "broadcast" (i.e., undefinable and potentially universal) community of witnesses. Just as the printing press five centuries before had begun to democratize learning, now the television set would democratize experience, incidentally changing the very nature of what was newly shared.

Before, the desire to share experience had brought people out of their homes gathering them together (physically as well as spiritually), but television would somehow separate them in the very act of sharing. While TV-democratized experience would be more equal than ever before, it would also be more separate. TV segregation confined Americans by the same means that widened their experience. Here was a kind of segregation that no Supreme Court ruling could correct, nor could it be policed by any federal commission. For it was built into the TV set.

This was again the familiar consequence of having a centralized and enlarged source, now not merely for running water or running electricity. Just as Rebecca no longer needed to go to the village well to gather her water (and her gossip), so now, too, in her eighth-floor kitchenette she received the current of hot and cold running images. Before 1970, more than 95 percent of American households had television sets. Now the normal way to enjoy a community experience was at home in your living room at your TV set.

In earlier times, to see a performance was to become part of a visible audience. At a concert, in a church, at a ball game or a political rally, the audience was half the fun. What and whom you saw in the audience was at least as interesting as and often humanly more important than what you saw on the stage. While she watched her TV set, the lonely Rebecca was thrust back on herself. She could exclaim or applaud or hiss, but nobody heard her except the children in the kitchen or the family in the living room, who probably already knew her sentiments too well. The others at the performance took the invisible form of "canned" laughter and applause. The mystery of the listening audience which had already enshrouded radio now became the mystery of the viewing audience. The once warmly enveloping community of those physically present was displaced by a world of unseen fellow TV watchers. Who else was there? Who else was watching? And even if they had their sets turned on, were they *really* watching?

Each of the millions of watching Americans was now newly segregated from those who put on the program and who, presumably, were aiming to please him. Television was a one-way window. The viewer could see whatever *they* offered, but nobody except the family in the living room could know for sure how the viewer reacted to what he saw. Tiny island audiences gathered nightly around their twinkling sets, much as cave-dwelling ancestors had clustered around their fires for warmth and safety, and for a feeling of togetherness. In these new tribal groups, each child's television tastes were as intimate a part of family lore as whether he preferred ketchup or mustard on his hamburger. With more and more two-TV families (even before 1970 these were one third of all American households) it became common for a member of the family to withdraw and watch in lonely privacy. Of course, broadcasters made valiant and ingenious efforts to fathom these secrets, to find out what each watcher really watched, what he really liked and what he really wanted. But the broadcasters' knowledge was necessarily based on samples, on the extrapolation of a relatively few cases, on estimates and guesses—all merely circumstantial evidence.

There was a new penumbra between watching and not-watching. "Attending" a ball game, a symphony concert, a theatrical performance or a motion picture became so casual that children did it while they wrote out their homework, adults while they played cards or read a magazine, or worked in the kitchen or in the basement. The TV watcher himself became unsure whether he was really watching, or only had the set on. Experience was newly befogged. The most elaborate and costly performances ceased to be special occasions that required planning and tickets; they became part of the air conditioning. Radio, too, had become something heard but not necessarily listened to, and its programming was directed to people assumed to be doing something else: driving the car, working at a hobby, washing the dishes. Car radios, which numbered 15 million in 1950, exceeded 40 million by 1960. With the rise of the transistor, miniaturized radio sets were carried about on the person like a fountain pen or a purse, to assuage loneliness wherever the wearer might be.

Newly isolated from his government, from those who collected his taxes, who provided public services, and who made the crucial decisions of peace or war, the citizen felt a frustrating new disproportion between how often and how vividly political leaders could get their messages to him and how often and how vividly he could get *his* message to them. Except indirectly, through the opinion polls, Americans were offered no new avenue comparable to television by which they could get their message back. Private telegrams began to become obsolete. The citizen was left to rely on the telephone (which might respond to his call with a "recorded message") or on a venerable nineteenth-century institution, the post office.

By enabling him to be anywhere instantly, by filling his present moment with experiences engrossing and overwhelming, television dulled the American's sense of his past, and even somehow separated him from the longer past. If Americans had not been able to accompany the astronauts to the moon they would have had to read about it the next morning in some printed account that was engrossing in retrospect. But on television, Americans witnessed historic events as vivid items of the present. In these ways, then, television created a time myopia, focusing interest on the exciting, disturbing, inspiring, or catastrophic instantaneous *now*.

The high cost of network time and the need to offer something for everybody produced a discontinuity of programing, a constant shifting from one sort of thing to another. Experience became staccato and motley. And every act of dissent acquired new dramatic appeal, especially if it was violent or disruptive. For this lost feeling of continuity with the past, the ineffective TV antidote was Old Movies.

* * *

Television, then, brought a new vagueness to everyday experience: the TV watcher became accustomed to seeing something-or-other happening somewhere-or-other at sometime-or-other, but all in Living Color. The common-sense hallmarks of authentic first-hand experience (those ordinary facts which a jury expected from a witness to prove that he had actually experienced what he said) now began to be absent, or only ambiguously present, in television experience. For his TV experience, the American did not need to go out to see anything in particular: he just turned the knob, and then wondered while he watched. Was this program live or was it taped? Was it merely an animation or a simulation? Was it a rerun? Where did it originate? When, if ever, did it really occur? Was it happening to actors or to real people? Was that a commercial?—a spoof of a commercial?—a documentary?—or pure fiction?

Almost never did the viewer see a TV event from a single individual's point of view. For TV was many-eyed, alert to avoid the monotony of any one person's limited vision. While each camera gave an image bigger and clearer than life, nobody got in the way. As the close-up dominated the screen, the middle distance dissolved.

The living-room watcher saw the player in left field, the batter at the plate, or rowdies in a remote bleacher more sharply than did the man wearing sunglasses in the stands. Any casual kook or momentary celebrity filled the screen, just like Humphrey Bogart or President Nixon. All TV experience had become theater, in which any actor, or even a spectator, might hold center stage. The new TV perspective made the American understandably reluctant to go back to his seat on the side and in the rear. Shakespeare's metaphors became grim reality when the whole world had become a TV stage.

In this supermarket of surrogate experience, the old compartments were dissolved. Going to a church or to a lecture was no different from going to a play or a movie or a ball game, from going to a political rally or stopping to hear a patent-medicine salesman's pitch. Almost anything could be watched in shirt sleeves, with beer can in hand. The experience which flowed through the television channels was a mix of entertainment, instruction, news, uplift, exhortation, and guess what. Successful programing offered entertainment (under the guise of instruction), instruction (under the guise of entertainment), political persuasion (with the appeal of advertising), and advertising (with the charm of drama). The new miasma, which no machine before could emit, and which enshrouded the TV world, reached out to befog the "real" world. Americans began to be so accustomed to the fog, so at home and solaced and comforted by the blur, that reality itself became slightly irritating because of its sharp edges and its clear distinctions of person, place, time, and weather.

As broadcasting techniques improved, they tended to make the viewer's experience more indirect, more controlled by unseen producers and technicians. Before, the spectator attending a national political convention would, simply by turning his head, decide for himself *where* he would look, but the TV watcher in the living room lacked the power to decide. Cameramen, directors, and commentators decided for him, focusing on this view of a brutal policeman or that view of a pretty delegate. As these conventions became guided tours by TV camera, the commentators themselves acquired a new power over the citizen's political experience, which was most vividly demonstrated at the Democratic National Convention in Chicago in

1968. Even as the American's secondhand experience came to seem more real and more authentic, it was more than ever shaped by invisible hands and by guides who themselves upstaged the leading performers and became celebrities.

Television watching became an addiction comparable only to life itself. If the set was not on, Americans began to feel that they had missed what was "really happening." And just as it was axiomatic that it was better to be alive than to be dead, so it became axiomatic that it was better to be watching *something* than to be watching nothing at all. When there was "nothing on TV tonight," there was a painful void. No wonder, then, that Americans revised their criteria for experience. Even if a firsthand experience was not worth having, putting it on TV might make it so.

Of all the wonders of TV, none was more remarkable than the speed with which it came. Television conquered America in less than a generation, leaving the nation more bewildered than it dared admit. Five hundred years were required for the printing press to democratize learning. And when the people could know as much as their "betters," they demanded the power to govern themselves. As late as 1671, the governor of Virginia, Sir William Berkeley, thanked God that the printing press (breeder of heresy and disobedience!) had not yet arrived in his colony, and he prayed that printing would never come to Virginia. By the early nineteenth century, aristocrats and men of letters could record, with Thomas Carlyle, that movable type had disbanded hired armies and cashiered kings, and somehow created "a whole new democratic world." Now with dizzying speed, television had democratized experience. It was no wonder that like the printing press before it, television met a cool reception from intellectuals and academics and the other custodians of traditional avenues of experience.

FROM PACKING TO PACKAGING:

The New Strategy of Desire

CHAPTER 49

I N THE UNITED STATES by the early twentieth century, all sorts of objects were being offered in newly attractive garb—creating a democracy of things. In the Old World, even after the industrial age had arrived, only expensive items were housed in their own box or elegantly wrapped. A watch or a jewel would be presented in a carefully crafted container, but the notion that a pound of sugar or a dozen crackers should be encased and offered for purchase in specially designed, attractive materials seemed outlandish. Essential to the American Standard of Living were new techniques for clothing objects to make them appealing advertisements for themselves. Industries spent fortunes improving the sales garb of inexpensive objects of daily consumption—a pack of cigarettes or a can of soup.

Just as the rise of factory-made clothing and the new American democracy of clothing leveled people and made it increasingly difficult to distinguish a man's occupation, his bank account, or the status of his family by what he wore, so it was with packaging. Here was a new way of democratizing objects, of leveling and assimilating their appearance. By looking at a newly designed machine-made package, it was hard to tell the quality of the inside object, and sometimes hard to tell even what the object was.

Packaging, which by the mid-twentieth century dominated the consciousness of the American consumer, had entered the lives of Americans unheralded and unchronicled for the very reasons which made it distinctive. The rise of packaging was a parable of the unnoticed, multiplex, anonymous sources of innovation. Packaging overcast experience with yet another pall of ambiguity and became the dominant new fact of everyday epistemology. Packaging fuzzied the edges of things, making it hard to know where the desired physical object ended and where its environment began.

* * *

Packing was, of course, as old as the making and moving of things. "To pack" meant "to put into a receptacle for transporting or storing." And the purpose of packing was to keep a thing safe and secure, to make it portable or preservable. The better a thing was packed, the less apt it was to be damaged, the farther it could travel, the longer it could be stored. Packing served transportation. It is not surprising, then, that in the nineteenth century the United States pioneered in techniques and materials of packing. The American factories that aimed to serve a national or international market, the department stores that drew their merchandise from all over, and the mail-order houses that shipped their goods to remote parts—all these required secure and durable ways of shipping.

The American distances, whether served by wagons, railways, automobiles, or airplanes, posed problems of preparing and encasing goods which were never faced by makers for a local market. Refrigerator cars and canning were, of course, ways of packing goods for markets distant in time or space. Americans also developed other materials and machinery for moving their products safely around the world. Before the Civil War, flour was shipped in cotton sacks (which found many other uses on the farm), for no one had yet made a paper bag that could do the job. But when the war stopped the supply of cotton for flour millers, a papermaker in upstate New York produced a paper bag sturdy enough to carry fifty pounds of flour. By 1875, American machinery for making metal boxes was being exported to Britain. But during these years, the design of a parcel was still dominated by the needs of shipping and storage. Containers were large and protective, suitable for the rural housewife's larder or for the floor of the country store.

Packaging (as it displaced *packing*) created whole new vistas for the consumer. For while packing was designed to transport and to preserve, packaging was designed to *sell*. Early in the twentieth century, "to package" had entered the American language as a verb. The story of packaging is the story of all the new things that Americans produced for sale. Packaging was a by-product of new American ways of selling, and the package itself became a new, and distinctively American, kind of salesman.

The wrapping of objects, naturally enough, had begun with the making of objects for sale. Gourds and banana leaves and baskets are still used in primitive markets. In western Europe in the days before mass production, wrapping itself was mostly a form of packing, designed to help the individual buyer carry home something he had bought. The package had not yet become part of the product for sale. There were a few exceptions. In the sixteenth century, German papermakers made wrappers for their own products. In the seventeenth century, quack medicines were sold in London in paper wrappers embellished with the signature of the inventor and an impressive coat of arms, and some tobacconists were using printed wrappers. Occasionally a wine bottle would bear the initialed seal of the tavern owner. But it was common in those days for a tea merchant's advertisement to remind customers to "bring a convenient Box." During the eighteenth century there was more packing of groceries, drugs, and cosmetics in forms convenient for the consumer. But still wrapping and labeling were less for sales appeal than for identification.

One reason for the slow progress of packaging was the scarcity of paper. In the seventeenth century the misjudgments of book publishers helped supply the lack. In those days it was not uncommon for a London bookseller to stock his books in the form of the unfolded, unbound printed sheets. When a customer wanted a book, the sheets would be put together, folded, and bound to his taste. The London bookseller's stock of sheets that remained unsold as books could then readily be sold for papers to grocers and apothecaries; a theological tract that could not elevate the mind would at least serve to wrap potatoes. In the early nineteenth century these indignities became less common with the invention of papermaking machinery.

Until then, paper had been made by hand, sheet by sheet, but in 1807 the Fourdrinier brothers in London patented a machine for making paper in continuous rolls. Within ten years Thomas Gilpin, using his own secret invention, produced in Delaware the first American machine-made paper, and others followed. Soon there were American machines that could turn out paper at the rate of forty-five feet per minute. New quick-drying machines made production independent of the weather, and every stage was speeded up. By 1830 the United States had become the greatest paper-producing and the greatest paper-consuming country in the world, and remained so.

With better machinery and increasing demand, there was a renewed search for raw materials to make paper cheaper and in larger quantity. The traditional European way of making paper required rags, and in colonial America the supply of rags had been especially scarce. After the middle of the seventeenth century, when people began papering their walls for decoration, the supply of rags became more inadequate than ever. Not until the early nineteenth century was paper made either from straw or wood pulp; by 1890 nearly all paper was being made from wood pulp. Then the paper supply was further increased by new ways of de-inking printed paper so that it could be re-pulped. This use of wood pulp for paper had the effect of denuding large tracts of the continent, transforming the beauties of primitive forests into tundras of unread newspapers. By 1934 a single machine operated by four men could turn out twenty tons of wood pulp a day. About this time a Georgia chemist discovered a new sulfate process by which Southern pine could be used for paper, and when this process was applied to other timbers it drastically reduced the cost of paper, besides providing a profitable use for Southern wastelands.

In the twentieth century the simplest and quickest form of packaging for the American shopper was, of course, the paper bag. But not until the mid-nineteenth century had ready-made paper bags come onto the market; an enterprising Englishman began to travel the English countryside peddling his handmade bags to grocers. In 1852 a primitive paper-bag-making machine was operating in Bethlehem, Pennsylvania. By 1860 an ingenious mechanic, Charles Hill Morgan, had designed a machine for making bags which finally showed commercial possibilities and which he used in his paper-bag factory in Philadelphia. By the 1870's Americans were in the business of selling bag-making machines.

American careers once again were to be made from commodities that had not even existed a half-century before. Luther Childs Crowell, the inventive son of a New England sea captain, was led somehow by his experiments with "aerial machines" (that never flew) to design a superior machine to make paper bags, for which he received a patent in 1867. A few years later he invented the square-bottomed paper bag (still used in the late twentieth century) and a machine for its manufacture. Following the pattern of other major innovations, his paper-bag patent was the subject of long and bitter litigation.

While paper bags were mostly for the customer's convenience, the new large-scale merchandisers were looking for new ways to speed their sales. A salesman could be making a second sale in the time it took to wrap a parcel in paper and twine. To cover their high overhead and make a profit, department stores needed to make volume sales to the big-city crowds who were in a hurry. It is not surprising, then, that soon after the Civil War, New York bag makers were beginning to prosper by selling their product to Macy's, Lord & Taylor, and other department stores. The bags themselves, when imprinted with the store's name, became advertisements. In 1889 the economist David Ames Wells, an enthusiast for American efficiency and himself the inventor of a device for folding paper on power presses, observed quite seriously that the cheap paper bag had been the most effective innovation during the preceding decade in speeding up American retail sales, especially the sale of groceries. By Wells's time, American factories each week were turning out millions of paper bags, which had begun to become standard equipment for the American retailer.

*   *   *

But even the improved paper bag was not versatile enough for all the tasks of packaging required by the novel mass-produced products of American factories. There was a need, too, for boxes of all shapes and sizes. And these would have to be machine-made, easy to store, easy to ship, and sturdy in use.

In England the early box makers were more akin to luggage manufacturers than to packagers. They made boxes to sell empty, for any use the buyer wished. The boxes were made by hand, mostly from wood, heavy paper, or cardboard. Since there was no easy way to make clean creases or sharp corners, many boxes were made round or oval, hand-shaped around a wooden form. But these products could not satisfy modern factory needs, because the containers, when empty, consumed so much space. The most important packaging inventions in the nineteenth century, after the flat-bottomed paper bag, were to be a more compact kind of box and the machine for its manufacture. If a way could only be found of making a box that would remain flat until it was filled with the product, factories could buy boxes in large numbers and stack them in a small space until needed. But to make folding boxes inexpensively there had to be a machine that would cut and crease cardboard.

By mid-century a Boston firm which had been making jewelers' boxes developed a machine that would crease and cut wood for boxes. The Dennisons had already been making "set-up" boxes, which the jeweler could unfold to display his merchandise on the counter or in a show window. But paper cartons were still made in the same laborious way, shaped one at a time by hand around wooden forms.

The crucial invention was made by Robert Gair, a clever Scotsman who had immigrated to New York City at the age of fourteen. After a tour in the Union Army, Gair set up a factory for paper bags, selling his product to department stores and other big-city shops. He enlisted in his firm the man who during the war had devised a sturdy paper bag for flour. Gair's catalogue soon offered a variety of bags for flour and buckwheat, grocers' bags, seed bags, and other bags imprinted with the merchant's name. But in his factory, bags were still made by hand in the laborious old way.

Gair saw that if cardboard cartons could be made quickly and cheaply in a form easy to store and easy to use, they would vastly enlarge the market for packaging. Then, in April 1879, one of Gair's workers who was tending a printing press for seed bags had care-lessly allowed a metal rule on the press to slip up so that the paper was not only printed but actually cut. This gave Gair the clue that he needed. He designed a multiple die which used a sharp metal rule set high to cut the cardboard while it used blunt rules set lower to do the creasing. From this simple invention came the machine-made fold-ing box. On a secondhand press which Gair bought for $30, he fitted the cutting and creasing rules; this paper-box machine could cut and crease 750 sheets an hour, each sheet providing ten carton blanks, amounting to an hourly production of 7,500 cartons.

Before the end of the nineteenth century there were nearly a thousand patents related to folding boxes and their machines. Amer-ican machines to make cartons helped popularize the folding box in England. In 1898, Wills' Three Castles cigarettes were being packed in machine-made folding cartons (three million a week) from a ma-chine that was made in Philadelphia. Folding cartons, run off the presses by the millions, provided a versatile new form of packaging. By the second decade of the twentieth century these cartons were being made for candles, candy, oats, breakfast foods, cookies, and almost every other machine-made product. And the packagers had already begun to play a role in manufacturing and advertising. When someone from the National Biscuit Company in New York came to Robert Gair's son and told him that they were planning a new, na-tionally advertised product, he said, "You need a name." Uneeda Biscuits were the result. These words also spelled the end of the cracker barrel.

The rise of American packaging produced a host of packages of new and ingenious design. Until 1841 such collapsible packaging as there was had been made from animal bladders. Then an American artist patented a collapsible metal tube for artists' colors, and in 1870 there appeared the first American tube-making machinery. By 1892 a Connecticut dentist was putting up toothpaste in tubes, and soon afterward, Colgate's pioneered in the large-scale marketing of toothpaste in this form. By 1912 Mennen's took the lead with tubes to market shaving cream, and this new convenience—the death of the shaving mug!—must have had something to do with the changing fashion of men's faces in the following years. The very first Mennen shaving-cream tube showed a man with a clean-shaven chin.

Packages themselves became an important new commodity, and the packaging industry grew. Manufacturers designed closures specially adapted to powder, paste, or liquid, and they designed easy-dispensing caps, measuring caps, and containers in all shapes and sizes. These were accompanied by improvements in lithography, which reduced the cost of reproducing pictures on boxes and labels, and by new ways of printing on wood, glass, steel, tin, and aluminum. Cellophane, invented by a Swiss chemist in 1912, was developed and first manufactured by a French firm that had been making rayon, and then was commercially produced in the United States by DuPont in 1924.

The endless possibilities of packaging were symbolized in the mid-twentieth century by "aerosol." This Americanism, made up from "aero" + "solution," which appeared in dictionaries in the late 1960's, described a push-button package. Although available before World War II, at first these packages were heavy and costly and were used mainly for insect repellents. It took a decade to perfect this can into a safe, inexpensive, light-weight device that properly combined the propellant which forced the product out of the pack, with the product itself. By 1955, about 240 million aerosols were produced annually for non-food purposes alone; by 1956 the figure was 320 million. The use of aerosols was spreading, and soon left an indelible public mark in the form of graffiti applied with aerosol paint cans. By the 1960's, packaging in the United States, valued at more than $20 billion a year, had become a major American industry.

* * *

But packaging was more than merely another industry. It pervaded American life and transformed the American's experience of nearly all the objects which he bought or wanted to buy or thought he wanted. It brought one of the most manifold and least noticed revolutions in the common experience.

At first many of the consequences of packaging were of a familiar sort: cleanliness, convenience, and economy. As late as 1925 the

American Sugar Refining Company was urging on its wholesale dealers the advantages of packaged, as against bulk, sugar:

> Do you know that it takes a man about an hour and three-quarters to weigh out a 350-pound barrel of granulated sugar in five-pound paper bags; that a man averages only about 69 five-pound bags when he weighs out a 350-pound barrel; that the five pounds lost by spillage and downweight represent 1.4 per cent of the cost price of the sugar; that, in addition to sugar wasted, bags, twine and labor amount to about forty cents added to the cost per cwt. of the sugar; and—that 350 pounds of Domino Package Sugars mean 350 pounds sold with a profit on every pound; that no time is lost and no material or sugar wasted; that, therefore, a retailer makes more money per pound when he sells Domino Package Sugars; and that he will appreciate your pointing out these facts to him, thereby enabling him to make more money on sugar. . . .
>
> Now, if the grocer must scoop his sugar, weigh it, wrap it, tie it, give downweight, lose some by spillage—then we acknowledge that the margin of profit is not worth the trouble. And that is why for years we have been urging the grocery trade to handle Domino Package Sugars. With this line you eliminate all handling costs, all expense, all losses. On that basis, 200 per cent profit is practically clear. Why not try it out?

But this was still a novel idea for the grocer. And in 1928 only 10 percent of household sugar was sold in package form.

Salt became a new, more profitable, item for the grocer. Before the age of packaging, salt was packed in cotton bags, retailing at from two to five cents each. The producer's profit margin was so narrow that it actually depended on the fluctuation in the price of cotton. Since the cotton bag gave no more protection against moisture than an ordinary salt shaker, much of the contents of a bag of salt might be unusable in humid weather or by the time the housewife needed it. When producers began marketing salt in convenient square wax-wrapped cartons or in round cartons with aluminum spouts, they found that housewives were willing to pay three or four times the price for the same quantity. When the Morton Salt Company made "When it rains it pours" into a household phrase, they were really selling a new kind of package.

But packaging was not merely a new way for the more profitable retailing of old products. Packaging created new uses, and opened wider markets, with the result that products themselves were transformed. Before 1900, tea was sold in bulk by the grocer, and perfume was ladled out by the druggist for each customer from his large bottle into smaller, plain bottles. Within two decades the tea bag had made it possible to make tea where there was no teapot, and luxury packaging transformed perfume into a gift parcel and a bedroom ornament. Matches, which formerly were items for the kitchen or the fireplace, or which had to be carried about the person in a matchsafe, were now packaged into compact books of matches and became a new advertising medium. Ice cream, too, became a newly portable commodity when it was put up in an edible package, like the ice-cream cone (an Americanism first recorded in 1909) or the Eskimo Pie (an American trade name introduced in 1921).

The growth of American mass-merchandising, along with the rise of national advertising and national branding, offered new opportunities for the ubiquitous selling of small quantities of all sorts of things. Packaging opened a new market for candy. Early in the twentieth century candy had been sold only at confectioners' and in few other stores, by the half-pound, pound, two-pound or five-pound box, or in bulk. It was messy and inconvenient to carry about just a few pieces. Then, in the 1920's, small packages of candy began to be displayed in drugstores, cigar stores, newsstands, grocery stores, and scores of other even more unlikely places, tempting people to pick up a nickel "candy bar" (an American expression, first recorded in print in 1943) for their pocket or desk drawer. One result was that even while the number of confectionary stores in the United States declined quite steadily, from some 63,000 in 1929 to fewer than 14,000 forty years later, during these years the opportunities for buying and consuming candy were becoming more widespread than ever. "Hershey," "Baby Ruth," "Oh Henry!," and "Mars" became colloquial expressions for units of candy—the products of small-unit packaging. The same story could be told of the spreading consumption of potato chips, nuts, and scores of other foods, newly distributed in small packages.

Some things could not have had a wide market at all without speedier, more attractive and more functional packaging. When two young businessmen bought the Mint Products company that produced Life Savers, the little round mints with the hole were packed in sturdy cardboard cartons that were held together by paste. After a few weeks on the dealer's shelf these Life Savers would lose their mint flavor and they absorbed the flavor of the paste. The new management at Life Savers discarded the old boxes and instead used tin foil, which did not absorb the flavor, which was easily sealed again after one mint was removed, and which looked attractive on the counter. Cigarettes and chewing gum too could hardly have found their universal market without machine-made packages. By the mid-1920's a single automatic wrapping machine could turn out 50 cigarette packages a minute. A single chewing-gum packaging machine wrapped gum in foil at the rate of 400 sticks a minute, 200 boxes (twenty packages per box) each hour, or 1,800 packages a day.

The new packaging machinery helped modify retailing in still another way, by providing contents to fill the newly perfected vending machines. Before the mid-twentieth century, in American everyday parlance the word "vendor" no longer meant a *person* who sold but "a machine that dispenses goods upon the deposit of a coin or coins." These new ways of merchandising gave a new importance to packaging and made new demands of the package. Packaging became an art of selling-without-salesmen. And after the rise of advertising itself, nothing did more to contribute to the decline of salesmanship than the improved technology of packaging.

By the 1950's, "packaging engineering" had become a new American occupation: larger firms had their own specialized staffs and smaller firms consulted packaging engineers. By the late 1960's, consumer products accounted for 70 percent of all packaging mate-

rials. Without anyone having intended it, and when few even noticed, everyone had become increasingly dependent on packaging.
Businessmen could well say, "No packaging, no brands—no brands,
no business."

*   *   *

The packaging revolution, like other transformations of American experience, came rapidly—within a third of a century. As late as
1920, few of the housewife's purchases were packaged. Of common
household groceries, packaged goods then included only a small proportion of sugar, salt, rice, flour, tea, or coffee. The unpackaged
products were seldom sold under brand names. But the growth of
national advertising and national brands (which had been both a
cause and an effect of department stores, five-and-tens, chain stores,
and the earliest self-service stores) produced still another new American institution: the supermarket. Dictionaries defined this new
Americanism as "a large retail market that sells food and other
household goods and that is usually operated on a self-service, cash-
and-carry basis." But by mid-century, merchandising specialists
were defining a supermarket as a store that did at least $1 million of
business annually.

While the self-service grocery store, as we have seen, had been
pioneered before World War I by Piggly Wiggly and others, the
supermarket became increasingly important only after World War
II. Giving a smaller role than ever to the salesman, it was preeminently a place of self-service. The widening spectacle of competing
items and competing brands displayed to the customer on open
shelves gave the package a newly seductive power.

During World War I, when labor was scarce, the large grocery
markets had turned to self-service, and the customer was provided a
basket to carry the purchases he selected off the shelves. One of the
first supermarkets, San Francisco's Crystal Palace, opened in 1923 in
a large steel-frame building on the site of a former baseball diamond
and circus ground with 68,000 square feet of selling area and parking
for 4,350 cars (one hour free). Offering food, drugs, tobacco, liquor
(after 1934), jewelry, a barber shop, a beauty parlor, and a cleaning

establishment, the store by 1937 had set sales records of 51,000 pounds of sugar in one hour, 5 carloads of eggs in a month; in a single year it sold 200 tons of lemons, 250 tons of oranges, and 300 tons of apples. By this time other supermarkets were beginning to show comparable sales.

An important accessory of the supermarket, which increased sales by making it easier for the customer to give in to his purchasing temptations, was the shopping cart. An employee of a Houston grocery store in the early 1920's removed the handle from a toy express wagon, fastened a shopping basket on the wagon, and then made the front wheels stationary so that the customer could guide the cart by the basket handle. By the later 1930's, similar carts were being manufactured for sale to grocery-store owners. In the 1950's, shopping carts came into use in self-service hardware stores, appliance stores, and discount department stores.

Department stores and supermarkets brought together many kinds of merchandise under one roof. During World War II the scarcity of certain goods had increased this tendency toward "scrambled" merchandising. When drugstores could not get some of their usual items, they stocked small appliances, food, luggage, and toys, while supermarkets carried clothing, kitchenware, hardware, drugs, and cosmetics, and department stores branched out into food, liquor and a variety of new services. The parking problem, more acute every year, made customers eager for "one-stop" or "one-parking" shopping.

While the differences between one kind of shop and another were dissolved, so too were the distinctions between shopping and nonshopping hours. As early as 1931, a Long Island supermarket was advertising, "Come in your Lincoln, Come in your Ford, Come with the Baby Carriage. Come with any old thing but come, come, come! Fri. 9 p.m., Sat. 10 p.m." Supermarkets, and then self-service hardware and department stores, and discount stores began to stay open nightly, including Sundays.

The increasing size of the stores, the increasing number of items, the increasing competition for the buyer's attention by items arrayed so the buyer could reach them for himself, made packaging into a newly sophisticated and self-conscious industry. The salesman was nowhere to be seen. The housewife-customer, equipped with a shopping cart, wandered without guidance and often without clear purpose through a wilderness of packages. Not unless she had trouble finding some particular item did she get advice or assistance (except from a fellow customer) until she reached the check-out counter. She had to make decisions for herself, based on her preferences for certain brands or on the appearance and appeal of the packages on the shelf. Once again, the American lived the public-private paradox. The flood of goods into these enormous channels of merchandising pushed the citizen-consumer back on himself. The decision to buy or not to buy had become more private than ever before.

The overwhelming new power of packaging, then, came from self-service. In 1928 the pioneer book, *Packages That Sell*, by Richard B. Franken and Carroll B. Larrabee, foreshadowed the new emphasis. "The package," they said, "should be merchandised . . . in the same way that the product is merchandised." This was the final stage in the attenuation of things. For while every object had a different purpose—to brush teeth, to comb hair, to please the palate, or whatever else—all packaging shared one purpose, namely *to sell*. Whatever the content of the package, whatever its other purposes, every package was shaped somehow toward that same end. And the new merchandising tended to put every package in competition with every other.

However well any package might protect or preserve its content, it failed if it did not sell. Therefore the important, the substantial and essential qualities of a package were the qualities that forced the reluctant or indifferent buyer to buy. From this new point of view, color, size, shape, material, and function had but one test for all packages: What impression did the package make on the prospective customer?

The important size of a package, for example, was its *apparent* size. Using the so-called Order-of-Merit Method, which an American psychologist, James McKeen Cattell, had used in 1902 to measure the relative brightness of two hundred shades of gray, Franken and Larrabee proposed a way to "obtain a quantitative measurement of a qualitative or subjective thing. In packaging this method will tell us beforehand which of a series of packages will help stimulate the sale of the product to the greatest extent, and will thus enable us to formulate principles upon which to build the future packages." As an illustration they showed, from the results of tests of consumer preference, why a certain shape of 10-ounce can was the best package for codfish cakes. "The apparent size of objects," they explained, "depends somewhat on their shape. . . . the flat 10-ounce can . . . was selected for Gorton-Pew's Ready-to-Fry Codfish Cakes because it looked larger than the tall can . . . although both cans had the same cubic capacity."

*   *   *

Now the package—as well as, or instead of, the product—was what was advertised. From a sampling study of large-circulation general magazines, Franken and Larrabee observed that while in 1900 only 7 percent of the advertisements of packaged products showed a picture of the package, by 1925 the proportion had reached 35 percent and was going up. "The primary function of advertising is to create a desire in the consumer's mind to buy a product. This desire, once created, must be carried to the point of sale. . . . Best of all . . . is to picture the package in the advertisement. Even if only a favorable impression has been created, without the desire to buy, the sight of the actual package may turn this impression into active desire on the part of the consumer." In stores, then, it was more important to display the distinctive brand-named carton than the usable object itself. The "dummy carton" began to play a leading role in store windows and on counters.

The supermarket offered new opportunities for "impulse buying"; and impulse buying was essentially the buying of packages. With the rise in the American Standard of Living, the increase of disposable income, and the multiplication of novel objects, more and more people went to the supermarket hoping to be seduced into buying something they "really wanted." In England and elsewhere in the Old World, it was still true in the late twentieth century that middle-class shoppers went to market to buy what they wanted, while Americans went increasingly to *see* what they wanted.

A series of studies by the DuPont Company, begun in 1949, showed that "impulse buying" was on the increase. As a large producer of packaging materials, the DuPont Company, of course, had a special interest in proving the growing importance of impulse buying, and so of packaging. But their conclusions were widely substantiated. By 1959 more than half the housewife's purchases in a supermarket were "unplanned"—that is, they were purchases that she had not intended to make before she entered the store; and less than a third of her purchases had been specifically planned before coming to the store. In the five years from 1954 to 1959, the DuPont study showed, the number of supermarkets in the United States had increased by nearly 40 percent (to some 30,000 stores), and the number of different items stocked in supermarkets had increased nearly 30 percent (to an average of 6,000 items and a high of 8,000 items in larger supermarkets). "The shopper is depending on the supermarket for more and more items she needs . . . she is spending 50% more time in the supermarket (27 minutes per trip against 18 minutes five years ago) and has increased the number of items purchased. . . . the supermarket has become her 'shopping center' rather than just a food store."

What did it mean, then, to speak of the "demand" for *products* when so large a proportion of what consumers bought was determined by the appeal of the packages? What was the meaning of "desire" when the housewife in the supermarket averaged fourteen (13.7) buying-decisions in twenty-seven minutes? Packaging, which at the end of the nineteenth century was still only a means to protect a product, had become a thing-in-itself. Now where did the package end and the product begin? Who could say?

Shrewd manufacturers and merchandisers could not fail to become adept at what Dr. Ernest Dichter, a psychoanalytic marketing consultant, called "the Strategy of Desire." A good *product* was not enough; success required a *package* that would stimulate desire. From one point of view, as Dr. Dichter explained in 1961, this was a result of the uniform and high quality of American products.

> When people buy soap, they know that they are going to get soap. They know they do not any more have to worry about getting a piece of chalk. But because our technological development has been so good and so fast, the fact is that almost all our products are uniformly good, so that there is in reality very little difference, in the same price category, between a product with one brand name and a product with another. What people actually spend their money on are the psychological differences, brand images permitting them to express their individuality. . . . We have reached . . . a psychoeconomic era. It is because of the improved quality and reliability of our merchandise that we can allow ourselves the luxury of making our decisions on the basis of more purely psychological factors.

To say that products were more and more standardized was to say that the consumer's world, like the world of the photograph and the phonograph, had also become a world of repeatable experience. Packaging and brand-naming had helped make the experience more reliably repeatable. The packaging of convenience foods, as a study by Arthur D. Little & Co. argued, plays "an important role in reducing the risks of non-repeatability in the preparation of food products. The ability of a housewife to repeat the quality of a given meal is increased." The familiar package justified the hope that it would be the same this time, too.

While the American consumer now had an unprecedented guarantee that the experience of a particular product was repeatable, other aspects of his experience were overcast by new penumbras. The package or the object? Form or content? Did he really want it, or had he been persuaded to buy it on impulse? Would he have bought it if it had been offered to him in a package of different size, shape, or color, or if it had been displayed on a different shelf or beside something else more attractive? Or if he had not had his shopping cart so handy? The anonymous product—the product without a brand name, which had dominated the stores a half-century before—had by the mid-twentieth century become slightly disreputable. Everything had a name, and packages were commonly bought because the name on the package had become familiar in print or on the television screen. Inevitably, then, the packaged world with its new strategy of desire brought a vagueness and uncertainty of desire. Had packaging, like clothing, become a badge of man's lost innocence?

FROM

THE
DISCOVERERS

> *"And take upon 's the mystery of things,*
> *as if we were God's spies."*
> SHAKESPEARE, *King Lear*

My hero is Man the Discoverer. The world we now view from the literate West—the vistas of time, the land and the seas, the heavenly bodies and our own bodies, the plants and animals, history and human societies past and present—had to be opened for us by countless Columbuses. In the deep recesses of the past, they remain anonymous. As we come closer to the present they emerge into the light of history, a cast of characters as varied as human nature. Discoveries become episodes of biography, unpredictable as the new worlds the discoverers opened to us. The obstacles to discovery—the illusions of knowledge—are also part of our story. Only against the forgotten backdrop of the received common sense and myths of their time can we begin to sense the courage, the rashness, the heroic and imaginative thrusts of the great discoverers.

This is a story without end. All the world is still an America. The most promising words ever written on the maps of human knowledge are *terra incognita*—unknown territory.

THE TEMPTATIONS OF THE MOON

CHAPTER 1

F ROM FAR-NORTHWEST GREENLAND to the southernmost tip of Patagonia, people hail the new moon—a time for singing and praying, eating and drinking. Eskimos spread a feast, their sorcerers perform, they extinguish lamps and exchange women. African Bushmen chant a prayer: "Young Moon! . . . Hail, hail, Young Moon!" In the light of the moon everyone wants to dance. And the moon has other virtues. The ancient German communities, Tacitus reported nearly two thousand years ago, held their meetings at new or full moon, "the seasons most auspicious for beginning business."

Everywhere we find relics of mythic, mystic, romantic meanings—in "moonstruck" and "lunatic" (Latin *luna* means moon), in "moonshine," and in the moonlight setting of lovers' meetings. Even deeper is the primeval connection of the moon with measuring. The word "moon" in English and its cognate in other languages are rooted in the base *me* meaning measure (as in Greek *metron*, and in the English *meter* and *measure*), reminding us of the moon's primitive service as the first universal measurer of time.

Despite or because of its easy use as a measure of time, the moon proved to be a trap for naïve mankind. For while the phases of the moon were convenient worldwide cycles which anybody could see, they were an attractive dead end. What hunters and farmers most needed was a calendar of the seasons—a way to predict the coming of

341

rain or snow, of heat and cold. How long until planting time? When to expect the first frost? The heavy rains?

For these needs the moon gave little help. True, the cycles of the moon had an uncanny correspondence with the menstrual cycle of women, because a sidereal month, or the time required for the moon to return to the same position in the sky, was a little less than 28 days, and a pregnant woman could expect her child after ten of these moon-months. But a solar year—the proper measure of days between returning seasons—measures 365¼ days. The cycles of the moon are caused by the moon's movement around the earth at the same time that the earth is moving around the sun. The moon's orbit is elliptical, and departs by an angle of about five degrees from the earth's orbit about the sun. This explains why eclipses of the sun do not occur every month.

The discomfiting fact that the cycles of the moon and the cycles of the sun are incommensurate would stimulate thinking. Had it been possible to calculate the year, the round of seasons, simply by multiplying the cycles of the moon, mankind would have been saved a lot of trouble. But we might also have lacked the incentive to study the heavens and to become mathematicians.

The seasons of the year, as we now know, are governed by the movements of the earth around the sun. Each round of the seasons marks the return of the earth to the same place in its circuit, a movement from one equinox (or solstice) to the next. Man needed a calendar to find his bearings in the seasons. How to begin?

*   *   *

The ancient Babylonians started with the lunar calendar and stayed with it. Their obstinacy in sticking with moon cycles for their calendar-making had important consequences. In search of a way to measure the cycle of the seasons in multiples of moon cycles, they eventually discovered, probably around 432 B.C., the so-called Metonic cycle (after an astronomer Meton) of nineteen years. They found that if they used a nineteen-year cycle, assigned to seven of the years thirteen months, and assigned to the other twelve years only twelve months, they could continue to use the conveniently visible phases of the moon as the basis of their calendar. Their "intercalation," or insertion of extra months, avoided the inconvenience of a "wandering" year in which the seasons wandered gradually through the lunar months, so that there was no easy way of knowing which month would bring the new season. This Metonic calendar with its nineteen-year clusters was too complicated for everyday use.

The Greek historian Herodotus, writing in the fifth century B.C., illustrated these complications in a famous passage when he reported how the wise Solon answered the rich and irascible Croesus, who asked him who was the happiest of mortals. To impress on Croesus the vast unpredictability of fortune, he calculated according to the Greek calendar then in use the number of days in the seventy years which he regarded as the limit of the life of man. "In these seventy years," he observed, "are contained, without reckoning intercalary months, 25,200 days. Add an intercalary month to every other year, that the seasons may come round at the right time, and there will be, besides the seventy years, thirty-five such months, making an addition of 1,050 days. The whole number of the days contained in the seventy years will thus be 26,250, whereof not one but will produce events unlike the rest. Hence man is wholly accident. For yourself, Croesus, I see that you are wonderfully rich, and the lord of many nations; but with respect to your question, I have no answer to give, until I hear that you have closed your life happily."

* * *

The Egyptians somehow escaped the temptations of the moon. So far as we know, they were the first to discover the length of the solar year and to define it in a useful, practical fashion. As with many other crucial human achievements, we know the *what*, but remain puzzled still about the *why*, the *how*, and even the *when*. The first puzzle is why it was the Egyptians. They had no astronomical instruments not already well known to the ancient world. They showed no special genius for mathematics. Their astronomy remained crude compared with that of the Greeks and others in the Mediterranean and was dominated by religious ritual. But it seems that by about 2500 B.C. they had figured out how to predict when the rising or setting sun would gild the tip of any particular obelisk, which helped them add a glow to their ceremonies and anniversaries.

The Babylonian scheme, which kept the lunar cycles and tried to adjust them to the seasonal or solar year by intercalation, was inconvenient. Local whims prevailed. In Greece, fragmented by mountains and bays and fertile in landscape loyalties, each city-state made its own calendar, arbitrarily intercalating the extra month to mark a local festival or to suit political needs. The result was to defeat the very purpose of a calendar—a time scheme to hold people together, to ease the making of common plans, such as agreements on the planting of crops and the delivery of goods.

The Egyptians, even without the Greek yen for mathematics, solved the practical problem. They invented a calendar that served everyday needs throughout their land. As early as 3200 B.C., the whole Nile Valley was united with the Nile Delta into a single kingdom which lasted for three thousand years, until the Age of Cleopatra. Political unity was reinforced by nature. Like the heavenly bodies themselves, the Nile displayed a regular but more melodramatic natural rhythm. The longest river in Africa, the Nile stretches four thousand miles from its remote headstream, gathering the rainfall and snowmelt of the Ethiopian highlands and all the northeastern continent into a single grand channel to the Mediterranean. The pharaoh's realm was aptly called the Empire of the Nile. The ancients, taking Herodotus' cue, called Egypt "the gift of the Nile." The search for the sources of the Nile, like the search for the Holy Grail, had mystic overtones, which stirred death-defying explorers into the nineteenth century.

The Nile made possible the crops, the commerce, and the architecture of Egypt. Highway of commerce, the Nile was also a freightway for the materials of colossal temples and pyramids. A granite obelisk of three thousand tons could be quarried at Aswan and then floated two hundred miles down the river to Thebes. The Nile fed the cities that clustered along its banks. No wonder that the Egyptians called the Nile "the sea" and in the Bible it is "the river."

The rhythm of the Nile was the rhythm of Egyptian life. The annual rising of its waters set the calendar of sowing and reaping with its three seasons: inundation, growth, and harvest. The flooding of the Nile from the end of June till late October brought down rich silt, in which crops were planted and grew from late October to late February, to be harvested from late February till the end of June. The rising of the Nile, as regular and as essential to life as the rising of the sun, marked the Nile year. The primitive Egyptian calendar, naturally enough, was a "nilometer"—a simple vertical scale on which the flood level was yearly marked. Even a few years' reckoning of the Nile year showed that it did not keep in step with the phases of the moon. But very early the Egyptians found that twelve months of thirty days each could provide a useful calendar of the seasons if another five days were added at the end, to make a year of 365 days. This was the "civil" year, or the "Nile year," that the Egyptians began to use as early as 4241 B.C.

Avoiding the seductively convenient cycle of the moon, the Egyptians had found another sign to mark their year: Sirius, the Dog Star, the brightest star in the heavens. Once a year Sirius rose in the morning in direct line with the rising sun. This "heliacal rising" of Sirius, which occurred every year in the midst of the Nile's flood season, became the beginning of the Egyptian year. It was marked by a festival, the five "epagomenal days" (days outside the months), celebrating in turn the birthday of Osiris, of his son Horus, of his Satanic enemy, Set, of his sister and wife, Isis, and of Nephthys, the wife of Set.

Since the solar year, of course, is not precisely 365 days, the Egyptian year of 365 days would, over the centuries, become a "wandering year" with each named month gradually occurring in a different season. The discrepancy was so small that it took many years, far longer than any one person's lifetime, for the error to disturb daily life. Each month moved through all the seasons in fourteen hundred and sixty years. Still, this Egyptian calendar served so much better than any other known at the time that it was adopted by Julius Caesar to make his Julian calendar. It survived the Middle Ages and was still used by Copernicus in his planetary tables in the sixteenth century.

* * *

While the Egyptians for their everyday calendar succeeded in declaring their independence of the moon, the moon retained a primeval fascination. Many peoples, including the Egyptians themselves, kept the lunar cycle to guide religious festivals and mystic anniversaries. Even today people dominated by their religion let themselves be governed by the cycles of the moon. The daily inconvenience of living by a lunar calendar becomes a daily witness to religious faith.

The Jews, for example, preserve their lunar calendar, and each Jewish month still begins with the appearance of a new moon. To keep their lunar calendar in step with the seasonal year the Jews have added an extra month for each leap year, and the Jewish calendar has become a focus of esoteric rabbinical learning. The Jewish year was made to comprise twelve months, each of 29 or 30 days, totaling some 354 days. In order to fill out the solar year, Jewish leap years—following the Metonic cycle of Babylonia—add an extra month in the third, sixth, eighth, eleventh, fourteenth, seventeenth, and nineteenth year of every nineteen-year period. Other adjustments are required occasionally to make festivals occur in their proper seasons—for example, to ensure that Passover, the spring festival, will come after the vernal equinox. In the Bible most of the months retain their Babylonian, rather than the Hebrew, names.

Christianity, following Judaism for most religious anniversaries, has kept its tie to the lunar calendar. "Movable feasts" in the Church were moved around in the solar calendar because of the effort to keep festivals in step with the cycles of the moon. They still remind us of the primeval charm of the most conspicuous light in the night sky. The most important of these Christian, moon-fixed festivals is, of course, Easter, which celebrates the resurrection of Jesus. "Easter-Day," prescribes the English Book of Common Prayer, "is always the first Sunday after the Full Moon which happens upon, or next after the Twenty-first day of March; and if the Full Moon happens upon a Sunday, Easter-Day is the Sunday after." At least a dozen other Church festivals are fixed by reference to Easter and its lunar date, with the result that Easter controls about seventeen weeks in the ecclesiastical calendar. The fixing of the date of

Easter—in other words, the calendar—became a great issue and a symbol. Since the New Testament recounted that Jesus was crucified on the Passover, the anniversary of the Easter resurrection would obviously be tied to the Jewish calendar. The inevitable result was that the date of Easter would depend on the complicated lunar calculations by which the highest Jewish council, the Sanhedrin, defined the Passover.

Many of the early Christians, following their own literal interpretation of the Bible, fixed the death of Jesus on a Friday, and the Easter resurrection on the following Sunday. But if the anniversary of the festival was to follow the Jewish lunar calendar, there was no assurance that Easter would occur on a Sunday. The bitter quarrel over the calendar led to one of the earliest schisms between the Eastern Orthodox Church and the Church of Rome. The Eastern Christians, holding to the lunar calendar, continued to observe Easter on the fourteenth day of the lunar month, regardless of the day of the week. At the very first ecumenical (worldwide) council of the Christian Church, held at Nicaea in Asia Minor in 325, one of the world-unifying questions to be decided was the date of Easter. A uniform date was fixed in such a way as both to stay with the traditional lunar calendar and to assure that Easter would always be observed on Sunday.

But this did not quite settle the matter. For community planning someone still had to predict the phases of the moon and locate them on a solar calendar. The Council of Nicaea had left this task to the bishop of Alexandria. In that ancient center of astronomy he was to forecast the phases of the moon for all future years. Disagreement over how to predict those specified cycles led to a division in the Church, with the result that different parts of the world continued to observe Easter on different Sundays.

The reform of the calendar by Pope Gregory XIII was needed because the year that Julius Caesar had borrowed from the Egyptians, and which had ruled Western civilization since then, was not a precise enough measure of the solar cycle. The actual solar year—the time required for the earth to complete an orbit around the sun—is 365 days, 5 hours, 48 minutes, and 46 seconds. This was some 11 minutes and 14 seconds less than the 365¼ days in the Egyptian year. As a result, dates on the calendar gradually lost their intended relation to solar events and to the seasons. The crucial date, the vernal equinox, from which Easter was calculated, had been fixed by the First Council of Nicaea at March 21. But the accumulating inaccuracy of the Julian calendar meant that by 1582 the vernal equinox was actually occurring on March 11.

Pope Gregory XIII, though notorious now for his public Thanksgiving for the brutal massacre of Protestants in Paris on Saint Bartholomew's Day (1572), was in some matters an energetic reformer. He determined to set the calendar straight. Climaxing a movement for calendar reform which had been developing for at least a century, in 1582 Pope Gregory ordained that October 4 was to be followed by October 15. This meant, too, that in the next year the vernal equinox would occur, as the solar calendar of seasons required, on March 21. In this way the seasonal year was restored to what it had been in 325. The leap years of the old Julian calendar were readjusted. To prevent the accumulation of another 11-minute-a-year discrepancy, the Gregorian calendar omitted the leap day from years ending in hundreds, unless they were divisible by 400. This produced the modern calendar by which the West still lives.

Simply because the reform had come from Rome, Protestant England and the Protestant American colonies obstinately refused to go along. Not until 1752 were they persuaded to make the change. The Old Style calendar year that governed them till then had begun on March 25, but the New Style year began on January 1. When the necessary eleven days were added, George Washington's birthday, which fell on February 11, 1731, Old Style, became February 22, 1732, New Style.

Back in 1582, when Pope Gregory took ten days out of the calendar, there had been grumbling and confusion. Servants demanded their usual full monthly pay for the abridged month; employers refused. People objected to having their lives shortened by papal decree. But when Britain and the American colonies finally got around to making the change, Benjamin Franklin, aged forty-six when he lost the ten days of his life, with his usual cheery ingenuity gave readers of his *Poor Richard's Almanack* something to be thankful for:

> Be not astonished, nor look with scorn, dear reader, at such a deduction of days, nor regret as for the loss of so much time, but take this for your consolation, that your expenses will appear lighter and your mind be more at ease. And what an indulgence is here, for those who love their pillow to lie down in peace on the second of this month and not perhaps awake till the morning of the fourteenth.

The world never entirely accepted the Gregorian reform. The Eastern Orthodox Church, wary of subjecting itself to any Romish rule, has kept the Julian calendar for its own calculation of Easter. And so the Christian world, supposedly held together by a Prophet of Peace, has not been able to agree even on the date to celebrate the resurrection of their Savior.

* * *

Still, for everyday secular affairs, the whole Christian world has shared a solar calendar which serves the convenience of the farmer and the merchant. But Islam, insisting on literal obedience to the words of the prophet Muhammad and to the dictates of the holy Koran, continues to live by the cycles of the moon.

The crescent, the sign of the new moon, appears on the flag of Muslim nations. Despite scholarly dispute about the origin of the crescent symbol, there can be no doubt of its appropriateness for the peoples who have obediently submitted the schedule of their lives to the divinely commanded measure of the moon. And it is doubly significant as a conspicuous exception to the Muslim ban on representing natural objects. At least as early as the thirteenth century, the crescent became the military and religious symbol of the Ottoman Turks. There is reason to believe that its adoption and its survival as a sign of Islam came from the dominance of the new moon, which not only is a signal of the beginning and end of the month-long Muslim season of fasting, but is the regular punctuation for the whole calendar.

The new moons, declares the Koran, "are fixed times for the people and for the pilgrimage." The Muslim world, with orthodox scrupulosity, has tried to live by the moon. Just as Caesar had decisively committed his world to the convenience of the solar year, with the months serving as indices of the seasons, so Muhammad committed his everyday world to the cycles of the moon. These lunar cycles would guide the faithful to the divinely ordained dates for the prime religious duties—the pilgrimage to Mecca and the Ramadan month of fasting. The Muslim year consists of twelve lunar months, of alternately 29 and 30 days. The fractional correction to keep the months in step with the moon was secured by varying the length of the twelfth month in the year. A cycle of thirty Muslim years was defined, in nineteen of which the final month had 29 days, with 30 days in the others.

Since the Muslim calendar contains only 354 or 355 days, the months have no regular relation to the seasons. Ramadan, the ninth month—the month of fasting, the observance which marks the true Muslim—and Dhu'l-Hijja, the twelfth month, during the first two weeks of which the faithful are to make their pilgrimage to Mecca, may occur in summer or in winter. In each year the festival of Ramadan and the Pilgrimage occur ten or eleven days earlier than in the previous year. The everyday inconveniences of this kind of calendar are simply another reminder of the good Muslim's surrender to the will of Allah. The calendar itself, for others a mere schedule of worldly affairs, the Muslim makes an affirmation of faith.

The Muslim's literal submission to the moon cycle has had some interesting consequences. To live by the God-given visible phases of the moon (and not by some human calculation of when the new moon is expected) has meant, of course, that celebration of a festival must await the actual sight of the moon. Most Muslims hold to this view, following a traditionally accepted utterance of the prophet Muhammad, "Do not fast until you see the new moon, and do not break the fast until you see it; but when it is hidden from you [by cloud or mist] give it its full measure." If clouds or mist prevent the new moon from being seen in certain villages, those villages will observe the beginning and the end of Ramadan at different times from their neighbors.

One of the most hotly debated issues in Islam is whether it is permissible to define the beginning and end of festivals not by observation but "by resorting to calculation." The members of the Ismaili sect, who separated themselves in this way, failed to persuade most of their fellow Muslims, who still stand by the need to *observe*, that is, actually to see the new moon. Strict adherence to the lunar calendar has become a touchstone of loyalty to traditional Islam. "Resort to calculation"—the appeal to the sophisticated mathematics of a solar year rather than to the simple, visible dictates of the lunar cycle—has marked the modern revolts against tradition. In 1926, when Kemal Atatürk (Mustapha Kemal) proclaimed the end of the sultanate in Turkey and "modernized" the nation by adopting a new code of laws, by making civil marriage compulsory, and by abolishing the fez for men and the veil for women, he also abandoned the lunar calendar of Islam and adopted the solar calendar of the West.

While for many in the West the calendar may seem nothing more than a system of chronological bookkeeping, it has proved to be one of the most rigid of human institutions. That rigidity comes partly from the potent mystic aura of sun and moon, partly from the fixed boundaries of the seasons. Revolutionaries have frequently tried to remake the calendar, but their success has been short-lived. The National Convention of the French Revolution set up a committee on calendar reform—made up of mathematicians, an educator, a poet, and the great astronomer Laplace—which produced a new calendar of charming rational symmetry. In 1792 their decimal calendar replaced the 7-day week by a 10-day week called a *décade*, each day of which was given a Latin numerical name, three of which comprised a month. The day was divided into ten hours, each consisting of 100 minutes, each minute of 100 seconds. In addition to the 360 days of these twelve months, the extra 5 or 6 days were given edifying names: Les Vertus, Le Génie, Le Travail, L'Opinion, Les Récompenses, with a leap day called Sans-culottide dedicated to holidays and sports. This calendar, designed to loosen the grip of the

Church on daily life and thought, lasted uneasily for only thirteen years. When Napoleon became ruler of France, he restored the Gregorian calendar with its traditional saint's days and holidays, for which he received the Pope's blessing.

In China the Revolution of 1911 brought a reform, which introduced the calendar of the West, alongside the traditional Chinese calendar.

In 1929 the Soviet Union, aiming to dissolve the Christian year, replaced the Gregorian with a Revolutionary calendar. The week was to have 5 days, 4 for work, the fifth free, and each month would consist of six weeks. The extra days needed to make up each year's complement of 365 or 366 would be holidays. The Gregorian names of the months were kept, but the days of the week were simply numbered. By 1940 the Soviet Union had returned to the familiar Gregorian calendar.

THE WEEK:

Gateway to Science

CHAPTER 2

S O LONG AS man marked his life only by the cycles of nature—
the changing seasons, the waxing or waning moon—he remained a prisoner of nature. If he was to go his own way and
fill his world with human novelties, he would have to make his own
measure of time. And these man-made cycles would be wonderfully
varied.

The week—or something very like it—was probably the earliest
of these artificial time clusters. Our English word "week" seems to
come from an Old High German word meaning to change, or turn
about (like the English "vicar" and the German *Wechsel*). But the
week is no Western invention, nor has it everywhere been a cluster
of seven days. Around the world, people have found at least fifteen
different ways, in bunches of five to ten days each, of clustering their
days together. What is planet-wide is not any particular bouquet of
days but the need and the desire to make some kind of bouquet.
Mankind has revealed a potent, pressing desire to play with time, to
make more of it than nature has made.

Our own Western seven-day week, one of the most arbitrary of
our institutions, came into being from popular need and spontaneous agreement, not from a law or the order of any government. How
did it happen? Why? When?

Why a *seven*-day week?

The ancient Greeks, it seems, had no week. Romans lived by an eight-day week. Farmers who worked in the fields for seven days came to town for the eighth day—the market day (or *nundinae*). This was a day of rest and festivity, a school holiday, the occasion for public announcements and for entertaining friends. When and why the Romans fixed on eight days and why they eventually changed to a seven-day week is not clear. The number seven almost everywhere has had a special charm. The Japanese found seven gods of happiness, Rome was set on seven hills, the ancients counted seven wonders of the world, and medieval Christians enumerated seven deadly sins. The Roman change from eight to seven seems not to have been accomplished by any official act. By the early third century A.D. Romans were living with a seven-day week.

There must have been some popular new ideas afloat. One of these was the idea of the Sabbath, which appears to have come to Rome through the Jews. "Remember the sabbath day, to keep it holy," says the Fourth Commandment. "Six days shalt thou labor, and do all thy work but the seventh day is the sabbath of the Lord thy God; in it thou shalt not do any work, thou, nor thy son, nor thy daughter, thy manservant, nor thy maidservant, nor thy cattle, nor the stranger that is within thy gates. For in six days the Lord made heaven and earth, the sea, and all that in them is, and rested the seventh day; wherefore the Lord blessed the sabbath day, and hallowed it" (Exodus 20:8–11). Every week God's creatures reenacted His Creation. The Jews made their week a memorial too of their liberation from slavery. "And remember that thou wast a servant in the land of Egypt, and that the Lord thy God brought thee out thence through a mighty hand and by a stretched out arm: therefore the Lord thy God commanded thee to keep the sabbath day" (Deuteronomy 5:15). When the Jews observed the Sabbath, they dramatized the Again-and-Again quality of their world.

There were other, less theological forces at work, such as the human need to refresh body and mind. The idea of a seventh day of rest, the very name Sabbath (from the Babylonian *Sabattu*) appears to have survived from the years when the Jews were in Babylonian captivity. The Babylonians observed certain enumerated days—the seventh, fourteenth, nineteenth, twenty-first, and twenty-eighth days of the month—when specific activities were forbidden to their king.

We find another clue in the name Saturday, which the Jews and the Romans and others after them came to use for their Sabbath day. Among the Romans, Saturn's Day, or Saturday, was a day of evil omen when all tasks were ill-starred, a day when battles should not be fought, nor journeys begun. No prudent person would want to risk the mishaps that Saturn might bring. According to Tacitus, the Sabbath was observed in honor of Saturn because "of the seven stars which rule human affairs Saturn has the highest sphere and the chief power."

By the third century the seven-day week had become common in private life throughout the Roman Empire. Each day was dedicated to one of the seven planets. Those seven, according to the current astronomy, included the sun and the moon, but not the earth. The order in which planets governed the days of the week was: sun, moon, Mars, Mercury, Jupiter, Venus, and Saturn. This order was *not* that of their then supposed distance from the earth, which was the "normal" order in which Dante, for example, later described the zones in the heavens, and in which the names of the planets were recited in the schools down to the time of Copernicus.

Our familiar order of the names for the days of the week came from this order of the planets that the Romans thought "governed" the first hour of each day in turn. The astrologers of the day did make use of the "order" of the planets according to their supposed distance from the earth, to calculate the "influence" of each planet on worldly affairs. They believed that each planet would govern an hour, then in the next hour would give way to the influence of the next planet nearer the earth, and so on through the cycle of all seven planets. After each cycle of seven hours, the planetary influences would begin all over again in the same order. The "governing" planet for each day, then, was the planet that happened to preside over the first hour of that day, and each day of the week thus took its name from the planet that governed its first hour. The result of this way of calculating was to name the days of the week in their now familiar order.

The days of our week remain a living witness to the early powers of astrology. We easily forget that our days of the week really are named after the "planets" as they were known in Rome two thousand years ago. The days of the week in European languages are still designated by the planets' names. The survival is even more obvious in languages other than English. Here, with the dominant planet, are some examples:

English	French	Italian	Spanish
Sunday (Sun)	dimanche	domenica	domingo
Monday (Moon)	lundi	lunedì	lunes
Tuesday (Mars)	mardi	martedì	martes
Wednesday (Mercury)	mercredi	mercoledì	miércoles
Thursday (Jupiter)	jeudi	giovedì	jueves
Friday (Venus)	vendredi	venerdì	viernes
Saturday (Saturn)	samedi	sabato	sábado

When peoples have tried to extinguish ancient idolatry, they have replaced the planetary names with simple numbers. So the Quakers call their days First Day, Second Day, and so on up to Seventh Day. They hold their religious meetings not on Sunday but on First Day. In modern Israel, too, the days of the week are given ordinal numbers.

One of the more unexpected examples of the power of the planetary idea is the Christian change of the Sabbath from Saturday, or Saturn's day, to Sunday, or Sun's day. When Christianity first took root in the Roman Empire, pious Church Fathers worried over the survival of the pagan gods in the names of the planets that governed the Christian week. The Eastern Church had some success in exterminating this pagan influence: the names of the days in both modern Greek and Russian ceased to be planetary. But Western Christianity proved more willing to turn Roman beliefs and prejudices to their own purpose. The Church Father Justin Martyr (c. 100–c. 165) shrewdly explained to the Emperor Antoninus Pius and his sons (c. 150) why the Christians chose their particular day for Gospel reading and to celebrate the Eucharist. "It is on what is called the

Sun's day that all who abide in the town or the country come together. . . . and we meet on the Sun's day because it is the first day on which God formed darkness and mere matter into the world and Jesus Christ our saviour rose from the dead. For on the day before Saturn's day they crucified him, and on the day after Saturn's day which is the Sun's day he appeared to his apostles and disciples and taught them."

Saturn's day, the traditionally unlucky day when the Jews found it wise to abstain from work, somehow remained the pivot around which the weekly auspices would revolve. But there were still other influences. The Mithraists, followers of the Persian mystery religion who worshipped the sun-god Mithras, which was one of the strongest competitors of Christianity in the Roman Empire, adopted a seven-day week. They naturally felt special reverence for what everybody then called the Sun's day.

The Christians fixed their Lord's day, then, so that every week's passing would relive the drama of Jesus Christ. By taking Communion, every Christian would somehow become one of the Disciples at the Last Supper. The script for this mystic drama was, of course, the liturgy of the mass. The Eucharist, like the other sacraments, became a repeat performance of a crucial symbolic event in the history of the Church. What a happy coincidence that the Sun's day was already known as a day of joy and renewal! "The Lord's day is reverenced by us," a Church Father, Maximus of Turin, explained in the fifth century, "because on it the Savior of the world like the rising sun, dispelling the darkness of hell, shone with the light of resurrection, and therefore is the day called by men of the world the Sun's day, because Christ the sun of righteousness illumines it." The Sun's day, like the first David, prefigured the dazzling light of the sun in the true Savior. The Church Fathers made this coincidence further evidence that the world had long been preparing itself for the Savior's coming.

* * *

The making of our week was another forward step in man's mastery of the world, in his reach toward science. The week was man's own cluster, not dictated by the visible forces of nature, for the planetary influences were invisible. By seeking astral regularities, by imagining that regularly recurring forces at a distance, forces that could be judged only by their effects, might govern the world, mankind was preparing a new arsenal of thought, an escape from the prison of Again-and-Again. The planets, unworldly forces, would lead mankind out into the world of history.

The planetary week was a path into astrology. And astrology was a step toward new kinds of prophecy. The earlier forms of prophecy can give us a hint of why astrology was a step forward into the world of science. Ancient rituals brought with them a complicated "science" for using parts of a sacrificed animal to foretell the future of the person who offered the sacrifice. Osteomancy, for example, prophesied by examining a bone of the sacrificed animal. In the midnineteenth century, Sir Richard Burton reported from Sindh, in the valley of the Indus, the elaborate technique still widely used for divining from the shoulder blade of a sacrificed sheep. The osteomancers divided the bone into twelve areas, or "houses," each answering a different question about the future. If in the first "house" the bone was clear and smooth, the omen was propitious and the consulter would prove to be a good man. If, in the second "house," which pertained to herds, the bone was clear and clean, the herds would thrive, but if there were layers of red and white streaks, robbers must be expected.

And so it went. Hepatoscopy, which predicted by examining the sacrificed animal's liver, was one of the earliest popular techniques of prophecy among the Assyro-Babylonians. It seems to have been used in China in the Bronze Age. Then the Romans and many others continued the practice. The liver impressed the diviners by its large size, its interesting shape, and its heavy burden of blood. An elaborate bronze model of a sheep's liver, which survives from Piacenza, Italy, is covered with inscriptions indicating what was to be foretold by the condition of each party. Every conceivable human activity or experience—from the knotting of strings to the interpretation of dreams—has become an oracle, witnessing man's desperate eagerness for clues to his future.

By contrast with these other kinds of prophecy, astrology was progressive. Astrology differed in asserting the continuous, regular force of a power at a distance. The influences of heavenly bodies on the events on earth it described as periodic, repetitious, *invisible* forces like those that would rule the scientific mind.

It is not surprising that earliest man was awed by the heavens and enticed by the stars. These first night-lights which inspired the priests of ancient Babylonia also sparked the popular fancy. The changelessness of the rhythm of life on earth made the shifting fireworks of the sky into melodrama. The coming and going of the stars, their rising and falling, their moving about the heavens, became the conflicts and the adventures of the gods.

If the rising and setting of the sun made so much difference on earth, why not also the movement of the other heavenly bodies? The Babylonians made the whole sky a stage for their mythological imagination. Like the rest of nature, the heavens were a scene of living drama. Like the entrails of sacrificial victims, the heavens were divided into zones and then peopled with fantastic figures. The evening star, later called the planet Venus—the brightest heavenly object next to the sun and moon—became a luminous lion roaming the sky from east to west. The great god El, jealous of so bright and high-rising a luminary, put the lion to death again at every dawn. The Old Testament presents this fantasy in the vision of Lucifer cut down for his pride: "How art thou fallen from heaven, O Lucifer, son of the morning! . . . For thou hast said in thine heart, I will ascend into heaven, I will exalt my throne above the stars of God. . . . I will ascend above the heights of the clouds; I will be like the most High" (Isaiah, 14:12–14). This diurnal assassination was accomplished by the messenger of El, Michael (meaning "Who is like El?"). In the sky the gods fought battles, made love, formed alliances, and hatched conspiracies. How inconceivable that these cosmic events should not affect life on earth! Every farmer knew that the clouds in the sky, the warmth of the sun, and the heavenly gift of rain decided the fate of crops and so really governed his own life. Of course, the subtler, more obscure heavenly events required proper interpretation by priests.

This lure of the skies produced a fertile lore of the skies. The powers of sun and rain, the *correspondence* between happenings in the heavens and happenings on earth, stirred the search for other correspondences. The Babylonians were among the first who elaborated a mythological frame for these universal correspondences. Their vivid imaginings would be perpetuated by Greeks, Jews, Romans, and others over the following centuries.

The theory of correspondences became astrology, which sought new links between space and time, between the movements of physical bodies and the unfolding of all human experience. The growth of science would depend on man's willingness to believe the improbable, to cross the dictates of common sense. With astrology man made his first great scientific leap into a scheme for describing how unseen forces from the greatest distance, from the very depth of the heavens, shaped everyday trivia. The heavens, then, were the laboratory of mankind's first science, just as the interior of the human body, the intimate inward realm of his consciousness, and the Dark Continents in the atom, would be the scenes for his latest sciences. Man sought to use his growing knowledge of the patterns of repeating experience in his never-ending struggle to break the iron ring of repetition.

Social or wholesale prophecy flourished in Babylonia. It forecast the large events—battles, droughts, plagues, harvests—which affected the whole community. For centuries such astrology remained a lore rather than a doctrine. The Greeks made a science of it. Personal astrology—"judicial" astrology, or genethlialogy—which cast *a person's* fortune from the position of the heavenly bodies at the moment of his birth, developed more slowly. The person was called the "native," and the prophecy came to be called a "nativity," or horoscope.

The Greeks, too, were torn between wanting to know the good news and fearing to know the bad. Their medical astrologers divided the whole sky according to the signs of the zodiac, then assigned a particular stellar force to each part of the body. Then Greek anti-astrologers attacked the whole dogma of astral forces with arguments that would last into modern times. The names assigned to the stars, the anti-astrologers argued, were quite accidental. Why should this planet be called Mars and that Saturn or Venus? And why did the astrologers limit their horoscopes to human beings? Would not the same astral fortunes govern all animals? And how could astrologers explain the different fortunes of twins? The Epicureans, whose philosophy was built on the belief in each man's freedom to shape his destiny, attacked astrology as a way of making men think they were mere slaves of the stars.

In ancient Rome, astrology attained an influence seldom equaled in later centuries. Astrologers—called *Chaldaei* after the Chaldean or Babylonian origins of the science, or *Mathematici* from their astronomical calculations—were a recognized profession whose repute varied with the turbulent times. Under the Roman Republic they became so powerful and so unpopular that in 139 B.C. they were expelled not only from Rome but from all Italy. Afterwards, under the empire, when their dangerous prophecies had brought several astrologers to trial for treason, they were repeatedly banished. But the same emperor who would banish some astrologers for their ominous forebodings, would employ others to guide his imperial household. Some areas were declared off limits. In the late empire, even when astrologers were tolerated or encouraged, they were forbidden to make prophecies about the life of the emperor.

Christian emperors failed in their efforts to discourage astrology. "There are many," the historian Ammianus Marcellinus recounted in the late fourth century after Constantine officially converted the empire to Christianity, "who do not presume either to bathe, or to dine, or to appear in public, till they have diligently consulted, according to the rules of astrology, the situation of Mercury and the aspect of the moon. It is singular enough that this vain credulity may often be discovered among the profane sceptics, who impiously doubt or deny the existence of a celestial power." By that time the powers of the seven planets were attested by the quiet transformation of the eight-day week into the week of seven days, with each day now subordinate to one of the seven planets. When Romans attended the imperial circus, the astral powers were seen everywhere. Over each of the twelve stalls from which the chariots started their race, there appeared a sign of one of the twelve constellations of the zodiac. Each of the seven tracks of the racecourse was intended to represent a heavenly circuit of one of the seven planets.

THE RISE OF THE EQUAL HOUR

W HILE MAN ALLOWED his time to be parsed by the changing cycles of daylight he remained a slave of the sun. To
become the master of his time, to assimilate night into
the day, to slice his life into neat, usable portions, he had to find a
way to mark off precise small portions—not only equal hours, but
even minutes and seconds and parts of seconds. He would have to
make a machine. It is surprising that machines to measure time were
so long in coming. Not until the fourteenth century did Europeans
devise mechanical timepieces. Until then, as we have seen, the measuring of time was left to the shadow clock, the water clock, the sandglass, and the miscellaneous candle clocks and scent clocks. While
there was remarkable progress five thousand years ago in measuring
the year, and useful week clusters of days were long in use, the subdivided day was another matter. Only in modern times did we begin to
live by the hour, much less by the minute.

* * *

The first steps toward the mechanical measurement of time, the
beginnings of the modern clock in Europe, came not from farmers
or shepherds, nor from merchants or craftsmen, but from religious
persons anxious to perform promptly and regularly their duties to
God. Monks needed to know the times for their appointed prayers.

In Europe the first mechanical clocks were designed not to *show* the time but to *sound* it. The first true clocks were alarms. The first Western clockworks, which set us on the way to clockmaking, were weight-driven machines which struck a bell after a measured interval. Two kinds of clocks were made for this purpose. Probably the earlier were small monastic alarms, or chamber clocks—called *horologia excitatoria*, or awakening clocks—for the cell of the *custos horologii*, or guardian of the clock. These rang a small bell to alert a monk to summon the others to prayer. He would then go up to strike the large bell, usually set high in a tower, so that all could hear. About the same time much larger turret clocks began to be made and placed in the towers, where they would ring the large bell automatically.

These monastic clocks announced the canonical hours, the times of day prescribed by the Church's canons, or rules, for devotion. The number of these hours varied, of course, with the changing canons of the Church, with the varied customs from place to place, and with the rules of particular orders. In the sixth century, after Saint Benedict, the canonical hours were standardized at seven. Distinct prayers were specified to be said at the first light or dawn (Matins or Lauds), with the sunrise *(Hora Prima)*, at midmorning *(Hora Tertia)*, at noon *(Hora Sexta* or *Meridies)*, at midafternoon *(Hora Nona)*, at sunset (Vespers, or *Hora Vesperalis*), and at nightfall (Compline, or *Completorium*). The number of strokes of the bell varied from four at sunrise to one at noon and back to four again at nightfall. The precise hour, by our modern calculation, for each of these prayers depended in any given place on the latitude and the season. Despite the complexity of the problem, monastic clocks were adjusted to vary the time between bells according to the season.

Efforts to adapt earlier timekeeping devices to the making of sounds had never been quite successful. A clever Parisian fitted a lens into his sundial to act as a burning glass which precisely at noon focused on the touchhole of a small cannon, and so automatically saluted the sun at its apex. This elegant cannon clock, installed by the Duke of Orléans in the garden of the Palais Royal in 1786, is said to have fired the shot that started the French Revolution. Centuries before, complicated water clocks had been designed to mark passing time by tossing pebbles or blowing whistles. Some such devices were probably tried in monasteries.

But a new kind of timepiece, a mechanical timepiece that was a true clock, would be much better adapted to the new mechanical needs. The very word "clock" bears the mark of its monastic origins. The Middle English *clok* came from the Middle Dutch word for bell and is a cognate of the German *Glocke*, which means bell. Strictly speaking, in the beginning a timepiece was not considered to be a clock unless it rang a bell. It was only later that it came to mean any device that measured passing time.

These first mechanical clocks came into an age when sunlight circumscribed the times of life and movement, when artificial lights had not yet begun to confuse night with day. Medieval striking clocks remained silent during the dark hours. After the four strokes which announced Compline, the prayers at nightfall, the next bell was not sounded until the time for Matins, the prayers at dawn the next morning. But in the long run the unintended consequence of the making of mechanical clocks, and a hidden imperative of the machine itself, was to incorporate both hours of darkness and hours of sunlight into a single equal-houred twenty-four-hour day. The monastic clock, specially designed for *sounding* the time, pointed the way to a new way of thinking about time.

The sundial, water clock, and hourglass were all designed primarily to *show* the passing time, by the visible gradual flow of a shadow across a dial, of water from a bowl, of sand through a glass. But the mechanical clock, in its monastic origins, was made for a decisive mechanical act, a stroke of a hammer on a bell. The needs of mechanical timekeeping, the logic of the machine itself, imposed a new feeling. Instead of being synonymous with repeated cycles of the sun, which varied as the cycles of the seasons commanded, or with the shorter cycles of other flowing media, time now was to be measured by the staccato of a machine. Making a machine to *sound* the canonical hours required, and achieved, mechanical novelties which would be the foundation of clockmaking for centuries to come.

The force that moved the arm that struck the bell was provided by falling weights. What made the machine truly novel was the device that prevented the free fall of the weights and interrupted their drop into regular intervals. The sundial had shown the uninterrupted movement of the sun's shadow, and the sandglass operated by the free-falling of water or sand. What gave this new machine a longer duration and measured off the units was a simple enough device, which has remained almost uncelebrated in history. It was called an escapement, since it was a way of regulating the "escape" of the motive power into the clock, and it held revolutionary import for human experience.

With the simplicity of the greatest inventions, the "escapement" was nothing more than an arrangement that would regularly interrupt the force of a falling weight. The interruptor was so designed that it would alternately check and then release the force of the weight on the moving machinery of the clock. This was the basic invention that made all modern clocks possible. Now a weight falling only a short distance could keep a clock going for hours as the regular downward pull of the falling weights was translated into the interrupted, staccato movement of the clock's machinery.

The earliest simple form was the "verge" escapement. An unknown mechanical genius first imagined a way of connecting the falling weight by intersecting cogged wheels to a vertical axle which carried a horizontal bar, or verge, with weights attached. These weights regulated the movement. When they were moved outward, the clock beat slower; when moved inward, the clock went faster. The back-and-forth movement of the bar (moved by the large falling weights) would alternately engage and disengage the cogs on the clock's machinery. These interrupted movements eventually measured off the minutes and, later, the seconds. When, in due course, clocks became common, people would think of time no longer as a flowing stream but as the accumulation of discrete measured moments. The sovereign time that governed daily lives would no longer be the sunlight's smooth-flowing elastic cycles. Mechanized time would no longer flow. The tick-tock of the clock's escapement would become the voice of time.

Such a machine plainly had nothing to do with the sun or the movements of the planets. Its own laws provided an endless series of uniform units. The "accuracy" of a clock—which meant the uniformity of its measured units—would depend on the precision and regularity of the escapement.

*   *   *

The canonical hours, which had measured out the daylight into the appropriate elastic units between divine services, were registered on clocks until about the fourteenth century. It was around 1330 that the hour became our modern hour, one of twenty-four equal parts of a day. This new "day" included the night. It was measured by the time between one noon and the next, or, more precisely, what modern astronomers call "mean solar time." For the first time in history, an "hour" took on a precise, year-round, everywhere meaning.

There are few greater revolutions in human experience than this movement from the seasonal or "temporary" hour to the equal hour. Here was man's declaration of independence from the sun, new proof of his mastery over himself and his surroundings. Only later would it be revealed that he had accomplished this mastery by putting himself under the dominion of a machine with imperious demands all its own.

The first clocks did not have dials or hands at all. They did not need them, since their use was simply to *sound* the hour. An illiterate populace that might have trouble reading a dial would not mistake the sound of bells. With the coming of the "equal" hour, replacing the "temporary" or "canonical" hour, the sounding of hours was ideally adapted for measurement by a simple machine. Sun time was translated into clock time.

By the fourteenth century in Europe large turret clocks in the belfries of churches and town halls were sounding the equal hours, heralding a new time-consciousness. Church towers, built to salute God and to mark man's heavenward aspirations, now became clock towers. The *torre* became the campanile. As early as 1335, the campanile of the Chapel of the Blessed Virgin in Milan was admired by the chronicler Galvano della Fiamma for its wonderful clock with many bells. "A very large hammer . . . strikes one bell twenty-four times according to the number of the twenty-four hours of the day and night; so that at the first hour of the night it gives one sound, at the second, two strokes, at the third, three, and at the fourth, four; and thus it distinguishes hour from hour, which is in the highest degree necessary for all conditions of men." Such equal-hour clocks became common in the towns of Europe. Now serving the whole community, they were a new kind of public utility, offering a service each citizen could not afford to provide himself.

People unwittingly recognized the new era when, noting the time of day or night, they said it was nine "o'clock"—a time "of the clock." When Shakespeare's characters mentioned the time, "of the clock," they recalled the hour they had heard last struck. Imogen, Cymbeline's daughter, explains that a faithful lover is accustomed "to weepe 'twixt clock and clock" for her beloved. While the populace now began to know the "hour," several centuries passed before they could talk of "minutes." During the whole fourteenth century, dials were seldom found on clocks, for the clocks' function was still to *sound* the hours. They are not found on the Italian campaniles, though there may have been one on St. Paul's Cathedral (1344) in London. Early dials were not like ours. Some showed hours only from I to VI with hands that moved around the dial four times in twenty-four hours. Others, like the famous work of Giovanni de' Dondi (1318–1389), enumerated the full twenty-four hours.

It was not too difficult to improve clocks that already struck the hour so that they could strike the quarter-hour. A dial, marked 1 to 4, was sometimes added to indicate the quarters. Later these were replaced by the figures 15, 30, 45, and 60 to indicate minutes. There was still no minute hand.

By 1500 the clock at Wells Cathedral in England was striking the quarter-hours, but had no way to mark the minutes. To measure minutes you still had to use a sandglass. A separate concentric minute hand, in addition to the hour hand, did not come into use until the pendulum was successfully applied to clocks. The pendulum also made it possible to indicate seconds. By 1670 it was not unusual for clocks to have a second hand whose movements were controlled by a 39-inch pendulum with a period of just one second.

More than any earlier invention the mechanical clock began to incorporate the dark hours of night into the day. In order to show the right time at daybreak this time machine had to be kept going continuously all night.

When does a "day" begin? Answers to this question have been almost as numerous as those to the question of how many days should be in a week. "The evening and the morning were the first day," we read in the first chapter of Genesis. The very first "day" then was really a night. Perhaps this was another way of describing the mystery of Creation, leaving God to perform his miraculous handiwork in the dark. The Babylonians and the early Hindus calculated their day from sunrise. The Athenians, like the Jews, began their "day" at sunset, and carried on the practice through the nineteenth century. Orthodox Muslims, literally following Holy Script, continue to begin their day at sunset, when they still set their clocks at twelve.

As we have seen, for most of history, mankind did not think of a day as a unit of twenty-four hours. Only with the invention and diffusion of the mechanical clock did this notion become common. The early Saxons divided their day into "tides"—"morningtide," "noontide," and "eveningtide"—and some of the earliest English sundials are so marked.

Other widespread ways of dividing the day were much simpler than the system of "temporary" hours, which subdivided daylight and darkness. The seven canonical hours marked the passing time for Columbus and his crew.

Even after the arrival of the mechanical clock the sun left its mark on the measuring of the hours. The "double-twelve" system, by which Americans count the hours, is such a relic. When the *daylight* hours were measured off and subdivided, in contrast to the hours of night, the hours of each of the two parts were numbered separately. And so it remained, even after a machine required that time be measured continuously. The first 24-hour clocks—while substituting equal mechanical hours for the elastic canonical or "temporary" hours—still remained curiously tied to the sun. They normally used sunset as the end of the twenty-fourth hour.

To ask how we came to our day, hour, minute, and second takes us deep into the archaeology of everyday life. Our English word "day" (no relation to the Latin *dies*) comes from an old Saxon word "to burn," which also meant the hot season, or the warm time. Our "hour" comes from Latin and Greek words meaning season, or time of day. It meant one-twelfth part of the sunlight or the darkness—the "temporary," or seasonal, hour—varying with season and latitude, long before it acquired its modern meaning of one twenty-fourth part of the equinoctial day.

Why the twenty-four? Historians do not help us much. The Egyptians did divide their day into twenty-four "hours"—"temporary," of course. Apparently they chose this number because they used the sexagesimal system of numbers, based on multiples of sixty, which had been developed by the Babylonians. This pushes the mystery back into earlier centuries, for we have no clear explanation of why the Babylonians built their arithmetic as they did. But their use of the number sixty seems to have had nothing to do with astronomy or the movement of heavenly bodies. We have seen how the Egyptians fixed 360 days as the regular days of their year—12 months of 30 days each, supplemented by 5 additional days at the end of each year. They also marked off 360 degrees in a circle, perhaps by analogy to the yearly circuit of the sun. Sixty, being one-sixth of the 360 and so a natural subdivision in their sexagesimal system, became a convenient subdivision of the circle, and also of each "degree" or each hour. Perhaps the Chaldean Babylonians, noticing five planets—Mercury, Venus, Mars, Jupiter, and Saturn—multiplied 12 (the number of the months, and a multiple of 6) by the planetary 5, and so arrived at the significant 60.

An everyday relic of the primitive identification of the circuit of the sun with the full circle is our sign for a "degree." The tiny circle we now use to designate a degree is probably a hieroglyph for the sun. If the degree sign ° was a picture of the sun, then 360°—a full circle—would also properly mean a cycle of 360 days, or a full year. The degree as a way of dividing the circle was first applied by ancient Babylonian and Egyptian astronomers to the circle of the zodiac to designate the stage or distance traveled by the sun each day, just as a *sign* described for them the astronomical space passed through in a month.

Our "minute," from the medieval Latin *pars minuta prima* (first minute or small part), originally described the one-sixtieth of a unit in the Babylonian system of sexagesimal fractions. And "second," from *partes minutae secundae*, was a further subdivision on the base of sixty. Since the Babylonian arithmetic was based on that unit, it was their version of a decimal and was easier to handle in their scientific calculations than other "vulgar fractions" *(minutae)* would have been. Ptolemy used this sixty-unit system for subdividing the circle, and he also used it to divide the day. Not until much later, perhaps in the thirteenth century with the arrival of the mechanical clock, did the minute become a division of the hour. The language, again, is a clue to the needs and capacities of time-keeping machinery. The "second" was at first an abbreviation for "second minute," and originally described the unit resulting from the second operation of sexagesimal subdivision. Long used for subdivisions of a circle, seconds were not applied to timekeeping until clockmaking was refined in the late sixteenth century.

The clock did not entirely liberate itself from the sun, from the dictates of light and darkness. In Western Europe the hours of the clock continued to be numbered from noon, when the sun was at the meridian, or from midnight midway between two noons. In most of Europe and in America a new day still begins at midnight by the clock.

The archaeology of our everyday life leads us all over the world. The 365 days of our year acknowledge our debt to ancient Egyptian priests, while the names of months—January, February, March— and of the days of our seven-day week—Saturday, Sunday, Monday—remain our tie to the early Hebrews and to Greek and Roman astrologers. When we mark each hour of our 24-hour day, and designate the minutes after the hour, we are living, as a historian of ancient science reminds us, by "the results of a Hellenistic modification of an Egyptian practice combined with Babylonian numerical procedures."

*　*　*

The broadcasting medium of the medieval town was bells. Since the human voice could not reach all who needed to hear a civic announcement, bells told the hours, summoned help to extinguish a fire, warned of an approaching enemy, called men to arms, brought them to work, sent them to bed, knelled public mourning at the death of a king, sounded public rejoicing at the birth of a prince or a coronation, celebrated the election of a pope or a victory in war. "They may ring their bells now," Sir Robert Walpole observed in 1739 on hearing bells rung in London to announce the declaration of war against Spain, "before long they will be wringing their hands." Americans treasure a relic of that age of bells in the Liberty Bell, which announced Independence in Philadelphia.

There was supposed to be power and therapy in the sound of the bells that were rung to ward off an epidemic or to prevent a storm. Citizens of Lyons, France, in 1481 petitioned their town council that they "sorely felt the need for a great clock whose strokes could be heard by all citizens of all parts of the town. If such a clock were to be made, more merchants would come to the fairs, the citizens would be very consoled, cheerful and happy and would live a more orderly life, and the town would gain in decoration."

Community pride was a pride of bells. Churches, monasteries, and whole towns were judged by the reach and resonance of the peals from their towers. An inscription on an old bell boasted, "I mourn death, I disperse the lightening, I announce the Sabbath, I rouse the lazy, I scatter the winds, I appease the bloodthirsty" *(Funera plango, fulmina frango, Sabbath pango, Excito lentos, dissipo ventos, paco cruentos)*. Paul Revere, the messenger of the American Revolution, made a reputation, and a fortune, as a caster of bells for proud New England towns. The art of bell-casting and experiments with bell-ringing devices advanced the art of the clockmaker and encouraged the elaboration of clocks.

Widespread illiteracy helps explain why dials were slow to appear on the exterior of public clocks. Not everybody could read even the simple numbers on a clockface. The very same factors that delayed the production of calibrated dials also encouraged experiment, ingenuity, and playfulness with clockwork performances. The great public clocks of the Middle Ages did not much advance the precision of clockworks, which, before the pendulum, lost or gained as much as an hour a day. It was technically difficult to improve the escapement hidden inside the machinery, and that regulated the accuracy of the movement. But it was easy to add wheels to wheels to improve the automated public display.

Nowadays the calendrical or astronomical indicators on antique clocks seem superfluous ornaments on a machine that should only show us hours, minutes, and seconds. For at least two centuries after the great mechanical clocks began to be built in Europe, it was quite otherwise. The magnificent clock made about 1350 for the Cathedral of Strasbourg served the public as both a calendar and an aid to astrology. Also an instructive and entertaining toy, it performed a variety show as it tolled the hours. In addition to a moving calendar and an astrolabe with pointers marking the movement of sun, moon, and planets, in its upper compartment the Three Magi bowed in procession before a statue of the Virgin Mary while a tune played on the carillon. At the end of the procession of the Magi, an enormous cock made of wrought iron with a copper comb and set on a gilded base opened its beak and stuck out its tongue, crowing as it flapped its wings. When rebuilt in 1574, the Strasbourg clock included a calendar showing movable feasts, a Copernican planetarium with revolutions of the planets, phases of the moon, eclipses, apparent and sidereal times, precession of the equinoxes, and equations for translating sun and moon indicators into local time. A special dial showed the saint's days. Each of the four quarters of each hour was struck by a figure showing one of the Four Ages of Man: Infancy, Adolescence, Manhood, and Old Age. Every day at noon the twelve Apostles passed before Christ to receive His blessing. The days of the week were indicated by chariots among clouds, each carrying the appropriate pagan god. The burghers of Strasbourg boasted that they had produced one of the Seven Wonders of Germany. In the late nineteenth century, German immigrant clockmakers in the Pennsylvania Dutch countryside produced Americanized versions of these "apostolic clocks" which added to the traditional procession of Magi and Apostles a patriotic parade of presidents of the United States.

The most popular dramas of the Middle Ages did not occur on a theater stage, nor even at the fairs or in the courtyards of churches, but were broadcast from clock towers. When the great turret clocks were in full display, they performed every hour on the hour, and every day, including Sundays and holidays. The Wells Cathedral clock, first built in 1392 and improved in the following centuries, offered a widely appealing show. Dials indicated the hour, the age, and phases of the moon. Opposite the moon was a figure of Phoebus, for the sun, weighted to remain upright. Another dial showed a minute hand concentric with an hour hand that carried an image of the sun which made a full circle each twenty-four hours. In a niche above, two pairs of armored knights circled around in combat in opposite directions. As the bell struck the hour one of them was unhorsed and then, when out of view, regained his saddle. A conventional uniformed figure, "Jack Blandifet," struck each hour with a hammer but sounded the quarter-hours on two smaller bells with his heels.

Clockmakers lost no opportunity for drama. In place of a clapper hidden in the bell, they preferred vivid automata to strike the hours and the quarters. The striking figure became personified as "Jack," derived from Jacquemart, a shortened form of Jacques combined with *marteau* (hammer). This word later became generalized into "jack," meaning a tool that saved labor. A pair of such Jacks, two robust men of bronze, dating from 1499, still perform for us on the Piazza San Marco in Venice. Here was something for everyone. As the chronicler at Parma observed in 1431, to the whole populace *("al popolo")* the town clock told only the simple hours, while to the few who could understand *("agli intelligenti")* it showed the phases of the moon and all sorts of astronomical subtleties.

The clock dial, a convenience for the literate, and the first mechanical device for registering time visibly rather than aurally, is said to have been invented by Jacopo de' Dondi of Chioggia, Italy, in 1344. For this he was honored with the title of the Horologist *(Del Orologio)*, which became his family name. "Gracious Reader," his epitaph boasted, "advised from afar from the top of a high tower how you tell the time and the hours, though their number changes, recognize my invention. . . ." His son, Giovanni de' Dondi, completed in 1364 one of the most complicated clockworks ever built, combining a planetarium and a timepiece. Although the clock itself has disappeared, Dondi left detailed descriptions and complate drawings from which this famous "astrarium" has been reconstructed, and can now be viewed in the Smithsonian Institution in Washington, D.C. An elegant heptagonal machine of brass activated by falling weights, it stands about five feet high. In many respects it was centuries ahead of its time, for it took account of such subtleties as the slightly elliptical orbit of the moon. On its numerous dials, it recorded the mean hour and minute, the times of the setting and rising of the sun, conversion of mean time to sidereal time, the "temporary" hours, the day of the month and month of the year, the fixed feasts of the Church, the length of daylight for each day, the dominical letter of the year, the solar and lunar cycles, the annual movement of the sun and moon in the ecliptic, and the annual movements of the five planets. In addition, Dondi provided the means to predict eclipses, indicated the movable feasts of the Church, and devised a perpetual calendar for Easter. People from everywhere came to Padua to see the clock and meet the genius who had spent sixteen years making it.

In that age the boundary was much less sharp than it would become later between the data of the heavens and the needs of everyday life. Night was more threatening, and darker, and the modern mechanical antidotes to darkness, heat, and cold had not yet been invented. For people on the seacoast or on a river the tide times were crucial. Over everybody and everything, the influence of the planets—the astral powers—governed. The Strasbourg clock of 1352 used the data of the heavens to provide the community also with medical advice. A conventional human figure was surrounded by the signs of the zodiac. Lines were drawn from each sign to the parts of the body over which it ruled and which should be treated only when that sign was dominant. The clock then offered information about the changing dominance of the signs, helping citizens and doctors to choose the best times for medical treatment. The astrological indications on the public clock in Mantua, Italy, impressed a visitor in 1473 with its display of "the proper time for phlebotomy, for surgery, for making dresses, for tilling the soil, for undertaking journeys, and for other things very useful in this world."

WHY IT HAPPENED IN THE WEST

IN EUROPE THE clock very early became a *public* machine. Churches expected communicants to assemble regularly and repeatedly for prayers, and flourishing cities brought people together to share a life of commerce and entertainment. When clocks took their places in church steeples and town belfries, they entered on a public stage. There they proclaimed themselves to rich and poor, awakening the interest even of those who had no personal reason to mark the hours. Machines that began as public instruments gradually became some of the most widely diffused private instruments. But instruments that began their lives in private might never become diffused into the wants and needs of the whole community. The first advertisement for the clock was the clock itself, performing for new publics all over Europe.

No self-respecting European town would be without its public clock, which tolled all citizens together to defend, to celebrate, or to mourn. A community that could focus its resources in a dazzling public clock was that much more a community. The bell tolled for all and each, as the poet John Donne noted in 1623, and the tolling of the community's bells was a reminder that "I am involved in mankind."

Many communities, even before they had organized sewage disposal or a water supply, offered the town clock as a public service. In due course each citizen wanted his own private clocks—first for his household, then for his person. When more people had their private timepieces, more other people needed timepieces to fulfill their neighbors' expectations at worship, at work, and at play.

All the while, the clock was being secularized—another way of saying it was being publicized. The first European clocks, as we have seen, alerted cloistered monks for their regular prayers, but when the clock moved into the church steeple and then into the town belfry, it moved out to a secular world. This larger public soon required the clock for the whole schedule of daily life. In Europe the artificial hour, the machine-made hour, took the calculations of time out of the calendar-universe, out from the penumbra of astrology, into the bright everyday light. When steam power, electric power, and artificial illumination kept factories going around the clock, when night was assimilated into day, the artificial hour, the clock-marked hour became the constant regimen for everyone. The story of the rise of the clock in the West, then, is the story of new modes and widening arenas of publicity.

The contrast to China is dramatic and illuminating. There, circumstances conspired to prevent publicity. The first spectacular mechanical clockworks in China, as we have seen, were made not to mark the hour but to mark the calendar. And the science of the calendar—both of its making and of its meaning—was hedged in by government secrecy. Each Chinese dynasty was symbolized, served, and protected by its own new calendar. Between the first unification of the empire in the third century B.C. (c. 221) and the end of the Ch'ing, or Manchu, dynasty in 1911, about one hundred different calendars were issued, with a name identifying it with a particular dynasty or emperor. These were not required by advances in astronomy or in the technology of observation, but were needed to put the cachet of the heavens on the authority of a new emperor. Private calendar-making was punished as a kind of counterfeiting—as both a threat to the security of the emperor and an act of lèse majesté. The French Jesuit and translator of Ricci, Nicholas Trigault, reported in the early seventeenth century that the Ming emperors "forbad any to learn this Judiciall Astrology but those which by Hereditary right are thereto disigned, to prevent Innovations."

To find clues to why the mother of machines proved so unfertile there, we must recall some of the large features of life in ancient China. One of the first, most remarkable of Chinese achievements was a well-organized centralized government. As early as 221 B.C. the "Chinese Caesar," the precocious King Cheng, who had ascended the throne of Ch'in at the age of thirteen, had managed within twenty-five years to unify a half-dozen Chinese provinces into a single great empire, with a vast hierarchy of bureaucrats. He standardized the laws and the written language, established uniform weights and measures, and even fixed the length for carriage axles so they would fit into the wheel ruts.

The Chinese kings, as we have seen, had regulated the calendar, the state religion remained emphatically tied to the round of the seasons, and astronomy became "the secret science of priest-kings." Chinese farming depended on irrigation, and successful irrigation required predicting the rhythms of the monsoon rains and the melting of the snows to flood the rivers and fill the canals.

From earliest times in China an astronomical observatory was an essential part of the cosmological temple, the ruler's ritual headquarters. As the central government became stronger and better organized, Chinese astronomy, by contrast with astronomy in ancient Greece or medieval Europe, became more and more official and governmental. This meant, of course, that Chinese astronomy became increasingly bureaucratic and esoteric. There the technology of the clock was the technology of astrological indicators. Just as in the West the machinery for minting coins, for printing paper money, or for manufacturing gunpowder was tightly controlled, so in China were calendrical timepieces.

The imperial rites that survive from the era of the Chinese Caesar required the emperor to define the four cardinal points—north, south, east, and west—by observations of the polestar and the sun. The Imperial Astronomer, one of the highest-ranking hereditary officials, was expected to keep watch at night from the emperor's observatory tower. He "concerns himself with the twelve years [the sidereal revolutions of Jupiter], the twelve months, the twelve [double] hours, the ten days, and the positions of the twenty-eight stars. He distinguishes them and orders them so that he can make a general plan of the state of the heavens. He takes observations of the sun at the winter and summer solstices, and of the moon at the spring and autumn equinoxes, in order to determine the succession of the four seasons."

Another high hereditary official, the Imperial Astrologer, interpreted the message of the heavens for the destiny of the people.

> He concerns himself with the stars in the heavens, keeping a record of the changes and movements of the planets, the sun and the moon, in order to examine the movements of the terrestrial world, with the object of distinguishing good and bad fortune. He divides the territories of the nine regions of the empire in accordance with their dependence on particular celestial bodies. All the fiefs and principalities are connected with distinct stars, and from this their prosperity or misfortune can be ascertained. He makes prognostications, according to the twelve years [of the Jupiter cycle], of good and evil in the terrestrial world. From the colours of the five kinds of clouds, he determines the coming of floods or drought, abundance or famine. From the twelve winds he draws conclusions about the state of harmony of heaven and earth, and takes note of the good or bad signs which result from their accord or disaccord.

Incidentally these state astrologers produced the most remarkable continuous record of celestial phenomena before the rise of modern astronomy. The Chinese record of an eclipse in 1361 B.C. is probably the earliest verifiable eclipse reported by any people. Other Chinese records cover long periods for which we have no other accurate chronicle of celestial events. Twentieth-century radio-astronomers still use these records in their study of novae and supernovae.

While these state records survive, most of the ancient Chinese literature on astronomy has disappeared. Because astronomy was so state-oriented, so security-bound, and so secret, the old astronomy books have left few traces. By contrast, the early books on mathematics, which were used by merchants, directors of public works, and military commanders, have survived in considerable numbers. Repeated imperial edicts enforced state security for calendrical science, astronomy, and astrology. In A.D. 840, for example, when the empire had recently been disturbed by the appearance of several comets, the Emperor ordered all observers in the imperial observatory to keep their business secret. "If we hear of any intercourse between the astronomical officials or their subordinates and officials of other government departments or miscellaneous common people, it will be regarded as a violation of security regulations which should be strictly adhered to. From now onwards, therefore, the astronomical officials are on no account to mix with civil servants and common people in general. Let the Censorate look to it." The security concerns which so notoriously plagued atomic research centers at Los Alamos and Harwell in World War II had their Chinese antecedents.

The famous Heavenly Clockwork of Su Sung could not have been constructed if Su Sung had not been a high imperial official authorized to help the Emperor view the astrological destinies. This explains, too, why, within a few years, Su Sung's spectacular achievement had become only a dim legend. If Su Sung had built his clockwork not for the private garden of a Chinese emperor but for a European town hall, he would have been hailed as a heroic public benefactor. His work would have become a monument to civic pride—the object of widespread emulation.

* * *

The Emperor himself had an especially intimate need for calendrical timekeepers. For every night the Emperor in his bedchamber had to know the movements and positions of the constellations at every hour—in precisely the way Su Sung's Heavenly Clockwork made possible. In China the ages of individuals and their astrological destinies were calculated not from the hour of birth but from the hour of conception.

When Su Sung constructed his imperial clock, the Emperor had as attendants a large number of wives and concubines of various ranks. These women totaled 121 (one-third of 365, to the nearest round number), including one empress, three consorts, nine spouses, twenty-seven concubines, and eighty-one assistant concubines. Their rotation of duty, as described in the Record of the Rites of the Chou dynasty, was as follows:

> The lower-ranking [women] come first, the higher-ranking come last. The assistant concubines, eighty-one in number, share the imperial couch nine nights in groups of nine. The concubines, twenty-seven in number, are allotted three nights in groups of nine. The nine spouses and the three consorts are allotted one night to each group, and the empress also alone one night. On the fifteenth day of every month the sequence is complete, after which it repeats in reverse order.

By this arrangement, the women of highest rank would lie with the Emperor on the nights nearest to the full moon, when the Yin, or female, influence would be most potent, and so best able to match the potent Yang, or male, force of the Son of Heaven. So timely a combination, it was believed, would assure the strongest virtues in the children then conceived. The main function of the women of lower ranks was to nourish the Emperor's Yang with their Yin.

A corps of secretarial ladies kept the records of the Emperor's cohabitations with their brushes dipped in imperial vermilion. The proper order of these proceedings in the imperial bedchamber was believed essential to the larger order and well-being of the empire. In the disorderly days of the ninth century, writers lamented that the ancient tradition of "nine ordinary companions every night, and the empress for two nights at the time of the full moon" was no longer respected, with the result that "alas, nowadays, all the three thousand [palace women] compete in confusion."

The need for an accurate calendrical clock, to show the position of the heavenly bodies at each moment of the day or night, was then obvious, to ensure the best-qualified succession of emperors. The ruling houses of China did not follow the rule of primogeniture. In theory, only the sons of the empress could become emperor, but this usually left the emperor with a number of young princes from whom to choose his heir. A prudent emperor was bound to give close attention to the astrological omens at the precise moment when each prince was conceived. To record these facts accurately was the duty of the secretarial ladies with their vermilion brushes. The astronomical observations and mechanical calculations of Su Sung's Heavenly Clockwork provided the data for these records and prognostications, and so were of great political significance. But these curiosities of the imperial court had little to do with a farmer's life. The community as a whole was not expected, and did not dare, to plumb the depths of state astrology, nor to profit from the data of calendrical timepieces.

* * *

By contrast, the spread of the clock in the West came from community needs—which meant the need for publicity and portability. The crucial development, as we have seen, was the advance from the weight-driven to the spring-driven clock. Heavy weights and their accompanying pendulum rooted a clock in the site where it was first placed. But a portable spring-driven clock was versatile in its habitat. For Europeans the seafaring clock in the eighteenth century was an exploring machine—a catalyst to cartographers, travelers, merchants, botanists, and navigators, a device that encouraged sailors to go farther, helped them know where they were, and made it possible to come back again. Eventually the pocket watch, and then the wristwatch, would put a timepiece on the person of millions.

The first great Chinese clock, incarcerated in the precincts of the imperial court, was driven by a stream of water. Su Sung's escapement, the heart of his "heavenly clockwork," required a continuous stream of water, which, of course, firmly attached the machine to one site.

To confirm that there was nothing "Oriental" or "Asiatic" about the sterility of the clock in China, we have the interesting contrast of Japan. For while the Chinese remained obstinate isolationists, stubbornly suspicious of anything from outside, the Japanese combined a determination to preserve their own arts and institutions with a remarkable capacity for imitating and incorporating whatever came from abroad. Before the end of the seventeenth century the Japanese were producing their own copies of European clocks. In the next century the Japanese began to develop a clockmaking industry, turning out clocks of their own design with an adjustable "hour" plate and fixed hands. They perfected a double-escapement clock with one balance for the hours of the day and a second for hours of the night, since the "hours" of day and night were unequal.

Until 1873 the Japanese retained the "natural" sunlight day divided into six equal hours between sunrise and sunset. Their "hour" still varied from day to day, but they succeeded in making a clock that accurately marked these unequal hours throughout the year. Since the paper walls of Japanese houses were too fragile to hold up a heavy European wall clock, they devised a "pillar clock," which hung from the timber framing of a Japanese room and marked the hours on a vertical scale. Sliding indicators on a vertical scale could be readily moved to mark the proper changing intervals of the variable hour from day to day. The Japanese retention of a system long since abandoned in Europe actually proved an incentive to their ingenuity.

The difficulty of making mainsprings delayed the manufacture of spring-driven clocks in Japan until the 1830's. Before long the Japanese were making their own elegant *inro* watches to fit into the traditional Japanese *inro*, or pillbox case, which was attached to a cord, to be worn with the pocketless Japanese costume, around the neck or tucked into the obi. Since the Japanese customarily sat on the floor, they did not develop long-case, or "grandfather," clocks.

The congestion of Japan, with its flourishing urban centers and enterprising merchants, encouraged the publicity of arts and crafts, and kept people and things in motion. Numerous ports and a network of well-traveled roads circulated all sorts of commodities. Clockmaking developed earlier in Japan than in China. Local lords, daimyos and shoguns ordered clocks for their castles, but the public taste for clocks and the opportunity for the millions to buy them did not come until the nineteenth century.

THE AWE OF MOUNTAINS

CHAPTER 10

L ONG before men thought of conquering the mountains, the mountains had conquered men. Castle of the Higher Powers, the mountain long remained, in the words of Edward Whymper, the first conqueror of the Matterhorn, "an affront to man's conquest of nature." Every high mountain was idolized by people who lived in its shadow. Inspired by the Himalayas that they gazed at in awe, the people of north India imagined a still higher mountain farther north, which they called Mt. Meru. Hindus and, later, Buddhists made that mythical 84,000-mile-high mountain-above-the-mountains the dwelling place of their gods. Mt. Meru, central mountain of the universe and vertical axis of the egg-shaped cosmos, was surrounded by seven concentric mountain rings around which revolved the sun, the moon, and the planets. Between the seventh and an outer eighth ring were the continents of the earth.

On Mt. Meru, according to the sacred Hindu scriptures, "there are rivers of sweet water running in it, and beautiful golden houses inhabited by the spiritual beings, the Deva, by their singers the Gandharva, and their harlots the Apsaras." The later Buddhist tradition held "that Meru lies between four worlds in the four cardinal directions; that it is square at the bottom and round at the top; that it has the length of 80,000 yojana, one half of which rises into heaven, whilst the other half goes down into the earth. That side which is next to our world consists of blue sapphires, which is the reason why heaven appears to us blue; the other sides are of rubies, yellow and white gems. Thus Meru is the centre of the earth." The divine Himalaya—a range 1,600 miles long and 150 miles wide—were all that could be seen of the High Places. Peaks over 25,000 feet, including Everest, Kanchenjunga, Godwin Austen, Dhaulagiri, Nanga Parbat, and Gosainthan, defied human climbers even after the age of mountain climbing had arrived. They also inspired gratitude, for hidden high among them (prosaic geographers of a later age would call them the "watershed") were the secret sources of the life-giving Indus, the sacred Ganges, and the Brahmaputra.

* * *

The Japanese, too, had their Fujiyama, a goddess who dominated their landscape and never ceased to be celebrated in their art. Hokusai, the master of the popular Ukiyo-e prints, made *Thirty-six Views of Fuji* (1823–29), which showed the many faces of the sacred heights.

In the West, the Greeks had their Olympus, rising a sudden 9,000 feet above the Aegean. Often shrouded in clouds, the veiled summit of Olympus gave gods their privacy. Only between the clouds could mortals glimpse an amphitheater of tiers of boulders where the gods sat in council. "Never is it swept by the winds nor touched by snow," wrote Homer, "a purer air surrounds it, a white clarity envelops it and the gods there taste of a happiness which lasts as long as their eternal lives." The Greeks were confident that Olympus was the highest mountain on earth. In the beginning, after Cronus had completed his creation of the world, his sons drew lots to partition his empire, and Zeus won the ethereal heights, Poseidon received the sea, and Hades was awarded the dark depths of the earth. While Hades remained alone below, Zeus allowed the other gods to share his residence on Olympus.

On the heights of Mt. Sinai the God of the Jews gave Moses the tablets of the Law.

And on the third day in the morning, there was thunder and lightning and a dark cloud upon the mountain and a very loud trumpet blast, and all the people who were in the camp trembled. And Moses brought the people out of the camp to meet God and they assembled at the foot of the mountain. And Mount Sinai was all smoke because the Lord descended upon it in fire; and the smoke of it went up like the smoke of a kiln. And all the people trembled greatly. And as the trumpet blast grew louder and louder, Moses spoke and the Lord answered him in thunder. And Yahweh came down upon Mount Sinai to the top of the mountain. And Yahweh called Moses to the top of the mountain and Moses went up. . . .

[Exodus 19:16–20]

Where there were no natural mountains, people built artificial mountains. The oldest surviving examples are the stepped pyramids—the "ziggurats"—of ancient Mesopotamia, which go back to the twenty-second century B.C. "Ziggurat" meant both the summit of a mountain and a man-made stepped tower. The vast pyramidal pile in Babylon, 295 feet square and 295 feet high, became notorious as the Tower of Babel. While the effect from a distance was that of a stepped pyramid, the ziggurat, as Herodotus described it about 460 B.C., was a pile of solid towers, each slightly smaller than the one on which it rested. "In the topmost tower there is a great temple, and in the temple is a great bed richly appointed, and beside it a golden table. No idol stands there. No one spends the night there save a woman of that country, designated by the god himself, so I was told by the Chaldeans, who are the priests of that divinity."

When the ancient ziggurats were crumbling in the fourth century, an Egyptian reported the tradition that the ziggurat "had been built by giants who wished to climb up to heaven. For this impious folly some were struck by thunderbolts; others, at God's command, were afterwards unable to recognize each other; all the rest fell headlong into the island of Crete, whither God in His wrath had hurled them." A ziggurat, according to the sacred Babylonian texts, was a "Link of Heaven and Earth."

The Tower of Babel became a symbol of man's effort to reach the heavens, to trespass on the territory of the gods. The ziggurat was said to be the earthly shape of the ladder that the patriarch

Jacob, grandson of the Mesopotamian Abraham, saw. "And he dreamed, and behold a ladder set up on the earth, and the top of it reached to heaven: and behold the angels of God ascending and descending on it." All across flat Mesopotamia people felt the need for an artificial mountain to reach up to the gods, and to allow gods more easily to reach down to men. Every major city had at least one high-reaching ziggurat, probably the highest, as it was the most impressive, structure to be seen. Remains of thirty-three survived into the twentieth century. Perhaps the ziggurat was a burial mound from which the God-King Marduk could be resurrected. Or perhaps it was only a stairway from which the God could descend to the city, and on which people could ascend to make their requests.

In the Nile Valley in lower Egypt we can still see some of the most durable artificial mountains. The primeval hill, the place of the creation of life, was especially vivid to the Egyptians. Every year when the Nile flood receded, mounds of newly silted mud fertile with new life appeared above the water, and so every year Egyptians relived the story of the Creation.

The earliest Egyptian pyramid was a stepped pyramid, similar to the ziggurats of Mesopotamia. The great pyramid of Zoser (first king of the third dynasty: c. 2980 B.C.), at Sakkara in Lower Egypt, showed six steps. "A staircase to heaven is laid for him [the king] so that he may mount up to heaven thereby." The Egyptian word "to ascend" included the sign of a stepped pyramid. The later pyramids showed no steps, but took on the smooth pyramidal slope, the sacred sign of the sun-god. The God-King Pepi, the ancient Egyptians explained, "has put down this radiance as a stairway under his feet. . . . stairs to the sky are laid for him."

*   *   *

In Tibet, the lamas every day offered the Buddhas their own model of the earth: their little mound of rice was Mt. Meru. The Buddha instructed that his bones, after cremation, should be placed in a mound at the crossing of four highways, to symbolize the universal reign of his teachings.

During the long rule of Hinduism, countless "stupas"—

artificial-mountain replicas of Mt. Meru—had symbolized the vertical axis of the egg-shaped universe. When the emperor Asoka, who reigned from c. 273 to 232 B.C., made Buddhism the religion of his vast empire, he simply transformed the Hindu stupa into a stupa for Buddhists. Two of Asoka's stupas remain—the Great Stupa at Sanchi in central India and the Bodhnath Stupa at Katmandu in Nepal.

Like the Mesopotamian ziggurat, the Buddhist stupa was a model of the cosmos. Above a square or circular base rose the solid hemispherical dome, a replica of the dome of heaven enclosing the world-mountain that rose from earth to the sky. The world-mountain stuck up through the dome of heaven in the form of a small balcony at the summit; at the center of the dome arose a mast, the axis of the world, extending all the way up from the watery depths imagined to lie beneath.

The most impressive, largest, and most intricate of these artificial Buddhist mountains is the great stupa of Borobudur (c. eighth century A.D.) in Java. Above five walled rectangular terraces rise three round platforms bearing seventy-two small bell-shaped stupas, each containing a Buddha, and a larger solid capstone stupa surmounting all. We share the feeling of the Buddhist epic poet of Ceylon on the completion of the great stupa there: "Thus are the Buddhas incomprehensible, and incomprehensible is the nature of the Buddhas, and incomprehensible is the reward of those who have faith in the incomprehensible."

After Buddhism ebbed away from India and the Hindu faith returned, many great shrines were painted white to make more obvious their symbolic identity with the sacred snowcapped Himalaya. Hindu temples, like the Mesopotamian ziggurat, the Egyptian pyramids, and other reconstructions of the primal mountain, but unlike the Christian cathedral, were not shelters within which the faithful could gather. The artificial mountain, like the natural mountain, was an object of worship, the sacred earth at its most eminent, up which the faithful could ascend. *The builder*, who had imitated what the gods had made, was possessed of magical power.

The Hindu dynasties produced their many ornate versions of the primeval mountain—dome, spire, hexagonal or octagonal tower. The surfaces and panels, the niches and friezes of these stone monuments, bubble with images of plants, of monkeys and elephants, and of men and women in all conceivable postures. The grandest of them, the Hindu temple Kailasa ("Shiva's paradise") at Ellora, in south-central India, ingeniously used the mountain itself to make the effigy of a divine mountain. A mountain-carved-out-of-a-mountain, Kailasa was constructed by first cutting a trench into the mountain to isolate a mass of rock 276 feet long, 154 feet wide, and 100 feet high. By working from the top of the mass down, the rock cutters avoided the need for scaffolding. The product of two hundred years' labor was a worthy replica of Shiva's paradise, Mount Kailasa in the Himalaya. Hindu architects and sculptors down to their latest efforts, as at Khajraho in central India (c. 1000), never gave up their rebuilding of Mt. Meru, and spent their energy with ever greater profligacy in carving erotic images of the reunion of man and his gods. The *sikhara*, or spire, which topped the Hindu stupa also meant mountain peak.

Perhaps the most gigantic religious monument in the world is the stupa-temple complex of Angkor Wat, built by the Cambodian king Suryavarman II (1113–1150) as his sepulcher and the temple of his divinity. The stupa there, fantastically elaborated and multiplied, is a vast filigreed stepped pyramid, a sculptured mountain.

On the other side of the world simpler, starker pyramids were rising, symbols of the universal awe of mountains. In the Valley of Mexico, the Toltecs piled up their Pyramid of the Sun, two-thirds the height of the Tower of Babel, at Teotihuacán. On the flat peninsula of Yucatán, the Mayas set up their pyramid-temples at Uxmal and Chichén Itzá.

THE DISCOVERY OF ASIA

MARCO POLO excelled all other known Christian travelers in his experience, in his product, and in his influence. The Franciscans went to Mongolia and back in less than three years, and stayed in their roles as missionary-diplomats. Marco Polo's journey lasted twenty-four years. He reached farther than his predecessors, beyond Mongolia to the heart of Cathay. He traversed the whole of China all the way to the Ocean, and he played a variety of roles, becoming the confidant of Kublai Khan and governor of a great Chinese city. He was at home in the language, and immersed himself in the daily life and culture of Cathay. For generations of Europe, his copious, vivid, and factual account of Eastern ways was the discovery of Asia.

Venice at the time was a great center for commerce in the Mediterranean and beyond. Marco Polo was just fifteen years of age in 1269, when his father, Nicolò, and his uncle Maffeo Polo returned to Venice from their nine-year journey to the East. Another of Marco's uncles, also named Marco Polo, had trading houses in Constantinople and at Soldaia in the Crimea, where Nicolò and Maffeo had joined him in 1260 in his trading ventures. Marco Polo opens his own book with an account of these earlier travels in which he had no part. Nicolò and Maffeo laid in a stock of jewels at Constantinople which they took by sea to Soldaia, then north and east along the

Volga to the splendid court of Barka Khan, son of Genghis Khan. Barka Khan not only treated them courteously and with honor but, what was more to the point, bought their whole stock of jewels, as Marco Polo observes, "causing the Brothers to receive at least twice its value."

When a war between Barka Khan and a rival Tartar prince cut off the Polo brothers' return to Constantinople, they decided to take their trading ventures farther eastward. A seventeen-day journey across the desert took them to Bokhara, where they fell in with some Tartar envoys who were en route to the court of the Great Khan, Kublai Khan. These envoys persuaded the Polos that Kublai Khan, who had never before seen any Latins, intensely desired to see them, and would treat them with great honor and liberality. The envoys promised to guard them on the way. The Polo brothers took up this invitation, and after a full year's journey, "seeing many marvels of divers and sundry kinds," arrived at the court of Kublai Khan. The Great Khan, every bit as friendly as had been promised, proved to be a man of wide-ranging curiosity and alert intelligence, eager to learn everything about the West.

Finally he asked the two brothers to be his envoys to the Pope, requesting one hundred missionaries educated in all the Seven Arts to teach his people about Christianity and Western science. He also wanted some oil from the lamp at the Holy Sepulcher in Jerusalem. When Nicolò and Maffeo departed, they carried the Emperor's Tablet of Gold, his certificate of safe passage, ordering everybody en route to supply their needs. Arriving at Acre in April 1269, the two brothers learned that the Pope had died and his successor had not yet been named. They returned to Venice to await the result. When the new pope, Gregory X, was finally named, he did not offer the requested hundred missionaries, but instead only assigned two Dominican friars to accompany the Polos.

In 1271, when Nicolò and Maffeo Polo set out from Venice on their return journey to Kublai Khan, they took with them Nicolò's seventeen-year-old son, Marco, who was destined to make their trip historic. At Lajazzo on the eastern Mediterranean the two Dominicans left in panic. The three Polos, now alone, proceeded to Baghdad, then on to Ormuz at the mouth of the Persian Gulf, where they might have taken ship for a long journey through the Sea of India. Instead they chose to go north and east overland through the Persian Desert of Kerman to the frigid mountains of Badakhshan, noted for its rubies and lapis lazuli, and its fine horses. There used to be horses here, Marco tells us, which were "directly descended from Alexander's horse Bucephalus out of mares that had conceived from him and they were all born like him with a horn on the forehead." There they stayed a year to allow Marco to recover from an illness by breathing the pure mountain air.

Then up still higher, across a land of glaciers, with many peaks over twenty thousand feet—Pamir, which the natives accurately called "The Roof of the World." "Wild game of every sort abounds. There are great quantities of wild sheep of huge size [now known as *ovis Poli*, though William of Rubruck had noted them before]. Their horns grow to as much as six palms in length and are never less than three or four. From these horns the shepherds make big bowls from which they feed, and also fences to keep in their flocks." "No birds fly here because of the height and the cold. And I assure you that, because of this great cold, fire is not so bright here nor of the same colour as elsewhere, and food does not cook well." They then took the old southern caravan route through northern Kashmir, where no European would be seen again till the nineteenth century, then eastward to the edge of the Gobi Desert.

The party rested at Lop, a town at the western edge of the desert, where travelers usually took supplies to strengthen them against the terror of the crossing.

> Beasts and birds there are none, because they find nothing to eat. But I assure you that one thing is found here, and that a very strange one, which I will relate to you.
>
> The truth is this. When a man is riding by night through this desert and something happens to make him loiter and lose touch with his companions, by dropping asleep or for some other reason, and afterwards he wants to rejoin them, then he hears spirits talking in such a way that they

seem to be his companions. Sometimes, indeed, they even hail him by name. Often these voices make him stray from the path, so that he never finds it again. And in this way many travellers have been lost and have perished.

Across the desert they entered Tangut, in extreme northwestern China, traversed the Mongolian steppes and arrived in the court of the Great Khan after a trek of three and a half years.

Kublai Khan received the Venetians with great honor. Sensing the talents of the twenty-one-year-old Marco, the Khan at once enlisted him in his service, and sent him on an embassy to a country six months away. When we read Marco Polo's travels today, we all reap the fruits of the voracious curiosity of that thirteenth-century Mongol emperor.

Now he had taken note on several occasions that when the Prince's ambassadors returned from different parts of the world, they were able to tell him about nothing except the business on which they had gone, and that the Prince in consequence held them for no better than fools and dolts, and would say: "I had far liever hearken about the strange things, and the manners of the different countries you have seen, than hearing of the affairs of strange countries." Mark therefore, as he went and returned, took great pains to learn about all kinds of different matters in the countries which he visited, in order to be able to tell about them to the Great Khan. . . . Thereafter Messer Marco abode in the Khan's employment some seventeen years, continually going and coming, hither and thither, on the missions that were entrusted to him. . . . And, as he knew all the sovereign's ways, like a sensible man he always took much pains to gather knowledge of anything that would be likely to interest him, and then on his return to Court he would relate everything in regular order, and thus the Emperor came to hold him in great love and favour. . . . And thus it came about that Messer Marco Polo had knowledge of, or had actually visited, a greater number of the different countries of the World than any other man; the more that he was always giving his mind to get knowledge, and to spy out and enquire into everything in order to have matter to relate to the Lord.

It seemed, the Khan would exclaim, that only Marco Polo had learned to use his eyes!

We do not know how Nicolò and Maffeo Polo spent their time at the court of the Khan, except that, at the end of the seventeen years, they had "acquired great wealth in jewels and gold." Every year Kublai Khan became more reluctant to lose Marco's services. But in 1292 an escort was required for a Tartar princess who was to become the bride of the Ilkhan of Persia. Envoys of the Ilkhan had already failed in their efforts to deliver the seventeen-year-old bride overland. Returned to the court of Kublai Khan, they hoped to secure sea passage. Just then Marco had come back from an assignment that had taken him on a long sea voyage to India. The Persian envoys, who knew the seafaring reputation of Venetians, persuaded Kublai Khan to allow the Polos to accompany them and the bride by sea. The Khan outfitted fourteen ships, with an entourage of six hundred persons and supplies for two years. After a treacherous sea voyage through the South China Sea to Sumatra and through the Sea of India from which only eighteen of the six hundred survived, the Tartar princess was safely delivered to the Persian court. She had become so attached to the Venetians that she wept at the parting.

The Polos, returning home overland by way of Tabriz in northern Persia, Trebizond on the south coast of the Black Sea, to Constantinople, finally reached Venice in the winter of 1295, after their absence of twenty-four years. The Polo family had long since given them up for dead. A plausible tradition reports that when these three shabby strangers appeared, looking more like Tartars than Venetians, their noble relatives would have nothing to do with them. But the relatives' memories were quickly jogged when the unkempt wanderers ripped open the seams of their sordid garments and produced their secret treasure—a shower of rubies, diamonds, and emeralds. The returned travelers were affectionately embraced, and then entertained at a luxurious banquet, where music and jollity were mixed with exotic reminiscence.

Those were years of bitter rivalry between Venice and Genoa for the Mediterranean seafaring trade. On September 6, 1298, a climactic sea battle between Venice and Genoa at Curzola off the Dalmatian coast left the Genoese victors, with seven thousand prisoners. Among these was a "gentleman commander" of a Venetian galley, Marco Polo. Brought back in chains to a prison in Genoa, he became friendly with another prisoner, relic of an earlier Genoese victory over the Pisans. This Rustichello happened to be a writer of romances who already had a considerable reputation for his retelling of the tales of King Arthur and his Round Table. Not a literary genius, Rustichello still was master of his genre, industrious and persuasive. In Marco Polo's reminiscences he saw the raw material for a new kind of romance—"A Description of the World"—and he persuaded the Venetian to cooperate. Marco Polo must somehow have managed to secure his notes from home. Then, profiting from his enforced leisure and from their confinement together, the Venetian dictated a copious account of his travels to Rustichello, who wrote it all down.

If either Marco Polo or Rustichello had not fought in the wars against Genoa, we might have no record of Marco Polo's travels and might not even have heard his name. Luckily, Rustichello was a writer congenial to the great Venetian traveler, and he knew the makings of a romance to charm the world for seven hundred years. Of course he could not restrain himself from occasionally embellishing Marco Polo's facts with his own fancies. Some of the more colorful episodes are adapted from earlier writings by Rustichello or others. For example, the extravagant praise that Kublai Khan lavished on the young Marco when he first arrived at the court recalls what King Arthur said, according to Rustichello's own romance, when he received the young Tristan at Camelot. This was not the first or the last time a writer made the reputation of an adventurer. The formula, "as told to," which nowadays appears less often than it rightly should on title pages of books, has a surprisingly respectable history. Why did the energetic Venetian, who was literate in several languages, who must have written much to please Kublai Khan and extensive detailed notes for his own use, not write down for himself his personal adventures? Perhaps if promptly on his return to the commercial city of Venice in 1295 he had been tempted by a publisher's contract, he might have written his own book. But two centuries would pass before a publishing trade flourished.

Other great medieval travelers—Friar Odoric of Pordenone, Nicolo de' Conti, and Ibn Battuta—and the noted French chronicler and biographer of Saint Louis, Jean de Joinville (1224?–1317?), also dictated their books. The rewards of money or celebrity were not yet dangled before so many, nor was literacy required to get or to hold political power. The opening sentence of the prologue of Marco Polo's book exhorts: "Emperors and kings, dukes and marquises, counts, knights, and townsfolk, and all people who wish to know the various races of men and the peculiarities of the various regions of the world, take this book, take this book *and have it read to you.*"

Rustichello wrote Marco Polo's book in French, which in Western Europe in those days was current among the laity just as Latin was among the clergy. Before long it was translated into most European languages, and numerous manuscripts survive. Never before or since has a single book brought so much authentic new information, or so widened the vistas for a continent.

BEYOND THE THREATENING CAPE

UNLIKE Columbus, who would aim straight for the Indies, Prince Henry the Navigator had a larger, a vaguer, and more modern destination—true to his horoscope. "The noble spirit of this Prince," the admiring reporter Gomes Eanes de Zurara explained, "was ever urging him both to begin and to carry out very great deeds. . . . he had also a wish to know the land that lay beyond the isles of Canary and that Cape called Bojador, for that up to his time, neither by writings, nor by the memory of man, was known with any certainty the nature of the land beyond that Cape. . . . it seemed to him that if he or some other lord did not endeavour to gain that knowledge, no mariners or merchants would ever dare to attempt it, for it is clear that none of them ever trouble themselves to sail to a place where there is not a sure and certain hope of profit."

We have no evidence that Prince Henry had in mind the specific purpose of opening a sea-way around Africa to India. What beckoned him was the unknown, which lay west and southwest into the Sea of Darkness and southward along the uncharted coast of Africa. The Atlantic islands—the Azores (one-third of the way across the Atlantic Ocean!), the Madeiras, and the Canaries—had probably been discovered by Genoese sailors in the mid-fourteenth century. Prince Henry's efforts in that direction were less an enterprise of discovery than of colonization and development. But when his people landed in Madeira (*madeira* means wood) in 1420 and set about clearing the thick woods, they set a fire that raged for seven years. Although they never planned it that way, the potash left from the consumed wood would prove a perfect fertilizer for vineyards of the Malmsey grapes imported from Crete to replace those forests. The justly famous "Madeira" wine was the lasting product. Yet, as his stars foretold, Prince Henry was by nature and by preference not a colonizer but a discoverer.

When we look at a modern map of Africa, we look long and need a magnifying glass before we can find Cape Bojador (Portuguese for "Bulging Cape"), on the west coast, just south of the Canary Islands. Some thousand miles north of the continent's greatest westward bulge we see a tiny bump on the coastal outline, a "bulge" so slight that it is almost imperceptible on maps of the full continent. The sandy barrier there is so low that it can be seen only when one comes close, where there are treacherous reefs and unmanageable currents. Cape Bojador was no worse than a score of other barriers that skillful Portuguese sailors had passed and survived. But this particular Cape Bojador they had made their *ne plus ultra.* You dare not go beyond!

When we see the enormous risky promontories, the Cape of Good Hope or Cape Horn, that European seafarers would manage to round within the next century, we must recognize Bojador as something quite else. It was a barrier in the mind, the very prototype of primitive obstacles to the explorer. The eloquent Zurara tells us "why ships had not hitherto dared to pass beyond Cape Bojador."

> And to say the truth this was not from cowardice or want of good will, but from the novelty of the thing and the wide-spread and ancient rumour about this Cape, that had been cherished by the mariners of Spain from generation to generation. . . . For certainly it cannot be presumed that among so many noble men who did such great and lofty deeds for the glory of their memory, there had not been one to dare this deed. But being satisfied of the peril, and seeing no hope of honour or profit, they left off the attempt. For, said the mariners, this much is clear, that beyond this Cape there is

no race of men nor place of inhabitants . . . and the sea so shallow that a whole league from land it is only a fathom deep, while the currents are so terrible that no ship having once passed the Cape, will ever be able to return. . . . these mariners of ours . . . [were] threatened not only by fear but by its shadow, whose great deceit was the cause of very great expenses.

At home in Sagres Prince Henry knew that he could not conquer the physical barrier unless he first conquered the barrier of fear.

He would never reach farther into the unknown unless he could persuade his seamen to go beyond Cape Bojador. Between 1424 and 1434 Prince Henry sent out fifteen expeditions to round the inconsequential but threatening cape. Each returned with some excuse for not going where none had gone before. At the legendary cape the sea bounced with cascades of ominous red sands that crumbled from the overhanging cliffs, while shoals of sardines swimming in the shallows roiled the waters between whirlpools. There was no sign of life along the desert coast. Was this not the very image of the world's end?

When Gil Eannes reported back to Prince Henry in 1433 that Cape Bojador was in fact impassable, the Prince was not satisfied. Would his Portuguese pilots be as timid as those Mediterranean or Flemish sailors who plied only the familiar ways? Surely this Gil Eannes, a squire whom he knew well in his own household, was made of bolder stuff. The Prince sent him back in 1434 with renewed promise of reward for yet another try. This time, as Eannes approached the cape he steered westward, risking the unknown perils of the ocean rather than the known perils of the cape. Then he turned south and discovered that the cape was already behind him. Landing on the African shore, he found it desolate, but by no means the gates of hell. "And as he purposed," Zurara reported, "so he performed—for in that voyage he doubled the Cape, despising all danger, and found the lands beyond quite contrary to what he, like others, had expected. And although the matter was a small one in itself, yet on account of its daring it was reckoned great."

Having broken the barrier of fear "and the shadow of fear," Prince Henry was on his way. Year after year he dispatched expeditions, each reaching a bit farther into the unknown. In 1435, when he sent out Eannes once again, this time with Afonso Baldaya, the royal cupbearer, they reached another fifty leagues down the coast. There they saw footprints of men and camels, but still did not encounter the people. In 1436, when Baldaya went out again, with orders to bring back an inhabitant for the Prince to interview at Sagres, he reached what seemed to be the mouth of a huge river, which he hoped would be the Senegal of "the silent trade" in gold. They called it the Rio de Ouro, even though it was only a large inlet and not a river, for the Senegal actually lay another five hundred miles farther south.

The relentless step-by-step exploration of the west African coast proceeded year by year, although commercial rewards were meager. In 1441, from Prince Henry's household went Nuno Tristão and Antão Gonçalves, reaching another two hundred fifty miles farther to Cape Branco (Blanco) where they took two natives captive. In 1444 from that area Eannes brought back the first human cargo— two hundred Africans to be sold as slaves in Lagos. Zurara's eyewitness account of this first European episode in the African slave trade was a painful glimpse of the miseries to come. "Mothers would clasp their infants in their arms, and throw themselves on the ground to cover them with their bodies, disregarding any injury to their own persons, so that they could prevent their children from being separated from them."

But Zurara insisted that "they were treated with kindness, and no difference was made between them and the free-born servants of Portugal." They were taught trades, he said, were converted to Christianity, and eventually intermarried with the Portuguese.

The arrival of this human merchandise from Africa, we are told, caused a change in the public attitude toward Prince Henry. Many had criticized the Prince for wasting the public substance in his frolics of exploration. "Then those who had been foremost in complaint grew quiet, and with soft voices praised what they had so loudly and publicly decried." "And so they were forced to turn their blame into public praise; for they said it was plain the Infant was another Alexander; and their covetousness now began to wax greater." Everybody wanted a share of this promising Guinea trade.

When Dinis Dias rounded Cape Verde, the western tip of Africa, in 1445, the most barren coast had been passed, and the prosperous Portuguese trade with west Africa soon engaged twenty-five caravels every year. By 1457 Alvise da Cadamosto—a Venetian precursor of the Italian sea captains like Columbus, Vespucci, and the Cabots who served foreign princes—advancing down the coast for Prince Henry had accidentally discovered the Cape Verde Islands and then went up the Senegal and Gambia rivers sixty miles from the sea. This Cadamosto proved to be one of the most observant as well as one of the boldest of Prince Henry's explorers. By his engaging accounts of curious tribal customs, of tropical vegetation, elephants, and hippopotami, he enticed others to follow.

At the time of Prince Henry's death in Sagres in 1460 the discovery of the west African coast had only begun, but it was well begun. The barrier of groundless fear had been breached in what became the first continuous organized enterprise into the unknown. Prince Henry therefore is properly celebrated as the founder of continuous discovery. For him each new step into the unknown was a further invitation.

Prince Henry's death caused only a brief hiatus in the exploring enterprise. Then in 1469 King Alfonso V, Prince Henry's nephew, in financial difficulty, found a way to make discovery into a profitable business. In an agreement quite unlike any we have heard of before between sovereign and vassal, Fernão Gomes, a wealthy citizen of Lisbon, committed himself to discover at least one hundred farther leagues, about three hundred miles, of the African coast each year for the next five years. In return, Gomes obtained a monopoly of the Guinea trade, from which the King received a share. The rest of the story has the inevitability of a steadily rising curtain. Discovery of the whole west African coast by the Portuguese now was a question no longer of *whether* but of *when*.

The supposed Portuguese policy of secrecy poses tantalizing problems for the historian because the policy itself seems to have been kept secret. When we chronicle Portuguese advances into the hitherto unknown, we must wonder whether any particular Portuguese voyage was unrecorded because of this "policy of secrecy" or simply because it was never made. Portuguese historians have been understandably tempted to treat the absence of a record of pre-Columbian voyages to America as a kind of evidence that such voyages really were made. The Portuguese did have some diplomatic and compelling reasons to advertise their discoveries in America. In Africa, however, they had every reason to conceal both the knowledge they had gained of the actual shape of the coast and word of the treasure they were extracting there. The records that remain of these earliest Portuguese discoveries in Africa are probably only minimal notices of their exploits.

The Gomes contract, we know, produced an impressive annual series of African discoveries—around Cape Palmas at the continent's southwestern tip, into the Bight of Benin, the island of Fernando Po at the eastern tip of the Guinea coast and then down southward across the equator. It had taken Prince Henry's sailors thirty years to cover a length of coast that Gomes, under his contract, covered in five. When Gomes' contract expired, the King gave the trading rights to his own son, John, who became King John II in 1481, opening the next great age of Portuguese seafaring.

King John II had some advantages that Prince Henry had lacked. The royal treasury was now enriched by the feedback of imports from the west African coast. Cargoes of pepper, ivory, gold, and slaves had already become so substantial that they gave their names to the parts of the continent that faced the Gulf of Guinea. For centuries these would be called the Grain Coast (Guinea pepper was known as "Grains of Paradise"), the Ivory Coast, the Gold Coast, and the Slave Coast. King John protected Portuguese settlements by building Fort Elmina, "the mine," in the heart of the Gold Coast. He supported land expeditions into the interior, to the back-country of Sierra Leone and even as far as Timbuktu. And he pushed on down the coast.

As we have noted, when mariners advanced below the equator they could no longer see the North Star, and so had to find another way to determine their latitude. To solve this problem King John, like Prince Henry, collected experts from everywhere, and he set up a commission headed by two learned Jewish astrologer-mathematicians—a Portuguese dividend from the persecutions across the border in Spain. In 1492, when the Spanish inquisitor-general Torquemada gave Jews three months to convert to Christianity or leave the country, the brilliant Abraham Zacuto left the University of Salamanca and was welcomed to Portugal by King John II. Zacuto's disciple at Salamanca, Joseph Vizinho, had already accepted the King's invitation ten years before, and in 1485 had been sent out on a voyage to develop and apply the technique of determining latitude by the height of the sun at midday. He was to accomplish this by recording the declination of the sun along the whole Guinea coast. The most advanced work for finding position at sea by the declination of the sun, as would be necessary in sailing below the equator, was the *Almanach Perpetuum* which Zacuto had written in Hebrew nearly twenty years before. After Vizinho translated these tables into Latin, they guided Portuguese discoverers for a half-century.

Meanwhile King John, carrying on Prince Henry's work, kept sending his discovery voyages farther down the west African coast. Diogo Cão reached the mouth of the Congo (1480–84), and began the custom of setting up stone markers *(padroes)*, surmounted by a cross, as proof of first discovery and tokens of Christian faith.

These advances down the coast brought new rumors of the famous but still unseen Prester John. While Prince Henry's first objective was to move into the unknown, another objective, his chronicler Zurara reported, was "to know if there were in those parts any Christian princes, in whom the charity and the love of Christ was so ingrained that they would aid him against those enemies of the faith." This conjectural potential ally must have been Prester John, whose "letter," as we have seen, had been circulating in Europe for two centuries. By this time the locale of the legendary priest-king had been transferred from "furthest Asia" to Ethiopia. Whenever one of Prince Henry's voyages found another great river—the Senegal, the Gambia, the Niger—debouching on the west coast, he found new hope that this at last might be the "Western Nile" that would lead to Prester John's Ethiopian kingdom. When King John II's men reached Benin at the eastern tip of the Gulf of Guinea, he received the interesting report that the kings of Benin had sent gifts to a king called Ogané whose realm was twelve months' journey inland to the east, and who returned gifts inscribed with small crosses. Prince Henry had already unsuccessfully tried to make contact with Prester John by journeys inland, and King John II's own envoys to Jerusalem had also failed to find him.

By 1487 King John II had organized a two-pronged grand strategy for reaching the long-sought Christian ally. He would send one expedition southeastward overland and another by sea around the African coast. If there really should be a sea passage to India, a Christian ally was more desirable and more necessary than ever, not only for crusading but also to serve as a way station and supply base for future trading enterprises.

The overland expedition that left Santarém on May 7, 1487, like others before it, was characteristically small, consisting of only two men. After a considerable search, the King had chosen Pero da Covilhã (1460?–1545?) and Afonso de Paiva for the dangerous assignment. Covilhã, a married man with children, in his late twenties, had already proven himself bold and versatile. He had spent much of his life abroad, had taken part in ambushes in the streets of Seville, had served as the King's secret agent at the court of Ferdinand and Isabella, and had undertaken diplomatic missions to the Barbary States in north Africa. Covilhã's mission to Tlemcen, famous as "the Granada of Africa," and then to Fez, accustomed him to the Muslim ways, which did not vary much from Morocco to Calicut, and so equipped him to travel through Islam without rousing suspicion. While in those days knowledge of Arabic was not unusual in Portugal, his contemporaries praised Covilhã as "a man who knew all the languages which may be spoken by Christians, Moors, or the heathen." An attractive man of courage and decision, he also possessed the required powers of observation and of memory. Of his companion, Paiva, we know only that he was a gentleman of the court, and that he, too, spoke Spanish and Arabic.

Covilhã and Paiva had an audience with the King and were then briefed by the King's chaplain, his physicians and his geographers, in a session shrouded in secrecy. From the plans presented in Portugal some time before by Christopher Columbus, these experts had drawn information that was expected to be useful. A Florentine banker in Lisbon gave the travelers a letter of credit, which they drew on for expenses as they moved eastward through Spain and Italy. At Barcelona they took ship for Naples, then sailed to Rhodes. There, as they took off into Muslim territory, the knowledgeable Knights Hospitalers of Saint John of Jerusalem warned that they would now be no more than "Christian dogs." The prospering agents of Venice and Genoa whom they would encounter would want no Portuguese competition. They were urged therefore to dress and act the part of Muslim merchants, ostensibly dealing in a cargo of honey. In this guise they reached Alexandria, where they both nearly died of fever, then on to Cairo and Aden at the mouth of the Red Sea.

There they separated. Paiva was to make his way directly to Ethiopia and Prester John, while Covilhã would go on to India. Paiva disappeared, but Covilhã finally reached Calicut and Goa on the southwestern shores of India, where he witnessed the prosperous trade in Arabian horses, spices, fine cottons, and precious stones. In February 1489 Covilhã took ship westward to Ormuz at the entrance to the Persian Gulf, then to the east African port of Sofala opposite Madagascar and back north to Cairo. Having completed his mission of assessing the European trade with India, he was eager to return home. But there in Cairo he encountered two Jewish emissaries from King John II who carried a letter instructing Covilhã, if he had not already done so, to proceed at once to the realm of Prester John to collect information and promote an alliance.

Unable to disobey his sovereign, Covilhã took up the mission, meanwhile sending to King John a momentous letter with all he had learned about Arab seafaring and the commerce of India. In 1493, after a side trip to Mecca, six years after his departure from Portugal, he finally arrived in Ethiopia. In this Realm of Prester John, actually ruled by Alexander "Lion of the Tribe of Judah, and King of Kings," he became a Portuguese Marco Polo, so useful at court that the King would not let him leave. Convinced that he would never return home, Covilhã married an Ethiopian wife who bore him several children.

Meanwhile, Covilhã's letter, which has not survived and which is known only secondhand, would have a powerful influence on the future of Portugal and of Asia. For it appears to have informed King John II, from reports Covilhã had heard on the African coast, "that his [the king's] caravels, which carried on trade in Guinea, navigating from land to land, and seeking the coast of this island [Madagascar] and of Sofala, could easily penetrate into these Eastern seas and come to make the coast of Calicut, for there was sea everywhere."

"THE ENTERPRISE OF THE INDIES"

CHAPTER 30

"THAT noble and powerful city by the sea," Genoa, where Columbus spent the first twenty-two years of his life, had long struggled against Venice for maritime dominance of the eastern Mediterranean. The Venetian Marco Polo had dictated his travels from a Genoese prison. In Columbus' youth Genoa was a flourishing center of shipbuilding and seafaring enterprise whose map-makers dominated the market for portolano charts in the western Mediterranean. They were even making maps of the parts of the African coasts newly discovered by the Portuguese disciples of Henry the Navigator. It was in Genoa that Columbus very likely began to learn the arts of map-making, which he and his brother later practiced in Lisbon. While Genoa would remain a birthplace and nursery of individual explorers like Columbus (1451?–1506) and John Cabot (1450–1498), the grand seafaring enterprises required larger resources, a vaster hinterland, and, when the Muslims held so much of the eastern Mediterranean, a more western exposure.

In 1476, when Columbus was serving on a Flemish vessel in a Genoese convoy escorting a cargo through the Straits of Gibraltar and up to northern Europe, his ship was attacked and sunk by a French armada. Luckily this occurred near Lagos, off the coast of Portugal only a few miles from where Prince Henry the Navigator had made his headquarters. The twenty-five-year-old Columbus used one of the floating long oars as a life raft and propelled himself ashore.

In those years there could have been no happier or more providential landing for an ambitious young mariner. The friendly people of Lagos dried and fed Christopher, then sent him to join his younger brother Bartholomew in Lisbon. Henry the Navigator had made Portugal the exploring center of Europe, and perhaps of the world. By 1476 those exploits were paying off in rich cargoes of Negro slaves, ivory, malagueta pepper, and gold dust. The rewards of seafaring were visible all around. The Columbus brothers, Christopher and Bartholomew, went into the newly flourishing business of making and selling mariner's charts. In Lisbon they could update the old charts by adding the latest information brought back by the adventuring Portuguese ships. With sharper knowledge of new seacoasts arriving every month, the chart-maker had to be a kind of marine journalist.

When Columbus and his brother set up shop in Lisbon, Portuguese ships were still inching down the west coast of Africa and had only reached the Gulf of Guinea. But the full shape of Africa, which Ptolemy had hitched around to join southeast Asia, making a closed sea of the Indian Ocean, had not yet been traced by mariners. In late 1484, when Columbus offered what he called his "Enterprise of the Indies" to King John II of Portugal, it still seemed that a westward sea passage might be not only the shorter but perhaps the only maritime route to the Indies.

A full decade earlier a westward sea passage to the Indies seems to have been under consideration by King John's predecessor, Alfonso V. He had sought the expert opinion of a famous Florentine physician-astrologer-cosmographer Paolo dal Pozzo Toscanelli (1397–1482), who, in a letter dated June 25, 1474, proposed "a shorter way of going by sea to the lands of spices, than that which you are making by Guinea." Basing his argument mainly on Marco Polo's report of the vast eastward extent of Asia and the location of "the noble island of Cipangu," or Japan—"most fertile in gold, pearls and precious stones, and they cover the temples and the royal residences with solid gold"—supposedly some fifteen hundred miles off the Chinese coast, Toscanelli confidently urged a trial of the westward passage. "Thus by the unknown ways there are no great spaces of the sea to be passed." Toscanelli, himself one of the more advanced cartographers of his age, had actually drawn a nautical map of the Atlantic Ocean, a copy of which he sent along with his letter to Lisbon.

In late 1481 or early 1482, when Columbus heard of this letter, he wrote to Toscanelli in great excitement and asked for more information. In return he received an encouraging letter along with another chart, which he eventually carried with him on his trip to prove that Toscanelli was right.

While Columbus had already been convinced, he now became passionate for this grand untested opportunity. Those who could finance him were harder to persuade. To convince investors to put their treasure in so novel an enterprise, he had to be at home in the writings of travelers, cosmographers, theologians, and philosophers. For, as we have already seen, geography as a separate discipline was in neither the trivium nor the quadrivium, and still had no place in the medieval Christian gamut of knowledge. Genoese, the tongue to which Columbus was born, was a spoken dialect, not a written language, and so was no help in his effort to document his Enterprise of the Indies. But Italian, which was a written language, and might have helped him, was a language that Columbus could not speak or write. He had no formal schooling where he might have learned Italian, and when by his own efforts he became literate, he wrote Castilian, which was then the favorite language of the educated classes on the Iberian peninsula, including Portugal. When Columbus wrote Castilian, he used Portuguese spelling, which suggests that he first spoke Portuguese. He may have written Portuguese too, but we have nothing in that language from his hand. He did somehow learn to read Latin, which was essential for his efforts to persuade the learned.

In 1484 Columbus made his first formal presentation of the Enterprise of the Indies to King John. At first the King was much taken by the enthusiasm of the engaging young Genoese. Columbus, having "read a good deal in Marco Polo . . . reached the conception that over this Western Ocean Sea one could sail to this Isle Cypango and other unknown lands," and for this purpose he asked the King to man and equip three caravels. But the King "gave him small credit," finding Columbus to be "a big talker and boastful in setting forth his accomplishments, and full of fancy and imagination with his Isle Cypango."

Despite his own doubts, the King was enough persuaded by the fast-talking Columbus to refer the project to a committee of experts. This group, which included an eminent cleric and two Jewish physicians respected for their knowledge of celestial navigation, turned down Columbus. Contrary to vulgar legend, their rejection was not based on any disagreement about the shape of the earth. Educated Europeans by this time had no doubt about the earth's sphericity. But the committee seems to have been troubled by Columbus' gross underestimate of the sailing distance westward to Asia. And, in the end, their misgivings proved better founded than were Columbus' hopes.

Of course, Europeans had no notion that there might be a land barrier between Europe and Asia in the form of two vast continents. At the very most, some of them suspected that in the Western Ocean there might be islands like Antillia, the mythical Island of the Seven Cities, and possibly others, which could serve as way stations. Columbus' optimistic calculations indicated that the direct westward sea voyage from the Canary Islands to Japan would be only twenty-four hundred nautical miles. A tempting prospect! And by no means beyond the capacity of Portuguese vessels in that day. The furthest Portuguese venture down the west coast of Africa, Diogo Cão's discovery of the Congo River in that very year, 1484, was more than five thousand nautical miles from Lisbon. And there still was no sign of where, or whether, the African continent really could be rounded by ships en route to the Indies. If Portuguese ships could go out and return safely to a destination five thousand miles away, past treacherous shoals and hostile natives, surely they could reach out a mere half that distance due west across the friendly open ocean.

King John II's committee did not allow themselves to be persuaded by Columbus' will to believe. Still, in 1485, presumably with the committee's expert concurrence, the King authorized two Portuguese, Fernão Dulmo and João Estreito, to try to discover the island of Antillia in the Western Ocean. This expedition was to be at their own expense, and they would be hereditary captains of any land they discovered. But they promised that after they had sailed west for forty days they would return home whether or not they had found any islands. We know no more of that ill-fated expedition than that they set sail in 1487. And that, unlike Columbus, they made the mistake of setting out from the Azores, in the high latitudes where the strong westerly winds made their expedition nearly impossible. Seeking Antillia for forty days was one thing, to go all the way to farthest Asia, quite another. The King's committee of experts was, of course, much nearer the truth than was the enthusiastic Columbus. The actual air-line distance from the Canaries to Japan is ten thousand six hundred nautical miles, and their estimates were probably in that neighborhood. They dared not encourage their king to invest in so speculative an enterprise.

Fourteen eighty-five proved a bad year for Columbus in more ways than one. In that year his wife died, and with his five-year-old son, Diego, he left the country where he had spent most of his adult life. He moved on to Spain, hoping there for better luck in promoting his monomaniacal project.

Columbus' successful enterprise would be almost as much a feat of salesmanship as of seamanship. Helped by his brother Bartholomew, he spent most of the next seven years peddling the Enterprise of the Indies in the courts of western Europe. In Spain he first awakened the interest of the Count of Medina Celi, a wealthy Cádiz shipowner. Celi might have financed the three caravels for Columbus' voyage if the Queen had not refused her assent. Such an expedition, if it went out at all, should certainly be a royal enterprise. She let a year pass before she would receive Columbus in audience. Then she, too, appointed a commission, under Hernando de Talavera, her confessor, to hear Columbus' proposal in detail, and to make recommendations.

Columbus now suffered through dreary years of academic and bureaucratic palaver by Queen Isabella and her Spanish minions. Meanwhile the commission proved its academic qualifications by neither approving nor rejecting the project. The professors learnedly debated the width of the Western Ocean and kept Columbus on the string with the pittance of a tiny monthly royal grant.

As the Spanish negotiations dragged on he recalled that King John II of Portugal had been personally friendly to him back in 1484–85, and so he decided to go back to Lisbon and try again. From Seville Columbus wrote the King of Portugal telling of his hopes. But Columbus had left Portugal in dire financial straits with many unpaid bills behind. He dared not return to Lisbon unless the King guaranteed him safe-conduct and freedom from arrest for his debts. The King agreed, praising Columbus' "industry and good talent," and urged him, "our particular friend," to come ahead. The King's renewed interest was doubtless due to the fact that the voyage of Dulmo and Estreito to Antillia had been abortive. Also there was still no word from Bartholomeu Dias, who had been gone seven months seeking the eastward sea passage to India, in the twentieth Portuguese attempt in that direction.

As it turned out, Columbus could not have chosen a worse moment. For, as we have seen, when Christopher and his brother Bartholomew arrived in 1488, they were just in time to be on the dock to see Bartholomeu Dias and his three caravels triumphantly sail up the Tagus with the good word that he had rounded the Cape of Good Hope and found that there really was an open eastward sea passage to India. Dias' success and all that it promised naturally killed King John's interest in Columbus. If the eastward sea passage was open and clear, why speculate in the other direction?

The Columbus brothers desperately hoped that this very Portuguese success to the east would stimulate the interest of rivals in a competing project in the other direction. Bartholomew, it seems, went to England, where he tried unsuccessfully to awaken the interest of King Henry VII, then went on to France where he solicited King Charles VIII. The French king himself was at first not receptive, but Bartholomew, encouraged by the friendly support of the King's elder sister, stayed on in France and was there supporting himself as a map-maker when news finally came of Columbus' great discovery.

Meanwhile Christopher returned from Lisbon to Seville, where he found Ferdinand and Isabella still vacillating. In disgust, he was actually en route to take ship for France to help Bartholomew persuade King Charles VIII when Queen Isabella, urged on by her keeper of the privy purse, suddenly decided to stake Columbus. Columbus' advocate had pointed out that support of his enterprise would cost no more than a week's royal entertainment of a visiting dignitary. Perhaps Isabella was persuaded by the fact that Columbus had shown his intention to offer the bargain enterprise to her rival sovereign next-door. She would pledge her crown jewels if needed to finance the trip. Fortunately, this proved unnecessary.

In her melodramatic last-moment decision, the Queen sent a messenger to catch Columbus before he embarked for France. Not till April 1492, eight years after Columbus had made his first offer to the king of Portugal, were the contracts, the so-called Capitulations, between Columbus and the Spanish sovereigns finally signed. The years of persuasion and promotion were at an end. Now Columbus' element would be the sea, where personal charms would not help, for there were no friends at Neptune's court. Columbus had spent years collecting evidence and "expert witnesses" for the feasibility of a westward voyage to reach the Indies. The project, though surely not harebrained, was without doubt speculative. Yet its feasibility depended on two simple propositions that were not at all unorthodox.

The first, a Christian cartographic dogma, was that the surface of the earth was covered mostly by land. "Six parts hast thou dried up," declared the prophet Esdras (II Esd. 6:42). Among the orthodox it had become axiomatic that the surface of our planet was six-sevenths dry land and only one-seventh water. God's rationale for this seemed obvious, since He had set man above all the rest of Creation. "Nature could not have made so disorderly a composition of the globe," affirmed João de Barros, the Portuguese historian, who gives us our best account of Columbus' efforts to sell the king of Portugal on his project, "as to give the element of water preponderance over the land, destined for life and the creation of souls." If all the oceans together amounted to only one-seventh the surface of the earth and, as all the learned believed, the earth was a sphere, then there was not much sea available to separate Spain to the westward from the Indies, the Western Ocean could not be extensive, and Columbus' enterprise was feasible. *Q.E.D.*

The second proposition concerned the eastward extent of the land mass of Asia and the size of the whole earth. Obviously, the more extensive and eastward-reaching Asia was imagined to be, the narrower became the sea passage that Columbus proposed to make. On this subject the opinions of the most respected authorities varied wildly. Agreeing that the earth was a sphere encompassing all the way round 360 degrees of longitude, they expressed their estimates in the number of degrees of longitude between Cape St. Vincent in Portugal and the east coast of China. These estimates ranged from 116 degrees (in the Catalan Atlas of 1375) or 125 degrees (Fra Mauro, 1459) or 177 degrees (Ptolemy, A.D. 150), to maximum estimates of 225 degrees (Marinus of Tyre, A.D. 100) or 234 degrees (Martin Behaim, 1492). We now know that the correct figure is 131 degrees.

For a sailor going west, the practical meaning of any of these estimates in nautical miles depended on still another, even more important matter of opinion—the circumference of the earth. The length of one degree of longitude at the equator, ⅟₃₆₀ of the circuit of the earth, plainly varied with the size one assigned to the whole planet. Here, too, the most respected authorities widely, though not quite so wildly, disagreed. Their estimates of the circumference varied by some 25 percent, from the Catalan Atlas figure of about 20,000 miles to Fra Mauro's figure of about 24,000. Translating these figures into the length of a degree at the equator, they produced estimates that ranged from about 56 miles to about 66 miles. The correct figure is 69 miles.

Now it is easy to see that whether or not you thought Columbus' Enterprise of the Indies was feasible depended on which combination of figures you selected. If you believed that the land mass of Eurasia extended eastward from Cape St. Vincent to the coast of China only for some 116 degrees of longitude, that left the vast reach of 244 degrees for the westward oceanic distance between Portugal and China. And that made a sea voyage of 14,000 miles! We cannot be surprised that Columbus chose another set of figures.

We know a great deal about what Columbus read. For clues to Columbus' reaction to what he read, we have at least 2,125 of his "postils," his manuscript comments in the margins of his own copies of authoritative books. These books discussed the question of the eastward extent of Eurasia, the breadth of the Western Ocean, and the size of the earth. Of the books that Columbus owned, we have his copy of Plutarch's *Lives*, his copy of Ptolemy's *Geography* (1479) with no writing in it by Columbus, except his signature, and three other geographical works, all copiously annotated in Columbus' own hand.

Most extensively annotated was the *Imago mundi*, a world geography written about 1410, before the widespread revival of Ptolemy in Christian Europe. The author, the French theologian-astrologer Pierre d'Ailly, documented Columbus' hopes on the crucial questions of the eastward extent of Asia and the width of the Western Ocean. Columbus appears to have kept the *Imago mundi* by him for years, underlining passages in a variety of pens and inks, adding comments, summarizing points in the text, drawing an index finger to emphasize a sentence, with comments also in the hand of his brother Bartholomew. D'Ailly served Columbus well, not only because he adopted Marinus of Tyre's long stretch (225 degrees) for the eastward extent of Eurasia, but also because he made the Western Ocean conveniently narrow. More than that, d'Ailly explicitly refuted Ptolemy, whose shorter estimates of about 177 degrees for Eurasia made him a powerful witness against Columbus. "The length of the [Eurasian] land toward the Orient," the *Imago mundi* declared, "is much greater than Ptolemy admits . . . because the length of the habitable Earth on the side of the Orient is more than half the circuit of the globe. For, according to the philosophers and Pliny, the ocean which stretches between the extremity of further Spain (that is, Morocco) and the eastern edge of India is of no great width. *For it is evident that this sea is navigable in a very few days if the wind be fair* [Columbus' heavy underlining], whence it follows that the sea is not so great that it can cover three quarters of the globe, as certain people figure it."

Another heavily annotated work in Columbus' library—the *Historia rerum ubique gestarum* (1477) of Aeneas Sylvius (Pope Pius II, or Piccolomini)—collected scraps of enticing information about China, drawn from Marco Polo, Odoric of Pordenone, and others, with special emphasis on the Great Khan and the Emperor of China, along with tales of Amazons and anthropophagi. Then, of course, there was Marco Polo's *Travels*, which Columbus owned and extensively marked, and which had provided the basis for all the later estimates of the vast eastward extent of China.

The magic of the East that captured Columbus was concocted from the eloquent reminiscences of Marco Polo, the extravagant imaginings of Sir John Mandeville and others who had been inspired by them, the myths of Asian treasure, and the fables of fantastic animals and peculiar peoples. And by the despair over the Christians' failure to dislodge the infidel from the Holy Sepulcher which now diverted missionary efforts toward the heathens in Asia. Columbus must have been persuaded, too, by the axiom attributed to Aristotle, that one could cross from Spain to the Indies in a few days. And by the oft-repeated prophecy of Seneca, "An age will come after many years when the Ocean will loose the chain of things, and a huge land lie revealed; when Tiphys will disclose new worlds and Thule no more be the Ultimate."

FAIR WINDS, SOFT WORDS, AND LUCK

C HRISTOPHER COLUMBUS' single-minded devotion to his Enterprise of the Indies and all the treasure of Ferdinand and Isabella would have counted for naught if Columbus had not had fair winds and if he had not known how to harness the winds to carry him there *and back.* The long-past Age of Sail has taken away with it the wonder we should feel for Columbus' mastery of the winds. Columbus was, of course, grossly mistaken about the continents. He did not really know the lands, but he did know the sea, which in his time especially meant to know the winds.

When, at the age of forty-one, Columbus won his opportunity to try his great enterprise, he already had a wide-ranging seafaring experience behind him. Under the Portuguese flag he had sailed from above the Arctic Circle nearly to the equator, and from the Aegean westward to the outer Azores. One trip had been in a vessel engaged in trading wool and dried fish and wine between the far-north regions of Iceland and Ireland, the Azores, and Lisbon. Then for a while Columbus had lived in Porto Santo, in the Madeira Islands, where one of his sons was born. From there he had sailed, and once actually commanded, voyages to São Jorge da Mina, the flourishing Portuguese trading post on the Gold Coast of the Gulf of Guinea. His varied experience in sailing northern latitudes and encountering all the perils of the sea would now at last be turned to a single grand purpose.

Columbus might have set out from Cádiz, the main Spanish seaport on the Atlantic, but Cádiz was crowded on his appointed day, for it had been designated as the principal point of embarkation for departing Jews. His day of departure, August 2, 1492, had also been fixed by their Most Catholic Majesties, Ferdinand and Isabella, as the deadline for the expulsion of all Jews from Spain. Any who remained thereafter were to be executed unless they embraced the Christian faith. Thousands whose only crime was faith in their God were on that very day being crammed into the holds of ships that crowded the narrow Rio Saltés. Out of the Gulf of Cádiz they would be shipped to a well-known, unfriendly old Christian world. Some would seek refuge in the Netherlands, others in the more tolerant world of Islam.

In the early morning of August 3 the very same tide that carried the hapless Jews to an old world of persecutions carried Columbus' three vessels from Palos de la Frontera near the mouth of the Río Tinto toward their unwitting discovery of a new refuge for the persecuted.

Columbus' own journal recorded that his trip was ordered only after the realm had been cleansed of Jews. His Catholic sovereigns now dispatched him to the idolaters of India on another high Christian mission—"their conversion to our Holy Faith, and ordained that I should not go by land (the usual way) to the Orient, but by the route of the Occident, by which no one to this day knows for sure that anyone has gone." As we have seen, Columbus' was not the first voyage from the Iberian peninsula to try the way westward into the Atlantic. Dulmo and Estreito, who had set out in 1487 to find the fabled island of Antillia, had the bad judgment to set sail directly west from the Azores in the high latitudes, and had never been heard from since. They had not come to terms with the wind.

Instead of setting his course due west from Spain, Columbus first sailed southward to the Canaries and so prudently avoided the strong westerly winds of the North Atlantic. At the Canaries, after this useful week-long "shake-down cruise," he turned due west, exploiting the advantages at that season of the northeasterly trade winds, which would carry him direct to his destination. An incidental advantage of this route from Columbus' point of view was that the

Canary Islands happened to be on the same parallel of latitude as Cipangu (Japan), the particular destination that he had chosen from his reading of Marco Polo. He could run directly "westing," following his latitude until he reached his desired point in the Indies. It was on the parallel of the Canaries that Orient and Occident were said to come closest together, for there the islands of Japan, according to Marco Polo, lay fully fifteen hundred miles off the east coast of China.

Having set that course, Columbus found clear sailing. With a following wind, Columbus' ships scudded ahead. The strong following wind was so constant that Columbus' crew even began to fear that in those regions they might never find the westerly wind needed to take them home. They must actually have felt some relief, then, on September 19, when Columbus hove the deep-sea lead and still found no bottom at two hundred fathoms, that they ran temporarily into an area of variable winds. On October 5 the restless crew was encouraged by flocks of birds flying their way. Then, thirty-three days out, at two o'clock on the morning of October 12, a lookout on the *Pinta* claimed the announced 5,000-maravedi bonus, for he was the first to shout *"Tierra! Tierra!"*

For the homeward journey Columbus planned to go north, above the "horse latitudes," to the neighborhood of 35 degrees, where he would meet the westerly trades. While Columbus' plan for using the winds was quite correct, the homeward passage was troubled by storms.

In those days it was not for nothing that mariners were called "sailors," men of the sail. They were expected to fill their sails with the winds to take them where they wanted. "The wind bloweth where it listeth" was Saint John's way of describing the mystery of that world. "And thou hearest the sound thereof, but canst not tell whence it cometh, and whither it goeth: so is every one that is born of the Spirit" (John 3:8). For the skillful mariner, the Columbus, the winds were the mystery he had to master just as the steamer's captain must master the machinery of his ocean liner. Modern racing yachtsmen agree that a sailing vessel today, after all that has been learned in the last five centuries, could not do better than follow Columbus' route.

Was his course the product of solid knowledge of the winds or the dictate of a faultless seaman's instinct? Even before he set out, he already had personal experience of the ways of the winds in all the different latitudes where his voyage to the Indies would take him, and so he was well equipped to find the best course out and back. Acolytes of the sea (like Samuel Eliot Morison, whose *Admiral of the Ocean Sea* sings the mystique of seamanship) prefer to credit Columbus' intuition.

The "discovery" of America has overshadowed Columbus' other discoveries, which the passing of the Age of Sail has made it hard for us to appreciate. Even on his first voyage, as another seafaring historian, George E. Nunn, reminds us, Columbus really made *three* momentous discoveries. Besides finding land that Europeans had not found before, he discovered both the best westward sea passage from Europe to North America and the best eastward passage back. Columbus discovered the pathways necessary for ships whose source of energy was the wind. Although he might not have known where he really was going or where he had finally arrived, he was a knowledgeable master of the winds, which would make it possible for others to follow him.

Of course, he also had to manage his men, and keeping up the morale of a crew sailing into the unknown was no easy matter. Mutiny threatened on more than one occasion during the 33-day outward voyage. Passage to the Indies had to be accomplished before the patience of the crew wore thin. At the outset Columbus promised his men that they would find land when they had gone 750 leagues, or about 2,250 statute miles, west of the Canaries. They needed to be reassured that they were not going to some point of no return.

Columbus was not above using devious, even deceptive, techniques to keep his crew in good spirits and devoted to the common purpose. He did not forget his crew's concern for getting home, and in good time. To be sure that he would not discourage the men, he falsified his daily journal of the voyage. In noting down his estimates of distance traveled, "he decided to reckon less than he made, so that if the voyage were long the people would not be frightened and dismayed." For example, on September 25, Columbus himself believed that they had sailed a full 21 leagues, "but the people were told that 13 was the distance made good; for it was always feigned to them that the distances were less, so that the voyage might not appear so long." As it turned out, Columbus was deceiving them less than he intended. He did not realize that his own habit was to overestimate distance. The result was that the "phony" reckoning that he gave out to the crew turned out to be closer to the facts than his own "true" journal.

There were more than a few tricky moments during the outward passage. On September 21–23, for example, when they sailed into the Sargasso Sea, the vast oval area of the mid-South Atlantic which was blanketed with bright green and yellow sargassum gulfweed, the crew, who had never seen anything like this before, took alarm. Fearing their ships would be "frozen" in sargassum, they demanded that the captain change course to find open water. Columbus plowed straight ahead. Still today, however, sailors keep alive the superstitious fear of getting stuck in the Sargasso Sea.

Even the calm weather, lack of rain, and smooth seas became a cause for grumbling. If there was no rain, how to replenish the supply of fresh water on the salt ocean? If Columbus was to carry them endlessly westward, as some of the crew feared, perhaps their only hope of seeing their families again would be to toss him overboard. Columbus turned aside complaints with "soft words" and visions of the Indies' treasure which all would share. But he also reminded them of the dire consequences for the whole crew should they return to Spain without him. On his first outward voyage Columbus had that most precious additional ingredient, luck. The weather was beyond compare, so (in his own words) "that the savor of the mornings was a great delight." "The weather was like April in Andalusia, the only thing wanting was to hear the nightingales."

Not the least remarkable, though the least celebrated, of Columbus' achievements was his ability on his later voyages to return to the lands he had first so accidentally and unwittingly encountered. Doubly remarkable, too, because Columbus' navigating techniques were so rudimentary. In Columbus' time, celestial navigation was quite undeveloped. He was unable to use even so elementary an instrument as the astrolabe. Despite romanticized illustrations to the contrary, he probably never saw a cross-staff. With his simple quadrant he was unable to do any useful sighting until he had been ashore at Jamaica for a full year. Only many years after Columbus' death did celestial navigation become normal equipment for the professional European pilot.

To set his direction and find his bearings at sea, Columbus depended on dead reckoning. This was less a scientific technique than a practical skill. He used the magnetic compass to fix direction, then estimated distance by guessing the speed at which they were sailing, by watching the bubbles, gulfweed or some other object float by. His estimates were crude, because not until the sixteenth century did someone invent the chip log to measure speed.

Dead reckoning served well enough for going from one known location to another, where the landscape, shoals, and currents were familiar. But it gave you no bearings into the unknown. Columbus, we must recall, thought he was traveling to a known destination.

INTO "THE MISTS OF PARADOX"

CHAPTER 38

NOTHING could be more obvious than that the earth is stable and unmoving, and that we are the center of the universe. Modern Western science takes its beginning from the denial of this commonsense axiom. This denial, the birth and the prototype of science's sovereign paradoxes, would be our invitation to an infinite invisible world. Just as Knowledge was what led Adam and Eve to discover their nakedness and put on their clothing, so the guilty knowledge of this simple paradox—that the earth was not as central or as immobile as it seemed—would lead man to discover the nakedness of his senses. Common sense, the foundation of everyday life, could no longer serve for the governance of the world. When "scientific" knowledge, the sophisticated product of complicated instruments and subtle calculations, provided unimpeachable truths, things were no longer what they seemed.

* * *

Ancient cosmologies used picturesque and persuasive myths to embellish the verdicts of common sense, and to describe how the heavenly bodies moved. On the walls of the tombs of the Egyptian pharaohs in the Valley of the Kings we can find colorful caricatures of how above the Earth the God of Air supported the dome of heaven. There, too, we observe how every day the sun-god Ra rode his boat through the sky. Every night, riding another boat through the waters beneath the earth, he arrived back where he began his daily journey again. This mythic view, as we have seen, did not prevent the Egyptians from developing the most precise calendar of the solar year that was known for millennia. To the ordinary Egyptian such myths made sense. They did not contradict what he saw every day and every night with his naked eye.

The Greeks developed the notion that the earth was a sphere on which man lived while the heavens above were a rotating spherical dome that held the stars and moved them about. The spherical nature of the earth, as we have seen, was demonstrated by such commonsense experience as the disappearance of departing ships below the horizon. The spherical nature of the heavens was also confirmed by everybody's naked-eye experience, day and night. Outside that dome of stars, according to the Greeks, there was nothing, not space, nor even emptiness. Inside the sphere of the stars, the sun went around the earth in its daily and yearly courses. Plato described the creation of this two-sphere universe with his usual mythic felicity. "Wherefore he made the world in the form of a globe, round as from a lathe, having its extremes in every direction equidistant from the center, the most perfect and the most like itself of all figures; for he considered that the like is infinitely fairer than the unlike."

In his work *On the Heavens* Aristotle elaborated this commonsense vision into an attractive dogma. "Ether," transparent and weightless, was the pure material of the heavens and of the concentric nesting heavenly spheres that carried the stars and the planets. Though some of his disciples disagreed, Aristotle said that these ethereal shells numbered precisely fifty-five. The varying distance of each planet from the earth was explained by the movements of each planet from the innermost to the outermost edges of its own special sphere. For many centuries the speculations of leading Western astronomers, astrologers, and cosmologists were only modifications of this picture.

To understand the paradoxical beginnings of modern science, we must recall that this beautiful symmetrical scheme, much ridiculed in the modern classroom, actually served very well for both astronomer and layman. It described the heavens precisely as they looked and fitted the observations and calculations made with the naked eye. The scheme's simplicity, symmetry, and common sense made it seem to confirm countless axioms of philosophy, theology, and religion. And it actually performed some functions of a scientific explanation. For it fitted the available facts, was a reasonably satisfactory device for prediction, and harmonized with the accepted view of the rest of nature. In addition, it aided the astronomer's memory with a convenient coherent model, replacing the list of miscellaneous facts then known about the heavens. More than that, while this much maligned geocentric, or "Ptolemaic," scheme provided the layman with a clear picture to carry around in his head, it helped the astronomer reach out to the unknown. Even for the adventurous sailor and the navigator it served well enough, as Columbus proved. The modern advance to Copernicus' heliocentric system would be hard to imagine if the geocentric system had not been there available for revision. Copernicus would not change the shape of the system, he simply changed the location of the bodies.

Of course the traditional geocentric system of Aristotle and Ptolemy and so many others over centuries had its own weaknesses. For example, the system did not explain the irregularities observed in the motions of the planets. But the layman hardly noticed these irregularities, and anyway they seemed adequately described by the supposed movement of each planet within its own special ethereal sphere. Astronomers were adept at explaining away what seemed only minor problems by a variety of complicated epicycles, deferents, equants, and eccentrics, which gave them a heavy vested interest in the whole scheme. The more copious this peripheral literature became, the more difficult it became to retreat to fundamentals. If the central scheme was not correct, surely so many learned men would not have bothered to offer their many subtle corrections.

Why did Nicolaus Copernicus (1473–1543) go to so much trouble to displace a system that was amply supported by everyday experience, by tradition, and by authority? The more we become at home in the Age of Copernicus, the more we can see that those who would remain unpersuaded by Copernicus were simply being sensible. The available evidence did not require a revision of the scheme. Decades would pass before astronomers and mathematicians could gather new facts and find new instruments, a century or more before laymen would be persuaded against their common sense. To be sure, despite all the arcane modifications that astronomers and mathematicians devised, the old scheme did not quite fit all known facts. But neither would Copernicus' own simplification.

* * *

It seems that Copernicus was animated not by the force of facts but by an aesthetic, metaphysical concern. He imagined how much more beautiful another scheme could be. Copernicus possessed an extraordinarily playful mind and a bold imagination. But there was nothing extraordinary about his career. Although he never took holy orders, he led his whole working life comfortably in the bosom of the Church. In fact, it was the Church that made it possible for him to pursue his wide-ranging intellectual and artistic interests. He was born in 1473 in the busy commercial town of Thorn on the banks of the Vistula River in northern Poland. When he was only ten, his father, a prosperous wholesale merchant and city official, died. His uncle and guardian, who became bishop of Ermeland, a see in northern Poland, arranged for Nicolaus to be taken care of by Mother Church. In the Bishop's cathedral seat, the city of Frauenburg, his nephew Nicolaus was appointed canon at the age of twenty-four, and this post remained his worldly support until the day he died.

As an astronomer Copernicus was a mere amateur. He did not make his living by astronomy or by any application of astronomy. By our standards, at least, he was wonderfully versatile, which put him in the mainstream of the High Renaissance. He was born when Leonardo da Vinci (1452–1519) was in full career, and Michelangelo (1475–1564) was his contemporary. He began by studying mathematics at the University of Cracow, where he picked up enough skill at painting to be able to leave us a competent self-portrait. After receiving his convenient appointment as canon of Frauenburg he quickly took leave for an extended journey to Italy to study canon law at Bologna and Ferrara, to study medicine at Padua, and incidentally to hear some lectures in astronomy. Back in Frauenburg, he served as the Bishop's personal physician until his uncle's death in 1512. In those turbulent times his post as canon was no sinecure. He had to keep the accounts, to see that the chapter's political interests were protected, and serve as commissary of the whole diocese. Along the way he provided the Polish provincial Diet of Graudenz with a scheme for improving its currency. Copernicus developed his heliocentric theory as an avocation, and only the enthusiasm of friends and disciples induced him to have it published.

Copernicus was well aware that his system seemed to violate common sense. For that very reason his friends had "urged and even importuned" him to publish the work. "They insisted that, though my theory of the Earth's movement might at first seem strange, yet it would appear admirable and acceptable when the publication of my elucidatory comments should dispel the mists of paradox."

Copernicus' own first comprehensive sketch of his system, *Commentariolus* or "Sketch of his Hypotheses for the Heavenly Motions," was not printed during his lifetime. Only a few handwritten copies were circulated among his friends. Oddly enough, the first description to the world of Copernicus' revolutionary system was not by Copernicus himself but by a brilliant and erratic twenty-five-year-old disciple. This young Austrian, born Georg Joachim (1514–1574), had taken the name Rheticus to avoid bearing the stigma of his father, a town physician who had been beheaded for sorcery. Rheticus arrived in Frauenburg in the summer of 1539 to meet Copernicus and learn more about his new cosmology, still not available in print. He had just received his M.A. from the University of Wittenberg for a thesis which proved that the Roman law did not forbid astrological predictions, because like medical predictions they were based on observable physical causes. Rheticus was obviously a young man of some courage and considerable powers of persuasion. Although Copernicus had repeatedly refused to give in to requests that he himself publish his stirring new ideas, he now granted his young visitor permission to do the job for him.

Within a few months, by late September that same year, Rheticus had written his *First Report (Narratio Prima)* of Copernicus' system, in the form of a letter to his former teacher, which was printed in Danzig early in 1540. For Copernicus the advantages of such a trial balloon were obvious. If the reception was favorable, he could confidently publish his own amplified account. If not, he could leave it alone or modify his own statement. Copernicus' doubts were dispelled when the demand for Rheticus' *First Report* required a second edition in 1541. He then turned to revising for publication the manuscript of his own great work, which he had nearly completed a full decade before. Copernicus assigned to Rheticus the task of seeing the epochal book through the press. When, at the last moment, Rheticus, for personal reasons, could not finish the job, he unfortunately handed it over to an acquaintance Andreas Osiander (1498–1552). This militant, quarrelsome and Machiavellian Lutheran theologian believed that divine revelation was the sole source of truth, and, as we shall see, was determined to do all he could to cast Copernicus' suggestions in the image of his own orthodoxy. Copernicus, who lay dying in Frauenburg far from the site of publication, would be powerless to intervene.

The revolutionary suggestion of Copernicus was that the earth itself moved. If the earth moved around the sun, then the sun and not the earth was the center of the universe. Might not the whole scheme of the heavens become suddenly simpler if the sun, instead of the earth, were imagined at the center?

Copernicus' objective was not to devise a new system of physics, much less a new scientific method. His single revision—a moving earth no longer in the center—leaves the large features of the Ptolemaic system untouched. He stays with the doctrine of spheres, which was crucial to the Ptolemaic system, and avoids the debated question whether the celestial spheres were imaginary or real. He does not say whether the "spheres" (*orbes*) in which the planets and, according to his system, the earth too revolve are only a convenient geometric device for describing how they move, or whether each "sphere" really is a thick shell made of some ethereal transparent material. For Copernicus, *orbis* simply meant sphere, and he plainly keeps the traditional concept of spheres in his own system. The title of the climactic book in which he finally summed up his theory, *De*

Revolutionibus Orbium Caelestium, does not refer to planets, but means "Concerning the Revolutions of the Heavenly Spheres." On another crucial question, whether the universe is finite or infinite, Copernicus again decisively refuses to commit himself. He leaves this matter "to the discussion of the natural philosophers."

Just as Columbus relied on Ptolemy and the other traditional texts whose suggestions he thought had not been energetically enough pursued, so, too, Copernicus found his clues among the ancients. First of all, from Pythagoreanism, the influential doctrine of the followers of Pythagoras of Samos, a Greek philosopher and mathematician of the sixth century B.C. None of Pythagoras' own work has survived, but the ideas fathered on him by his followers would be among the most potent in modern history. Pure knowledge, the Pythagoreans argued, was the purification *(catharsis)* of the soul. This meant rising above the data of the human senses. The pure essential reality, they said, was found only in the realm of numbers. The simple, wonderful proportion of numbers would explain the harmonies of music which were the beauty of the ear. For that reason they introduced the musical terminology of the octave, the fifth, the fourth, expressed as 2:1, 3:1, and 4:3.

For astronomy the Pythagorean adoration of numbers carried an overwhelming message. "They say that the things themselves are Numbers," was Aristotle's succinct summary in his *Metaphysics*, "and do not place the objects of mathematics between Forms and sensible things." "Since, again, they saw that the modifications and the ratios of the musical scales were expressible in numbers—since, then, all other things seemed in their whole nature to be modelled on numbers, and numbers seemed to be the first things in the whole of nature, they supposed the elements of numbers to be the elements of all things, and the whole heaven to be a musical scale and a number. . . . and the whole arrangement of the heavens they collected and fitted into their scheme; and if there was a gap anywhere, they readily made additions so as to make their whole theory coherent." In Copernicus' time Pythagoreans still believed that the only way to truth was by mathematics.

The other fertile source for Copernicus' ideas and for the pragmatic foundations of modern science was just as surprising—Plato and his mystic followers, the Neoplatonists. Although Copernicus was to be the unconscious prophet of the scientific belief in the sovereignty of the senses, his godfather was Plato, who believed that all the data of the senses were mere unsubstantial shadows. Plato's "real" world was a world of ideal forms, and from his point of view geometry was more real than physics. Over the entrance to Plato's Academy, we are told, stood the warning, "Let no one destitute of geometry enter my doors."

Plato's Neoplatonist followers, too, built their whole view of the world on an ideal mathematics. Numbers offered the best human vision of God and the world-soul. "All mathematical species . . . have a primary subsistence in the soul," observed Proclus (A.D. 410?–485), the last and greatest of the Greek exponents of Neoplatonism, "so that, before sensible numbers, there are to be found in her inmost recesses, self-moving numbers . . . ideal proportions of harmony previous to concordant sounds; and invisible orbs, prior to the bodies which revolve in a circle. . . . we must follow the doctrine of Timaeus, who derives the origin, and consummates the fabric of the soul, from mathematical forms, and reposes in her nature the causes of everything which exists."

Neoplatonism, reborn in the Renaissance—the age into which Copernicus was born—took up battle against the frigid, prosaic spirit of the scholastics. Aristotle's hardheaded commonsense approach had been reinforced by the finding of new Aristotelian texts in the twelfth century. Against this the Neoplatonists championed poetry and the free-flying imagination. When Copernicus studied at Bologna, his teacher was Domenico Maria de Novara, an enthusiastic Neoplatonist who attacked the Ptolemaic system. Surely the heavenly scheme must be too simple to need all that pedantic apparatus of epicycles, deferents, equants, etc., etc. The astronomers must somehow have missed the essential charm of celestial numbers.

In Copernicus' own Preface to his *De Revolutionibus,* he spoke with the voice of his teacher and put himself squarely in the ranks of the Neoplatonists. The Ptolemaic system for explaining the motions of the planets, he said, required "many admissions which seem to violate the first principle of uniformity in motion. Nor have they been able thereby to discern or deduce the principal thing—namely the shape of the Universe and the unchangeable symmetry of its parts." Copernicus believed that his system actually accorded better than the older geocentric system with the way the universe *ought* to be. He believed he was describing the actual truths of an essentially mathematical universe.

Heavenly motions must be perfect circles. In Copernicus' time, all this reminds us, astronomy was still a branch of mathematics—in E. A. Burtt's phrase "the geometry of the heavens." Following Pythagorean and Neoplatonic doctrine, this carried implications too for mathematics itself, which, instead of being the deductive study of abstract constructs, purported to describe the actual world. It would be some time before this notion changed. Meanwhile, this proved to be a fruitful confusion, luring astronomers and others through the gateway to modern science.

Copernicus had some authorities, and some appealing assumptions, but he did not yet have the evidence to support his hunches. In this, too, he was like Columbus, who thought the westward voyage to the Indies worth trying even though direct evidence was still lacking, and though Gama had done well enough by going eastward. Similarly the Ptolemaic system had for centuries provided a usable calendar. The scheme that Copernicus now proposed, for all its aesthetic appeal, fit the observed facts no better. Nor could he predict the position of the planets with anything like the demonstrated accuracy of the older system.

*   *   *

How seriously did Copernicus take his own proposals? Did he think that he had finally solved the central problems of astronomy? Or was he merely offering a tentative suggestion for others to explore? The first printed edition of Copernicus' great work, the *De Revolutionibus* (1543), which reached him only on his deathbed, carried a lengthy unsigned introduction which seemed to answer this question beyond doubt.

Since the novelty of the hypotheses of this work has already been widely reported, I have no doubt that some learned men have taken serious offense because the book declares that the earth moves, and that the sun is at rest in the center of the universe; these men undoubtedly believe that the liberal arts, established long ago upon a correct basis, should not be thrown into confusion. But if they are willing to examine the matter closely, they will find that the author of this work has done nothing blameworthy. For it is the duty of an astronomer to compose the history of the celestial motions through careful and skillful observation. Then turning to the causes of these motions or hypotheses about them, he must conceive and devise, since he cannot in any way attain to the true causes, such hypotheses as, being assumed, enable the motions to be calculated correctly from the principles of geometry, for the future as well as for the past. The present author has performed both these duties excellently. For these hypotheses need not be true nor even probable; if they provide a calculus consistent with the observations, that alone is sufficient. . . . So far as hypotheses are concerned, let no one expect anything certain from astronomy, which cannot furnish it, lest he accept as the truth ideas conceived for another purpose, and depart from this study a greater fool than when he entered it. Farewell.

Only later was it discovered that this introduction was not written by Copernicus at all. In the cause of Lutheran orthodoxy, the unscrupulous Andreas Osiander had secretly suppressed Copernicus' own introduction and substituted this unsigned one, which he concocted himself. It was the great Johannes Kepler (1571–1630) who identified the anonymous author and defended Copernicus from Osiander's "most absurd fiction," the slander on his scientific integrity. Osiander had thought he was defending Copernicus, but his exercise in timidity proved superfluous. By the time the *De Revolutionibus* was spread abroad, Copernicus himself was dead and safely beyond reach of retribution by any church on earth. "He thought that his hypotheses were true," the outraged Kepler insisted, "no less than did those ancient astronomers. . . . He did not merely think so, but he proves that they are true. . . . Therefore Copernicus is not composing a myth but is giving earnest expression to paradoxes, that is, philosophizing, which is what you required in an astronomer."

Copernicus himself was no party to the theological compliance to which Osiander had tried to commit him. But Kepler, always an enthusiast, appears to have become more of a Copernican than Copernicus himself. Copernicus seemed to have realized that he had only pushed the door ajar. He enjoyed giving his contemporaries a glimpse of what might be in store for them. This itself required courage. He was not yet ready for a bold exploration of his New World. He did not and could not yet realize how new was the New World he had opened. For, again like Columbus, he was still relying heavily on ancient maps.

Copernicus described his system as "hypotheses." And in the language of the Ptolemaic Age a "hypothesis" was more than a mere experimental notion. It was, rather, the principle or the fundamental proposition (his synonyms were *principium* or *assumptio*) on which a whole system was based. This meant, according to Copernicus, that his propositions had two essential qualities. First, they must "save the appearances" *(apparentias salvare)*, which meant that the conclusions drawn from them must agree with the actual observations. Some interesting ambiguities in this simple phrase would surface within the next century, when the telescope supplied "appearances" not visible to the naked eye. In 1543 "saving the appearances" still seemed a self-evident and self-defining criterion. Yet, fitting what the eye saw was not enough. A second requirement was that a scientific proposition had to fit with and confirm the basic *a priori* notions accepted as the axioms of physics. For example, it must not be inconsistent with the axiom that all the motions of heavenly bodies are circular and that every such motion is uniform. While, according to Copernicus, the Ptolemaic system fitted well enough with observed appearances, it did not adequately provide for the required uniformity and circularity. A "true" system by Copernicus' standards would not merely satisfy the eye *(apparentias salvare)* but it would also have to please the mind.

If Copernicus had fears that his astronomic system would put him down as a heretic, these proved quite unfounded, not only during his lifetime but for a half-century after his death. His friends high in the Church, including a cardinal and a bishop, had long been urging him to publish his *De Revolutionibus*. He actually dedicated his great work to Pope Paul III, whose own mathematical education, he hoped, would arouse his special interest.

The prophets of Protestantism—Luther (1483–1546), Melanchthon (1497–1560), and Calvin (1509–1564)—all close contemporaries of Copernicus, carried a strong fundamentalist, anti-intellectual message. "An upstart astrologer," was Luther's epithet for Copernicus in his *Table Talk* in 1539. "This fool wishes to reverse the entire science of astronomy; but sacred Scripture tells us that Joshua commanded the sun to stand still, and not the earth." "Now, it is in want of honesty and decency," Luther's disciple Melanchthon added a few years after Copernicus' death, "to assert such notions publicly, and the example is pernicious. It is the part of a good mind to accept the truth as revealed by God and to acquiesce in it." Calvin seems never to have heard of Copernicus, but his fundamentalist bias made him and his disciples plainly unsympathetic. The Osiander who naïvely tried to cover Copernicus' theological flank with his forged apologetic introduction was a well-known Lutheran preacher with a Protestant notion of orthodoxy. This helps explain, too, why the *De Revolutionibus* was not published as we might have expected, in Wittenberg, where Rheticus was professor at the university. For Wittenberg, where Luther nailed his 95 Theses on the door of All Saints Church, had become the headquarters for the preachings of Luther and Melanchthon.

The Catholic Church took a more sophisticated and more tolerant view of speculations in secular science. After the fourteenth century the Church had not officially proclaimed any orthodox cosmology. Perhaps the follies and frustrations of Christian geography and the stirring secular revelations of the new seafaring age had something to do with this. But, whatever the reasons for this openness, Copernicus' *De Revolutionibus* was actually read in some of the best Catholic universities. The Church had survived many a secular novelty. Wiser heads continued to hope that the eternal truths of revelation and divine reason could be kept safely isolated from the shifting explanations of the practical world. It was decades after Copernicus' death before this separation had ceased to be possible.

* * *

In astronomy, more than in other sciences, there was a simple public test of any system. A perfect theory of the heavens would regularly and accurately forecast the dates of the summer and the winter solstice, the arrival of summer and winter. By Copernicus' time the discrepancy of the calendar offered public evidence that the generally accepted theory of the heavens was not quite right. When Julius Caesar drew on the Egyptian calendar to reform the Roman calendar in 45 B.C., as we have seen, he introduced the system of three years of 365 days followed by a leap year of 366 days. This produced a year of 365¼ days, which still proved to be some 11 minutes and 14 seconds longer than the actual solar cycle. Over the centuries, the accumulation of this error, like that of a clock that runs too slow, had produced a noticeable dislocation of the calendar. As a result, when Copernicus lived, the vernal equinox, which traditionally marks the beginning of spring in the northern hemisphere, had moved back from March 21 to March 11. Farmers could no longer rely on their calendar for the planting and the gathering of their crops, merchants could not depend on the calendar in signing contracts for the delivery of seasonal products.

Copernicus himself had used this disorder in the calendar as a reason for trying some alternative to the Ptolemaic system. "The mathematicians," he declared in his Preface to the *De Revolutionibus*, "are so unsure of the movements of the Sun and Moon, that they cannot even explain or observe the constant length of the seasonal year." Surely, Copernicus argued, there must be something the matter with a theory that had produced this calendar.

Meanwhile the Renaissance city-states and a seafaring commerce that reached around the world had brought new needs for a calendar that was precise and reliable. It is not surprising that Renaissance popes undertook calendar reform. But when they asked Copernicus to help with the project, he said the time was not yet ripe. While the old geocentric Ptolemaic system could not produce a calendar of the required accuracy, the evidence was not yet available to prove that his own heliocentric system would work any better. With the facts available at the time, as historians of astronomy remind us, Copernicus' revised scheme actually would not work as well.

Even so, Copernicus' notions were co-opted into the service of the Church to help Pope Gregory XIII produce the reformed calendar, which we still use. During the next half-century the only direct public application of Copernicus' theories was for this very practical purpose. Yet this "proof" of the truth of Copernicus' system was not by Copernicus himself and was presented in such a way as not to seem an endorsement of any risky cosmological shift.

The work on the calendar was done by another enthusiastic disciple of Copernicus with a genius and a passion for astronomical computation. At the age of twenty-five Erasmus Reinhold (1511–1553) was appointed professor of astronomy (*mathematum superiorum*) at the University of Wittenberg in 1536 by Luther's redoubtable lieutenant Philip Melanchthon. In the 1540's, when printing had made textbooks inexpensive enough to come into general use in universities, Reinhold produced popular versions of the standard works expounding the Ptolemaic system and the solid heavenly spheres. His colleague Rheticus, then also a professor at Wittenberg, had brought back an enthusiastic account of Copernicus. In Reinhold this awakened "a lively expectancy" and a hope that Copernicus would "restore astronomy." When the *De Revolutionibus* appeared, Reinhold began annotating his copy and was stimulated to prepare a set of astronomical tables fuller than any then available. After seven years of labor on "this huge and disagreeable task" (in Kepler's phrase), Reinhold finally published his calculations in 1551.

Reinhold's *Prutenic Tables*, named after his patron the Duke of Prussia, were so far superior to anything else at the time that they soon became the standard astronomical tables in Europe. To revise the older tables, Reinhold had freely used observations that Copernicus had included in his work. Of course he did not realize that Copernicus' notions of the positions and the movements of the planets, which he assumed to be combinations of simple circles, were far from the fact. Nevertheless Reinhold's product was an improvement and came into general use. While he generally acknowledged his debt to Copernicus, he did not even refer to the heliocentric system. The conjectural new arrangements of sun and planets seemed merely a means toward a better table of numbers, and were themselves of no special interest. When Pope Gregory XIII made his new calendar in 1582, he relied in turn on Reinhold's tables. Their superior accuracy seems to have been a bizarre historical coincidence, testimony to Reinhold's intuition rather than the truth of Copernicus' system.

NEW WORLDS WITHIN

T HE microscope was a product of the same age that made the telescope. But while Copernicus and Galileo have become popular heroes, prophets of modernity, Hooke and Leeuwenhoek, their counterparts in the microscopic world, have been relegated to the pantheon of the specialized sciences. Copernicus and Galileo played leading roles in the much publicized battle between "science" and "religion," Hooke and Leeuwenhoek did not.

We do not know who invented the microscope. The leading candidate is Zacharias Jansen, an obscure spectacle-maker of Middelburg. We do know that the microscope, like eyeglasses and the telescope, was in use long before the principles of optics were understood, and it was probably as accidental as the telescope. It could hardly have been devised by anyone eager to peer into a microscopic world still unimagined. Soon after the first telescopes were made, people simply tried using them to enlarge objects nearby. In the beginning the same Italian word, *occhialino*, or the Latin *perspicillum* served for both telescope and microscope. Galileo himself tried using his telescope as a microscope. "With this tube," Galileo reported to a visitor in Florence in November 1614, "I have seen flies which look as big as lambs, and have learned that they are covered over with hair and have very pointed nails by means of which they keep themselves up and walk on glass, although hanging feet up-

437

wards, by inserting the point of their nails in the pores of the glass."
He discovered to his dismay that while a telescope focused on the
stars needed to be only two feet long, to magnify small objects
nearby required a tube two or three times that length.

As early as 1625 a member of the Academy of the Lynxes, the
physician-naturalist John Faber (1574–1629), had a name for the
new device. "The optical tube . . . it has pleased me to call, after
the model of telescope, a microscope, because it permits a view of
minute things."

The same suspicions that made Galileo's critics unwilling to
look through his telescope, and then reluctant to believe what they
saw, also cursed the microscope. The telescope was obviously useful
in battle, but there were no battles yet where the microscope could
help. In the absence of a science of optics, sensible people were especially wary of "optical illusions" (deceptiones visus). This medieval distrust of all optical devices was the great obstacle to a science of
optics. As we have seen, it was believed that any device standing between the senses and the object to be sensed could only mislead the
God-given faculties. And to a certain extent the crude microscopes
in those days confirmed their suspicions. Chromatic and spherical
aberration still produced fuzzy images.

In 1665 Robert Hooke (1635–1703) published his *Micrographia*,
an enticing miscellany expounding his theory of light and color, and
his theories of combustion and respiration, along with a description
of the microscope with its uses. But the widespread suspicions of optical illusions would plague Hooke. At first the "new world" he
claimed to see through his lenses was the butt of ridicule—for example, in Thomas Shadwell's popular farce *The Virtuoso* (1676).

What Galileo's *Sidereus Nuncius* had done for the telescope and
its heavenly vistas, Hooke's *Micrographia* now did for the microscope. Just as Galileo did not invent the telescope, neither did
Hooke invent the microscope. But what he described seeing in his
compound microscope awakened learned Europe to the wonderful
world within. Fifty-seven amazing illustrations drawn by Hooke
himself revealed for the first time the eye of a fly, the shape of a bee's
stinging organ, the anatomy of a flea and a louse, the structure of
feathers, and the plantlike form of molds. When he discovered the

honeycomb structure of cork, he said it was made of "cells." Frequently reprinted, Hooke's illustrations remained in textbooks into the nineteenth century.

Just as the telescope had brought together the earth and the most distant heavenly bodies into a single scheme of thought, now microscopic vistas revealed a minuscule world surprisingly like that seen on a large scale every day. In his *Historia Insectorum Generalis* Jan Swammerdam (1637–1680) showed that insects, like the "higher" animals, possessed an intricate anatomy and did not reproduce by spontaneous generation. In his microscope he saw insects developing as man did, by epigenesis, the gradual development of one organ after another. Still, belief in other forms of spontaneous generation survived. As we shall see, it was not until Louis Pasteur's brilliant experiments with fermentation in the nineteenth century, and his practical application of his ideas for the preservation of milk, that the dogma ceased to be scientifically respectable.

The microscope opened dark continents never before entered and in many ways easy to explore. The great sea voyages had required large capital, organizing genius, talents of leadership, and the charisma of a Prince Henry or a Columbus, a Magellan or a Gama. Astronomic exploring required the coordinated observations of people in many places. But a lone man anywhere with a microscope could venture for the first time where there were neither experienced navigators nor skilled pilots.

Antoni van Leeuwenhoek (1632–1723) with his microscope pioneered this new science of other-worldly exploration. In Delft, where he was born, his father made baskets to pack the famous delftware for the world market. Antoni himself made a good living by selling silk, wool, cotton, buttons, and ribbons to the city's comfortable burghers, and had a substantial income as head of the City Council, inspector of weights and measures, and court surveyor. He was a close friend of Jan Vermeer, and on the painter's death was appointed trustee of Vermeer's bankrupt estate. He never attended a university, and during his whole ninety years he left the Netherlands only twice, journeying once to Antwerp and once to England.

Leeuwenhoek did not know Latin and could write only in the vernacular Dutch of his native Delft. But the modern instrument-aided experience of the senses was trans-lingual. No longer did one need Hebrew, Greek, Latin, or Arabic to join the community of scientists.

That age of bitter commercial rivalry between the Dutch and the British for the treasures of the East Indies saw their vigorous collaboration in science. Even while the guns of British and Dutch admirals were firing at each other, British and Dutch scientists were cordially exchanging information and sharing new scientific vistas. An international community of science was growing. In 1668 the *Philosophical Transactions* of the Royal Society of London published an extract from an Italian learned journal telling how an Italian lensmaker, Eustachio Divini (1610–1685), using a microscope, had discovered "an animal lesser than any of those seen hitherto." Five years later, in the heat of the Anglo-Dutch naval wars, Henry Oldenburg (who was born in Germany, educated at the University of Utrecht, and was now in London publishing the *Philosophical Transactions*) received a letter from the Dutch anatomist, Regnier de Graaf (1641–1673):

> That it may be the more evident to you that the humanities and science are not yet banished from among us by the clash of arms, I am writing to tell you that a certain most ingenious person here, named Leeuwenhoek, has devised microscopes which far surpass those which we have hitherto seen, manufactured by Eustachio Divini and others. The enclosed letter from him, wherein he describes certain things which he has observed more accurately than previous authors, will afford you a sample of his work; and if it please you, and you would test the skill of this most diligent man and give him encouragement, then pray send him a letter containing your suggestions, and proposing to him more difficult problems of the same kind.

With this "encouragement," Leeuwenhoek was drawn into a community of science where he enjoyed fifty years of communication with a world of unseen colleagues.

Careful drapers like Leeuwenhoek were in the habit of using a low-power magnifying glass to inspect the quality of cloth. His first microscope was a small lens, ground by hand from a glass globule and clamped between two perforated metal plates, through which an object could be viewed. Attached was an adjustable device for holding the specimen. All his work would be done with "simple" microscopes using only a single-lens system. Leeuwenhoek ground some five hundred fifty lenses, of which the best had a linear magnifying power of 500 and a resolving power of one-millionth of a meter. In the traditions of alchemy, of instrument-making, and of cartography, Leeuwenhoek was secretive. What visitors to his shop saw, he declared, was nothing compared with what he himself had seen with the superior lenses that he was not at liberty to show them. His fellow townsmen called him a magician, but this did not please him. He remained wary of the eager visitor from abroad who, he said, "was much rather inclined to deck himself out with my feathers, than to offer me a helping hand."

The Royal Society encouraged Leeuwenhoek to report his findings in one hundred ninety letters. Since he had no systematic program of research, a letter was his perfect format for reporting his unexpected glimpses of the innards of anything and everything. Some of his first chance observations proved to be his most startling. If Galileo was so excited by distinguishing stars in the Milky Way, and four new satellites of the planet Jupiter, how much more exciting to discover a universe in every drop of water!

Once Leeuwenhoek had a microscope he began looking for something to do with it. In September 1674, out of curiosity, he filled a glass vial with some greenish cloudy water, which the country folk called "honey-dew," from a marshy lake two miles outside of Delft, and under his magnifying glass he found "very many small animalcules." He then turned his microscope on a drop of pepper water:

> I now saw very plainly that these were little eels, or worms, lying all huddled up together and wriggling; just as if you saw, with the naked eye, a whole tubful of very little eels

and water, with the eels a-squirming among one another: and the whole water seemed to be alive with these multifarious animalcules. This was for me, among all the marvels that I have discovered in nature, the most marvellous of all; and I must say, for my part, that no more pleasant sight has ever yet come before my eye than these many thousands of living creatures, seen all alive in a little drop of water, moving among one another, each several creature having its own proper motion: . . .

In his famous Letter 18 to the Royal Society (October 9, 1678), he concluded that "these little animals were, to my eye, more than ten thousand times smaller than the animalcule which Swammerdam has portrayed, and called by the name of Water-flea, or Water-louse, which you can see alive and moving in water with the bare eye."

Like Balboa speculating on the extent of his great Southern Ocean, or Galileo delighting in the new infinity of the stars, so Leeuwenhoek luxuriated in the minuteness of these tiny creatures and their infinitely vast populations. He put into a slender glass tube an amount of water as big as a millet seed, marked off thirty divisions on the tube "and I then bring it before my microscope, by means of two silver or copper springs, which I have attached thereto . . . to be able to push it up or down." The visitor to his shop at the time was amazed. "Now supposing that this Gentleman really saw 1000 animalcules in a particle of water ⅓₀th of the bigness of a millet-seed, that would be 30000 living creatures in a quantity of water as big as a millet-seed, and consequently 2730000 living creatures in one drop of water." Yet, Leeuwenhoek added, there were much smaller creatures not revealed to the visitor, "but which I could see by means of other glasses and a different method (which I keep for myself alone)."

It is no wonder that those who read these reports were troubled by doubts. Some accused him "of seeing more with his imagination than with his magnifying glasses." To persuade the Royal Society, he produced signed testimonials of eyewitnesses, not fellow scientists but simply respectable citizens, notaries public, the pastor of the English congregation in Delft, and others. Each called himself a *testis oculatus*, who had seen the little animals with his very own eyes.

Having discovered the world of bacteria, Leeuwenhoek went on to dignify its inhabitants. Contradicting Aristotle's dogmas about the "lower animals," he declared that each of the animalcules had its full complement of the bodily organs needed for the life it led. Therefore there was no reason to believe that the small animals, insects and intestinal worms, would arise spontaneously out of filth, dung, dirt, and decaying organic matter. Rather, as the Bible hinted, each reproduced after its kind and was the offspring of a predecessor of the same species.

When Leeuwenhoek sent the report of his microscopic observations of human semen to the Royal Society, he discreetly apologized. "And if your Lordship should consider that these observations may disgust or scandalize the learned, I earnestly beg your Lordship to regard them as private and to publish or destroy them, as your Lordship thinks fit." Some years earlier, William Harvey, in his *De Generatione* (1651), had described the egg as the sole source of new life. The prevailing notion was that semen provided nothing more than fertilizing "vapors." When Leeuwenhoek, who equated motility with life, saw the lively spermatozoa swimming about, he went to the other extreme and gave them the dominant role in creating new life.

An irrepressible explorer, he went down many dead ends—explaining pepper's pungent taste by its spiny microscopic texture, and human growth by the "preformation" of organs in the sperm. But he also opened vistas into microbiology, embryology, histology, entomology, botany, and crystallography. His well-earned election as a Fellow of the Royal Society of London (February 8, 1680) delighted him beyond measure. It signaled a new world of scientists, international and unacademic, where knowledge would be advanced not only by the traditional custodians of knowledge. Mere "mechanicks," amateurs, would come into their own.

UNSEEN CURRENTS WITHIN

F OR fourteen centuries Galen dominated European physiology as well as anatomy. His persuasive account of the life process started from the three "souls," or *pneuma*, that Plato said governed the body. The rational in the brain ruled sensation and motion, the irascible in the heart controlled the passions, and the concupiscible in the liver gave nutrition. After being inhaled, air was transformed into *pneuma* by the lungs, and the life process transformed one kind of *pneuma* into another. The liver elaborated "chyle" from the alimentary tract into venous blood carrying the "natural spirit," which ebbed and flowed in the veins with a kind of tidal motion. Some of this natural spirit entered the left ventricle of the heart where it became a higher form of *pneuma*, the "vital spirit." Then the vital spirit was carried to the base of the brain where, in the *rete mirabile*, the blood was transformed into a still higher form of *pneuma*, the "animal spirit." This highest form of *pneuma* was diffused through the body by the nerves, which Galen supposed to be hollow.

Each aspect of the soul possessed its own special "faculty," corresponding to its *pneuma*-producing power. "So long as we are ignorant of the true essence of the cause which is operating," Galen explained, "we call it a *faculty*. Thus we say that there exists in the veins a blood-making faculty, as also a digestive faculty in the stomach, a pulsatile faculty in the heart, and in each of the other parts a special faculty corresponding to the function or activity of that part."

This, in brief, was the grand structure of Galen's physiology, which was essentially a *pneuma*-tology. He explained everything, yet no one could accuse him of pretending to more knowledge than he really had, for he freely admitted the elusive character of all the elements in his system. Appealing to the indefinable to explain the inexplicable, his vocabulary provided an arena of debate for philologically minded Doctors of Physick.

At the heart of Galen's system was a special theory about the human heart. For the *innate heat*, which, according to Hippocrates and Aristotle, pervaded the whole body and distinguished the living from the dead, had its source in the heart. Nourished by the *pneuma*, the heart naturally was the hottest organ, a kind of furnace that would have been consumed by its own heat if it had not been conveniently cooled by air from the lungs. The heat that came with life itself was therefore *innate*, the hallmark of the soul.

Since the heart was plainly the citadel of Galenic physiology, before doctors could discard their "spirits" and their *pneuma* someone would have to provide another persuasive account of how the heart functioned. This would be accomplished by William Harvey (1578–1657). Born near Folkestone, England, into a family of substance, he would have every advantage that an aspiring physician could have desired. After attending King's School in Canterbury, he went on to Gonville and Caius College at Cambridge.

The college had become a unique center of medical education since it was refounded by John Caius (pronounced "Keys"; 1510–1573), a man of dynamic energy who had championed medical professionalism in an earlier generation. As a student at Padua, Caius actually lived with the great Vesalius, who was still teaching anatomy there. But he remained a devotee of Galen. "Except for certain trivial matters," Caius insisted, "nothing was overlooked by him, and all those things that recent authors consider important could have been learned solely from Galen." As president of the College of Physicians in London, Caius asserted the power of the college to license physicians and to banish quacks. In order to raise the level of medical

education he persuaded the judges, following their similar grant to
the United Company of Barber-Surgeons in 1540, to provide every
year the bodies of four executed criminals for dissection, two of
which were to go to his college at Cambridge. While Caius was physician to Edward VI, Mary, and Elizabeth he made a fortune, with
which he rebuilt his old Cambridge college as "Gonville and Caius"
and funded the first scholarships in the university for the study of
medicine.

When the fifteen-year-old Harvey came to Gonville and Caius
in 1593, he had been awarded a scholarship in medicine to support
him for six years. Then, in 1599, following Caius' own example,
Harvey went to Padua, where he won the confidence of his fellow
students, and became the representative of the "English Nation" on
the university council. Of course, the lectures were in Latin, which
Harvey could read and speak. Student life was turbulent without
being intellectually exciting. Harvey usually wore a weapon and was
"too apt to draw out his dagger upon every slight occasion." But
luckily one stimulating professor pointed the way for Harvey's life in
medicine.

The famous Fabricius ab Aquapendente (1533–1619), who had
once treated Galileo as his patient, was an indefatigable researcher,
but still a devotee of Galen. When a group of students rebelled
against his mocking manner, he managed to conciliate them with a
precious cadaver for their very own dissection. The anatomical theater that Fabricius constructed in 1595 made it possible for the first
time to perform teaching anatomies indoors. Five flights of wooden
stairs wound up to six circular galleries above a narrow pit. From all
these galleries students could lean on the balustrades as they peered
down through the darkness at a table in the center where students
held up candelabras to illuminate the cadaver as it was dissected.
This provided three hundred students at one time with a clear view.
The scarcity of cadavers and the infrequency of anatomies made this
a signal advance in medical education. Here Harvey witnessed Fabricius' theatrical anatomies. For a while Harvey lived with Fabricius
in his country house, with a pleasure garden attached, just outside
Padua.

About 1574, long before Harvey came to Padua, in the course of his dissections Fabricius had noticed that the veins of the human limbs contained tiny valves that allowed the blood to flow in one direction only. He noted that such valves were not found in the large veins of the trunk of the body which took blood directly to the vital organs. Fabricius aptly fitted these new facts into Galen's old theories of the centrifugal movement of blood outward to feed the viscera:

> My theory is that Nature has formed them [the valves] to delay the blood to some extent, and to prevent the whole mass of it from flooding into the feet, or hands and fingers, and collecting there. Two evils are thus avoided, namely, undernutrition of the upper parts of the limbs, and a permanently swollen condition of the hands and feet. Valves were made, therefore, to ensure a really fair distribution of the blood for the nutrition of the various parts. . . .

The memory of these wonderful valves, which Fabricius demonstrated to the young Harvey at Padua, would remain vivid in Harvey's mind to trouble and stimulate him.

When Harvey returned to England, he married the daughter of the doctor who had been physician to Queen Elizabeth, became a Fellow of the College of Physicians and acquired a prosperous, aristocratic medical practice. At the same time he regularly gave the lectures on surgery at the college from 1615 to 1656. And he served as the royal physician, first to James I and then to Charles I, in times when it was politically risky to befriend the king. Harvey's circle included the philosopher-scientist Francis Bacon, the Rosicrucian Robert Fludd, the lawyer John Selden, and Thomas Hobbes, and his interests covered the universe.

* * *

Galen had diffused the vital processes into separate organs, each satisfying a particular bodily need. In Galen the blood played no unifying role, for the unity of life processes was in the collaboration of the several "spirits" or *pneuma*. The blood, concocted in the liver, was only another specialized vehicle carrying a nourishing cargo out to certain organs. Harvey went in search of a unifying vital phenomenon. The success of his quest he revealed in his *De Motu Cordis et Sanguinis in Animalibus* (On the Motion of the Heart and of Blood in Animals), a poorly printed tract of seventy-two pages published in 1628.

When we read Harvey's little book today, we are still impressed by its cogency. Step by step he leads us to his conclusion that the heart propels the blood, and that the movement of the blood is circular throughout the whole body. First he marshals the available facts about the arteries, veins, and the heart, their structure and operation. All along the way his observations are "gauged from dissection of living animals."

When Harvey began to study the heart, doctors were not yet agreed on whether the heart was at work when it expanded, which seemed to coincide with the expansion of the veins, or when it contracted. He starts with a rudimentary description of how the heart works.

> In the first place, then, in the hearts of all animals still surviving after the chest has been opened and the capsule immediately investing the heart has been divided, one can see the heart alternating between movement and rest, moving at one time, devoid of movement at another. . . . Muscles in active movement gain in strength, contract, change from soft to hard, rise up and thicken; and similarly the heart. . . .
>
> At one and the same time, therefore, the following events take place, namely, the contraction of the heart, the beat of the apex [of the heart] (felt outside through its striking against the chest), the thickening of the heart walls, and the forcible expulsion of the contained blood by the constriction of the ventricles.
>
> Thus the exact opposite to the commonly accepted views is seen. The general belief is that the ventricles are being distended and the heart being filled with blood at the

time when the apex is striking the chest and one can feel its beat from the outside. The contrary is, however, correct, namely, that the heart empties during its contraction. Hence the heart movement which is commonly thought to be its diastole is in fact its systole. And likewise its essential movement is not diastole [expansion] but systole [contraction]; and the heart does not gain in strength in diastole but in systole—then indeed is when it contracts, moves, and becomes stronger.

Harvey goes on to describe the movement of the arteries, how they expand when the heart contracts and pumps blood into them. "An idea of this generalized pulsation of the arteries consequent upon the expulsion of blood into them from the left ventricle can be given by blowing into a glove, and producing simultaneous increase in volume of all its fingers." "Hence," he explains, "the pulse which we feel in the arteries is nothing but the inthrust of blood into them from the heart."

Harvey then traces the blood as it leaves the right chamber of the heart. From the right ventricle the blood is carried through the lungs on its way into the left auricle, and from there it is expelled through the left ventricle. This implied another new notion—the "lesser," or pulmonary, circulation of the blood, the circulation of the blood through the lungs.

This notion, which proved essential to Harvey's larger system, had already been expounded by Realdo Colombo (1510–1559), who was no deep student of Galen but a bold experimentalist, and successor to Vesalius at Padua. The Italian physician and botanist Andrea Cesalpino (1519–1603) had described the cardiac valves and the pulmonary vessels connected to the heart. It also happened that the Spanish virtuoso, Michael Servetus, whom Calvin burned at the stake for heresy in 1553, had incidentally described the pulmonary circulation of the blood in his most culpable theological tract, *Christianismi Restitutio* (1553), of which only a few copies survive. And as early as the thirteenth century the Arab physician Ibn al-Nafis seems also to have had this idea.

It was Colombo who supplied Harvey with the essential facts.

Two crucial sets of his observations were missing pieces in Harvey's cardiovascular puzzle. The first was the fact, which had not been known to Vesalius, that the blood passed from the right ventricle of the heart into the left by way of the lungs. The second was the accurate description of the workings of the heart, and the proper meaning of systole and diastole. Colombo insisted that the heart did its work when it contracted, in systole. He listed the rhythm of the heart among "things which are most beautiful to behold. You will find out that while the heart is dilating the arteries are constricted, and again, while the heart is constricting that the arteries are dilated." This simple fact, as Harvey himself noted, gave him a clue he needed on how to use vivisections, rescuing him in "the task so truly arduous and full of difficulties, that I was almost tempted to think, with Fracastorius, that the motion of the heart was only to be comprehended by God."

When Harvey brought together Colombo's insights into the heart's pumping action with Fabricius' descriptions of valves in the veins which permitted the flow in only one direction, he began to see the light. The heart was not a furnace but a pump, and the blood flowed out to nourish the organs. But still other facts were needed to prove the *circularity* of the blood's movement. Harvey had to take the momentous step from the mere *circulation* of the blood—which even Galen had suggested after his fashion—to the *circularity* of the movement, which became the foundation concept of modern physiology. The reasoning that made this step possible was momentous in a larger sense. It opened the way from qualities to quantities—from the ancient world of "humors" and vital spirits to the modern world of thermometers and sphygmomanometers, electrocardiograms, and countless other measuring machines.

Having described the paths of the blood into and out of the heart and the function of the heart in constantly propelling the flow, Harvey had posed the essential question. He had found an Amazon within and the force that kept the current flowing. But he had not yet charted the full course of the rivers and rivulets of the blood. "The remaining matters, however," Harvey explained in his crucial Chapter 8, "(namely, the amount and source of the blood which so crosses through from the veins to the arteries), though well worthy of consideration, are so novel and hitherto unmentioned that, in speaking of them, I not only fear that I may suffer from the ill-will of a few, but dread lest all men turn against me. To such an extent is it virtually second nature for all to follow accepted usage and teaching which, since its first implanting, has become deep-rooted; to such extent are men swayed by a pardonable respect for the ancient authors."

Here he posed a novel *quantitative* question, "How much blood passes from the veins into the arteries?"—to which he was determined to give a quantitative answer. "I also considered the symmetry and size of the ventricles of the heart and of the vessels which enter and leave them (since Nature, who does nothing purposelessly, would not purposelessly have given these vessels such large size)." By opening the arteries of living animals he hoped to find his answer. He examined "how much blood was transmitted and in how short a time." "*So great a quantitie* cannot be furnished from those things we eat, and . . . it is far greater than is convenient for the nutrition of the parts [italics added]." If the filling of the bloodstream was being constantly replenished only by the juice from newly ingested food, the result would be both the quick emptying of all the arteries and the bursting of the arteries by the excessive inrush of the blood.

What was the answer? Within the bodily system there was no explanation, "unless the blood somehow flowed back again from the arteries into the veins and returned to the right ventricle of the heart. In consequence, I began privately to consider if it had a movement, as it were, in a circle."

This explanation was beautiful in its simplicity. Having in his own mind confirmed his hypothesis against all the objections that he himself could raise, Harvey then tried to persuade his colleagues by marshaling ancient authorities in his support. He quoted at length the sovereign Galen—"that divine man, that Father of Physicians"—to support his own view of the relation of arteries and veins to the lungs. He repeatedly and respectfully cited Aristotle, whose anatomical ideas had been somewhat eclipsed since the dissemination of printed texts of Galen in the sixteenth century.

Harvey had long felt a kinship with Aristotle's way of looking at living processes. For Aristotle, too, saw life as the single process of the whole living organism—not as something that occurred when "spirits," or *pneuma*, were added to bodily organs. Aristotle's view of the unity of the life process was an incentive to this quest, and finally a justification of Harvey's conclusions. Harvey explained in Chapter 8, where he first expounded the circular movement of the blood:

> We have as much right to call this movement of the blood circular as Aristotle had to say that the air and rain emulate the circular movement of the heavenly bodies. The moist earth, he wrote, is warmed by the sun and gives off vapours which condense as they are carried up aloft and in their condensed form fall again as rain and remoisten the earth, so producing successions of fresh life from it. In similar fashion the circular movement of the sun, that is to say, its approach and recession, give rise to storms and atmospheric phenomena. . . .
>
> This organ deserves to be styled the starting point of life and the sun of our microcosm just as much as the sun deserves to be styled the heart of the world.

We are naturally tempted to seek a connection between Harvey's belief in the circular movements of the blood, with the heart at the center, and Copernicus' heliocentric theory, with planets going around the sun at the center. There is no evidence to support this seductive surmise. Galileo was teaching at Padua when Harvey was a student, but so far as we know, none of his students was a physician. And anyway, in his lectures at that time, Galileo was still faithfully expounding the Ptolemaic system.

Harvey repeatedly insisted that what he described was only simple fact, neither the application nor the embroidering of a philosophy. "I do not profess to learn and teach Anatomy from the axioms of the Philosophers," he explained in the introduction to his *De Motu*, "but from Dissections and the Fabrick of Nature." And near the end of his life he recalled, "I would say with Fabricius, 'Let all reasoning be silent when experience gainsays its conclusion.' The too familiar vice of the present age is to obtrude as manifest truths, mere fancies, born of conjecture and superficial reasoning, altogether unsupported by the testimony of sense."

Still there was a gap in Harvey's circle which he could not bridge. The large quantities of blood were always being speedily propelled from the heart into the arteries, then to the veins, and so back to the heart. But the whole system would not work unless blood was constantly being transmitted from arteries to veins.

Harvey finally had no answer as to how that happened. Yet his faith in the large simple circle of the blood made him confident that the last crucial link in the pathway must be there. He never could find the connecting passageways ("anastomoses," the doctors later would call them), but he expressed his fervent belief that the connection was actually accomplished by some still undiscovered "admirable artifices." Though Harvey occasionally used a magnifying lens, he had no microscope, and that would be required to discover the capillaries. Ultimately, he had to rest his theory on his faith that Nature had not failed to complete the circle.

PRIORITY BECOMES THE PRIZE

T HE salute to Newton was a thoroughly modern gesture, for
Europe had only lately learned to value the new. "Is it not
evident," John Dryden asked in 1668, "in these last hundred years (when the study of philosophy has been the business of all
the Virtuosi in Christendom), that almost a new Nature has been
revealed to us? . . . more noble secrets in optics, medicine, anatomy,
astronomy, discovered, than in all those credulous and doting ages
from Aristotle to us?" In this new age of "revelations," honors would
be heaped on him who was reputed to be the *first* to unveil a truth of
nature. For now the printing press, by speedily spreading word of a
new discovery, finally made it possible to define priority. And priority brought a kudos it never could have had before.

Europe's ancient institutions of learning, colleges and universities, had been founded not to discover the new but to transmit a heritage. By contrast, the Royal Society and other parliaments of
scientists, with their academies in London, Paris, Florence, Rome,
Berlin, and elsewhere, aimed to increase knowledge. They were a
witness not so much to the wealth of the past as to what Bishop Sprat
called "the present Inquiring Temper of this Age." Robert Boyle put
it in a nutshell in the title of his *Essay of men's Great Ignorance of the
Uses of Natural Things, or there is scarce any one thing in Nature whereof
the Uses to human Life are yet thoroughly understood.*

In earlier times, to possess an idea or a fact meant keeping it secret, having the power to prevent others from knowing it. Maps of treasure routes were guarded, and the first postal services were designed for the security of the state. Physicians and lawyers locked their knowledge in a learned language. The government helped craft guilds exclude trespassers from their secrets. But the printing press made it harder than ever to keep a secret. More than that, the press changed radically, and even reversed, what it meant to "own" an idea. Now the act of publishing could put a personal brand on a newly discovered fact or a novel idea.

We cannot be surprised at Bishop Sprat's defense of the Royal Society:

> If to be the Author of new things, be a crime; how will the first Civilizers of Men, and makers of Laws, and Founders of Governments escape? Whatever now delights us in the Works of Nature, that excells the rudeness of the first Creation, is New. Whatever we see in Cities, or Houses, above the first wildness of Fields, and meaness of Cottages, and nakedness of Men, had its time, when this imputation of Novelty, might as well have bin laid to its charge. It is not therefore an offense, to profess the introduction of New things, unless that which is introduc'd prove pernicious in itself; or cannot be brought in, without the extirpation of others, that are better.

Established tradesmen and artisans of course were suspicious of the new, for "they are generally infected with the narrowness that is natural to Corporations, which are wont to resist all new comers, as profess'd Enemies to their Privileges."

In organizing the Royal Society, the shrewd Henry Oldenburg had seen the new significance of priority. He sensed that members might be reluctant to send their discoveries to the society for fear that others might steal their claims to be the first. So he proposed "that a proper person might be found out to discover plagiarys, and to assert inventions to their proper authors." To protect the rights of priority to investigations still in progress, Oldenburg moved that "when any Fellow have any philosophical notion or invention not yet made out, and desired the same, sealed in a box, to be deposited with one of the secretaries till perfected, this might be allowed, for better securing inventions to their authors." The progress of science would be haunted by the specter of priority. Even the most eminent scientists would seem more concerned to claim the credit than to prove the truth of their discoveries.

*   *   *

The heroic Isaac Newton would embody the spirit of modern science in this as in so many other ways. Soon after his death, Newton's character was idealized as much as his work, and no less misunderstood. The poet William Cowper (1731–1800) described the Godlike Newton:

> Patient of contradiction as a child,
> Affable, humble, diffident, and mild,
> Such was Sir Isaac.

The real Newton was anything but affable. The student who served as Newton's assistant for five years, from 1685 to 1690, declared that in all that time he had heard Newton laugh only once—when someone rashly asked him what benefit there might be in studying Euclid.

Before he was thirty and without the incentive or the rewards of public recognition, Newton was well on the way to his great discoveries. By 1672 he had shaped his theory of fluxions which would be the basis of the calculus, but London booksellers, who usually lost money on mathematical treatises, were not eager to publish it. A passion for priority clouded his later years when he was in a unique position to assert his claims. A concern for priority in his invention of the reflecting telescope, described in Newton's earliest surviving letter, dated February 1669, first brought him into the public community of scientists. The instruments used by Galileo and others before Newton were all "refracting" telescopes, employing lenses to magnify the image and bring the light rays to a focus. But these had to be

inconveniently long and suffered from chromatic aberration. Newton's invention, which used concave mirrors instead of lenses, could
be much shorter and could produce a greater magnification without
chromatic aberration. In the long run they would have still other
advantages which did not occur to Newton.

There would be a natural limit to the size of a refracting telescope because a lens can be supported only at the edge and the
weight of the lens itself tends to distort its shape. But a mirror can be
supported from behind and so can be made much larger without
risking distortion. Newton had made and coated the mirrors and the
tools for making the mirrors for his telescope with his own hands. "If
I had staid for other people to make my tools & things for me," he
exclaimed, "I had never made anything of it." His first reflecting
telescope, though only six inches long, had a magnification of forty
times, which, he boasted, was more than that of a refractor six feet
long. When word of Newton's invention reached members of the
Royal Society, there was general astonishment, which produced a
letter to him in January 1672 from Henry Oldenburg, enclosing a
drawing of Newton's telescope:

> Your Ingenuity is the occasion of this addresse by a hand
> unknowne to you. You have been so generous, as to impart to
> the Philosophers here, your Invention of contracting Tele-
> scopes. It having been considered, and examined here by
> some of the most eminent in Opticall Science and practise,
> and applauded by them, they think it necessary to use some
> means to secure this Invention from the Usurpation of for-
> reiners; And therefore have taken care to represent by a
> scheme that first Specimen, sent hither by you, and to de-
> scribe all the parts of the Instrument, together with its effect,
> compared with an ordinary, but much larger, Glasse . . . in a
> solemne letter to Paris to M. Hugens, thereby to prevent the
> arrogation of such strangers, as may perhaps have seen it
> here, or even with you at Cambridge; it being too frequent,
> that new Invention and contrivances are snatched away from
> their true Authors by pretended bystanders. . . .

Newton replied promptly, with a show of modesty that would become rarer with the passing years, that he "was surprised to see so much care taken about securing an invention to me, of which I have hitherto had so little value. . . . who, had not the communication of it been desired, might have let it still remained in private as it hath already done some yeares." Elected a Fellow of the Royal Society the following week, early in February he sent them his first contribution, his paper on the theory of colors fulfilling his hope that "my poore & solitary endeavours can effect towards the promoting your Philoso-phicall designes."

By a gradual progression, Newton became councillor, and then in 1703 president—in effect, dictator—of the Royal Society for the quarter-century until his death. As his prestige grew, so did his dyspepsia, his unwillingness to give credit to others or share credit for his great discoveries. To assert his primacy in every branch of science that he touched, he marshaled his full powers over what has been called the first scientific "establishment" in the modern world. A martinet in conducting meetings of the society, he never tolerated any sign of "levity or indecorum," and actually ejected Fellows from the meetings for misbehavior. Election to Fellowship, worth honor and money, required his support. When William Whiston, his former assistant in mathematics at Cambridge and his successor in the Lucasian chair, but a man of unorthodox theology, was proposed in 1720, Newton threatened to resign as president if Whiston was elected. In 1714, when Parliament was deliberating on the prize for a way to find longitude at sea, Newton pontificated that no clock would serve the purpose. This probably delayed acceptance of Harrison's clock, which, as we have seen, really did solve the problem. As scientific adviser and pundit, he disposed of coveted government posts—chiefs of observatory and members of scientific commissions—which multiplied with the years. He himself left his Lucasian Professorship of Mathematics for the powerful and remunerative government post as Warden, and later Master of the Mint, during which time his income sometimes came to a then spectacular £4,000 a year. He supervised the great recoinage, hounded out counterfeiters, and seemed to delight in their draconian punishment.

In 1686, when Newton sent to the Royal Society the completed manuscript of Book I of the *Principia*, Robert Hooke immediately claimed that the basic ideas had been plagiarized from his communications to Newton a dozen years before. "Philosophy is such an impertinently litigious Lady," Newton responded to Oldenburg in exasperation, "that a man had as good be engaged in Law suits as have to do with her. I found it so formerly & now I no sooner come near her again but she gives me warning." And his contempt for the presumptuous Hooke grew without bounds. "Now is this not very fine? Mathematicians that find out, settle & do all the business must content themselves with being nothing but dry calculators and drudges & another that does nothing but pretend & grasp at all things must carry away all the invention as well of those that were to follow him as of those that went before." Far from acknowledging Hooke's priority, Newton went back to his manuscript and deleted references to Hooke's work. Halley and others who mildly took Hooke's part so aroused Newton's ire that he threatened to suppress the whole Book III of his great work. They dissuaded him from this act of self-immolation, but Newton still nursed his fury. He kept Hooke as his favorite enemy for the next seventeen years, and to express his pique he refused to publish his *Opticks* or to accept the presidency of the society until after Hooke's death in 1703. The sober verdict of an eighteenth-century French admirer of Newton recognized that Hooke's claims were not entirely without merit but showed "what a distance there is between a truth that is glimpsed and a truth that is demonstrated."

Newton's later years, when he had become the idol of "Philosophic" London, could be chronicled in his acrimonious quarrels with subordinates and his vindictive plots against any who threatened to become his equal. In a first sordid episode he maliciously deprived the unlucky Astronomer Royal, John Flamsteed (1646–1719), of the satisfaction of publishing the scientific products of his lifetime. Though plagued by ill health, Flamsteed had invented new techniques of observation, had improved micrometer screws and calibrations, had spent £2,000 of his own, and finally constructed the best instruments of the age for his work at Greenwich. In a dozen years he made twenty thousand observations, which far excelled Tycho Brahe's in accuracy. But the scrupulous Flamsteed would not yet publish his figures. "I want not your calculations but your Observations only," the imperious Newton badgered Flamsteed. In pique, Newton threatened to drop his own "moon's theory" and blame it on Flamsteed if Flamsteed did not speedily deliver. When the miserable Flamsteed complained that Newton's "hasty artificial unkind arrogant" letters had aggravated his splitting headaches, Newton advised that the best way to cure headaches was "to bind his head strait with a garter till the crown of his head was nummed." The impatient Newton had all Flamsteed's uncorrected observations at the Greenwich Observatory gathered together, then compiled and published them. Appalled to see his lifework garbled, Flamsteed petitioned the Lords of Treasury, managed to buy up three hundred of the four hundred original copies, carefully removed the ninety-seven pages that he had prepared for publication and burned the rest. Flamsteed died before he could complete his work. But his vindication was accomplished by two friends who published his three-volume star catalogue in 1725 which became a landmark in modern astronomy as the first to take advantage of the telescope.

The spectacle of the century in the newly public scientific arena was Newton's battle with the great Baron Gottfried Wilhelm von Leibniz. Now the stakes were one of the greatest scientific priority prizes of any age—the glory of inventing the calculus. The calculus was something that few even of the scientists of that age understood. But the priority issue was easy enough to grasp. Educated laymen recognized that the calculus was an important new way to calculate velocities and rates of change, and that it promised to multiply the uses of scientific instruments and measuring devices. We, too, can understand the priority issue without an expert's knowledge of the calculus. The priority debate, however unedifying, widened the audience for science. What was this "differential calculus" over which great men enjoyed insulting one another in public? The very question was news when the King, his mistress Henrietta Howard, Princess Caroline, and the whole diplomatic corps became interested and discussed ways of settling the dispute.

Newton's antagonist, Leibniz (1646–1716), was himself one of the profoundest philosopher-scientists of modern times. At the age of six he began reading in the copious library of his father, who was a professor of moral philosophy at the University of Leipzig, and by fourteen he was well acquainted with the classics. Leibniz, according to De Quincey, was unlike the great thinkers who were planets revolving in their own orbits, for Leibniz was a comet "to connect different systems together." Before he was twenty-six, Leibniz had devised a program of legal reform for the Holy Roman Empire, had designed a calculating machine, and had developed a plan to divert Louis XIV from his attacks on the Rhineland by inducing him to build a Suez Canal. In 1673, when he visited London on a diplomatic mission, he met Oldenburg and was elected to the Royal Society. Leibniz's European travels put him in touch with Huygens, Spinoza, Malpighi, and Galileo's pupil Viviani. He met the Jesuit missionary Grimaldi, who was about to leave for Peking to become the Chinese court mathematician.

Frederick the Great called Leibniz "a whole academy in himself." Even so, in 1700 the King of Prussia had founded the Berlin Academy. Unlike its counterparts in Paris and London, this was not a spontaneous community of scientific enthusiasts, but was largely the creature of Leibniz himself. The government monopoly of printing and of the newly reformed calendar would be used to fund the academy and its observatory and to make science the property of the whole community. Naturally enough, Leibniz opposed the use of Latin and he championed the vernacular.

Our learned men have shown little desire to protect the German tongue, some because they really thought that wisdom could only be clothed in Latin and Greek; others because they feared the world would discover their ignorance, at present hidden under a mask of big words. Really learned people need not fear this, for the more their wisdom and science come among people, the more witnesses of their excellence they will have. . . . On account of the disregard of the mother tongue, learned people have concerned themselves with things of no use, and have written merely for the bookshelf; the nation has been kept from knowledge. A well-developed vernacular, like highly-polished glass, enhances the acuteness of the mind and gives the intellect transparent clearness.

When Georg Ludwig, the elector of Hanover, ascended the English throne in 1714 as George I, Leibniz hoped the King would take him along to London as court historian. But the King refused until Leibniz had completed his genealogical history of George's family, and the great Leibniz spent the last two years of his gout-ridden life trying to finish this trivial assignment. When he died in 1716, he had been abandoned by the princes whom he had spent his life trying to please.

For our story the crucial connection in Leibniz's life was his life-long relation to the Royal Society, first fruitful, but finally fatal. The dramatic climax came with the publication in 1712 of the official report of the august committee of the society that had been appointed to adjudicate the priority dispute between Leibniz and Newton. Technically the occasion was Leibniz's complaint that he had been insulted by John Keill, a Fellow who had accused Leibniz of plagiarizing Newton and claiming to have been the first inventor of the differential calculus.

Though actually charged only with deciding the decorum of Keill's behavior, the committee had seized the opportunity to defend Newton's priority. They summarized the "facts," including numerous conversations and prolific correspondence among the society's Fellows, to show that Keill's statements were not gratuitous insults but simply a recognition of Newton's right to his invention. Through Oldenburg, the committee explained, Leibniz had first been in touch with another Fellow of the Society, John Collins (1625–1683), who had devoted himself to promoting the exchange of mathematical discoveries. Back in 1672 Collins had sent a letter to Leibniz in Paris telling him about Newton's invention of a method of "fluxions" which was essentially what Leibniz now claimed as his own. According to the committee, Leibniz had never done anything more than restate Newton's method, which he had already learned about from Collins' letter, "in which letter the method of fluxions was sufficiently described to any intelligent person." *Commercium epistolicum* (a commerce of letters) was the name they gave to their report, which plainly declared that the opportunities for plagiarism stemmed from the new community of scientific correspondents. So the committee triumphantly convicted Leibniz and awarded the laurel of "first inventor" to Newton. A century and a half after the trial of Leibniz, in 1852 the accomplished mathematician Augustus De Morgan (1806–1871) established that Leibniz had never received the incriminating document but only a copy from which the suggestive passages had been removed.

If the facts had been more widely known, the proceedings would have discredited Newton himself, who at the time was the undisputed dictator of the Royal Society. There was never a direct confrontation between Newton and Leibniz, for all Newton's moves were backstage. Behind the scenes the unsavory role of chief instigator was played by Fatio de Duillier, a half-mad Swiss amateur mathematician and enthusiastic meddler, with whom Newton had a long and curious relationship. Newton had been Fatio's devoted patron, and Fatio, twenty-two years Newton's junior, had occasionally lived with Newton. When the Newton-Leibniz duel held public attention, Fatio had become a religious crank, secretary to a riotous sect of "Prophets" who foretold a second burning of London, for which Fatio had been punished in the pillory at Charing Cross and at the Royal Exchange.

Back in 1699 Newton himself had sent the Royal Society a communication accusing Leibniz of plagiarism. As president of the society, Newton, to humble Leibniz and vindicate his own priority, set up "a numerous Committee of Gentlemen of several Nations" to make an impartial decision on the evidence. The members, all of course appointed by Newton, were five certified Newtonians, plus the Prussian ambassador and a Huguenot refugee. We now know, what was not known at the time, that Newton himself wrote the committee's "impartial" report. Then Newton took the further trouble of writing an anonymous review and summary of the report, which he included in later reprints of the *Commercium epistolicum*. In addition, he was the author of hundreds of other documents "exposing" Leibniz and extolling the originality of his own discovery of the calculus. His most astonishing display of academic overkill was his devotion of the whole of the *Philosophical Transactions* for January and February 1715 (except for three pages) to yet another polemic against Leibniz—and a further backdating of Newton's discovery into the 1660's. Still Newton was not satisfied. Further to humiliate his enemy and to publicize the committee's verdict, he convened a special meeting at the Royal Society to which he invited the whole diplomatic community. Newton "once pleasantly" reported to a disciple that "He had broke Leibniz's Heart with his Reply to him."

The unfortunate Leibniz's Berlin Academy provided no troops nor any arsenal comparable to Newton's Royal Society. Leibniz had hoped to find a champion in the willful Princess Caroline of Anspach, who had accompanied her father-in-law, George I, from Hanover to London, for she was the center of a brilliant salon. After witnessing the sordid quarrel, the philosophical princess, who kept her power in British politics by connivance at her husband George II's amours, concluded that "great men are like women, who never give up their lovers except with the utmost chagrin and mortal anger. And that, gentlemen, is where your opinions have got you." Leibniz died in 1716, before Newton had exhausted his rage. But Leibniz did win a posthumous victory. The mathematical world adopted Leibniz's symbols—the letter *d*, as in *dx* or *dy*, and the long *s* written as { (the initial letter of *summa*)—and the name *calculus integralis* (which had been suggested to Leibniz by Jakob Bernoulli I in 1690) and these dominated mathematics textbooks into the late twentieth century.

* * *

Of course there were priority battles before Newton, and these would become normal afterwards. At the opening of the modern era, Galileo had attacked a host of rivals—one for pretending to have invented the telescopic uses of astronomy "which belongs to me," another for claiming to have preceded him in observing sunspots, others for attempting "to rob me of that glory which was mine, pretending not to have seen my writings and trying to represent themselves as the original discoverers of these marvels," and still another who "had the gall to claim that he had observed the Medicean planets which revolve about Jupiter before I had" and who then devised "a sly way of attempting to establish his priority." Other notorious quarrels erupted later between Torricelli and Pascal, between Mouton and Leibniz, and between Hooke and Huygens. As the pace of invention and discovery accelerated, so did the bitterness and frequency of priority disputes.

Eighteenth-century Europe saw a vaudeville series of such bouts. Who had first demonstrated that water was not an element but a compound? Was it Cavendish, Watt, or Lavoisier? Each had fervent champions. There was John Couch Adams versus Urbain Jean Leverrier in the case of who first predicted the position of Neptune. Who was first to discover the vaccination against smallpox? Was it really Jenner—or Pearson or Rabaut? As the means of publicity multiplied and with increasing literacy and the rise of the daily newspaper, stakes seemed higher and arguments became more heated. Should the credit for introducing antisepsis go to Lister—or perhaps to Lemaire? The great Michael Faraday (1791–1867), who had worked with Sir Humphry Davy (1778–1829) and had become his intimate, as we shall see, found his election to the Royal Society opposed by Davy (who had earlier fought for his own priority). Davy alleged that William Hyde Wollaston (1766–1828) had preceded Faraday in discovering electromagnetic rotation.

The printing press and the academies made every priority a national victory. Modern rulers in Europe, who had long been patrons of astrologers and alchemists, now became patrons of scientists and technicians. Medieval condottieri had done penance by founding a Balliol College at Oxford or a Trinity College in Cambridge to ensure their entrance into heaven. Modern condottieri founded institutes and prizes. Alfred Nobel (1833–1896) tried to atone for his fortune earned from manufacturing dynamite for warmakers by establishing the prizes first awarded in 1901 for peacemakers and for the great innovators of techno-science. The Nobel prizes, the most coveted of international awards, offer celebrity and money to the winners of the priority race in the sciences. One of the lucky winners, James Watson, in his confession, *The Double Helix* (1968), gave us at long last a frank and unashamed account of how modern scientists scheme for the kudos of priority.

PATHS TO EVOLUTION

CHAPTER 59

"THE year which has passed," Thomas Bell, eminent president of the Linnean Society of London reported at the end of 1858, "has not, indeed, been marked by any of those striking discoveries which at once revolutionize . . . the department of science on which they bear; it is only at remote intervals that we can reasonably expect any sudden and brilliant innovation." The select Linnean Society (of which Joseph Banks was a founder) had been created in 1788 to preserve the library, herbarium, and manuscripts which Linnaeus had left to his son, and which on his son's death had been bought for them by an English botanist. Despite Bell's observation, the three papers read to the society on July 1 of that year bore more revolutionary implications than any other offerings to the forum of scientists since Sir Isaac Newton's day.

Those papers (which came to only seventeen pages in the society's *Journal*), "On the Tendency of Species to form Varieties; and on the Perpetuation of Varieties and Species by Natural Means of Selection," had been communicated to the society by two of its most accomplished fellows, Sir Charles Lyell, the geologist, and J. D. Hooker, the botanist. The sponsors offered "the results of the investigations of two indefatigable naturalists, Mr. Charles Darwin and Mr. Alfred Wallace. These gentlemen having, independently and unknown to one another, conceived the same very ingenious theory to account for the appearance and perpetuation of varieties and of specific forms on our planet, may both fairly claim the merit of being original thinkers in this important line of inquiry." The three items were: extracts from a manuscript sketched by Darwin in 1839 and revised in 1844; the abstract of a letter from Darwin to Professor Asa Gray of Boston, Massachusetts, in October 1857, repeating his views on species stated in the earlier manuscript; and an essay by Wallace written at Ternate in the East Indies in February 1858, which he had sent to Darwin with instructions to forward it to Lyell if he found it sufficiently novel and interesting.

In later years historians would note July 1, 1858, as the date of the first public statement of the modern theory of evolution. But at the time the Darwin-Wallace papers made hardly a ripple. Neither Darwin nor Wallace was present, and there was no discussion by the thirty fellows who were there. A scheduled paper with a contradictory thesis was not even given. The reading of these articles was a rite of priority, required by the new etiquette of science.

In the progress of the idea of evolution we witness a distinctly modern phenomenon in the progress of science. Modern times brought new instruments of publicity, the printing press with its new powers of diffusion, scientific societies with their wider and more public forums. All this meant a new mobility for scientific ideas and for scientists themselves. Of course, the new incrementalism of science did not spell an end to revolutions in thought, but it did change the pace and the character of these revolutions. Now novel ideas could be introduced piecemeal, unobtrusively, even perfunctorily. And who could tell when one of these ideas might signal a revolution in thought? On that July day in London the Linnean Society prepared to publish observations made by Darwin twenty years earlier on his round-the-world voyage on the *Beagle* alongside complementary observations made by Wallace a few months before in Ternate in the distant Moluccas.

When Darwin, a young man of twenty-two, had sailed out on December 27, 1831, on the five-year voyage of the *Beagle*, he took with him the just published first volume of Charles Lyell's *Principles of Geology*, a going-away gift from his Cambridge professor of botany. Lyell (1797–1875) would provide the background for all Darwin's thinking about the processes of nature and so make it possible for modern evolutionary thought to bear the name of Darwinism. Lyell's crucial insight, documented with copious evidence in his book, was that the earth had been shaped from the beginning by uniform forces still at work—erosion by running water, accumulation of sediment, earthquakes, and volcanoes. Since such forces through millennia had made the earth what it was in his day, there was no need to imagine catastrophes. This doctrine, christened by the English philosopher William Whewell, came to be known as Uniformitarianism.

Lyell had tried to avoid the shoals of theology and cosmology simply by refusing to discuss the origins of the earth. Speculative theories of a Creation, he said, were unnecessary and unscientific. The implications for plants and animals were obvious. If the present activity of Vesuvius or Etna explained changes in the surface of the earth, could not other forces equally visible today show us how species and varieties of plants and animals had come into being? The Cambridge professor of botany who gave Darwin the copy of Lyell which he read and cherished on the *Beagle* warned him not to believe everything in it. The few other books he took along included the Bible, Milton, and Alexander von Humboldt's travels in Venezuela and the Orinoco basin.

In the mystery story of how Darwin came to his notions of evolution, the voyage of the *Beagle* was, of course, a crucial episode. An essential link in the chain of people and ideas was John Stevens Henslow (1796–1861), the teacher who first inspired the young Darwin with enthusiasm for the study of nature. From the chair of botany the handsome magnetic Henslow single-handedly stirred a botanical renaissance in the university. He initiated field trips to observe plants in their natural habitat and required his students to make independent observations, training a new generation of botanists interested less in Linnaean taxonomy than in plant distribution, ecology, and geography. The Cambridge Botanical Garden became a teaching laboratory.

Henslow's historic accomplishment was to transform the Cambridge playboy Darwin from a listless student of theology into a passionate naturalist. At the age of sixty-seven, Darwin still recalled "a circumstance which influenced my career more than any other":

> This was my friendship with Prof. Henslow. Before coming up to Cambridge, I had heard of him from my brother as a man who knew every branch of science, and I was accordingly prepared to reverence him. He kept open house once every week, where all undergraduates and several older members of the University, who were attached to science, used to meet in the evening. I soon got through Fox an invitation and went there regularly. Before long I became well acquainted with Henslow, and during the latter half of my time at Cambridge took long walks with him on most days; so that I was called by some of the dons "the man who walks with Henslow"; and in the evening I was very often asked to join his family dinner. His knowledge was great in botany, entomology, chemistry, mineralogy and geology. His strongest taste was to draw conclusions from long-continued minute observations.

In 1831, when the Admiralty asked Henslow to recommend a naturalist to serve on the *Beagle*'s voyage to map the coasts of Patagonia, Tierra del Fuego, Chile, and Peru and to set up chronometric stations, he recommended his favorite pupil.

Charles was eager to accept. But his father, already irritated by Charles' false start at Edinburgh in the study of medicine, was dead set against any more such casual adventures. "You care for nothing but shooting, dogs, and rat-catching," the elder Darwin had complained, "and you will be a disgrace to yourself and all your family." Now he was determined to keep the vagrant Charles on the path to the clergy, and the dutiful son would not join the *Beagle* without his father's permission. Luckily, Professor Henslow and Charles' uncle, Josiah Wedgwood II, succeeded in persuading Charles' father to let Charles go. "The pursuit of Natural History," Wedgwood argued, "though certainly not professional, is very suitable to a clergyman."

Henslow kept in close touch with his pupil during the five-year voyage of the *Beagle*. They corresponded regularly, and Henslow looked after the specimens that Darwin sent back to London. When the *Beagle* arrived at Montevideo a copy of Lyell's second volume was awaiting, and at Valparaiso on the other side of the South American continent Darwin received the third volume, just off the press. Throughout his trip Darwin was applying Lyell's principles. And at the coral-encrusted rims of submerged volcanic craters in the Indian Ocean, he concluded that the Kelling Atoll had been built up over at least a million years.

The second volume of Lyell went beyond physical geology and applied his Uniformitarianism to biology. Throughout geological time, Lyell explained, new species had been emerging, and others had become extinct. Survival of a species depended on certain conditions of its environment, but geological processes were constantly changing those conditions. Failure in competition with other species in the same habitat might extinguish a species. The success of one prosperous species might crowd out others to extinction. Lyell's survey of the geographic distribution of plants and animals suggested that each species had come into being in one center. Similar habitats on separate continents seemed to produce quite different species equally adapted to their habitats. Environment, species—everything was in flux.

Lyell's interest in these problems had been piqued by the French naturalist Lamarck (1744–1829). But Lamarck, insisting on the inheritance of acquired characteristics, had really abandoned the concept of species. For him a species was only a name for one set of generations while the animal was adapting to its environment. And if every species was infinitely plastic, then no species would ever have to become extinct. While Lyell had kept species as the essential units in his processes of nature, he could not explain how a new species would originate.

The impressionable Darwin was tantalized by Lyell's suggestions. Everywhere in South America he encountered plants and animals he had never seen before. In the Galápagos he was enticed by the variations of bird species on widely separated islands in the same latitude. Meanwhile, Henslow had been so much impressed by Darwin's letters that he had read some of them to the Philosophical Society of Cambridge, and even printed some of them for private distribution. When the *Beagle* returned in 1836, Henslow joined with Lyell in securing for Darwin a grant of £1,000 to help him compile his five-volume report, and then managed his election as Secretary of the Geological Society of London.

During the next few years Darwin, by his own account, saw more of Lyell than of any other man. "His delight in science was ardent," Darwin recalled, "and he felt the keenest interest in the future progress of mankind. He was very kind-hearted, and thoroughly liberal in his beliefs or rather disbeliefs." Still Lyell would be slow in coming around to Darwin's own theories. "What a good thing it would be," the young Darwin had complained to Lyell when older geologists refused to follow Lyell, "if every scientific man was to die when 60 years old, as afterwards he would be sure to oppose all new doctrines." But in his late sixties the courageous Lyell's *Antiquity of Man* (1863) would finally abandon his opposition to evolution and begin to embrace Darwin's views of the origin of species. "Considering his age, his former views, and position in society," observed Darwin, "I think his action has been heroic."

Lyell, twelve years Darwin's senior, and at the height of his fame, remained Darwin's mentor. After the Darwins moved to Down in Kent, the Lyells would come visit for days at a time. As Darwin recalled:

It appeared to me that by following the example of Lyell in Geology, and by collecting all facts which bore in any way on the variation of animals and plants under domestication and nature, some light might perhaps be thrown on the whole subject. My first note-book was opened in July 1837. I worked on true Baconian principles, and without any theory collected facts on a whole-sale scale, more especially with respect to domesticated productions, by printed enquiries, by conversation with skilful breeders and gardeners, and by extensive reading. When I see the list of books of all kinds which I read and abstracted, including whole series of Journals and Transactions, I am surprised at my industry. I soon perceived that Selection was the key-stone of man's success in making useful races of animals and plants. But how selection could be applied to organisms living in a state of nature remained for some time a mystery to me. In October 1838, that is fifteen months after I had begun my systematic enquiry, I happened to read for amusement "Malthus on Population," and being well prepared to appreciate the struggle for existence which everywhere goes on from long-continued observation of the habits of animals and plants, it at once struck me that under these circumstances favourable variations would tend to be preserved and unfavourable ones to be destroyed. The result of this would be the formation of new species.

Here in a nutshell was what Darwin had to add to the thinking about species.

Still, Darwin was "so anxious to avoid prejudice" from the premature exposure of his ideas, that he held back. In June 1842, for his own satisfaction, he penciled a brief abstract of his theory in 35 pages, which he then enlarged in 1844 to another "abstract" of 230 pages. In 1856, when Lyell advised Darwin to expand his treatment, he began at once "to do so on a scale three or four times as extensive as that which was afterwards followed in my Origin of Species."

*   *   *

Then, early in the summer of 1858, as Darwin recorded, all his "plans were overthrown." He received from the Moluccas Wallace's essay "on the tendency of varieties to depart indefinitely from the original type." Wallace asked him, if he thought well of the essay, to send it on to Lyell, and, as we have seen, the scrupulous Darwin did just that. If Wallace's paper was to be published, what would Darwin do with his own labored product of twenty years? Darwin was torn.

Again Lyell, the statesman in the new parliament of science, played a crucial role. Determined to preserve Darwin's claim to priority and at the same time to give Wallace his due, Lyell urged that the three items be promptly offered to the Linnean Society. "I was at first very unwilling to consent," Darwin confessed, "as I thought Mr. Wallace might consider my doing so unjustifiable, for I did not then know how generous and noble was his disposition. The extract from my M.S and the letter to Asa Gray had neither been intended for publication and were badly written. Mr. Wallace's essay, on the other hand was admirably expressed and quite clear. Nevertheless our joint productions excited very little attention, and the only published notice of them which I can remember was by Prof. Haughton of Dublin, whose verdict was that all that was new in them was false, and what was true was old."

Alfred Russel Wallace (1823–1913), whom history would recognize as co-author of the idea of natural selection, offered a vivid contrast to Darwin. Born into an impoverished family of nine children in Monmouthshire in South Wales, he attended a grammar school for a few years, dropped out at fourteen, and educated himself by reading. As a boy visiting London he frequented the "Hall of Science" in Tottenham Court Road, a workmen's club for advanced teachers where he was converted to Robert Owen's socialism and "secularism," a skepticism of all religions. He supported himself as an apprentice-surveyor with his brother, then read up enough on his own to qualify as a schoolmaster in Leicester. There he had the good luck to meet Henry Walter Bates (1825–1892), who had been working thirteen hours a day drearily apprenticed to a local hosiery manufacturer, but was finding his refuge in Homer, Gibbon, and amateur entomology. Bates and Wallace became fast friends, and joined in beetle-collecting expeditions into the countryside.

A voracious reader, the young Wallace discovered an inspiring assortment of books on science, natural history, and travel, including Malthus' *On Population*, Darwin's journal of the *Beagle*, and Lyell's *Geology*. One of the books that impressed him most was a stimulating book on evolution by another amateur naturalist, Robert Chambers (1802–1871). *Vestiges of the Natural History of Creation* (1844) was so controversial that Chambers had to publish it anonymously to avoid damage to his publishing business, but it went through four editions in seven months and soon sold twenty-four thousand copies. Though condemned as godless by respectable scientists, it irrevocably popularized the ideas of organic and cosmic evolution, and the evolution of species.

Alexander von Humboldt's dramatic personal account of his travels in Mexico and South America emboldened Wallace to enlist Bates on an expedition to gather specimens along the Amazon. Four years (1848–52) of collecting there earned young Wallace a reputation as a field naturalist. On his return voyage to England his ship caught fire and sank, along with his specimens, but he was not discouraged from collecting. He set out promptly for the Malay Archipelago. There and in the Moluccas he spent eight years exploring and gathering specimens, and formulated the theory of natural selection in the paper that Darwin received early in 1858.

If a Greek dramatist had contrived two characters to show how fate could bring men by opposite paths to the same destination, he could hardly have done better than invent Darwin and Wallace. Darwin, the elder by a dozen years, had been dedicated by his wealthy family to a career in the Church. All his life Darwin did his best to follow Lyell's advice "never to get entangled in a controversy, as it rarely did any good and caused a miserable loss of time and temper." Tediously gathering specimens and evidence over two decades, Darwin seemed led to his theory of natural selection almost against his will. The impoverished Wallace, inspired early with a suspicion of religion and all established institutions, was hasty to embrace theories and plunge into controversy. When he was only twenty-two, Chambers' popular *Vestiges* had converted Wallace to an unshakable conviction that species arose through a process of evolution, and his trip to the Amazon was for facts to convince others. By his later trip through the Malay Archipelago covering fifteen thousand miles and gathering some 127,000 specimens, he aimed to gather conclusive evidence. From his arrival there he kept a notebook on evolution, which he called his "Species Notebook." Wallace's essay "On the Law which Has Regulated the Introduction of New Species" (1855) was published three years before the paper he sent to Darwin.

During the 1860's, the very years when the elementary notions of evolution were being publicly tested, Wallace spread himself over the most miscellaneous causes. He became a passionate convert to Spiritualism, pursuing his interest in socialism he was elected the first president of the Land Nationalization Society (1881), and he was an outspoken advocate of women's rights. Curiously, his passion for controversy drew him into the movement against vaccination for smallpox. His pamphlet *Forty-five Years of Registration Statistics, Proving Vaccination to Be Both Useless and Dangerous* (1885) was followed by three days of testimony before the Royal Commission where he argued that more patients died from vaccination than from the disease.

Seeking a wider arena for controversy, Wallace reached into outer space. The eminent astronomer Percival Lowell (1855–1916) argued in *Mars and Its Canals* (1906) that there must have been intelligent inhabitants on Mars, who had made the channels now visible by building a system of irrigation—using water from the annually melting polar ice caps—which created bands of cultivated vegetation. Wallace, though no astronomer, at the age of eighty-four entered the lists. In *Is Mars Habitable?* (1907) he insisted that life could not exist elsewhere in the universe. And twentieth-century evidence has proved that the expert Lowell was probably farther from the truth than the amateur Wallace. Science and reform had produced what Wallace enthusiastically christened *The Wonderful Century* (1898).

The facts of geographical distribution that provided the cautious Darwin with questions supplied the brash Wallace with answers. Seeing natural selection led Darwin away from religious faith. Late in life he recalled that the grandeur of the Brazilian forest had once reinforced his "firm conviction of the existence of God and of the immortality of the soul. . . . But now the grandest scenes would not cause any such convictions and feelings to rise in my mind. It may be truly said that I am like a man who has become colour-blind." "There seems to be no more design to the variability of organic beings and in the action of natural selection, than in the course which the wind blows."

But Wallace's passion for evolution led him more and more toward a belief in a "Higher Intelligence." Increasingly he needed a God to explain what he saw in nature. "I hope," Darwin told Wallace when Wallace's review of Lyell's books in 1869 laid bare his resurgent faith in a God, "you have not murdered too completely your own and my child."

* * *

Just as the voyages of Gama and Magellan had been preceded by uncelebrated pioneers on trading voyages across the Mediterranean and by those who inched down around the coast of Africa, so too there were countless pioneers in the voyages toward evolution. But while Columbus knew there was a Japan to be reached, Gama that India was there, the pioneers of evolution were en route to an unknown destination.

To describe amply all who contributed to Darwin's mature theory of evolution would require volumes on the rise of modern biology, geology, and geography. We would have to recount ancient Greek foreshadowings, Saint Augustine's suggestion that while all species had been created by God in the Beginning, some were mere seeds that would appear at a later time, medieval notions of an organic world, Montesquieu's hints of the multiplication of species from the discovery in Java of flying lemurs, the French mathematician Maupertuis's speculations on the chance combinations of elementary particles, Diderot's suggestions that higher animals may all have descended from "one primeval animal," Buffon on the development and "degeneration" of species, Linnaeus' gnawing doubts that species might not be immutable, the metaphoric fancies of Charles' grandfather Erasmus Darwin on the urges of plants and animals sparked by "lust, hunger, and danger" to develop into new forms— and countless others.

Among earlier contemporaries of Darwin we would have to include Lamarck's bold exploration of the hazy borderland between species and varieties and his evolutionary "tree." Nor could we omit Georges Cuvier's grand systematic arrangement of all classes of the animal kingdom. "These diverse bodies may be looked upon as a kind of experiment performed by nature," Cuvier ventured in 1817, "which adds or subtracts from each of these different parts (just as we try to do the same in our laboratories) and itself shows the results of these additions and subtractions." Many others who, like Cuvier, denied the evolution of species, still detected progress in the sorts of creatures found in the more recent levels of the earth.

Cuvier's *bête noire*, the indomitable Etienne Geoffroy Saint-Hilaire (1772–1844), took up Napoleon's invitation to join the scientific expedition to Egypt and at the risk of his life collected specimens from the tombs. He translated "evolution" from a word for the embryonic development of the individual into a word for the emergence of species. For Geoffroy, the structural similarity of all vertebrates suggested the evolution of mammals from fishes, and he declared the evolution of the whole animal kingdom. But he said that the innovator, like Christ, must be willing to wear a crown of thorns.

The data for evolution were an unanticipated by-product of a seafaring expedition which had a clearly defined assignment. The *Beagle*, as we have seen, had been sent by the British Admiralty to chart the coast of South America and to fix longitude more accurately by a world-encircling chain of chronological calculations. But the modern parliaments of science—the Royal Society, the Linnean Society, and their counterparts across Europe and the Americas—had made natural history a deliberate forum for the unexpected.

The triumph of evolution was a victory not merely of ideas but of printed matter, which in its European typographic form was a revolutionary new device for spreading grand ideas to the most unlikely places. *An Essay on the Principle of Population* (1798), by Thomas Robert Malthus (1766–1834), which Darwin had read in October 1838, would also catalyze Wallace. In his *Autobiography*, Wallace recalled that when he was a schoolteacher in Leicester in 1844–45 passing many hours in the town library, "perhaps the most important book I read was Malthus's 'Principles of Population,' which I greatly admired for its masterly summary of facts and logical induction to conclusions. It was the first work I had yet read treating any of the problems of philosophical biology, and its main principles remained with me as a permanent possession and twenty years later gave me the long-sought clue to the effective agent in the evolution of organic species." And he recorded vividly the moment when Malthus reappeared on his horizon and changed his life. In January 1858 Wallace had just arrived at Ternate in the Moluccas to collect butterflies and beetles, "bitten by the passion for species and their description, and if neither Darwin nor myself had hit upon 'Natural Selection,' I might have spent the best years of my life in this comparatively profitless work." His thinking had reached a dead end.

I was suffering from a sharp attack of intermittent fever, and every day during the cold and succeeding hot fits had to lie down for several hours, during which time I had nothing to do but to think over any subjects then particularly interesting me. One day something brought to my recollection Malthus's "Principles of Population," which I had read twelve years before. I thought of his clear exposition of "the positive checks to increase"—disease, accidents, war, and famine—which keep down the population of savage races to so much lower an average than that of more civilized peoples. It then occurred to me that these causes or their equivalents are continually acting in the case of animals also; and as animals usually breed much more rapidly than does mankind, the destruction every year from these causes must be enormous in order to keep down the numbers of each species . . . as otherwise the world would long ago have been densely crowded with those that breed most quickly. . . . Why do some die and some live? And the answer was clearly, that on the whole the best fitted live. From the effects of disease the most healthy escaped; from enemies, the strongest, the swiftest, or the most cunning; from famine, the best hunters or those with the best digestion; and so on. Then it suddenly flashed upon me that this self-acting process would necessarily *improve the race*, because in every generation the inferior would inevitably be killed off and the superior would remain—that is, *the fittest would survive*. . . . I waited anxiously for the termination of my fit so that I might at once make notes for a paper on the subject.

The following two evenings he spent writing the paper that he sent to Darwin by the next post, with the results we have already seen.

Malthus' ideas on population had been a reaction against his father's admiration for the utopian ideas of Rousseau and William Godwin. Though destined for the clergy and actually ordained, the young Malthus at Cambridge had done brilliantly in mathematics. "Population, when unchecked," he gave as the heart of his "principle," "increases in a geometrical ratio. Subsistence increases only in arithmetical ratio." And despite his frequent old-fashioned moralizing, his book had the ring of quantitative social science. Malthus had an eminently practical purpose—to reshape the Poor Laws so that the leaders of England "would not be open to the objection of violating our promises to the poor." And in the long run he would influence economic thinking. Karl Marx learned from him, and John Maynard Keynes would credit Malthus with the idea that effective demand was a way of avoiding depressions. But Malthus' influence on biology was quite unpredicted. The struggle for existence, Darwin explained in the *Origin of Species*, "is the doctrine of Malthus applied with manifold force to the whole animal and vegetable kingdom." The cogency of Malthus' style had much to do with the remarkable impact of his small book, which went through six editions before his death and increased in power with the years.

Publication was often the crux of the matter. Whether readers agreed or disagreed, what mattered was that the published book sparked discussion as it sold copies. When Darwin's *Origin of Species* was offered to the shrewd John Murray (who had published a revised *Voyage of the Beagle* and Herman Melville's tales of the South Seas after several others had refused), he was far from enthusiastic. The cautious Darwin asked Lyell on March 28, 1859, how he should approach Murray:

P.S. Would you advise me to tell Murray that my book is not more *un*-orthodox than the subject makes inevitable. That I do not discuss the origin of man. That I do not bring in any discussion about Genesis, &c., &c., and only give facts, and such conclusions from them as seem to me fair.

Or had I better say *nothing* to Murray, and assume that he cannot object to this much unorthodoxy, which in fact is not more than any Geological Treatise which runs slap counter to Genesis.

Finally, all that Murray objected to were the words "Abstract" and "Natural Selection" in the title. Seeing only the chapter titles, and on Lyell's recommendation, Murray agreed to publish, giving Darwin two-thirds of the net profit.

The Reverend Whitwell Elwin, editor of the prestigious *Quarterly Review*, in a reader's report, which would become a classic in the trade, advised Murray that it was unwise to publish anything that called itself only an "abstract." Since the subject was so controversial, Elwin urged that, instead, Darwin should write a book on pigeons, on which he was known to have some ingenious observations. "Everyone is interested in pigeons," he added. "The book would be reviewed in every journal in the kingdom and would soon be on every library table." Darwin was not persuaded.

A lawyer friend of Murray's encouraged him to print 1,000 copies instead of the planned 500, and the number was raised to 1,250 before publication on November 24, 1859. Until the last moment Darwin feared that Murray was overcommitted, and even offered to pay the cost of his proof corrections. When all copies were taken by booksellers, another 3,000 were printed. The result was beyond expectations. "Sixteen thousand copies have now (1876) been sold in England," Darwin noted in his *Autobiography*, "and considering how stiff a book it is this is a large sale. It has been translated into almost every European tongue, even into such languages as Spanish, Bohemian, Polish, and Russian. It has also, according to Miss Bird, been translated into Japanese and is there much studied. Even an essay in Hebrew has appeared on it, showing that the theory is contained in the Old Testament!" He proudly counted more than 265 reviews, and numerous essays. Darwin attributed the publishing success (not large, for popular novels were equaling Darwin's boasted total in a single year) to his bringing together "innumerable well-observed facts," and to the moderate size of the book, which he said he owed to help from Wallace's essay.

The initial hostile reception of the *Origin of Species*, and especially the ignorant and contemptuous attack by Bishop Samuel Wilberforce, has become proverbial. But contempt rapidly gave way to acclaim. Within a decade of publication, questions for the natural science tripos at Cambridge, instead of asking for "evidence of design" in nature, required an analysis of the concept of the struggle for existence. When even the ill-tempered Bishop Wilberforce reluctantly confessed his error, Darwin's champion, Thomas Henry Huxley, remained unsatisfied. "Confession unaccompanied by penitence . . . affords no ground for mitigation of judgment; and the kindliness with which Mr. Darwin speaks of his assailant, Bishop Wilberforce, is so striking an exemplification of his singular gentleness and modesty, that it rather increases one's indignation against the presumption of his critic." Huxley called Darwin's book "the most potent instrument for the extension of the realm of natural knowledge which has come into men's hands, since the publication of Newton's Principia." "It was badly received by the generation to which it was first addressed, and the outpouring of angry nonsense to which it gave rise is sad to think upon. But the present generation will probably behave just as badly if another Darwin should arise, and inflict upon them what the generality of mankind most hate— the necessity of revising their convictions."

The long-term influence of Darwinism and its fruitful ambivalence for science and religion was embodied in Huxley's invention of the word "agnostic" to describe the limits and the promise of scientific knowledge. Huxley took his clue from Saint Paul's encounter with the Athenians worshipping at an altar inscribed "To the Unknown God." On the urging of twenty members of Parliament, when Darwin died in 1882 he was buried in Westminster Abbey.

THE LOST ARTS OF MEMORY

BEFORE the printed book, Memory ruled daily life and the occult learning, and fully deserved the name later applied to printing, the "art preservative of all arts" (*Ars artium omnium conservatrix*). The Memory of individuals and of communities carried knowledge through time and space. For millennia personal Memory reigned over entertainment and information, over the perpetuation and perfection of crafts, the practice of commerce, the conduct of professions. By Memory and in Memory the fruits of education were garnered, preserved, and stored. Memory was an awesome faculty which everyone had to cultivate, in ways and for reasons we have long since forgotten. In these last five hundred years we see only pitiful relics of the empire and the power of Memory.

The ancient Greeks gave mythic form to this fact that ruled their lives. The Goddess of Memory (Mnemosyne) was a Titan, daughter of Uranus (Heaven) and Gaea (Earth), and mother of all the nine Muses. In legend these were Epic Poetry (Calliope), History (Clio), Flute playing (Euterpe), Tragedy (Melpomene), Dancing (Terpsichore), the Lyre (Erato), Sacred Song (Polyhymnia), Astronomy (Urania), and Comedy (Thalia). When the nine daughters of King Pierus challenged them in song, the King's daughters were punished by being changed into magpies, who could only sound monotonous repetition.

Everyone needed the arts of Memory, which, like other arts, could be cultivated. The skills of Memory could be perfected, and virtuosi were admired. Only recently has "memory training" become a butt of ridicule and a refuge of charlatans. The traditional arts of Memory, delightfully chronicled by historian Frances A. Yates, flourished in Europe over the centuries.

The inventor of the mnemonic art was said to be the versatile Greek lyric poet Simonides of Ceos (c. 556–468?B.C.). He was reputed also to be the first to accept payment for his poems. The origins were described in the work on oratory by Cicero, who was himself noted for his mnemonic skill. Once at a banquet in the house of Scopas in Thessaly, Simonides was hired to chant a lyric in honor of his host. But only half of Simonides' poem was in praise of Scopas, as he devoted the other half to the divine twins Castor and Pollux. The angry Scopas therefore would pay only half the agreed sum. While the many guests were still at the banquet table a message was brought to Simonides that there were two young men at the door who wanted him to come outside. When he went out he could see no one. The mysterious callers were, of course, Castor and Pollux, who had found their own way to pay Simonides for their share of the panegyric. For at the very moment when Simonides had left the banquet hall the roof fell in, burying all the other guests in the ruins. When relatives came to take away the corpses for the burial honors, the mangled bodies could not be identified. Simonides then exercised his remarkable memory to show the grieving relatives which bodies belonged to whom. He did this by thinking back to *where* each of the guests had been seated. Then he was able to identify by place each of the bodies.

It was this experience that suggested to Simonides the classic form of the art of Memory of which he was reputed to be the inventor. Cicero, who made Memory one of the five principal parts of rhetoric, explained what Simonides had done.

He inferred that persons desiring to train this faculty must select places and form mental images of the things they wish to remember and store those images in the places, so that the order of the places will preserve the order of the things, and the images of the things will denote the things themselves, and we shall employ the places and images respectively as a wax writing-tablet and the letters written on it.

Simonides' art, which dominated European thinking in the Middle Ages, was based on the two simple concepts of places *(loci)* and images *(imagines)*. These provided the lasting elements of Memory techniques for European rhetors, philosophers, and scientists.

A treatise (c. 86–82 B.C.) by a Roman teacher of rhetoric known as *Ad Herennium*, after the name of the person to whom his work was dedicated, became the standard text, the more highly esteemed because some thought it had been written by Cicero. Quintilian (A.D. c. 35–c. 95), the other great Roman authority on rhetoric, made the classic rules memorable. He described the "architectural" technique for imprinting the memory with a series of places. Think of a large building, Quintilian said, and walk through its numerous rooms remembering all the ornaments and furnishings in your imagination. Then give each idea to be remembered an image, and as you go through the building again deposit each image in this order in your imagination. For example, if you mentally deposit a spear in the living room, an anchor in the dining room, you will later recall that you are to speak first of the war, then of the navy, etc. This system still works.

In the Middle Ages a technical jargon was elaborated on the basic distinction between the "natural" memory, with which we were all born and which we exercise without training, and the "artificial" memory, which we can develop. There were different techniques for memorizing things or words. And differing views about where the student should be when he worked at his memory exercises and what were the best kinds of places to serve as imaginary storage houses for the *loci* and images of memory. Some teachers advised the student to find a quiet place, where his imagined impressions of the *loci* of memory would not be weakened by surrounding noises and passing people. And, of course, an observant and well-traveled person was better equipped to provide himself with many varied Memory-places. In those days one could see some student of rhetoric walking tensely through a deserted building, noting the shape and furnishing of each room to equip his imagination with places to serve as a warehouse for his memory.

The elder Seneca (c. 55 B.C.–A.D. 37), a famous teacher of rhetoric, was said to be able to repeat long passages of speeches he had heard only once many years before. He would impress his students by asking each member of a class of two hundred to recite a line of poetry, and then he would recite all the lines they had quoted—in *reverse* order, from last to first. Saint Augustine, who also had begun life as a teacher of rhetoric, reported his admiration of a friend who could recite the whole text of Virgil—backwards!

The feats and especially the acrobatics of "artificial" memory were in high repute. "Memory," said Aeschylus, "is the mother of all wisdom." "Memory," agreed Cicero, "is the treasury and guardian of all things." In the heyday of Memory, before the spread of printing, a highly developed Memory was needed by the entertainer, the poet, the singer, the physician, the lawyer, and the priest.

The first great epics in Europe were produced by an oral tradition, which is another way of saying they were preserved and performed by the arts of Memory. The *Iliad* and the *Odyssey* were perpetuated by word of mouth, without the use of writing. Homer's word for poet is "singer" (*aoidos*). And the singer before Homer seems to have been one who chanted a single poem, short enough to be sung to a single audience on one occasion. The surviving practice in Muslim Serbia, which is described by the brilliant American scholar-explorer Milman Parry, is probably close to the custom of Homeric antiquity. He shows us how in the beginning the length of a poem was limited by the patience of an audience and a singer's remembered repertoire. Then the achievement of a Homer (whether a he, she, or they) was to combine hour-long songs into a connected epic with a grander purpose, a larger theme, and a complicated structure.

The first manuscript books in the ancient Mediterranean were written on papyrus sheets glued together and then rolled up. It was inconvenient to unroll the book, and frequent unrolling wore away the written words. Since there were no separate numbered "pages," it was such a nuisance to verify a quotation that people were inclined to rely on their memory.

Laws were preserved by Memory before they were preserved in documents. The collective memory of the community was the first legal archive. The English common law was "immemorial" custom which ran to a "time whereof the memory of man runneth not to the contrary." "In the profound ignorance of letters which formerly overspread the whole western world," Sir William Blackstone noted in 1765, "letters were intirely traditional, for this plain reason, that the nations among which they prevailed had but little idea of writing. Thus the British as well as the Gallic druids committed all their laws as well as learning to memory; and it is said of the primitive Saxons here, as well as their brethren on the continent, that *leges sola memoria et usu retinebant.*"

Ritual and liturgy, too, were preserved by memory, of which priests were the special custodians. Religious services, often repeated, were ways of imprinting prayers and rites on the youth of the congregation. The prevalence of verse and music as mnemonic devices attests the special importance of memory in the days before printed textbooks. For centuries the standard work on Latin grammar was the twelfth-century *Doctrinale*, by Alexander of Villedieu, in two thousand lines of doggerel. Versified rules were easier to remember, though their crudity appalled Aldus Manutius when he reprinted this work in 1501.

Medieval scholastic philosophers were not satisfied that Memory should be merely a practical skill. So they transformed Memory from a skill into a virtue, an aspect of the virtue of Prudence. After the twelfth century, when the classic treatise *Ad Herennium* reappeared in manuscripts, the scholastics seemed less concerned with the technology than with the Morality of Memory. How could Memory promote the Christian life?

Saint Thomas Aquinas (1225–1274), his biographers boasted, memorized everything his teachers ever told him in school. In Cologne, Albertus Magnus helped him train his memory. The sayings of the Church Fathers that Aquinas collected for Pope Urban IV after his trips to many monasteries were recorded not from what he had *copied* out but from what he had merely *seen*. Of course he remembered perfectly anything he had ever read. In his *Summa Theologiae* (1267–73) he expounded Cicero's definition of Memory as a part of Prudence, making it one of the four cardinal virtues, and then he provided his own four rules for perfecting the Memory. Until the triumph of the printed book, these Thomist rules of memory prevailed. Copied again and again, they became the scheme of textbooks. Paintings by Lorenzetti and Giotto, as Frances A. Yates explains, depicted virtues and vices to help viewers apply the Thomist rules of artificial Memory. The fresco of the Chapter House of Santa Maria Novella in Florence provides memorable images for each of Aquinas' four cardinal virtues and their several parts. "We must assiduously remember the invisible joys of paradise and the eternal torments of hell," urged Boncompagno's standard medieval treatise. For him, lists of virtues and vices were simply "memorial notes" to help the pious frequent "the paths of remembrance."

Dante's *Divine Comedy*, with his plan of Inferno, Purgatorio, and Paradiso, made vivid both places and images (following the precepts of Simonides and Aquinas) in an easily remembered order. And there were humbler examples, too. The manuscripts of English friars in the fourteenth century described pictures—for example, of Idolatry in the role of a prostitute—not meant to be seen with the eye, but rather to provide invisible images for the memory.

Petrarch (1304–1374) also had a great reputation as an authority on the artificial memory and how to cultivate it. He offered his own helpful rules for choosing the "places" where remembered images were to be stored for retrieval. The imagined architecture of Memory, he said, must provide storage places of medium size, not too large or too small for the particular image.

By the time the printing press appeared the arts of Memory had been elaborated into countless systems. At the beginning of the sixteenth century the best-known work was a practical text, *Phoenix, sive Artificiosa Memoria* (Venice, 1491), which went through many editions and was widely translated. In that popular handbook, Peter of Ravenna advised that the best memory *loci* were in a deserted church.

When you have found your church, you should go around in it three or four times, fixing in your mind all the places where you would later put your memory-images. Each locus should be five or six feet from the one before. Peter boasted that even as a young man he had fixed in his mind 100,000 memory *loci*, and by his later travels he had added thousands more. The effectiveness of his system, he said, was shown by the fact that he could repeat verbatim the whole canon law, two hundred speeches of Cicero, and twenty thousand points of law.

* * *

After Gutenberg, realms of everyday life once ruled and served by Memory would be governed by the printed page. In the late Middle Ages, for the small literate class, manuscript books had provided an aid, and sometimes a substitute, for Memory. But the printed book was far more portable, more accurate, more convenient to refer to, and, of course, more public. Whatever was in print, after being written by an author, was also known to printers, proofreaders, and anyone reached by the printed page. A man could now refer to the rules of grammar, the speeches of Cicero, and the texts of theology, canon law, and morality without storing them in himself.

The printed book would be a new warehouse of Memory, superior in countless ways to the internal invisible warehouse in each person. When the codex of bound manuscript pages supplanted the long manuscript roll, it was much easier to refer to a written source. After the twelfth century some manuscript books carried tables, running heads, and even rudimentary indexes, which showed that Memory was already beginning to lose some of its ancient role. But retrieval became still easier when printed books had title pages and their pages were numbered. When they were equipped with indexes, as they sometimes were by the sixteenth century, then the only essential feat of Memory was to remember the order of the alphabet. Before the end of the eighteenth century the alphabetic index at the back of a book had become standard. The technology of Memory retrieval, though of course never entirely dispensable, played a much smaller role in the higher realms of religion, thought, and knowledge. Spectacular feats of Memory became mere stunts.

Some of the consequences had been predicted two millennia earlier when Socrates lamented the effects of writing itself on the Memory and the soul of the learner. In his dialogue with Phaedrus reported by Plato, Socrates recounts how Thoth, the Egyptian god who invented letters, had misjudged the effect of his invention. Thoth was thus reproached by the God Thamus, then King of Egypt:

> This discovery of yours will create forgetfulness in the learners' souls, because they will not use their memories; they will trust to the external written characters and not remember of themselves. The specific which you have discovered is an aid not to memory, but to reminiscence, and you give your disciples not truth, but only the semblance of truth; they will be hearers of many things and will have learned nothing; they will appear to be omniscient and will generally know nothing; they will be tiresome company, having the show of wisdom without the reality.

The perils that Socrates noted in the written word would be multiplied a thousandfold when words went into print.

The effect was beautifully suggested by Victor Hugo in a familiar passage in *Notre-Dame de Paris* (1831) when the scholar holding his first printed book turns away from his manuscripts, looks at the cathedral, and says "This will kill that" *(Ceci tuera cela)*. Print also destroyed "the invisible cathedrals of memory." For the printed book made it less necessary to shape ideas and things into vivid images and then store them in Memory-places.

The same era that saw the decline of the everyday empire of Memory would see the rise of Neoplatonism—a mysterious new empire of the hidden, the secret, the occult. This revival of Platonic ideas in the Renaissance gave a new life and a new realm to Memory. Plato had made much of the soul and its "memory" of ideal forms. Now a galaxy of talented mystics developed a new technology of Memory. No longer the servant of oratory, only an aspect of rhetoric, Memory became an arcane art, a realm of ineffable entities. The

Hermetic art opened secret recesses of the soul. The bizarre Memory Theater of Giulio Camillo, exhibited in Venice and Paris, provided Memory-places not just for convenience but as a way of representing "the eternal nature of all things" in their "eternal places." The Neoplatonists of Cosimo de' Medici's Platonic Academy in Florence—Marsilio Ficino (1433–1499) and Pico della Mirandola (1463–1494)—built an occult art of Memory into their elusive philosophies.

The most remarkable explorer of the Dark Continent of Memory was the inspired vagrant Giordano Bruno (1548–1600). As a young friar in Naples, he had been inducted into the famous Dominican art of Memory, and when he abandoned the Dominican order, laymen hoped he would reveal the Dominican secrets. He did not disappoint them. For his work *On the Shadows of Ideas, Circe* (1582) explained that Memory-skill was neither natural nor magical but was the product of a special science. Introducing his Memory-science with an incantation by Circe herself, he showed the peculiar potency of images of the decans of the zodiac. The star images, Shadows of Ideas, representing celestial objects, are nearer to the enduring reality than are images of this transient world below. Bruno's system for "remembering" these "shadows of ideas contracted for inner writing" from the celestial images brought his disciples to a higher reality.

> This is to form the inform chaos. . . . It is necessary for the control of memory that the numbers and elements should be disposed in order . . . through certain memorable forms (the images of the zodiac). . . . I tell you that if you contemplate this attentively you will be able to reach such a figurative art that it will help not only the memory but also all the powers of the soul in a wonderful manner.

A guaranteed way to the Unity behind everything, the Divine Unity!

But the everyday needs for Memory were never as important as they had been in the days before paper and printed books. The kudos of Memory declined. In 1580 Montaigne declared that "a good memory is generally joined to a weak judgment." And pundits quipped, "Nothing is more common than a fool with a strong memory." In the centuries after printing, interest has shifted from the technology of Memory to its pathology. By the late twentieth century, interest in Memory was being displaced by interest in aphasia, amnesia, hysteria, hypnosis, and, of course, psychoanalysis. Pedagogic interest in the arts of Memory came to be displaced by interest in the arts of learning, which were increasingly described as a social process.

And with this came a renewed interest in the arts of forgetting. When Simonides offered to teach the Athenian statesman Themistocles the art of Memory, Cicero reports that he refused. "Teach me not the art of remembering," he said, "but the art of forgetting, for I remember things I do not wish to remember, but I cannot forget things I wish to forget."

The study of forgetting became a frontier of modern psychology, where mental processes were first examined experimentally and subjected to measurement. "Psychology has a long past," Hermann Ebbinghaus (1850–1909) observed, "yet its real history is short." His beautifully simple experiments, which William James called "heroic," were described in *Memory: A Contribution to Experimental Psychology* (1885) and laid the foundation for modern experimental psychology.

Ebbinghaus invented meaningless raw materials for his experiments. Nonsense syllables. By taking any two consonants and putting a vowel in between, he devised some twenty-three hundred rememberable (and forgettable) items, and he put them in series. For his experiments the syllables had the advantage of lacking associations. For two years he used himself as the subject to test the powers of retaining and reproducing these syllables. He kept scrupulous records of all his trials, of the times required for recollection, and of the intervals between his efforts. He also experimented in "relearning." His efforts might have been of little use without his passion for statistics.

Now, Ebbinghaus hoped, not mere sense perceptions (which Gustav Fechner [1801–1887] had already begun to study and to whom he dedicated his work) but mental phenomena themselves could be submitted to "an experimental and quantitative treatment." Ebbinghaus' "forgetting-curve" related forgetting to the passage of time. His results, still significant, showed that most forgetting takes place soon after "learning."

In this unexpected way the inward world of thought began to be charted with the instruments of modern mathematics. But other explorers, in the Neoplatonist tradition, kept alive an interest in the mysteries of memory. Ebbinghaus himself said that he had studied "the non-voluntary re-emergence of mental images out of the darkness of memory into the light of consciousness." A few other psychologists rashly plunged into that "darkness" of the unconscious, but even as they did so they claimed to have invented a whole new "science."

The founders of modern psychology were increasingly interested in forgetting as a process in everyday life. The incomparable William James (1842–1910) observed:

> In the practical use of our intellect, forgetting is as important a function as remembering. . . . If we remembered everything, we should on most occasions be as ill off as if we remembered nothing. It would take as long for us to recall a space of time as it took the original time to elapse, and we should never get ahead with our thinking. All recollected times undergo . . . foreshortening; and this foreshortening is due to the omission of an enormous number of facts which filled them. "We thus reach the paradoxical result," says M. Ribot, "that one condition of remembering is that we should forget. Without totally forgetting a prodigious number of states of consciousness, and momentarily forgetting a large number, we could not remember at all. . . ."

In a century when the stock of human knowledge and of collective memories would be multiplied, recorded, and diffused as never before, forgetting would become more than ever a prerequisite for sanity.

But what happened to "forgotten" memories? "Where are the snows of yester-year?" In the twentieth century the realm of memory was once again transformed, to be rediscovered as a vast region of the unconscious. In his *Psychopathology of Everyday Life* (1904) Sigmund Freud (1856–1939) started from simple examples, such as the forgetting of proper names, of foreign words, and of the order of words. The new arts of Memory for which Freud became famous had both the scientific pretensions of Simonides and his followers and the occult charm of the Neoplatonists. Of course, people had always wondered at the mystery of dreams. Now Freud found the dream world also to be a copious secret treasury of Memories. Freud's *Interpretation of Dreams* (1900) showed how psychoanalysis could serve as an art and a science of Memories.

Others, stirred by Freud, would find still more new meanings in Memory. Latent Memory, or the unconscious, became a new resource of therapy, anthropology, and sociology. Might not the tale of Oedipus record everyone's experience? Freud's own mythic metaphors hinted at our inner inheritance of ancient, communal experience. Carl Jung (1875–1961), more in the Hermetic tradition, popularized the "collective unconscious." Now Freud, his disciples and dissidents, as we will see, had again rediscovered, or perhaps after their fashion reconstructed, the Cathedrals of Memory.

"TO WAKE THE DEAD"

CHAPTER 73

A FULL CENTURY passed before Winckelmann found his Vespucci to show and tell the world what had really been discovered. Although Heinrich Schliemann (1822–1890), too, rose from poverty to celebrity, in almost every other way he was Winckelmann's opposite. Schliemann personally financed all his exploits. He was his own patron. He imported into archaeology the enterprise and love of action that had made him his fortune in commerce. For him, exploring the past became an athletic feat and an adventure in diplomacy, to feed a newly news-hungry age. And his love of a beautiful woman helped keep the public spotlight on his digging.

Son of a poor Protestant minister in a village in north Germany, Heinrich Schliemann's "natural disposition for the mysterious and the marvellous" was fired by his father's passion for ancient history.

He often told me with warm enthusiasm of the tragic fate of Herculaneum and Pompeii, and seemed to consider him the luckiest of men who had the means and the time to visit the excavations which were going on there. He also related to me with admiration the great deeds of the Homeric heroes and the events of the Trojan war, always finding in me a warm defender of the Trojan cause. With great grief I heard

from him that Troy had been so completely destroyed, that
it had disappeared without leaving any traces of its existence.
My joy may be imagined, therefore, when, being nearly
eight years old, I received from him, in 1829, as a Christmas
gift, Dr. Georg Ludwig Jerrer's *Universal History*, with an
engraving representing Troy in flames, with its huge walls
and the Scaean gate, from which Aeneas is escaping, carrying his father Anchises on his back and holding his son As-
canius by the hand; and I cried out, "Father, you were
mistaken: Jerrer must have seen Troy, otherwise he could
not have represented it here." "My son," he replied, "that is
merely a fanciful picture." But to my question, whether ancient Troy had such huge walls as those depicted in the
book, he answered in the affirmative. "Father," retorted I,
"if such walls once existed, they cannot possibly have been
completely destroyed: vast ruins of them must still remain,
but they are hidden away beneath the dust of ages." He
maintained the contrary, while I remained firm in my opinion, and at last we both agreed that I should one day excavate
Troy.

His mother died when he was nine. Since his father's poverty left
him little hope of going to the university, he dropped out of the
Gymnasium, where he might have pursued his classical interests, and
instead went to the vocational Realschule. At fourteen Schliemann
was apprenticed to a grocer and spent five years working from five in
the morning till eleven at night, grinding potatoes for the whiskey
still, packaging herring, sugar, oil, and candles. He escaped by
becoming cabin boy on a ship bound for Venezuela. When the ship
was wrecked in the North Sea, he found a post as messenger and
later bookkeeper for a trading firm in Amsterdam.

Through these drab years Heinrich never lost his romantic ambition. Determined someday to unearth the real Troy, every spare
minute, even as he ran errands or waited in line at the post office, he
improved himself by reading. By his own system he acquired a score
of languages, never missing an opportunity to learn or to practice

what he learned. "This method consists in reading a great deal aloud, without making a translation; devoting one hour every day to writing essays upon subjects that interest one, correcting these under a teacher's supervision, learning them by heart, and repeating in the next lesson what was corrected on the previous day." Within six months, he reports, he had acquired "a thorough knowledge of the English language," as part of the process having "committed to memory the whole of Goldsmith's *Vicar of Wakefield* and Sir Walter Scott's *Ivanhoe*." In only six weeks devoted to each, he learned to write "and to speak fluently" French, Dutch, Spanish, Italian, Portuguese, and some others. When he traveled through the Middle East, he acquired a practical knowledge of Arabic.

The spoken word interested him most. He never forgot the cadence of spoken Greek, which he first heard when a drunken miller, a dropout from the Gymnasium, came into the grocery store where Schliemann was working and melodiously recited lines from Homer. But he waited till middle life to turn to his beloved Greek. "Great as was my wish to learn Greek, I did not venture upon its study till I had acquired a moderate fortune; for I was afraid that this language would exercise too great a fascination upon me and estrange me from my commercial business."

Schliemann followed an arduous and devious road to fortune. When he was a young man in Amsterdam, Russian merchants were coming there for the indigo auctions. Except for the Russian vice-consul, Heinrich found no one in Amsterdam who knew Russian, and when the vice-consul refused to be his teacher, he employed his usual system in a crash program to teach himself. He hired an old Dutchman to be his audience as he declaimed Russian two hours each evening. When the tenants of his boarding house complained, Heinrich did not change his system but he had to change lodgings twice before he was satisfied with his fluency in the language.

The trading firm where he worked had dealings in St. Petersburg and sent him there as their agent. In St. Petersburg, trading in indigo, dyewoods, and war materials like saltpeter, brimstone, and lead, he soon, to his own surprise, made a fortune. Then he no longer feared the glorious distraction of the classical language. He spent six weeks learning modern Greek and in another three months plunged into the ancient authors. After the Crimean War, he traveled the world pursuing his historical interests. His childhood love was a playmate, Minna Meincke, who had shared his fantasy of pursuing the quest for Troy. And when he was established in business he went in search of her. He did find Minna Meincke, but alas she was already married. In 1852 he made the mistake of marrying a Russian beauty who wanted only his money. She refused even to share his home, much less his archaeological interests. Meanwhile, having become an American citizen by the accident that he was traveling in California when it became a state of the Union, he went to Indiana to benefit from its loose divorce laws and there divested himself of his Russian wife.

Determined not to make the same mistake again, he asked an old friend, his Greek teacher who had since become the archbishop of Athens, to find him a suitable young Greek wife. The Archbishop obliged by suggesting his relative, Sophia Engastromenos, a bright and beautiful seventeen-year-old schoolgirl. In Athens, before he decided to marry Sophia, Schliemann visited her classroom incognito to hear how she recited Homer. Her mellifluous Greek brought tears to his eyes, and clinched his determination to marry her. The polylingual Heinrich, at forty-seven, made Sophia his life-long student. At their marriage she knew only ancient and modern Greek, but he promised that she would learn four more languages in the next two years. He trudged her about the capitals of Europe and the Near East, expounding history and archaeology, testing her knowledge, pressing her not to lag behind. After an interval of headaches, nausea, and fevers, she survived to become his colleague when he finally began his digging at Hissarlik in 1871. She went into the archaeological trenches, something astonishing at the time for a woman, and managed to direct a crew of Turkish workmen in the excavations.

Schliemann, unlike Winckelmann, believed his vocation to be digging. His proper province was not words but things. But the work he loved required that he supervise laborers who spoke exotic languages. And his gift of tongues, which helped him manage his digs, enabled him to convert doubters and advertise his finds.

A quixotic archaeologist with a beautiful wife directing a hundred and fifty rebellious workmen on the exotic Turkish landscape could hardly prevent his work becoming public, even in those early salad days of the sensational press. The open-air archaeologist would become the public property of the newspaper audience. Now the explorer of the past had to forsake the library and the museum, go to distant places, and move heavy objects up and out into public view. His success would be judged not only by academicians but by impatient millions.

Schliemann could not be budged from his faith that Homer's Troy was at the obscure modern village of Hissarlik in northwestern Turkey on the Asian side just four miles from the mouth of the Dardanelles. When he compared the site with Bunarbashi, several miles south of there, where other scholars had placed it, his conviction became stronger than ever. But Schliemann's chosen site was privately owned. The bureaucratic, autocratic, and corrupt Turkish officials first tried to block him, then blackmailed him before granting the required digging permit. Excavation at Troy would be paid for entirely by Schliemann, who considered it a privilege to spend his fortune in this way. He never complained of the expense, but was prudent and businesslike.

In September 1871, hiring a crew of eighty laborers, he began digging into the mound at Hissarlik. Precisely according to plan, he found layer after layer of cities and fortifications, one below another. He knew that as he dug he was destroying monuments of a more recent era, but his destination was Troy! Twenty-three feet below the surface and stretching down to thirty-three feet, he found ruins of a city he believed to be Troy. He impulsively identified everything he had hoped to find—remnants of the Temple of Athena, the main altar for sacrifices, the Great Tower, houses, and streets—all just as described in the *Iliad*.

In early May 1873, as his workmen were digging out the top of the ancient wall, Schliemann himself spied a shiny gold object. As he recalled seven years later in his own melodramatic account:

> In order to secure the treasure from my workmen and save it
> for archaeology, it was necessary to lose no time; so, al-

though it was not yet the hour for breakfast, I immediately had *païdos* (rest-time) called. . . . While the men were eating and resting, I cut out the Treasure with a large knife. This required great exertion and involved great risk, since the wall of fortification, beneath which I had to dig, threatened every moment to fall down upon me. But the sight of so many objects, every one of which is of inestimable value to archaeology, made me reckless, and I never thought of any danger. It would, however, have been impossible for me to have removed the treasure without the help of my dear wife, who stood at my side, ready to pack the things I cut out in her shawl, and to carry them away.

Keeping his secret for the moment, he successfully smuggled the gold treasure (eventually nine thousand objects) out of Turkey. His cautions proved justified, for the workman who later found a gold object in the excavations quickly had it melted down by a local gold-smith. The gold, and not Homer's Troy, was what interested Turkish officials. They blocked his further excavations and sued for return of the treasure.

While Schliemann's story of his digging was substantially correct, recent historians raise an eyebrow at this example of how his feeling for drama sometimes overshadowed the fact. His "dear wife," who according to him was catching the treasure in her shawl, appears at that moment to have been not in Hissarlik but in Athens. Still, such trivial embellishments increased public interest in the new romance of archaeology.

Schliemann returned to Greece, where, by intervention of the British prime minister Gladstone and the British ambassador, he had secured permission to dig, and he plunged into another sensational adventure. This time Schliemann was pursuing his hunches about the treasure still to be found at the fabled site of ancient Mycenae. There, he insisted, was the buried treasure of Agamemnon. And there, too, he had been guided by his reading to dissent from the accepted scholarly view. Scholars generally had agreed that the tombs of Agamemnon and Clytemnestra must be outside the walls of the citadel. But Schliemann, a confidant of the ancients, put his faith in Pausanias, the famous second-century traveler who described "the heroes' graves . . . in the midst of the meeting-place." To Schliemann this meant inside the city walls. At Mycenae when he found stelae arranged in a circle suggesting the ancient agora, he began digging. In December 1876 he found the first of five shaft graves. For forty-five days Schliemann and Sophia, their hands numbed by cold and using only fingers, a penknife, and a small shovel, dug within the grave circle.

Their reward—the richest treasure ever yet excavated from the past—was a find of bodies "literally covered with gold and jewels." The faces, distinguishable when unearthed, quickly disintegrated in the air, but each gold mask still had its own character. By intuition, learning, expertise, and good luck, the Schliemanns had found this fabulous prize: "the mask of Agamemnon," gold diadems, gold and silver statuettes, gold sword handles, precious necklaces and bracelets, stone and gold and alabaster vases, goblets of gold and silver, and scores more of dazzling jewels. Not one to hesitate at a moment of drama, Schliemann telegraphed to King George of Greece, "It is with extraordinary pleasure that I announce to your Majesty my discovery of the graves which, according to tradition, are those of Agamemnon, Cassandra, Eureymedon, and their comrades, all killed during the banquet by Clytemnestra and her lover Aegisthus." He declared that no comparable treasure had ever been unearthed. "All the museums of the world taken together," he boasted, "do not have one-fifth as much."

Despite his enthusiasm, faith, and scholarship, Heinrich Schliemann's discoveries were not quite what he thought. He was not off the mark as far as the earlier explorer who aimed for Japan, who thought he had reached Cathay but had merely discovered America. We now know that the city that Schliemann chose as Homer's Troy from superimposed strata of "the five prehistoric cities" was the wrong one. The spectacular find that he called the treasures of Priam, dug from the second and third layers above bedrock, actually came from a thousand years before Priam. With funds supplied in Schliemann's will, his heir, Wilhelm Dörpfeld (1853–1940),

proved Homer's Troy to be the sixth level up from the bottom which
Schliemann had cut through in his haste. His conclusions at Mycenae, too, were off the mark. He had not, as he proclaimed, found the
tomb of Agamemnon. The tomb he found was many centuries older.

When classical scholars ridiculed his identification of King
Priam with his Troy, Schliemann still insisted on "Priam"—"because he is so called by the tradition of which Homer is the echo; but
as soon as it is proved that Homer and the tradition were wrong, and
that Troy's last king was called Smith, I shall at once call him so."
His instinct for the flamboyant, his melodramatic appeal to ancient
heroes, awakened the historical curiosity of millions. Even in error,
Heinrich and Sophia grandly advanced public knowledge. People
everywhere were fascinated by the Schliemanns' courage and determination. The vast watching public came to believe that the earth
held relics and messages from real people in the distant past.

Heinrich's contribution to the techniques of field archaeology
was not inconsiderable. When twentieth-century archaeologists attack him for destroying en route relics he had not planned to discover, they forget the primitive state of archaeology in his day. In
stratigraphy he pioneered by applying to human relics the principles
that others had already applied to geology. Homer's *Iliad* was not
mere "humanized sun myths," as the oversubtle German scholars
were then insisting. Even by his mistakes Schliemann proved the reality of a Homeric civilization by unearthing the pre-Homeric civilization out of which it grew. To the canonical four civilizations:
Babylonia, Egypt, Greece, and Rome, he added two more from
"prehistory." If there were these two, then why not many more?

Schliemann's successor, Sir Arthur Evans, who took up his clues
to unearth still another scintillating civilization at Knossos in Crete
in 1900, acknowledged his debt:

> Less than a generation back the origin of Greek civiliza-
> tion, and with it the sources of all great culture that has ever
> been, were wrapped in an impenetrable mist. That ancient
> world was still girt round within its narrow confines by the
> circling "Stream of Ocean." Was there anything beyond?

The fabled kings and heroes of the Homeric Age, with their palaces and strongholds, were they aught, after all, but more or less humanized sun myths?

One man had faith, accompanied by works, and in Dr. Schliemann the science of classical antiquity found its Columbus. Armed with the spade, he brought to light from beneath the mounds of ages a real Troy; at Tiryns and Mycenae he laid bare the palace and the tombs and treasures of Homeric Kings. A new world opened to investigation, and the discoveries of its first explorer were followed up successfully by Dr. Tsountas and others on Greek soil. The eyes of observers were opened, and the traces of this prehistoric civilization began to make their appearance far beyond the limits of Greece itself.

But jealousy of scholarly competitors and the needs of sensational journalism made the glitter of Trojan and Mycenaean gold seem an indictment. Was Schliemann only a mercenary treasure hunter, like others less celebrated? Did he care less to enrich knowledge than to fill his own coffers? Even these accusations had the advantage of focusing public interest on the new worlds of archaeology. But they were unfounded. If Schliemann had not quickly removed the Trojan treasure from Turkey, there would have been little left for historians to study. To the Greek nation he gave all the treasure he unearthed at Mycenae and elsewhere, now splendidly displayed in the museum at Athens. For all his labors and risks, financed by him personally, he had no compensation except his celebrity and the satisfaction of kindling enthusiasm for his beloved Greece.

In the new world of publicity, others did Schliemann's work for him. Back in Winckelmann's time, to be stirred by his enthusiasm for classical Greece you had to read his books. But now, with Schliemann's own shrewd assist, every turn of the archaeologist's spade became news. The reading public did not have to wait for heavy tomes to enjoy the adventures of excavation. Newspaper readers held their breath, watching daily for Schliemann's dispatches to *The Times* of London, the *Daily Telegraph*, and *The New York Times*.

The Turkish government's refusal of a permit or the arrogance of a petty official became an international cause célèbre, advertised in letters from Schliemann himself, or in lengthy reports with others' by-lines but later revealed to be his work. Of course, he was made a Fellow of honorary and learned societies, and even the London Grocers' Association invited him to lecture and elected him to membership. His portrait by an artist of the *Illustrated London News* was reprinted across the world, making a trademark of Schliemann's broad forehead and heavy moustache, and reporters inventoried his dandyish wardrobe of fifty suits, twenty hats, forty-two pairs of shoes, thirty walking sticks and fifteen riding crops.

When Dom Pedro II, emperor of Brazil, a devotee of the classics, came with his Empress to visit Turkey, Schliemann, using his fluent Portuguese, toured them through the digs at Hissarlik, after which the Emperor declared himself fully persuaded that this was the true site of Homer's Troy. At Mycenae the Emperor's party was served a sensational luncheon in the depths of the famous Treasury of Atreus, to the delight of the avid press corps. Sophia, of course, added a touch of living romance not commonly found at prehistoric diggings. Heinrich and Sophia became the royal family of archaeology. The young Greek beauty was a welcome variant on the stereotype of fragile Victorian femininity. "The part I have taken in the discoveries is but small," she modestly confessed, "in Troy as well as in Mycenae. I have only superintended thirty workmen." After the upper layer of pebbles was removed from the tombs in Mycenae, "from thence it was exceedingly difficult, because, on our knees in the mud, my husband and I had to cut out the pebbles, to cut away the layer of clay, and to take out one by one the precious jewels."

In London the Royal Archaeological Institute held a special meeting on June 8, 1877, to honor Heinrich and Sophia. The spotlight was on the glowing Sophia, doubly escorted into the hall on the arm of Lord Talbot, the president, and of William E. Gladstone, who had requested the privilege. The address was given by Sophia. Lord Talbot had praised her "as the first lady who has ever been identified in a work so arduous and stupendous, you have achieved a reputation which many will envy—some may emulate—but none can ever surpass." The address of the twenty-five-year-old Sophia dazzled by its erudition and eloquence. In her admiration for Britain she archly confessed that the sin of the ancient Greeks was "envy." Then she read a paean to the Greek sky and the Greek mind, and recalled that the Greek language was so beautiful that "the mere sound filled my husband with wild enthusiasm at a time when he did not know yet a word of Greek." She concluded with "an appeal to the English ladies to teach their children the sonorous language of my ancestors, so that they may be enabled to read 'Homer' and our other immortal classics in the original." At the end she was saluted by a standing ovation. "As I heard and saw the ovation given to my Sophithion by such a notable assemblage," Heinrich wrote, "I could only wonder why the great gods of Olympus had given me this woman as a wife, friend, colleague and lover. My eyes ran with tears so I could barely see."

The press corps that followed the Schliemanns made their own demands. When, as at Tiryns, the digging was slow, *The New York Times* correspondent immediately announced that Heinrich's luck had run out—only days before one of his most spectacular finds, the remains of a palace rivaling that at Troy or Mycenae. In those primitive decades of the daily press, cameras were still cumbersome, and only barely portable. When Schliemann unearthed the remarkably preserved bodies in the tombs at Mycenae, he had no photographer along and so sent urgently for an artist to paint likenesses before the bodies disintegrated. His books on his excavations still contained no photographs, though some of the drawings were copied from photographs. The first report on archaeological excavation to include photography was not Schliemann's but the German archaeologist Alexander Conze's report on his diggings in Samothrace (1873). When we compare these photographs with the rude line illustrations of earlier reports, we see how much the camera has increased the vividness of history, making millions eager to see more.

THE DISCOVERY OF PREHISTORY

I N the eighteenth century, when Buffon stretched the calendar of nature into tantalizing eons, pious Christians still found the Biblical chronology by which Archbishop Ussher had fixed the creation at 4004 B.C. too comforting to abandon. For them the whole course of early history seemed to run from Eden through Jerusalem, and was amply chronicled in the Bible. The ancient events that concerned Christians had occurred exclusively in and around the Mediterranean, and the human heritage was the heritage of Greece and Rome. When Newton made the voyage of the Argonauts the base line for his chronology, he too kept Biblical events in sharpest focus.

But what had happened *before* Bible times? Today we may be amazed that so few Christians asked that question. Yet for believing Christians the question seemed meaningless: What happened *before* history? Before anything really happened? Not until the mid-nineteenth century did the word "prehistory" enter European vocabularies. Meanwhile thoughtful Europeans had somehow excluded from their historical ken most of the earthly past.

Along with the plants and animals and minerals brought back to Europe by missionaries, merchants, explorers, and naturalists came human artifacts for "cabinets of curiosities," familiar features of the households of the rich and the powerful. In the Middle Ages such curious, ancient, and precious objects had been occasionally exhibited too in churches, monasteries, colleges, and universities. In the Renaissance, regal collections including the booty of battle, the gifts of ambassadors, and the works of court artists adorned the palaces of popes and Medicis. So were born the great Vatican collections, the Uffizi and the Pitti in Florence, the Louvre in Paris, the Escorial near Madrid, and others in ducal capitals like Dresden, where Winckelmann was first inspired. These were for the delight of a privileged few.

The eighteenth century in Europe saw a new kind of collection, a novel institution, the *public* museum. The British government pioneered by acquiring the collections of Sir Hans Sloane in 1753, which were opened to the public in 1759. Some private collections, like the Vatican museums, were voluntarily opened to the public. Others, like the Louvre, were seized by revolutionaries for the whole citizenry. Across Europe a new museum public expected to learn, to be delighted, to be entertained. The word "tourist" entered the English language after 1800 for the mobile community of transient spectators. The hopes of breathless museum-explorers were exaggerated by the distances they had traveled.

In the United States and wherever there had not been palaces or royal collections, the public had to start from scratch. New World counterparts appeared: Peale's Museum (1784) in Philadelphia, the Smithsonian Institution (1846) in Washington, and others in South America. Across Asia—in India, Siam, China, Japan—the great collections generally remained the preserve of princely courts or went into the inner sanctums of temples. Only revolutions of one kind or another would open these treasures to public view. From conquered lands—from Egypt, Greece, Rome, and Persia—works of painting and sculpture, and even whole buildings, were transported to the great museums in London, Paris, Amsterdam, or Berlin.

As the European museums grew, at first they showed only the sorts of objects that aristocratic dilettantes had collected for prestige or out of curiosity. Objects of beauty held the spotlight, with occasional items of historical association, such as old crowns, scepters, and orbs, or a rare scientific instrument like an orrery. Objects that were not obviously beautiful or conspicuously strange aroused little interest. Yet, as it turned out, it was precisely these crude anonymous objects that would open prehistoric vistas and give the public a new vocabulary for all history. As we have seen, surviving *objects* had a special power to help people grasp the past. But the buried relics in Rome and Greece simply documented a past familiar from sacred or classical literature. The discovery of prehistory through objects would reach back far beyond the written word and vastly extend the dimensions of human history.

A strange series of coincidences gave the leading role in this discovery to a Danish businessman, Christian Jürgensen Thomsen (1788–1865). Without the erudition of a Scaliger or the mathematical genius of a Newton, he was a man of superlative common sense, richly endowed with the virtues of the dedicated amateur. His passion for curious objects was matched by his talent for awakening the curiosity of the new museum public. Born in Copenhagen, the eldest of six sons of a prosperous shipowner, he was trained for business. He came to know the family of a Danish consul who had served in Paris during the French Revolution, and who had brought back collections purchased from the panicked aristocracy. When young Christian, still only fifteen, helped his friends unpack their treasures, they gave him a few old coins to begin his own collection, and by the time he was nineteen he was a respected numismatist. In 1807, when the British fleet bombarded Copenhagen harbor to keep the Danish fleet from Napoleon, buildings went up in flames, and Christian joined the emergency fire brigade. Working through the night, he rescued the coins of a leading numismatist whose house was hit, and carried them to safety with the Keeper of the Royal Cabinet of Antiquities.

Copenhagen's newly established Royal Commission for the Preservation of Danish Antiquities was being flooded by miscellaneous old objects sent in by public-spirited citizens. The aged secretary of the commission could not face the accumulating pile. It was time for a younger man—and an opportunity made to order for Thomsen, then twenty-seven and known for his own beautifully organized collection of coins. "Mr. Thomsen is admittedly only a dilettante," the bishop on the commission conceded, "but a dilettante with a wide range of knowledge. He has no university degree, but in the present state of scientific knowledge I hardly consider that fact as being a disqualification." Accordingly, young Thomsen was honored with the post of unpaid nonvoting secretary. As it turned out, Thomsen's lack of academic learning equipped him with the naïveté that archaeology needed at that moment.

The dusty shelves of the commission's storerooms overflowed with unlabeled odd bundles. How could Thomsen put them in order? "I had no previous example on which to base the ordering of such a collection," Thomsen confessed, nor had he money to hire a professor to classify objects by academic categories. So he applied the commonsense procedures learned in his father's shipping warehouse. Opening the parcels, first he separated them into objects of stone, of metal, and of pottery. Then he subdivided these according to their apparent use as weapons, tools, food containers, or religious objects. With no texts to guide him, he simply looked at the objects, then asked himself what questions would be asked by museum visitors who saw them for the first time.

When Thomsen opened his museum to the public in 1819, visitors saw the objects sorted into three cabinets. The first contained objects of stone; the second, objects of bronze; the third, objects of iron. This exercise in museum housekeeping led Thomsen to suspect that objects made of similar materials might be relics of the same era. To his amateur eye it seemed that the objects of stone might be older than similar metal objects, and that the bronze objects might be older than those of iron. He shared this elementary suggestion with learned antiquarians, to whom he later modestly gave credit for the idea.

His notion was not entirely novel, but the similar notions found in classical authors were fanciful and misleading. In the Beginning, according to Hesiod, Cronos created men of the Golden Age who never grew old. Labor, war, and injustice were unknown. They eventually became guardian spirits on earth. Then in the Silver Age, when men lost their reverence for the gods, Zeus punished them and buried them among the dead. The Bronze Age, which followed (when even houses were made of bronze), was a time of endless strife. After the brief interlude of a Heroic Age of godlike leaders in their Isles of the Blessed, came Hesiod's own unfortunate Iron Age. Yet worse was still in store for mankind, a future of men born senile, and of universal decay.

Thomsen was not well enough educated to try to fit his museum objects into this appealing literary scheme. He was more interested in objects than in words. There were already "too many books," he complained, and he was not eager to add his own. But finally, in 1836, he produced his practical *Guide to Scandinavian Antiquities*, which outlined his famous Three-Age System. This, his only book, translated into English, French, and German, and spread across Europe, was an invitation to "Pre-History."

It was hard for European scholars at the time to imagine that human experience before writing could have been divided into the epochs that Thomsen suggested. It seemed more logical to assume that stone tools were always used by the poor, while their betters always used bronze or iron. Thomsen's commonsense scheme did not please the pedants. If there was a Stone Age, they scoffed, then why not also an Age of Crockery, a Glass Age, and a Bone Age? Thomsen's scheme, refined but not abandoned by scholars in the next century, proved to be more than an exercise in museum management. It carried the plain message that human history had somehow developed in homogeneous stages that reached across the world. And he arranged the objects in his museum according to his "principle of progressive culture."

Thomsen showed how much was to be learned, not only from those ancient sculptures that embodied Winckelmann's ideal of beauty but even from the simple tools and crude weapons of anonymous prehistoric man. Opening his collections free to everybody, Thomsen offered lively talks about the everyday experience of people in the remote past. A deft lecturer, he would hide some interesting little object behind his coattails, then suddenly produce it at the point in his story when that kind of object—a bronze utensil or an iron weapon—first appeared in history.

Following Thomsen's hints, archaeologists discovered and explored the trash heaps of the past. Their paths into history no longer ran only through the gold-laden tombs of ancient kings, but also through the buried kitchen middens ("middens," from an Old Scandinavian word for muck or dunghill). The first excavation of these unlikely sources was the work mainly of Thomsen's disciple Jens Jacob Worsaae (1821–1885). At the age of fifteen he had become Thomsen's museum assistant and during the next four years spent his holidays digging into the ancient barrows of Jutland with the aid of two laborers paid by his parents. With his athletic temperament and his outdoor enthusiasms he was the ideal complement to the museum-oriented Thomsen. In 1840, when he was only nineteen, using stratigraphy and the field evidence from Danish barrows and peat bogs, he published an article confirming Thomsen's Three-Age theory and assigning prehistoric objects to a Stone Age, a Bronze Age, or an Iron Age. He, too, was suggesting latitudes of time, throughout Denmark and beyond. A dozen years later, in 1853, the Swiss archaeologist Ferdinand Keller (1800–1881), when exploring the lake dwellings of Lake Zurich, concluded that "in Switzerland the three ages of stone, bronze, and iron, are quite as well represented as in Scandinavia."

Some obvious difficulties plagued these prophets of prehistory. How could you stretch human experience to fill the thousands of years of the past opened by Buffon and the geologists? How much neater to fit all pre-Christian history into the comfortable 4004 years B.C. defined by Archbishop Ussher! And then there were new problems created by the geologists, who now revealed that northern Europe had been covered by ice when Stone Age men were living in caves in southern France. To correlate all these facts required a still more sophisticated approach to the early human past. If the Stone Age people of southern Europe advanced northward only after the retreat of the glaciers, then the three universal stages were reached at different times in different places.

To make the Three-Age scheme fit the whole human past in Europe was not easy. The so-called Age of Stone in Thomsen's museum was represented by polished stone artifacts of the kind people would be tempted to send in as curios. Meanwhile, Worsaae, out in the field, was hinting that the Age of Stone was far more extensive and more ancient than was suggested by these skillfully polished stone implements. On the digging sites each object unearthed could be studied not as an isolated curio but among all the remains of a Stone Age community. And these too might provide clues to other Stone Age communities across the world.

Worsaae's opportunity came in 1849, when a wealthy Dane named Olsen was trying to improve his large estate called Meilgaard on the northeast coast of Jutland. Building a road, he sent his workmen in search of gravel for surfacing material. When they dug into a bank a half-mile from the shore, they found no gravel but luckily hit an eight-foot layer of oyster-shells, which was even better for their purpose. Mixed with the shells they found pieces of flint and animal bones. One small bone object two and a half inches long caught their attention. Shaped like a four-fingered hand, it was plainly the work of human craft. Perhaps it had been made for a comb.

Olsen, the proprietor, sharing the popular interest in antiquities which had been stimulated by Thomsen, sent the object to the museum in Copenhagen, where Worsaae's curiosity was aroused. Shell heaps recently turned up elsewhere in Denmark had brought to light flaked flint, odd pottery fragments, and crude stone objects similar to the Meilgaard comb. Perhaps this mound of oyster shells "had been a sort of eating-place for the people of the neighborhood in the earliest prehistoric times. This would account for the ashes, the bones, the flints and the potsherds." Perhaps here, at long last, modern man might visit an authentic Stone Age community. And actually imagine Stone Age men and women at their everyday meals. Worsaae observed that the shells had all been opened, which would not have been the case if they were merely washed up from the shore.

When other scholars disagreed, each with his own theory, the Danish Academy of Sciences appointed a commission. Worsaae, with a zoologist and a geologist, was assigned to interpret these shell heaps found along the ancient Danish shore. These "shell middens," the commission concluded, were really kitchen middens, which meant that now for the first time the historian could enter into the daily life of ancient peoples. Trash heaps might be gateways to prehistory. Such a discovery could not have been made indoors in a museum, but only on the spot in the field. Since the crudely crafted artifacts of the kitchen middens were never polished, unlike the polished stone artifacts of a later Stone Age, they were not likely to be noticed by laymen or sent to a museum. The kitchen middens opened another vast epoch of human prehistory—an early Stone Age, which extended behind the later Stone Age of polished stonework.

Thomsen and his museum collaborators had done their work of publicizing archaeology so well that the question now raised—whether the Stone Age really should be divided into two clearly defined stages—was no longer an arcane conundrum for university professors. The issue was hotly debated in the public proceedings of the Danish Academy. Worsaae's opponents insisted that the shell heaps were only the picnic sites of the Stone Age visitors who had left their best implements elsewhere. The king of Denmark, Frederick VII, who shared the growing interest in antiquities, had excavated middens on his own estate and even wrote a monograph with his interpretation. In 1861, to "settle" the issue, he summoned the leading scholars to a full-dress public meeting at Meilgaard, where he would preside. This royal conclave, no routine academic conference, would be celebrated with the panoply of a coronation. Besides hearing a debate, all those invited would witness the ritual excavation of a new portion of the mound. In the mid-June heat, archaeologists dug into the celebrated mound from eight in the morning till six in the evening, wearing their official "archaeologist's" uniform out of respect for the King. When King Frederick had appointed Worsaae curator of his private collection of antiquities in 1858, he had playfully designated this archaeologist's uniform (high collar and tight-fitting jacket, topped off by a pillbox hat), which was now de rigueur at the diggings.

The lords of surrounding estates entertained the King and his party with banquets and dancing to band music every night. In honor of their royal visitor the neighbors created triumphal arches, and the King was accompanied everywhere by his mounted guard in full livery. A royal welcome to the Old Stone Age!

Early in the meeting it was agreed that Worsaae had won his

scholarly point, which now would be proclaimed in royal company and for the whole nation. "I had the especial satisfaction," Worsaae wrote, "of seeing that, among the many hundred stone implements discovered among the oysters, not a single specimen was found with any traces of polishing or of superior culture." And he reported with relish how a human fillip was added to the formal splendor. "Only at the last minute, after we had frequently remarked on this fact, did two polished axes turn up, of a completely different type, which some practical joker had inserted in the heap to cheat us." The practical joker, it was widely assumed, was King Frederick himself.

Seldom has so drab an epoch of history been so splendidly inaugurated. But now, to the royal Danish imprimatur was added the near-unanimous agreement of scholars across Europe. What came to be called the Culture of Kitchen Middens (c. 4000–c. 2000 B.C.) was discovered in due course across the northern European coasts, and in Spain, Portugal, Italy, and North Africa. In southern Africa, northern Japan, in the islands of the Pacific, and in the coastal regions of both Americas, Kitchen Middens cultures seemed to have persisted into a later era. Once identified and placed in the chronicle of human development, the middens provided revealing latitudes of time—and a new vividness for the prehistoric past.

Worsaae, who became professor of archaeology at Copenhagen, and then succeeded Thomsen as director of the museum, is often called "the first professional archaeologist." His mentor Thomsen called him a "heaven stormer." Worsaae accurately praised Thomsen's Three-Age System as "the first clear ray . . . shed across the Universal prehistoric gloom of the North and the World in general." Not in the heavily documented realms of recent history but in the dark recesses of earliest times would mankind first discover the "universality" of history. The first discovery of the community of all human experience in eras and epochs, the worldwide phenomena of human history, was made when "prehistory" was parsed into the three ages: Stone, Bronze, and Iron. And as Worsaae explored the boundaries between the three ages, he began to raise some profound questions that were explosive for fundamentalist Christians. One of these was the problem, still agitated by anthropologists: independent invention or cultural diffusion?

The disturbing notion, suggested by bold thinkers from Buffon to Darwin—that man had existed long before the Biblical date of Creation in 4004 B.C.—was beginning to be accepted by the scientific community. But the remote antiquity of man was popularized not so much by a theory as by the discovery of a vast and undeniable subject matter, a new dark continent of time, prehistory. More persuasively than a theory, the artifacts themselves seemed to bear witness to a chronology of prehistory that argued the evolution of man's culture.

Gradually, as the word "prehistory" came into use in the European languages, the idea entered popular consciousness. The exhibition in Hyde Park in 1851, which purported to survey all the works of humankind, still gave no glimpse of prehistory. Then, at the Universal Exhibition in Paris in 1867, the Hall of the History of Labor showed an extensive collection of artifacts from all over Europe and from Egypt. The official guide to Prehistoric Walks at the Universal Exhibition offered three lessons from the new science: the law of the progress of humanity; the law of similar development; and the high antiquity of man. In that same year the announcement of the first Congrès International Préhistorique de Paris brought the first official use of the word "prehistoric."

Prehistory entered the curriculum of public education along with the companion ideas of evolution. Charles Darwin's disciple and leading popularizer, John Lubbock (Lord Avebury, 1834–1913), made a European reputation by fitting prehistory into evolution. His *Pre-Historic Times* (1865), which coined the words "Paleolithic" and "Neolithic" for the "Polished Stone Age," was widely read by laymen, who imbibed prehistory and evolution in a single delightful read. *The Origin of Civilization* (1871) drew on widely separated evidences of centers of the Three Ages to argue that the crucial inventions had arisen independently. All of which seemed to support Herbert Spencer's argument that "Progress is not an accident but a necessity. It is a fact of nature."

When Schliemann came to London in 1875, William E. Gladstone saluted him by recalling that when they were growing up, "prehistoric times lay before our eyes like a silver cloud covering the whole of the lands that, at different periods of history, had become illustrious and interesting. . . . Now we are beginning to see through this dense mist and the cloud is becoming transparent, and the figures of real places, real men, real facts are slowly beginning to reveal to us their outlines." The pioneer anthropologist Edward B. Tylor optimistically announced in 1871 that prehistory finally had "taken its place in the general scheme of knowledge"—extending the vistas of human history a thousandfold.

*   *   *

The Three Ages, the worldwide epochs of prehistory, made it easier to imagine other epochs that transcended city, region, or nation. By defining latitudes of history, man had enlarged his view of the world's past and present. The invention of grand historical "Eras," "Epochs," or "Ages" which overreached political bounds would provide time receptacles ample enough to include the whole data of past communities of culture, yet small enough for persuasive definition. Few other concepts have done so much to deprovincialize man's thinking. The Ages of history would dominate (and sometimes tyrannize) the modern historian, focusing his vision on clusters of past experience—the Great Age of Greece, the Middle Ages, the Age of Feudalism, the Renaissance, the Enlightenment, Modern Industrialism, the Rise of Capitalism, etc.

These notions were to time what the "species" were to nature, a way of classifying experience to make it useful. They were the taxonomy of history. Of course, just as with "species," there was the danger that the label would be taken for the thing, the mere name of an "epoch" might somehow become a force governing interpretation of the events. Still, the advantages of the epochal way of thinking far outweighed the risks. The convenient groupings of men, events, achievements, and institutions helped bring some order into the puzzling miscellany of the past. The six "world periods" (*aetates*) into which the early Church Fathers had divided all time before the coming of Christ were not historical but prophetic and theological. They did not characterize the past, but were categories of prophecy, stages toward the Incarnation.

"The 'spirit of the age,'" John Stuart Mill (1806–1873) explained in 1831, "is in some measure a novel expression. I do not believe that it is to be met with in any work exceeding fifty years in antiquity. The idea of comparing one's own age with former ages, or with our notion of those which are yet to come, had occurred to philosophers; but it never before was itself the dominant idea of any age. Before men begin to think much and long on the peculiarities of their own times, they must have begun to think that those times are, or are destined to be, distinguished in a very remarkable manner from the times that preceded them." The idea of homogeneous epochs in history, he added, was consistent either with the notion of cycles, or with "the idea of a trajectory or progress." Mill plumped for "the progressiveness of the human race . . . the foundation on which a method of philosophizing in the social science has been of late years erected." How could one imagine "progress" without some notion of the coherence of events in each epoch?

Now a host of new influences—museums, archaeological excavations, international expositions, along with the daily press and the periodical press—was spreading a consciousness of history beyond academic circles, preparing people to believe that they lived in an Age of Progress. "There is a progressive change," John Stuart Mill concluded from his study of history, "both in the character of the human race, and in their outward circumstances so far as moulded by themselves . . . in each successive age the principal phenomena of society are different from what they were in the age preceding, and still more different from any previous age."

A vivid reminder of these newly drawn latitudes of time was the invention in the mid-nineteenth century of the "Age of the Renaissance" to describe an era in Europe from about the fourteenth to the seventeenth century. The French nationalist historian Jules Michelet entitled the seventh volume of his History of France *The Renaissance* (1855), and saw the era dominated by "the discovery of the world and the discovery of man." Then the Swiss historian Jacob Burckhardt's *Civilization of the Renaissance in Italy* (1860) offered a classic portrait of the men and institutions that gave the era its character and made it the "mother" of modern European civilization. So a student, confident in the jargon of historical epochs, could characterize Dante as "a man who stood with one foot in the Middle Ages and with the other saluted the rising star of the Renaissance." In our century much of the scholarly debate over the nature of the Renaissance has concerned the latitudes of time: When did the Renaissance begin? Was it the same phenomenon in different parts of Europe?

Two grand assumptions, which lay beneath talk of the Renaissance, shaped future thinking about man's role in all history. First, belief that every age somehow exuded a prevailing spirit—what German scholars called the *Zeitgeist*, what Carl Becker called the "Climate of Opinion"—which favored certain notions and institutions. Second, that within these limits, men had the power to make history. Renaissance men made a Renaissance. If, as Burckhardt explained, they made the state "a work of art," in later ages, too, men could accomplish the unprecedented.

THE INFINITE AND THE
INFINITESIMAL

F ROM Hiroshima on August 6, 1945, the world received the
shocking discovery that man had opened the dark continent
of the atom. Its mysteries would haunt the twentieth century.
Yet for two thousand years the "atom" had been the most arcane of
philosophers' concerns. The Greek word *atomos* meant the smallest
unit of matter, supposed to be indestructible. Now atom was a
household word, a threat and a promise without precedent.

The first atomic philosopher was a legendary Greek, Leucippus,
suspected to have lived in the fifth century B.C. Democritus, his
pupil, who gave to atomism its classic form as a philosophy, was so
amused at human follies that he was known as "the laughing philosopher." Yet he was one of the first to argue against mankind's decline
from a mythical Golden Age and to preach a gospel of progress. If
the whole universe consisted only of atoms and void, it was not infinitely complex but somehow intelligible, and there might be no limit
to man's power.

In one of the greatest Latin poems, *De rerum natura*, Lucretius
(c. 95 B.C.–c. 55 B.C.) perpetuated ancient atomism. Aiming to free
people from fear of the gods, he showed that the whole world was
made of void and atoms that moved by their own laws, that the soul
died with the body, and that therefore there was no reason to fear
death or supernatural powers. Understanding nature, he said, was

the only way to peace of mind. The Church Fathers, committed to the Christian afterlife, attacked Lucretius, and he was ignored or forgotten during the Middle Ages but became one of the most influential figures in the Renaissance.

So atomism first entered the modern world as a system of philosophy. Just as the Pythagorean symmetry provided a framework for Copernicus, just as geometry enticed Kepler, and as the Aristotelian perfect circle charmed Harvey, so the philosophers' "indestructible" atoms appealed to chemists and physicists. "The theory of Democritus relating to atoms," Francis Bacon observed, "is, if not true, at least applicable with excellent effect to the exposition of nature." Descartes (1596–1650) invented his own notion of infinitely small particles moving through a medium he called the ether. Another French philosopher, Pierre Gassendi (1592–1655), seemed to confirm Democritus and offered still another new version of atomism, which Robert Boyle (1627–1691) adapted to chemistry, proving that the proverbial "elements"—earth, air, fire, and water—were not elementary at all.

The prophetic insights of a Jesuit mathematician R. G. Boscovich (1711–1787) charted paths for a new science of atomic physics. His bold notion of "point-centers" abandoned the old concept of an assortment of different solid atoms. The fundamental particles of matter, he suggested, were all identical, and matter was the spatial relations around these point-centers. Boscovich, coming to these notions from mathematics and astronomy, foreshadowed the increasingly intimate connection between the structure of the atom and the structure of the universe, between the infinitesimal and the infinite.

The experimental path into the atom was charted by John Dalton (1766–1844), a self-educated Quaker amateur, who picked up a suggestive notion from Lavoisier (1743–1794). A founder of modern chemistry, Lavoisier brought atomic theory back to earth when he finally made the atom a useful laboratory concept by defining an "element" as a substance that could not be broken down into other substances by any known method. Born to a family of weavers in Cumberland in the English Lake District, Dalton carried the mark of his modest origins all his life. At twelve he had taken charge of the Quaker school in his village. When he went on to teach in nearby Kendal, in the school library he found copies of Newton's *Principia*, Boyle's *Works*, and Buffon's *Natural History*, along with a two-foot reflecting telescope and a double microscope. There he came under the spell of a phenomenal blind natural philosopher, John Gough, who, Dalton wrote a friend, "understands well all the different branches of mathematics. . . . He knows by the touch, taste, and smell, almost every plant within twenty miles of this place." He would be celebrated by Wordsworth in his *Excursion*. From Gough, Dalton received his basic education in Latin, Greek, and French, his introduction to mathematics, astronomy, and all observational science. Following Gough's example, Dalton began keeping a daily meteorological record, which he continued until the day he died.

When Dissenters set up their own New College in Manchester, Dalton became professor of mathematics and natural philosophy. In the Manchester Literary and Philosophical Society he found an eager audience for his experiments. To them he offered his "Extraordinary Facts Relating to the Vision of Colours," probably the first systematic work on color blindness, from which John and his brother Jonathan both suffered. "Having been in my progress so often misled by taking for granted the results of others, I have determined to write as little as possible but what I can attest by my own experience." He observed the aurora borealis, suggested the origins of the trade winds, the causes of clouds and of rainfall, and incidentally made improvements in rain gauges, barometers, thermometers, and hygrometers. Dalton's interest in the atmosphere provided the approach to chemistry that led him to the atom.

Newton had expected the smallest invisible bodies to follow the quantitative laws governing the largest heavenly bodies. Chemistry would recapitulate astronomy. But how was man to grasp and measure the movements and mutual attractions of these invisible particles? In his *Principia*, Newton had speculated that phenomena of nature not described in that book "may all depend upon certain forces by which the particles of bodies, by some causes hitherto unknown, are either mutually impelled towards one another and cohere in regular figures, or are repelled and recede from one another."

Dalton went in search of "these primitive particles," seeking some experimental way to encompass them in a quantitative scheme. Since gases were the loosest, most mobile form of matter, Dalton focused on the atmosphere, the mixture of gases that comprised the air, which provided the point of departure for all his thinking about atoms. "Why does water not admit its bulk of every gas alike?" he asked his colleagues in 1803 in the Manchester Literary and Philosophical Society. "I am nearly persuaded that the circumstance depends upon the weight and number of the ultimate particles of the several gases—those whose particles are lightest and single being least absorbable, and the others more, according as they increase in weight and complexity." Dalton had discovered that contrary to the prevailing view the air was not a single vast chemical solvent but a mixture of gases, each of which remained distinct and acted independently. The product of his experiments was his epoch-making *TABLE: Of the Relative Weights of Ultimate Particles of Gaseous and Other Bodies.* Taking hydrogen as 1, he itemized twenty-one substances. Depicting the invisible "ultimate particles" as tiny solid balls, like pieces of shot but much smaller, he proposed to apply to them the Newtonian laws of the attractive forces of matter. He aimed at "a new view of the first principles of elements of bodies and their combinations," which "I doubt not . . . will in time . . . produce the most important changes in the system of chemistry, and reduce the whole to a science of great simplicity, and intelligible to the meanest understanding." When he showed a "particle of air resting on 4 particles of water," like "a square pile of shot" with each tiny globe touching its neighbors, he provided the ball-and-spoke model for organic chemistry in the century to come.

For his popular lectures Dalton invented his own "arbitrary marks as signs chosen to represent the several chemical elements or ultimate particles," displayed in a table of atomic weights. Of course, Dalton was not the first to use a shorthand for chemical substances— the alchemists had theirs. But he was probably the first to use such symbolism in a quantitative system of "ultimate particles." Making an atom of hydrogen his unit, he calculated the weight of molecules as the sum of the weights of component atoms, and so supplied a modern syntax for chemistry. The actual abbreviations using the first letter of each element's Latin name (H_2O, etc.) were designed by the Swedish chemist Berzelius (1779–1848).

The first reception of Dalton's atomic theory was anything but enthusiastic. The great Sir Humphry Davy quickly dismissed his notions as "rather more ingenious than important." But Dalton's ideas, elaborated in *A New System of Chemical Philosophy* (1808), were so persuasive that he was awarded the Royal Medal in 1826. Never forgetting his plebeian origins, he still remained aloof from the Royal Society in London, but was elected without his consent in 1822. Suspicious of the Society's aristocratic, dilettante tone, he felt more at home in Manchester, where he did most of his work, and he joined with Charles Babbage and helped found the British Association for the Advancement of Science to bring science to all the people. Theologically orthodox Newtonians would not believe that God had necessarily made His invisible "ultimate particles" invariable or indestructible. They shared Newton's suspicion that God had used His power "to vary the laws of Nature, and make worlds of several sorts in several parts of the universe."

Dalton's indestructible atom became the foundation of a rising science of chemistry, providing elementary principles—its laws of constant composition and of multiple proportions, its combination of chemical elements in the simple ratio of their atomic weights. "Chemical analysis and synthesis go no farther than to the separation of particles one from another, and their reunion," Dalton insisted. "No new creation or destruction of matter is within the reach of chemical agency. We might as well attempt to introduce a new planet into the solar system or annihilate one already in existence, as to create or destroy a particle of hydrogen." He continued to use the laws of visible heavenly bodies as his clues to the infinitesimal universe. The prophetic Sir Humphry Davy still remained unconvinced. "There is no reason," he said, "to suppose that any real indestructible principle has yet been discovered."

Dalton was only a Columbus. The Vespuccis were still to come, and when they came they would produce some delightful surprises and some terrifying shocks. Meanwhile, for a half-century, Dalton's indestructible solid atom served chemists well and was usefully elaborated. A French scientist, Gay-Lussac, showed that when atoms combined, it was not necessarily in the one-to-one fashion described by Dalton but might be in some other arrangement of simple integers. An Italian chemist, Avogadro (1776–1856), showed that equal volumes of gases at the same temperature and pressure contained equal numbers of molecules. And a Russian chemist, Mendeleyev, proposed a suggestive "periodic law" of the elements. If elements were arranged in the order of increasing atomic weight, then groups of elements of similar characteristics would recur periodically.

The dissolution of the indestructible solid atom would come from two sources, one familiar, the other quite novel—from the study of light and the discovery of electricity. Einstein himself described this historic movement as the decline of a "mechanical" view and the rise of a "field" view of the physical world, which helped put him on his own path to relativity, to new explanations and new mysteries.

On the wall of his study, Albert Einstein kept a portrait of Michael Faraday (1791–1867), and there could have been none more appropriate. For Faraday was the pioneer and the prophet of the grand revision that made Einstein's work possible. The world would no longer be a Newtonian scene of "forces at a distance," objects mutually attracted by the force of gravity inversely proportional to the square of the distance between them. The material world would become a tantalizing scene of subtle, pervasive "fields of force." This was just as radical as the Newtonian Revolution, and even more difficult for the lay mind to grasp.

Like the Copernican Revolution in astronomy, the "Field" Revolution in physics would defy common sense and carry the pioneer scientists once again into "the mists of paradox." If Michael Faraday had been trained in mathematics, he might not have been so ready for his surprising new vision. The son of a poor blacksmith on the outskirts of London, Faraday had to earn his own way from an early age, and when wartime prices were high in 1801, he was said to have lived on a loaf of bread for a week. His parents were members of the Sandemanian Church, a small fundamentalist and ascetic Scottish Protestant sect, which, like the Quakers, believed in a lay clergy and opposed the accumulation of wealth. He attended Sunday meetings regularly and remained an elder until his last years. In his much thumbed Bible the most marked passages were in the Book of Job. He had almost no formal education—"little more than the rudiments of reading, writing, and arithmetic at a common day-school" —but at the age of thirteen he luckily found employment with a friendly French émigré printer and bookbinder, a M. Riebau. At first he delivered the newspapers that Riebau loaned out and then he picked them up to be delivered again.

Among the books that came to Riebau's shop for binding was *The Improvement of the Mind,* by the hymn writer Isaac Watts, whose system of self-improvement Faraday followed by keeping the commonplace book that would eventually become his famous laboratory notebook. One day he received for rebinding the volume of the *Encyclopaedia Britannica* (3d. ed., 1797) that contained the article of 127 double-column pages on Electricity by an erratic "Mr. James Tytler, chemist." Demolishing the prevailing one-fluid and two-fluid theories of electricity, Tytler proposed that electricity was not a material flow at all but a kind of vibration, akin to light and heat. This tantalizing suggestion was the beginning of Faraday's pursuit of science.

In 1810 he began attending public lectures offered by the City Philosophical Society and then Humphry Davy's lectures at the Royal Institution. In December 1811 Faraday had impressed Davy by sending him the neatly bound and beautifully penned notes he had taken at Davy's lectures, along with his request for a post as his assistant. That October, Davy had been temporarily blinded by an explosion in his laboratory, and he now needed an amanuensis. Davy hired Faraday for one guinea a week and the use of two rooms at the top of the Institution with fuel and candles, laboratory aprons, and freedom to use the apparatus. At twenty, Faraday found himself in the laboratory of one of the greatest chemists of the age, where he could experiment at will. A dream come true!

Sir Humphry and Lady Davy rounded off Faraday's education by taking him along on their tour of the Continent in 1813–14, visiting France and Italy, meeting scientists, and sharing the talkative Davy's hopes and doubts. When Faraday returned to England in April 1815, Davy had inoculated him against easy generalizations and had renewed his passion for experiment. Back in the laboratory, he tested heating and lighting oils, and finally discovered benzene. He made the first known compounds of chlorine and carbon, which became ethylene, resulting from the first known substitution-reaction. He pioneered in the chemistry of steel alloys. What eventually proved crucial in his life was the commission from the Royal Society that led him to produce a new "heavy" optical glass with a high refractive index especially useful for experiments in polarized light.

Faraday's sanguine temperament was reinforced by a happy marriage to the sister of someone he had met at the City Philosophical Society. Sarah Bernard never shared the scientific interests that kept him awake nights, but said she was happy to be "the pillow of his mind."

In the new world of priority prizes his early successes even aroused the jealousy of his famous mentor. In 1824, when Faraday was proposed as a Fellow in the Royal Society for his feat of liquefying chlorine, Davy opposed his election and claimed that he himself was entitled to the credit. But Faraday was elected anyway.

Davy had been intrigued by recent theoretical efforts to adapt Newton's ideas to the needs of the chemist in the laboratory. The most attractive of these was Boscovich's "point-center" theory, which had described the atom not as a tiny billiard ball of impenetrable matter but as a center of forces. If the "ultimate particles" of matter should have this character, it might explain the interaction of chemical elements, their "affinities" and the ways of making stable compounds.

Boscovich had limited his radical suggestion to the chemical elements. When Faraday's passion for experiment was focused by chance on the uncharted realm of electricity, he was newly attracted by Boscovich's theory. In 1821 a friend asked Faraday to write for the *Philosophical Magazine* a comprehensive article explaining electromagnetism to the lay public. Current interest had been awakened when, just the previous summer, the Danish physicist Hans Christian Oersted (1777–1851) during the demonstration for an evening lecture showed that a current-carrying wire would deflect a magnetic needle. Following Oersted's clues, Faraday devised a simple apparatus of two beakers containing mercury, a current-carrying wire, and two cylindrical bar magnets. With this he elegantly demonstrated electromagnetic rotation, proving both that a current-carrying wire would rotate around the pole of a magnet and that the pole of a magnet would rotate around a current-carrying wire. Perhaps Faraday began to suspect that somehow surrounding a current-carrying wire there were circular lines of force. And perhaps the forces of magnetism and of electricity were somehow convertible. At this point it was lucky that Faraday was not a sophisticated mathematician. For then he might have followed the conventional path, like that taken by the French mathematical prodigy André Marie Ampère (1775–1836), and have tried to explain electromagnetism simply by a mathematical formulation of Newtonian centers of force. Faraday's naïve vision saw something else.

Without intending it, Faraday had already made the first recorded conversion of mechanical into electric energy. This was, of course, the crucial step toward the electric motor and the electric generator with all their transformations of daily life. Once again a revolution in science would depend on the defiance of common sense. Surprising though it might seem, the power of a magnet, unlike the Newtonian force of gravitation, was not focused in a massy object emanating straight lines of force-at-a-distance. In numerous experiments after 1821 Faraday was beginning to glimpse a bizarre phenomenon, and the possibility that the magnet and the electric current somehow created a "field of force."

Faraday, blessed with the amateur's naïve vision, was not seduced by the revered Newton's mathematical formulae. Faraday's experiments over the next twenty-five years—from his first wires and magnets rotating in beakers of mercury to his grand prophetic outlines of a modern field theory—eventually would open the way to a new vision of the universe. Through it all Faraday would be drawn by his simple Sandemanian faith in the unity and coherence of God's creation.

In 1831, when Faraday learned that Joseph Henry in Albany,

New York, had reversed the polarity of electromagnets by reversing the direction of the electric current, he set up his own experiments. He aimed to show how a moving magnet could generate a current of electricity. By an astonishingly simple experiment, which passed an electrostatic discharge through a wet string, he managed to show that static electricity was essentially not different from other kinds, and hence that all known kinds of electricity were identical. Then with his experiments in electrochemistry he showed that the decomposing power of electricity was directly proportional to the quantity of electricity in solution, and hence that electricity must somehow be the force of chemical affinity. Using a piece of blotting paper soaked in potassium iodide, he effected an electrostatic discharge into the air, so disposing of the Newtonian-based theory that electricity, like gravitation, was a force exerted from one "pole" to another. All these were clues to the existence of electric particles and to electric fields—openings toward fields of force with hints of the convertibility of forces and the unity of all phenomena.

By 1838 Faraday had the basis for a new theory of electricity. He developed a whole new vocabulary of such terms as "electrode," "cathode," and "electrolysis." Perhaps, he ventured, electric forces were intermolecular and electricity somehow transferred energy without transferring matter. Wary of using the term "current" because of its mechanical connotations, he described this transfer as a process in which minute particles were put under a strain, which was then conducted from particle to particle.

After a trying five-year interlude when his mind seemed hopelessly fatigued from these early years of relentless experiment, Faraday bounced back for a crucial next step in his chain of experiments. At this moment the young William Thomson (1824–1907), later famous as Lord Kelvin, had been puzzling over the nature of electricity and the difficulty of fitting it into the Newtonian scheme. In August 1845 Thomson wrote to Faraday describing his initial success in giving mathematical form to Faraday's notion of lines of force, and suggesting some further experiments. None of the eminent physicists of the day had been persuaded by Faraday.

But Thomson, then only twenty-one, was open to even wilder

possibilities. If there really were lines and fields of forces, might not experiment conceivably prove a kinship between electricity and light? Faraday determined to pursue the outlandish suggestion. At first the difficulties seemed insuperable. "Only the very strongest conviction that Light, Magnetism and Electricity must be connected . . . led me to resume the subject and persevere." On September 13, 1845, Faraday tried passing a ray through a piece of the "heavy glass" with a high refractive index that he had made fifteen years before, and in the field of a strong electromagnet. "There was an effect produced on the polarized ray," he recorded with satisfaction, "and thus magnetic force and light were proved to have relation to each other. This fact will most likely prove exceedingly fertile." He was reassured by finding that the angle of rotation of the ray of light was directly proportional to the strength of the electromagnetic force.

Faraday now found his earlier metaphor of interparticulate "strain" inadequate, and went on to suggest a "flood of power"—the electromagnet being a "habitation of lines of force." From comparing the action of different substances on the passage of magnetic force he contrasted "paramagnetics," which conducted the force well, with "diamagnetics," which conducted poorly. He then showed that his "lines of force" were not polar (directed to the nearest pole) as the old Newtonian theories would have suggested, but were continuous curves. His crucial conclusion, the axiom of modern "field" theory in physics, was that the energy of the magnet was not in the magnet itself but in the magnetic field.

Faraday had sketched the outline of a surprising new invisible world. Among these infinitesimal fields of forces exerted by mysterious minute entities modern physicists would find their New Worlds and their Dark Continents, with secrets of a still wider unity and mystery of phenomena. "I have long held an opinion, almost amounting to conviction," Faraday wrote to the Royal Society in 1845, "in common I believe with many other lovers of natural knowledge, that the various forms under which the forces of matter are made manifest have one common origin; or, in other words, are so directly related and mutually dependent, that they are convertible as it were, one into another, and possess equivalents of power in their action. In modern times the proofs of their convertibility have been accumulated to a very considerable extent, and a commencement made of the determination of their equivalent forces."

The succession of proofs that Faraday had prophesied moved with accelerating momentum in the next century. Communications among scientists were more continuous, and their achievements more collaborative than ever before. Sometimes it became a matter of chance who took (or was given) the credit for taking, the next step. Faraday's discoveries had been the product of an unmathematical mind. But the persuasiveness of the field theory would still depend on its being given a mathematical form. This was accomplished by Faraday's admirer James Clerk Maxwell (1831–1879), who translated Faraday's "lines" or "tubes" of force into a mathematical description of a continuous field. Just as Newton had given mathematical form to Galileo's insights, so, Einstein noted, Maxwell's equations performed a similar function for Faraday. "The formulation of these equations," Einstein and his collaborator Leopold Infeld called "the most important event in physics since Newton's time, not only because of their wealth of content, but also because they form a pattern for a new type of law." The features of these equations would appear "in all other equations of modern physics." These equations would become a basis, too, for Einstein's own theory of relativity. The next great step after Faraday in the revision of Newtonian physics and the dissolution of the "indestructible" atom came with the discovery of cathode rays, X-rays, and radioactivity. The clues to the electron were followed up by J. J. Thomson (1856–1940), who discovered minute invisible particles of uniform mass, only one eighteen-hundredth that of the hydrogen atom, which till then was the lightest known object. In 1911, Ernest Rutherford (1871–1937) discovered an atomic nucleus for the next generation of physicists to explore, as their predecessors had explored the electron.

The mysteries of the atom multiplied with every new discovery. The limits of mathematics were increasingly disclosed. In the mind of Einstein the unity of phenomena—the quest of Dalton and Faraday—brought "scientific" problems and paradoxes beyond the earlier ken of any but Hermetic philosophers. Just as physicists illustrated their atom by planetary and celestial systems, so the infinitesimal offered clues to the infinite. Time and space came together in a single tantalizing riddle, which led Einstein to conclude that "the eternal mystery of the world is its comprehensibility."

FROM

THE
CREATORS

"And, as imagination bodies forth
The forms of things unknown, the poet's pen
Turns them to shapes, and gives to airy nothing
A local habitation and a name."
SHAKESPEARE, *A Midsummer Night's Dream*

The pursuit of knowledge is only one path to human fulfilment. This companion book, also a view from the literate West, is a saga of Heroes of the Imagination. While *The Discoverers* told of the conquest of illusions—the illusions of knowledge—this will be a story of visions (and illusions) newly created. For this is a story of how creators in all the arts have enlarged, embellished, fantasized, and filigreed our experience. These creators, makers of the new, can never become obsolete, for in the arts there is no correct answer. The story of discoverers could be told in simple chronological order, since the latest science replaces what went before. But the arts are another story—a story of infinite addition. And each of us alone can experience how the new adds to the old and how the old enriches the new, how Picasso enhances Leonardo and how Homer illuminates Joyce.

THE SILENCE OF THE BUDDHA

THE Buddha had no answer to the riddle of creation. Much of his appeal to millions around the world for twenty-five hundred years came from his commonsense refusal to try to answer unanswerable questions. "Is the universe eternal or not eternal, or both?" "Is the universe infinite in space or not infinite, or both or neither?" The Buddha listed these among the fourteen questions to which he allowed no reply.

"Have I ever said to you," the Buddha asked, "come, be my disciple and I will reveal to you the beginning of things?" "Sir, you have not." "Or, have you ever said to me I will become your pupil for you will reveal to me the beginning of things?" "Sir, I have not." His only object, the Buddha reminded his disciple, was "the thorough destruction of ill for the doer thereof." "If then," the Buddha went on, "it matters not to that object whether the beginning of things be revealed . . . what use would it be to have the beginning of things revealed?"

This hardheaded approach may surprise us in the West, where we commonly think of Buddhism as a mystic way of thought. But a wholesome reticence entered the mainstream of Buddhism, and came to be called the Silence of the Buddha. Confucius, too, had his own list of things "about which the master never spoke"—"weird things, physical exploits, disorders, and spirits." Inquiry for its own sake, merely to know more, philosophy on the Greek model, had no

place either in the Buddhist tradition. Greek philosophers, beginning with Thales, were men of speculative temperament. What is
the world made of? What are the elements and the processes by
which the world is transformed? Greek philosophy and science were
born together, of the passion to know.

The Buddha's aim was not to know the world or to improve it
but to escape its suffering. His whole concern was salvation. It is not
easy for us in the West to understand or even name this Buddhist
concern. To say that the Buddhists had a "philosophy" would be
misleading. Not only did the Buddha remain silent when asked
about the first creation. He despised "speculations about the creation of the land or sea" as "low conversation," which was like tales
of kings, of robbers, of ministers of state, talk about women and
about heroes, gossip at street corners, and ghost stories. He urged
disciples to follow his example and not fritter away their energy on
such trifles.

He offered an original, if slightly malicious, explanation of how
the idea of a single Creator had ever got started. He said it began as
only a rumor, invented by the conceit of a well-known figure inherited from the prolific Hindu mythology. The culprit was none other
than Brahma, of wondrous and various genealogy. Originally associated with the primeval Prajapati, whom we have met, Brahma
was said to have been born from a golden egg. Some credited him
with creating the earth, others said that he had sprung from a lotus
that issued from the protector-god Vishnu's navel. In the Buddha's
lifetime Hindus still worshiped Brahma as a creator god.

The Lord Buddha explained how, at one stage in the endless cycles of the universe, this character had cast himself in the role of
Creator:

> Now there comes a time when this world begins to
> evolve, and then the World of Brahma appears, but it is
> empty. And some being, whether because his allotted span is
> past or because his merit is exhausted, quits his body in the
> world of Radiance and is born in the empty World of
> Brahma, where he dwells for a long, long time. Now, be-
> cause he has been so long alone he begins to feel dissatisfac-

tion and longing, and wishes that other beings might come and live with him. And indeed soon other beings quit their bodies in the World of Radiance and come to keep him company in the World of Brahma.

Then the being who was first born there thinks: "I am Brahma, the mighty Brahma, the Conqueror, the Uncon-quered, the All-seeing, the Lord, the Maker, the Creator, the Supreme Chief, the Disposer, the Controller, the Father of all that is or is to be. I have created all these beings, for I merely wished that they might be and they have come here!" And the other beings . . . think the same, because he was born first and they later. And the being who was born first lived longer and was more handsome and powerful than the others. . . .

That is how your traditional doctrine comes about that the beginning of things was the work of the god Brahma.

Following the Buddha, the Buddhist scriptures repeatedly boasted their freedom from such silly personal conceits as belief in a Creator.

*   *   *

The indifference of the Buddha to the tantalizing questions of creation had a source in the experience of the Gautama Buddha him-self. His career was quite the opposite of that which led Confucius to his own kind of indifference. Confucius was uninterested in the ori-gin of the world because it had no current bearing on the reforma-tion of man or of government. The Buddha was interested in escaping the world and so aimed to make life on earth irrelevant. Both men were teachers. While Confucius offered maxims for the politician, the Buddha's life was raw material for legends, folklore, and fairy tales.

The obscure Confucius was frustrated in his unsuccessful search for the power to reform society. The Gautama Buddha (561?–483? B.C.) willfully abandoned power and glory. Confucius lived among sordid intrigues of bedroom and palace. The Buddha's life was over-cast with sublime mysteries.

Prince Siddhartha, later to be the Gautama Buddha, was born in

Kapilavastu in northeastern India on the border of present-day Nepal. A prince of the Kingdom of the Bakyas, he was raised in fabled Oriental luxury. The legend of his life reveals the archetype of the Buddha, the essence of Buddhism, which grew over the centuries after his death. But the early Buddhists, like the Hindu Brahmins, believed that religious knowledge was too sacred to be written down. For four centuries after his death, facts and legends about the Buddha, his dialogues and sayings were preserved only in the memories of monks. The surviving accounts of his life are the accumulated product of disciples over generations.

This composite character is revealed in the very name of the Buddha. For *buddha* (past participle of Sanskrit *buddh*, to awaken or to know) is not a personal name but a term of praise, like messiah or christ (the anointed one). The proper name of the founder was Gautama. In his time he was known as Sakyamuni, the Sage from the tribe of the Sakyas. Unlike the founder of Christianity or of Islam, the Gautama Buddha was not thought to be unique. He represented a kind of person who recurred, but only rarely, over the aeons. The Gautama Buddha was not the first nor would he be the last. He was another in an endless series of Enlightened Ones. For us the historical Sakyamuni is lost in the historic Buddha.

He had not appeared on earth first as Gautama. For his perfect enlightenment could not have been attained in only one life. It must have been the result of his repeated earlier efforts in numerous incarnations. Only then had he become a Bodhisattva, a Bodhi-being in the person of the Prince Siddhartha. The explanation in the Buddhist scriptures of how this came about directs us to the Buddhist view of history. And their endless cycles of time also help us understand why the mystery of creation did not trouble them.

> Someone is called a Bodhisattva if he is certain to become a Buddha, a "Buddha" being a man who has first enlightened himself and will thereafter enlighten others. . . . This change from an ordinary being to a Bodhi-being takes place when his mind has reached the stage when it can no longer turn back on enlightenment. Also he has by then

gained five advantages; he is no more reborn in the states of woe, but always among gods and man; he is never again born in poor or low-class families; he is always male, and never a woman; he is always well-built, and free from physical defects; he can remember his past lives, and no more forgets them again.

(Translated by Edward Conze)

This full enlightenment was reached gradually, during three "incalculable aeons." "In the first incalculable aeon he does not yet know whether he will become a Buddha or not; in the second he knows he will be a Buddha, but does not dare to say so openly; in the third he knows for certain that one day he will be a Buddha, and fearlessly proclaims that fact to the world." With charming inconsistency, the same Buddhists who admired the Lord Buddha for his commonsense refusal to answer the fourteen unanswerable questions could not resist a temptation to calculate the "incalculable." Some figured it as a vast number increased by multiples, others by squares. One of the more precise scholars offered a number designated by 1 followed by 352 septillions of kilometers of zeros, allowing that one zero occupies a length of 0.001 meter.

In the endless cycles of the World, in each Great Period, or Kalpa, there were four Ages, comparable to the four ages of the Greeks and the Hindus. Each Great Period began with an Age of Destruction by fire, wind, and water, followed by a gradual reformation and re-population of the world. In none of these did a Creator appear nor were His works required. The Great Periods were not all the same. In some no Buddha would appear and these are called "void." In others one or many Buddhas might appear. In each cycle of recovery the primordial water slowly receded and a solid world of dry land emerged. Where the sacred tree of the Buddha would be, a lotus appeared. There were as many lotuses as there would be Buddhas in the Period.

During each Great Period, life carried on by transmigration (*samsara*) of souls from one creature to another. Schools of Buddhism disagreed on points of doctrine, but they agreed that there was no beginning to the process of transmigrations. And there would surely be no end. Since there were an infinite number of souls, how could there ever be a time when they all would have attained Nirvana?

Attaining Nirvana was, of course, everyone's hope. For the transmigrations of a soul finally dissolved the self, and so ended the suffering that came with all existence. The arrival of the Gautama Buddha on earth as Prince Siddhartha about 561 B.C. was just another stage in the countless processes of his reincarnation. And his previous lives provided some of the most appealing passages in the Buddhist scriptures. They chronicle how his soul had stored up merit toward his reward of ever-higher incarnations and final fulfillment in Buddhahood and Nirvana.

The tale of the hungry tigress told how Gautama, in an earlier incarnation as Prince Mahasattva, had gone walking in the jungle. There he encountered a weary tigress who a few days before had been delivered of seven cubs. Since she could find no meat or warm blood to feed them, they were all about to die of hunger. Mahasattva thought, "Now the time has come for me to sacrifice myself! For a long time I have served this putrid body and given it bed and clothes, food and drink, and conveyances of all kinds. . . . How much better to leave this ungrateful body of one's own accord and in good time! It cannot subsist for ever, because it is like urine which must come out. To-day I will use it for a sublime deed. Then it will act for me as a boat which helps me to cross the ocean of birth and death." With those words the prince threw himself down in front of the tigress. But she was too weak to move. Mahasattva, being "a merciful man," had carried no sword. So he cut his throat with a sharp piece of bamboo and fell near the tigress, who soon ate all his flesh and blood, leaving only bones. "It was I," the Buddha explained to his disciple, "who at that time and on that occasion was that Prince Mahasattva."

Finally, as Prince Siddhartha, he had been born again into a life of luxury. For the young prince the King provided three palaces, one for winter, one for summer, and one for the rainy season. During the rainy season the prince was entertained by beautiful dancing girl-musicians, as his father did not want him to be tempted to leave the palace. Shuddhodana had reason to take special measures to keep his son Gautama at his princely station. For Gautama's birth, Buddhist scriptures reported, had been most unusual. When the birth approached, Queen Maya accompanied the King to Lumbini, "a delightful grove, with trees of every kind, like the grove of Citraratha in Indra's Paradise."

> He came out of his mother's side, without causing her pain or injury. His birth was as miraculous as that of . . . heroes of old who were born respectively from the thigh, from the hand, the head, or the armpit. . . . He did not enter the world in the usual manner, and he appeared like one descending from the sky. . . . With the bearing of a lion he surveyed the four quarters, and spoke these words full of meaning for the future: "For enlightenment I was born, for the good of all that lives. This is the last time that I have been born into this world of becoming."
>
> (Translated by Edward Conze)

Seven Brahmin priests predicted that if the boy stayed at home he would eventually become a universal monarch, but if he left home he would become a Buddha.

He was married off at the age of sixteen to his cousin Yashodhara, "chaste and outstanding for her beauty, modesty, and good breeding, a true Goddess of Fortune in the shape of a woman." And in due time Yashodhara bore him a son. "It must be remembered that all the Bodhisattvas, those beings of quite incomparable spirit, must first of all know the taste of the pleasures which the senses can give. Only then, after a son has been born to them, do they depart to the forest."

On his pleasure excursions the young Gautama was awakened to human suffering. The gods dismayed him by images of old age and of disease. Finally they showed him a corpse. And at the sight of death his heart was again filled with dismay. "This is the end," he exclaimed, "which has been fixed for all, and yet the world forgets its fears and takes no heed! . . . Turn back the chariot! This is no time or place for pleasure excursions. How could an intelligent person pay no heed at a time of disaster, when he knows of his impending destruction."

Now, at the age of twenty-nine, Prince Siddhartha (not yet a Buddha) began his experimental search for truth, which meant a way out of the sufferings of the world. For himself and all mankind he sought escape from Creation. When, why, and how suffering had first been brought into being was not his concern. Would it not be enough to show the way out of the suffering that plagued mankind every day?

After the vision of the corpse, the gods sent a vision of a religious mendicant to remind Gautama of his mission to deliver mankind. In the long past this apparition had seen other Buddhas. Now he exhorted Gautama to follow in their path. "O Bull among men, I am a recluse who, terrified by birth and death, have adopted a homeless life to win salvation! Since all that lives is to extinction doomed, salvation from this world is what I wish and so I search for that most blessed state in which extinction is unknown." With these words the being rose like a bird into the sky. Gautama, amazed and elated, was now fully convinced of his mission of salvation. "Then and there," Buddhist scriptures report, "he intuitively perceived the Dharma [the ultimate reality; The Way], and made plans to leave his palace for the homeless life."

In the middle of the night, before setting out "to win the deathless state," Gautama took a parting look at his beautiful wife and his infant son asleep in their palace bedchamber. He did not awaken them for fear they might dissuade him from his flight. Gautama's next years of relentless search for Enlightenment and Salvation rivaled the range of William James's *Varieties of Religious Experience*. Baffling episodes of mysticism and satanism were interrupted by blinding flashes of common sense.

For a while he sat at the feet of renowned sages, learning their systems for escaping selfhood by entering "the sphere of neither-perception-nor-non-perception" through the ecstasy of mystic trances. They still did not lead him to Enlightenment.

Then he turned to a monkish life of self-denial. He starved himself until his buttocks were like a buffalo's hoof, his ribs like the rafters of a dilapidated shed, the pupils of his eyes sunk deep in their sockets "as water appears shining at the bottom of a deep well," and the skin of his belly cleaved to his backbone. We see the emaciated Gautama in the unforgettable Greco-Gandhara sculpture of the second century. "This is not the Dharma which leads to dispassion, to enlightenment, to emancipation," he concluded, ". . . Inward calm cannot be maintained unless physical strength is constantly and intelligently replenished."

When his five companion ascetics abandoned him, he returned to a normal diet, his body became fully rounded again and "he gained the strength to win enlightenment." When he walked toward the roots of a sacred fig tree (now called the *bodhi* tree, *Ficus religiosa*) intent on his high purpose, Kala, "a high-ranking serpent, who was as strong as a King elephant," was awakened by "the incomparable sound of his footsteps" and saluted Gautama, who seated himself cross-legged in the most immovable of postures and said he would not arise until he had received Enlightenment. "Then the denizens of the heavens felt exceedingly joyous, the herd of beasts, as well as the birds, made no noise at all, and even the trees ceased to rustle when struck by the wind."

Now he suffered his final trial, the siege of the satanic Mara, Lord of Passions. Mara's demonic army, including his three sons (Flurry, Gaiety, and Sullen Pride) and three daughters (Discontent, Delight, and Thirst), attacked the impassive Gautama. He speedily dispersed Mara's hordes, who fled in panic. The great seer, "free from the dust of passion, victorious over darkness' gloom," using his skill at meditation entered a deep trance. In the first watch of the night (6:00 P.M. to 10:00 P.M.) he recalled all his own former lives, the thousands of births he had been through. "Surely," he concluded, "this world is unprotected and helpless, and like a wheel it turns round and round." He saw that the world of samsara, of birth and death, was "as unsubstantial as the pith of a plantain tree." In the second watch (10:00 P.M. to 2:00 A.M.) he attained "the perfectly pure heavenly eye" and saw that the rebirth of beings depended on the merit of their deeds, but "he found nothing substantial in the world of becoming, just as no core of heartwood is found in a plantain tree when its layers are peeled off one by one." In the third watch (2:00 A.M. to 6:00 A.M.) he saw the real nature of the world, how greed, delusion, and ignorance produced evil and prevented getting off the wheel of rebirth.

The climax of his trance was Enlightenment, the state of all-knowledge. "From the summit of the world downwards he could detect no self anywhere. Like the fire, when its fuel is burnt up, he became tranquil." "The earth swayed like a woman drunken with wine . . . and the mighty drums of thunder resounded through the air. Pleasant breezes blew softly, rain fell from a cloudless sky, flowers and fruits dropped from the trees out of season—in an effort to show reverence for him."

Gautama now at the age of thirty-five had become a Buddha. He arose and found the five ascetic monks who had abandoned him. To them he preached the middle way to Enlightenment, which became the essential doctrine of Buddhism: the Holy Eightfold Path—right views, right intentions, right speech, right conduct, right livelihood, right effort, right mindfulness, and right concentration, and the Four Holy Truths. These Truths were: first, that all existence—birth, decay, sickness, and death—is suffering; second, that all suffering and rebirth are caused by man's selfish craving; third, that Nirvana, freedom from suffering, comes from the cessation of all craving; and fourth, that the stopping of all ill and craving comes only from following the Holy Eightfold Path. These steps to the extinction of self were the way of the Buddha, the way of Enlightenment.

Is it any wonder that the Buddha dismissed those who asked when and how the world was created? That he aimed at them "the unbearable repartee" of silence? What soul en route to Buddhahood would waste energy on the mystery of creation? The Buddha aimed at Un-Creation. The Creator, if there was one, was plainly not beneficent. The Buddha charitably had not conjured up such a Master Maker of Suffering, who had imposed a life sentence on all creatures. If there was a Creator, it was he who had created the need for the extinction of the self, the need to escape rebirth, the need to struggle toward Nirvana. The Lord of the Buddhists was the Master of Extinction. And no model for man the creator.

THE INNOVATIVE GOD OF
SAINT AUGUSTINE

C HRISTIANITY, turning our eyes to the future, played a leading role in the discovery of our power to create. The ancient Greeks, adept at poetic and philosophic speculation about the past, seldom speculated about the future. And the typical Greek thinker has been called a "backward-looking animal." The dominant figure in this modern Christian story, after Jesus and Saint Paul, was Saint Augustine. He would help us to Janus-Vision.

We have seen how Hesiod's myth of a Golden Age, popularized by poets and dramatists, had depicted the decline of practically everything. His Paradise Lost was a tale of man's fall from the primitive Age of Innocence down into the present Age of Iron. Empedocles' cycles of creation, destruction, and re-creation also made progress inconceivable.

To Plato, too, nothing new seemed possible. Confined by his theory of forms, the only progress he could imagine was to come closer to the ideal models that had existed from eternity. And Aristotle in his own way denied the possibility of the new. His preexisting "appropriate forms" prescribed the limits within which any institution like the city-state could develop. Greek hopes for mankind, imprisoned in the mold of their idealism, prevented their imagining that man's power to create might be infinite.

The Greeks saw the advance of civilization bringing new ills. Their sour parable of technological progress was the familiar myth of Prometheus. Punished for affronting the gods by stealing fire for men's use, Prometheus was chained to a rock so an eagle could feed on his liver, which grew back each night. According to Lucretius, necessity had led men to invent, and then inventions spawned frivolous needs that equipped and encouraged them to slaughter one another in war. Strabo (63 B.C.?–A.D. 24?) complained that cultivated Greeks had brought decadence to innocent barbarians. According to the geographer-historian Trogus, the Scythians had learned more from nature than the Greeks had learned from all their philosophers.

With meager historical records, the Greeks naturally credited the great inventions to gods or ancient heroes. The benefactors of mankind, they thought, must have been superhuman. But Euhemerus of Messene (c.300 B.C.), in an ingenious travel fantasy, debunked the gods as mere idealized fabrications based on heroes who had really lived. His theory—"Euhemerism"—attracted Roman skeptics, menaced pagan faith, and appealed to pious Christians.

Then Christian writers themselves opened the ways. The very idea of Gospels (Good News) was new. Early Christian writers attacked the idea of cycles. The Church Fathers reminded people that every day they were witnessing changes and not a mere repetition of earlier events. Origen (185?–254) of Alexandria dismissed the absurd notion that "in another Athens another Socrates will be born who will marry another Xanthippe and will be accused by another Anytus and another Meletus." "In your clothing, your food, your habits, your feelings, finally even in your language," Tertullian (160?–230?) told the citizens of Carthage, "you have repudiated your ancestors. You are always praising antiquity, but you renew your life from day to day." "If you look at the world as a whole, you cannot doubt that it has grown progressively more cultivated and populated. Every territory is now accessible, every territory explored, every territory opened to commerce." The full Christian armory was targeted on the repetitive view of history.

But it was one thing to ridicule a simplistic dogma, quite another to create something in its place. This would be the grand achievement of Saint Augustine. He would offer an all-encompassing view of man's place in the unfolding drama of time, which made plausible man's own creative powers in a novelty-laden future.

Augustine came to his faith in mid-life, and his enduring writings were inspired by the traumas of his time. Born of middle-class parents in 354 in Tagaste, a small town on the coast of Algeria, he showed such promise in school that his family sent him to study in Carthage hoping to qualify him for government service. His father was a pagan, but his mother was a devout Christian, who yearned to see Augustine converted to her faith. Teaching rhetoric in Carthage, Augustine became unhappy with his rowdy students and their irregular fees and went to Rome. There Symmachus, the influential leader of the pagan party, was charmed by Augustine's eloquence and good nature. Symmachus became his patron and secured his appointment as professor of rhetoric in Milan, then the residence of the Western Roman Emperor. When the thirty-year-old Augustine arrived in Milan in 384, where Symmachus was the prefect, his career prospects were bright. As professor of rhetoric he delivered the regular eulogies of the emperor and the consuls of the year, and so had the opportunity to ingratiate himself with men in power. He was the closest thing to a minister of propaganda for the imperial court.

The young Augustine's tasks at court were clear enough and challenging. But he was torn by inner uncertainties. His travail during these crucial years Augustine would record in his *Confessions*, which William James in the twentieth century still found the most eloquent and vivid account of the troubles of the "divided soul." Although Augustine never was at home in Greek, he was captivated by classical philosophy and inspired by reading Cicero to turn away from rhetoric. "An exhortation to philosophy . . . altered my affections. . . . Every vain hope at once became worthless to me; and I longed with an incredibly burning desire for an immortality of wisdom." At the same time his mother, Monica (332?–387; later canonized), a woman of simple Christian faith, harassed him with her pleas for his instant conversion.

In his impatient quest, Augustine had earlier joined the Manichaeans, who had much to attract a young man of twenty. Appealing to "reason" against faith or authority, they offered their own simple dualist dogma. The conflict between the Kingdom of Light and the Kingdom of Darkness, they said, solved the riddle of Creation, the origins of evil, and all other knotty problems. A secret society, with much of the appeal of the Communist Party in the troubled capitalist society of the 1930s, and with cells all over the Roman world, the Manichaeans enjoyed the aura of "the happy few." Emphasizing self-knowledge, they divided their members into the Elect, who followed a rigorous discipline of fasts and rites and would speedily enter paradise at death, and the Hearers, who supported the Elect and would enter paradise only after reincarnation. Their founder, a Persian sage Mani (or Manes, 216?–276?) claimed to be God's final prophet. Since the Manichaeans included Jesus among their prophets, Christians treated them as a heresy, while the Manichaeans called themselves the purest of all faiths. They became a religion of their own, the more feared and abominated by both respectable pagan Romans and orthodox Christians because they had foreign ties and their numbers were never publicly known. Historians have called them the Bolsheviks of the fourth century. For nine years before coming to Milan, Augustine had been a Hearer. But now the Manichaeans' easy certainties no longer satisfied him.

And there were other considerations. His pious mother, still pressing him to convert, was arranging his marriage to a Christian heiress. The emperor whom he served was a Christian, and Bishop Ambrose of Milan was militantly orthodox. Soon after his arrival in the city Augustine became a catechumen, a person seeking instruction in the Church. He recorded in his *Confessions* how he was overwhelmed by Ambrose the charismatic preacher, who revealed the Hebrew origins of Greek philosophy, destroyed the Manichaean materialist dogma of light and darkness, and opened new ways of thinking about the future. "So I was confounded and converted." Simplicianus, whom he had asked to instruct him as he had instructed Ambrose, baptized Augustine on Easter Eve, 387. His mother, extravagantly pleased, said she was now ready to die.

Abandoning a worldly career, Augustine returned in 391 to his native Tagaste. "I was looking for a place to set up a monastery, to live with my 'brethren.' I had given up all hope in this world. What I could have been, I wished not to be; nor did I seek to be what I am now. For I chose to be humble in the house of my God rather than to live in the tents of sinners." The small Christian congregation of neighboring Hippo needed an assistant for their aging Bishop Valerius. The hostile Manichaeans were numerous and the bishop of the heretical Donatists forbade local bakers to bake bread for the Christians. The orthodox needed a native voice, for Valerius was a Greek, not at home in Latin, and ignorant of the community's rural Punic dialect. One day when Augustine stopped casually to pray in the basilica, the others there turned suddenly to him, pushed him to the apse, and forcibly ordained him as their priest. The astonished Augustine felt himself "condemned" by his God, who thus had "laughed him to scorn."

For the rest of his life Augustine remained in Hippo, which he would make famous in the annals of Christendom. When Valerius died, Augustine became bishop of Hippo. "I feared the office of a bishop to such an extent," he recalled, "that, as soon as my reputation came to matter among 'servants of God,' I would not go to any place where I knew there was no bishop. I was on my guard against this: I did what I could to seek salvation in a humble position rather than be in danger in high office. But . . . a slave may not contradict his Lord. I came to this city to see a friend, whom I thought I might gain for God, that he might live with us in the monastery. I felt secure, for the place already had a bishop. I was grabbed. I was made a priest . . . and from there, I became your bishop." The position of bishop made daily demands on Augustine as administrator, judge, teacher, and preacher.

Still, during these years in Hippo, Augustine's literary output, with the aid of his staff of stenographers, was phenomenal. Four hundred sermons and two hundred letters (some amounting to treatises on great issues) have survived—also books on Christian Doctrine (c.397–428), on the Trinity (c.400–416), and on countless other theological topics.

Augustine's two masterworks expounding human destiny in two contrasting dimensions are very much alive today. His *Confessions* (c.400), a saga of his inward life, and its successors and imitators over the centuries, would allow the world to share the spiritual travail and posturings of the most restless men and women. In this tradition of the internal Odyssey, Rousseau a millennium and a half later would stir poets, novelists, dramatists, and revolutionaries. The *City of God* (413–426), Augustine's scheme of universal history, as we shall see, helped man off the "wheel" of again-and-again, toward a new view of the Creator. Providing a vocabulary for Christian thinking in the West for centuries, his work was occasioned by the trauma of his own lifetime.

*   *   *

At midnight on August 24, 410, as the gates of Rome were opened, and the city was awakened by Gothic battle trumpets sounding their victory, Alaric and his hordes poured in. "Eleven hundred and sixty-three years after the foundation of Rome, the Imperial City, which had subdued and civilized so considerable a part of mankind," Gibbon records, "was delivered to the licentious fury of the tribes of Germany and Scythia." Rome had fallen!

For the people of that age this event, which for us is only another episode in the long barbarian invasions, was apocalyptic. "When the brightest light on the whole earth was extinguished," wrote Saint Jerome, who heard the news in Bethlehem, "when the Roman empire was deprived of its head and when, to speak more correctly, the whole world perished in one city, then 'I was dumb with silence, I held my peace, even from good, and my sorrow was stirred.' " "Who would believe," he asked "that Rome, built up by the conquest of the whole world, has collapsed, that the mother of nations has also become their tomb?"

There is no modern counterpart for that catastrophe, for no modern city has the mystique of Rome. Following Virgil's prophecy in the *Aeneid* that Romans would have "dominion without end," Rome had been known as the Eternal City. Obeying Jesus' exhortation to "render unto Caesar the things which are Caesar's" and Saint Paul's warning that "the powers that be are ordained of God," good Christians saw no sacrilege in submitting to the secular authority of Rome. Some had actually seen the hand of Providence in the rise of the Roman Empire. Augustus (27 B.C.–A.D. 14) and Jesus were contemporaries, and the rising empire seemed a bulwark of the faith. So Tertullian (160?–230?) justified Christian prayers for the health of

Roman emperors. "For we know that only the continued existence of the Roman Empire retarded the mighty power which threatens the whole earth, and postpones the very end of this world with its menace of horrible afflictions." When the Romans tired of civil war, Ambrose recalled, they conferred the imperium on Augustus Caesar, "thus bringing to an end their intestine strife. But this also made it possible for the Apostles to travel throughout the whole world as the Lord Jesus had bidden them: 'Go forth and teach all nations,' " "Let the Church march on!" intoned Augustine, "The Way is open; our road has been built for us by the emperor."

For the strong pagan party the Fall of the City seemed proof that Christianity was destroying Rome. But Bishop Augustine in Hippo made it the point of departure for his Christian view of history. Now in his mid-fifties, having spent much of his life attacking heresies, he "did not wish to be accused of having merely contradicted the doctrine of others, without stating my own." The thirteen years (413–426) he spent on his *City of God* created a new kind of defense of the new religion.

First he aimed to correct rumors about what really happened when Alaric entered Rome. A sign of divine Providence was Alaric's respect for the treasure of the Church and the persons of Christians. When one of his men discovered the hiding place of the consecrated gold and silver vessels of Saint Peter, Alaric ordered their return to the church in the Vatican. Alaric was reported as saying that he waged war against the Romans but not against the Apostles. And, because of the Christians, Rome—unlike Sodom—was not totally destroyed. The first chapter of *The City of God* observed that "all their headlong fury curbed itself, and all their desire of conquest was conquered . . . this ought they to ascribe to these Christian times, to give God thanks for it, and to have true recourse by this means unto God's name. . . ."

Even if the barbarians had not shown such mercy, their entry into Rome would not have been an argument against Christianity. "The truth is that the human race has always deserved ill at God's hand . . . ," as Tertullian observed, "the very same God is angry now, as he always was, long before Christians were so much as spoken of."

The first half of *The City of God* sang this familiar exonerating litany of the catastrophes before Jesus Christ. To support his case against the pagans, Augustine would commission his disciple Orosius to catalog the misfortunes that came before there was a Christianity. Not lacking material, Orosius produced his *Seven Books of Histories against the Pagans*, which a thousand years later could still be distinguished by Petrarch as the classic summary of "the evils of the world."

Having disposed of the gross libels on the role of Christianity in history, Augustine went on to create his own philosophy of history, which would dominate Western thought for the next millennium. And he provided the most potent weapon against historical pessimism and the classic cycles. His ideas would show an uncanny power to be transformed into a modern idea of progress.

Awed by man's ingenuity, Augustine exclaimed:

> ... man's invention has brought forth so many and such rare sciences and arts (partly necessary, partly voluntary) that the excellency of his capacity makes the rare goodness of his creation apparent, even then when he goes about things that are either superfluous or pernicious, and shows from what an excellent gift he has those inventions and practices of his. What varieties has man found out in buildings, attires, husbandry, navigation, sculpture, and painting! What perfection has he shown in the shows of theatres, in taming, killing, and catching wild beasts! What millions of inventions has he against others, and for himself in poisons, arms, engines, stratagems, and such like! What thousands of medicines for the health, of meat for the palate, of means and figures to persuade, of eloquent phrases to delight, of verses for pleasure, of musical inventions and instruments! How excellent inventions are geography, arithmetic, astrology, and the rest! How large is the capacity of man, if we should dwell upon particulars! Lastly, how cunningly and with what exquisite wit have the philosophers and heretics defended their very errors—it is strange to imagine!
>
> (Bk. XXII, Ch. XXIV, translated by John Healey)

Yet all these remarkables, he warned, were no proper measure of the advance of mankind, no promise of endless progress on earth. They only revealed "the nature of man's soul in general as man is mortal, without any reference to the way of truth whereby he comes to the life eternal."

Augustine did offer a promise of novelty and uniqueness in human experience. The coming of Jesus Christ, he declared, had disposed of the cyclical view once and for all. Redesigning the shape of history from the wheel to the line, Augustine gave man's life direction. The familiar words of Ecclesiastes (I, 9, 10)—"there is no new thing under the sun, nor any thing whereof one may say, behold this is new: it hath been already in the time that was before us"—only described the recurrence of "successive generations, the sun's motions, the torrents' falls, or else generally all transitory creatures . . . trees and beasts." "Far be it from the true faith that by these words of Solomon we should believe are meant these cycles by which . . . the same revolutions of time and of temporal things are repeated. . . . God forbid, I say, that we should swallow such nonsense! Christ died, once and for all, for our sins." Christianity took man off the wheel, "which, if reason could not refute, faith could afford to laugh at." The Christian God opened the vistas of infinity, "whereas His wisdom being simply and uniformly manifold can comprehend all incomprehensibility by his incomprehensible comprehension." Now history was revealed not as an "eternal return" but as an eternal movement, to fulfill the promise announced by the coming of Christ.

Classical thinkers had, one way or another, put the motive force of history outside the individual man. For Plato and Aristotle, we have seen, history reproduced eternal ideas or fulfilled preexisting natural forms. In the early Roman Empire the power of Fortune attained the dignity of a cult. Others assigned the decisive role to Chance or the Fates. But for Christians, in Ambrose's phrase, the material world offered "not gods but gifts," a catalog of opportunities for mankind. Euripides had accused bold inventors or grand discoverers of "imagining themselves wiser than the gods." When the ancients deified benefactors into Promethean deities, they were refusing to see the creative powers in man himself. Man's destiny, no longer wholesale, had become retail. The crucial questions now concerned the individual soul.

The City of God offered its own way of measuring man's fulfillment. Symmachus and his pagan party in Rome had defended the old religion by its proven usefulness and challenged Christianity as a novelty unproven by its uses. But Augustine's test rose above the visibly useful.

All mankind he divided into two "cities"—two vast communities that encompass the whole earth of past, present, and future. "That which animates secular society (*civitas terrena*; the earthly city) is the love of self to the point of contempt for God; that which animates divine society (*civitas caelestis*; the heavenly city) is the love of God to the point of contempt for self. The one prides itself on itself; the pride of the other is in the Lord; the one seeks for glory from man, the other counts its consciousness of God as its greatest glory."

The earthly city, Augustine the realist explained, was a world of conflict. "By devoting themselves to the things of this world, the Romans did not go without their reward" in victories, "deadly or at any rate deathly." Yet victory did not go to the virtuous. "God grants earthly kingdoms both to the good and to the evil, yet not haphazard . . . nor yet by fortune, but in accordance with the order of times and seasons, an order which, though hidden from us, is fully known to Him. . . . Felicity, however, He does not grant except to the good." "The greatness of the Roman empire is not therefore to be ascribed either to chance or fate. Human empires are constituted by the providence of God." The foundation of the earthly city was laid "by a murderer of his own brother, whom he slew through envy, and who was a pilgrim upon earth of the heavenly city." Just as Cain slew Abel, so Romulus murdered his brother Remus. "The strife therefore of Romulus and Remus shows the division of the earthly city itself; and that of Cain and Abel shows the opposition of the city of men and the city of God."

Augustine's story begins with the Creation and will end with the Last Judgment. Every event is unique, and every soul follows its own destiny, to survive in Hell or in Heaven. History mysteriously marshals citizens of the City of God toward their reward of eternal life. "And I, John," said he, "saw that holy city, New Jerusalem, coming down from God out of heaven, prepared as a bride adorned for her husband. . . . And he that sat upon the throne said, Behold, I make all things new." No one could know when fulfillment would come, for History was a continuous unfolding of man's mysterious capacities—for creation, for love of God, for joining the Eternal City. The climactic event for the world was the coming of Christ. But the climactic event for each man still lay in the promise of history, which had transported the classical Golden Age from the remote past into the remote but certain future. In a historic coup d'état men had seized the powers of their Creator.

CASTLES OF ETERNITY

O F THE SEVEN Wonders of the World, famous in antiquity, only the oldest, the Pyramids, has survived. The ancient Egyptians have won their battle against time. We wonder that monuments elsewhere outlast the centuries, but the Egyptian world seems changeless. The perpetual sun and the annual rhythm of the rising Nile declare continuity of life as vivid to us as it was to the ancient Egyptians. Their message from 2700 B.C. still comes in the Pyramids. Why could not man himself be changeless, and go on living forever? They built cities of the dead for people who would never die. Where we see the lifeless dead, ancient Egyptians saw endless life. "O King N thou art not gone dead," reads the Pyramid text, "Thou art gone alive."

Eternal life needed an eternal dwelling. The earliest Egyptians built houses of reeds. And by the period of the Pyramids, their houses were built of sun-dried brick, which also have gone with the wind. But now we see those Egyptians as great stone builders. Their indestructible dwellings for the dead became castles of eternity.

While the words of their optimism, their belief in life everlasting, remain arcane and elude us, their stones still publish their faith in the equality of the dead with the living. Egyptian tomb paintings make their daily life more vivid than that of any other ancient people. We see them eating and drinking, irrigating their fields,

cultivating and harvesting, hunting and fishing; we see them dancing and sculpting and building. We see their children playing four
thousand years ago. Sepulchral stele ask prayers for the deceased
from all passersby. "O ye who live and exist, who love life and hate
death. . . ."

Abhorrence of death somehow did not lead them to fear the
dead or worship ancestors. Tomb robbery could hardly have been so
prevalent in all periods if the Egyptians had been haunted by fear of
the dead. Excavators almost never find an unrobbed tomb. The
Egyptian way was not to fear death but to deny it. They insisted on
the similarity of the needs of "men, gods, and dead." Like the living
prince's royal "house of the living," the temple was "the god's castle," and the tomb was everyman's castle. There the owner lived on
and his possessions were stored.

Because the dead had reason to fear the living, the jewel-adorned
mummies were hidden in deep tomb shafts. Inscribed on the walls of
the chamber and the sides of the sarcophogus were spells against intruders. Even the hieroglyphs of men and animals drawn to protect
and serve the deceased might be threatening. To make these harm-
less, the ambivalent tomb artists of the Old Kingdom sometimes
would take off legs or bodies, or even chop them in half. To feed the
tenants of these hidden apartments, tomb architects of the Age of the
Pyramids built over the burial shaft another structure, a mastaba,
with a false door leading to a life-sized statue of the deceased to receive the food offerings. To ensure a continuous supply of food after
death, noblemen set aside land as an endowment for priests to feed
them. The better-furnished tombs of the Second Dynasty even contained washbasins and privies.

The relations of the dead to the living were sometimes too intimate for comfort. Since the invisible spirit "comes in darkness and
enters slinking in," the malicious dead could do their mischief un-
detected. But the loving dead could continue to help. Ancient Egyptians wrote letters to deceased parents asking their support and their
protection. To the unfriendly dead they wrote letters begging
them to go away. In a touching letter from the Twentieth Dynasty,
a distressed widower recalls how faithful he had been during his

life and begs his dead wife to stop her mischievous tricks. "I did not give thee pain through anything that I did. Nor didst thou find me flouting thee by behaving like a peasant and entering into a strange house. . . . I did the thing that a man in my position usually does as regards thy ointment, thy provisions and thy clothes, and I did not dispose of them elsewhere on the pretext that 'the woman is away.' " In her last illness he had employed a master physician, on her death had mourned for eight months, had limited his food and drink, and then for three years remained celibate. Why, since her death, had she inflicted all sorts of evil on him? He begged the gods to judge between them. A letter like this would be inscribed on an earthenware dish with a food offering. After nostalgic recollection of good times together came the grievance or the request for aid. Death, it seems, had not extinguished the deceased, but had only increased the distance between the writer and the addressee.

In the Old Kingdom, the most ancient period of historic Egypt, only the Pharaoh seems to have enjoyed eternal life. But passing centuries brought "the democratization of the hereafter." Magical pyramid texts on the coffins of nobles helped them become deified into eternal life. In the "Western" regions of the afterlife there was little distinction between pharaohs and nobles. Eventually this opportunity for eternal life reached down the social scale to anyone—even artisans, peasants, and servants—who could afford the necessary ritual and magic. But before then, since servants were the property of their masters, they somehow, through their masters, enjoyed a vicarious immortality.

Naturally enough, to prepare for continuing life, the ancient Egyptians tried to preserve the living form. Techniques for protecting the body from decay improved to provide nobles and commoners as well as pharaohs with the body for an eternal life. Mummification, beginning as a science, increasingly became an art. After removing the brain of the deceased, the intestines were taken out and put in four alabaster vases. The heart, believed to be the seat of the intellect, was separated, wrapped, and reinserted in the body. The empty abdomen was stuffed with linen, sawdust and aromatic spices. Seventy days of soaking in natron (hydrated sodium carbonate) prevented the rest of the body from decaying. The natron-dried body was wrapped in rolls of linen steeped in gum. There were sixteen such layers on the mummy of Tutankhamon. Between the layers they inserted small stone charms, fetishes, and papyrus scraps with magic texts.

Early efforts aimed only to prevent decay. But gradually the priestly embalmers became cosmeticians. They used resinous pastes to flesh out the corpse, inserted artificial eyes, and added metal sheaths to hold fingers in place. Though the body was no longer so skillfully preserved, now it was wrapped in garish painted linen rolls. The deteriorating art of the embalmer after the Twenty-first Dynasty symbolized the decay of ancient Egyptian civilization.

But the mystique of the mummification survived and its medicinal powers became proverbial. In the Middle Ages "mummy," the powder made (really or reputedly) from ground-up mummies, was a staple of European apothecary shops. "These dead bodies," the English traveler Hakluyt complained in 1599, "are the Mummie which the Phisitians and Apothecaries doe against our willes make us to swallow." Originally the word "mummy" did not refer to the dead body, but came from the Arabic *mumiyah*, meaning bitumen or tar, and was based on the misconception that the black appearance of mummies came from their having been dipped in pitch.

* * *

What the mummification did for the Pharaoh's body, the pyramid and its surrounding stone temples created for his house. Both showed ancient Egyptian optimism, faith that they could conquer time. How and why their unexcelled techniques for building in stone were so quickly perfected still puzzles historians. Only about a century elapsed between the first notable Egyptian structures of stone and the triumphant masonry of the Great Pyramid. How did they quarry huge blocks of limestone, transport them for miles, then raise, place, and fit them with a jeweler's precision? All without the aid of a capstan, a pulley, or even a wheeled vehicle!

Modern engineers find mathematics their indispensable tool. Yet the mathematics of the ancient Egyptians, compared with that of other ancient peoples, was crude. Egyptian arithmetic in the Age of the Pyramids was based wholly on a knowledge of the "two times" table and we can wonder whether in the modern sense it should even be called mathematics. Multiplication and division were cast in the form of addition. They multiplied a number by duplicating it the required times, and then added the sums, and their system of division was similar. Oddly enough, this "dyadic" principle would be used again in the twentieth-century computer, but for most of history it was a dead end. Their rudimentary system of "unit-fractions" left them no way of expressing complex fractions.

Still, the Great Pyramid (the Pyramid of Cheops), covering 13.1 acres with six and a quarter million tons of stone, whose casing blocks averaged two and a half tons each, showed a micrometric accuracy of design. The squareness of its north and south sides had a margin of error of only 0.09 percent, and of the east and west sides only 0.03 percent. The vast dressed-rock pavement on which this enormous mass was resting, when surveyed from opposite corners deviated from a true plane by only 0.004 percent. And there is no evidence that their techniques or designs were borrowed from abroad.

The oldest surviving architectural structure of stone masonry, the Step Pyramid of Zoser, appeared suddenly in the Third Dynasty of the Old Kingdom (c. 2700 B.C.). The refinement of its masonry casing is already remarkable. Imhotep, the man reputed to be the architect, their pioneer tactician in the battle against time, was deified as Founding Father of Egyptian culture. Celebrated as chief minister, astrologer, and magician to the great Third Dynasty pharaoh Zoser (c.2686–c.2613 B.C.), he became the patron of writing. Scribes would pour a libation to him from their writing jar before beginning work. His proverbs were repeated for centuries, and he became the mythical founder of Egyptian medicine. Two thousand years after his death he was still remembered and given fully divine status. Ailing devotees prayed at temples built to him in Memphis and on the island of Philae in the Nile, where they went hoping that Imhotep would reveal cures in their dreams. The Greeks adapted him as their god of medicine, whom they called Asklepios.

At Saqqara, overlooking the ancient capital of Memphis south of modern Cairo, we can still see Imhotep's solid claim to fame. His Step Pyramid, the world's oldest surviving creation of hewn stone, is a birthplace of the architectonic spirit. What we see today is a rectangular stone structure of six steps, at the base measuring 597 yards from north to south and 304 yards from east to west, reaching a height of 200 feet. Excavations suggest that it was larger when it was first completed. Before the weathering of centuries and the removal of fragments to build other buildings, it must have contained 850,000 tons of stone and was part of a vast complex of walls and temples. The surrounding buildings, so far as we know, were also without precedent. When cased with freshly hewn white Tura limestone rising above the tawny sands they were a dazzling spectacle.

The Step Pyramid was man's first skyscraper. Even in ancient Egypt, where it would soon be overtowered by taller, grander monuments, it never ceased to inspire awe, recorded in graffiti by pilgrims in the age of Rameses II, fifteen hundred years later. A monument to the newly discovered creative powers of man the architect, it was a monument, too, to man the organizer and to the power of community. Zoser's pyramid, as we shall see, was one of the earliest signs of the constructive power of the state.

Still, the uses of the pyramid are obscure. Part of a funerary monument complex, the Step Pyramid was probably intended to be Zoser's tomb. Perhaps the buildings surrounding the Pyramid were stone replicas of the royal palace in Memphis, to serve the Pharaoh's needs in his later life.

The time between the building of this first large structure known to history and the triumphs of the Great Pyramid of Cheops was a little more than a century. We are not accustomed to think of the Egyptians as paragons of progress, but few great advances in human technique have been so sudden and so spectacular. A new technology of creation! Not until the modern skyscraper in the midnineteenth century, four thousand years later, was there another comparable leap in man's ability to make his structures rise above the earth. Then the technology of the skyscraper, too, as we shall see, arrived with a comparable speed.

The new art and technology of hewn-stone building was suddenly revealed in gargantuan scale, with a wonderful new-rounded perfection of craft. The Step Pyramid was a work of small-block masonry. Its stones, about nine inches square, were small enough to be managed by hand without mechanical devices. Within another half-century at the so-called temple of the Sphinx, Egyptians were handling boulders of thirty tons. The increase in scale was matched by improvements of technique.

Zoser's successor Sekhemkhet built a step pyramid, but it disintegrated. The first "true" pyramid, with a square base and flat sides sloping to a point at the summit, appears to have been the pyramid of Meidum (about thirty miles south of Memphis) built by Huni, the last king of the Third Dynasty. This disintegrated pyramid of Meidum revealed a step-pyramid core of several stages cased with six thick coatings of local Tura limestone. Additional fillings and facings of stone produced a geometrically true pyramid. Only at the bottom do traces of this shape remain, disintegrated above by gravity, by weather, and by the pilfering of stone for use elsewhere. The limestone casing, poised inward at an angle of 75 degrees, was not bonded together, but depended entirely on its angle of incline for solidity.

The pyramid at Meidum was not the last unsuccessful effort to build a durable perfect pyramid. The problems of the first architect-engineers in stone remain vividly portrayed in the so-called Bent Pyramid, twenty-eight miles north of Meidum, built by King Seneferu (c.2650 B.C.) of the Fourth Dynasty. On a square ground plan measuring 620 feet at the base, the smooth mountain of stone rises at first at an angle of 54 degrees and 31 minutes for about half its height, then, abruptly and symmetrically, the angle decreases to 43 degrees and 21 minutes until the top of the pyramid is reached at 303 feet (101 meters). Various explanations have been offered for the change to a less steep angle of construction. It is most likely that, in mid-project, the builders decided to avoid another catastrophe like the collapse of the pyramid at Meidum, and so left us a bizarre monument to architectural discretion.

We see another evidence of that discretion at Dahshur within sight of the Bent Pyramid and a short distance to the north. This so-called Red Pyramid, which takes its color from the underlying blocks of local limestone now exposed, was the earliest tomb known to have been completed as a true pyramid. It seems flat compared with the later pyramids of the Giza group. And so it is, for the collapse at Meidum had revealed the perils of the steeper angle at the first stage of the Bent Pyramid. The builders cautiously inclined this pyramid at an angle (43 degrees and 36 minutes) almost the same as that of the upper half of the Bent Pyramid. Their caution was justified, for their basic structure has withstood the millennia. But the gentle slope made it an easy quarry for stone robbers. Piece by piece over the centuries they removed the original covering of dressed white limestone, which once gave it a dazzling finished elegance, leaving it now with a distinctive color never intended by the architects.

Where else can we see, within less than a hundred miles, in full scale, so comprehensive an open-air museum of one of the great ages of architecture? These two monuments at Dahshur, the Bent Pyramid and the Red Pyramid, show a transition from the small-stone masonry of the Step Pyramid and Meidum to the magnificent megaliths of the Great Pyramid at Giza. The pyramid builders had now learned how to increase stability by laying the stones of the inner limestone base at a slope, and in other ways, too. Still to come was the gargantuan scale of Giza—the megalithic blocks (two and a half tons to fifteen tons), and the bold steep angle of about 52 degrees. Future pyramids with their still-steeper gradient survived because of improvements in structural design.

The climax of this first great age of architecture still rises above the desert near Cairo at Giza, on the west bank of the Nile. There three grand stone monuments of perfect pyramid design reveal our legacy from Pharaohs Cheops (Khufu), Khaf-Re, and Man-kau-Re, all of the Fourth Dynasty (c.2650–2500 B.C.). Of these, the Great Pyramid of Cheops, commonly dignified as the Great Pyramid (rising to some 482 feet), is the oldest, the largest, and the best built. The exact quantity of hewn stone inside remains one of its many secrets. Its outer structure of huge limestone blocks rests on an inner core of rocks. Without dismantling the pyramid we cannot know the size of that core. What we do know allows us to estimate that it contained about 2,300,000 hewn stone blocks with an average weight of two and a half tons. This gargantuan mass and its desert site frustrate any effort to compare the architectural power of the Great Pyramid with anything else in the world. The 13.1 acres covered by its base would be room enough for the cathedrals of Florence, Milan, and St. Peter at Rome, with space to spare for Westminster Abbey and London's St. Paul's.

*   *   *

Two thousand years after their construction, the tourist-historian Herodotus (c.425 B.C.) visited the Pyramids and put together his unforgettable concoction of fact, myth, and fantasy, explaining how and why they were built. The Egyptians, he said, were the first people "to broach the opinion that the soul of man is immortal." The Great Pyramid, according to Herodotus, was the work of the forced labor of a hundred thousand men, relieved every three months by a fresh lot. By ten years' oppression Cheops produced the sixty-foot-wide causeway of polished stone covered with carvings of animals to convey the stones the five-eighth mile from the Nile to the building site. On a sort of island, Cheops built fantastic underground chambers. Twenty years of oppression produced the Great Pyramid itself, "the stones of which it is composed are none of them less than thirty feet in length." Herodotus imagined a machine for hoisting the stones. Awed by the vast numbers employed, he noted "an inscription in Egyptian characters on the pyramid which records the quantity of radishes, onions, and garlic consumed by the labourers who constructed it; and I perfectly well remember that the interpreter who read the writing to me said that the money expended in this way was 1600 talents of silver . . . then . . . what a vast sum must have been spent on the iron tools . . . and on the feeding and clothing of the labourers."

Cheops plunged his country into "all manner of wickedness" to finance his project. When he needed more treasure, Herodotus recounts, he sent his daughter to the public brothels to sell her favors.

But she, too, wanted to leave a memorial pyramid. To accumulate her "hope chest" she required each man to make her a present of a stone "towards the works which she contemplated." The monument to her charms (which Herodotus saw, and so can we) was a good deal smaller than the Great Pyramid. Measuring one hundred and fifty feet along each side, it is the midmost of the three small pyramids in front of the Great Pyramid.

We still know little about the ancient Egyptian technology for handling the large blocks of stone. There is no evidence that they had anything like the capstan (familiar on shipboard for hoisting the anchor) or the pulley. Perhaps they had no kind of lifting tackle. For moving blocks they must have depended on sleds, rollers, and levers. They did leave us pictures of temporary brick and earth embankments constructed to provide ramps up which they dragged stones to their desired height. Of course these would have added substantially to the task of construction. A pyramid provided natural support for such an embankment, which may help explain the appeal of this shape for their high-rise monuments.

Uninhibited by evidence, awed visitors have enjoyed making up their own accounts of how and why pyramids were built. Some said the pyramids were granaries. Medieval Arab legends told of an ancient king who foresaw the Great Flood and built pyramids to store the secrets of astronomy, geometry, physics, and technology. The traveler Ibn Batuta (1304–1377) reported that Hermes Trismegistos (the Greek name for the Egyptian god Thoth) "having ascertained from the appearance of the stars that the deluge would take place, built the pyramids to contain books of science and knowledge and other matters worth preserving from oblivion and ruin." This belief in a hidden relation between the Great Pyramid and the truths of science and religion never died.

But why did ancient Egyptians create their monuments in the shape of pyramids? The word "pyramid," purely Greek in origin, gives us no clue. A similar word in Greek means "wheaten cake," and perhaps the Greeks thought that from a distance the pyramids looked like cakes resting on the desert. "Obelisk," another Greek word of architectural interest, had a comparable flippant origin because it was the Greek word for "little spit" or "skewer." We know that the ancient Egyptians called a tomb a Castle of Eternity. In the Egyptian language their word for pyramid may have meant "place of ascension." This would square with the fact that the earliest such structures were step pyramids, and such step cores were found within later pyramids.

For ascent to the heavens, a step pyramid served as well and perhaps more conveniently than the smooth-surfaced later true pyramids, whose construction was vastly more difficult and labor-consuming. Building a true pyramid required a single long high embankment or a series of low ramps. What spiritual, magical, and aesthetic benefits were great enough to justify so heavy an additional cost?

To the ancient Egyptians, any mound—mastaba, step pyramid, or true pyramid—could be a symbol of life. It was on a primeval mound emerging from the waters of chaos (like the mounds that emerged annually from the Nile when its water receded) that Atum the god of creation first appeared to create the universe. Any mound might have magic power to promote continuing life for the entombed deceased. But why the smooth, the "true," pyramid?

We do have some clues. The Age of the Pyramids saw the rise of the Heliopolitan priesthood, a thriving cult of the sun. When the sun rose on the Valley of the Nile, what its rays first touched was the tip of the Pyramid long before it reached the humbler dwellings below. How natural, then, that the king, the likeness of the sun-god Re, should live perpetually in a dwelling like the primeval hill! And in the very material of the first solid substance, the Benben, which was a stone. Just as in this life, so in the hereafter, the king must survive to protect his people. And what better image than a true pyramid, spreading symmetrically from a heavenward point, like the rays of the sun shining down on the earth?

The king, according to the pyramid texts, mounts to the heavens on the rays of the sun. May not the true pyramid have represented these rays on which the king could ascend? If so, then the design of the true pyramid would have been every bit as practical for the ever-living pharaoh as the steps of the Step Pyramid. To ease the king's ascent and for accompanying the sun-god Re in daily journeys around the earth, they sometimes provided the king with a wooden boat, like that found near the Great Pyramid in its chamber lined with Tura limestone. In the Fourth Dynasty, the Age of the Pyramids, the Pharaoh was the circumnavigating heavenly companion and the earthly image of the sun-god Re. Gradually the pharaohs incorporated the name of the sun-god into their own.

*   *   *

The meanings and benefits of the Pyramids were not all otherworldly. They would also be monuments of community, of the awesome power of the state. Centuries of travelers' tales, of legends and the fantasies of Haggadah illustrators have created the misleading stereotype of a tyrannical Pharaoh with gangs of sweating slaves driven by heartless overseers. While we idealize the pious craftsmen and humble laborers who built Amiens, Mont-St.-Michel, and Chartres over centuries, and we extol a society that could put so much of its capital into enduring monuments of faith, we have not been generous to the pyramid builders.

The advance of Egyptology has helped us see similarities in the monument builders of all ages. Many ancient Egyptian images survive to show laborers moving heavy stones and shaping sculpture, and foremen directing the work. We do not see whips or any other evidence of forced labor. Egyptologists now are agreed that the pyramids were not the work of slaves. Perhaps, they suggest, ancient Egyptians, like other people since, were proud of their grand public works. Firm in their shared loyalties and religious faith, might they not have been proud too, to join in works of community? During the months of inundation of the Nile, peasants who were unable to work at their crops could come to a pyramid site, always near the river. At this time every year the water transport of people and building materials was easiest. Meanwhile, in the off-season, small groups of workers would be quarrying the building stone.

At least seventy thousand workers at a time must have been engaged during the three months of inundation in the Age of the Pyramids. In the absence of other evidence and before the age of firearms, it is hard to imagine how such a crew could have been forcibly drawn from distant villages and brutally kept at work over many decades. Increasing evidence suggests that the pyramids were built by voluntary labor. In Old Kingdom Egypt there appear to have been few slaves except for some prisoners of war. If the pyramids overwhelm and dazzle us as great public works, might they not also have impressed the people who built them? Might they not have been proud of their part in so great a work? We have some clues in the tally marks that we can still read on the casing stones. Some inscriptions—"Boat Gang" or "Craftsmen Crew"—mark special tasks, while others—"How vigorous is Snofru" or "The White Crown of Khufu"—mark the reign when the work was done. And others—"Vigorous Gang," "Enduring Gang," or "Sound Gang"— declare the workers' pride. Can we not imagine that pyramid builders, returning each season to their villages, boasted to their amazed fellow villagers of the scale and grandeur of the work in which they had a small part?

The pyramids are the only great public works we know from the Fourth Dynasty. They appear to have transformed Egypt from a country of scattered villages into a strong centralized nation. How spectacular a first demonstration of what an organized state could accomplish! What unprecedented supplies of food, what mass transport, shelter, and sanitation! The power of the state was now revealed. While the primeval state created the pyramids, the pyramids themselves helped create the state in a focus of communal effort, of common faith in the living sun-god. The enormous task over many years must have brought into being a numerous bureaucracy, which could be enlisted for other purposes. In the Age of the Pyramids the word "pharaoh" itself meant "great house," not the person of the ruler but the place where the divine ruler dwelled. Pyramid builders, affirming their faith and their community, were making an eternal dwelling place for their ruler. After the Fourth Dynasty we witness the speedy decline of the central state. Nobles who had once built their tombs around the great pyramid of the Pharaoh now built them out in the provinces where they lived and ruled. And this, too, marked the decline of pyramid building and the deterioration of the quality of stone monuments.

We begin to see how crude it is to ask whether the pyramids were a "useful" creation. For they were grand public works, creatures and creators of community. Perhaps sensing this, when the founders of the United States sought, for the new nation's Great Seal, a fitting symbol of America's hopeful unknown future, they chose an unfinished pyramid (still found on the dollar bill). A modern physicist, Kurt Mendelssohn, has helped us put the Fourth Dynasty pyramid building in a modern perspective:

> There is only one project in the world today which, as far as one can see, offers the possibility of being large enough and useless enough to qualify eventually for the new pyramid. And that is the exploration of outer space. . . . In the end, the results of space exploration are likely to be as ephemeral as the Pharaoh accompanying the sun. The effort—will be gigantic. No other incentive will be provided than the satisfaction of man to make a name for himself by building a tower that reaches unto planetary space. Five thousand years ago the Egyptians, for an equally vague reason, accepted a monstrous sacrifice of sweat and toil. . . .

May not future generations puzzle over why late-twentieth-century man, at astronomical cost, went shooting off into outer space?

However inscrutable their motives, in their aim to conquer time the ancient Egyptians succeeded. They still carry the plain message of man's power as communal creator. In 1215, according to the Arab chronicler Abd al Latif, Caliph Malek al Azis Othman was offended by these monuments of idolatry. As a work of piety he assembled a large crew to destroy one of the smaller pyramids, the pyramid of Menkaure at Giza. After eight months' labor, his crew had made so little impression that he gave up. The mark of that hopeless effort is still visible in a small scar on the north slope of that pyramid. Since then, only the exploits of tomb robbers and the frolics of boisterous tourists tossing stones down from the summits have marred the pyramids' simple grandeur.

A ROAD NOT TAKEN:

The Japanese Triumph of Wood

W ESTERN belief in a Creator-God and creator man has carried with it belief that nature is to be mastered. But the Japanese, for example, who did not have a Creator-God or a myth of beginnings like ours in the West, found another path and have made nature their ally. Their world, like Hesiod's, is a product of procreation. The male and female deities, Izanagi and Izanami, stood on the Floating Bridge of Heaven and thrust down the Heavenly Jeweled Spear into the ocean below. Brine dripping from the spear coagulated into an island on which they lay together. Then Izanami gave birth to the islands of Japan along with the deities of nature—mountains, rivers, trees, and crops.

Their reverent, friendly, and intimate Japanese feelings toward nature have been expressed in an attitude to mountains very different from ours in the West. Japanese country folk have viewed mountain peaks and even smoking volcanoes as collaborating spirits. Hunters revered the mountain *kami*, whom farmers saw protecting them and supplying the water to make their rice grow. It is in the mountains, says Shinto myth, that the purified ancestral spirits dwell after thirty-three or fifty years of waiting in the nearby cemetery. Eventually these ancestral mountain spirits themselves became helpful *kami*, coming down to the rice paddies in spring and returning to their high habitats in the fall.

Cults of the mountain *kami* as early as the Nara period (710–794) nourished the supernatural powers by mountain asceticism and bred belief in mountain magic. The flourishing cult of Mount Fuji (now with more than thirteen hundred shrines) made its majestic volcanic cone the nation's symbol. An ancient folktale reports the contest between Japan's three sacred mountains.

> In ancient times Yatsu-ga-take [Mount Haku] was higher than Mt. Fuji. Once the female deity of Fuji [Asama-sama] and the male deity of Yatsu-ga-take [Gongen-sama] had a contest to see which was higher. They asked the Buddha Amida to decide which was loftier. It was a difficult task. Amida ran a water pipe from the summit of Yatsu-ga-take to the summit of Fuji-san and poured water in the pipe. The water flowed to Fuji-san, so Amida decided that Fuji-san was defeated.
>
> Although Fuji-san was a woman, she was too proud to recognize her defeat. She beat the summit of Yatsu-ga-take with a big stick. So his head was split into eight parts, and that is why Yatsu-ga-take (Eight Peaks) now has eight peaks.

Loyal pilgrims to Mount Fuji, who wanted to see their favorite mountain win, used to leave their sandals at the top to raise its height.

The European fear of mountains delayed the climbing of Mont Blanc, western Europe's highest mountain, till 1786. But there is no period of recorded history when the Japanese were not climbing Mount Fuji. Its symmetrical cone was one of the oldest subjects of their art and poetry. The ascent of Mount Fuji with its ten stations early became a ritual, and the circuit of the crater's rocky peaks carried a high ceremonial meaning of Japanese affinity with nature.

Surprisingly, this feeling has not been shaken by frequent earthquakes. Every year nearly 10 percent of the energy released in the world by earthquakes is concentrated around Japan. In the last century Japan has suffered twenty-three destructive earthquakes. The most disastrous, in 1923, left one hundred thousand dead. Still, the

myth of Shinto—the indigenous Japanese religion with its cultic devotion to the deities of nature and its veneration of the emperor as a
descendant of the sun goddess—managed even to make earthquakes
a token of good cheer. In the very beginning, we are told, when the
sun goddess, sister of Susanowo, came out of her cave and brightened the earth, the eight million dancing deities of nature were so
delighted that they shook the earth with their shouts of joy, as they
still do from time to time.

The omnipresent expression of the traditional Japanese relation
to nature is the Shinto belief in *kami*. The Japanese term *kami*, of
uncertain origin, is not properly defined by any familiar Western
term. According to Motoori Norinaga (1730–1801), the prophet of
Shinto in the Edo period, *kami* are found in "such objects as birds,
beasts, trees, plants, seas, mountains and so forth. In ancient usage,
anything whatsoever which was outside the ordinary, which possessed superior power, or which was awe-inspiring was called kami."
Their omnipresence and the need to worship them attest an overarching reverence—equally for the bud of the flower, for the veins
and wrinkles on the tiny stone, for the snowcapped Mount Fuji, for a
chrysanthemum bush, for a giant cypress, or for ideas like growth or
creation. Ancient Shinto, awed by the specificity and uniqueness of
all natural objects, gave each its own *kami*, and dared not homogenize the blowing wind and the immobile mountain into any single
pallid abstraction.

"So God created man in his own image . . . male and female
created he them. . . . and God said unto them, Be fruitful, and multiply, and replenish the earth, and subdue it: and have dominion over
the fish of the sea, and over the fowl of the air, and over every living
thing that moveth upon the earth." And God made plants for man's
sustenance. In Christian theology the "natural" man is evil, because
he has not been redeemed from his original sin.

Nothing could be more different from the traditional Japanese
view. In the mythology of the *Nihon Shoki*, men and women are the
brothers and sisters of all objects in nature. Man has no "dominion"
over nature, because he is part of it. He cannot be the master of other
creatures, for all are members of the same family. The *kami* are

man's collaborators. So landscape painting, which comes only late and slowly in Western art, is an ancient form in Japan, as we have seen that it was in China. There man is an inseparable aspect of the landscape, as the landscape is part of man.

While Western architects would battle the elements, the Japanese, admiring their power, have sought ways to exploit their charms. Western architects used stone to resist the ravages of time, but the Japanese would win by submitting. Conquest by surrender has been familiar in Japanese life. Some say that is the weapon of Japanese women. It is the way of judo (derived from a Chinese word meaning "gentle way"), a sport that aims "to turn an opponent's force to one's own advantage rather than to oppose it directly." By contrast with the belligerence of Western boxing and wrestling, judo promotes an attitude of confidence and calm readiness. The great works of early Western architecture—Stonehenge, the Pyramids, the Parthenon, the Pantheon, Hagia Sophia—were created to defy the climate, the seasons, and the generations. But Japanese architecture became time's collaborator. The Western concern was for survival, the Japanese concern was for renewal. Nature was composed of myriad *kami*, self-renewing forces. Shinto celebrated the reviving seasons, whose omnipresent symbols were flowers and trees.

* * *

This Japanese way was revealed in traditional Japanese architecture by the dominance of wood (as in China and Korea), when much of the rest of the world chose the way of stone. Even today the oldest surviving buildings in Japan are made of wood. A facile explanation is that wooden structures were less vulnerable to earthquakes. But history has shown that wooden structures are easy victims of earthquake in addition to being far more vulnerable to fire, typhoon, and hurricane. Where stone was used in the castles of Nagoya and Osaka, apparently in response to European firearms, it survived earthquakes better than wood.

The interior construction of ancient Japanese tombs showed advanced techniques of stone construction (found also in China and Korea), which have survived in some castle walls and stone bridges.

And there are impressive examples of early Japanese stone sculpture. But there is not a single surviving ancient Japanese building of stone. The precocious development of Japanese metallurgy may help us understand their early uses of wood. Stone can be fashioned with stone, as it must have been to shape the mortise-and-tenon stone joints of Stonehenge. Woodworking, fashioning and fitting timbers for large buildings, required tools of iron. And with such tools, however primitive, wood construction was much easier than construction in stone. Other modern civilizations emerged during a Bronze Age before they had iron woodworking tools. Western cultures understandably began their architecture in stone and brick and then stayed with these materials. But even in the primitive Yayoi era (300 B.C.–A.D. 300), when Japanese architecture was born, they had plenty of the iron tools that made the crafting of wood feasible.

In Japan, too, the terrain, the climate, and the rainfall produced flourishing forests. The large stands of the blessed cypress (Japanese "hinoki," *Chamaecyparis obtusa*) proved a happy coincidence. Carpenters' tools of those early times did not include a crosscut saw or the familiar modern plane, and cypress, with its grain running straight along the length of the timber, was suited to these limitations of their tool-chest. From the very beginning the appealing soft texture of cypress and its fragrance encouraged the Japanese to enjoy the unadorned surface. Probably, too, the influence of China, where wood architecture was highly developed, had an effect.

There are of course some advantages to wooden buildings, which we in the West forget. As Edward S. Morse (1838–1925), the pioneer Western student of Japanese culture, explained in 1885, before the epidemic of Westernization:

> . . . the Japanese house . . . answers admirably the purposes for which it was intended. A fire-proof building is certainly beyond the means of a majority of these people, as indeed it is with us; and not being able to build such a dwelling, they have from necessity gone to the other extreme, and built a house whose very structure enables it to be rapidly demolished in the path of a conflagration. Mats, screen-partitions,

and even the board ceilings can be quickly packed up and carried away. The roof is rapidly denuded of its tiles and boards, and the skeleton framework left makes but slow fuel for the flames. The efforts of the firemen in checking the progress of a conflagration consist mainly in tearing down these adjustable structures; and in this connection it may be interesting to record the curious fact that oftentimes at a fire the streams are turned, not upon the flames, but upon the men engaged in tearing down the building!

Wood, being an organic material, even after it is cut from the growing tree responds to the weather. The architects of the splendid Shosoin, the imperial treasure repository at Nara, took account of this. The triangular cypress logs stacked horizontally gave a smooth surface on the interior and a corrugated surface on the outside. In wet weather the logs expand to seal the building, but when it is hot and dry they shrink and create ventilating cracks so the air can circulate within.

The classic examples of Japanese traditional architecture are found at Ise, the most famous Shinto shrine on the south coast of Honshu. Here, better than anywhere else, we witness the distinctive Japanese conquest of time by the arts of renewal. Here, too, we can see how Japanese architecture has been shaped by the special qualities of wood, and how wood has carried the creations of Japanese architects on their own kind of voyage through time. Stone by its survival and its crumbling has often carried messages never intended. But few relics of wood survive the centuries. Those we inherited intact from Egypt were sealed in the bowels of stone tombs and pyramids. Wooden ruins inspire us with a desire to clear them away. They are the makings not of romantic landscapes but of fire hazards and slums. What landscape architect ever decorated a garden with a dilapidated structure of wood? Where are the Piranesis of wooden ruins?

What the wooden shrines at Ise offer us are not architectural relics. These are not the remains of the past. They are not even "monuments" as the Parthenon on the Acropolis, the Temple at

Paestum, the Colosseum in Rome are monuments. Though the visitors to Ise match the numbers of tourists who throng the Acropolis in Athens or the Forum in Rome, most come not as tourists. To Ise they can still come for a living experience, to worship at these shrines as their ancestors did when the shrines were first built centuries ago.

Ironic twists of history, and even acts of plunder and of war, have preserved stone relics. If Lord Elgin had not removed (1801–1803) sculptures and architectural fragments from the Parthenon on the Acropolis in Athens and transformed them into the "Elgin Marbles," museum models of classical art, none might ever have survived. But there was a price to pay, for his first shipment was lost at sea and only the second found a home in the British Museum, where we can see them today.

Western visitors to pre-Westernized Japan were struck by the absence of those architectural stone monuments so characteristic of European countries. But the classic examples of traditional Japanese architecture, the shrines at Ise, are not really monuments either. Not mere reminders of the past, they are rather its revivals. For the Ise shrines are always new, or at least never more than twenty years old. The Inner Shrine (Naiku) and the Outer Shrine (Geku) are both rebuilt on nearby land from the ground up every twenty years. This ceremony of reconstruction has been repeated since about A.D. 690 for the Naiku shrine to the supreme goddess Amaterasu-Omikami and also for the Geku shrine to the goddess of foodstuffs, clothing, and other necessities of life, Toyouke-no-Omikami. It has remained a continuous rhythmic feature of Japanese life over these centuries. During the civil wars of the fifteenth and sixteenth centuries the ceremonial reconstruction was sometimes neglected. After the seventeenth century the cycle for a while became twenty-one years. When the fifty-ninth renewal, scheduled for 1949, was postponed as a consequence of war, special ceremonies were held at Ise praying for forgiveness for the delay. The postponed renewal was accomplished in October 1953. The next, the sixtieth renewal, was completed after ten years of preparation in October 1973, with food, ritual, and traditional dance.

In the West we have revered the past by costly works of architectural restoration. We patch up falling columns and prop up failing buttresses. In Venice we struggle to prevent the sinking of palaces and churches of earlier centuries. All in our stony struggle for survival. For three years scaffolding and derricks overshadowed the west front of our national capitol to restore the stone façade. The restoration of the Statue of Liberty in New York Harbor, which took years and cost millions, became a flamboyant expression of national pride and international goodwill.

Ise is another story, not of restoration but of renewal. There every effort ensures that the renewed structure will be as elegant as the one replaced. First the new site is purified by priestly ceremonies. Selection of the hinoki from a special forest begins ten years in advance. These sixteen thousand cypress timbers, chosen with accompanying prayers, are hauled on wagons drawn by local residents in ceremonial white robes. After the timber-hauling pageant the neighboring townsfolk are privileged to strew white pebbles on the inner precincts of the two main shrines that the dedication will make off-limits.

Acquiescence to the forces of nature is revealed in countless ways. Each shrine's supporting columns, much thicker than needed to hold up the structure, are the shape and thickness of the live tree. Stuck in the ground as they once grew, they respond to the moisture of the earth. The finished shrine displays the variegated beauty of the hinoki's natural texture—not the dead uniformity of a painted surface but the nuanced grain of natural growth.

It is not surprising that the skills and the standards of the ancient Japanese carpenter-joiner have survived these fifteen hundred years. For each generation has had the opportunity and the need to match the work of the first builders. In the Ise tradition, the Japanese do not waste their energies repairing the great works of the past. Instead, they do the same work over and over again themselves. They build their Chartres anew in each generation. "Herein alone," Edward S. Morse observed, "the Japanese carpenter has an immense advantage over the American, for his trade, as well as other trades, have been perpetuated through generations of families. The little children have been brought up amidst the odor of fragrant shavings. . . ."

The Japanese carpenters' tools, it seems, were at first made from prototype iron implements brought in ancient times (c.300 B.C.–A.D. 300) from the Asian mainland. Though refined over the centuries, these still show their early origins. They are designed for the Asian stroke—sawing and planing toward the body, rather than, as in the West, away from the body. Japanese wooden structures used few nails, for they were carpenter-joined. Love of the unadorned wood surface produced a variety of tools for different woods and different finishes that astonished Western observers who wondered if the perfect swallow-tail joints at the corners of door and window frames could have been the product of magic. By 1943, before hand-operated power tools were widely used, the customary tool-chest of a Japanese carpenter included 179 items. His nine chisels had cutting edges that increased by increments of 3 millimeters (0.12 in.). The Japanese carpenter lavished on the frames of shrines and houses a micrometric elegance that Westerners have reserved for their most elegant cabinets. Their shrines and houses of wood became their prized furniture. And almost their only furniture!

Respect for the uniqueness of each piece of wood is assured when lumber for these structures is not sold in random pieces. To provide timbers that match one another in grain and color, the segments of cut logs are tied back together in the positions they filled in the living trunk. How different from the stock of a Western lumberyard! The very word "lumber" (which in English first referred to miscellaneous stored items) betrays the difference. For the Japanese carpenter every timber has its claim to a continuing life.

*   *   *

In countless little ways the Ise shrines are still intimately tied to nature and the seasons. The cakes and sake for the renewal celebrations are made from rice ceremonially transplanted in the same seven-acre rice paddies that have been used for two thousand years. This field is irrigated with the clean waters of the river Isuzu, and fertilized not by night soil but only by dried sardines and soy bean patties. In late April trees are cut for the new hoes to be used in sowing the seed. In late June young men and women, wearing white garments tucked in with red cords, transplant the seedlings to the tune of sacred drum and flute music, and join in a procession to the nearby shrine of the deity who owns the paddy, where they dance and pray for the harvest.

Classical Shinto buildings do not dominate the surrounding nature but fit in. They are nonmonumental in every sense of the word. Made of wood and not of stone, they do not defy the elements. And they do not rise above the surrounding trees. Unlike Gothic cathedrals or Greek temples, they are not structures complete in themselves that could be set in cities or on mountaintops. Japanese shrines do not overwhelm or aspire. The buildings at Ise acquiesce in the landscape and become part of it, renewable as the seasons.

In their "modest" scale they differ too from the sacred buildings of other great world religions. Hindus, Buddhists, Jews, Christians, and Muslims have built their temples, synagogues, churches, and mosques in grand dimensions. In Japan, if you see a work of sacred architecture from before the Meiji era that rises on a monumental scale, it is apt to be a Buddhist or Chinese import. Grand pagodas like those at Yakushiji were probably transformations of the Indian stupa. Even on these imported forms the Japanese medium of wood leaves its special mark. While the oldest *stone* pagodas in Japan come only from the twelfth century, much older pagodas there that date back to the eighth century (730) were made of wood. Buddhism, to house enormous statues of the seated or reclining Buddha, imported an alien taste for the colossal. What is thought to be the largest wooden building under a single roof is the Daibutsuden, the Hall of the Great Buddha of Todaiji at Nara. First built in 751, it has been several times destroyed by fire and rebuilt, once in the twelfth century and again in the early eighteenth century. But all the while classical Shinto architects have obstinately preserved the human scale.

The great works of Western architecture live in our mind's eye in hefty Greek columns, in the overwhelming domes of the Pantheon and St. Peter's, in the national capitols, and of course in Gothic spires. In the last century, too, we have declared our architectural war on nature in the very name of our skyscraper. "An instinctive taste," Samuel Taylor Coleridge wrote, "teaches men to build their churches in flat countries with spire steeples, which, as they cannot be referred to any other object, point as with silent finger to the sky and stars." This Western taste that Coleridge noted infected Japan only in the last century, an import from the West.

Even when Western architecture was not dramatized by a spire, it has commonly emphasized the vertical. During the European Renaissance, which gave ancient Greek and Roman motifs their modern vitality, the featured decorative element was the wall. A cornice sometimes revealed where the roof had been. But the roof itself, except when made into a dome or spire, disappeared from the approaching spectator's view. And since the dominance of steel and concrete and glass, modern Western architecture has remained an architecture of walls, façades, and invisible roofs.

Japanese classical architecture has offered a delightful contrast. The most expressive element is the roof, and the emphasis is on the horizontal. The small scale of the traditional buildings makes it possible for the approaching pedestrian to envision the whole roof, including the ridge, even as he begins to enter. The beauty of the building is most conspicuously the beauty of the roof, with its curves and sweeps and sculptural modeling. The styles of Shinto architecture, then, are distinguished by their roofs, and the hierarchy of Japanese buildings is fixed not by their height but by their roof design.

By contrast to the cornerstone laying, the customary dedication of a Western building, in Japan it is the placing of the decorative and symbolic ridgepole that dedicates the whole. This ceremony calls for divine protection, gives thanks for having completed the most difficult part of the work, and prays for safety and durability. Not only symbolically but functionally the Japanese roof holds the building together. The ridge, with its heavy timbers at right angles, emphasizes the horizontal, and the weight of the roof keeps the whole structure in place. The heavier the roof, Japanese carpenters have said, the more stable the structure. In earthquakes that are not too severe, this design has advantages. A building not resting on deep foundations but on columns at ground level, and held together by the roof, may bounce and sway without collapsing.

The Japanese concern for the form of the roof, both inside and out, discouraged the use of one of the most common structural features of Western architecture, and still further emphasized the horizontal. The familiar truss, a most un-Japanese device, is made of straight pieces to form a series of rigid triangles. It dates from Western pre-history and has had a long and useful career. Timber trusses, like those used by the ancient Greeks for roofing, were common in the Middle Ages and the Renaissance. The ancient Greeks also knew the arch, but found its shape so unappealing that they used it mainly for sewers. So the Japanese, who knew well enough the engineering principle of the truss, must have found that its crossed emphasis and its explicit rigidity violated their vision of simple elegance and flexibility for a sacred building. The truss was not widely used by the Japanese until their architecture was Westernized.

The stable wetland-farming communities of the world of Shinto offered a horizontal perspective on the universe. The Shinto divinities came not from the heavens but from beyond the horizon. The primary form of Shinto worship was not prayers sent upward to the heavens but food grown in the surrounding lands and offered on altars at the human level. While the inspiring vistas from a Greek temple are upward to the open sky, and the Gothic cathedral silhouettes its gargoyles and spires against the sky, the classical Japanese building offered a view from or through the building out to the surrounding landscape.

Apart from the roof, the most interesting feature of a classic Japanese building is its horizontal plan. For interest and variety Western architects achieved their modular arrangements in the vertical, in the differing heights and diverse decoration of a building's stories. But the Japanese architects achieved this in the horizontal. The famous Ninomaru Palace of Nijo Castle in Kyoto, built for shoguns who came to visit the capital, became a model that we can still see. There an appealing asymmetric arrangement of squares and rectangles attached at corners and edges unfolds as we move through the building or along its exterior. We enjoy a spectrum of visual surprises, far more suspenseful than what is offered by the vertical stacking of stories that can be encompassed at a glance outside a Western building. Incidentally, this same scheme multiplies the corner rooms with their broad horizontal vistas. The tatami (a straw floor mat about six by three feet), which became the standard Japanese measure of floor area, reinforced the geometric design and further emphasized the horizontal.

The horizontal view, bringing together indoors and outdoors, minimizes the boundaries in between. The mingling of inner and outer space, achieved in the modern West only laboriously and expensively by the use of glass, comes naively in classic Japanese architecture. The approaching visitor can see through the building to the garden on the other side. And the occupant seated before the opened or half-opened fusuma and shoji (movable paper screens) encompasses the house-scape and landscape in a single sweep of the eye.

The Japanese house, never complete in itself, was part of the landscape, and the garden was one with the house. When transplanted into the city, the Japanese house still called for its own miniaturized piece of landscape. The forest was sampled indoors by bonsai, the art of dwarfing trees. The classic Japanese garden had little in common with the Mughal gardens of India, the fountained landscapes of Rome, or the geometrical vistas of Versailles. Nor with the familiar informal Western gardens of colorfully patterned flowers in bloom. The Japanese garden was designed for all seasons, acquiescing in their changes and making the most of them.

The great ancient capitals of the West—Athens with her Acropolis, Rome with her seven hills—used the profile against the sky for buildings on undulating terrain. The Parthenon or a Capitoline temple punctuated the high points. But, like Nara before it, Kyoto (Heian-kyo), on the Chinese model, was laid out as a flat rectangle (three and a half miles north to south, three miles east to west) divided by a great north-south highway, and was subdivided by parallel avenues into checkerboard units. This city-model of clarity was surrounded by mysterious mist-covered mountains on the horizon. The "borrowed view" in garden design was a way to incorporate distant forested hills, the horizontal view, into the design for the house and garden.

Shinto, even when overlaid with Buddhist and Chinese elements, as in Ryoanji and other famous Zen temples, still speaks affinity with nature, reaching outward, not upward. The Japanese garden adds a whole new dimension to our Western view. It is not merely a product but a microcosm of nature. Mountains, oceans, islands, and waterfalls are all there in small horizontal compass. The *kami* can be as easily revered in a rock garden as on a mountainside. Rocks, a prominent foil to the fragility of growing trees and shrubs and mosses, affirm the unchanging. They are not an architect's effort to defy the forces of time and nature, but another way of acquiescing. The Japanese garden renews what dies or goes dormant, and reveres what survives.

In all these ways the Japanese declared a truce with the menaces of nature and of passing time. However belligerent were Shinto's political teachings, for man's relation to nature Shinto offered conquest by surrender. Their pact with nature was written in timbers of hinoki. Uncompromising Western architects in stone again and again boasted that though their lives might be short, their works would be eternal. The Japanese architects in wood could not be so deceived. At Ise they could see that if the life of art is short, life and the creators of art are eternal.

THE SPECTATOR REBORN

CHAPTER 35

I T was for a new audience in a newly flourishing art form that Shakespeare produced his version of the human comedy. Now again a writer could reach his whole community with a sustained work of literary art. The drama born in ancient Greece as we have seen was a community art. Begun as ritual with the whole community dancing in the "orchestra" together, it became a spectacle in which some citizens participated only as spectators. But in the European Middle Ages the literary arts became either immured in monastic libraries or elaborated for the entertainment of courtly audiences. The troubadours (from *trobar*, to find or invent), who flourished in Provence into the thirteenth century singing the langue d'oc vernacular, were expected to entertain the noble ladies. While supposed to "invent," in fact they only elaborated conventional tales of kings and queens, shepherds and shepherdesses, of adulterous and unrequited love. The folk music and folklore, which no one could inhibit, remained a world apart from writers and readers.

The Renaissance city and the city theaters somehow furnished a community of spectators like that which had inspired and acclaimed the great Greek dramatists. Now the spectator was reborn. "Citizens"—inhabitants of the city—became a full-spectrum theater audience. This community became the opportunity and the inspiration for Shakespeare too, whose great works were written to be acted, not to be read.

The theater had risen in London during Shakespeare's youth. The suddenness with which the new pastime had appeared raised the alarm of the learned and the pious. Like television in our time, theater acquired its frightening popularity within a half century. Playwrights and actors had been amateurs and the first players made their living by touring their troupes around the country. When they came to London they acted in the bear-baiting rings or in the courtyards of inns. But in 1576, when Shakespeare was a twelve-year-old schoolboy in Stratford, James Burbage built the first theater in London, and within forty years there were at least five others. The Globe, the Rose, the Swan, the Red Bull, the Fortune, and Blackfriars, specially designed for their purpose, were attracting Londoners of both sexes and all classes to an appealing and time-consuming new kind of professional entertainment. Travelers from the Continent were surprised at this feature of London life.

"By the daily and disorderly exercise of a number of players and playing houses erected within this City," the lord mayor of London wrote to the Archbishop of Canterbury in 1592, "the youth thereof is greatly corrupted and their manners infected with many evils and ungodly qualities by reason of the wanton and prophane devices represented on the stages by the said players, the apprentices and servants withdrawn from their works." It was no wonder that in 1596 the Privy Council assented to an order "to thrust those Players out of the Citty and to pull downe the Dicing houses." Playhouses were forced out to the suburbs, beyond the city walls, to the north and west, or, like the Globe, southward to the other side of the Thames.

When many buildings had been specially constructed for presenting plays, audiences had to be attracted. Paying from a penny to half a crown for admission, they filled the daily performances. An Englishman visiting a playhouse in Venice in 1611 found "the house very beggarly and base in comparison of our stately playhouses in England; neither can their actors compare with us for apparel, shews and music."

The building that James Burbage appropriately christened the Theatre still had the large round open-air arena of the baiting pit, now paved and with drains to carry off rainwater. Surrounding the arena were three superimposed rows of galleries. The spectators numbered altogether about three thousand. Most paid a penny to stand in the yard, others paid twopence or more for a seat in the galleries or boxes. The players, no longer crowded onto an improvised booth on stage, now enjoyed a large permanent stage with changing rooms behind, and a gallery above for a lord's room and musicians. The roofed changing rooms supported a "hut" on its fourth story to hold suspension gear so angels or other players could fly down to the stage. An open-air arena on this plan was called a "public" theater. The alternative, the "private" theater, with a usual capacity of about seven hundred, was an indoor structure like the great halls of the Inns of Court and the Oxford and Cambridge colleges, adapted from the Tudor domestic hall. A low stage protruded into the room where benches accommodated the spectators. In the larger of these "private" playhouses there were three galleries around the sides and the end. Spectators would be seated in the pit, in galleries, or in boxes, and paid sixpence or more. Until about 1606, only private playhouses were found within the City of London, and public playhouses only in the suburbs.

Playhouses were open to all who had the price of admission. But while public theaters attracted everyone, and drew mainly from the lower classes, the private theaters with higher admission prices appealed to the better educated. Publishers of plays tried to give their printed dramas a sophisticated tone by indicating on the title page that the work had been prepared for a "private" theater. The theater had its origins in performances at court, as the continuing control by the Master of the Revels indicated, but the audiences at the new theaters were anything but courtly. A sharp observer in 1579 reported:

> In our assemblies at plays in London, you shall see such heaving, and shoving, such itching and shouldering to sit by women . . . that it is a right comedy to mark their behaviour, to watch their conceits. . . . Not that any filthiness in deed is committed within the compass of that ground, as was done in Rome, but that every wanton and his paramour, every man and his mistress, every John and his Joan, every knave and his queen, are there first acquainted and cheapen the

merchandise in that place, which they pay for elsewhere as they can agree.

The frequent changes of program encouraged Londoners to come back to the same theater again and again. As Shakespeare observed in the opening chorus of *Henry V*:

> O! for a Muse of fire, that would ascend
> The brightest heaven of invention;
> A kingdom for a stage, princes to act
> And monarchs to behold the swelling scene.
> . . . . But pardon, gentles all,
> The flat unraised spirits that hath dar'd
> On this unworthy scaffold to bring forth
> So great an object: can this cockpit hold
> The vasty fields of France? or may we cram
> Within this wooden O the very casques
> That did affright the air at Agincourt?

In two weeks during the 1596 season a Londoner could have seen eleven performances of ten different plays at one playhouse, and on no day would he have had to see a repeat performance of the day before.

The burgeoning city theaters no longer provided profitable employment for amateurs. Playwriting had quickly become a growth industry and a profession. Of the twelve hundred plays offered in London theaters in the half century after 1590, some nine hundred were the work of about fifty professional playwrights.

Into this world came the young William Shakespeare (1564–1616) from Stratford-on-Avon. Son of a prominent and prosperous alderman, he seems to have had a solid elementary education at the grammar school, but he had not gone to the university. At the age of eighteen he married Anne Hathaway, twenty-six, of a substantial family in the neighborhood. They had a daughter and then twins, a boy and a girl. By 1592 he was acting in London, and was well enough known to invite the often-quoted sarcasm of Robert Greene, a prominent rival playwright. "There is an upstart crow, beautified with our feathers, that with his *Tygers heart wrapt in a Players hide* supposes he is as well able to bombast out a blank verse as the best of you, and, being an absolute Johannes Fac totum, is in his own conceit the only Shake-scene in a country." The first publication of this jack-of-all trades (fac totum) "upstart crow," William Shakespeare, was *Venus and Adonis* (1593), in the courtly mythological tradition, and dedicated to the Earl of Southampton.

> Call it not love, for Love to heaven is fled,
> Since sweating Lust on earth usurp'd his name;
> Under whose simple semblance he hath fed
> Upon fresh beauty, blotting it with blame;
>   Which the hot tyrant stains and soon bereaves,
>   As caterpillars do the tender leaves.
>
> Love comforteth like sunshine after rain,
> But Lust's effect is tempest after sun;
> Love's gentle spring doth always fresh remain,
> Lust's winter comes ere summer half be done.
> Love surfeits not, Lust like a glutton dies;
> Love is all truth, Lust full of forged lies.

He followed it the next year with his "graver labour," *The Rape of Lucrece*, another long poem dedicated to the earl. His best poetry, outside the plays, would be found in his 154 sonnets, published in 1609 and dedicated to a cryptic "Mr. W. H." But Shakespeare was most committed to the newly flourishing entertainment art. Despite his not entirely respectable occupation he became a gentleman in 1596, when the College of Heralds finally granted his father a coat of arms.

We know little else about Shakespeare's private life during these twenty years when he wrote the great body of drama and poetry against which all later creators of English literature would be measured. He prospered, and very soon, at his new occupation in London. By 1597 he was well enough off to buy the Great House of New Place, the second largest dwelling in Stratford. It was three stories high with five gables, on a city lot sixty by seventy feet. Within the next few years he also purchased a 137-acre tract near town for £230 cash, and invested the considerable sum of £440 in the lease of tithes. In 1613 he bought for speculation the Blackfriars Gate-House property in London. His remunerative loans and continuing litigation proved him a man of substance. Shakespeare became for a time the most popular playwright of the London stage. Prudent investments and his good reputation would enable him to leave his heirs a solid estate.

* * *

When the First Folio of Shakespeare's thirty-six plays was published in 1623, seven years after his death, eighteen plays appeared in print for the first time. Printing a play was a way of squeezing some profit from a playwright's work when it could not be acted because of the plague or when the stage version had failed. Players' companies guarded successful scripts against competitors. In 1598, when Sir Thomas Bodley began building the collection for the great Oxford library that still bears his name, he persuaded the Stationers' Company in London, which had a monopoly of English printing, to agree to send his library in perpetuity a copy of every book. But he cautioned his librarian in Oxford against collecting the "many idle books and riff-raffs . . . almanacs, plays, and proclamations," of which he would have "none, but such as are singular." Of plays, he explained, "hardly one in forty" was worth keeping.

Printing the texts of plays was a way of giving the theater and the new profession of playwright an aura of respectability. In 1616, when Ben Jonson, Shakespeare's rival, published a folio of his *Workes* it was the first time the collected plays of an English author had been published. The First Folio of Shakespeare in 1623 was only the second. Jonson was ridiculed for dignifying his plays as if they were serious literary "Workes." Plays printed before 1616 appeared in the unbound form common for almanacs and joke books. To print plays in a large handsomely bound folio as was done with collections of sermons or ancient classics claimed a new longevity for the playwright's work.

Shakespeare's contemporary public were not readers but listeners. While our age of omnipresent print, and of photographic and electronic images, relies on the eye, Elizabethans were experienced and long-suffering listeners. Once in 1584, when Laurence Chaderton, Master of Emmanuel College, Cambridge, the town's preacher for a half century, had preached for only two hours the disappointed congregation cried out, "For God's sake, sir, go on! we beg you, go on!" He and others urged that listening was more profitable than reading. The spoken word brought "the zeale of the speaker, the attention of the hearer, the promise of God to the ordinary preaching of His Word . . . and many other things which are not to be hoped for by reading the written sermons." Those who lived by the spoken word made every sermon a performance. Reading the classic sermons of Shakespeare's contemporary John Donne (1573–1631), we miss the histrionic talent that kept his audiences on edge for hours.

Shakespeare could prosper only by pleasing these audiences. As Dr. Samuel Johnson would note on the opening of the Drury Lane Theater in 1747, "we that live to please must please to live." Shakespeare's posthumous fame proved a surprising coincidence of the vulgar taste of his time with the sophisticated taste of following centuries. For Shakespeare the claims of immortality were not pressing. It was more urgent to please contemporary London playgoers. Beginning in London as the actor who annoyed Robert Greene in 1592, he appeared as a "principal comedian" in Ben Jonson's *Every Man in His Humour* in 1598, and a "principal tragedian" in Jonson's *Sejanus* in 1603, and he continued to act until he retired to Stratford in 1611.

His acting talent also gave him an advantage in selling his plays. An Elizabethan playwright usually wrote a play to the order of a playing company, then read it to the actors for their approval. If his work was approved he was paid six pounds and his role was over. Some playwrights, like George Chapman, did not even go to see their plays performed. But Shakespeare, we are told, paid close attention to the production. By 1594 he was an acting member of the Lord Chamberlain's Company, which had its problems. In 1597 a seditious comedy, *The Isle of Dogs*, by Thomas Nashe and Ben Jonson led the Privy Council to shut all playhouses. Jonson and two of the actors were sent to prison. In 1598, when the theaters reopened, Shakespeare enjoyed a great success with *Henry IV*, Part One, introducing Falstaff. The company also did well with Jonson's *Every Man in His Humour*, in which Shakespeare acted.

When the company lost their lease at the Theatre they pooled the actors' resources to build a new theater across the Thames south of London. With timbers from Burbage's dismantled historic Theatre they erected the new Globe Playhouse in July 1599. Taking the motto *Totus mundus agit histrionem* (A whole world of players), the Lord Chamberlain's Company flourished with its rich repertory by Shakespeare, Jonson, and others, despite increasing competition from new theaters and the boys' companies. Shakespeare himself held an investor's share and as an actor was entitled to another portion of the company's receipts, adding up to about 10 percent. His share fluctuated over the years. For the first time these actors had financed the building of their own theater. And the greatest English dramatist acquired a substantial stake in the popularity of his work in his own day. The public was becoming a patron.

On his accession, King James designated the former Lord Chamberlain's Company as the King's Company. Letters patent (May 19, 1603) expressly authorized nine of its members (including William Shakespeare and Richard Burbage) "freely to use and exercise the art and faculty of playing Comedies, Tragedies, Histories, Interludes, Morals, Pastorals, stage plays . . . as well for the recreation of our loving subjects as for our solace and pleasure." The company acted before the court six times during the next Christmas holidays.

Shakespeare continued to write and act for the King's Company at the Globe and in the Blackfriars, their "private" playhouse during winter. The Age of Shakespeare at the Globe had a dramatic end on June 19, 1613. During a gala performance there of Shakespeare's *Henry VIII* "with many extraordinary circumstances of pomp and majesty," the cannon discharged from the thatched roof to announce the entry of the king set fire to the thatch. "Where being thought at first but an idle smoke, and their eyes more attentive to the show, it kindled inwardly, and ran round like a train, consuming within an hour the whole house to the very ground. This was the fatal period of that virtuous fabric; wherein yet nothing did perish but wood and straw, and a few forsaken cloaks; only one man had his breeches set on fire, that would perhaps have broiled him, if he had not by the benefit of a provident wit put it out with bottle ale." By the following spring the prosperous members of the King's Company, including Shakespeare, had paid for having the Globe "new builded in a far fairer manner than before." But Shakespeare, who now owned a fourteenth share in the enterprise, had retired to Stratford. Within his twenty-year London career he had produced the poems and plays that made him the idol of English literature. The English-speaking community in all future centuries would be united by familiarity with "the Bible and Shakespeare."

*　*　*

Shakespeare had arrived at a crucial moment for a creator's collaboration with the city audience. The city theater, as we have seen, had just now provided new incentives and opportunities to reach out to a listening public hungry for entertainment. The reborn spectator offered the literary man a new chance for feedback, which meant a new stimulus and a new resource for creators. In the soliloquy itself, a newly developed literary convention, the actor shared his private thoughts with the audience. We hear the hesitating Hamlet blame himself:

> O! that this too solid flesh would melt,
> Thaw and resolve itself into a dew;
> Or that the Everlasting had not fix'd
> His canon 'gainst self-slaughter! O God! O God!
> How weary, stale, flat, and unprofitable
> Seem to me all the uses of this world.
> Fie on it! O fie! 'tis an unweeded garden
> That grows to seed; things rank and gross in nature
> Possess it merely. . . .
>
> （I, ii)

The sense of nationhood, inspired by a vigorous virgin queen and by a generation of world explorers, challenged by a formidable Spanish rival, was enriched by a national vernacular recently conscious of itself. As John of Gaunt boasts in *Richard II*:

> This royal throne of kings, this scepter'd isle,
> This earth of majesty, this seat of Mars,
> This other Eden, demi-paradise,
> This fortress built by Nature for herself
> Against infection and the hand of war,
> This happy breed of men, this little world,
> This precious stone set in the silver sea,
> Which serves it in the office of a wall,
> Or as a moat defensive to a house,
> Against the envy of less happier lands,
> This blessed plot, this earth, this realm, this England.
>
> (II, i)

By reaching recklessly out to imaginary creations of other times and places the Elizabethan stage violated the traditional canons of Aristotle's *Poetics*, which still insisted on the duty of all artists to imitate nature. "Art imitates nature as well as it can," observed Dante, "as a pupil follows his master, thus it is a sort of grandchild of God." These Aristotelian unities of time, place, and action would make the unreality of the stage less disturbing. And a play *read*, it was said, "hath not half the pleasure of a Play *Acted:* for . . . it wants the pleasure of Graceful Action."

Sir Philip Sidney expressed the liberated Elizabethan spirit in his *Apologie for Poetrie* (1580; published, 1595):

> Only the poet, disdaining to be tied to any such subjection, lifted up with the vigor of his invention, doth grow in effect another nature, in making things either better than nature bringeth forth, or, quite anew, forms such as never were in nature. . . . Nature never set forth the earth in so rich tapes-

try as divers poets have done. . . . Her world is brazen, the
poets only deliver a golden.

And he translated the plain biblical theology into literature: man the
creator fulfilling the image of his Creator. "Neither let it be deemed
too saucy a comparison to balance the highest point of man's with
the efficacy of nature; but rather give right honor to the heavenly
Maker of that maker, who, having made man to his own likeness, set
him beyond and over all the works of that second nature: which is
nothing he showeth so much as in poetry."

The dramatist, no longer to be blamed for "deceiving" his audience by misrepresenting nature, should be applauded, for "that
which they do, is not done to *Circumvent*, but to *Represent*, not to
Deceive others, but to make others *Conceive*." In the next century
John Dryden would actually defend the dramatist's mission as a welcome kind of "deception." Sidney's *Apologie for Poetrie* had been a
prophetic defense of the poet's power to reach *in*, to carry the listener into the playground of his personal imagination. For the poet
mere imitation (*mimesis*) was not enough. Writing before any of
Shakespeare's plays had appeared, while still defending the Aristotelian unities, he deplored the poor products on the London stage.

We do not know that Shakespeare ever read Sidney. But Sidney's declaration of independence from the imprisoning archetype
of nature spoke for Shakespeare, too, and opened a world for the
adventuring word. This new stage, this new scene of collaborative
conception and deception, Shakespeare peopled beyond even Sidney's imagining. The poet and his audience would journey inward to
bizarre new worlds where creation somehow preceded conception.
The spectator was no longer a mere victim but a full collaborator,
without whom the poets' work was unfulfilled. The vast new world
within, a new "nature" of the poets' own creation, stretched infinitely in all directions.

With prodigious energy Shakespeare used all the conventions of
his age in this joint exploring-creating expedition. He started with
light comedy, *The Comedy of Errors*, *The Taming of the Shrew*, *Love's
Labour's Lost*, and the tragedy of *Romeo and Juliet*. He explored the

recent history of the Wars of the Roses in the three parts of *Henry VI*. He depicted the tragedies of earlier English history in *Richard II* and *Richard III*, in the adventures of *Henry IV* and *Henry V*. He mined the grandeur, romance, and tragedy of ancient Rome in *Julius Caesar*, *Antony and Cleopatra*, and *Coriolanus*. He elaborated comedies from the Italian—*The Merchant of Venice* and *Much Ado about Nothing*—and invented the fantasy of *A Midsummer Night's Dream*. He reshaped fragments of history and folklore into triumphant tragedies—*Hamlet*, *Othello*, *King Lear*, and *Macbeth*.

The limits imposed by Elizabethan society Shakespeare somehow made into his opportunity. For the dramatist still dared not comment explicitly on the politics or mores of his own age. Not until the theater would be freed from the whims of the Master of the Revels and the Privy Council could there be serious dramas of contemporary life on the London stage. Ironically, Hamlet and Lear and Macbeth would remain alive for alien centuries, precisely because Shakespeare's inhibitions saved him from recounting topical problems in familiar settings. He would reach out to us, and take us inward with him to enjoy the Human Comedy in exotic costumes and on remote scenes, equally enticing to the Elizabethan theatergoer and to us.

* * *

While we can never solve the mystery of Shakespeare, we do know enough about him and his work to dispose of some easy generalizations. For example, the temptation bred on the Left Banks of the world to identify the creator's genius with instability, or even with madness. Shakespeare's life makes us pause at Proust's self-serving declaration that "everything great comes from neurotics. They alone have . . . composed our masterpieces." Shakespeare's contemporaries seemed agreed on his good-natured equanimity. It is hard to believe he was bland. But Charles Lamb and others have found it "impossible to conceive a mad Shakespeare." Did he have "the sanity of true genius"? Among quarrelsome competing playwrights, he avoided the acrimony that drew his rival Ben Jonson into a murderous duel with a fellow actor and sent him to prison for a seditious play. Called the amiable "English Terence," he was widely praised for "no railing but a reigning wit." Still, during Shakespeare's lifetime, Ben Jonson exceeded him in reputation and it was Jonson, not Shakespeare, whom the king appointed poet laureate with a substantial pension in 1616.

Had Shakespeare not enjoyed the affection of his fellow actors his plays might not have survived. About three fourths of the prolific output of playwrights in his lifetime has disappeared. But Shakespeare's fellow actors, as a token of friendship to him, did us the great service of preserving the texts of his plays when they arranged publication of the First Folio in 1623. What other playwright of that age was so well served by his fellows? The First Folio Shakespeare, the compilers explained, was published not for profit but "only to keep the memory of so worthy a friend and fellow alive as was our Shakespeare." In his Ode addressed "to the Memory of My Beloved Master William Shakespeare," Jonson's praise for the "Sweet Swan of Avon" expressed a general view. Shakespeare's professional life, in a turbulent age, was conspicuously placid. Except for the "dark lady of the sonnets," we know of no unrequited loves, no Beatrice or Fiammetta!

Still, amiable legends circulated which had the ring of truth and the appeal of Shakespearean wit, and which idolatrous biographers would have trouble explaining away. One was a stage-door anecdote noted for March 13, 1601, in the diary of a London student:

> Upon a time when [Richard] Burbidge played Richard III there was a citizen grew so far in liking with him that, before she went from the play, she appointed him to come that night unto her by the name of Richard the Third. Shakespeare, overhearing their conclusion, went before, was entertained and at his game ere Burbidge came. Then, message being brought that Richard the Third was at the door, Shakespeare caused return to be made that William the Conqueror was before Richard the Third.

Shakespeare's proverbial fluency was praised by his fellow actors in their preface to the Folio. "His mind and hand went together, and what he thought, he uttered with the easiness that we have scarce received from him a blot in his papers." But Jonson, a laborious writer who left only a fraction of Shakespeare's output, years later still nursed resentment that the players should have "mentioned it as an honor to Shakespeare, that in his writing . . . he never blotted out a line. My answer hath been, 'Would he had blotted a thousand!' "

Unlike other great creators of the human comedy, Shakespeare never left his home country. Even in England he traveled little, and had no public life outside his profession. He had a meager formal education, "small Latin and less Greek," and showed no learned idiosyncrasy in his reading habits. His best resource was probably in the classic curriculum of the Elizabethan grammar school he attended, reinforced by the reading habits of any literate Elizabethan. Like Boccaccio and Chaucer before them, the writers of Shakespeare's age did not aim at "originality." They were accustomed to borrow, embellish, elaborate, and revise Homer, Ovid, Cicero, Virgil, Plutarch, among others, and the abundant classical myths and legends. None of Shakespeare's plays told a thoroughly original story. As an actor, Shakespeare made his living and stocked his memory with works of other playwrights. He seems to have been well read too in contemporary English authors. The narrow scope and traditions of his elementary education focused his imagination. He felt no uneasiness at drawing on these others and on his own earlier works, or simply translating into blank verse Holinshed's *Chronicles* or North's *Plutarch*. His *Julius Caesar, Coriolanus*, and *Antony and Cleopatra* showed a faithfulness to their Plutarchean source that might worry later pursuers of originality. When Ben Jonson ridiculed Shakespeare's lack of classical learning, one of Shakespeare's champions retorted "That if Mr. Shakespeare had not read the Ancients, he had likewise not stollen any thing from 'em; (A Fault the other made no Conscience of)."

The better-documented Ben Jonson provided a perfect foil for our Shakespeare. The robust and irritable Jonson, insecure stepson of a bricklayer, was proud of his learning, and of the sponsorship of the pedantic William Camden. In his plays he took up and developed the popular psychology of "humours." With explicit theories he professed to do his best to follow the classical rules and apologized, as in *Sejanus*, when he violated them. His most durable play, *Volpone*, applied the simplistic theory that each character should express a dominant humour. While Shakespeare, too, briefly experimented with this theory (in *Timon of Athens*), his achievement was to liberate the theater from such conventions and formulas. Jonson explained in the Prologue to *Every Man in His Humour*,

> Though need make many poets, and some such
> As art and nature have not bettered much;
> Yet ours, for want, hath not so loved the stage,
> As he dare serve th' ill customs of the age. . . .
> One such, today, as others plays should be;
> Where neither chorus wafts you o'er the seas,
> Nor creaking throne comes down the boys to please . . .
> But deeds and language such as men do use,
> And persons such as Comedy would choose,
> When she would show an image of the times,
> And sport with human follies, not with crimes. . . .

Shakespeare's characteristic response was an *Antony and Cleopatra*, which violated all classical rules and offered thirty-two changes of scene across the remote and ancient world.

*   *   *

Nothing was more remarkable about Shakespeare than his afterlife. Within a half century after his death, in 1668, John Dryden intoned the paean of posterity.

> . . . he was the man who of all Modern and perhaps Ancient Poets, had the largest and most comprehensive Soul. All the Images of Nature were still present to him, and he drew them not laboriously, but luckily: when he describes any thing, you more than see it, you feel it too. Those who accuse him to have wanted learning, give him the greater commendation: he was naturally learned; he needed not the spectacles of Books to read Nature: he looked inwards, and found her there.

"I am proud," Coleridge boasted in 1811, "that I was the first in time who publicly demonstrated . . . that the supposed irregularities and extravagances of Shakespeare were the mere dreams of a pedantry that arraigned the eagle because it had not the dimensions of the swan." And he saw that "on the Continent the works of Shakespeare are honoured in a double way; by the admiration of Italy and Germany, and by the contempt of the French."

For the cult of Shakespeare, which has had its ups and downs but never died, George Bernard Shaw in 1901 invented the word "bardolatry." The cult flourished too in Tocqueville's America, this land of the equality of conditions, where frontier wits made burlesques of Shakespeare a staple for raw communities. "The literary inspiration of Great Britain darts its beams into the depths of the forests of the New World," Tocqueville noted in 1839. "There is hardly a pioneer's hut which does not contain a few odd volumes of Shakespeare. I remember reading the feudal drama of Henry V for the first time in a log cabin."

THE MUSIC OF INSTRUMENTS:

From Court to Concert

THE arts of instrument-created music changed the relation of performer to audience. Western drama had been born in the separation of ancient Greek spectators from the participants, and the "orchestra," once a dancing place for community ritual, became a site where some danced while others looked on. So, too, modern music climaxing in the symphony would separate the audience from the music makers in a new way. Since Gregorian chants had been sung by the clergy only, Luther's emphasis on congregational music aimed to allow all to affirm their faith by the very act of singing. But the elaboration of musical instruments, increasingly specialized and requiring increasing skill, opened a widening gulf between performer and listener. Now the audience heard someone else's affirmation.

A product of this rise of instrumental music, a grand creation of Western music, was the symphony. The word "sonata" (from Latin *sonare*, to sound) as opposed to "cantata," a composition for voices (from Latin *cantare*, to sing), first comes into English about 1694, for a musical composition for instruments. The great creators of symphony had at hand a new musical form along with a newly elaborated array of instruments in an orchestra—in communities eager to support their work. All these elements came into being slowly after the Renaissance, the product of some people we know and of more who remain anonymous.

The "sonata" in the baroque period (1600–1750; the era of Monteverdi, Purcell, and J. S. Bach) came to denote a new type of instrumental work in the "abstract" style. This meant music without words, and referring to nothing outside itself. By the end of the seventeenth century the sonata had emerged and begun to be standardized in the works of the Italian violinist and composer Arcangelo Corelli (1653–1713). His two versions were classified not by their music form but by their social function. One was the *sonata da chiesa*, or church sonata (with a slow introduction, a loosely fugal allegro, a cantabile slow movement, and a melodic "binary" finale), the other was the *sonata de camera*, or chamber sonata mainly of dance tunes. A classical style was foreshadowed in the solo sonatas for keyboard instruments of Domenico Scarlatti (1685–1757) and Carl Philipp Emanuel Bach (1714–1788).

The term "symphony" and its variants were first used in the seventeenth century simply for the various forms of instrumental music. But it came to be used mainly for the Italian opera overture of three movements (fast, slow, fast). These overtures began to be played in concerts apart from their operas. Meanwhile the three-movement (or four-movement) symphony for orchestra became a form all its own for the classical symphony, quite separate from the overture, with a unique dignity. "Symphony" now came to mean a sonata for orchestra. It would have been impossible without the new wealth of musical instruments.

In Western Europe the practice began, about the fifteenth century, of building whole "families" of instruments. A typical family, like the shawms (double-reed woodwind instruments), would be made in instruments from the smallest to the largest size. The social role of music was revealed by the fact that instruments were differentiated mainly into *haut* (loud) and *bas* (soft). Loud instruments were for outdoor music and soft were for more intimate, usually indoor, occasions. The shawm came to be known as the *hautbois* (loud wood), which left its trace on the modern version of this same instrument, the oboe (a correct transcription of how the French word was pronounced in the eighteenth century).

A clue to the newly flourishing technology of musical instruments was the piano. "Pianoforte" (later abbreviated to "piano") first appears in English about 1767. An abbreviation of *piano e forte*, meaning "soft and strong," "pianoforte" named a new instrument that, unlike the harpsichord, could vary its tone. The harpsichord could only be plucked. But the sound of the piano was made by hammers operated from a keyboard and striking metal strings. The varying force of the hammer, controlled by dampers and pedals, made the gradations of tone. The first successful piano, about 1726, was the work of an Italian harpsichord maker, Bartolomeo Cristofori (1655–1731). Described at the time as a "harpsichord with soft and loud," it had all the essentials of modern piano action. Haydn's active life as a musician spanned the years from the piano's invention nearly to its modern form. He had decided tastes in pianos, preferring the Viennese to the English. Mozart, too, was interested in the mechanics of the piano, still developing in his lifetime, and he contributed to its improvement. He had a pedal constructed for his piano that he used when improvising and for the basso continuo of his concerti. Beethoven believed the musical possibilities of the piano were still imperfectly understood and helped reveal them.

When cast iron replaced wooden frames to hold the strings, it increased their tension and the loudness of their music. The piano was designed in various shapes and sizes as the Industrial Revolution brought mass production. Within a century the piano in the living room became a symbol of middle-class gentility, and eligible young ladies needed their piano lessons. As the audiences of music lovers multiplied, the power and versatility of the piano enlisted the talents of the best composers.

But the piano was only one of a wide array of new instruments and of newly perfected ancient instruments that would make the modern symphony orchestra. The violin, originating in the medieval fiddle and developed during the Renaissance, was much improved by Antonio Stradivari (1644–1737), Giuseppe Guarneri (1698–1744), and others. The modern bow was invented by François Tourte (1747–1835), and the violin had its modern form by the early nineteenth century. Trumpets and horns were elaborated and made more versatile by added lengths of tubing; clarinets became respectable in the woodwind section by 1800. There was hardly any instrument of the modern orchestra, from the trombone to the harp, that did not acquire greater volume and subtlety in the late eighteenth and early nineteenth century.

As the elaborated sonata was matched by the elaborating instruments of all kinds, the modern large orchestra emerged—a collection of instruments equipped to play symphonies. Mid-eighteenth-century orchestras were commonly solo ensembles with one player in each part and little interdependence of the parts. The large orchestra for a public concert hall needed other music. Meanwhile chamber music, in the form developed by Haydn, Mozart, and Beethoven, attained an intimacy and expressive range it lacked when it was merely synonymous with instrumental music. "Chamber music" acquired an elite and even arcane tone by contrast with the newly flourishing public music.

* * *

The "orchestra," a grand new instrument of instruments, was itself a creation of these "classical" Western composers and a by-product of their symphonies. Slowly after the Renaissance, with the rise of "wordless" music, there developed the arts of "orchestration," of using instruments for their special music properties. Until then music, not generally composed for particular instruments, would be played by whatever instruments were available. An organist of St. Mark's in Venice, Giovanni Gabrieli (1557–1612), may have been the first Western composer to designate particular instruments for the parts. The rise of opera in Italy about 1600, and the coming of the opera orchestra reinforcing dramatic effects, led to more specific scoring and greater reliance on strings to balance winds and percussion. And the *Orfeo* of Claudio Monteverdi (1567–1643), performed in Mantua in 1607 with an orchestra of some forty instruments, is said to be the first occasion when a composer specified which instruments were to be used at which moments.

Not until the eighteenth century did the word "orchestra" cease to have only its ancient Greek meaning for the space in front of the stage where the community had once danced and where dramatic choruses danced and sang. Now it meant a company of musicians

performing concerted instrumental music. And now Byron conde-
scended to "the pert shopkeeper, whose throbbing ear aches with
orchestras which he pays to hear." "To orchestrate" would not enter
our language until the late nineteenth century.

The modern symphony orchestra arose out of the Italian opera
orchestra and English and French court orchestras, which at first
had only strings, but gradually added woodwinds and other instruments. By the mid-eighteenth century the basic modern symphony
orchestra had its four sections—woodwinds, brass, percussion, and
strings. Surprisingly, these features of the modern symphony orchestra took shape not in a great capital but in the phoenix-city of
Mannheim on the right bank of the Rhine in southwestern Germany. Founded in 1606 on a checkerboard pattern of rectangular
blocks, Mannheim was destroyed in 1622, during the Thirty Years'
War, rebuilt and then again destroyed by the French in 1689. But
the irrepressible community at the convenient confluence of the
Rhine and the Neckar rose again. It became a cultural center for the
electors palatine in the mid-eighteenth century. The elector Karl
Theodor (ruled 1743–59; in Mannheim, 1743–78) had a personal
passion for music that attracted some of the best performers and
composers, creating an orchestra that became a prototype for the
modern symphony. This Mannheim School, which flourished until
the abrupt removal of the court to Munich in 1778, adapted the dramatic Italian overture to the new form of the concert symphony, and
devised novel instrumental effects. Musicians across Europe came to
recognize the "Mannheim sign" (a melodic appoggiatura) and the
"Mannheim rocket" (a controlled orchestral crescendo making a
swiftly ascending melodic figure).

Here the classical symphony acquired the form that would be
elaborated by Haydn, Mozart, and Beethoven. And Mannheim announced the age of public concerts, when symphony orchestras
would become symbols and catalysts of civic pride. As these orchestras multiplied in the next century the public appetite for music became more historical and more cosmopolitan. Now concerts not
only offered works commissioned for the occasion or sacred or traditional music. They reached back to revive earlier works. The Con-

certs of Ancient Music held in London (1776–1848) pointed the way to this "historicism," dramatized by Felix Mendelssohn's 1829 centennial performance of parts of Bach's *Saint Matthew Passion*. Mannheim was destined to be destroyed again in World War II, but again showed its capacity to be reborn. Did the city's shallow past help explain its openness to new ways in music?

The founder of the improbable Mannheim School of symphonists was the vigorous Johann Stamitz (1717–1757), whose leadership made it famous across Europe. His orchestra, large for its day, included twenty violins, four each of violas, violoncellos, and double basses, two each of flutes, oboes, and bassoons, four horns, one trumpet, and two kettledrums. The musical traveler-historian Charles Burney (1726–1814) was so impressed that he called this orchestra "an army of generals." Stamitz achieved new melodramatic effects with the full range of these instruments for crescendo, diminuendo, sforzando, tremolo, and virtuoso violin performances, expanding from the whispery pianissimo to the explosive fortissimo. He added a contrasting second theme to the sonata's allegro movements, and increased movements from three to four by adding a fast finale after the minuet. While these four movements would become standard for the symphonies of Haydn and Mozart, Beethoven would replace the minuet with a scherzo.

* * *

The symphony orchestra, increasing in size and cost, needed patrons. It required new complex musical compositions, along with organization, leadership, and a responsive audience. In Beethoven's lifetime a new creative role was beginning to be revealed for the conductor. The arts of drama and architecture also required leadership, organization, and community participation. But the writer, painter, or sculptor could create for himself, needed no other performer and no stage but paper, canvas, or stone. Music shared with painting, sculpture, and architecture the peculiarity that it too could be a "background" or ambient art. The classification of instruments as "loud" (for outdoors) or "soft" (for indoors) revealed this role. Music transformed the atmosphere as other things were happening.

While the book required a focused reader, music allowed variant degrees of inattention. This ambient nature of music, which made it useful for worship, ritual, festival, nuptials, and coronations also explained its long subordination to the needs of church and court. And this wonderfully protean character explains Walter Pater's observation that "all art constantly aspires towards the condition of music."

Just as the Gregorian chant enlisted music for the church, the symphony and its orchestra signaled the emergence of instrumental music as an art in its own right, becoming dependent not on prince or church but on a public of music lovers. In this story Haydn, Mozart, and Beethoven played crucial roles in their creation of the modern symphony. Their lives overlapped, they knew and influenced each other, but their careers and their products were spectacularly distinctive. In their lives they dramatized the changing resources and opportunities for Western music.

Joseph Haydn (1732–1809), often called the father of the symphony, found his opportunity and his challenge in a small but rich principality in western Hungary. His career showed how much could be done within the narrows of princely patronage, where he spent his thirty maturing years.

> My prince was always satisfied with my works. Not only did
> I have the encouragement of constant approval, but as conductor of an orchestra I could make experiments, observe
> what produced an effect and what weakened it, and was thus
> in a position to improve, to alter, make additions or omissions, and be as bold as I pleased. I was cut off from the
> world; there was no one to confuse or torment me, and I was
> forced to become original.

The story of Haydn's life is how he secured and used this playground for his music. Then how he finally reached out to the wider world.

Born in 1732 into the family of a wheelwright in an eastern Austrian village near the Hungarian border, he fortunately impressed the choirmaster of the Cathedral of St. Stephen in Vienna, who toured the countryside to find choristers. The beauty of the eight-year-old Haydn's voice and his remarkable ability to trill his notes brought him the reward of a pocketful of cherries, which he never forgot, and an invitation to the choir school of St. Stephen. There he acquired a wide musical experience but no education in musical theory. When his voice changed, he was dropped from the school and at seventeen had to shift for himself in the big city. He took young pupils, and made music for dances and serenades while he taught himself musical theory in the works of C.P.E. Bach and others. Recommended by his aristocratic pupils, in 1758 he became music director in the chapel of a minor Bohemian nobleman, Count Morzin. When Morzin found he could not afford a sixteen-piece orchestra, it was lucky for young Haydn. His first symphony composed for Count Morzin had already charmed a grander patron, Prince Paul Anton Esterhazy.

Along with his title of prince of the Holy Roman Empire, Prince Paul Anton (1710–1762) inherited a family tradition of hospitality and patronage. His baroque castle at Eisenstadt, outside Vienna, offered two hundred rooms for the guests who provided the audience for his concerts, the visitors to his picture gallery, the readers for his library, and walking companions on the countryside of grottoes and artificial waterfalls. The prince himself played the violin and cello and admired the young Haydn, whom he engaged as assistant conductor of his large and active orchestra. The contract, dated May 1, 1761, obliged Haydn "to conduct himself in an exemplary manner, abstaining from undue familiarity and from vulgarity in eating, drinking, and conversation," to preserve the harmony of the musicians, and "to instruct the female vocalists, in order that they may not forget in the country what they have been taught with much trouble and expense in Vienna." His musical duties required him to "appear daily in the antechamber before and after midday, and inquire whether His Highness is pleased to order a performance of the orchestra," to "compose such music as His Serene Highness may command . . . and not compose for any other person without the knowledge and permission of His Highness."

The prince's brother Nicholas "the Magnificent," who succeeded to the title and the family tradition of patronage in 1762, put competing princes in the shade. Returning from France, he decided to build his own Versailles. To prove his power over nature, he purposely chose an insect-infested swamp, which he had drained and cleared, as the site of his fantasy castle, which he called Esterhaza. Prince Nicholas's own illustrated book recalled its charms. Besides the usual country amenities of parks, grottoes, and waterfalls, there was a library of "seventy-five hundred books, all exquisite editions, to which novelties are being added daily," manuscripts, "old and new engravings by the best masters," a picture gallery "liberally supplied with first-class original paintings by famous Italian and Dutch masters," a marionette theater "built like a grotto," and a luxurious opera house that would hold four hundred people.

> Every day, at 6 PM, there is a performance of an Italian *opera seria* or *buffa* or of German comedy, always attended by the prince. Words cannot describe how both eye and ear are delighted here. When the music begins, its touching delicacy, the strength and force of the instruments penetrate the soul for the great composer, Herr Haydn himself, is conducting. But the audience is also overwhelmed by the admirable lighting and the deceptively perfect stage settings. At first we see the clouds on which the gods are seated sink slowly to earth. Then the gods rise upward and instantly vanish, and then again everything is transformed into a delightful garden, an enchanted wood, or, it may be, a glorious hall.

In 1776, when Esterhaza was completed and Haydn was named musical director, Prince Nicholas fully deserved his title as "the Magnificent."

Haydn helped make Esterhaza famous by attracting the best singers from Italy and musicians from all over for his celebrated orchestra (from sixteen to twenty-two players). "If I want to enjoy a good opera," said Empress Maria Theresa (1717–1780), "I go to Esterhaza." For one of her visits Haydn wrote a symphony (No. 48) and produced his opera, *Philemon and Baucis*, in the marionette theater. After a masked ball and sensational fireworks came a finale of a thousand colorfully costumed folk-dancing peasants. Haydn's proudest present for the empress's table was three grouse that he had miraculously felled with one shot.

He was expected to plan similar celebrations at least once a year, and most of Haydn's operas were written for such occasions. The robust festivities sometimes included mock country fairs and performances by whole villages with their own bands and dancing troupes. Haydn's musicians, engaged for the season without their families, were exhausted by the frequent performances and endless rehearsals that stretched their stay deep into the autumn. "Papa" Haydn looked after them and tried to persuade the prince to send musicians on furlough back to their families. Hoping the prince would get the message, he even wrote a "Farewell" symphony in which the sounds of one instrument after another ceased as each player put out his candle.

Haydn spent some thirty years—most of his adult life—in this gilded prison, not lacking performers or appreciative audiences for his compositions. His family life was unhappy. During his early days teaching music in Vienna he had fallen in love with a pupil, the daughter of a hairdresser, but she would not have him, and entered a convent. He then allowed her family to persuade him to marry her unattractive and quarrelsome elder sister. They had no children, and she did not "care a straw whether her husband [was] an artist or a cobbler." Which encouraged Haydn to compose a canon for the familiar poem by Lessing:

> If in the whole wide world
> But one mean wife there is,
> How sad that each of us
> Should think this one is his!

He sought relief hunting and fishing in the countryside he loved. No wonder it is impossible to make an edition of Haydn's works that includes all his ephemera. As his fame grew, calls for new compositions multiplied, even exceeding his fantastic powers of creation. His good-natured desire to satisfy admirers tempted him to sell the same work to several different persons or (as with his Paris symphonies) to publishers in different countries.

* * *

Liberation from Esterhaza, the widening of Haydn's vistas and his audience to match his growing fame, did not come from his own initiative. If Prince Nicholas the Magnificent had lived on, Haydn might have spent the rest of his life in Esterhaza. In September 1790 Haydn's patron of twenty-eight years died, succeeded by his son Prince Anton, who had no interest in music and dismissed all the musicians except Haydn himself and a few others to carry on the chapel services. With a pension, now feeling free to leave Esterhaza, Haydn moved so hastily to Vienna that he left many of his belongings behind. Flattering invitations from the king of Naples and others came in. At last Haydn, nearly sixty, was being tempted out into the world. Luckily the winning invitation was from John Peter Salomon (1745–1815) a German-born violinist and concert organizer who had settled in London. He brought an attractive commission— an opera for the king's theater, six symphonies and twenty new smaller compositions—for fees of twelve hundred pounds. While the London orchestras then led Europe in instrumental music, Haydn still showed courage when he chose London over Naples. In place of the cloistered security of the court of the king of Naples, Haydn risked the fickle public. He was at home in Italian but knew not a word of English. And then to brave the horrendous Channel crossing, which, even a century later, led Brahms to refuse an honorary degree from Cambridge! "Oh, Papa," Mozart warned, "you have had no education for the wider world, and you speak so few languages." "But my language," Haydn replied, "is understood all over the world."

Arriving on New Year's Day, 1791, he found "this mighty and vast town of London, its various beauties and marvels," a cause of "the most profound astonishment." His reach to the world would enlarge his music, for his London symphonies showed a mastery of instruments, a melody and wit, that excelled his earlier output. English audiences responded with frenzied enthusiasm. He was lion-ized by royalty and awarded an honorary degree in Oxford. These eighteen months produced a new Haydn. On his way back to Vienna he stopped at Bonn, where he met the twenty-two-year-old Beethoven, whom he advised to move to Vienna for his instruction. In his letter to the elector in Bonn urging him to support Beethoven's stay in Vienna, he testified, from the work he had already heard, "that Beethoven will eventually reach the position of one of Europe's greatest composers, and I will be proud to call myself his teacher."

After less than a year in Vienna Haydn was tempted back to London and to another triumph. There he produced the last of his brilliant twelve "London" symphonies. The king and queen tried to persuade him to make his home in England. When his London apotheosis as the God of Musical Science did not persuade him to stay, the British were offended. Meanwhile Prince Nicholas II, who had succeeded to the House of Esterhazy, brought Haydn home to Vienna for a dream revival of the prince's family's orchestra.

Somehow Haydn was not quite ready to take his chances with the public. But the English experience had stimulated him to compose some eight hundred pages of music, and widened his hopes for himself. He had been moved by the oratorios at the Handel commemoration in Westminster Abbey in 1791 and, back in Vienna, tried his hand again at that form. The product was two oratorios, both derived from English texts. Composing *The Creation*, with a libretto based on Milton's *Paradise Lost* and the Book of Genesis, he said, put him in closer touch than ever with his Creator, and it was a public success when performed in 1798. By 1801 he had completed another oratorio on the text of James Thomson's long poem *The Seasons*. In these works Haydn grandiosely celebrated the rural delights that he had enjoyed in thirty years around Esterhaza. To lift his countrymen's morale during their siege by Napoleon, he composed on the English model of "God Save the King" an Austrian national anthem, "Gott erhalte Franz den Kaiser," the melody of which was later adopted by the Germans for "Deutschland über Alles." Haydn used the theme for his "Emperor Quartet," and played the anthem on his piano three times when he felt death approaching.

Haydn's last years were filled with accolades. At the Vienna concert on his seventy-sixth birthday, Beethoven acknowledged his teacher by kneeling before him and kissing his hand. When Napoleon occupied Vienna he stationed a guard of honor before Haydn's house, and when Haydn died in 1809 the French army of occupation joined in honoring him. The numerous legacy of false attributions also attested to his fame. His authentic legacy was enormous—108 symphonies, 68 string quartets, 60 piano sonatas, 25 operas (of which 15 survive), and 4 oratorios.

In his symphonies Haydn gave form to what would be called the classical style, to be reshaped and fulfilled by Mozart, Beethoven, and others. His triumph, the twelve "Salomon" symphonies that he wrote for London, showed a new range of orchestration, new uses for trumpets, timpani, clarinets, cellos, and woodwinds. Re-creating the sonata in its symphonic form, he was creating the orchestra into a new composite instrument.

*   *   *

The career of Haydn, the last fine fruit of the community of princely patronage, offered stark contrast to that of his successor in creating the classical style. Haydn did not attain fame and fortune until he was nearly forty. Mozart's talents were exploited and displayed across Europe when he was six. Haydn spent most of his life under comfortable patronage; Mozart never ceased searching for a patron. Yet they collaborated in shaping the symphony and its new orchestral resources into a classical style. Toward the end of his life, Haydn himself did test the new public world of concertgoers, but Mozart lived in that world. As admirers of each other they saw rising European communities of musical creators, amateurs, and concertgoers.

Leopold Mozart described his son, Wolfgang Amadeus, as the "miracle which God let be born in Salzburg." There was no better place than Salzburg, Austria, in which a musical prodigy could have been born in 1756. Nor a more effective father for such a prodigy. Competent violinist and author of a famous treatise on violin playing, Leopold Mozart was expert enough to discern the genius of his son yet shrewd and self-effacing enough to spend himself cultivating his son's genius. His domineering nature would painfully inhibit Wolfgang's personality, but would nurture his talent and sense of mission. An active composer himself, Leopold ceased composing in deference to his precocious son. After Wolfgang's first public appearance at Salzburg University in 1762, his father began a ceaseless round of tours, showing off the boy and his talented but less precocious sister, Nannerl (five years his senior). A sensation at the imperial court in Vienna, they then visited towns in southern Germany, the Rhineland, Brussels, Paris, Munich, Holland, Berne, and Geneva. Three Italian tours touched the principal cities from Milan to Naples. Between the ages of six and fifteen Wolfgang was on tour more than half the time, impressing audiences by virtuoso performances on the keyboard instruments, on the organ, and the violin, playing on sight, and improvising variations, fugues, and fantasias. Most astonishing was Wolfgang's ability to write music, at an age when others had only begun to read it. At six he had composed minuets, before his ninth birthday his first symphony, at eleven his first oratorio, and at twelve his first opera. These contributed to the more than six hundred compositions eventually cataloged in 1862 and numbered by an Austrian scholar Ludwig von Köchel (1800–1877), who christened each with a "K" number.

While Wolfgang was a sight to be seen and a talent to be heard, the boy himself saw and heard a great deal that enriched his own work. His tours introduced him to the range of music composed and heard across Europe, when there were distinctive Italian and German styles. Bach had never visited Italy, nor had Haydn who spent most of his life in an Austrian village. Mozart would be able to combine the lightness of Italian vocal music and opera buffa and the seriousness of German instrumental music, sonata and symphony. No other composer so succeeded in marrying Italian homophony with German polyphony to make a European music.

It is not easy to separate the public astonishment at the child from admiration for his music. At Schönbrunn, where the imperial family played musical instruments, they delighted in the little boy who kissed the empress and jumped in her lap asking, "Do you really love me?" Goethe, then fourteen, remembered hearing music from the "little man, with powdered wig and sword." At Louis XV's Versailles only Madame de Pompadour was not impressed. "The Empress kisses me," Wolfgang announced. "Who is this that does not want to kiss me?" In England George III satisfied himself by setting the boy difficult tests on the keyboard, and Queen Charlotte's music master, J. C. Bach, engaged him in musical games. The London concerts were a box-office success, and the Royal Society received for its Philosophical Transactions the "Account of a very remarkable young Musician" with documentary proof of Wolfgang's age, and anecdotes of how he would "sometimes run about the room with a stick between his legs by way of horse."

After the tours, commissions came in—music for the marriage of Archduke Ferdinand in Milan, and for the enthronement of Hieronymus Colloredo as archbishop of Salzburg. But this new archbishop was less tolerant of his concertmaster Leopold's absences to tour with his son. In Salzburg in a few months in 1772, the sixteen-year-old Mozart composed eight symphonies, four divertimentos, and some sacred works. He was appointed an honorary concertmaster, but the archbishop made unreasonable demands. In Salzburg from 1774 to 1781 Wolfgang ceaselessly composed while both Mozarts sought refuge anywhere else from the tyrannical archbishop. Wolfgang still was not allowed to tour alone and Leopold assigned Frau Mozart to accompany him to Mannheim and Paris. En route Wolfgang fell in love with Aloysia Weber, a sixteen-year-old soprano, but his father forbade marriage. Frau Mozart died in Paris, and Wolfgang returned gloomily to Salzburg. When Aloysia refused to marry Wolfgang, he pursued her younger sister, Constanze. "She is not ugly," he observed, "but at the same time far from beautiful. Her whole beauty consists in two small black eyes, and a handsome figure. She has no wit, but enough sound sense to be able to fulfil her duties as a wife and mother." The successful premiere of *Die Entführung aus dem Serail* on July 12, 1782, in Vienna encouraged Mozart to believe he could afford a wife and he outraged his father by marrying Constanze three weeks later.

Despite his growing fame and multiplying commissions, Mozart never became rich. He remained improvident and extravagant, lived hand-to-mouth, and never in relaxed comfort. In 1781, when Mozart quit the service of the archbishop who had made him eat with the servants, his resignation was confirmed "with a kick on my arse . . . by order of our worthy Prince Archbishop." That year, too, he met Haydn. During the next four years Mozart composed the six quartets that he dedicated to Haydn. We do not know how intimately they knew each other, but Mozart freely admitted his debt to his "most dear friend," from whom "I first learned how to compose a quartet." After meeting Haydn and receiving his accolades, Mozart was stimulated to produce some symphonic novelties all his own, such as the "Haffner Symphony," without a patron. During these years he also developed and perfected the classical concerto for piano and orchestra.

Mozart's estrangement from the archbishop of Salzburg left him living on the income from his performances or sale of his music. This was risky, and no major composer since Handel had ventured it. Now he wrote memorable concertos (most of those from K. 413 to K. 595) for his own performances in Vienna. At long last, and after a strenuous pursuit, in 1787 Emperor Joseph II engaged Mozart as chamber composer. But while his predecessor Gluck had received twelve hundred gulden annually, Mozart received only eight hundred. In these last years, being otherwise occupied, Mozart composed few symphonies, but the three he produced in the summer of 1788—the symphonies in E Flat (K. 543), G Minor (K. 550) and C (the "Jupiter," K. 551)—were unexcelled in symphonic brilliance and in new uses of the orchestra.

In Vienna finally, from age thirty to thirty-six, Mozart produced some of his most durable music on the flightiest themes and showed his ability to respond to passing tastes. *Le Nozze di Figaro* (1786), *Don Giovanni* (1787), and *Così fan tutte* (1790) were based on comic librettos by Lorenzo da Ponte (1749–1838), a man of many talents. Da Ponte had taken the name of the bishop who converted him from Judaism to Catholicism. He was said to have consulted Casanova himself for an authentic Don Giovanni. He eventually came to America, became professor of Italian in Columbia College in New

York City, and the leading exponent of Dante and Italian opera here. In 1791 Mozart adopted a plot supplied by an old Salzburg acquaintance for *Die Zauberflöte*.

In July 1791 a stranger came to Mozart and commissioned a requiem. The fee was large, and the only condition was that the transaction never be revealed. The ailing and hypochondriac Mozart wondered whether this request was an omen of his own funeral. The requiem remained unfinished at Mozart's death on December 5, 1791. Constanze gave the manuscript to be completed by Mozart's friend Franz Xaver Süssmayr, who delivered it to the stranger as a finished work by Mozart. The stranger, the perverse Count Franz von Walsegg-Stuppach, then had it performed as a work of his own, which made it a "double forgery." Eventually Constanze allowed it to be published under Mozart's name. And the ghostwritten *Requiem* was performed at the memorial service for Beethoven on April 3, 1827, a week after his death.

Mozart had for some time had the notion that he was being poisoned by his relentless rival Antonio Salieri. But this proved quite groundless, and Salieri himself took the trouble on his deathbed to make an official denial. Mozart seems to have died of several recurring ailments, aggravated by overwork and malnutrition. "I have finished before I could enjoy my talent," Mozart declared at thirty-six. According to Viennese custom, he was buried unceremoniously in a mass grave in a churchyard outside the city.

THE PAINTED MOMENT

THE story that begins with the reach to eternity climaxes in our time with the effort to capture the elusive moment. The power of stone enticed the builders of Stonehenge, the Pyramids, and the Parthenon. But it was the power of light that produced the most modern art forms, for light, the nearly instantaneous messenger of sensation, is the speediest, the most transient. Light, after the heavens and the earth, God's first creation in Genesis (1:3), remains the Judeo-Christian symbol of the presence of God. John the Baptist announced Jesus as light (John 1:4ff.), affirmed by Jesus himself. Candles are lit on the Jewish Sabbath and mark holy festivals. And in modern times light has played surprising new roles for those who would re-create the world.

"Modernity," said Baudelaire, "is the transitory, the fugitive, the contingent, one half of art of which the other half is the eternal and the immutable." For this modern half, light is the vehicle and the resource. It was the Impressionists who made an art of the instantaneous, and Claude Monet (1840–1926) who showed how it could be done. To shift the artist's focus from enduring shapes to the evanescent moments required courage. It demanded a willingness to brave the jeers of the fashionable salons, a readiness to work speedily anywhere, and an openness to the endless untamed possibilities of the visual world. Cézanne summed it up when he said, "Monet is only an eye, but my God what an eye!"

The son of a prosperous grocer, Monet was born in Paris in 1840 and as a child of five moved with his family to Le Havre on the north side of the Seine estuary on the Normandy coast. That city, it was said, was "born of the sea," and so too was Monet the Impressionist. In the weather of Normandy, as generations of Channel passengers have painfully learned, the proverbially unpredictable sun, clouds, rain, and fog transform the sky and its sea reflections from moment to moment. Young Monet, impatient to flee the "prison" of school, eagerly explored beaches and cliffs. Until 1883 he was frequently refreshing his vision with visits to the French coast, north or south. Then he found in the Seine, in the Thames, and in his ponds at Giverny other water mirrors for his ever-changing world. "I should like to be always near it or on it," he said of the sea, "and when I die, to be buried in a buoy."

The first signs of his talent were his caricatures of teachers and other local characters in his school copybooks. By the time he was fifteen he was selling these in the shop of the local picture framer. There a chance encounter would shape Monet's life as an artist and the future of Western painting. Eugène Boudin (1824–1898), a painter and son of a pilot, had worked on an estuary steamer before opening the picture-framing shop patronized by some of the leading artists of the age. They urged him to try his hand at landscapes. With Millet's encouragement Boudin went to Paris, where he rebelled against the studio style of the Beaux-Arts by painting natural scenes in the open air. Back in Normandy he painted vivid seascapes.

The fifteen-year-old Monet later recalled that when he first saw Boudin's seascapes he disliked them so much—they were not at all in the "arbitrary color and fantastical arrangements of the painters then in vogue"—that he did not want to meet the man who painted them. But one day in the shop, about 1856, Monet ran into Boudin, who praised the young man's caricatures. "You are gifted; one can see that at a glance," he said, "But I hope you are not going to stop there . . . soon you will have had enough of caricaturing. Study, learn to see and to paint, draw, make landscapes. The sea, the sky, the animals, the people, and the trees are so beautiful, just as nature made them, with their character, their genuineness, in the light, in the air, just as they are." Painting outdoors was still unusual for artists when Boudin took it up. Constable and Corot had done outdoor sketches, but painting had been an art of the studio, where the artist could control the subject and the light. The introduction of metal-tube pigments in the 1840s in place of the laborious studio process of mixing colors had made outdoor painting practical.

"The exhortations of Boudin," Monet recalled, "had no effect ... and when he offered to take me with him to sketch in the fields, I always found a pretext to decline politely. Summer came—my time was my own—I could make no valid excuse; weary of resisting, I gave in at last, and Boudin, with untiring kindness, undertook my education. My eyes were finally opened and I really understood nature; I learned at the same time to love it." That summer Monet went on an outdoor excursion with Boudin to Rouelles, near Le Havre. "Suddenly, a veil was torn away. I had understood—I had realized what painting could be. By the single example of this painter devoted to his art with such independence, my destiny as a painter opened out to me." Boudin preached the need to preserve "one's first impression." "Everything that is painted directly on the spot," he insisted, "has always a strength, a power, a vividness of touch that one doesn't find again in the studio." Boudin was urging him to capture the moment of light.

The artist's move out of doors was not only a change of place. As Monet would show, it changed the "subject" of his painting and the pace of his work, leaving a predictable studio world of walls and windows and artificial light for scenes of evanescent light. Monet would create new ways of capturing that light and that evanescence.

At the age of eighteen, encouraged by Boudin, Monet applied to the Municipal Council of Le Havre for a grant to study art in Paris. The council turned him down on the grounds that "natural inclinations" for caricature might "keep the young artist away from the more serious but less rewarding studies which alone deserve municipal generosity." Still his father sent him to Paris for advice from established artists and a tour of the salons where artists' reputations were made. Originally sent for only a month or two, he was quickly seduced by the city and decided to remain indefinitely. He was fas-

cinated by the artists' café world, by the debates between the romantic "nature painters" and the "realists" known for their still lifes and
workers' scenes.

*   *   *

The headstrong young Monet refused to enroll in the École des
Beaux-Arts, citadel of the establishment, though it would have
pleased his father and assured a parental allowance. Instead he joined
the offbeat Académie Suisse, where there were no examinations and
no tuition. For a small fee artists could work from a living model.
The "academy" had been started by a former model in a decrepit
building where a dentist had once pulled teeth for one franc each.
The free atmosphere and low cost had attracted some great talents.
Courbet and Manet had worked there. Pissarro still stopped in occasionally to paint or to meet friends, and Monet found him a kindred
spirit. Perhaps the most intellectual and self-conscious of the Impressionist circle, Pissarro (1830–1903) introduced Monet to the
scientific rationale for their new approach to painting.

Monet's parents in Le Havre were alarmed at the rumors of his
bohemian life in Paris, and in 1860, when young Monet was unlucky
enough to have his number called for the obligatory seven years of
military service, they thought they had him cornered. Monet's father
offered to "buy" a substitute if Monet would commit himself to the
career of a respectable artist. But they had misjudged their son.

> The seven years of service that appalled so many were full of
> attraction to me. A friend, who was in a regiment of the
> Chasseurs d'Afrique and who adored military life, had com-
> municated to me his enthusiasm and inspired me with his
> love for adventure. Nothing attracted me so much as the
> endless cavalcades under the burning sun, the *razzias* [raids],
> the crackling of gunpowder, the sabre thrusts, the nights in
> the desert under a tent, and I replied to my father's ultima-
> tum with a superb gesture of indifference. . . . I succeeded,
> by personal insistence, in being drafted into an African regi-
> ment. In Algeria I spent two really charming years. I inces-

santly saw something new; in my moments of leisure I attempted to render what I saw. You cannot imagine to what an extent I increased my knowledge, and how much my vision gained thereby. I did not quite realize it at first. The impressions of light and color that I received there were not to classify themselves until later; they contained the germ of my future researches.

He had long admired Delacroix's paintings of Algeria, which had first awakened him to the wonders of the North African sun.

When he fell ill with anemia and was granted sick leave, his parents bought him out of the Chasseurs. And in the summer of 1862 he had another lucky encounter, this time with a half-mad Dutch painter, Johan Barthold Jongkind (1819–1891), who would inspire Monet's later work by his bold outdoor sketches and watercolors not so much of the ships and windmills but of the changing atmosphere. "He asked to see my sketches, invited me to come and work with him, explained to me the why and wherefore of his manner and thereby completed the teaching I had already received from Boudin. From that time he was my real master; it was to him that I owe the final education of my eye."

The very "sketchiness" of Monet's drawings that so much appealed to Jongkind was what troubled his artist aunt in Le Havre. "His sketches are always rough drafts, like those you have seen; but when he wants to complete something, to produce a picture, they turn into appalling daubs before which he preens himself and finds idiots to congratulate him." His father let him go back to Paris on the firm understanding "that this time you are going to work in dead earnest. I wish to see you in a studio under the discipline of a well-known master. If you resume your independence, I will stop your allowance without more ado." Through family connections he found a place in the studio of Charles Gleyre, who was both reputable and conventional enough to satisfy his father. "When one draws a figure," Gleyre advised, "one should always think of the antique. Nature . . . is all right as an element of study, but it offers no interest. Style, you see, is everything." Another student was the young Renoir

(1841–1919), whom Gleyre lumped together with Monet as misguided spirits and so encouraged a lasting friendship. They also felt kinship with another Gleyre pupil, Frédéric Bazille (1841–1870), whose wealthy family had allowed him to have his fling at art and who more than once would be a lifesaver for Monet.

By the summer of 1864, Monet had left Gleyre's studio and begun his staccato life of painting-excursions to the forests near Paris and the seacoasts of Normandy and elsewhere. It was during these twenty years that Monet developed as the Arch-Impressionist. Outside the familiar line of development of Western painting, with new ways of depicting the solid outer world, Monet instead aimed to report whatever the alert artist self could make of the moments of light that came to it. As Monet's biographer William C. Seitz puts it, he was "shucking off the image of the world perceived by memory in favor of a world perceived momentarily by the senses."

Monet came to this freedom of re-creation by stages. His early success at the Salon of 1865 with a harbor seascape *(Pointe de la Hève, Sainte-Adresse)* and in the Salon of 1866 with his life-size portrait of Camille Doncieux showed that he had the competence to satisfy the Academicians. Zola praised the portrait ("a window open on nature") for its "realism," and extolled Monet as "a man amid this crowd of eunuchs." But Manet was irritated when, through the similarity of their names, he was praised for a work by that "animal" Monet. Despite such minor premature triumphs more than twenty years would pass before Monet was widely recognized or could make a comfortable living. Meanwhile, he suffered all the pangs of the bohemian, which would provide Zola's painful details for his novels about the egoism and frustrations of the Impressionist artists. When Zola published *L'Oeuvre* (The Masterpiece) in 1886, it ended his thirty-year friendship with Cézanne, and deeply offended Pissarro and Renoir. Monet still confessed "fanatical admiration" for Zola's talent, but would never forgive him. "I have been struggling fairly long and I am afraid that in the moment of succeeding, our enemies may make use of your book to deal us a knockout blow."

Nor was Monet exaggerating the pain of those years. In the gloomy summer of 1866, when all his possessions were about to be seized by his creditors, Monet slashed two hundred of his canvases to save them from that fate, which explains why so few of his early works survive. In those years he was continually on the move, avoiding creditors and seeking a home he could afford. For lack of any other place, in 1867 he had to go back to his family in Le Havre. There he was temporarily rescued by his wealthy artist friend Bazille who bought Monet's *Women in the Garden* for twenty-five hundred francs to be paid out in fifty monthly installments of fifty francs each. This work had been refused at the Salon of 1867. When the Franco-Prussian War broke out in 1870, despite his financial difficulties Monet took Camille Doncieux, his mistress, whom he had just married, and their son born three years before, to London, and then to Holland—painting all the while. Returning to France in 1871, he found the enterprising dealer Paul Durand-Ruel willing to pay good prices for his paintings. He included Monet's works in his catalog, which unfortunately was never published because of the financial crash of 1873 and the following six-year depression.

What is remarkable is not that Monet's talents were not recognized sooner, but that, even without powerful patrons, his new vision was recognized during his lifetime. Unlike many other pioneer artists of his generation, he would end his life prosperous and acclaimed. For twenty years, meanwhile, he migrated from one seacoast or river site to another, with occasional forest and urban interludes.

* * *

When the jury of artists for the annual Paris Salon of 1863 had rejected three fifths of the paintings submitted, there was such an outcry that the politically sensitive Napoleon III "wishing to leave the public as judge of the legitimacy of these complaints has decided that the rejected works of art be exhibited in another part of the Palais de l'Industrie. This exhibition will be elective . . ." This historic Salon des Refusés included pictures by Monet's friends, Jongkind, Pissarro, and Cézanne. The center of interest and of controversy was Manet's *Le Déjeuner sur l'herbe*, a large canvas (six by nine feet) of two fully dressed male artists and two fully undressed

female models decorously picnicking in the woods. A painting by
Courbet had also been rejected for "moral reasons." When the emperor publicly labeled Manet's painting as "immodest," he attracted
the crowds. The young Monet had none of his works in this salon.
But it heralded a new spirit among Paris artists, of which Monet
himself would be one of the brightest stars.

As Manet had adapted his shocking *Le Déjeuner sur l'herbe* from
works of Giorgione and Raphael, now Monet, who had seen Manet's
work at the Salon des Refusés, decided in 1863 to have his own try at
the familiar theme. His work, he hoped, would be more true to nature. The surviving central fragment is now in the Louvre, and a
smaller replica he made in 1866 can be seen in the Pushkin Museum
in Moscow. Monet was already beginning to use his characteristic
Impressionist technique of flat colors, bright patches, and broken
brushwork.

During these years Monet was developing into the bold Impressionist. On a visit to Le Havre in 1872 he painted a view of the harbor, *Impression: Sunrise*, which in 1874 was one of his twelve works
(five oils, seven pastels) in a historic private group exhibit. The 165
works also included Degas, Pissarro, Cézanne, Renoir, Sisley, and
Morisot, among others. Monet's painting became the eponym for
the school and for a decisive movement in Western arts (not only
painting). Monet's painting of Le Havre harbor viewed from his
window showed a small brilliant red disk of a sun reflected in broken
brushwork on the waters, with shadowy masts and hulls enveloped in
damp vapors of a nebulous atmosphere. "I was asked to give a title
for the catalogue; I couldn't very well call it a view of Le Havre. So I
said: 'Put *Impression*.' "

The month-long exhibition attracted a large paying audience.
But more seem to have come to laugh than to admire. One pundit
praised these painters for inventing a new technique: load a pistol
with some tubes of paint, fire at the canvas, then finish it off with a
signature. The critic Louis Leroy's sarcastic article in the *Charivari*
(April 5, 1874) noted the "cottony" legs of Renoir's dancers. He
made Monet's painting the hallmark of the show, which he called
Exhibition of the Impressionists. He reported a puzzled conversation before Monet's painting:

"What does the canvas depict? Look at the catalogue."

" '*Impression, Sunrise.*' "

"*Impression*—I was certain of it. I was just telling myself that, since I was impressed, there had to be some impression in it . . . and what freedom, what ease of workmanship! Wallpaper in its embryonic state is more finished than that seascape."

The Impressionist label stuck, and was adopted by the painters themselves. But the laughter died away. "They are being attacked— and with good reason," some friends responded, "because they resemble each other a bit too much (they all derive from Manet) and because sometimes they happen to be shapeless, so predominant is their desire of exclusively sketching reality."

This was only the first of a series of brilliant group exhibits every year from 1876 to 1882. In 1877 Mary Cassatt was invited to join. Their last group exhibit was held in Paris in 1886, and a selection by Durand-Ruel was taken to New York. Monet was regularly represented, with fifty works in the New York show. Collectors became interested in his work, and Durand-Ruel had taken him up again.

Monet's family life was not untroubled. His romance with Camille Doncieux, *The Woman in the Green Dress*, painted in 1866, began in Paris in 1865 and she bore him their first child in 1867, just before he returned penniless to Le Havre. Constantly short of money, in June 1875 he appealed to Manet to lend him twenty francs, for Camille's money was used up. Then during an 1876 visit seeking support from the wealthy collector Ernest Hoschedé at his chateau, Monet formed a liaison with Hoschedé's wife, Alice. The winter of 1877 was desperate for Monet back in Paris. Camille was ill and Monet had no money for food or rent. (Zola would later depict his straits in *L'Oeuvre*.) Again, he sought help from friends, and Manet again responded. Driven out of his Argenteuil house by debts, with Manet's financial assistance he rented a house farther from Paris at Vétheuil, also on the Seine but near open country. Before this move he offered Dr. Gachet a painting in exchange for a loan to pay for the imminent delivery of his second child. He asked Zola for money to cover the cost of moving his furniture to the house that Manet had helped him rent. Disaster piled on disaster. When the celebrated singer Jean-Baptiste Faure, who had collected Monets on speculation, now put them on auction they brought depressingly small prices. Hoschedé, financially ruined, was suddenly forced to sell his collection of Monets at sacrifice figures.

Mme. Hoschedé left her husband in that summer of 1878, about the time of her husband's disastrous sale of Monets. With her six children she moved in with the Monets at Vétheuil. There she also cared for the ill Camille and the two young Monet children. Monet still had no money for paint or canvas. "I am no longer a beginner," he wrote a friend on December 30, 1878, "and it is sad to be in such a situation at my age [thirty-eight], always obliged to beg, to solicit buyers. At this time of the year I feel doubly crushed by my misfortune and 1879 is going to start just as this year ends, quite desolately, especially for my loved ones to whom I cannot give the slightest present." Despite all, the indomitable Monet kept up his spirits by painting fields of poppies and views of the Seine. He had to pawn everything to pay for Camille's last illness. She died in September 1879, ending their thirteen troubled years together. At her death Monet wrote again to the friend asking him to retrieve from the pawnshop "the locket for which I am sending you the ticket. It is the only souvenir that my wife had been able to keep and I should like to tie it around her neck before she leaves forever." Though broken in spirit, he remained the almost involuntary servant of optical impressions. Seeing Camille on her deathbed, he could not prevent himself from capturing on canvas the blue, gray, and yellow tones of death on her face. Appalled, he compared himself to an animal that could not stop turning a millstone, for he was "prisoner of his visual experiences." The painting now hangs in the Louvre.

The life Monet shared with Alice Hoschedé for the next thirty years, despite its pains, had many sunny days. After the impoverished Ernest Hoschedé had withdrawn from his family to a bachelor life in Paris, Monet and Alice lived together with their combined eight children. In the 1880s, Alice by looking after the children made possible Monet's frequent painting excursions around France and abroad. They moved to Giverny in 1883 in rented quarters. Ernest died in 1891, and they married the next year. As Monet developed the now-famous Giverny properties, this became an artist's mecca and a model bourgeois household. In the 1890s Monet traveled much less. With Alice taking a strong hand, they both developed the astonishing gardens at Giverny. Alice died in 1911.

*　*　*

While "impressionist" painters flourished separately, Impressionism as a group movement disintegrated. By 1881 the original group of the first Impressionist Exhibit of 1874 had dispersed, and pristine Impressionism had no group exhibits after 1886. With the aid of enterprising dealers and increasingly adventurous collectors, including many Americans, Monet became a self-supporting painter. By the 1890s he was a recognized master. And Monet experimented ever more boldly with his optical self. He offered more than a new style in his way of re-creating the artist's visual world. Monet's early experience of the volatile atmosphere of Normandy, and of the dazzling sunshine of North Africa, as we have seen, had prepared him for the fireworks of light. He had the courage to give up the publicly agreed-on world of the known for the world seen only by the artist himself.

This was a revolutionary shift in focus, a change both in the resources of the artist and the demands made on the artist. For while the descriptive artist had his tasks limited by the observed world out there, the Impressionist's assignments were infinite. And this way of re-creating the world came close to abolishing "subject matter." The Impressionist artist's "motifs" had no other purpose than to call attention to the painting and give the viewer his bearings in the artist's world of impressions. Gone was the need for mythological, historical, religious, patriotic, or epoch-making subject matter. The optical impressions of an artist-self at a given moment were quite enough. Monet tended toward landscape or seascape, not because of their special significance, nor from a romantic love of nature. His motifs were not so much Nature as the Out-of-Doors, a world of ambient atmosphere, of ever-changing light and infinite iridescence. No object had a fixed color and even shadows could contain the whole spectrum.

Impressionists were prophets of the new, prototypical re-creators. As the young poet-critic Jules Laforgue observed of them, "The only criterion was newness. . . . it proclaimed as geniuses, according to the etymology of the word, those and only those who have revealed something new." Every Impressionist painting was of a new "subject," which was the visual world of the artist at that evanescent moment. For novel subjects Monet found nothing more fertile than water—in the sea or the river, and in the snow, constantly changing and reflecting. And so he said "the fog makes London beautiful."

The outdoor painter worked under stringent time limits. While the studio painter could take four years for a Sistine ceiling and another five to paint the wall behind the altar, an impression by Monet had to be painted with near-photographic speed. Monet sometimes painted for only fifteen minutes at a time on a canvas. If the light was sufficiently similar on another day he might return. Atmosphere, sun, shadow and the time of day were all crucial. "One day at Varengeville," the French dealer and collector Ambroise Vollard reported, "I saw a little car arriving in a cloud of dust. Monet gets out of it, looks at the sun, and consults his watch: 'I'm half an hour late,' he says, 'I'll come back tomorrow.' "

This was an age of focused interest in optics, in the theory of light and color and the burgeoning art and science of photography. At no time since Newton had physicists made such advances or been so adventurous in their theories of light. In Germany Hermann Helmholtz (1821–1894) had invented the ophthalmoscope (1850) and a new theory of color vision, the Scotsman James Clerk Maxwell (1831–1879) was investigating color perception and the causes of color blindness, while Ogden N. Rood (1831–1902), an American professor at Columbia University, was developing a flicker photometer for comparing the brightness of light of different colors, and producing *Modern Chromatics* (1879). The kaleidoscope and the stereoscope had entered living rooms. Joseph Nicéphore Niepce (1765–1833), Louis Daguerre (1787–1851), and William Henry Fox Talbot (1800–1877) had already pioneered the age of photography. It was impossible for men and women of culture not to know this magical new graphic art.

Of special interest to painters was the work of the French chemist Michel Eugène Chevreul (1796–1889) who, besides doing pioneer research in animal fats to improve the candle and soap industry, had been experimenting with color contrasts at the Gobelin tapestry works. Charged with preparing dyes at the Gobelin works, Chevreul discovered to his surprise that the major problems were less those of chemistry than of optics. If a color did not register its proper effect, it was apt to be due not to a deficiency of the pigment but to the influence of neighboring colors. His researchers produced his "law of simultaneous contrast," published in 1839. While Chevreul built on Newtonian theory, he discovered his own "law" by observation. "Where the eye sees at the same time two contiguous colors," he noted, "they will appear as dissimilar as possible, both in their optical composition and in the height of their tone." Any color therefore would influence its neighbor in the direction of that color's complementary (those elements of white light absorbed by the given color). Thus red would tend to make adjacent surfaces appear greener, green would be enhanced by juxtaposed red, as red in turn would be enhanced by a neighboring green.

The intellectual Pissarro became an enthusiast for Chevreul and for the new science of color. "We could not pursue our studies of light with much assurance," he observed, "if we did not have as a guide the discoveries of Chevreul and other scientists." Neo-Impressionists, he urged, should aim "to seek a modern synthesis of methods based on science, that is, based on M. Chevreul's theory of color and on the experiments of Maxwell and the measurements of O. N. Rood. To substitute optical mixture for mixture of pigments. In other words, the breaking up of tones into their constituents. For optical mixture stirs up more intense luminosities than mixture of pigments does." Chevreul provided the basis of the "divisionist" technique of painting. He charted the way to the *pointillisme* of Seurat and Signac and for Pissarro himself. And Pissarro enlisted a group he called "scientific impressionists" for whom the optical sciences were to be steps toward the liberation of man.

Monet may have known the work of Chevreul. He could hardly have avoided hearing of it from his talkative friend Pissarro. Even while Monet professed to abhor theory, he found ways of applying the emerging theories of color, and he became the archprophet of an impressionism based on bold new juxtapositions of light and color. Just as Giotto had found his way to a kind of linear perspective ahead of the modern theories of Brunelleschi and Alberti, so Monet seems intuitively to have been led to the techniques that would be justified and explained by the new science of light and color. The influence of photography, which had ceased to be arcane, was quite another matter, for it seemed to provide the equivalent of a momentary Impressionist's sketch, a scientific and foolproof grasp on instantaneity. Baudelaire had warned that photography and poetry were incompatible. But it is likely that some of the Impressionists made clandestine use of photography. It is hard not to suspect that the blurred image of photographed objects in motion had some effect on paintings like Monet's *Boulevard des Capucines* (1873). Perhaps the photographers' earnest quest to record the instantaneous encouraged painters like Monet to outdo them in color.

The Impressionist painter had accelerated the pace of his work to match the pace of modern life. Monet was in search of the *now*, and capturing a short-lived motif required a spontaneous style. Monet himself described the challenge of making a laborious art serve the aim of "instantaneity." Momentarily frustrated by the too-rapid changes of light as he painted his haystack series (October 1890), he wrote:

> I'm grinding away, sticking to a series of different effects, but the sun sets so early at this time that I can't go on. . . . I'm becoming so slow in working as to drive me to despair, but the more I go on, the more I see that I must work a lot to succeed in rendering what I am looking for: "Instantaneity," especially the envelope, the same light spread everywhere, and more than ever I am disgusted by easy things that come without effort.

This kind of painting required its own kind of patience, to wait for the precise moment and come again and again in search of that moment. Monet's friend Guy de Maupassant, who sometimes accompanied him in his search for that moment, compared Monet's life to that of a trapper.

If the bohemian artist had to survive the rigors of hunger and unheated studios, the Impressionist had to brave wind and rain and snow. A journalist in 1868 at Honfleur, opposite Le Havre, described Monet in his neighborhood. "We have only seen him once. It was in the winter during several days of snow, when communications were virtually at a standstill. It was cold enough to split stones. We noticed a foot-warmer, then an easel, then a man, swathed in three coats, his hands in gloves, his face half-frozen. It was M. Monet, studying a snow effect."

Of all painters' works those of Monet are the hardest to describe in words, precisely because they had no "subject" but the momentary visual impression on a unique self. Though suspicious of all prescribed "forms," Monet did create a spectacular new form of painting. In the "series" he found a way to incorporate time in the artist's canvases by capturing a succession of elusive moments. Monet's series were his way of making peace between the laborious painter and the instant impression of the eye. In his early years Monet had sometimes painted more than one picture of the same scene, and so revealed the changing light and atmosphere. But now he planned extensive series of the same subject under variant light, season, and atmosphere. Here was a new use of time and atmosphere, a new epic form, in which the differences between paintings were part of the plot. Monet had done something of this sort in his paintings of London in 1870. The series concept flourished and grew as Monet in his fifties finally put poverty behind him. Now a prosperous celebrity, he could elaborate his ideas at will, as repetitively and outrageously as he wished, with no worry of having to appeal to the market. Back in 1874 he had begun a surprising series of smoke and fog at the Gare St. Lazare, and had done paintings of the same fields of poppies. In the 1890s he threw himself into his series with passion and in profusion.

Monet's first great series seemed to have a most unpromising subject. But for this haystack (*meule*) series the haystack was not really his subject. "For me," he explained, "a landscape does not exist as a landscape, since its appearance changes at every moment; but it lives according to its surroundings, by the air and light, which constantly change." In May 1891 he exhibited fifteen paintings of this haystack series, showing the same motif under varying conditions of atmosphere, sun and snow, sunrise and sunset. It was this series that had inspired Maupassant's characterization and Monet's own complaints of the painful elusiveness of "instantaneity." Another series, "Poplars on the Epte" (1891), followed, depicting the variations of vertical shapes just as the haystacks pursued the rounded bulk of a haystack against the flat landscape.

Then, as if to show that even man's works could nourish the most subtle impressions, Monet did a series of impressions of the façade of Rouen Cathedral seen from the window of a shop opposite. When twenty of the Rouen series were exhibited in the Durand-Ruel gallery in 1895, they sold for the high price of fifteen thousand francs each, a price Monet had insisted on. Monet's friend Georges Clemenceau acclaimed the series as a *"Révolution de Cathedrales"*—a new way of seeing man's material works, a hymn celebrating the cathedral as a mirror for the unfolding works of light in time. Here, he said, was a new kind of temporal event. Two more great series still remained on Monet's agenda. A series on the Thames, begun in 1900, had produced more than a hundred canvases by 1904. Then, after Monet had settled down in Giverny in 1900, he began his water-garden series, which he was still elaborating at the time of his death in 1926.

It is difficult to grasp the grandeur of any of these series when we see only individual canvases in different museums. The delight of each haystack painting comes also from our view of its Impressionist companions. Monet's fascination with the gardens at Giverny and his attention to their care were another witness to his obsession with visual change. His small home territory—Giverny, its paths, arbors, trees, and flowers and its Japanese bridge—provided inexhaustible motifs for Monet in his last years. He delighted in the daily opening and closing of pond-lily blossoms and in the moving clouds mirrored in the shifting surface of the ponds. In 1977 the Académie des Beaux-

Arts, which he had spurned a century before, took possession of Giverny and made it a national Monet shrine. Clemenceau, as a politician less attracted by evanescence than was Monet, proposed that despite failing eyesight and depression at the loss of his wife, Alice, Monet should paint an encircling mural for a new studio. These dazzling murals became a monument to Monet, dedicated two years after his death, in the Orangerie of the Tuilleries and would be christened by some the Sistine Chapel of Impressionism.

Still, no encircling mural could properly celebrate Monet the Impressionist. His achievement was not in the durable but in the elusive moment. He conquered time by capturing light, the speediest messenger of the senses. "I love you," Clemenceau wrote to Monet, "because you are you, and because you taught me to understand light."

THE RISE OF THE SKYSCRAPER

T HE NEXT CREATION of Western architecture was a new collaboration of man and the machine. For centuries Western architecture had been dominated by only two styles—the classical Greco-Roman legacy and the Gothic legacy of the Middle Ages. Modern times would add another, the joint product of architect and engineer, of the "poetry and prose" of the building arts, which allowed creators to conjure with upward space. It would come from the heart of America and would be more than a style—a design for a new kind of building. The Greco-Roman borrowed from temples, the Gothic adapted from churches. The skyscraper was created for the tall office building. Excelling all others in height, it would add a new scale and dimension to man's architectural creations. Its gesture was not to the gods, nor to God, but simply to the sky. Before the rise of the skyscraper, the American cityscape was commonly dominated by a church spire. In Lower Broadway in New York City in 1880 the tallest building was the spire of Trinity Church.

Chicago was to be the birthplace, the Athens or St.-Denis, of the architecture that took businessmen into the sky, where they could look down on the steeples of their churches. And Chicago itself was a phenomenon, in the intensity, speed, and magnitude of its growth. In 1833 the city had barely acquired the 150 population required to incorporate, which fifteen years later reached 20,000, by 1870 counted more than 300,000. In 1890 its 1.1 million made it the nation's second city. A Chicago novelist declared it was "the only great city in the world to which all of the citizens have come for the avowed object of making money." "The lightning city" thrived on growth and expansion, on the movements of people and what they produced.

Focus and terminus of every then-known form of transportation, at the northern end of a canal connecting the Great Lakes with the Mississippi River, Chicago commanded the greatest inland waterway system in the world, which the steamboat made more fluent than ever. From Chicago, a rail network reached the Atlantic, Gulf, and Pacific coasts. The center for gathering, processing, and distributing the produce of a burgeoning continental-agricultural nation, for a century Chicago remained the livestock and meatpacking capital of the world. In Chicago, even before the Civil War the need for quickly built, easily demounted, and readily transported buildings had produced a bizarre architectural novelty. The widely ridiculed "balloon frame house" was displacing the traditional heavy mortise and tenon frame with lightweight planks of milled lumber quickly nailed together. Some objected that such flimsy houses would be blown away by the first wind. But in this community with few skilled carpenters and no restrictive guilds a new technology won the day. The balloon frame would house millions in American cities and suburbs to come.

Meanwhile, in the nation's largest city, New York, there was pressure to provide offices for the growing financial empires headquartered there. In the 1880s and 1890s the first tall buildings still fitted somehow into the city scene. Not until 1892 did a secular building, the 309-foot-tall Pulitzer Building, overshadow Trinity Church (284 feet). For centralized business administration, to bring businesses that dealt with one another close together, and to fit them into the congested downtown, New York builders began building tall. Elevators were necessary, but at first the public was put off by fears of falling. The ingenious Elisha Graves Otis (1811–1861), who had been working in a bedstead factory, invented a safety device that prevented the elevator from falling if the lifting chain broke. He set up his factory in Yonkers, in 1861 patented and manufactured the steam elevator, and so made the tall building convenient. These "vertical railways" were first generally used in hotels. They were the uncelebrated essential engineering feature that made possible the modern skyline.

While adopting the new elevators New York architects still used traditional materials in the traditional way for their high buildings. What is sometimes called the first tall office building was erected (1868–70) at 120 Broadway. Though rising to a height of 130 feet, it contained only five working stories. Except for its height, there was nothing novel in its construction, which was of masonry with some brick and some wrought-iron beams in the interior. The fear of fire, which might cause the exposed metal frame to buckle and collapse, prevented the use of iron framing throughout. But new ways of fire-proofing ironwork by cladding with fireproof tile as well as speedier and safer elevators encouraged more high buildings in the next five years. The Western Union Building rose to 230 feet, the Tribune Building to 260. Despite their unusual height, they still relied on masonry walls and partitions, with supporting wrought-iron beams.

Masonry, however, was ill-suited to tall buildings. The outside walls at the bottom would have to be made thicker to support the great weight of the masonry and the increasing weight of beams and floors for each added story. As a result the entrance floors to a tall masonry office building would require the lower walls of a medieval fortress. Before electric lighting, which was not practical till the 1880s, illumination was also a problem. The space allowed for windows in such structures would be more suited for shooting arrows out than for admitting sunlight, while the most valuable shop and office space near the ground would be consumed with thick masonry.

For the upreaching modern skyscraper some other kind of construction was required. New York was not to be the place. Two centuries old at the time of the Civil War, it was ancient by American standards, and had accumulated countless building regulations. Its architects, dominated by the Beaux-Arts academic tradition, imagined monuments to outshine their French or British counterparts. But Chicago was a young city bursting with new arrivals. There in 1880 the median age of architects active in designing large buildings was only thirty. More often than not they were engineers rather than architects. With few exceptions they were not infected by the Beaux-Arts tradition, and were prepared to create new structures for new needs. And the newest need was office space for expanding American enterprise in the congested city.

To these Chicago advantages an inscrutable providence added a traumatic incentive, one of the great urban catastrophes of modern times. In America, unlike the Old World, destructive catastrophes such as earthquakes, floods, and invasions had not generally been required to provide a clean slate for innovation. But the Chicago fire of October 8–10, 1871, destroyed within two days much of the physical product of the city's forty years. The city had been built with no thought of fire. Even the sidewalks were of resinous pine. The cause of the great Chicago fire remains unknown, but the legend of Mrs. O'Leary's cow knocking over a lantern persists. Between nine o'clock Sunday evening, October 8, and ten-thirty the following night, three and a half square miles of the central city were burned out. Although there was a confirmed loss of only three hundred lives, eighteen thousand buildings were incinerated and one hundred thousand people were left homeless. Local moralists, comparing it with the ancient destruction of Babylon, Troy, and Rome, called it a modern apocalypse. "Very sensible men," Frederick Law Olmsted reported from the scene, "have declared . . . that it was the burning of the world." In sober fact, the catastrophic fire offered American architects an opportunity like that seized by Nero in ancient Rome.

The phoenix would become the appropriate symbol of the city, for a new Chicago arose speedily from the ashes. "Oh it was an enlivening, inspiring sight," only five months later a visitor exclaimed, "to look out each morning, upon a brave wall of solid masonry, which one had not noticed before! . . . the constant stream of vehicles that went plunging through the streets, like fire engines bent on saving a city from destruction; and, indeed, their errand was of equal moment—the building up of the New, since the Old could no longer be saved!" The speed and magnitude of the catastrophe were said to be another confirmation of the city's uniqueness. Like the settlers starting over at Plymouth Rock, they found new reason to see Chicago as the archetypal American city. Within a month, five thousand cottages were being built, and real estate prices rose above prefire levels. The stage was set for a building boom—and architectural creation—without precedent.

*　*　*

Chicago, the New World's new city, had become perforce a scene for the first American urban renewal. And on what a scale! Frontier engineer-architects, at home in building iron bridges, were open to new ways. Steel-frame construction, the additional element needed for the skyscraper, was created in Chicago within a dozen years after the fire. This "cage construction" had obvious essential advantages over masonry. A steel-frame skeleton supporting a tall building would not have to be thick at the base, and so would free the valuable rentable space near the ground. A conventional eleven-story masonry building required thick bearing walls at the bottom that would leave clear interior room widths of only sixteen feet. A steel frame would open up the interior of the building, regardless of its height, and at the same time would open the outer walls for large windows and natural light, which now could penetrate the interior.

The first building of true skyscraper design—or "cage construction"—the Home Insurance Company Building, was built in Chicago (1884–85) by William LeBaron Jenney (1832–1907). Major Jenney, father of the skyscraper, was a New Englander who, at seventeen, had sailed in one of his father's whalers around the Horn in 1849 to join the gold rush to California. After three years at the Lawrence Scientific School studying engineering and eighteen months in Paris studying art and architecture, he served as engineer building the trans-Panama railroad, then as engineer for General Sherman in the Civil War. After the war he settled in Chicago. The assignment that made history was his commission to design for the Home Insurance Company a fire-resistant building with the greatest number of well-lighted small offices. A piece of folklore circulated by the contractor for this building helps us understand the simple virtues of the "cage" construction. One evening, it seems, when Jenney came home depressed at his inability to solve his problem, his wife happened to be reading a heavy book. Casually putting it aside, she laid it on top of a nearby birdcage. With a Eureka flash, Jenney suddenly saw that if the flimsy wire frame of the birdcage would support a heavy book, a similar metal cage might support the weight of a tall building. By creating steel-skeleton construction he opened the era of the skyscraper.

The nine-story Home Insurance Company Building, finished in 1885, proved that a steel skeleton could support a high structure. Architects had feared that in case of fire the different rates of thermal expansion between iron and masonry might buckle the metal and crack the masonry. And Jenney had planned to use heavy granite piers to bear some of the weight of the frame, which was to be cast-iron columns. Before these cast-iron columns were delivered, the Carnegie-Phipps Steel Company perfected a way of rolling steel columns. Jenney substituted these for the iron above the sixth floor, and so, finally, steel entered buildings. This was fifteen years after steel had been used in an American bridge. The lightness of steel compared with wall-bearing masonry, together with the new processes of riveting, opened up the building to sunlight and allowed grand increases in height. The greater strength of steel columns made it possible to space the columns farther apart inside the building, leaving the interior space flexible for movable partitions. Steel-skeleton construction where the enclosing walls had no load-bearing function would eventually make possible increasingly dramatic use of glass. The steel frame not only created an enormous new demand for steel. It allowed the architect's imagination to soar upward as well as outward. Now the sky would be the limit.

This was not the first time that Americans had added a new material for the architect. The versatile James Bogardus (1800–1874), trained as a watchmaker, improved the striking parts of clocks, devised new machines for engraving, and a metal-cased pencil that was "forever pointed." In Italy in 1840, "contemplating rich architectural designs of antiquity," he had first conceived the idea of emulating them in modern times by the use of cast iron. His own five-story factory (1850) was said to be the first complete cast-iron building in the world. He patented his "Improvements in the Methods of Constructing Iron Houses" (1850), and made whole buildings, including the frames, floors, and supports, of cast iron. Such buildings could be erected speedily at all seasons "by the most ignorant workman," could easily be taken to pieces and removed, making possible thinner walls, "fluted columns and Corinthian capitals, the most elaborate carvings, and the richest designs" at little cost. All of which "would greatly tend to elevate the public taste for the beautiful, and to purify and gratify one of the finest qualities of the human mind." Bogardus's cast-iron buildings never became popular, but his concept was prophetic. His 175-foot-high tower (1855) for the McCullough Shot and Lead Company in New York, with its octagonal cast-iron frame of true skeletal construction and nonbearing curtain walls, may have been known to Jenney.

Once Jenney had shown that it could be done, many others followed. Chicago became a living museum of the new American architecture and a forum for its prophets. The most eloquent of these was Louis Henri Sullivan (1856–1924). Born in Boston, son of an immigrant Irish dancing master, he attended public schools. At the age of thirteen, impressed that anyone could make up a building out of his head, he decided to become an architect. At sixteen he entered the course in architecture at the Massachusetts Institute of Technology, where he learned to draw, and was offered the classical orders "in a sort of misch-masch of architecture theology." He left impatiently after a year. In New York he met the famous Richard Morris Hunt, who told him that to become an architect he must go to Paris. He found employment in an architectural office in Philadelphia. When he lost this job in the disastrous panic of 1873, he joined his dancing-master father in Chicago. At the age of seventeen, he arrived there on the day before Thanksgiving, a month after the Great Fire. He found a city in ashes, and architects measuring their commissions by the mile. He later exuberantly reported his impressions:

> Louis thought it all magnificent and wild: a crude extravaganza, an intoxicating rawness, a sense of big things to be

done. . . . The elevated wooden sidewalks in the business district with steps at each street corner, seemed shabby and grotesque; but when Louis learned that this meant that the city had determined to raise itself three feet more out of the mud, his soul declared that this resolve meant high courage; that the idea was big; that there must be big men here. The shabby walks now became a symbol of stout hearts. . . . The pavements were vile, because hastily laid; they erupted here and there and everywhere in ooze. Most of the buildings, too, were paltry. . . . But in spite of the panic, there was stir; an energy that made him tingle to be in the game.

Young Louis found a job with the warm and generous Major Jenney, who had begun practice only five years before. "The Major was a free-and-easy cultured gentleman but not an architect except by courtesy of terms. His true profession was that of engineer."

Following Hunt's advice, after six months the restless Sullivan set off for the École des Beaux-Arts in Paris. To prepare himself in six weeks for the rigorous entrance examination he studied eighteen hours a day (with an hour off for exercise at the gymnasium), he wore out three successive tutors in French, engaged a tutor in mathematics, and read widely in history. The three-week-long examination—written, drawn, and oral—he passed brilliantly. To recover from the strains of the examination he went to Italy. There the high point was the two days he spent in the Sistine Chapel in Rome, and so at eighteen he discovered Michelangelo, who would be his lifelong idol. "Here Louis communed in silence with a Super-Man. Here he felt and saw a great Free Spirit. Here he was filled with the awe that stills. . . . Here was power as he had seen it in the mountains, here was power as he had seen it in the prairies, in the open sky, in the great lakes stretching like a floor toward the horizon, here was the power of the forest primeval."

At the Beaux-Arts, as at MIT, the problems posed to students were purely academic, unrelated to the real world. The history of architecture taught there focused on abstractions called "styles." But Sullivan saw architecture "not merely as a fixation here and there in time and place, but as a continuous outpouring never to end, from the infinite fertility of man's imagination evoked by his changing needs." And here was a clue to his principle "so broad as to admit of no exception," which became his "holy grail" for architecture.

After about a year in Paris, Sullivan returned to Chicago in 1875 seeking work as an architect. Fascinated by the great bridge recently completed (1867–74) by James B. Eads (1820–1887) across the Mississippi at St. Louis, he spent his spare time reading up on engineering, and discovered engineer heroes. When he entered the firm of Dankmar Adler in 1879, which became Adler and Sullivan in 1881, the urgent architectural problem in the congested city was how to provide light for offices and how to build higher. The new sciences of Spencer, Huxley, and Tyndall reinforced Sullivan's revulsion against an architecture of historic styles.

The quest for an American architecture had found a prophetic voice a half century before Sullivan. The New England sculptor Horatio Greenough (1805–1852) had scandalized patriots by his gigantic statue of a half-naked George Washington in the guise of a Roman warrior, but his plea for an "American Architecture" (1843) was acclaimed by Emerson and others. Greenough dared to mock Thomas Jefferson's use of a Roman temple as a model for an American State House. Even while the Washington Monument was being constructed he ridiculed the "palpable absurdity" of the original design, "the intermarriage of an Egyptian monument—whether astronomical, as I believe, or phallic, as contended by a Boston critic, matters not very much—with a Greek structure or one of Greek elements."

* * *

Louis Sullivan was to be the spokesman as well as the exemplar of an American architecture. The professional architects of his day, grateful legatees of Vitruvius and Suger, were sitting ducks for this Walt Whitman of the building arts:

> You are ill. Your eye wanders. This is no Roman temple built by a motley crowd of organ-grinders—spook-creatures of your fertile brain—it's a bank; just a plain, ordinary, every-day American bank, full of cold hard cash and other

cold things. I know all about it, I read about it in the papers. I saw it built, I know the president. . . . The Roman temple can no more exist in fact on Monroe Street, Chicago, U.S.A., than can Roman civilization exist there. Such a structure must of necessity be a simulacrum, a ghost. . . . But Roman does not mean American, never did mean American, never can mean American. Roman was Roman; American is, and is to be, American. The architect should know this without our teaching, and I suspect that he does know it very well in his unmercenary moments.

Sullivan's brief article, "The Tall Office Building Artistically Considered," in *Lippincott's Magazine* (March 1896) became the manifesto of a modern and an American architecture. This was no Vitruvian Ten Orders for modern architects but an eloquent defense of what was already visible in the pioneer American skyscrapers. The word "skyscraper" had already entered the American language in a *Chicago Tribune* article (January 13, 1889) entitled "Chicago's Skyscrapers" to describe this new kind of tall building.

"The architects of this land and generation," Sullivan began, "are now brought face to face with something new under the sun—namely, that evolution and integration of social conditions, that special grouping of them, that results in a demand for the erection of tall office buildings." On the ground floor there must be "a main entrance that attracts the eye to its location," and spaces suitable for stores and banks, a story below ground for the services of power, heating, and lighting, and an attic space on top for the machinery of the circulatory system. Rising above the ground floor should be "an indefinite number of stories of offices piled tier upon tier, one tier just like another tier, one office just like all the other offices—an office being similar to a cell in a honey-comb, merely a compartment, nothing more. . . . We, without more ado, make them look all alike because they are all alike." Tall buildings in New York and Chicago had been plastered with imported ornaments—classical architraves, Gothic windows and gargoyles—that bore no relation to the modern structure.

To his earthy empiricism Sullivan added "the imperative voice of emotion." "It demands of us, what is the chief characteristic of the tall office building? And at once we answer, it is lofty. This loftiness is to the artist-nature its thrilling aspect. It is the very open organ-tone in its appeal. . . . It must be tall, every inch of it tall." Sullivan, no master of understatement, generalized his inspiring prescription for the skyscraper into a universal law.

> Whether it be the sweeping eagle in his flight or the open apple-blossom, the toiling work-horse, the blithe swan, the branching oak, the winding stream at its base, the drifting clouds, over all the coursing sun, form ever follows function, and this is the law. Where function does not change form does not change. The granite rocks, the ever-brooding hills, remain for ages; the lightning lives, comes into shape, and dies in a twinkling.

In his wordy Whitmanesque manifesto for functionalism Sullivan exhorted American architects to "cease struggling and prattling handcuffed and vainglorious in the asylum of a foreign school" and produce a democratic art "that will live because it will be of the people, for the people, and by the people." But the architect of the future would be tempted by "the art of covering one thing with another thing to imitate a third thing, which, if genuine, would not be desirable."

Early skyscrapers irked city-neighbors by blocking their sunlight and their view of the heavens. The Equitable Life Building completed in 1915 at 120 Broadway in New York City covered a full block and rose without setbacks to thirty-nine stories. Its 1.2 million feet of rentable space made it the world's largest office building, but its east-west mass deprived adjacent buildings of light, and cast long, broad shadows. The neighbors' protests sparked the first zoning ordinance in the United States, in 1916, which limited a skyscraper's total floor area to twelve times the size of its plot. The Equitable had provided inside floor space more than thirty times the size of the land it covered. The perils of the skyscraper to city life were being revealed.

The American half century after the first building of true skyscraper design, William LeBaron Jenney's Home Insurance Company Building in Chicago in 1885, was one of the most productive in
the history of architecture. As distinct an architectural type as the
Greek temple or the Gothic cathedral, the skyscraper showed the
same uncanny capacity for variation, adaptation, camouflage, and
embellishment. But while those earlier types stayed on the ground
and only occasionally punctuated the skyline, the skyscraper reached
relentlessly upward, and created a new heaven-bound delineation for
the modern city. American cities came to be identified less by their
street plans than by their recently created "skylines."

The skyscraper leitmotif was elaborated in three overlapping
phases: the classic, the theatrical, and the international. The classic
phase appeared in the first prototypes of skeleton-frame construction in the 1880s and 1890s built in Chicago, or mostly by Chicago
architects. While they overshadowed other city buildings by going
up over ten stories, in silhouette they still seemed a squarish piling of
story on story. The revolutionary skeleton of the Home Insurance
Company Building was so well hidden that not until the original was
demolished to make way for a higher building in 1931 did three expert investigating committees establish its claim to be the first building of skeleton-frame skyscraper design. Sullivan's masterpieces in
this classic skyscraper style were the Wainwright Building in St.
Louis (with Adler, 1891), the Chicago Stock Exchange (with Adler,
1894), the Guaranty Building in Buffalo (with Adler, 1895), and the
Carson Pirie Scott store (1901–4) in Chicago.

When the leading architecture critic of the day, Montgomery
Schuyler (1843–1914), assessed "The Sky-Scraper Up to Date" in
1899, he attacked American architects for aiming at all costs at
"originality" instead of "shining with new grace through old forms."
He reminded Americans of the enduring wisdom of Aristotle, "the
father of criticism, that a work of art must have a beginning, a middle, and an end." The best skyscrapers, he noted, had followed "the
Aristotelian triple division . . . the more specific analogy of the column." Just as the ancient Greek column had a base, a smooth supporting body, and a decorated capital, so the skyscraper should

visibly distinguish these elements—decorated treatment on the ground floor, an ornamented cornice at the top, and in the body of the building an unbroken repetition of the "tiers of similar cells" like the column itself. Despite his protestations, Sullivan's own most esteemed early "skyscrapers" like the Wainwright Building seemed to follow this Aristotelian model.

* * *

The liberation of the American skyscraper came not in Chicago but in New York in what the architecture critic Paul Goldberger has called the "theatrical" phase. The different layouts of cities encouraged giving a different aspect to their tall buildings. The streets of recently settled Chicago had marked out symmetrical square blocks, providing sites for squat squarish buildings. But in New York the narrow crooked lanes and varied angular intersections inherited from two centuries of history gave a different challenge to its architects. "As the elephant . . . to the giraffe, so is the colossal business block of Chicago to the skyscraper of New York," the novelist William Archer observed. "There is a proportion and dignity in the mammoth of Chicago which is lacking in most of those which form the jagged skyline of Manhattan Island. . . . They are simply astounding manifestations of human energy and heaven-storming audacity." These dramatic architectural experiments had special appeal for Edward Steichen and Alfred Stieglitz and their new art of photography. On the curious triangular plot (only six feet wide at its apex) at the intersection of Broadway and Twenty-third Street in 1903 rose Chicago architect Daniel Burnham's Flatiron Building, which was the subject of one of Stieglitz's most dramatic photographs. Its surrounding downdrafts added human sensations to the architectural by flapping up the petticoats of long-skirted women as they passed by. Bizarre towers rose across the city—the Metropolitan Life tower (1909) had a replica of the campanile in St. Mark's Square in Venice, while the Woolworth Building (1913), the world's tallest at the time, adapted Gothic motifs (gargoyles and all) to ornament the top of its 792 feet and even to embellish entrances of its twenty-nine speedy elevators.

Skyscraper theatrics provided a new American kind of advertisement. Across the land in the Old World big buildings had always advertised the power of prince and Church. Now skyscrapers wrote their commercial message in the sky—advertising life insurance, sewing machines, or five-and-tens. F. W. Woolworth paid $13.5 million in cash for his building, an expensive advertisement but well worth it. On April 24, 1913, President Woodrow Wilson turned the opening switch from the White House, and the eminent Methodist clergyman S. Parkes Cadman proclaimed it "The Cathedral of Commerce," sending a brand-name message around the world. "Just as religion monopolized art and architecture during the Medieval epoch, so commerce has engrossed the United States since 1865. . . . Here, on the Island of Manhattan . . . stands a succession of buildings without precedent or peer. . . . Of these buildings, the Woolworth is Queen, acknowledged as premier by all lovers of the city . . . by those who aspire toward perfection, and by those who use visible things to obtain it."

By 1930 another theatric advertisement had overtaken the Woolworth Building. The seventy-seven-story Chrysler building, rising to 1,048 feet, was the world's tallest when completed in 1930. It also combined a romantic spire of jazzy stainless-steel arches with ornamental trim and gargoyles fashioned after the device on the hood of the 1929 Chrysler car, and earned its architect William Van Alen the sobriquet of "the Ziegfeld of the profession." It was wonderful how rapidly the skyscraper sweepstakes were lost or won. The very next year the Empire State Building rose to 102 stories and 1,200 feet. With former Governor Alfred E. Smith as the front man, it proved a better advertisement for American architecture than for the American economy. When it opened in the midst of the Depression, it had so few tenants that it was called the Empty State Building. Still, it became rich in news and folklore. In 1933 it proved a convenient perch for King Kong, who made a spectacular climb to the top. But in 1945, when a small plane rammed into its seventy-sixth floor, killing the pilot and thirteen others, some said it proved that God never intended that there should be such tall buildings.

Chicago entered the theatric sweepstakes when the Chicago

Tribune Company in 1922 announced a competition for the design of its skyscraper office in the heart of the city. Of the 160 architects from all over, the competition was won by Chicago architects John Mead Howells and Raymond Hood with their Gothic tower crowned by a circle of buttresses. In New York's Woolworth tradition it succeeded as an advertisement for "the world's greatest newspaper" but had little influence on the future of architecture. In sharp contrast, the second-prize design by the Finnish architect Eliel Saarinen for a clean stepped-back central tower with no cornices or belt courses separating the floors and with no imitation of classical or Gothic themes provided the model for future American skyscrapers. "It goes freely in advance," Louis Sullivan acclaimed, "and with the steel frame as a thesis, displays a high science of design such as the world up to this day had neither known nor surmised." Saarinen immigrated to the United States to become one of the most influential city planners of the generation.

*   *   *

The next phase of the American skyscraper, like other triumphs of American culture, would become international. No longer in the tones of a Walt Whitmanesque muscular America, the skyscraper celebrated the technology that was bringing the world together. The provincial, rural-minded Thomas A. Edison in 1926 prophesied doom. "If . . . New York keeps on permitting the building of skyscrapers, each one having as many people as we used to have in a small city, disaster must overtake us." And Thomas Hastings (1860–1929), an American Beaux-Arts disciple, foresaw "the city of dreadful height." But on seeing the city, the bold French-Swiss architect Le Corbusier declared, "The skyscrapers of New York are too small and there are too many of them." Others, too, like Raymond Hood, saw new opportunities. "Congestion is good," he insisted, "New York is the first place in the world where a man can work within a ten-minute walk of a quarter of a million people. . . . Think how this expands the field from which we can choose our friends, our co-workers and contacts, how easy it is to develop a constant interchange of thought."

The flamboyant Frank Lloyd Wright (1869–1959), from rural Wisconsin, shared Edison's fear of the congested overbuilt city. His practice had been mainly in domestic architecture, but he had been entranced by the skyscraper since his early years as apprentice to Sullivan. He let his imagination soar, offered thin-slab designs long before Rockefeller Center, pioneered in glass for tall buildings with his plan for a Luxfer Prism Skyscraper (1895), which was never built, and topped the competition with his grand solution (1956) to congestion on the ground, a Chicago Mile-High Skyscraper (never built). His tall-building designs, some said, were nothing but small Wright houses blown up to skyscraper scale. His successes would eventually be buildings of a smaller scale hugging the ground.

The later triumphs of the American skyscraper, appropriately for a nation of nations, would be called the International Style and invited architects from all over the world. Its first great monument, cleansed of classical and Gothic frippery, was Rockefeller Center. Conceived in 1927 as a new home for the Metropolitan Opera Company, its planning was interrupted by the Depression of 1929, but was carried on by John D. Rockefeller, Jr., as the first great privately financed mixed-use urban project. The product (1932–40) of Raymond Hood and a team of architects, its seventy-story skyscraper, surrounded by lower buildings with an open plaza in the center, became a delightful focus of pedestrian life. The thin skyscraper slab, a dramatically simple form, did not require the setbacks customary in other tall buildings. The lower surrounding buildings and the open central plaza showed respect for community light and air and provided social amenities. For the first time it offered larger and smaller skyscrapers as a group.

The International Style was dramatized again in the slender thirty-nine-story slab of the United Nations Secretariat building (1952), which was created by a Rockefeller Center architect, Wallace K. Harrison, around a sketch by Le Corbusier. Its unbroken vertical line, a response to Sullivan's plea, was the vivid opposite to the theatrical Woolworth or Chrysler Building. Sheer walls of green glass faced east and west and narrower stretches of white marble rose on north and south. This International Style, so chaste in steel and glass that it could hardly be called a style, found its apostle in the colorful Mies van der Rohe (1886–1969), a refugee from the German Nazis. In Chicago he made the Illinois Institute of Technology a nursery of modernism. His masterpiece in 1958, the Seagram Building at 375 Park Avenue in New York City, was a thirty-eight-story tower of bronze and glass (with no setbacks and no classic or Gothic adornment at top or bottom) set in its own inviting plaza with two fountains in the foreground and a site for an elegant restaurant in the rear. This plain tower became a prototype for Miesian architecture, a simple structure boasting its simplicity. Some critics objected that Mies was not as honest as he seemed, for his buildings really depended on hidden supports. One admirer called the Seagram Building "a beautiful lady in hidden corsets." But Miesian simplicity prevailed—in the Lever House (1952) in New York, the Inland Steel Building (1957) in Chicago by Skidmore, Owings, and Merrill, the CBS Building (1965) by the Finnish architect Eliel's son Eero Saarinen, in I. M. Pei's John Hancock Tower in Boston (1975), in Kevin Roche's United Nations Plaza Building (1976), and in the twin 110-story towers of the World Trade Center (1976) in lower Manhattan, the city's tallest buildings, which added height, without adding much interest, to the skyline.

Just as steel had made the skyscraper possible, now quite unpredictably the magic of glass incorporated sun and light and all surroundings into buildings in ways the Gothic acolytes could not have imagined, and added a new ambiguity to "structural honesty." The walls of windows made buildings like the Lever House look as if they were made of glass by the deceptive use of spandrel glass to cover the external steel structure between the floors. Glass, this newly versatile ancient material, brought together indoors and outdoors, with new problems of heating and cooling and extravagant demands for energy. Ironic for those who preached that "form follows function," glass varied the appearance of tall buildings without revealing their structure or function.

* * *

In architecture of all the arts it would be most difficult to abandon the secure and familiar forms in which people had lived and worshiped and been governed. But in 1890, when the Congress of the United States authorized a World's Columbian Exposition in Chicago to celebrate the four hundredth anniversary of the "discovery" of America, it might have been assumed that the exposition would display the wonders of this new American architecture in its birthplace. Left to themselves Chicagoans had been bold and original. The skyscraper had already made its dramatic appearance. But, facing the Old World art world, frontier Americans became insecure and apologetic. A commission of the city's best architects and landscape designers produced a "white city" of 686 acres to be recovered from the swamps of the city's south side, embellished with lagoons. Its buildings, though newly lit by electricity, were a grandiose array of classical and neo-Renaissance designs. With twenty-eight million visitors from May through October in 1893, it would be acclaimed as the most successful and influential of all world's fairs in the United States.

The Columbian Exposition set a new fashion in urban boosterism, for it "put Chicago on the map." It was also part of the City Beautiful Movement that resulted in the invitation to Daniel Burnham (1846–1912), who was in charge of the construction in Chicago, to become a designer of the Mall in Washington, D.C., under the McMillan Plan, sponsored by Senator James McMillan of Michigan. This plan, which restored the almost forgotten L'Enfant plan of 1792, was adopted in 1901, and eventually made the capital a city of parks and vistas. So the skyscraper found its place as a separate facet of urban design alongside the "horizontal city" that preserved human scale and warmth in otherwise cold city environments.

Burnham also was the Chicago champion of the classical revival. "The influence of the Exposition," he prophesied, "will be to inspire a reversion toward the pure ideal of the ancients. We have been in an inventive period, and have had rather contempt for the classics." In this competition between the Wild West and the Cultured East, the East won hands down. The White City of columns, temple fronts, arches, and domes showed little that was Chicago American. But the only building admired abroad was Louis Sullivan's Transportation Building, not in the classical mold. Burnham's prediction was on the mark. The Exposition, displacing the fashionable Romanesque of H. H. Richardson, heralded a revival of classical forms.

Louis Sullivan, prophet of an American architecture, deplored this triumph of "good taste" and academic pallor. He stigmatized as dangerously contagious "the virus of the World's Fair." Thus Architecture died in the land of the free and the home of the brave.

> ... the architectural generation immediately succeeding the classic and Renaissance merchants are seeking to secure a special immunity from the inroads of common sense, through a process of vaccination with the lymph of every known European style, period, and accident. ... There is now a dazzling display of merchandise, all imported. ... We have Tudor for colleges and residences; Roman for banks, and railway stations and libraries—or Greek if you like—some customers prefer the Ionic to the Doric. We have French, English, and Italian Gothic, classic and Renaissance for churches. In fact we are prepared to satisfy, in any manner of taste. Residences we offer in Italian or Louis Quinze. We make a small charge for alterations and adaptations.

Architects, Thorstein Veblen explained, were again playing their familiar role, for "the office of the leisure class in social evolution is to retard the movement and to conserve what is obsolescent."

While Americans remained charmed by the obsolescent, Sullivan paid the prophet's price. The spectacle of the World's Columbian Exposition left him embittered, in a slough from which he never recovered. His remaining years were an undocumented nightmare, too frustrating to be recorded in his autobiography. The economic depression of 1893 made architectural commissions scarce. His longtime partner, Dankmar Adler, left him briefly in 1895 for a lucrative post with an elevator company. Then his assistant of many years left him. By 1909, desperate for lack of commissions, Sullivan had to sell his library and household effects, and then he migrated from one cheap hotel to another. In 1918 he had to give up his office in the Auditorium Tower, which had brought him fame, and move to a small office on the second floor. His marriage in 1899 had ended in separation and divorce. In 1918 he tried unsuccessfully to obtain work for the war. By 1920 he had no office, was living in one bedroom and depended on donations from friends. But he did collect his thoughts, published numerous articles, and in 1918 composed his *Kindergarten Chats*, a meandering Whitmanesque manifesto of American architecture, for which no publisher could be found at the time. Then he wrote his *Autobiography of an Idea* and collected a series of nineteen plates of his designs for ornaments, which a friend placed in his hands as he was dying in his lonely hotel room in 1924.

INVENTING THE ESSAY

CENTURIES passed in Western literature before authors let themselves be themselves in what they wrote. Dominated by classical conventions, the literati found no forms in which to describe themselves freely and randomly. We should not be shocked, then, by Oscar Wilde's paradox "Being natural is only a pose." Saintly epiphanies and confessions like Saint Augustine's had recorded the search for salvation. A letter addressed to a particular person, usually not intended for publication, was governed by the candor and the good manners of the writer. But how could an author show himself naked, unboastful and unashamed?

For literary self-portrait a new form was created by a French provincial landowner of the Renaissance. Michel de Montaigne (1533–1592) christened his creation "Essays." From the French *essayer*, "to try," the name itself revealed that the task Montaigne had set himself seemed difficult and uncertain. He dared claim only that he had made some "tries" in this new exercise of self-revelation. Montaigne's preface to his 1580 *Essays* declared:

> This, reader, is an honest book. . . . I want to appear in my simple, natural, and everyday dress, without strain or artifice; for it is myself that I portray. My imperfections may be read to the life, and my natural form will be here in so far

as respect for the public allows. Had my lot been cast among those people who are said still to live under the kindly liberty of nature's primal laws, I should, I assure you, most gladly have painted myself complete and in all my nakedness.

So, reader, I am myself the substance of my book, and there is no reason why you should waste your leisure on so frivolous and unrewarding a subject.

(Translated by J. M. Cohen)

Despite this uninviting invitation the book survived to become a model for our most popular, most influential, and most widely imitated form of nonfiction.

Yet in contrast to the "forms" of rhetoricians, the essay was not really a form at all. Rather it was a way of literary freewheeling, a license to be random and personal. Aldous Huxley, himself a brilliant practitioner, explained: "By the time he had written his way into the Third Book he had reached the limits of his newly discovered art. . . . Free association artistically controlled—this is the paradoxical secret of Montaigne's best essays. One damned thing after another—but in a sequence that in some almost miraculous way develops a central theme and relates it to the rest of human experience." The "central theme" that held his *Essays* together, Montaigne repeatedly reminds his reader, was nothing but Montaigne himself.

Personal reflections had previously been cast in certain recognized molds, tamed and domesticated into familiar paths. Some, like the *Moralia* of Plutarch (c.46–120), were treatises on moral conduct—"How to Discern Between a Flatterer and a Friend," or "How to Restrain Anger." Others, like the *Meditations* of Marcus Aurelius (121–180), offered aphorisms and moral precepts. Montaigne knew these works. And his focus, not on morality but on the elusive, ever-changing, contradictory self, was courageously new. Not as a prescription for the Good Life, but for the sheer joy of exploration and self-discovery. Offering not the Good, but the Unique. Here was a landmark in man's movement from the complacency of divine certitude to the piquancy of experience and human variety.

How did Montaigne, who boasted only of his ordinariness, become the creator of a momentous new form of literary freedom and literary creation? Montaigne's ancestry and education were well designed to sharpen his sense of personal uniqueness. His father, Pierre Eyquem, sometime mayor and prosperous merchant of Bordeaux, bore the name "de Montaigne" because Pierre's grandfather had bought the Montaigne château and feudal territory that came with it. His mother descended from a Spanish Jewish family, the Lopez de Villeneuva, who lived in Aragon at the height of the Inquisition in the late fifteenth century. Three members of the family, including Michel's great-great-great-grandfather Micer Pablo (in 1491) were burned at the stake. They were prominent Marranos, Spanish Jews who had gone through the motions of conversion to escape persecution, but who continued to practice Judaism secretly. The Marrano memory could not have been lost on Michel. He frequently expressed his sense of the injustice done to the Jews, which confirmed his doubts of force as an effective agent of persuasion. "Some turned Christians," he wrote, "of their faith, or of that of their descendants, even today, a hundred years later, few Portuguese are sure, though custom and length of time are far stronger counselors than any other compulsion." The Marranos remained suspect in both the Jewish and the Christian world.

Michel was born in the Château de Montaigne, thirty miles east of Bordeaux. The oldest of eight surviving children, he yet enjoyed close attention from "the best father there ever was." To widen the noble child's sympathies, he "had me held over the baptismal font by people of the lowest class, to bind and attach me to them." And Montaigne recalls in his *Essays* that, instead of bringing in a nurse, as many noble families did, his father sent Michel

> from the cradle to be brought up in a poor village of his, and kept me there as long as I was nursing, and even longer, training me to the humblest and commonest way of life. . . . His notion aimed . . . to ally me with the people and that class of men that needs our help; and he considered that I was duty bound to look rather to the man who extends his

arms to me than to the one who turns his back on me. . . . His plan has succeeded not at all badly. I am prone to devote myself to the little people, whether because there is more vainglory in it, or through natural compassion, which has infinite power over me.

(Translated by Donald M. Frame)

Believing that the "tender brains" of children were shocked by being rudely awakened from sleep, "he had me suddenly awakened by the sound of some instrument, and I was never without a man to do this for me." As a painless way of teaching the boy Latin, still the language of European learning, his father hired a German tutor who spoke good Latin but no French, and decreed that no one should speak anything but Latin in Michel's presence.

"Altogether we Latinized ourselves so much that it overflowed all the way to our villages on every side, where there still remain several Latin names for artisans and tools that have taken root by usage." He was six before he knew French, his mother tongue and the language of the neighborhood. He was taught Greek "artificially, but in a new way in the form of amusement and exercise. We volleyed our conjugations back and forth, like those who learn arithmetic and geometry by such games as checkers and chess." In this domestic Athenaeum, it is remarkable that Michel grew up to be even as normal as he was.

Sent off to school in Bordeaux, he completed the twelve-year course in seven. His teachers feared he would show up their imperfect Latin, and he declared himself lucky that at least they did not teach him the "hatred of books" that they somehow instilled in other noblemen. His own philosophy of education would be shaped by seeing the brutal discipline that made the school "a jail of captive youth. They make them slack, by punishing them for slackness before they show it. Go in at lesson time; you hear nothing but cries, both from tortured boys and from masters drunk with rage."

After studying law at the university, Michel through family connections became a magistrate. For the next dozen years (1554–70) he experienced the world of affairs, the venality and injustices of the law. He saw one fellow judge tear a scrap from the paper on which he had sentenced an adulterer, to write a love note to the wife of a colleague on the same bench. Lawless France, he complained, had "more laws than all the rest of the world together."

* * *

One crucial experience, not the kind that could be prescribed generally for the preparation of an author, marked Montaigne's path to become an essayist. In 1559, soon after he had joined the Bordeaux Parlement, he met a brilliant fellow magistrate two years his elder whose person would inspire and haunt him for the rest of his life. This was Étienne de la Boétie (1530–1563).

> Some inexplicable power of destiny . . . brought about our union. We were looking for each other before we met, by reason of the reports we had heard of each other, which made a greater impression on our emotions than mere reports reasonably should. I believe that this was brought about by some decree of Heaven. We embraced one another by name. And at our first meeting, which happened by chance at a great feast and gathering in the city, we found ourselves so familiar, so bound to one another, that from that time nothing was closer to either than each was to the other.
>
> (Translated by J. M. Cohen)

This friendship lasted till La Boétie's death from dysentery in 1563. Since 1554 La Boétie had been happily married to an older woman of an eminent local family, the widowed mother of two children. She had no children with La Boétie.

Again and again, Montaigne described his intense relationship with La Boétie. But he does not detail the erotic element. Unlike the Greeks, he writes, "our morality rightly abhors" a homosexual relationship. Still, in the chapter "On Friendship" and elsewhere in his *Essays* he discloses feelings not usual in accounts of friendship between men. Taking his relationship with La Boétie as his prototype of friendship, Montaigne contrasts marriage. "Not only is it a bargain to which only the entrance is free, continuance in it being constrained and compulsory, and depending upon other things than our will, but it is a bargain commonly made for other ends." Acquaintanceship can be enjoyed with many. "But that friendship which possesses the soul and rules over it with complete sovereignty cannot possibly be divided in two. . . ." For nearly five years, he tells us, communications with this alter ego satisfied his need to reveal himself.

The death of La Boétie, who was only thirty-three, hit him hard. On the wall of the entrance to the study he recorded his debt to "the tenderest, sweetest, and closest companion, than whom our age has seen no one better, more learned, more charming, or indeed more perfect, Michel de Montaigne, miserably bereft of so dear a support of his life . . . has dedicated this excellent apparatus for the mind." He recalled with satisfaction "not having forgotten to tell anything" to his friend. The sudden deprivation of this uninhibited friendship and its opportunities for self-revelation left a vacuum. "Hungry to make myself known," Montaigne sought a way to replace his conversations with his best friend. And later generations must be grateful for this premature death of La Boétie, for Montaigne himself suggests that if La Boétie had lived, instead of the essays he might only have written letters.

> Letter writing . . . is a kind of work in which my friends think I have some ability. And I would have preferred to adopt this form in which to publish my sallies, if I had had someone to talk to. I needed what I once had, a certain relationship to lead me on, sustain me, and raise me up. . . . I would have been more attentive and confident, with a strong friend to address, than I am now, when I consider the tastes of a whole public. And if I am not mistaken, I would have been more successful.
>
> (Translated by Donald M. Frame)

But writing letters to imaginary correspondents, to "traffic with the wind, as some others have done," would not satisfy Montaigne. With his "humorous and familiar style . . . not proper for public business, but like the language I speak, too compact, irregular, abrupt, and singular" he had to create a form of his own. And so came the *Essays*, which marked a new path for authors in future centuries.

This synopsis of Montaigne's personal incentives to create the modern essay leaves out the broad currents of life in his time and the frustrations of public life that also played their part. From his grief at the death of La Boétie, Montaigne sought relief in marriage. "Needing some violent diversion to distract me from it, by art and study I made myself fall in love, in which my youth helped me. Love solaced me and withdrew me from the affliction caused by friendship." The object of this factitious love was the twenty-year-old daughter of an eminent Catholic family of Bordeaux. He boasted that the decision was not made by himself. "We do not marry for ourselves, whatever we say; we marry just as much for our posterity, for our family. . . . Therefore I like this fashion of arranging it rather by a third hand than by our own, and by the sense of others rather than by our own. How opposite is all this to the conventions of love!" In 1565, two years after he lost his friend, he married Françoise de la Chassaigne. By conventional standards it seemed a good marriage, although of the six children she bore him only one survived more than a few months after birth. Montaigne still insisted that friendship, not love, should be the bond of marriage.

Meanwhile, life in Montaigne's France did not encourage a firm religious faith. In religious wars tainted by political intrigue and dynastic feuds it was seldom clear whether the parties were fighting for their king or for their God, and they were inclined to confuse the two. Just as Montaigne's relation to La Boétie had bred habits of honest self-revelation, so the spectacle of the "wars of the three Henrys" bred a skeptical frame of mind. The word "Huguenot" now entered the French language for the Protestant sect that was widening its appeal, especially to the nobility of southwestern France. The year when Montaigne began writing his essays, 1572, was the year of the Saint Bartholomew's Day Massacre. The devious Catherine de' Medici took advantage of the assemblage of nobles in Paris for the wedding of her daughter to Henry of Navarre (later

Henry IV) to order the assassination of the Huguenot leader Coligny and many others. The butchery in Bordeaux, too, was terrifying, and nobody knows how many thousands were massacred across the provinces. For this bloody victory of the faith Pope Gregory XIII celebrated a thanksgiving Mass in Rome.

The volatile religious spirit was symbolized in Henry IV, a Protestant who vainly tried to pacify the country and save his life by his pretended conversion to Catholicism (1593). His conciliatory Edict of Nantes (1598) which offered Huguenots in some places political and religious freedom only sparked another cycle of civil wars, and led to his own assassination. Still, Montaigne's father, an enemy of forced convictions, had been tolerant in the family, allowing his children to follow their own faiths. Two of Michel's brothers were Protestant. Montaigne himself, though professing to be a Catholic, was a trusted adviser and chamberlain to Henry, the leading Protestant. The moderation of his faith made him suspect on both sides.

Even before the Saint Bartholomew's Day Massacre, Montaigne had decided to withdraw from public life. He had served thirteen years in the Bordeaux Parlement and had spent much of the last seven years reverently tracking down and editing the writings of La Boétie. He marked the occasion of his retirement, on his thirty-eighth birthday, with a Latin inscription near the entrance to his library-study:

> . . . Michel de Montaigne, long weary of the servitude of the court and of public employments, while still entire, returned to the bosom of the learned Muses, where in calm and freedom from all cares he will spend what little remains of his life. . . . and he has consecrated it to his freedom, tranquility, and leisure.

The pleasures of the library were, of course, not new to Montaigne. The past year, as a task of filial piety, he had worked at translating from Latin into French a little-known work of theology. The Spanish scholar Raymond Sebond's *Book of Creatures, or Natural Theology,* published some one hundred fifty years before, had caught his father's fancy as an antidote to Protestantism. His father had instructed Michel to translate it, and he dedicated the translation to his father on the very day of his father's death.

The enduring product of this act of piety was not what the elder Montaigne had hoped for. Michel's own "Apology for Raymond Sebond," became the longest and most philosophically explicit of his essays. While exploring the role and the limits of reason and pretending to defend Sebond, Montaigne expounded his own skepticism. Ironically, his act of filial piety had provided him with a way to dispose of his father's faith. Montaigne's message here too is still in the spirit of the *Essays*, which he sums up in his famous motto "What do I know?" *(Que sais-je?)* Montaigne purports to prove that "Man is nothing without God," but the burden of his argument is that since Man has no knowledge, skepticism is the only wisdom.

He reveals man's delusion of superiority over other animals. Yet reason, knowledge, and imagination, which seem to distinguish man from the other animals, seldom add to his happiness. Our memory is as often a pain as a comfort. "For memory sets before us, not what we choose, but what it pleases. Indeed, there is nothing that imprints a thing so vividly on our memory as the desire to forget it." Montaigne divides philosophers into three classes: those who claim to have found the truth; those who deny that truth can be found; and those like Socrates who confess their ignorance and go on searching. Only the last are wise. All others make the mistake of believing that truth and error can be measured by man's capacities. Our senses are our only contact with the world, and they tell us nothing but what the senses can tell. How can we know what is really out there? Montaigne still professes that he supports the Catholic religion, which is beyond the reach of reason or the senses. Yet his father would not have been happy to see that he was supporting the Faith "as the rope supports the hanging man."

*　*　*

Montaigne was not as successful as he had hoped in his efforts to withdraw completely from public life. He continued to be enlisted in the battles and diplomacy of the religious wars. But he had begun writing essays soon after his retirement in 1571. By 1578 he had found, or invented, "Essays" as the title for his literary creation. Perhaps it came, somehow, from a literary competition in 1540 at the Floral Games in Toulouse, his mother's hometown. To break the tie among the leading competitors in the poetry contest, a last line would be supplied to which each contestant "tried" to supply the best opening lines. The idea of "trial" or "experiment" is essential to Montaigne's new literary creation. He is aiming not to construct a philosophy or prescribe a morality, but only "to spy on himself from close up. This is not my teaching, this is my study; and it is not a lesson for others, it is for me." "These are my humors and opinions; I offer them as what I believe, not what is to be believed."

The ninety-four essays of varying length published in his first two volumes in 1580 were delightfully miscellaneous, with all the charm of randomness. "I am myself the substance of my book," his Preface explained. "Whatever these absurdities may be, I have had no intention of concealing them, any more than I would a bald and graying portrait of myself, in which the painter had drawn not a perfect face, but mine." Their very heterogeneity testified to frankness. "Of Idleness" is followed by "Of Liars" and "Of Prompt or Slow Speech." "Of the Uncertainty of Our Judgment" precedes "Of War Horses," and "Of Smells" before "Of Prayers." "Of the Greatness of Rome" comes just before "Not to Counterfeit Being Sick," and "Of Thumbs." There is no effort at chronology, at the development of arguments, ideas, or narrative, no attempt to deny the flux, or to insist that flux can know flux. "I do not portray being: I portray passing . . . from day to day, from minute to minute. . . . This is a record . . . of irresolute and, when it so befalls, contradictory ideas; whether I am different myself, or whether I take hold of my subjects in different circumstances and aspects." With his *Essays*, Montaigne had discovered and begun to explore himself, then he created a self in words. When these volumes were published in Bordeaux he observed with his usual self-deprecation that the farther away the readers were, the better they would like his work. At home "they think it droll to see me in print."

One of his most outlandish and most influential essays revealed

that Montaigne could use his self-explorations to help others illuminate the world. "Of Cannibals" urges caution before we stigmatize
any people as "barbarous," a term that the Greeks indiscriminately
applied to all strange ways. "We see from this how chary we must be
of subscribing to vulgar opinions; we should judge them by the test
of reason; and not by common report." He describes the savagery of
torturing heretics, prisoners, and criminals, which really seems to
him a way of "eating a man alive." "I consider it more barbarous to
eat a man alive than to eat him dead; to tear by rack and torture a
body still full of feeling, to roast it by degrees, and then give it to be
trampled and eaten by dogs and swine—a practice which we have not
only read about but seen within recent memory, not between ancient
enemies, but between neighbours and fellow-citizens, and what is
worse, under the cloak of piety and religion—than to roast and eat a
man after he is dead." But his reflections on cannibals would have a
more cheerful afterlife when Shakespeare, who probably read this
passage in Florio's translation, himself translated these charitable
sentiments into *The Tempest*.

It was at the conclusion of this work of nine years that Montaigne wrote his familiar self-disparaging preface. His book was only
"to amuse a neighbor, a relative, a friend." He sought his well-
earned respite in Italy, where he visited the watering places seeking
relief from the kidney stone that never ceased to plague him. At
Rome, where "every man shares in the ecclesiastical idleness," he
was courteously received by the same Pope Gregory XIII who had
celebrated the grateful Mass for the Massacre of Saint Bartholomew's Day. His *Essays*, which had been reviewed by a papal censor
who could not read French, were, to his surprise, only mildly "corrected." Gone only a year, he received an urgent message to return
to Bordeaux, where he had been elected mayor. A Catholic loyalist
respected by the Protestants who now surrounded Bordeaux, he
might be useful in trying to keep the peace. He reluctantly accepted
the call, and after serving creditably he was allowed to return to his
study in 1585. There he revised Books I and II of his essays and
worked on Book III. The religious war heated up again, with the
Holy Catholic League in the ascendant. Now Montaigne, suspect

for not having joined the Catholic army, and with a Protestant brother and sister and friends among the heretics, was in constant peril. "I incurred the disadvantages that moderation brings in such maladies. I was belabored from every quarter: to the Ghibelline I was a Guelph, to the Guelph a Ghibelline. . . . It was mute suspicions that were current secretly."

An epidemic of the plague that drove him and his family for six months from his château decimated the neighborhood. Wherever they went, the terror followed them, "having to shift their abode as soon as one of the group began to feel pain in the end of his finger."

The first two volumes of the *Essays*, which had gone through four editions in Bordeaux, were finally being published in Paris, and were respectfully received by scholars. This encouraged him to go on. His third volume with thirteen essays appeared in 1588, with additions to the earlier volumes. Volume III offered more in the "essay" spirit. "This essay of myself" is more emphatic in his opinions and more self-conscious. "I would rather be an authority on myself than on Cicero." Again he is free with self-doubts and self-criticism. "Stupidity is a bad quality" he observes in "On the Art of Conversation," "but to be unable to bear it, to be vexed and fretted by it, as is the case with me, is another kind of disease that is hardly less troublesome." "I often risk some intellectual sallies of which I am suspicious, and certain verbal subtleties, which make me shake my head. But I let them go at a venture. I see that some are praised for such things; it is not for me alone to judge. I present myself standing and lying down, front and back, facing left and right, and in all my natural attitudes." "Our follies do not make me laugh, our wisdom does."

Montaigne never ceased to yearn for another living partner in his conversations about himself. His *Essays* still seemed only a substitute for spoken revelations to his departed friend. In 1588, in this third volume, a quarter century after the death of La Boétie, he is still plaintively reaching out:

> Amusing notion: many things that I would not want to tell anyone, I tell the public; and for my most secret knowl-

edge and thoughts I send my most faithful friends to a bookseller's shop. . . .

   If by such good signs I knew of a man who was suited to
me, truly I would go very far to find him; for the sweetness
of harmonious and agreeable company cannot be bought
too dearly, in my opinion. Oh, a friend!

                                 (Translated by Donald M. Frame)

Nor would he reach in vain.

   The answer to his prayer was almost as surprising and puzzling
as his relationship with La Boétie. Early in 1588, when he was in
Paris on one of his diplomatic missions, he met the brilliant and
learned Marie de Gournay (1566–1645), a young woman of twenty-
two who had so admired his *Essays* that she had written asking to
meet him. As her father had died ten years before, she now became
his *fille d'alliance*, his informally adopted daughter. The term had no
legal significance but described a soul mate to whom one had no
blood tie. The adoration may have been more on her side than on
his, but ailing and "friendless" he welcomed her literary intimacy.
He lived at her house for some months while he dictated passages of
the *Essays* to her, and he designated her his literary executor. After
painful bouts with a kidney stone and other ailments, when Montaigne died in his château in 1592, his wife and family welcomed de
Gournay and embraced her. She was responsible for the belated
shorter 1635 edition of the *Essays*, incorporating some of her own
omissions and some new passages she attributed to him.

   Marie de Gournay took the occasion in her 1635 edition to tone
down Montaigne's references to her. But her emendations revealed
her desire to obscure a relationship that may have been more than
filial. Montaigne had written that he loved her "more than a daughter" but she substituted "as a daughter." She omitted, among others,
his statement that "she is the only person I still think about in the
world." The rest of her life (she died in 1645) she spent editing, "improving," and defending Montaigne's works.

                            * * *

Montaigne's enduring legacy was not a philosophy, however appealing his tolerant skepticism has remained. His afterlife was a rare creation, a new form for literature, a new catalyst for literary conversation, self-exploration, and doubt. "A loose sally of the mind"; Dr. Johnson defined "essay" in his *Dictionary* (1755), "an irregular indigested piece; not a regular and orderly composition." No other Western author unwittingly created so vivid a witness as did Montaigne to the congenital rigidity of thought and the power of artistic archetypes. How astonishing that anyone should have had to "create" a literary form to dignify the loose sallies of the mind!

Few literary creators, Western adventurers of the word, have had so widespread or so interstitial an influence as Montaigne. The spirit of the essay has survived the obsolescence of Montaigne's faiths and the irrelevance of his doubts. He lived on in the courageous freedom of his example. His essay quest to put in words the self in all its vagueness and contradiction has become ever more appealing.

"Essay," which for Montaigne was a term of self-deprecation, for confessions of the elusive self, in later centuries became a banner for assertions, declarations, and bold exploration. Like the novel and biography, it would become a vehicle and a catalyst of modernity. The essay would be at once a vehicle of self-discovery, an affirmation of the writing individual, and a way of sharing the individuality of others. Every essay implied the need for experiment, for incremental random thoughts.

It is no accident that the pioneer English essayist Francis Bacon (1561–1626) was also a pioneer in the experimental, incremental approach to science. Bacon's political ambitions and his temperament led him to make his essays "Counsells, Civil and Morall" (1597, 1612, 1625). This put him in the tradition of Plutarch's *Moralia*, lacking the whimsicality and randomness of Montaigne. The essay became more intimately tied to everyday concerns by the new vogue of periodical publications, facilitated by printing presses and a reading public. Richard Steele's *Tatler* (1709–11) appeared three times a week, and the *Spectator* (1711–12), with Joseph Addison, appeared daily. Journalism, the current press, was the essayist's natural ally.

The journalist had to be an essayist, in every new issue hoping to make a better try, needing to shift subjects continually, to treat topics briefly, and to compete for the attention of impatient readers. The newspaper would be a bundle of essays, now not about the self but about the world.

The flood and variety of essays and essayists increased with the multiplication of magazines and newspapers. The essay provided a versatile and appealing form for the literary criticism and moral reflections of Dr. Johnson and Sainte-Beuve (1804–1869), for the political and philosophical speculations of John Locke and the Federalist papers, for the labored whimsies of Charles Lamb. Emerson (1803–1882) made the essay his own vehicle for an American substitute for a philosophy. And the essay was providentially suited to the existential philosophy of Camus, the random insights of Lafcadio Hearn, the tentative judgments of Thomas Mann, the opinions of G. K. Chesterton, the fantasies of George Orwell, the playfulness of E. B. White.

While the essay became a respectable form, its novelty was in its celebration of the self. Its reason for being was the belief that the thoughts, feelings, uncertainties, certitudes, and contradictions of a person merited statement and then attention by others. Experience of the doubting self became more intriguing than the fervency of belief. "When I play with my cat," Montaigne asked, "who knows if she does not amuse herself more with me than I with her."

"I TOO AM HERE!"

CHAPTER 69

BESIDE the Mystery of Time, with its staccatos and its continuities, there is the Mystery of Woman. Virginia Woolf's novels of consciousness let us share her wonder at the feminine self. Sometimes she can take refuge from time in the instantaneity of her "moments of being," which fill her writer's diary. Or she can follow the self through time—for centuries in *Orlando*, years in *To the Lighthouse*, and hours in *Mrs. Dalloway*. But for her there is no refuge from being a woman. She writes a great deal about women writers and their inhibitions in the England of her day, their endless "confinements" in pregnancy, their deprivation of education to play "the Angel in the House." She knows there is a unique feminine perception, but its definition eludes her. A woman needs *A Room of One's Own* (1929) to make her free. "In fact, as a woman, I have no country. As a woman I want no country. As a woman my country is the whole world."

Virginia Woolf's feat was finding, like Joyce, so many different ways to reveal "the flickerings of that innermost flame which flashes its messages through the brain." Called a pioneer of the "stream of consciousness," she was properly a pioneer of *streams* of consciousness. Proust and Joyce created their great works around one master consciousness. But each of Virginia Woolf's novels is a new experiment with the self. Unlike Proust or Joyce, she produced no copious masterpiece but numerous cogent experiments. Unlike Dickens or Balzac, who created new vistas of experience, she was concerned not with narrative but with reflection. Nor did she seem impoverished by her lack of experience. Any country house could be her Dublin.

Women had not the raw materials in their own lives for chronicles of worldly conflict and adventure, of struggles for wealth and power. The few who enriched English literature in the eighteenth and nineteenth centuries, when women were becoming an increasing part of the reading public, had the talent to embroider their limited experience.

Jane Austen (1775–1817), whose stature has increased with the years, led an uneventful life on the English countryside in her father's parsonage and in the Hampshire cottage to which the family retired. As she grew up she suffered no Dickensian poverty, nor did she witness the troubled city scene. Her family life was a caricature of the respectable literate middle class, with the six boys and two girls being inducted into literature by their father. While she never married, she seems to have had suitors, and her novels explored the provincial quests for propertied husbands for marriageable daughters. She made a human comedy of provincial manners. In her forty-two years, with *Pride and Prejudice* (1813), *Emma* (1816), and other novels, she earned a secure place in English literature. The most dramatic event in Jane Austen's own life was accepting the offer of marriage by the heir of a neighboring Hampshire family, then changing her mind overnight to refuse him after all.

Women were not to expose themselves to public view as authors, and in her lifetime her name never appeared on the title page of her works. Only after her death was her authorship publicly noted. Other women authors, such as Charlotte and Anne Brontë, sought the cover of a male pseudonym to avoid the condescension reserved for female authors. And Mary Ann Evans adopted the male nom de plume of George Eliot. The young Brontë sisters took refuge in the fairy-tale kingdoms of Angria and Gondal. Mrs. Radcliffe's *Mysteries of Udolpho* and Mrs. Shelley's *Frankenstein* and other Gothic novels sought escape from feminine confinements in tales of fear and fantasy.

The conspicuous disproportion until recently between the numbers of male and female authors reflected the narrowness of women's lives. Women wrote about what they were allowed to know about—the manners they witnessed in country houses, the follies and ironies of the marriage market. Or they reacted into exotic imaginings of horror. Ironically, English women writers of the early nineteenth century who were still conventionally confined by female proprieties became pioneers of realism in the modern novel. They made their own way. Sir Walter Scott acclaimed the "nameless author" of Jane Austen's *Emma* as a prophet of modern realism, and praised her "exquisite touch which renders commonplace things and characters interesting." Charlotte Brontë's *Jane Eyre* (1847) was censured for dealing too freely with subjects not proper for young ladies even to read about. Then there was the scent of scandal because she was rumored to have had an affair with Thackeray, to whom the second edition of *Jane Eyre* was dedicated. Like the hero of the book, Thackeray also had an insane wife. George Eliot (1819–1880), sometimes called the first practitioner of psychological realism in the English novel, defied convention by living with G. H. Lewes, a married man. And Virginia Woolf praised *Middlemarch* (1871–72) as "one of the few English novels written for grown-up people."

Important women novelists in the English language suddenly increased in the twentieth century. The "women's movement" was bearing fruit. Also the inward resources of the self had finally become the novelists' raw material. For these explorations, women needed no male passport. Women writers then pioneered in novels of the self, which liberated literary women from the private audience of their diaries and letters.

"I too am here!" Jane Welsh Carlyle (1801–1866) wrote plaintively to her friend John Sterling on June 15, 1835. The problems of literary women were eloquently revealed in her life. She had married the domineering Thomas Carlyle—"a warm true heart to love me, a towering intellect to command me, and a spirit of fire to be the guiding star—light of my life." Jane Welsh's uncommon literary talent was revealed in her letters, which survived. A letter directed expressly to her, she explained:

. . . was sure to give me a livelier pleasure, than any number
of sheets in which I had but a secondary interest. For in spite
of the honestest efforts to annihilate my I-ity, but merge it in
what the world doubtless considers my better half; I still find
myself a self-subsisting and alas! self-seeking *me*. Little
Felix, in the Wanderjahre [of Goethe], when, in the midst of
an animated scene between Wilhelm and Theresa, he pulls
Theresa's gown, and calls out, "Mama Theresa I too am
here!" only speaks out, with the charming truthfulness of a
child, what I am perpetually feeling, tho' too sophisticated
to pull people's skirts, or exclaim in so many words; Mr.
Sterling "I too am here."

While she dared not compete with the "towering intellect" of her
husband in the public literary form, the letter was perfect for her, as
it had served frustrated literary women for centuries. Whenever she
and Carlyle were separated she sent him a daily letter, "which must
be written dead or alive," and she expected the same from him.
When he once apologized for the length of a letter, she replied,
"Don't mind length, at least only write longly about yourself. The
cocks that awake you; everything of that sort is very interesting. I
hasten over the cleverest descriptions of extraneous people and
things, to find something 'all about yourself, all to myself.' "

* * *

After Jane Welsh Carlyle nearly a century passed before Virginia
Woolf (1882–1941) made the novel her versatile medium for exploring the self. The even tenor of her life, as lacking in worldly adventures as that of Jane Austen or Franz Kafka, forced her to wreak her
literary talent on herself as her raw material. She wrote of the world
within her, which she imagined also to be within others.

She was born in London in 1882 into a numerous family dominated by her father, Sir Leslie Stephen. A leading intellectual and
editor of the monumental *Dictionary of National Biography*, to which
he contributed some four hundred articles, he gave her "the free run
of a large and quite unexpurgated library." Her father's first wife was

Thackeray's daughter, her godfather was the poet James Russell Lowell, then American minister to England, and she was tutored in Greek by Walter Pater's sister. The eminent Victorians, one way or another, swam into her sedentary bookish ken. She longed for the life of the university that her brothers had enjoyed at Cambridge, but which her sex had denied her. She and her sister, Vanessa, were allowed to spend only the mornings studying Greek or drawing, but afternoons and evenings had to be given to proper womanly activities—looking after the house, presiding at tea, or being agreeable to other people's guests. To brother Thoby at Cambridge she wrote:

> I dont get anybody to argue with me now, & feel the want. I have to delve from books, painfully all alone, what you get every evening sitting over your fire smoking your pipe with [Lytton] Strachey, etc. No wonder my knowledge is but scant. Theres nothing like talk as an educator I'm sure. Still I try my best with Shakespeare. I read Sidney Lee's life. . . .

She never lost her sense of being ill-educated, which she blamed on the feminine stereotype.

Her evenings out remained a painful memory. For example, when she accompanied her half brother George Duckworth and Lady Carnarvon to dinner and theater, she made the terrible mistake, as they talked of art, of asking Lady Carnarvon if she had read Plato. If she had, Lady Carnarvon said, she surely would remember it. Virginia's question had spoiled the evening and appalled George, for Plato could lead to subjects unsuitable for a young lady to think about, much less discuss in public. He reminded her that "they're not used to young women saying *anything*."

But George showed less respect for the proprieties in his brazen sexual advances to his two half sisters, which they found impossible to repulse. He tried to smother their pain and disgust with ostentatious courtesies, presents, and invitations to parties and excursions, but Virginia and Vanessa freely expressed their venomous detestation of him to the puzzlement of friends. Virginia's first distasteful experience of sex and of child abuse, from her sixth year, affected her profoundly. "I still shiver with shame," she wrote in the last year of her life, "at the memory of my half brother." She was also abused by her other half brother, Gerald Duckworth. There is no evidence that Virginia was sexually abused by her father, but he did nothing to protect her. Victorian modest reticence and her mother's insensitivity prevented her seeking protection. Her recurrent "madness" may have been a reaction to these traumatic childhood experiences.

She had a number of passionate and sometimes troubling love affairs with women, not only with Vita Sackville-West, whom she admired. Being hotly pursued in 1930 by the aging Ethel Smyth (who sometimes wrote her twice a day) she found less pleasant, for Ethel blew her red nose in her table napkin, and her table manners were repulsive. "It is at once hideous and horrid and melancholy-sad. It is like being caught by a giant crab." In her letters Virginia casually refers to her own frigidity and wonders why people "make a fuss about marriage & copulation?" She never had children, presumably on her doctor's advice, but there may have been other reasons. "Never pretend," she wrote in 1923, "that the things you haven't got are not worth having. . . . Never pretend that children, for instance, can be replaced by other things." Still, her unsavory childhood experiences with George may also have nourished her willingness to rebel against the male-dominated literary world.

To be the writer she wanted to be, she recalled in 1931, she had to conquer a "phantom" hovering over her:

> And the phantom was a woman, and when I came to know her better I called her after the heroine of a famous poem [by Coventry Patmore (1823–1896)]. The Angel in the House . . . It was she who bothered me and wasted my time and so tormented me that at last I killed her. You who come of a younger and happier generation may not have heard of her. . . . She was intensely sympathetic. She was immensely charming. She was utterly unselfish. She excelled in the difficult arts of family life. She sacrificed herself daily. If there was chicken, she took the leg; if there was a draught she sat in it—in short she was so constituted that she never had a

mind or a wish of her own, but preferred to sympathise always with the minds and wishes of others. Above all—I need not say it—she was pure. Her purity was supposed to be her chief beauty—her blushes, her great grace. . . . And when I came to write I encountered her with the very first words. The shadow of her wings fell on my page; I heard the rustling of her skirts in the room.

Having killed the Angel in the House, what was the woman writer to do? She need only be herself! "Ah, but what is 'herself'? I mean, what is a woman? I assure you, I do not know. . . . I do not believe that anybody can know until she has expressed herself in all the arts and professions open to human skill."

Despite the world's inhibitions Virginia Woolf found in herself the resource for her creations. Her birth, her father's "unexpurgated" library, her female loves, and the circle of leading male intellectuals all helped. But she missed the stimulus of her own generation that she might have had at the university, even as she observed the galaxy of Victorian men of letters whom her father attracted. Seeing Thomas Hardy, John Ruskin, John Morley, and Edmund Gosse over the teacups must have cured any awe of the literary establishment and encouraged her to make new literary connections of her own. On her father's death in 1904, with her sister and brothers she moved to 46 Gordon Square in the Bloomsbury district of London. There they attracted a galaxy of their own generation, including Lytton Strachey, Clive Bell, Roger Fry, John Maynard Keynes, and E. M. Forster.

On Thursday evenings, guests gathered at about ten o'clock and stayed till two or three making conversation over whiskey, buns, and cocoa. The Bloomsbury Group—an anti-university of artists, critics, and writers from the universities—were notorious rebels against Victorian inhibitions in art, literature, and sex. By 1941, in wartime London the prim *Times* accused them of producing "arts unintelligible outside a Bloomsbury drawing-room, and completely at variance with those stoic virtues which the whole nation is now called upon to practise." The Cambridge philosopher G. E. Moore (1873–1958) had taught them that "by far the most valuable things . . . are . . . the pleasures of human intercourse and the enjoyment of beautiful objects . . . the rational ultimate end of social progress."

Virginia Woolf became the presiding genius of the group. Among them everything was discussable and seems to have been discussed, including whom Virginia should marry. Dismissing other possibilities, she married Leonard Woolf, whom she described as "a penniless Jew." At Cambridge he, too, had been a follower of G. E. Moore and a member of the elite Apostles. Woolf had entered the colonial civil service and served in Ceylon for eight years before marrying Virginia in 1912. They had no children, but otherwise this proved an idyllic match, with their shared passion for literature and ideas. Leonard gave up writing novels, but was a prolific editor and author of works of politics, philosophy, and memoirs. Unfailingly attentive to Virginia, he seemed eager to nurture a literary talent superior to his own. Vita Sackville-West noted Virginia's dislike of "the possessiveness and love of domination in men. In fact she dislikes the quality of masculinity."

Leonard and Virginia moved out of the Bloomsbury salon and began new collaborations. She had not yet completed her first novel at the time of their marriage. In 1917 at their house in Richmond they founded the Hogarth Press, which consumed much of their energies in following years. Their first publication was *Two Stories*, one by Leonard, one by Virginia. They aimed to publish only experimental work, which included stories by Katherine Mansfield, T. S. Eliot's *Poems* (1919), poems by Robinson Jeffers and E. A. Robinson, translations of Russian novelists, and Virginia's own works. They did the typesetting and press work themselves with the occasional help of a friend. At the insistence of Harriet Weaver, the American patron of poets, and through the good offices of T. S. Eliot, the manuscript of Joyce's *Ulysses* was submitted to them for publication. They were tempted, but found it beyond their capacities. They would have had to employ professional printers, and the ones they consulted objected that printing such a work would surely lead to their prosecution. Virginia was especially troubled because she and Joyce were pioneering on the same paths of exploring the self. But, as her nephew and perceptive biographer explains, "it was as though the pen, her very own pen, had been seized from her hands so that someone might scrawl the word fuck on the seat of a privy." Joyce's "smoking-room coarseness" must have revived the hovering phantom of The Angel in the House.

While there were limits to Virginia's defiance of convention, her Bloomsbury Group enjoyed tweaking the establishment with pranks in the undergraduate tradition. Most notorious was their Dreadnaught Hoax on February 10, 1910, planned by Virginia's brother Adrian, to outwit the British Navy and its formidable security with a tour of the most secret vessel of the fleet. A forged telegram from the "Foreign Office" to the commander of the Home Fleet announced a visit of the "emperor of Abyssinia." The Bloomsbury company, wearing blackface and costumes of imaginary Abyssinian nobility, arrived at Weymouth, were grandly welcomed and given a steam-launch tour of the fleet. Virginia herself, as aide to the emperor, wore actors' black greasepaint, false mustache and whiskers, but found it hard not to burst out laughing when she ceremoniously shook hands with the admiral of the fleet, who happened to be her cousin. For the "Swahili" they were expected to speak, "Emperor" Adrian concocted phrases from pig Latin and half-remembered lines of Virgil. The London press had a field day, and the House of Commons discussed the matter on the floor. When the pranksters apologized to the first lord of the admiralty, he treated them as schoolboys and told them not to do it again. The press had been especially attracted to the bewhiskered young lady, "very good looking, with classical features," reputed to be in the party, and Virginia gave them her story. Naval regulations were tightened, especially on telegrams, making it hard to repeat the joke and Virginia recalled, "I am glad to think that I too have been of help to my country."

* * *

Despite her lively sense of humor Virginia's life was one long bout with "madness," a vague, emotion-laden label then attached to all sorts of mental illnesses, especially those of women. In Virginia's own circle, cases of madness were familiar. Thackeray's wife, the mother of Leslie Stephen's first wife, had been a victim. Her half-sister Stella had been pursued by a "mad" cousin. The wife of Virginia's close friend, the painter and critic Roger Fry, was said to be going mad, and had just been committed to an asylum when Virginia joined the tour of Byzantine art in Constantinople that Fry had organized in 1911. Some may have thought Fry himself should be committed for championing the works of Cézanne and others in the first Postimpressionist Exhibition in November 1910.

Virginia Woolf's first signs of mental illness, at the age of thirteen, came just after her mother died in May 1895. She had a "breakdown" that summer, when she heard "horrible voices" and became terrified of people. All her life she was haunted by fears of recurrence of her madness and of the painful treatment that she suffered. For example, in June 1910, soon after the Dreadnaught Hoax, she fell ill with the "acute nervous tension" that later afflicted her whenever she neared the end of writing a novel. For the "complete rest" that her doctor recommended, she was incarcerated in Miss Thomas's private nursing home at Burley Park, Twickenham, known as "a polite madhouse for female lunatics." There two months of penal "rest cure" kept her in bed in a darkened room, eating only "wholesome" foods, while Miss Thomas limited her letters, her reading, and her visitors. Of course she was kept from all London society. After a bad bout in 1913 Leonard feared she would throw herself from the train on their return from the country, and she did attempt suicide with a mortal dose of Veronal, from which she was barely saved by a stomach pump.

Friends wondered that with Virginia's constant threats of suicide, Leonard too did not go mad during her two years of "intermittent lunacy." In 1915 one morning at breakfast she suddenly became excited and incoherent, talking to her deceased mother, with spells of violence and screaming, ending in an attack on Leonard himself. She was taken to a nursing home, then to their new home at Hogarth House where they expected to install their printing press. Under the care of four psychiatric nurses, she gradually became lucid and rational, and by the end of 1915 was as much back to normal as she would ever be.

But she never fully recovered, and her "madness" would bring on her death. In late March 1941 Leonard had taken the despondent Virginia to Brighton to consult a doctor in whom she had confidence. Having recently finished *Between the Acts*, she wrote to her publisher saying she did not want the book to be published. On a bright cold morning she wrote two letters, one to Leonard, the other to her sister, Vanessa. She explained that she was once again hearing voices and was sure she would never recover. She would not go on spoiling Leonard's life for him. "I feel certain," she wrote Leonard, "I am going mad again. You have given me the greatest possible happiness. . . . I don't think two people could have been happier till this horrible disease came. I can't fight any longer." She took her walking stick and walked across the meadow to the River Ouse. Once before she had made an unsuccessful effort to drown herself, and this time she had taken the precaution of forcing a large stone into the pocket of her coat. As she walked into the water to her death, her regret, she had already explained to her friend Vita, was that this is "the one experience I shall never describe."

* * *

Virginia Woolf's whole experience had driven her inward. To write about the affairs of the world, the struggles for power and place, or the grand passions, she had little to go on. Her world, a friendly critic put it, was the little world of people like herself, "a small class, a dying class . . . with inherited privileges, private incomes, sheltered lives, protected sensibilities, sensitive tastes." Instead of pretending to know people whom she had never known, she accepted her limits, and explored the mystery within. She had the advantage over other pilots on the stream of consciousness of a clear critical style that helped her describe where she was going. And where her predecessors had failed to go.

She had no patience with those who only looked outward, chronicling mere externals. Her literary manifesto, "Mr. Bennett and Mrs. Brown," replied to Arnold Bennett's strictures on her for being "obsessed by details of originality and cleverness." He had insisted that "the foundation of good fiction is character-creating and

nothing else." The Edwardian novelists whom she now targeted—
Arnold Bennett, H. G. Wells, and John Galsworthy—"laid an enormous stress upon the fabric of things. They have given us a house in
the hope that we may be able to deduce the human beings who live
there." Such novelists had abandoned their mission.

> Look within and life, it seems, is very far from being
> "like this." Examine for a moment an ordinary mind on an
> ordinary day. The mind receives a myriad impressions—
> trivial, fantastic, evanescent, or engraved with the sharpness
> of steel. From all sides they come, an incessant shower of
> innumerable atoms . . . so that if a writer . . . could write what
> he chose, not what he must . . . there would be no plot, no
> comedy, no tragedy, no love interest or catastrophe in the
> accepted style, and perhaps not a single button sewn on as
> the Bond Street Tailors would have it. Life is not a series of
> gig lamps symmetrically arranged; but a luminous halo, a
> semi-transparent envelope surrounding us from the begin-
> ning of consciousness to the end. Is it not the task of the
> novelist to convey this varying, this unknown and uncircum-
> scribed spirit, whatever aberration or complexity it may dis-
> play, with as little mixture of the alien and external as
> possible?

James Joyce and T. S. Eliot were on a new track, but they had "no
code of manners." "Their sincerity is desperate, and their courage
tremendous; it is only that they do not know which to use, a fork or
their fingers. Thus if you read Mr. Joyce and Mr. Eliot you will be
struck by the indecency of the one, and the obscurity of the other."
After two early novels in conventional style, she began her own
experiments with *Jacob's Room* (1922), about a young man killed in
the World War. T. S. Eliot applauded, "you have freed yourself
from any compromise between the traditional novel and your original gift." Others objected that the book had no plot. In *Mrs. Dalloway* (1925), her first accomplished novel in the style she would bring
to life, nothing momentous "happened." Its opening pages, like

Molly Bloom's reflections at the end of *Ulysses*, would become a classic of "stream of consciousness." For a single day we share the consciousness of the fashionable wife of a member of Parliament as she is planning and hosting a party.

> Mrs. Dalloway said she would buy the flowers herself.
>
> For Lucy had her work cut out for her. The doors would be taken off their hinges; Rumpelmayer's men were coming. And then, thought Clarissa Dalloway, what a morning— fresh as if issued to children on a beach.
>
> What a lark! What a plunge! For so it had always seemed to her when, with a little squeak of the hinges, which she could hear now, she had burst open the French windows and plunged at Bourton into the open air. How fresh, how calm, stiller than this of course, the air was in the early morning; like the flap of a wave; the kiss of a wave. . . .

We follow her thoughts and feelings through all that June day's trivia, from her shopping for flowers to greeting the guests at the party, which ends the book.

Mrs. Dalloway's reminiscent experience recalls her encounters with a former suitor who for the last five years has been in India, flavored with gratification and regret at her chosen life. The specter of death interrupts her party with news of the suicide of a young man, a victim of wartime shell shock, who had seen "the insane truth" and hurled himself from a window. We are not led down a narrative path but only share staccato "moments of being." Constantly reminded of the mystery of time, even on a single day, we are reminded too of the elusiveness of "our self, who fish-like inhabits deep seas and plies among obscurities threading her way between the boles of giant weeds, over sun-flickered spaces and on and on into gloom, cold, deep inscrutable; suddenly she shoots to the surface and sports on the wind-wrinkled waves; that is, has a positive need to brush, scrape, kindle herself, gossiping."

To the Lighthouse (1927), reflections of quiet family holidays on an island in the Hebrides, is often considered her best work. We follow the interrelations of the consciousness of the central figure, the charming, managing Mrs. Ramsay, wife of an egocentric professor of philosophy, their eight children, and miscellaneous guests, who include a woman painter and a mawkish young academic. The first section, "The Window," fills more than half the book with "moments of being" on one summer day. The second, "Time Passes," admits the outer world by noting the death of Mrs. Ramsay and a son killed in the war, revealed in the sad abandonment of the once-cheerful holiday house.

> So with the lamps all put out, the moon sunk, and a thin rain drumming on the roof a downpouring of immense darkness began. Nothing, it seemed, could survive the flood, the profusion of darkness which, creeping in at keyholes and crevices, stole round window blinds, came into bedrooms, swallowed up here a jug and basin, there a bowl of red and yellow dahlias, there the sharp edges and firm bulk of a chest of drawers. Not only was furniture confounded; there was scarcely anything left of body or mind by which one could say, "This is he" or "This is she." Sometimes a hand was raised as if to clutch something or ward off something, or somebody groaned, or somebody laughed aloud as if sharing a joke with nothingness.

The last section, "The Lighthouse," reports the painter Lily Briscoe's final success in a painting, "making of the moment something permanent." "In the midst of chaos there was shape; this eternal passing and flowing (she looked at the clouds going and the leaves shaking) was struck into stability. Life stands still here." Fulfilling Mrs. Ramsay's promise, after petty squabbles and despite Mr. Ramsay's misgivings, the remnants of the family finally reach the Lighthouse.

Having admitted time to interrupt the inward life of the Ramsay family, Virginia Woolf then plays with time as the interrupter of consciousness in *Orlando* (1928). In October 1927 she was suddenly taken by the idea, which first interested her as a dinner-table joke, of tracing the literary ancestors of her lover Vita Sackville-West. The product was "a biography beginning in the year 1500 and continuing to the present day called Orlando: Vita; only with a change about from one sex to another. I think, for a treat, I shall let myself dash this in for a week." And she explained to Vita how the idea had captured her—"my body was flooded with rapture and my brain with ideas. . . . But listen; suppose Orlando turns out to be Vita." She could think of nothing else, and wrote rapidly.

Just as *To the Lighthouse* had been fashioned of her own youth, *Orlando*, from items already noted in Virginia's diary, turned out to be an adventure in consciousness through time. A beautiful aristocratic youth from the Elizabethan court lives on until October 11, 1928, through various incarnations. As King Charles's emissary to the Court of the Sultan in Constantinople, suddenly and unaccountably—

> The sound of the trumpets died away and Orlando stood stark naked. No human being, since the world began, has ever looked more ravishing. His form combined in one the strength of a man and a woman's grace. . . . Orlando had become a woman—there's no denying it. But in every other respect, Orlando remained precisely as he had been. The change of sex, though it altered their future, did nothing whatever to alter their identity. . . . Orlando herself showed no surprise at it. Many people . . . have been at great pains to prove (1) that Orlando had always been a woman. (2) that Orlando is at this moment a man. Let biologists and psychologists determine. It is enough for us to state the simple fact; Orlando was a man till the age of thirty; when he became a woman and has remained so ever since.
>
> But let other pens treat of sex and sexuality; we quit such odious subjects as soon as we can.

On finishing the book she had her usual spell of doubts, and thought that it too was not worth publishing.

To the Lighthouse had made her a writer whom the literati had to know, and now *Orlando*, a simple fantasy, could reach others. While the earlier book had sold less than four thousand copies in its first year, *Orlando* sold more than eight thousand in its first six months. Leonard called *Orlando* the turning point in her career, for Virginia Woolf could now support herself as a novelist.

Though tempted to write another *Orlando*, she did not take the easy path. She continued to experiment, sometimes cryptically, with streams of consciousness. *The Waves* (1931), which some call her masterpiece, is a contrived interweaving of selves—six not very extraordinary people from childhood through middle age, telling their own thoughts about themselves and others. Self-revelations are divided by passages of lyrical prose on how the rising and declining sun transforms the landscape and the waves. Again there is a haunting interruption at word of the death of a young friend in India.

She deferred to the *Orlando* audience again with *Flush* (1933), which purported to enter the animal consciousness in a biography of Elizabeth Barrett Browning's spaniel. Virginia Woolf was not a dog lover, but she liked to imagine herself as an animal—a goat, a monkey, a bird, and now a dog, and then wonder what this would have done to her self.

Her impatience with any one way of viewing the self prevented her writing a monumental book. Never so confident of the mainstream of consciousness as was Proust or Joyce, she sought the many possible streams.

> . . . a novelist's chief desire is to be as unconscious as possible . . . imagine me writing a novel in a state of trance . . . a girl sitting with a pen in her hand, which for minutes and indeed for hours, she never dips into the inkpot. The image that comes to mind when I think of this girl is the image of a fisherman lying sunk in dreams on the verge of a deep lake with a rod held out over the water. She was letting her imagination sweep unchecked round every rock and cranny of the world that lies submerged in the depths of our unconscious being. Now came the experience . . . that I believe to be far commoner with women writers than with men. The line

raced through the girl's fingers. Her imagination had rushed away. It had sought the pools, the depths, the dark places where the largest fish slumber. And then there was a smash. There was an explosion. There was foam and confusion. The imagination had dashed itself against something hard. The girl was roused from her dream. . . . Men, her reason told her, would be shocked. The consciousness of what men will say of a woman who speaks the truth about her passions had roused her from her artist's state of unconsciousness.

MYSTERIES OF A PUBLIC ART

W HILE writers went inward, creating and probing the self, there developed in the twentieth century a surprising new public art focused on the outward visible shape of the world in motion. It, too, had the power to re-create the world, to conjure with time and space. And soon it was to have the power to bring the world into everyone's living room. The film artist, newly freed from the bondage of nature, was in thrall to a vast audience. A painter or sculptor could create at will in the studio or out of doors, the writer in his study, the composer at his piano. Even the architect could do great work for a private patron or a Medici pope. And a stage for theater could be improvised anywhere. But this art of film was on a grand scale that dwarfed the imperial extravagance of opera and served patrons across the world.

Emerging and flourishing in America, land of conquest of space and time, film art was newly democratic and popular in the very age when literature was newly arcane. Within the first century, the art of film showed a novelty appropriate to the democratic New World, a reach and a versatility unlike any art before. No earlier art was so widely and so complexly collaborative, so dependent on the marriage of art and technology, or on the pleasure of the community.

Other arts—architecture since ancient Egypt and drama since classic Greece—have been communal, focusing the energies, hopes,

686

and beliefs of many. But the art of film would be vastly public, and have the public as its patron. Its future was full of mystery and of promise suggested in the early twentieth century, when it suddenly became the most popular American art. The "movies" (which entered our written language about 1912) recreated all the world's dimensions with bold abandon. Giving a new immortality to life in all times and places, its medium was the very antithesis of stone, the static material in which man from the beginning of history had tried to make his work immortal. Light, the unlikely medium of man's newly created immortality, was the most elusive, most transient, most ephemeral of all phenomena. Recently revealed as "the pencil of nature" with the power to create durable images, light—when properly managed, captured, and focused in a camera and then in the human eye—had the power to make moving images that could be mistaken for the real world. The movies, it was said, had the power of "making us walk more confidently on the precarious ground of imagination."

The novelties and mysteries of the new art were numerous—in its process of creation, in its audience, in its powers to re-create the world, and to probe, create, and reveal the self.

The "motion" picture phenomenon was a discovery of a versatile and ingenious English doctor, Peter Mark Roget (1779–1869), best remembered for his still-useful *Thesaurus* (1852). One day as he looked out through the Venetian blinds in his study, he noticed that the cart moving through the street seemed to be proceeding by jerks. He suspected that it was a series of stationary impressions joined together that gave the eye the impression of a cart in motion. In 1824 he offered the Royal Society his paper on "Persistence of Vision with Regard to Moving Objects." So casually he had noted what would make possible the motion pictures. Sir John Herschel had observed it too when spinning a coin on a table he found it "possible to see both sides of the coin at once." Inventors applied this phenomenon to toys. With pretentious names—Thaumatrope, Fantoscope, etc.—these gadgets viewed a series of still drawings of an object in motion placed on a disk and seen through a slit in another disk on the same axis. Thus the animated "moving picture" preceded photography.

With photography it became possible to make "moving pictures" of the natural world. But this first required images of objects in motion, which was not possible in the early days of photography. Then the most famous of these was made in 1877 by Eadweard Muybridge of a galloping horse to help Leland Stanford, governor of California, to win his bet that at some moment all four hooves of a galloping horse are off the earth. When the cumbersome glass plate was replaced by the celluloid film improved by George Eastman with perforations fitted on sprocket wheels, it was possible to make ten pictures a second from a single camera. In 1888 an Englishman, William Kennedy Laurie Dickson, working in Thomas Edison's laboratory, made a Kinetograph and shot the first film on celluloid— *Fred Ott's Sneeze*, of a worker in Edison's factory. The first feasible projector, the Vitascope, was the work of Thomas Armat, but when bought out by Edison it was advertised as "Thomas A. Edison's latest marvel." By 1912 Edison boasted, "I am spending more than my income getting up a set of 6,000 films to teach the 19 million school children in the schools of the United States to do away entirely with books."

In Europe, inventors were improving the apparatus for an audience dazzled by the mere spectacle of pictures in motion. The Lumière brothers impressed Parisians with their film of workers leaving a factory and a train arriving in a station. Among their spectators in 1895 was a professional magician, George Meliès (1861–1938), who saw the film's magical promise. In the next fifteen years he made more than four hundred films, which exploited the camera with stop motion, slow motion, fade-out, and double exposure to show people being cut in two, turning into animals, or disappearing. From trick shots he went on to simple narrative, filming *Cleopatra*, *Christ Walking on the Waters* (1899), *Red Riding Hood* (1901), and his renowned *A Trip to the Moon* (1902). But he kept the camera fixed like the eye of a spectator seated in the audience, and did not move it for long shots or close-ups. The unlucky Meliès was put out of business by pirates who sold copies of his works, and he ended his life selling newspapers in the Paris Métro.

* * *

By the opening of the twentieth century, the basic technology of the silent films had developed, but the art was yet to be created. Americans had their first glimpse of film art in the work of Edwin S. Porter (1870–1941), the uncelebrated pioneer of the movie narrative of suspense. After his discharge from the navy Porter worked as handyman and mechanic in Edison's skylight studio on East Twenty-first Street in New York City. And he had the inspired idea—which now seems quite obvious—of using the camera not just to take photographs of actors on a stage but to put together moving picture "shots" of actions at different times and places to make a connected story. In what is called the first American documentary, *The Life of an American Fireman* (1903), he showed the dramatic possibilities of replacing the theatrical "scene" of actors on a stage by the "shot" created by the motion picture camera. In this six-minute film he brought together twenty separate shots (including stock footage from the Edison archive and staged scenes of a dramatic rescue from a burning building) by dissolves or cuts, to make a suspenseful story.

Porter himself made film history with the twelve minutes of *The Great Train Robbery* later that year. Using fourteen separate shots (not scenes), quickly shifting from one to another, without titles or dissolves, he left the spectator to connect this story of desperadoes who rob a mail train, shoot a passenger, and finally die in a shoot-out with the posse sent to pursue them. Conjuring with time, Porter showed his shots not necessarily in chronological order, and pioneered in "parallel editing," which invited the viewer to understand the jumps back and forth in time. He demonstrated that the camera, unlike the theater, did not have to carry out each scene to its end. His success temporarily set the single reel (eight to ten minutes) as the standard length for American films. At the same time he liberated the movies from the studio by providing a model for the American Western, with action, pursuit, and outdoor glamour. The biggest box-office success in its day, it drew audiences for ten years.

While making *Rescued from an Eagle's Nest* (1907), a hair-raising thriller of a baby snatched from a cradle by an eagle and then rescued by a brave mountaineer, Porter enlisted David Wark Griffith (1875–1948) to play the hero. A young man of limited experience and meager education, Griffith had been born on a farm in rural Kentucky. His earliest memories were of "my father Colonel Jacob Wark Griffith of the Confederacy," returning from the war, a wounded and beaten man, and of his father's flamboyant gestures with his officer's saber. Griffith's whole life would be overcast by nostalgia for his idealized Old South. He happened into the theater as an actor in the Louisville theater, and pieced together a living as a book salesman for Britannica, picking hops in California, with occasional roles in a traveling stock company. In his first film role at Biograph he had wrestled convincingly with a stuffed eagle manipulated by wires, and so came into the art that he would transform in the next decade. Obsessed by a past that never was, he became the shaper of an art that would reshape the American imagination.

From acting, Griffith moved into directing and at the Biograph Company in the next five years he directed more than four hundred films, most on one reel. In these gestation years of motion picture technique Griffith would liberate the movies from the theater.

> I found that the picture-makers were following as best they could the theory of the stage. A story was to be told in pictures, and it was told in regular stage progression; it was bad stage technique to repeat; it would be bad stage technique to have an actor show only his face; there are infinite numbers of things we do in pictures that would be absurdities on the stage, and I decided that to do with the camera only what was done on the stage was equally absurd.

Griffith proceeded to show what could be done with the new dramatic art.

When he left Biograph in 1913, his advertisement in *The New York Dramatic Mirror* described how his "innovations" had been "revolutionizing Motion Picture Drama and founding the modern technique of the art"—by "the large or close-up figures, distant views . . . , the 'switchback,' sustained suspense, the 'fade-out,' and restraint in expression, raising motion picture acting to the higher plain which has won for it recognition as a genuine art." What he had done, in a word, was to lift the spectator out of his seat and put him among the actors, or at any other vantage point to serve the story. There was no longer a standard distance between the audience and the actor.

While Porter had gambled on the spectator's ability to piece the movie "shots" together into a connected narrative, Griffith created a whole syntax. The movie viewer would soon be at home in a new language, adept at putting together a disconnected succession of close-ups, medium shots, panoramas, fade-ins, fade-outs, switch-backs, switchforwards, masked shots, iris-in shots, and the moving perspectives of tracking shots. The art of film, Griffith observed, "although a growth of only a few years, is boundless in its scope, and endless in its possibilities. The whole world is its stage, and time without end its limitations."

But his employers at Biograph were shocked when they saw his version of Tennyson's *Enoch Arden* (*After Many Years*, 1908), with its parallel shots of Annie Lee at the seaside and of Enoch shipwrecked on a desert island, each thinking of the other. "How can you tell a story jumping about like that? The people won't know what it's about." "Well," Griffith replied, "doesn't Dickens write that way?" "Yes, but that's Dickens; that's novel writing; that's different." "Oh, not so much," Griffith retorted, "these are picture stories; not so different." That very night he went home, reread one of Dickens's novels, and came back next day to tell his employers they could either use his idea or dismiss him. Griffith had been led by the Vanguard Word to lift the spectator from his seat in the theater and put the camera into the consciousness of characters—and viewers.

The power of the new art was proved in *The Birth of a Nation*, in which film historians see Griffith's creation of the grammar and syntax of the modern film. Its three hours on the screen pioneered the long feature film. And it was a box-office bonanza. Budgeted at $40,000 (four times the usual cost for a feature at the time), it finally came to $110,000, which included Griffith's savings and investment by his friends. Within five years after its release in 1915 it would earn $15 million, thirty years later had grossed some $48 million, and it went on earning. Its popular success, despite a banal and vicious message, was an ominous sign of the hypnotic power of the technology of the new art to overwhelm its content. Taken from a play by a bigoted North Carolina minister, the movie told a nostalgic tale idealizing the Old South and the institution of slavery, extolling the heroism of the Ku Klux Klan in saving white Southerners from bestial Negroes and their white political accomplices, and exhorting against racial "pollution."

Griffith had prophesied that "in less than ten years . . . the children in the public schools will be taught practically everything by moving pictures. Certainly they will never be obliged to read history again." *The Birth of a Nation* proved that there was substance in his grim prophecy. In the 1920s the film helped spark a revival of the Ku Klux Klan, which reached a membership of five million by the 1940s, and it continued to be used for recruiting and indoctrination into the 1960s. Thorstein Veblen hailed the movie as a triumph of "concise misinformation." Organized protests by enlightened citizens who labeled it "a deliberate attempt to humiliate ten million American citizens and portray them as nothing but beasts" and the refusal of eight states to license the film for exhibition did not prevent its spectacular box-office success.

Griffith himself tried to make the censorship of his film a patriotic issue, and cast himself as a martyr for "free speech" rather than for bad history. He launched into another blockbuster film, *Intolerance* (1916), which outdid its predecessor in scale and use of his new film syntax to tell the story (in four scenes) of intolerance through the ages: Babylon falling from the "intolerance" of a priest, Christ forced to the Cross by intolerant Pharisees, the massacre of Huguenots by intolerant Catholics on Saint Bartholomew's Day, and modern intolerance forcing poor women into prostitution and sending innocent men to the gallows. A single scene, of Belshazzar's feast, cost $250,000, more than twice the whole budget of *The Birth of a Nation*. But the audience, put off by the abstract thread and shrieking polemics, did not share Griffith's enthusiasm. The film was withdrawn from circulation after only twenty-two weeks and reedited into two separate films. At his death in 1948 Griffith was only a decayed celebrity, still paying off his debts on *Intolerance*.

Meanwhile, Griffith's work had gathered influence abroad. On Lenin's instructions it was widely shown in the Soviet Union. While Sergei Eisenstein (1898–1948) called himself a disciple of Griffith, his life and career could hardly have been more different. Born in Riga, Latvia, into a prosperous Christianized family of Jewish descent, Eisenstein had been a student of engineering in Petrograd when the Revolution approached in February 1917. He enlisted in the Red Army and in 1920 joined the Proletkult Theater producing plays in the new proletarian spirit. Eisenstein read widely, and had a talent for abstraction, which he cultivated in arcane Marxist disputes between Stanislavsky's acting "method," Meyerhold's theory of "biomechanics," and the vagaries of the futurist Mayakovsky, the "tireless one-man communist manifesto." Eisenstein, saying it was like trying to perfect "a wooden plough" to imagine a theater independent of the Marxist "revolutionary framework," elaborated his own mechanistic theory of film. The film, too, was admirably suited for his Marxist "collective hero," since it was possible to accumulate many more people on the screen than on the stage, and he embraced the opportunity to produce mass epics.

Eisenstein found his inspiration in Griffith and made a conscious technique of what Griffith, with his intuitive practical sense for visual drama, had been practicing. For Eisenstein *Intolerance* seemed "a brilliant model of his method of montage." This was a name for the distinctive feature of the new art, which the intellectual Eisenstein explained and demonstrated in his writing and his films. "Montage" (which did not come into the English language until 1929) from the French word for "assembly" meant bringing together film images not in chronological order but for their psychological and emotional stimulus. And it described the new role of the film editor. Eisenstein, with materialist bias, emphasized its origin in "engineering and electrical apparatus." And he saw Griffith as the pioneer. "This was the montage whose foundation had been laid by American film-culture, but whose full, completed, conscious use and world recognition was established by our [Soviet] films."

In montage Eisenstein saw both the creation of the film art and a newly creative role for the spectator. He found a similarity to the

Japanese ideogram that combined the character for "dog" with that for "mouth" to mean not "dog's mouth" but "bark." Similarly he noted that child + mouth = scream, bird + mouth = sing, water + eye = weep, etc. Thus, by juxtaposing concrete images in montage the moviemaker could lead the viewer to create his own abstractions. Eisenstein found montage similar to "the method of parallel action," which Griffith had seen in Dickens. He too was amazed at "Dickens's nearness to the characteristics of cinema in method, style, and especially in viewpoint and exposition."

In his masterpiece *Battleship Potemkin* (1925), commissioned by the Communist Party to celebrate the twentieth anniversary of the 1905 Revolution, Eisenstein gave classic form to his theory of montage. Minutely dissected and extravagantly praised, as late as 1958 it was acclaimed by an international poll of film critics as the best film ever made. A story of mutiny in the czarist navy against tyranny and filth, it produced the famous "Odessa steps sequence," showing the massacre by imperial troops of innocent Russian civilians who had come to pay their respects to an assassinated leader of the mutiny. This became the classic textbook sequence of montage—a baby carriage rolling slowly down the steps over massacred bodies, past a pair of crushed eyeglasses, and blood-soaked arms and legs. Going far beyond Griffith in multiplying shots for montage, this film, which ran to only 86 minutes, contained 1,346 shots, while *The Birth of a Nation*, which ran 195 minutes, had only 1,375 shots. While it was predictably attacked by the Party as another example of bourgeois "formalism," the film's appeal was not confined to Russia. Its emotional antiestablishment message led it to be banned in some European countries and it had to be shown underground. "After seeing *Potemkin*" the famous theater director Max Reinhardt confessed that "the stage will have to give way to the cinema."

* * *

The new public art of film, in curious ways, would reunite the community that millennia before had seen ritual transformed into drama on the slopes of the Athenian Acropolis. As the film art grew, it multiplied puzzling elements in the mystery of creation. It became more and more uncertain who was creating what, from what, and for whom. In Shakespeare's London, drama required a theater, of which only six would be flourishing. The live drama needed a stage, but the new art was conveyed in a machine that could project its message anywhere. The extent of this mystery was dazzling. By 1948 *The Birth of a Nation* had been seen by 150 million people all over the world.

Cinema art became collaborative on a scale and in a manner never before imagined. Griffith observed that in *The Birth of a Nation* "from first to last we used from 30,000 to 35,000 people." Producing a film resembled commanding and supplying an army more than any earlier kind of art. The set for *Intolerance* included a full-scale model of ancient Babylon rising three hundred feet aboveground on a scene that stretched across ten acres. With sixty principal players and eighteen thousand extras, it sometimes had a payroll of twenty thousand dollars a day. The commanders, besides Griffith, included eight assistant directors. The rough cut of the film ran for eight hours. There was a creating role, too, for the cinematographer and all who helped provide lighting, color, sound, and music. Reaching popular audiences never imagined for the opera, films provided vast audiences for composers and countless spectators for the dance, creating new forms of musical drama. When sound came to film in the late 1920s the movies could vie with opera as a union of the arts, ironically satisfying Wagner's hope for a *Gesamtkunstwerk*.

To all its other charms, the movies, by the 1950s, added the intriguing question of who really was the "maker" of the hypnotic products of the new art. The brilliant French moviemaker and critic François Truffaut (1932–1984) insisted that the director was a new kind of "author" *(auteur)* in this modern audiovisual language. So, he said, the director (or *auteur*) really was the person who created the film, and so should be given the major credit. This plausible suggestion itself sparked a lively controversy over the "auteur" theory, which debated who if anyone should be considered the prime creator of the complex collaborative product.

Over the actors, too, there came a new ambiguity and a new aura. Griffith had boasted "raising motion-picture acting to the

higher plane which has won for it recognition as a genuine art."
Now that all spectators could see the actor's face close up, it removed
the temptations to mug, and encouraged a subtler, "more restrained" style of acting. But there was a colossal irony in what the
new art did to these "more restrained" actors in the new art. Biograph had at first banned the names of actors from credits in their
films, and insisted on their anonymity. But film gave a vivid unique
personality to every actor as a person who could not be denied and
became a magnet for its audience. By 1919 "movie star" had entered
our written language for this new human phenomenon of awesome
dimensions. The celebrity of movie actors overshadowed even that
of eminent statesmen, baseball heroes, and notorious criminals. Gargantuan film creations became only vehicles for a Douglas Fairbanks, Greta Garbo, Humphrey Bogart, or Marilyn Monroe, whose
off-screen lives became news.

While movies gave actors a newly vivid role, they obscured the
"author," who often disappeared from the scene. Even while movie
rights to books sold for astronomical sums, films "based on" them
often had scant resemblance to the original. Some of the best authors, despairing at the scenes, the characters, and the ideas mangled
out of their works, refused to participate in their "story conferences," and became refugees from Hollywood.

An increasingly technological and industrial art, the movies gave
technicians, lighting experts, and cinematographers crucial roles in
making every film, just as the collaboration and enthusiasm of bankers, movie moguls, and executives were essential. By the 1920s there
developed in Hollywood a "studio system," with companies like
Warner Bros., M-G-M, and Universal organized to focus vast investment and countless collaborators. How did the popular products
emerge from this technological-industrial-artistic maelstrom? Some
suggested that there was a Genius of the System, which, like the
Muses of ancient Greece, somehow converged and balanced all the
elusive elements. But by the 1950s the colossi of the studio system
were themselves in decline, and "independent" producers were producing some of the most successful films. While this diffused the
powers of movie creation, it did not dissolve the mystery.

The heart of the mysteries of this new art was the audience. While Dickens could await public response to one number of his novel before shaping the next, the moviemakers could not so easily test their costly product as it was being created. From the beginning there was a hint of mystery in the movie audience. Since stage drama required light, the early Elizabethan theaters were in the open air, and performances were limited by the climate and the season. The movie house required darkness, where spectators could hardly see one another. Still, the public had become the patron and had to be pleased.

And who was the public? Moviemakers had the box-office test of whether they were pleasing their audience. But every step in the rise and diffusion of film drama deepened the mystery of the audience, who became less and less dependent on a theater. Now anyplace could be a theater. In every living room, television viewers could choose the film to be played and replayed at their pleasure. The creators of the newest art were in bondage to a spectral master.

ESSAYS

I

SEARCH FOR COMMUNITY

"A WRESTLER WITH THE ANGEL"

from HIDDEN HISTORY, *1987*

THE HISTORIAN is both discoverer and creator. To the uniqueness of his role we have a clue in the very word "history," which means both the course of the past and the legible account of the past. The historian is always trying to reduce, or remove, that ambiguity. If he is successful, he leads his readers to take—or mistake—his account for what was really there.

The historian sets himself a dangerous, even an impossible, task. In the phrase of the great Dutch historian J. H. Huizinga, he is "A Wrestler with the Angel." It is the angel of death who makes his work necessary yet destined never to be definitive. If man were not mortal, we would not be deprived of the living testimony of the actors, and so required to give new form to the receding infinity. From my own experience I will describe the historian's quest. I will suggest both the universal obstacles to recovery of the past, and some special resources, opportunities, and temptations for the historian in our own time. And finally, I will recall some qualities of historians whose works of discovery and creation I have found most satisfying and most durable.

THE LIMITS OF DISCOVERY: THE BIAS OF SURVIVAL

The historian can rediscover the past only by the relics it has left for the present. Historians of all ages have worked under these limitations. Their mission requires that they make the most of whatever they can find. They try to convince us that the relics they have examined and interpreted in their narrative are a reliable sample of the experience that men really had. But how reliable are the remains of the past as clues to what was really there?

My own experience as a historian has brought me vivid reminders of how partial is the remaining evidence of the whole human past, how casual and how accidental is the survival of its relics. One of my first shocks came, while exploring the American Experience in colonial times, in my effort to recapture the meaning of religion to the settlers of early New England. Their basic vehicle of religious instruction was the *New England Primer*. This, the chief text of compulsory education in early Massachusetts, carried a full rhymed alphabet—from "Adam" ("In Adams Fall we sinned all") to "Zaccheus" ("Zaccheus, he, did climb the tree, his Lord to see")—along with moral aphorisms, fragments of the Old Testament, and the text of prayers, including the familiar "Now I lay me down to sleep. . . ." This influential work, which first appeared about 1690, became the best-selling New England schoolbook, and had sold some 3 million copies within the next century. Benjamin Franklin, who knew a commercial opportunity when he saw one, made a tidy profit publishing his own secularized version.

For the flavor of New England religion, I went in search of original copies of the *Primer*, but they were hard to find. By contrast, I found it easy to consult the heavy tomes of Puritan theology, the lengthy sermons and treatises, like those of Thomas Shepard, finally collected into three volumes in 1853. These volumes, kept in the rare-book rooms of university libraries, were often in mint condition, sometimes even with uncut pages. Modern scholars pore over such works in plush bibliophilic comfort to discover what the early Puritans were "really thinking" about religion.

This experience set me thinking about the limits of historical discovery. I had a similar experience when I came to the early nineteenth century, trying to learn about American heroes of the age and what people thought of them. I turned at once to the popular "Crockett Almanacs." These were pamphlets of wide appeal published in the name of Davy Crockett (1786–1836), the man of little education and little respect for book learning, who said the rules of spelling were "contrary to nature." Crockett died a martyr's death at the Alamo in the fight for Texas independence in 1836. Besides recipes, and useful everyday hints for health and crops, they recounted Crockett's astonishing feats wrestling men and alligators, along with legends of other frontier prodigies like Mike Fink, Daniel Boone, and Kit Carson. The earliest of these almanacs in 1835 offered an "autobiography," which Crockett supposedly wrote soon before his death.

Between 1835 and 1856 some fifty such almanacs poured out of Nashville, New York, Boston, Philadelphia, and elsewhere by the ten thousands, in the name of Davy Crockett or his "heirs." Embellished by crude woodcuts on cheap paper, these almanacs were carried in saddlebags, slipped into hip pockets, handed about Western inns and bars, and around campfires as Americans moved west. The appetite for them seemed inexhaustible. But in late twentieth century they have become rare and costly collectors' items.

A dramatic contrast for the historian of American hero worship was the monumental official life of George Washington, authorized by his nephew Bushrod Washington and written by Chief Justice John Marshall. The work came to five volumes, sold by subscription at the then considerable price of $3.00 a volume. Even the flamboyant Parson Weems, who put his best efforts into it, could not make it sell. And when the first volume of the much-touted project reached subscribers in 1804 it quickly established itself as the publishing catastrophe of the age. John Adams charitably characterized this as not a book at all but rather "a Mausoleum, 100 feet square at the base and 200 feet high." History justified Adams' description because the volumes survived, as unread as they were unreadable. And even now complete sets in mint condition are not hard to come by, sometimes in secondhand furniture stores. Today, of course, it is much more convenient, and more tempting for the scholar, to mine the elegant bound volumes of Marshall, than to handle the ragged half-legible fragments of Davy Crockett. These two episodes of my own research led me to a rather troubling hypothesis.

The Law of the Survival of the Unread. If there is a natural and perhaps inevitable tendency toward the destruction and disappearance of the documents most widely used, this poses a discomfiting problem for the historian. For he inevitably relies heavily on the surviving printed matter. Is the historian, then, the victim of a diabolical solipsism? Is there an inverse relation between the probability of a document surviving and its value as evidence of the daily life of the age from which it survives?

To this troublesome "law" of historical evidence there are, as we shall see, countless exceptions. But the exceptions themselves are also reminders of the casual and accidental causes of preservation, survival, and accessibility. These only confirm our doubts that there is any necessary positive correlation between probabilities of survival and importance as clues of past thought and ways of life. Survival is chancy, whimsical, and unpredictable. Yet it is not impossible to list some of the Biases of Survival. These themselves do not tell us anything substantial about the human past. But they do provide us some helpful cautions. They may save us from jumping to wrong conclusions. They remind us of how the very accidents of survival may skew our vision of the past, exaggerating certain kinds of human activity, concealing or dissolving others. The limits of historical discovery come from the physical qualities of objects as much as from the human activities which they suggest. They apply not only to documents and printed matter but to all kinds of relics.

Survival of the Durable, and That Which Is Not Removed or Displaced. While this has the sound of tautology, its consequences are not always noticed—the tendency toward emphasis on the monumental, on experience recorded in writing or in books. Since religions are a deliberate effort to transcend the transience of the individual human life, monuments of religion are often more durable than other monuments. Tombs, burial objects, mummies, temples, churches, and pyramids tend to skew our view of the past. They give a prominence to religion in the relics of the past which it may not actually have had in the lives people lived. A contrast with monumental houses of religion are the simple dwellings of the people who did (or did not) worship there. Chartres Cathedral survives in its solid thirteenth-century glory, but the mud and wattle and wood houses of the citizens of Chartres surrounding it have been many times replaced.

In the United States this bias obscures some of the peculiar achievements of a mobile and technologically progressive civilization. One of the most characteristic architectural innovations in the United States is the balloon-frame house. This American invention, which appeared in Chicago about 1833, was notable not for the durability of its product, but for its ease and speed of construction and removal. Houses built by nailing together light timbers (instead of by the mortise-and-tenon of heavy beams) were put up quickly by people without the carpenter's skill. Such houses were taken down, and their frames transported by wagon or riverboat to the next stopping place in the transient, booming West. In Omaha in 1856 General William Larimer lived in a balloon house that had been framed in Pittsburgh and shipped out by steamboat. Then, when Omaha grew beyond his taste, he took down his house and moved it to another site. While the country mansions of the Dutch patroons of New York and plantation mansions of Virginia and Maryland survive, where are the balloon frames? This momentous American invention, whose twentieth-century products surround us today, has hardly entered the historical record.

Incidentally, we have lost two of the most vivid dimensions of past experience—color and odor. For us "classical architecture" means the chaste elegance of weathered marble. But in fact when the Parthenon was completed in Athens' great age, it was a garish polychrome, more resembling the extravagance of a twentieth-century World's Fair than our cliché of Greek elegance. And as we admire the venerable yellow patina of Amiens, Canterbury, or Chartres Cathedrals, we again forget the original vision. As Le Corbusier reminds us, "The cathedrals were white because they were new. The freshly cut stone of France was dazzling in its whiteness as the Pyramids of Egypt had gleamed with polished granite."

In the ages before running water and modern plumbing, the characteristic odors of bodies and places intruded in daily experience. The perfumes, today a dispensable luxury, were then a common necessity for pleasant conversation. It is not only automobiles that corrupt the atmosphere by their excrement. We easily forget that smog is the price of the freedom of our streets from manure, and from the flies and diseases it brought. The American industry in deodorants thrives, but where are the odors of the past?

Survival of the Collected and the Protected: What Goes in Government Files. We emphasize political history and government in the life of the past partly because governments keep records, while families and other informal groups seldom do. Yet informal groups—for example the anonymous wagon trains into which Americans organized themselves to go west or cross the continent—were among the most remarkable and most characteristic of American communities. Much of the peculiarly American experience, which has had this voluntary, spontaneous character, has eluded historians. The foundings of colleges and universities in England and Europe are recorded in the government chartering of corporations, in the orders of central ministries of education or ancient religious foundations. But in the United States the efforts of local boosters to form colleges to attract settlers, the volunteer enthusiasms of ministers and their congregations, and the haphazard philanthropy of wealthy citizens leave few official records. A democratic society like ours, a community of voluntary mobile communities, leaves a random record of its past.

Survival of Objects Which Are Not Used or Which Have a High Intrinsic Value. It is not only in printed matter that rarity and scarcity induce survival. Illuminated manuscripts, the treasures of palaces and monasteries, survive, while pamphlets, leaflets, and broadsides which made revolutions and reformations disappear. Sometimes they were incriminating, almost always they were crudely printed on paper of poor quality, easily disintegrated by the weather to which they were exposed. Nowhere is this bias more evident than in the numismatic relics of the distant past. The hoards (from the Old English word, "to cover or conceal") of coins which survived the raids of bandits and conquerors were, naturally enough, collections of the most valuable coins and other precious objects. No one troubled to bury the everyday coins of small denomination and base metals, which therefore are unlikely to survive for our examination today. European palaces, churches, and now their museums, display the jeweled and filigreed clocks and watches of early modern times. But the special timekeeping triumph of nineteenth-century America was the inexpensive household clock and then the "dollar watch," the wonder of European visitors. These dollar watches were not made for ease of repair and seemed not worth repairing. They seldom find their way into museums. Similarly, the elegantly engraved muskets with which European princes and their hunting companions enjoyed their leisure can be admired in many European museums of the arts. But the plain Kentucky Rifle, which was the early westward-moving pioneer's weapon of defense and staff of life, was not preserved as an object of beauty.

Survival of the Academically Classifiable and the Dignified. Teachers teach the subjects in which they have been instructed. The trivium (grammar, logic, and rhetoric) and quadrivium (arithmetic, geometry, astronomy, and music), which composed the Seven Liberal Arts of the medieval universities, were an exhaustive catalogue of what students were expected to learn, and what these students, when they became professors, were expected to teach. Geography for example had no place in the medieval scheme. We must piece together their notions of the earth, its shapes and its dimensions, from works of theology, along with the ephemeral maps, portolans, and planispheres used by navigators, traders, pirates, and empire builders. In the early ages of exploration, when geographic knowledge was one of the most valuable kinds of merchandise, the cartographic secrets of shorter, safer passages to the remote treasure troves of pepper, spice, and precious gems were classified information. Now they are hidden from us, as they once were from imperial and commercial competitors. In the field of literature, this academic conservatism has perpetuated the study of familiar classics but left much of what many people read stigmatized as "subliterature," beneath the interest of serious students.

Survival of Printed and Other Materials Surrounding Controversies.
What has passed for the study of the history of religion in America
should more accurately be described as the history of religious controversies. The silent or spoken prayers of the devout leave few records behind. But the disputations of theologians, the acrimony of the
religious academies, and the resolutions of church councils pour out
print. Then it is these disputes that command the interest and the
ingenuity of religious historians, while the passions of the heart and
the yearnings of the God-struck spirit, however constant and universal, remain private and invisible. Similarly, if we go in quest of the
daily eating and drinking habits of early Americans, it is not easy to
find records. At the same time the organized polemics of vegetarians
and food faddists leave a readable detritus. We know little about
what and how much earlier Americans drank. Yet the history of the
temperance movement and the prohibition of alcoholic beverages
has left an abundant literature to arrest the attention of historians.
The currents of daily life which flow smoothly, as Tolstoy noted,
leave a meager record. It is the eddies, whirlpools, and cross-currents
that attract notice. The daily sexual habits of those who conform to
the prevalent mores are seldom recorded for future historians and
have rarely been chronicled. The history of sexual conduct has
tended to become a record of deviants, of contraception and abortion, of polygamy and homosexuality. In the United States we have
had few adequate histories of family life and marriage, but abundant
monographs on the history of divorce and the movements for
women's rights. The history of law enforcement and obedience to
law eludes us while our shelves are filled with detective stories and
the chronicles of crime.

*Survival of the Self-Serving: the Psychopathology of Diarists and Let-
ter Writers.* Historians in professional training are urged to seek records by participants in events, preferably those made at the time or
soon after. So there is a natural tendency to rely on diaries and letters.
The thoughts, feelings, and affairs of the family and neighbors of Sir
John Fastolf (c. 1378–1459) live on in a thousand so-called Paston
Letters which happened to survive and so seem to record the fifteenth

century for us. The quirks and quiddities of the obsessive diarist Samuel Pepys (1633–1703) loom in the foreground of the social history of England in the seventeenth century. In America we inevitably lean heavily on the diaries and letters of William Byrd (1674–1744), a witty but atypical planter-politician, and on the memoirs of the articulate plantation tutor Philip Vickers Fithian. And we make much of the copious nineteenth-century diary written in the barely legible minuscule hand of the observant New Yorker George Templeton Strong, or the gargantuan "confessions" of the eccentric Arthur Inman. Of course intimate feelings interest the historian. But does not our hunger for the recorded word exaggerate the unusual point of view of those who happened to be diarists and letter writers? Are we victims, willingly or not, of a Casanova syndrome, which puts us at the mercy of the most articulate self-servers and boasters of the past? To correct our vision we still need an ample study of the psychopathology of diarists and perhaps of letter writers too. We are also at the mercy, and eagerly put ourselves at the mercy, of egotists. Perhaps autobiographies are a record only of those who thought too well of themselves, from Benvenuto Cellini, Casanova, and Benjamin Franklin to the self-serving political memoirists of our age.

How will the rise of the telephone and the decline of letter writing and the postal service "correct" or newly distort our recorded past? When President Thomas Jefferson wanted to instruct his Secretary of State, James Madison, he would commonly write him a note, which remains for us. But when President Lyndon Johnson wanted to instruct Secretary of State Dean Rusk, he would more often have used the telephone. Consequently when historians find a memorandum from President Johnson to Secretary Rusk, they will wonder whether the record was made, not to guide action but to convey a desired impression to future historians. President Nixon's notorious effort to use the new electronic technology to provide a taped chronicle of his work in the Oval Office reveals the new biases, opportunities, and risks—and reminds us of how much we lack of the earlier historical record. Meanwhile the flood of press releases and pseudo-events, expressly created to be reported, further dilutes and confuses the record.

Survival of the Victorious Point of View: The Success Bias. The history of inventions which we read today seems to have become the story of successful inventors. Eli Whitney, Isaac Merritt Singer, Henry Ford, Thomas A. Edison, and other lucky ones leave a vivid record. But the countless anonymous experimenters, the frustrated tinkerers who nearly made it, disappear. How many of their efforts ought to be part of the story? Occasionally, as in the lengthy litigations over who was the "first inventor" of the sewing machine, of the mechanical reaper, of barbed wire, of the telephone, of the automobile, and of the phonograph, we glimpse at least a few of the competitors for the money, the spotlight, and the glory. An unsung, but surely not unpaid, service of the legal profession has been to provide documentary evidence of the struggles of the also-rans and the near-successful.

American history as a whole presents a spectacle of this bias. A dominant theme in the writing of American history has been the filling of the continent, the consolidating of a great nation. But the desire to secede, to move *away* from the larger political community might have become the leitmotif. Just as the Puritans came to America as seceders from Britain, so the westward movers in the nineteenth century were seceders from the heavily settled, increasingly urban Atlantic coastal nation. If the South had won the Civil War, if the Bear Flag Republic of 1846 had survived, if the Republic of Texas had remained independent, the earlier American settlers too would have continued to shine not as nation builders but as courageous seceders. During the Vietnam War an unwilling American draftee, impressed by this aspect of American history, responded to his draft notice by informing the President that, in a great American tradition, instead of going into the United States Army, he would secede and become a nation all by himself.

A delightful irony in the earliest historical record arises from the difference between the survival powers of organic and of inorganic materials. For while organic material (what we now call biodegradable) is quick to disintegrate, inorganic materials survive, and so our evidences of prehistory come mainly from flint and stone implements. The bodies of people who used them were not apt to survive if they were not embalmed or, like the rare surviving hunter of the Stone Age, chemically preserved by nature in the bogs of Denmark. "It is a paradox," Grahame Clark reminds us, "that the best chance of organic material surviving in the ordinary way is that it should be destroyed by fire, but such remains, in being converted into carbon, acquire enormously enhanced powers of resistance." In the search for details of Early Iron Age culture in Jutland, it was found that houses abandoned to the processes of natural decay disappeared. Yet those destroyed by fire remained clearly defined by their charred stumps, by traces of carbonized roofing material found lying on the floor, and traces of wattle impressed on burnt daub. Charred wooden utensils also left archaeologically useful fragments. The bizarre moral is that while the houses of the victors vanished without a trace, gradually conquered by insects and weather and time, an Early Iron Age village had a better chance of earning a place in "history" if it was invaded and burned to the ground.

Survival of the Epiphenomenal. Often people write books and read them because they cannot personally experience what is described. We often remain uncertain whether writers were recording their experience or escaping it. In my own efforts to describe American manners and household customs I have been tantalized by this ambiguity. Emily Post's *Etiquette*, first published in 1922, and frequently revised thereafter, was so popular that her name became a synonym for proper behavior. Her books, like the New England Primers, were used up, so that now a complete set is not readily available. Emily Post described proper behavior: the kind of silver to be set, the tablecover and glassware to be used, the role of servants. The style of private entertaining she prescribed during the Great Depression in the lean 1930s still resembled what Scott Fitzgerald depicted in the luxuriant age of the Great Gatsby (1925). And her books remained the popularly accepted guides. Was this because people expected to follow her economically obsolete impractical advice or because they enjoyed fantasizing about how they never could, or could no longer, afford to entertain? The answers to these inward, private questions may be beyond the historian's ken.

Knowledge Survives and Accumulates, but Ignorance Disappears. A medieval folktale reports that a young alchemist was once told that, if he recited a certain formula, he could transform lead into silver and copper into gold. The only condition was that while reciting his formula, he must never be thinking of a white elephant. He learned the formula and tried reciting it. Unfortunately he could never make it work—for all the while he was earnestly trying not to think of a white elephant. The problem of latter-day historians is much like that of the young alchemist. For our minds are furnished with all the accumulated knowledge and experience of the ages since the period of the past we are trying to recapture. The modern globe of the earth is so firmly fixed in our vision that we find it hard to imagine the three-continent planet with a surface only one-seventh water, on which Columbus thought he was sailing. As we try to relive the experience of Americans hastening across the continent in the early nineteenth century, we see them traversing the fertile Great Plains, destined to be the granary of a great nation. But they thought they were crossing what on their maps was the Great American Desert. Some even sought camels to help their passage. How can we recapture their ignorance? Yet if we do not, we cannot really share their fears and their courage.

* * *

If this incomplete list of the biases of survival seems random and disorderly, it is because any neat and orderly catalog would be misleading. Every reader can add his own items to the list. The preservative and disintegrating processes of time are vagrant. The randomness of our list suggests both the unpredictable effects of the toll of time and the bizarre miscellany which is our inheritance from our past.

It is the sheerest folly to believe that we, Wrestlers with the Angel, can ever know the extent or the boundaries of our ignorance. Or that we can conquer the biases of survival by some new technology. We transfer inflammable, self-destructive nitrate motion picture films of the years before 1950 to acetate film and so avoid the immediate catastrophes of combustion. But how long will the acetate film survive? We have less than a century of use to guide us. We avoid the fragility of early phonograph discs by transferring them to sturdy plastic; we avoid the needle's wear by compact discs touched only by the laser's beam. But how long will these survive?

We should be chastened in our hope to master the whole real past by the ironic comprehensiveness of the oldest surviving records of civilization. We know more about some aspects of daily life in the ancient Babylon of 3000 B.C. than we do about daily life in parts of Europe or America a hundred years ago. By a happy accident, ancient Babylonians wrote not on paper or on wood, but on the clay which they found underfoot. "A little brick of clay," Edward Chiera reminds us, "if in pure condition and well kneaded may lie buried in the moist ground for thousands of years and not only retain its shape but harden again, when dried, to the same consistency as before. If it is covered with writing, as is generally the case with Babylonian tablets, one can take the small unbaked tablet and brush it vigorously with a good stiff brush without the slightest fear of damaging its surface. . . . If the salt encrustations should be too many and render decipherment impossible, then all one has to do is bake the tablet thoroughly. After baking, it can be immersed in water, subjected to acids, or even boiled, and it will be as fine and clean as on the day it was first made and written upon." Our grand dividend—the copious relics of this set of coincidences—is thousands of clay tablets recording everything from codes of laws and religious texts to teachers' copybooks, the notes of schoolchildren, the records of war booty, recipes, scientific works, diaries, and receipts for the sale of slaves and cattle. The messages we receive from that remote past were neither intended for us, nor chosen by us, but are the casual relics of climate, geography, and human activity. They, too, remind us of the whimsical dimensions of our knowledge and the mysterious limits of our powers of discovery.

* * *

The last two centuries in the West have seen a vast increase of the historian's resources and a multiplication of his physical and conceptual instruments of discovery. The modern social sciences have tried to overcome the limitations of the evidence, to extrapolate from the facts, to fill in gaps, and speculate productively about what is not or cannot be known. These additions to the historians' equipment have been a product and a by-product of two overwhelming enthusiasms of the modern West. The first is an enthusiasm for social reform. The second is an enthusiasm for science, and its application to society. The passion for reform was rooted in a growing belief that men had the right and should have the power to govern themselves, that inherited inequalities and privileges were unjust, that it was the scholar's and the ruler's duty to reduce human suffering. The passion for science was rooted in a similarly growing belief that there were no phenomena in nature, man, or society that could not be grasped, interpreted, predicted, and perhaps controlled, by human reason, if enlightened by facts and guided by science. These enthusiasms, nourished in the European Renaissance and in the Age of Exploration and Discovery, grew together. Social sciences and social reform were Siamese twins.

Of course, both movements had deep roots in classical antiquity, in the writings of Plato and Aristotle, in medieval science and theology, in Thomas Aquinas and Roger Bacon, as well as in the early modern writings of Machiavelli, Hobbes, Locke, and Rousseau. Although the expression "social sciences" did not enter the recorded English language until 1846 (as a translation of Comte), the social sciences had begun to find their separate identities by the later seventeenth century. An ample account of the rise of the social sciences would be nothing less than a survey of modern European history. In their origins and their applications, in the dogmas which grew out of them and the crusades for or against their dogmas, were the seeds of revolution, reformation, and reaction, of legislation and jurisprudence, of a wide assortment of political movements, and a fallout of countless pundits, agitators, saboteurs, dictators, celebrities, and national heroes.

By the mid-nineteenth century the English language had added a whole new vocabulary, a modern taxonomy of facts and theories about society, drawn from economics, political science, jurisprudence, anthropology, sociology, psychology, social psychology, statistics, and social and economic geography. The genealogy of these disciplines shows how each tried to declare its independence, and then its dominance over social thought. This is a tangled tale, another parable of how man's efforts to learn tempt him to arrogant belief that he knows more than he really does. Social scientists sought skeleton keys to human experience. Each of their dominant theories dramatized the hopes and frustrations of efforts to encapsulate and dogmatize human experience.

Of course, all these new "sciences" rested, or pretended to rest, on the solid data of "history." The accumulated facts about the past became the basis for newly discovered laws presumed to govern the present and offer confident predictions of the future. One of the most influential prophets of the new social science, Jean Jacques Rousseau (1712–1778), opened his potent treatise on the Social Contract with a single outrageous generalization about the whole human past and present: "Man is born free, and everywhere he is in chains." I will not recount the familiar story of the rise of each of the separate social sciences. Some of the biases of interpretation shared by these social sciences have affected the work of the historian. New knowledge and new disciplines have spawned new temptations.

Futuristic. The social sciences tend to study and interpret the past with an aim to changing the future. The founding fathers of the social sciences were prophets of progress. Condorcet (1743–1794) made important contributions to the theory of probability, and his most influential work was *A Sketch for a Historical Picture of the Progress of the Human Mind* (1795). After his historical survey of human development through its nine stages down to the French Revolution, he projected the future tenth epoch which would bring the final perfection of mankind. Adam Smith's *Wealth of Nations* (1776), the pioneer work of modern economics, offered many policy suggestions. He ended his views of the past with a prophetic look at the future.

The rulers of Great Britain have, for more than a century past, amused the people with the imagination that they possessed a great empire on the west side of the Atlantic. This empire, however, has hitherto existed in imagination only. It has hitherto been, not an empire but the project of an empire; not a gold mine, but the project of a gold mine. . . . It is surely now time that our rulers should either realize this golden dream . . . or that they should awake from it themselves, and endeavour to awaken the people. . . . If any of the provinces of the British empire cannot be made to contribute towards the support of the whole empire, it is surely time that Great Britain should free herself from the expense of defending those provinces in time of war, and of supporting any part of their civil or military establishments in time of peace, and endeavour to accommodate her future views and designs to the real mediocrity of her circumstances.

Normative. The social sciences tend to seek laws or norms of experience, past, present, and future. Having founded knowledge in experience, English philosophers treated history as no more than "philosophy teaching by example." David Hume, in his *Enquiries Concerning Human Understanding* (1777), generalized from experience that "a miracle can never be proved, so as to be the foundation of a system of religion." His "Natural History of Religion" described the "normal" or natural course of the events surrounding all religions. In the same empiric tradition which dominated much of thinking about society in the English-speaking world, Jeremy Bentham provided one of the most extreme, most dogmatic, and most influential statements of the normative social sciences. His *Principles of Morals and Legislation* (1780; 1823) began from the "principle of utility" and described how the measurement of pleasures and pains and their allotment as incentives and punishments could be used to produce the greatest happiness of the society. His dogmas led to the reform of prisons and the rewriting of criminal laws around the world. He might have considered his greatest triumph the English Reform Bill of 1832.

John Stuart Mill's classic *Utilitarianism* (1863) gave his version of the "happiness principle," and elaborated its applications in government, while his *Principles of Political Economy* (1848) provided a handbook for modern liberal politicians. Even law, once thought to

be the most characteristic of a society's institutions, was encapsulated in catchy generalizations. One of the most influential was Sir
Henry Maine's assimilation (*Ancient Law*, 1861) of the institutions of
ancient Rome, contemporary India, and Anglo-Saxon England into
the convenient rule that society progresses from custom to law
(using, in turn, fictions, equity, and legislation), and "from status to
contract."

Quantitative. The social sciences tend to become quantitative, to
reduce experience to numbers. In 1791 Sir John Sinclair had introduced the word "statistics" into the English language with the first
of the twenty-one volumes of his *Statistical Account of Scotland.* We
know of no public national census in the West before the eighteenth
century, when the counting of people and resources became an institution. The connection between social reform, representative institutions, and a numerical approach to society was dramatized in the
Constitution of the United States, which required a regular counting
of the population every ten years to insure a proportionate voice in
the Congress for every free citizen.

The Belgian pioneer of statistical science, Adolphe Quételet
(1796–1874), took for his slogan Laplace's exhortation, "Let us
apply to the political and moral sciences the method founded on observation and mathematics that has served us so well in the natural
sciences." "We can judge of the perfection toward which a science
has come by the facility, more or less great, with which it may be
approached by calculation."

To provide grist for the statistical mills of the social scientists,
the "questionnaire" was developed. (The word first appears in print
in English in 1901.) It became the basis of Lewis Henry Morgan's
(1818–1881) pioneer anthropology—his studies in kinship, sponsored by the Smithsonian Institution, which made common generalizations about the customs of American Indians and the peoples of
Asia. Morgan's *Ancient Society* (1877) tracing "the Lines of Human
Progress, from Savagery through Barbarism into Civilization" became a basis for the explosive generalizations, prophecies, and revolutionary dogmas of Karl Marx and Friedrich Engels.

The questionnaire was a forerunner, too, of a still newer device

for quantifying social facts—the public opinion poll. Market research, seeking out customers for American industry, elaborated a
new science of opinion polling. In the early twentieth century "public opinion" entered the American vocabulary, and by the 1930s
Elmo Roper, Archibald M. Crossley, and George Gallup and their
competitors were producing a new social science and the thriving
new enterprise of "opinion polling." With it came a refined science
of voting (psephology) and a growing tendency for Americans to
think of elections and predict outcomes in percentages. These tendencies were of course compounded and dramatized by the fantastic
new capacities of the computer to calculate rapidly and extrapolate
indefinitely.

Fragmented. The social sciences tend to become professional-
ized. One result is an ever sharper definition of boundaries among
the social science specialties. The early age of the modern sciences
had been marked by Royal Societies, National Academies, and in the
United States by the American Philosophical Society, where scholars pooled miscellaneous observations and personal speculations.
The new age of professionalization created a host of specialized associations, each of which focused on its own proper province and defended its right to professional separatism and its prerogatives of
employment against all trespassers. In the gregarious United States,
long marked by insecurity about its humanistic culture, and by enthusiasms for voluntary organization, these new professions flourished and multiplied.

A rising American standard of living, improved means of transportation, and the growing interests of city boosters, Chambers of
Commerce, travel agents, and hotel owners accelerated the trend to
national and regional meetings. The chronology of the founding of
these organizations attests the specialization and the fragmentation
of the study of society: the American Statistical Association (1839),
American Ethnological Society (1842), American Social Science Association (1865), American Library Association (1876), American
Historical Association (1884), American Economic Association
(1885), American Psychological Association (1892), American An-

thropological Association (1902), American Political Science Association (1903), American Sociological Society (later Association; 1905), American Society for Applied Anthropology (1941). This short list gives only a hint of the proliferation of the separate professions interested in the human past. Each organization published its own periodicals and monographs, sponsored lectures and symposia, and gave prizes for the best work in the field. Even if each did not actually issue a professional code of ethics, they all aimed at explicit standards of professional competence in their specialty. Organizations have multiplied and divided into countless subspecialties.

The rise of the social sciences, dramatized in these and other learned associations, has of course produced a vast and growing resource of facts, concepts, and hypotheses, along with a growing community of experts to assist the historian in his effort to discover the past. Scholarly professionals have recognized the need to bring together their findings and pool their resources in such organizations as the American Council of Learned Societies (1919), which federated forty-three national scholarly groups, and has sponsored such publications as the *Dictionary of American Biography* (1928–   ) and the *Dictionary of Scientific Biography* (1970–1980). "Behavioral Sciences" became the name in the late 1950s for a new enthusiasm and a renewed effort to consolidate the study of mankind and make it still more scientific. Meanwhile, the multiplication of American colleges and universities increased the widening flood of knowledge about the human past, in channels not even imagined a century ago. The raw materials for the American historian in the late twentieth century are rich, diverse, and authentic beyond the wildest dreams of his predecessors.

*   *   *

Yet the historian's purpose today remains not much different from that of his earliest and greatest forebears. "These are the researches of Herodotus of Halicarnassus, which he publishes in the hope of thereby preserving from decay the remembrance of what men have done, and of preventing the great and wonderful acts of the Greeks and the barbarians from losing their due meed of glory;

and withal to put on record what were their grounds of feud." "My conclusions," wrote Thucydides, "have cost me some labour from the want of coincidence between accounts of the same occurrences by different eye-witnesses, arising sometimes from imperfect memory, sometimes from undue partiality for one side or the other. The absence of romance in my history will, I fear, detract somewhat from its interest; but if it be judged useful by those inquirers who desire an exact knowledge of the past as an aid to the interpretation of the future, which in the course of human things must resemble if it does not reflect it, I shall be content. In fine, I have written my work, not as an essay which is to win the applause of the moment, but as a possession for all time."

When we think of survival, as Herodotus and Thucydides surely did, we must note the striking fact that works of the classic ancient historians are still read with pleasure by a vast audience for whom the physics of Aristotle, the botany of Theophrastus, the *Almagest* and *Geography* of Ptolemy, and the medical treatises of Galen have scant appeal. While the works of science and technology correct and displace their predecessors, the works of historians stay with us.

Perhaps the explanation is not so difficult. For the historian there is an uncanny continuing identity between his subject matter and his audience. Nowhere is this stated more eloquently than in the familiar words of Pericles' Funeral Oration (431 B.C.), as reported by Thucydides himself:

> Fix your eyes on the greatness of Athens as you have it before you day by day, fall in love with her, and when you feel her great, remember that this greatness was won by men with courage, with knowledge of their duty, and with a sense of honor in action. . . . So they gave their bodies to the commonwealth and received, each for his own memory, praise that will never die, and with it the grandest of all sepulchers, not that in which their mortal bones are laid, but a home in the minds of men, where their glory remains fresh to stir to speech or action as the occasion comes by. For the whole earth is the sepulcher of famous men; and their story is not

graven only on stone over their native earth, but lives on far away, without visible symbol, woven into the stuff of other men's lives. For you now it remains to rival what they have done and, knowing the secret of happiness to be freedom and the secret of freedom a brave heart, not idly to stand aside from the enemy's onset.

In a word, historians are always writing about us. Not because they extrapolate "laws" of social science. But because they write for people about people, than whom nothing is more interesting or more inscrutable.

New temptations for the twentieth-century historian are the by-product of his new resources and his new instruments of discovery. Biases of the social sciences can seduce the historian into attitudes at odds with his role as a literary artist. We are unwilling victims of the Biases of Survival, grateful for whatever the past happens to leave us. But to the enthusiasms, dogmas, and academic fashions of the social sciences we have become willing victims. We embrace their emphases in the hope of sharing the scientific kudos of the social scientists.

While the modern social sciences are inevitably futuristic, the historian must remain oriented to the past. He is primarily a narrator. His suspense comes from the wonder of the past itself. The romantic philosopher's description of the historian as "the prophet in reverse" is true only when the historian shares the prophet's sense of mystery, as he too reaches into the unknown. While social sciences are normative, looking for rules and laws, the historian must sacrifice none of the idiosyncrasy of the past. His unique mission is to discover the uniqueness of people and places and moments. He dare not sacrifice this to his contemporaries' will to master the present and future. Similarly, the quantitative hopes of the social sciences, their appetite for the fungible, for whatever can be counted and classified, is alien to the historian's search for nuance, flow, and the elusiveness of experience.

Finally, the modern making of history into one of the most respectable, most fragmented, and most self-conscious of the social sciences has its perils. Organized professional historians become the target of every group with political or reformist objectives, urging positions on foreign policy, championing movements for minorities, for women or the handicapped. However morally desirable, these positions reinforce the social science biases. Yet, at the same time, the profession itself becomes the main, sometimes the only, audience for its publications. Inevitably the language of history tends to become the jargon of historians speaking to one another. The profession becomes preoccupied with its own "classic controversies" on which members write articles and monographs, or deliver polemics.

Still, we must remain wary of generalizing about the historian-creator. His hallmark is his originality. While the discoverer focuses our vision anew on something already out there, the creator, of whom the historian is a peculiar breed, makes the object for us to see. He does it with words, and so is inhibited, guided, and fulfilled by language. But his limitations are at least as restricting as the hardness of the sculptor's marble. Like other writers who seek a voluntary audience—like the poet and the novelist—he must give delight. His accents must give pleasure. If his periods are not Gibbonian, he must have his own way with words. This we find from Parkman, Prescott, and Henry Adams to Samuel Eliot Morison, in all historians who live. He shares this qualification with other men of letters. But in addition he labors under two other necessities.

Credibility. His work must be true according to the prevalent standards of truth in his age, but his standards of truth must transcend the ephemeral or fashionable demands of academic or political or religious or racial dogma. Though scholars have learned much about ancient Rome since Gibbon wrote, and the schools of Marx, Pareto, and Freud have had their day, Gibbon still tells a credible tale. This is partly, of course, from his good luck in having been born away from the tyranny of orthodoxy or totalitarianism. But it is also from his courage to resist the tyranny of passing opinion, of political sycophancy, of religious orthodoxy, and to create an original vision.

Suspense and Surprise. This is the most paradoxical and the most demanding of the arts of the historian. While the poet and the novelist can hold off the reader's knowledge of how it all turned out, and entice him by the promise of telling, where the historian labors we already know the last chapter. His greatest challenge, while conforming to the facts as best determined in his age, is to provide his reader with a new access of surprise at how and why and when and who. The successful historian at his best demands and secures a willing suspension of knowledge. He asks the reader to pretend that he does not already know, so that the historian can add suspense to the true course of events. He can do this by his more vivid portrait in detail, by his network of surprising connections, and his array of unexpected consequences. The great historian, the historian-creator, adds a new drama to everything we thought we already knew. Everybody knew that the Roman Empire declined and fell. Gibbon made his readers feel that they had not really known.

The historian-creator refuses to be defeated by the biases of survival. For he chooses, defines, and shapes his subject to provide a reasonably truthful account from miscellaneous remains. Of course he must use the social sciences, but he must transcend the dogmas and theories. Like other literary artists, creators in the world of the word, and unlike the advancing social scientist, he is not engaged merely in correcting and revising his predecessors. He adds to our inheritance. At his best he is not accumulating knowledge which becomes obsolete, but creating a work with a life of its own. While Adam Smith survives in the reflected light of Ricardo and Marx and Keynes, Gibbon shines with a light all his own. The truth which the historian in any age finds in the past becomes part of our literary treasure. Inevitably the historian is torn between his efforts to create anew what he sees was really there, and the urgent shifting demands of the living audience. His motto could be Tertullian's rule of faith, *Credo quia impossibile*, I believe because it is impossible. At his best he remains a Wrestler with the Angel.

THE JEFFERSONIAN CIRCLE

from THE LOST WORLD OF THOMAS JEFFERSON, *1948*

JEFFERSON and his circle unwittingly accomplished for American civilization something like what St. Augustine did for medieval Christendom. Of course the fragments of the Jeffersonian literature are not to be compared with St. Augustine's greatest work. But if we consider the writings of the Jeffersonian circle as a whole, we will discover that they had a scope and function quite analogous to that of St. Augustine's *City of God.* Writing in the years just after the fall of Rome in 410, St. Augustine had a vision of an eternal city: his vision provided much of the theology and the political theory on which medieval Europe built its alternative to the earthly city. It was such a compelling vision that it remained vivid for centuries after the decay of Rome. The Jeffersonians, in the late eighteenth and early nineteenth centuries, were actually writing before their Rome had been built—before the American continent had been exploited or even explored. And their vision was of that *earthly* city which could and should be built here.

In the years between the founding of the republic and the death of Jefferson, there centered about Jefferson himself a few intellectuals who were sufficiently agreed on their task to give their philosophic adventure the character of a common expedition. These men, whom we are about to describe, were not so much a school of philosophy as a community of philosophers. While "my country" still meant something different to men in each state of the Union, even before the artificial bonds of political union were well forged, these Americans already felt united by the common challenge of their natural environment. Astronomer, botanist, anthropologist, physician, theologian, and political scientist spoke the same language, and thought in the same cosmos. They did not profess an explicit system of philosophy, nor did they publish Articles of Faith; yet their agreement was no less definite than if it had been formally declared.

The intellectual energies of this circle were organized by an institution framed on republican principles—the American Philosophical Society. This Society traced its origin back to the year of Jefferson's birth. "The first Drudgery of Settling new Colonies, which confines the Attention of People to mere Necessaries, is now pretty well over," Benjamin Franklin had announced in his circular letter of 1743 which proposed the organization, "and there are many in every Province in Circumstances that set them at Ease, and afford Leisure to cultivate the finer Arts, and improve the common Stock of Knowledge." Franklin accurately sketched the scope of the enlarged intellectual life which he was proposing, and predicted the direction of Jeffersonian interests when he described the proper concerns of such a new society:

All new-discovered Plants, Herbs, Trees, Roots, their Virtues, Uses, &c.; Methods of Propagating them, and making such as are useful, but particular to some Plantations, more general. Improvements of vegetable Juices, as Cyders, Wines, &c.; New Methods of Curing or Preventing Diseases. All new-discovered Fossils in different Countries, as Mines, Minerals, Quarries; &c. New and useful Improvements in any Branch of Mathematicks; New Discoveries in Chemistry, such as Improvements in Distillation, Brewing, Assaying of ores; &c. New Mechanical Inventions for Saving labour; as Mills and Carriages, &c., and for Raising and Conveying of Water, Draining of Meadows, &c.; All new Arts, Trades, Manufactures, &c. that may be proposed or thought of; Surveys, Maps and Charts of particular Parts of the Sea-coasts, or Inland Countries; Course and Junction of Rivers and great Roads, Situation of Lakes and Mountains, Nature of the Soil and Productions; &c. New Methods of Improving the Breed of useful Animals; Introducing other Sorts from foreign Countries. New Improvements in Planting, Gardening, Clearing Land, &c. . . .

The unifying purpose of these miscellaneous activities could not have been better stated than in Franklin's summary phrase: "all philosophical Experiments that let Light into the Nature of Things, tend to increase the Power of Man over Matter, and multiply the Conveniences or Pleasures of Life." In 1769, the Junto which grew out of Franklin's earliest effort was merged with a younger American Philosophical Society to form a new and energetic "American Philosophical Society, held at Philadelphia for promoting useful Knowledge." Consciously modeled on the Royal Society of London, from which it borrowed its rules, the young organization was nonetheless characteristically American in its interests. Members were classed into one or more of the following committees:

1. Geography, Mathematics, Natural Philosophy and Astronomy.
2. Medicine and Anatomy.
3. Natural History and Chymistry.
4. Trade and Commerce.
5. Mechanics and Architecture.
6. Husbandry and American Improvements.

The Preface of the first volume of the Society's *Transactions*, having explained that merely speculative knowledge might prove of little use, declared that members would "confine their disquisitions, principally, to such subjects as tend to the improvement of their country, and advancement of its interest and prosperity."

Including an intellectual élite from every corner of British North America, the American Philosophical Society was truly continental in catholicity and influence. By the time of the Revolution, it had become the main institution through which Americans collaborated to comprehend and master their environment, and the focus, not merely of "scientific" activity, but of intellectual life on the continent. "A treasure we ought to glory in," was Paine's praise in 1775. "Here the defective knowledge of the individual is supplied by the common stock." Its meetings were appropriately held at Philadelphia, the political capital until 1800, and for many years the most populous city in the Union. John Adams accurately (if somewhat enviously) described the city as "the pineal gland" of the continent. In the years between the death of Franklin in 1790 and the end of Jefferson's presidency in 1809, the South showed no comparable intellectual metropolis. New England was on the intellectual periphery; those were dull days for Harvard College and for the theology which she represented. The American Academy of Arts and Sciences (the Boston counterpart of the Philosophical Society) founded by John Adams in 1780 never attained the stature of a rival. It surely was in the Jeffersonian spirit that the center of American action should be the center of thought.

The meaning of "philosophy" under American conditions had been vividly exemplified in Franklin himself, who was the first president of the Philosophical Society. The model of the American philosopher, he was neither a profound nor a reflective man, but preeminently observant and inventive. Serving liberty and philosophy as a single master, he never doubted that a healthy and prosperous America would also be wise and moral. To cast up the national debt, to collect fossils, to experiment with electricity, to measure an eclipse, to shape a constitution or a moral creed—all were part of a single "philosophic" enterprise. The sheer joy of activity, of physical and social adjustment, and of material achievement seemed to supply some coherence for the miscellaneous practical energies of Franklin's age.

A full generation senior to Jefferson, who was not born until 1743, Benjamin Franklin (1706–1790) had grown old in a colonial America. As Franklin's had been perhaps the most energetic and catholic mind of the last age of our colonial existence, Jefferson's was to be the leading mind of the first age of our national life, and therefore in a powerful position for shaping the American intellectual character. When Franklin died in 1790, it was difficult to see who if not Jefferson should rightfully inherit the mantle of the American philosopher.

While it is Jefferson's political thought that has become familiar to us, the sum of Jeffersonian thought was more than a number of political maxims. And the breadth of Jeffersonian interests was not a mere personal idiosyncrasy. It was Jefferson's intellectual comradeship with his contemporaries that provided the incentive and resource for cementing his discrete observations into a whole. We must therefore allow him and a few of his closest and ablest fellow philosophers to collaborate for us, as they did for each other. The Jeffersonian circle with whom we shall be mainly concerned, although of course only a fraction of the Philosophical Society's membership, was the heart of the organization. The investigations of Rittenhouse, Rush, Barton and Priestley—and the popularizations of Paine and Peale—will all be seen focused through Jefferson himself on the central issues of man and society. Before trying to reconstruct the philosophy of this Jeffersonian circle we must examine briefly the characters and careers of these principal collaborators.

DAVID RITTENHOUSE (1732–1796), Jefferson's idol, was elected Franklin's successor as president of the American Philosophical Society in 1791. While lacking the flexibility, the culture, and the breadth of others of the Jeffersonian circle, Rittenhouse showed a brilliance and an inventive genius which made him the intellectual prodigy of his day. The son of a Germantown farmer, born eleven years before Jefferson, he had virtually no formal schooling. Yet before he was forty, he had built the famous "Orrery" or planetarium which came to be considered the first mechanical wonder of the American world. Rittenhouse's work was the subject of the first article in the first volume of *Transactions* of the Philosophical Society. "When the machine is put in motion, by the turning of a winch, there are three indexes, which point out the hour of the day, the day of the month and the year, (according to the *Julian* account) answering to that situation of the heavenly bodies which it then represented; and so continually, for a period of 5000 years, either forward or backward." By applying a small telescope to the ball representing the earth, and directing it to any planet, one could register on a dial the longitude and the latitude of that planet (as seen from the earth). The clock mechanism was contrived to produce music while the spheres revolved. Jefferson was so struck by the ingenuity of the machine that he thought it proved Rittenhouse's rightful place in a trio of American genius which included besides him only Washington and Franklin. "Second to no astronomer living," was Jefferson's praise. "In genius he must be the first, because he is self taught. As an artist he has exhibited as great a proof of mechanical genius as the world has ever produced. He has not indeed made a world; but he has by imitation approached nearer its Maker than any man who has lived from the creation to this day."

Rittenhouse was no secluded genius. He was a successful man of affairs and a consistent fighter for republican causes. By the time the Revolution arrived, he had helped survey the boundaries of half the colonies. After 1775 he was engineer of the Committee of Safety, and it was he who substituted iron for lead clockweights throughout Philadelphia in order to secure lead for Revolutionary bullets; he devised chain protections for American harbors and personally supervised much of the munitions manufacturing for the rebel cause. He served in the General Assembly of Pennsylvania and was a member of the Pennsylvania state constitutional convention of 1776. He was Jefferson's chief adviser on the troublesome problem of defining American units of weights and measures. And after urging by both Jefferson and Hamilton, Rittenhouse accepted appointment in 1792 as the first director of the United States Mint.

DR. BENJAMIN RUSH (1745–1813) was elected to deliver the Society's public eulogy upon the death of Rittenhouse in 1796. Rush himself was one of the most versatile men of the age. His eminence as a physician rivaled Rittenhouse's as an astronomer; and no one excelled him as a promoter of humanitarian projects. Rush's long friendship with Jefferson, amply attested in their correspondence, began in Revolutionary days and continued intimate until death. It was Rush's letter in 1811 that succeeded in reconciling Jefferson with John Adams; the fruit of this reconciliation was the voluminous

Adams-Jefferson correspondence which remains among the most revealing intellectual confessions of the age. Born two years after Jefferson, on a farm near Philadelphia, Rush was to acquire the best medical training offered by the English-speaking world in his time. After studying at the College of New Jersey (later called Princeton), he heard the first medical lectures of Dr. William Shippen and Dr. John Morgan at the College of Philadelphia; he then went to Edinburgh, where he imbibed the latest theories of medicine along with an enthusiasm for republicanism. Returning to Philadelphia, he took up the practice of medicine in 1769. His professorship of chemistry at the College of Philadelphia was the first in the colonies, and his *Syllabus of a Course of Lectures on Chemistry*, the first American textbook on the subject. A prosperous medical practice still left him time for active membership in the Philosophical Society and for an energetic part in founding the Pennsylvania Society for Promoting the Abolition of Slavery.

After meeting the newly arrived Thomas Paine in a Philadelphia bookshop in February, 1775, Rush made the fateful proposal that Paine write an appeal for American independence; Rush himself suggested the title "Common Sense." It was Rush who heard the early drafts of the famous pamphlet, chapter by chapter as Paine composed them. If he had done nothing more for the rebel cause, this bit of literary promotion would have been an ample service. Actually he attended the Continental Congress, signed the Declaration of Independence, and served as a surgeon-general in the Revolutionary Army. Through a series of articles for Philadelphia newspapers in the years just after the Revolution, Rush, still writing in the revolutionary spirit, persuasively argued for many humanitarian reforms. His essays, collected in a volume in 1798, condemned capital punishment, urged penal reform, called for a temperance movement, proposed a system of education especially suited to American conditions, and demanded the abolition of Negro slavery. Rush's great organizing talents enabled him to establish the first free medical dispensary in the country, to make more humane the treatment of the insane, and to aid James Wilson in securing Pennsylvania's ratification of the Federal constitution.

Rush's original contribution to American thought lay in medical science where he was distinguished as writer, teacher, and practitioner. After the death of Dr. John Morgan, he filled the chair of the Theory and Practice of Medicine in the new University of Pennsylvania. If sometimes dogmatic—for example in his uncompromising use of bleeding—Rush often showed courage in opposing the prejudices of the medical profession and the lay public. His theory that the yellow-fever epidemic of 1793 was caused partly by poor sanitation shocked patriotic Philadelphians and caused him to be ostracized by his profession. In that year Rush endangered his life by remaining in the city to help the dying and to learn more about the disease. He pioneered in relating dentistry to physiology and helped found veterinary medicine in America. His remarkable *Medical Inquiries and Observations upon the Diseases of the Mind* anticipated the approach of modern psychiatry. Perhaps greater than all his particular reforms was his vigorous attack on an antiquated medical terminology. Under his leadership Philadelphia became the center of medical education for the continent. Jefferson remarked at his death in 1813, "A better man could not have left us, more benevolent, more learned, of finer genius, or more honest."

BENJAMIN SMITH BARTON (1766–1815), another member, was for some years curator, and then vice-president during Jefferson's leadership of the Philosophical Society. The curiosity which had attracted Rittenhouse to the heavens, and stirred Rush's interest in the human mind and body, had drawn Barton toward the largely unknown botanical products of the continent. He was the greatest American botanist of his age. Barton's *Elements of Botany* (1803), the first important American treatise on the subject, went through several American and English editions and was even translated into Russian. When not yet twenty, he had accompanied his uncle, David Rittenhouse, on the surveying expedition to draw the western boundary of Pennsylvania which then divided it from Virginia. "I well recollect," wrote Barton many years later of the influence which his uncle had exerted on him, "how great were his pleasure and satisfaction, in contemplating the *Flora* of the rich hills of Weeling, and other branches of the Ohio, when I accompanied him into those parts of our Union, in the year 1785. In this wilderness, he first fostered my love and zeal for natural history." After a trip to Edinburgh, London, and Göttingen, Barton returned to Philadelphia to practice medicine and teach in the College of Philadelphia as professor first of natural history and botany, and later of *materia medica*. On Rush's death in 1813, Barton succeeded him as Professor of the Theory and Practice of Medicine in the University of Pennsylvania.

Barton's interests were in many ways characteristically American. While he devoted most of his life to *materia medica* (especially the uses of American plants for American diseases), his writings on natural history included observations on the pernicious insects of the United States, the Falls of Niagara, the geographical distribution of trees and shrubs, a new species of lizard, the American turkey, the function of absorption in amphibians, the origin of the boundaries of Lake Ontario, the generation of fishes, and the qualities of American honey. He made a beginning in cultural anthropology: his studies of the origin, history, and development of the American Indian were summarized in his widely read *New Views of the Origin of the Tribes and Nations of America*, which he dedicated to Jefferson.

JOSEPH PRIESTLEY (1733–1804), the great chemist now remembered for his discovery of oxygen, arrived from England in 1794 to join this circle of American philosophers. Next to Paine, Priestley was the most vivid symbol of the cosmopolitan republican spirit; and while still abroad he had become a close collaborator of the Jeffersonians. At the beginning of trouble between England and her colonies, Priestley had made American friends by his pamphlets favoring the rebel cause. Later his open advocacy of the French Revolution had drawn the wrath of a Birmingham mob, which on Bastille Day, 1791, burned his library and all his personal belongings. In the next year the French people made him a citizen of their republic. Driven from his native England at the age of sixty, Priestley came to Philadelphia as the appropriate asylum for his republican sentiments and philosophic interests.

It was David Rittenhouse who welcomed Priestley on behalf of American philosophy. Barton tells us that in the brief period between Priestley's arrival and the death of Rittenhouse, he often met Priestley at his uncle's house. Priestley's interest in nature went back to his youth in England when he had experimented with spiders; as tutor at an English school he had taken his students on country walks to collect fossils and botanical specimens. In America he was impatient with city life, and after negotiating with Rush (who in addition to all else was a land speculator), Priestley moved into the "wilderness" of the central part of Pennsylvania at Northumberland. Jefferson was disappointed, for he had tried to interest Priestley in settling near Monticello.

Replying to Rittenhouse's welcoming address, Priestley explained that he had left his native land principally "for the sake of pursuing our common studies without molestation." A member of the Philosophical Society since 1785, he had long shared the intellectual life of the Jeffersonian circle by correspondence. After settling in this country, he wielded an even greater influence. While Rittenhouse regarded the planets and Rush examined the mind and shape of man, while Barton studied anthropology and explored the world of vegetables and lower animals, Priestley's eye was on another aspect of nature. His principal concern was the composition and behavior of inanimate matter: though best known today for his experiments with gases, his physical researches were numerous and varied. Many years before, when Priestley was in London promoting the American cause, he had formed a friendship with Franklin, who stimulated his interest in electricity. At Franklin's suggestion, he had written *The History and Present State of Electricity*. Priestley recorded from Franklin's own mouth the only account which survives of the famous experiment of the electrical kite. Even before Priestley arrived in America, the Philosophical Society had received his manuscript notes of "Experiments on Phlogiston and the seeming concoction of water into air." After his arrival he gave them more of his experiments. The Society heard his observations on spontaneous generation, and received his diary of the weather during the sea voyage to America. Like Rush, Priestley had numerous practical interests and a fluent pen from which came essays on history and political science, diatribes against the slave trade, and projects of education. Jefferson relied heavily on his advice for the projected University of Virginia.

Priestley possessed still another qualification for rounding out the American philosopher's view of the world. He had been trained and had long made his living as a nonconformist minister, and throughout his life he remained a preacher. Priestley was perhaps the most influential and articulate exponent of Unitarianism during the first years of the republic. His extensive knowledge of languages, theology, and church history enabled him to supply the artillery to defend the Jeffersonian view of religion and metaphysics. *A History of the Corruptions of Christianity*, written before Priestley came to America, was a work which Jefferson read again and again and never ceased to admire. The friendship between Priestley and Jefferson deepened, and their philosophic harmony became closer with the years; with no other theologian did Jefferson feel equally at home. Priestley's extraordinary union of the theologian and the physicist qualifed him to expound the materialism on which Jefferson, Rush, and others rested their faith. There was surely no hyperbole when Jefferson described him as unexcelled for service "in religion, in politics, in physics."

Besides Jefferson himself, Rittenhouse, Rush, Barton, and Priestley comprised the major thinkers in that Jeffersonian circle with which we are concerned. Within the circle were two other men—Peale and Paine—who themselves lacked profundity but were admirably equipped for giving popular expression to the ideas which other men understood more profoundly.

CHARLES WILSON PEALE (1741–1827) served the Jeffersonian circle as its illustrator and showman. Raised in Maryland, where he had received little formal schooling, Peale early agitated against the Stamp Act. When Loyalist merchants cut off his credit, he was forced to abandon his trade of saddle maker, and he turned his amateur hand to painting portraits in order to support his family. Peale soon became one of those itinerant artists who in the days before photography went from village to village, providing town halls with local landscapes and filling commissions for family likenesses. In this way he grew intimately acquainted with the American scene, traveling from Newburyport in Massachusetts south to Virginia. A brief apprenticeship in London under Benjamin West qualified him on his return to America to paint a remarkable series of portraits of the

Revolutionary soldiers whom he came to know while serving as a captain of infantry; his numerous paintings of George Washington (including the earliest known) are still considered the most comprehensive and perceptive records of the General and President. The republican enthusiasm which qualified him for membership in the Committee of Public Safety and for active service in the Revolution stayed with him. In the Pennsylvania Assembly he voted for the abolition of slavery; and he himself freed the slaves he had brought from Maryland.

After Peale had settled in Philadelphia in 1776, his association with the leading men of the city gave a philosophic turn to his interests. When Dr. Morgan (Rush's predecessor as Professor of Medicine) gave Peale some mammoth bones from the Ohio, when Franklin presented him with a French Angora cat, and when he received a paddle fish from the Allegheny River, he conceived a plan for a museum of natural history which he founded in 1784. Peale's Museum, of which Jefferson accepted the presidency, was a storehouse and exhibiting place for many curious and interesting objects. Peale was among the first museum makers to reconstruct the natural habitat: sky and landscape were painted behind the animals, and birds' nests were shown as they appeared on the banks of rivers. In 1794, Peale displayed his characteristic showmanship when he made a parade of the removal of the museum from his studio on Lombard Street into the building of the Philosophical Society. At the head of the procession were men carrying an American buffalo, panthers, and tiger cats, followed by a long line of boys carrying smaller animals. Until 1802 the Museum remained in the Philosophical Society Hall where it occupied all but the two rooms reserved for meetings, but it prospered and outgrew even these quarters. In 1802 the Legislature offered the free use of Independence Hall. The visitor to the Museum could see a mammoth's tooth from the Ohio, an electrical machine, pieces of asbestos and belts of wampum, stuffed birds, and a large number of Peale's own portraits of heroes of the Revolution.

Peale's talents as artist and artisan qualified him to serve for many years as curator of the Philosophical Society. He arranged and drew the fossil bones presented by Jefferson, he pieced together a skeleton of an Asiatic elephant, and won the prize for the best method of warming rooms. The Society's memorial portraits of Franklin and Rittenhouse were done by Peale. His interests, while less deep than those of his fellows, were no less broad, ranging from natural history to dentistry and engineering. Although not a great naturalist, Peale was well known for his lectures on natural history which were accompanied by poetry and music. Jefferson, whose friendship with Peale went back to early Revolutionary days, continually assisted him in his scientific ventures. During Jefferson's presidency, pumps were loaned by the Navy Department to help Peale excavate the mammoth skeletons discovered at Newburgh, New York. It was Peale who engraved the animals discovered by Lewis and Clark. Jefferson frequently suggested objects for the Museum, and when in 1815 Peale finally wished to retire, he sought Jefferson's advice.

THOMAS PAINE (1737–1809), a friend of Rittenhouse, Rush, and Jefferson, possessed a rare talent for reducing to simple language and memorable phrase the ideas which other Jeffersonians stated in diffuse and sophisticated fashion. "No writer," Jefferson observed, "has exceeded Paine in ease and familiarity of style, in perspicuity of expression, happiness of elucidation, and in simple and unassuming language." His career is so familiar that any detailed account here is superfluous. But we should recall that Paine's association with the Jeffersonian circle remained a strong thread throughout his erratic career. An English expatriate like Priestley, Paine did more with his pen than any other man, not excepting Jefferson or Sam Adams, to hasten the Revolution and give heart to the rebels. No works were more effective than *Common Sense* and *The American Crisis* in building Revolutionary morale. While Jefferson was in Paris, he kept in close touch with Paine, exchanging observations on the French National Assembly and the French Declaration of the Rights of Man. Paine's *Rights of Man*, a defense of world republican revolution, which he wrote after the impending French Revolution had attracted him to Paris, was a work which made Jefferson rejoice; for by it he saw "the people confirmed in their good old faith." The storm raised by Jefferson's endorsement of this work, and even the notorious reputation for "atheism" which Paine had secured by his *Age of Reason*, did not deter Jefferson in 1801 from offering a government ship to bring Paine back to America. In Paine, Jefferson never failed to see the great popular champion of orthodox revolutionary principles: "In these it will be your glory to have steadily labored, and with as much effect as any man living."

While Paine was preeminently a publicist—and in this he was unexcelled—he also possessed a truly Jeffersonian versatility. His political writings overflowed political science, into economics, theology, and natural history. He showed talent as engineer and inventor. Perhaps his best known project was his plan for an iron bridge of a single arch, concerning which he frequently corresponded with Jefferson, and a model of which he actually sent to Peale's Museum. He never was elected to membership in the Philosophical Society but he shared the interests of his friends in it, and corresponded with them on numerous scientific problems. Upon his first arrival in America he urged the fuller exploration of the mineral resources of the country, and proposed "that were samples of different soils from different parts of America, presented to the [Philosophical] Society for their inspection and examination, it would greatly facilitate our knowledge of the internal earth, and give a new spring both to agriculture and manufactures." During the Revolution, Paine collaborated with Rittenhouse on a flame-carrying arrow of iron intended to disable the British Army on the other side of the Delaware River. He was full of practical projects, such as the design for a smokeless candle which he communicated to Franklin. Paine's letters to Jefferson include plans for a "geometrical wheelbarrow," a new explanation of the cohesion of matter, a method for estimating the amount of cut timber to be had from standing trees, a design for a motor wheel to be revolved by the explosion of gunpowder (said by Paine to excel the steam engine because of its greater simplicity and its cheaper operation), a new design for the roofs of houses, an improved method of constructing carriage wheels, and a scheme for making one gunboat do the work of two. He developed his own theory of the causes and cure of yellow fever, and shared his experiments in this field with his friend Rittenhouse.

It was Paine's extraordinary practical sense and his impatience with metaphysics that qualified him to give a lucid and popular (if sometimes vulgarized) expression to Jeffersonian ideas. He brought the Jeffersonians down to earth when they veered toward the doctrinaire or the esoteric. Paine's humble origins and his association with men of many nations gave his journalistic writings a humanity which still shines through his crude phrases.

The group of philosophers whose thought will concern us we have christened the Jeffersonian Circle, for THOMAS JEFFERSON (1743–1826) stood at the center of this philosophical community. He was the human magnet who drew them together and gave order and meaning to their discrete investigations. As astronomer and mechanic he was surely inferior to Rittenhouse; as physician and psychologist, beneath Rush; as botanist and anthropologist, not the equal of Barton; and as physicist and theologian below Priestley; for he lacked the unbalance of mind required to excel as a specialist. But he possessed a mind more catholic than theirs and better able to see nature as a whole. Being a statesman, he persistently demanded the human implications of their science.

On the death of Rittenhouse in 1796, the American Philosophical Society chose Jefferson for its president. Since he was not a Philadelphian but a Virginian, the choice signified the national character of the Society. Jefferson's reelection for nearly twenty years as president of the body which according to him "comprehends whatever the American World has of distinction in Philosophy & Science," was simple recognition of his leadership in American intellectual life. He had become a member of the Society in 1780, a councillor in 1781, and for years had been exchanging observations with fellow philosophers. From Jefferson the Society received an original design for a moldboard plough, observations on weights and measures, and communications on a variety of subjects ranging from meteorology to fossils. Through him were transmitted many interesting communications which he received from correspondents all over the world. After the removal of the capital to Washington, Jefferson no longer lived near the Society's headquarters, but year after year and over his frequent protest, American science honored him as its leader. The

Society refused his resignation of the presidency in 1808 when he was about to move from Washington to Monticello; not until 1815 was he permitted to retire.

The most impressive single monument of Jefferson's scientific achievement is his *Notes on Virginia*, which he prepared in response to a request by the French Government in 1781. The little volume collected his observations on every aspect of the Virginia environment: flora, fauna, mountains, rivers, population, laws, manufacturers, Indians, and Negroes. Even this remarkable work is no full measure of his interests, which we can see only in the wealth of his letters. During his busy political mission to France from 1784 to 1789, he naturally recorded day by day the progress of the Revolution there. But he also found time to note the rivers and the planets, to seek new species of rice, and to find fossil shells.

For Jefferson the Louisiana Purchase was at once a political, an economic and a "philosophical" event; he congratulated the Society "on the enlarged field of unexplored country lately opened to free research." Having initiated the famous Western Expedition (1804–1806) of Lewis and Clark, he took trouble to see that it bore scientific fruit. In his personal instructions to Captain Meriwether Lewis in 1803, Jefferson characteristically listed the kinds of useful information to be collected:

> Other objects worthy of notice will be, the soil and face of the country, its growth and vegetable productions, especially those not of the United States, the animals of the country generally, and especially those not known in the United States; the remains and accounts of any which may be deemed rare or extinct; the mineral productions of every kind, but particularly metals, limestone, pitcoal and saltpetre; salines and mineral waters, noting the temperature of the last, and such circumstances as may indicate their character; volcanic appearances; climate, as characterized by the thermometer, by the proportion of rainy, cloudy, and clear days, by lightning, hail, snow, ice, by the access and recess of frost, by the winds prevailing at different seasons, the dates

at which particular plants put forth or lose their flower or leaf, times of appearance of particular birds, reptiles or insects.

Among his contemporaries who were qualified to judge, Jefferson had a considerable reputation as a naturalist. When Barton described to the Philosophical Society a new plant, which he christened *Jeffersonia Virginica*, he declared that Jefferson had few peers among natural historians in America. Jefferson exchanged observations on eclipses with Rittenhouse, discussed anatomy and the theory of medicine with Rush, *materia medica* and the habits of plants and animals with Barton, chemistry and theology with Priestley, and engineering and architecture with Paine. He complained that for much of his life public duties interfered with those "philosophical evenings in the winter, and rural days in the summer" which were always his delight.

SELF-LIQUIDATING IDEALS

from DEMOCRACY AND ITS DISCONTENTS, *1969*

WORRYING ABOUT OUR values is more than a characteristic headache of our time. It is a by-product of long and potent forces in our history and of many peculiarities of American life. More perhaps than any other people, we Americans have tended to talk and think or (more precisely) to worry about our values. In our own time this tendency is a by-product of the American concept of a standard of living, of the American attitude to technology, and of American success in technology. We can better understand (though I suspect we can never cure) this American habit if we notice a peculiarity of the ideals to which we have been led by our geography, our wealth, our know-how, and our history.

We Americans have been led to the pursuit of some self-liquidating ideals. Myriad circumstances of our history have led us in this direction. A self-liquidating ideal is an ideal which is dissolved in the very act of fulfillment. Many of our most prominent and dominant ideals have had just this quality.

* * *

The earliest example is in the very first appeal of America—as a new world. The first charm of the continent was its newness. But when the new nation in a new world flourished and endured, it became old. By the later twentieth century we were among the oldest

743

of the new nations of modern times. Our federal Constitution, which in 1787 seemed so uncertain an experiment, is now the oldest written Constitution in working order.

How to stay young? This problem plagues nations as well as individuals. But it plagues us more than other nations.

How can we keep alive the experimental spirit, the verve and vitality, the adventure-lovingness of youth? Nations which glory in their antiquity—an Italy which traces its founders back and into the heavens to Romulus and Remus, the twin sons of Mars, and to a semimythic Aeneas; a France which reaches back to a Saint Louis and Saint Joan; a Britain whose genealogy includes a legendary King Arthur—those nations have other special problems. Despite occasional revolutions and pretended revolutions, in modern times those nations, even when they have gloried in newness, have tried to sanctify it with the aura of antiquity. They have aimed to historicize their myths.

Our nation, founded in the glaring light of history, from the beginning set itself a task of renewal. Our Pilgrim Fathers and Founding Fathers hoped to give the men of older worlds a second chance. But could any world—even this brave New World—stay forever new?

It is not only this first and most obvious of American ideals which has seemed to be self-liquidating. The newness of our nation would come, we were told, from the fact that the United States would be as varied and as multiplex as mankind. We would be (in Whitman's phrase) "a Nation of Nations." Our nation was to be (as Emma Lazarus proclaimed in her inscription on the base of the Statue of Liberty)

> Mother of Exiles. From her beacon-hand
> Glows world-wide welcome. . . .

The whole earth would be our womb. Our wealth and strength would be in our variety.

Of course, there were other regions of the world—the Balkans, the Middle East, South Asia—which also were a mélange of peoples and languages and religions. What would distinguish the United States was that we would give our varied peoples the opportunity to become one. As they were dissolved in the American "melting pot" they would become part of a single community.

But suppose we actually succeeded. Suppose we brought all the immigrant world into one great new nation. Suppose we managed to Americanize and assimilate the varied peoples of the world. What then?

Inevitably—and ironically—success would mean a new homogeneity. If the nation really succeeded in drawing together all these peoples, giving them a chance to discover their common humanity and to forget the feuds and ancient hatreds that had held them apart, how could it fail to dissolve much of that rich variety, that pungency which itself justified building a "Nation of Nations"?

This danger was not purely theoretical. The nineteenth century, which brought us tens of millions of varied immigrants—from Ireland, Italy, Poland, the Balkans, the Middle East, and elsewhere—concluded in a paroxysm of fear and puzzlement. Old settlers (themselves, of course, descended from immigrant Americans), once they became comfortable here, began to fear that the nation might not be homogeneous enough. The Immigration Restriction League, founded in the 1890's by a group of bright Harvard graduates, soon included many of the nation's most respectable political leaders, industrialists, labor leaders, educators, scholars, and authors. Congressional hearings on the "problem" of immigration then produced forty-odd published volumes on the evils of immigration. The popular "remedy" for the nation's variety was to assimilate the immigrant, and different ethnic groups were rated according to the ease and speed with which they "became" American. The new immigration policy of the 1920's proclaimed the dissolving of the adventurously pluralist ideal.

The pluralist ideal was being abandoned, not merely because some people believed it was wrong, or that it could never succeed. A better explanation of what was happening was that the effort to build a strong, nationalist, community-conscious people from this international miscellany had substantially succeeded. Millions, whose immigrant parents had arrived within the preceding century, came to believe in a newly consolidated Americanism, which left no place for later immigrants—or for others who were conspicuously, if superficially, unlike themselves. The organized labor movement, which included immigrants and was led by immigrants and the children of immigrants, had joined with New England bluebloods to demand an end to the opportunities for others which had made their own lives possible.

The years from about 1880 to about 1930 witnessed the greatest confusion in the shaping of an American ideal of nationhood. First- and second-generation immigrants collaborated with the descendants of earlier, more respectable and more prosperous immigrants, to define 100 percent Americanism. At the same time a new American sociology, which was substantially a Science of Minorities, arose to give respectability and aggressiveness to pluralism.

By the 1930's many Americans had moved from the older ideal of assimilation ("Americanize the immigrant") to the newer ideal of integration (allow each group to remain integral, and to glory in its distinctness). That was the first heyday of the balanced ticket. It was the age of the second Ku Klux Klan, with its white racism and anti-Semitism and anti-Catholicism. And, in response, it became an age of aggressive ethnicity. The grandchildren of immigrants, in search of their roots, fabricated a newly assertive and chauvinistic sense of separateness. Many otherwise respectable Americans were surprisingly tolerant of the racism of the Ku Klux Klan. This confusion survives into our own age, and helps explain the aggressive ethnicity and racism of groups like the Black Panthers, and the shocking toleration of destructive and illegal acts committed under the cover of racial separatism. The battle over immigration left scars among ethnic minorities not unlike the sectional scars left by the Civil War.

How can we fulfill the American ideal of pluralism without liquidating it? If we build a single strong "Nation of Nations," will not our nationality inevitably overshadow our ethnicity? When we must (however facetiously) urge our fellow Americans to "Be Ethnic," do we not declare that the price of success in our pluralistic nation has been to make us less plural? Perhaps some of the ethnic pangs of our age come from the discovery that this cherished ideal may be self-liquidating.

* * *

Other examples of our self-liquidating American ideals arise from our success in building a high standard of living, from our efforts to bring the best material things to everybody. "Every man a King"—Huey Long's extravagant slogan—is not far from the sober American hope. When before has a nation set itself the ideal of bringing to every citizen the delights of advanced technology?

I will offer two commonplace examples of how we have tended to be frustrated by our remarkable success in approaching this ideal.

1. *A Wilderness Holiday for Everybody: the Problem of our National Parks.* There is no more distinctive or more successful American institution than our National Parks. The National Park Service, within the Department of Interior, has demonstrated an efficiency, an imagination, and a democratic largeness of spirit to inspire all of us. Yet, despite their best efforts, and even because of their brilliant success, we face here again the troublesome paradox.

A purpose of our National Parks, beginning with the establishment of Yellowstone National Park in 1872, has been to preserve our wilderness for the benefit of all the American people. Rocky Mountain National Park, Grand Teton National Park, Glacier National Park, Yellowstone, and Yosemite, among others, aim to make accessible to all Americans the delights of the pristine continent. Our National Parks now comprise over fifteen million acres and receive some fifty-four million visitors each year. Their reach to the American public would have been impossible, of course, without the American Standard of Living, which includes the improvement and diffusion of the automobile, an unexcelled network of highways, and a high standard of leisure, with regular and extensive paid vacations.

The National Parks, themselves part of the American Standard of Living, have made it possible to democratize the wilderness. An American, then, does not need to be wealthy, to own a large estate, or to afford a retinue of servants to reach and enjoy thousands of acres of the most remote, most unspoiled, and most spectacular landscapes in the nation.

But, as Robert Cahn of *The Christian Science Monitor* has asked, "Will success spoil the national parks?" Our wilderness acres, simply because they are so attractive and so accessible, have begun to become traffic jams. Living conditions in the campsites of Yosemite Valley and around Lake Yellowstone—with laundry lines hanging from tent to tent and one camper unwittingly putting his elbow in his neighbor's soup—begin to resemble the congested cities from which these campers have fled. In 1967, for example, serious crimes in National Parks rose 67 percent, compared with a 16 percent rise in the crime rate in American cities.

The democratization of the automobile and the democratization of the wilderness countryside threaten to destroy the very landscapes that we want everybody to have access to. Is a wilderness holiday for all Americans a self-liquidating ideal?

2. *The Democracy of Things: From Model T to the Annual Model.* Henry Ford's dream was to make a new and better kind of family horse—a car which everybody could afford and which would last forever. Essential to his plan, of course, was perfecting his Model T. Although he was experimental in developing his car, he believed that once the design was fixed, the object was simply to find ways to make it by the millions.

It was essential to his ideal that all the cars should be alike. As he saw it, mass production (what he called "the democratization of the automobile") required standardization, and standardization meant turning out a single uniform product. "The way to make automobiles," Henry Ford explained in 1903, "is to make one automobile like another automobile, to make them all alike, to make them come through the factory just alike; just as one pin is like another pin when it comes from a pin factory, or one match is like another when it comes from a match factory."

To Ford this meant finding ways to turn out millions of Model T's. He was confident that he could succeed. In 1909 a friend warned Ford that the automobile would create a "social problem" by frightening all the horses on the highway. "No, my friend," Ford replied, "you're mistaken. I'm not creating a social problem at all. I am going to democratize the automobile. When I'm through everybody will be able to afford one, and about everyone will have one. The horse will have disappeared from our highways, the automobile will be taken for granted, and there won't be any problem."

Toward this end Ford focused his efforts on making his car as cheap as possible, making repairs inexpensive and easy. He continued to believe it was his mission to mass-produce copies of the same durable product. In 1922 he still insisted:

> We cannot conceive how to serve the consumer unless we make for him something that, as far as we can provide, will last forever. We want to construct some kind of machine that will last forever. It does not please us to have a buyer's car wear out or become obsolete. We want the man who buys one of our products never to have to buy another. We never make an improvement that renders any previous model obsolete. The parts of a specific model are not only interchangeable with similar parts on all other cars of that model, but they are interchangeable with similar parts on all the cars that we have turned out.

He meant what he said, and he had the power to make his dream come true.

Ford had begun producing his Model T in 1908. On May 27, 1927, the fifteen-millionth Model T was produced. And in that year, the number of Model T's still registered (and therefore still presumably on the road) came to 11,325,521. But the Model T was in trouble.

By 1920, Henry Ford's success in democratizing the automobile, in building an inexpensive car that would last forever, had produced a vast secondhand car market. Dealers faced a new kind of competition, no longer from the horse but from the millions of still-usable used Fords. At the same time, the American buying public was stirred by a rising standard of living, by rising expectations (encouraged, incidentally, by Ford's $5-a-day wage which he hoped would make it possible for still more workers to buy Fords), and by a love of speed and a love of newness. They demanded something new.

But Henry Ford's spectacular success was in producing a static model. The problems of style and consumer taste had hardly occurred to him. He was a genius at production. And with the help of his own brilliant staff, aided by the pioneer factory designer Albert Kahn and others, he had developed the assembly line and so had taken a giant step forward in elaborating the mass production which Eli Whitney had pioneered a century before.

Ironically, his faith in the Model T was an Old World faith. His belief in the perfectible product rather than the novel product, his insistence on craftsmanship and function rather than on consumer appeal eventually left him behind. His genius had heralded a new age beyond his imaginings—and not at all to his taste.

This spirit of the new age was expressed in what Charles K. Kettering and Allan Orth in 1932 called "the new necessity." "We cannot reasonably expect to continue to make the same thing over and over," they predicted. "The simplest way to assure safe production is to keep changing the product—the market for new things is infinitely elastic. . . . One of the fundamental purposes of research is to foster a healthy dissatisfaction." The leader toward the new ideal was Alfred P. Sloan, Jr., who shifted the point of view from the maker to the buyer. After Sloan went to General Motors, he developed a new and characteristically American institution. It is so familiar now that we hardly think of it as an institution. This was the annual model.

The spirit and purpose of the annual model were, of course, quite the opposite of those of Ford and his Model T. "The great problem of the future," Sloan wrote to Lawrence P. Fisher (of Fisher Body) on September 9, 1927, "is to have our cars different from each other and different from year to year." The annual model, then, was part of a purposeful, planned program. And it was based on creating expectations of marvelous, if usually vague, novelties-always-to-come.

Sloan and his able collaborators at General Motors set up a special new styling department, which soon employed over fourteen hundred people. General Motors showed a new concern for color, and even invented enticing, aphrodisiac names for old colors. Now for the first time the automobile designers included women. "It is not too much to say," Sloan explained, "that the 'laws' of the Paris dressmakers have come to be a factor in the automobile industry—and woe to the company which ignores them."

The invention of the annual model did, of course, create a host of new problems of planning and of production. How much novelty would the consumer tolerate? How to titillate and attract the buyer without frightening him by too much novelty too soon? The bulgy Buick of 1929 (nicknamed "the pregnant Buick"), which was an admirably functioning car but a disaster on the market, was, according to Sloan, the result of a design mistake of not over 1¾ inches in excess body curve.

* * *

The effort to democratize the automobile proved self-defeating —and illustrated the problem of self-liquidating ideals—in at least two other ways.

The ladder of consumption. When the Model T became cheap and reliable and almost universal, cheapness and reliability were no longer enough. To keep the automobile industry and General Motors flourishing, Sloan then devised what I would call a "ladder of consumption."

When Alfred P. Sloan, Jr., went to General Motors, the company was manufacturing numerous makes of cars. The makes had confused and overlapping markets. Sloan aimed to clarify the appeal of each General Motors make so that, for example, the Buick would plainly be a more desired car than a Chevrolet. He aimed to design a car for every purse, and to create a clear price gap between different makes. The gap, however, was not to be so great that many Chevrolet owners might not hope someday to be in the Buick class, or so that many Buick owners might not hope someday to be in the Cadillac class.

This ladder of consumption began to dominate production

plans. Starting with a price schedule, Sloan then had automobiles designed to fit the prices. This required a vast and unprecedented feat of coordination. Sloan aimed at what he called the "mass-class" market. And Sloan's annual model (with the accompanying ladder of consumption) came closer than any earlier American institution to creating a visible and universal scheme of class distinction in the democratic United States of America.

The attenuation of novelty. By the late twentieth century the newness of new models had begun to consist in dubious minutiae such as concealed windshield wipers and multiple taillights. To devise every year an automobile (or rather a line of automobiles) so spectacularly different from their annual predecessors that buyers would rush to the latest model—this taxed the ingenuity of style-conscious designers and imaginative production engineers. They racked their brains. They ran the gamut of human and diabolical ingenuity. As a result, some Chevrolets looked more impressive than some Cadillacs. The economy luxury car and the luxurious economy car were beginning to be confused. The few manufacturers—mostly foreign makers like Volkswagen and Mercedes-Benz—who did not visibly change their annual product found that they had a new sales appeal.

We cannot help recalling Henry Ford's plaint: "Change is not always progress. . . . A fever of newness has been everywhere confused with the spirit of progress." Ford himself had not imagined that the frenetic quest for annual novelty might make novelty itself pall. The success of the static model (the Model T) had itself created a demand for an annual model. The annual model ideal was itself being dissolved by success. What next?

* * *

All these are only parables of a peculiarly interesting feature of the relation of our American society to what sociologists call our values. (I prefer the commoner word, "ideals.") Anyone can think of many other comparable stories. For example, we pursue the ideal of universalizing the opportunity to travel (which makes all places more alike, and hence less worth the trouble of going to), or the ideal of indefinitely increasing leisure (which leads people to try to keep life interesting by making leisure into work), or the ideal of indefinitely increasing the means and improving the modes of communication (which leads people to communicate more and more of what is not worth communicating).

Perhaps the explanation for self-liquidating ideals is inherent in the idea of increase (which inevitably becomes excess), which has been so popular here. Perhaps it is even inherent in the ideal of democracy itself, which aims at the very same time to fulfill each unique individual and to abolish distinctions among individuals. Perhaps it is only another example of the universal tendency of love to destroy its object.

But whatever the deeper, cosmic causes, the phenomenon is, I think, obvious enough. The fact of self-liquidating ideals may help us understand some of the peculiar recurrent strains, and some of the peculiar challenges, of life in the United States today.

Old World cultures have tended to be *cumulative*—and to think of themselves as cumulative. Aristocratic cultures tended to appeal to ancient orthodoxies. To believe in the glories of France is to believe in the possibility of adding up all the disparate, conflicting achievements of different epochs of French history. Their glory is to widen the spectrum of their achievements. This requires the adding up of opposites—adding the achievements of a revolutionary republic to those of an *ancien régime*.

Old World revolutions have tended to produce explicit orthodoxies which aim to define the Good Society for all time to come.

But, starting in a new world, as a new nation, we remain a *renovating* culture. The federal experimental ideal was to make it possible to try new objectives. One of the most remarkable, and least heralded, features of our Constitution was its explicit provision for amendments.

Our recurrent need for renewal gives us some peculiarly American headaches and opportunities. For in our history there seem to be natural cycles of self-flagellation. Perhaps such recurring cycles do not come from the total failure which the self-flagellants insist upon. Perhaps they mark another age when ideals which have been substantially achieved have begun to be liquidated.

Perhaps we are witnessing an age of the self-liquidation of the ideal of the American democracy of things. Perhaps more and more Americans, surfeited by objects, many of which actually remove the pungency of experience, now begin to see the ideal—the ideal of everybody having the newest things—being liquidated before their very eyes. Perhaps the annual model has begun to lose its charm. People who are so frequently and so insistently reminded of the supposedly desirable differences between indistinguishable products, who hear the blaring of trumpets to herald a revolutionary new cold-water detergent—these people begin to be cynical about all novelty.

When the getting of more and more comes to mean less and less, when more and more Americans begin to worry about the comparative merits of their increasingly elaborate automatic appliances performing ever-more-trivial functions, is it any wonder that more and more Americans become skeptical of the salvation that lies in wealth? Is it any wonder that more Americans should begin to rediscover the basic uses of American wealth at the lowest levels of consumption? Who can doubt the satisfaction of having things or giving things when they relieve starvation or undernourishment? The poverty-Americans (who in recent years have been given the new dignity of a recognized "minority group") are perhaps the only Americans for whom the American consumption ideal has not been self-liquidating. They have not participated in either its benefits or its frustrations. Is it surprising, then, that Americans nowadays show so striking and sometimes even so militant a concern for poverty in America?

A second characteristic and growing concern of our age is the focus on environment. The word has suddenly become so popular that people act as if the very concept of environment were a creature of the mid-twentieth century, as if there had been no "environment" before. May not our new concern for the environment perhaps be another symptom of our discovery that the ideal of everything for everybody is somehow self-liquidating? By concern for environment these days we mean, of course, a concern over pollution of water and air, over congestion and crime and urban disorder—in other words for the unpredicted and uncalculated costs of building a democracy of things. So we concern ourselves less with the exhilarating prospect of making more things for everybody than with an effort (in President Nixon's phrase) to "restore nature." And we aim to cancel out some of the consequences of making so many things for everybody.

In the perspective of our history it is not surprising that we should find ourselves seeking to redefine ideals for the American nation. Perhaps it would be more comfortable to live in an age when the dominant purposes were in full flood, when the hope for fulfillment had not been overshadowed by the frustrations of fulfillment.

But may not much of the peculiar greatness of our nation consist in its uncanny and versatile powers of renewal? Again and again our nation has shown an astonishing capacity for setting itself hitherto-unimagined ideals, and then proving that these ideals can be fulfilled. And then setting still others. The burden and the challenge of being an American consist in these recurrent tests of our power of renewal. Paradoxically, this is our most distinctive and most potent tradition.

HOW BELIEF IN THE EXISTENCE
OF AN AMERICAN THEORY HAS
MADE A THEORY SUPERFLUOUS

from THE GENIUS OF AMERICAN POLITICS, *1953*

T HE American must go outside his country and hear the voice of America to realize that his is one of the most spectacularly lopsided cultures in all history. The marvelous success and vitality of our institutions is equaled by the amazing poverty and inarticulateness of our theorizing about politics. No nation has ever believed more firmly that its political life was based on a perfect theory. And yet no nation has ever been less interested in political philosophy or produced less in the way of theory. If we can explain this paradox, we shall have a key to much that is characteristic—and much that is good—in our institutions.

In this chapter I shall attempt an explanation. I start from the notion that the two sides of the paradox explain each other. The very same facts which account for our belief that we actually possess a theory also explain why we have had little interest in political theories and have never bothered seriously to develop them.

For the belief that an explicit political theory is superfluous precisely because we already somehow possess a satisfactory equivalent, I propose the name "givenness." "Givenness" is the belief that values in America are in some way or other automatically defined: *given* by certain facts of geography or history peculiar to us. The notion, as I shall outline it in the present chapter, has three faces, which I shall describe in turn. First is the notion that we have received our values as a gift from the *past;* that the earliest settlers or Founding Fathers equipped our nation at its birth with a perfect and complete political theory, adequate to all our future needs.

The second is the notion that in America we receive values as a gift from the *present,* that our theory is always implicit in our institutions. This is the idea that the "American Way of Life" harbors an "American Way of Thought" which can do us for a political theory, even if we never make it explicit or never are in a position to confront ourselves with it. It is the notion that to Americans political theory never appears in its nakedness but always clothed in the peculiar American experience. We like to think that, from the shape of the living experience, we can guess what lies underneath and that such a guess is good enough—perhaps actually better than any naked theory. While according to the first axiom of "givenness" our values are the gift of our history, according to the second they are the gift of our landscape.

The third part of "givenness" is a belief which links these two axioms. It is a belief in the *continuity* or homogeneity of our history. It is the quality of our experience which makes us see our national past as an uninterrupted continuum of similar events, so that our past merges indistinguishably into our present. This sense of continuity is what makes it easy for us to accept the two first axioms at the same time: the idea of a preformed original theory given to us by the Founding Fathers, and the idea of an implicit theory always offered us by our present experience. Our feeling of continuity in our history makes it easy for us to see the Founding Fathers as our contemporaries. It induces us to draw heavily on the materials of our history, but always in a distinctly nonhistorical frame of mind.

I. Values Given by the Past: The Preformation Ideal

Now I shall begin by trying to explain what I have called the first axiom of "givenness": the idea that values are a gift from our past. Here we face our conscious attitude toward our past and toward our way of inheriting from it. This particular aspect of the "givenness" idea may be likened to the obsolete biological notion of "preformation." That is the idea that all parts of an organism preexist in perfect miniature in the seed. Biologists used to believe that if you could look at the seed of an apple under a strong enough microscope you would see in it a minute apple tree. Similarly, we seem still to believe that if we could understand the ideas of the earliest settlers—the Pilgrim Fathers or Founding Fathers—we would find in them no mere seventeenth- or eighteenth-century philosophy of government but the perfect embryo of the theory by which we now live. We believe, then, that the mature political ideals of the nation existed clearly conceived in the minds of our patriarchs. The notion is essentially static. It assumes that the values and theory of the nation were given once and for all in the very beginning.

What circumstances of American history have made such a view possible? The first is the obvious fact that, unlike western European countries, where the coming of the first white man is shrouded in prehistoric mist, civilization in the United States stems from people who came to the American continent at a definite period in recent history. For American political thought this fact has had the greatest significance. We have not found it necessary to invent an Aeneas, for we have had our William Bradford and John Winthrop, or, looking to a later period, our Benjamin Franklin and James Madison. We have needed no Virgil to make a myth of the first settlement of our land or the first founding of the Republic; the crude facts of history have been good enough.

The facts of our history have thus made it easy for us to assume that our national life, as distinguished from that of the European peoples who trace their identity to a remote era, has had a clear purpose. Life in America—appropriately called "The American Experiment"—has again and again been described as the test or the proof of values supposed to have been clearly in the minds of the Founders. While, as we shall see, the temper of much of our thought has been antihistorical, it is nevertheless true that we have leaned heavily on history to clarify our image of ourselves. Perhaps never before, except conceivably in the modern state of Israel, has a nation so firmly believed that it was founded on a full-blown theory and hence that it might understand itself by recapturing a particular period in its past.

This idea is actually so familiar, so deeply imbedded in our thinking, that we have never quite recognized it as a characteristic, much less a peculiarity, of our political thought. Nor have we become aware of its implications. "Four score and seven years ago," Lincoln said at Gettysburg in 1863, "our fathers brought forth on this continent, *a new nation, conceived in Liberty, and dedicated to the proposition that all men are created equal.*" We have forgotten that these words are less the statement of a political theory than an affirmation that an adequate theory already existed at the first epoch of national life. As we shall see in a later chapter, this belief itself helps account for the way in which the traditional, conservative, and inarticulate elements of our Revolution have been forgotten. A few slogans have been eagerly grasped as if they gave the essence of our history. While the conservative and legal aspect of our Revolution has remained hidden from popular view, schoolboys and popular orators (who seldom read beyond the preambles of legal documents) have conceived the Declaration of Independence as written primarily, if not exclusively, to vindicate man's equality and his "inalienable rights to life, liberty, and the pursuit of happiness."

Our determination to believe in a single logically complete theory as our heritage from the earliest settlers has thus actually kept us from grasping the *facts* of the early life of our nation. Strenuous efforts have been made to homogenize all the fathers of our country. A great deal of the popular misunderstanding of the New England Puritans, for example, can be traced to this desire. Tradition teaches us to treat the history of our nation from 1620 to 1789 as a series of labor pains, varying only in intensity. The Puritans, we are taught, came here for religious and political liberty; and the American Revolutionaries are supposed to have shown a pilgrim-like fervor and clarity of purpose.

If we compare our point of view with that of the historically conscious peoples of Europe, we shall begin to see some of its implications. The Europeans have, of course, had their interludes of nostalgia for some mythical heroic age, some Wagnerian Götterdämmerung. Mussolini sought to reincarnate the Roman Empire, Hitler to revive some prehistoric "Aryan" community. But such efforts in Europe have been spasmodic. Europeans have not with any continuity attributed to their nameless "earliest settlers" the mature ideals of their national life. In contrast, we have been consistently primitivistic. The brevity of our history has made this way of thinking easy. Yet that is not the whole story. We find it peculiarly congenial to claim possession of a perfect set of political ideas, especially when they have magical elusiveness and flexibility. Their mere existence seems to relieve us of an unwelcome task.

Our firm belief in a perfectly preformed theory helps us understand many things about ourselves. In particular, it helps us see how it has been that, while we in the United States have been unfertile in political theories, we have at the same time possessed an overweening sense of orthodoxy. The poverty of later theorizing has encouraged appeal to what we like to believe went before. In building an orthodoxy from sparse materials, of necessity we have left the penumbra of heresy vague. The inarticulate character of American political theory has thus actually facilitated heresy-hunts and tended to make them indiscriminate. The heresy-hunts which come at periods of national fear—the Alien and Sedition Acts of the age of the French Revolution, the Palmer raids of the age of the Russian Revolution, and similar activities of more recent times—are directed not so much against acts of espionage as against acts of irreverence toward that orthodox American creed, believed to have been born with the nation itself.

Among the factors which have induced us to presuppose an orthodoxy, to construct what I have called a "preformation" theory, none has been more important than the heterogeneous character of our population. Our immigrants, who have often been the outcasts, the déclassés, and the persecuted of their native countries, are understandably anxious to become part of a new national life. Hence they are eager to believe that they can find here a simplicity of theory lacking in the countries from which they came. Immigrants, often stupidly blamed for breeding "subversive" or "un-American" ideas, have as much as any other group frenetically sought a "pure" American doctrine. Where else has there been such a naïve sense of political orthodoxy? Who would think of using the word "un-Italian" or "un-French" as we use the word "un-American"?

The fact that we have had a written constitution, and even our special way of interpreting it, has contributed to the "preformation" notion. Changes in our policy or our institutions are read back into the ideas, and sometimes into the very words, of the Founding Fathers. Everybody knows that this had made of our federal Constitution an "unwritten" document. What is more significant is the way in which we have justified the adaptation of the document to current needs: by attributing clarity, comprehensiveness, and a kind of mystical foresight to the social theory of the founders. In Great Britain, where there is an "unwritten" constitution in a very different sense, constitutional theory has taken for granted the *gradual* formulation of a theory of society. No sensible Briton would say that his history is the unfolding of the truths implicit in Magna Charta and the Bill of Rights. Such documents are seen as only single steps in a continuing process of definition.

The difference is expressed in the attitudes of the highest courts in the two countries. In Great Britain the highest court of appeal, the House of Lords, has gradually come to the conclusion that it must be governed by its own earlier decisions. When the House of Lords decides a point of the constitution, it is thus frankly developing the constitution, and it must follow the line which it has previously taken, until the legislature marks out another. Not so in the United States. Our Supreme Court considers itself free to overrule its earlier decisions, to discover, that is, that the constitution which it is interpreting really has all along had a different meaning from what had been supposed.

The American view is actually closer to the British view during the Middle Ages, when the very idea of legislation was in its infancy and when each generation believed that it could do little more than increase its knowledge of the customs which already existed. In the United States, therefore, we see the strange fact that the more flexible we have made our constitution, the more rigid and unexperimental we have made our political theory. We are haunted by a fear that capricious changes in theory might imperil our institutions. This is our kind of conservatism.

Our theory of society is thus conceived as a kind of exoskeleton, like the shell of the lobster. We think of ourselves as growing *into*

our skeleton, filling it out with the experience and resources of recent ages. But we always suppose that the outlines were rigidly
drawn in the beginning. Our mission, then, is simply to demonstrate
the truth—or rather the workability—of the original theory. This
belief in a perfect original doctrine, one of the main qualities of
which is practicality, may help us understand that unique combination of empiricism and idealism which has characterized American
political life.

If we turn from our constitution to our political parties, we observe the same point of view. The authority of a particular past generation implies the impotence of later generations to reconstruct the
theoretical bases of our national life. Today it is still taken for
granted that the proper arena of controversy was marked off once
and for all in the late eighteenth century: we are either Jeffersonians
or Hamiltonians.

In no other country has the hagiography of politics been more
important. The lives of our national saints have remained vivid and
contemporary for us. In no other country—except perhaps in Soviet
Russia, where people are called Marxists, Leninists, or Trotskyites—
do statesmen so intimately embrace the image of early national
heroes. Would an Englishman call himself a Walpolean or a Pittite?
Yet in the United States the very names of our political parties—
Republican and Democratic—are borrowed from the early age of
our national life. This remarkable persistence of early labels offers
the sharpest contrast to what we see in continental western Europe.
There new parties—and new party labels—come and go with the
seasons, and most of the parties, with double- or triple-barreled
names, draw on the novel vocabulary of the nineteenth and twentieth centuries. It is a commonplace that no fundamental theoretical
difference separates our American political parties. What need has
either party for an explicit political theory when both must be
spokesmen of the *original* American doctrine on which the nation
was founded?

Political theory has been little studied in the United States. For
example, departments of political science in many of our universities
show more interest in almost anything else than in political theory.

This, too, can be explained in part by the limitations imposed by the "preformation" point of view. If our nation in the beginning was actually founded on an adequate and sufficiently explicit theory revealed at one time, later theorists can have only the minor task of exegesis, of explaining the sacred texts. Constitutional history can, and in many ways has, become a substitute for political theory.

The unique role which our national past has played in constructing our image of ourselves and our standards for American life has made us hypersensitive about our own history. Because we have searched it for the substance of a political philosophy, we have been inclined to exaggerate its contemporary relevance. When Charles A. Beard in his *Economic Interpretation of the Constitution* in 1913 showed that members of the Constitutional Convention had a financial interest in the establishment of a stable federal government, he scandalized respectable scholars. Leaders of opinion, like Nicholas Murray Butler, thought the book a wholesale attack on the American creed. The explosive import of such a book would have been impossible, had not the facts of political history already been elevated into an axiom of political philosophy. Any innuendo against the motives of the Founding Fathers was therefore seen as an implied attack on the American way of life. The British have never been so disturbed by the suggestion that the barons had a personal interest in extracting from King John the concessions written into Magna Charta.

During the 1930's, when the Communist party made a serious effort to appear a native American growth (using the slogan "Communism Is Twentieth-Century Americanism"), it too sought to reinterpret the American past. It argued that the American Revolution had really been a class war and not merely a colonial rebellion. The radical attack on the doctrine of judicial review, which then seemed to obstruct change in our institutions, was made by way of a labored two-volume historical treatise, Louis Boudin's *Government by Judiciary*. He sought to prove that the Founding Fathers had never intended the Supreme Court to have the power to declare federal laws unconstitutional.

The lives of our great men have played a peculiarly large role in our attempt at self-definition. Some of our best historical talent has in recent years gone into biography: Beveridge's *Marshall*, Van Doren's *Franklin*, Malone's *Jefferson*, and Freeman's *Washington*. We have also the long filial tradition of Sparks's or Weems's or Marshall's *Washington* or Wirt's *Patrick Henry*. Such works are a kind of hybrid between what the lives of the saints or of the Church Fathers are for Catholics and what the lives of gods and goddesses were for the ancient Greeks. For us, biographies have taken on a special importance, precisely because we have had so little dogmatic writing. And our national history thus has a primary significance for Americans which is without parallel in modern nations. The quest for the meaning of our political life has been carried on through historical rather than philosophical channels.

It is not surprising, then, that much of our self-criticism has taken the form of historical reinterpretation. In periods of disillusionment we have expressed ourselves not so much in new philosophies, in dogmas of dictatorship or existentialism, as in earnest, if sometimes tortured, reinterpretations of the American past. In the 1920's and 1930's, for example, people who would not have looked twice at a revolutionary political theory or a nihilist metaphysic eagerly read W. E. Woodward's *New American History*, James Truslow Adams' *Founding of New England*, Edgar Lee Masters' *Lincoln*, or the numerous other iconoclastic works about Washington or Grant. The sharpest criticisms of contemporary America were the works of Sinclair Lewis and H. L. Mencken, which were hardly theoretical.

The mystic rigidity of our "preformation" theory has been consistent with great flexibility in dealing with practical problems. Confident that the wisdom of the Founding Fathers somehow made provision for all future emergencies, we have not felt bound to limit our experiments to those which we could justify with theories in advance. In the last century or so, whenever the citizens of continental western Europe have found themselves in desperate circumstances, they have had to choose among political parties, each of which was committed to a particular theoretical foundation for its whole program—"monarchist," "liberal," "catholic," "socialist," "fascist," or "communist." This has not been the case in the United States. Not even during the Civil War: historians still argue over what, if any, political theory Lincoln represented. In the crisis which followed the great depression, when Franklin D. Roosevelt announced his program for saving the American economy, he did not promise to implement a theory. Rather, he declared frankly that he would try one thing after another and would keep trying until a cure was found. "The country demands bold, persistent experimentation. It is common sense to take a method and try it: if it fails, admit it frankly and try another." Neither he nor his listeners doubted that whatever solution, within the limits of common-law liberties, might prove successful would also prove to have been within the prevision of the Founding Fathers. The people balked only when a proposal—like the Court-packing plan—seemed to imperil the independence of the judiciary, an ancient principle of the common law.

On second thought, it is not surprising that we who have been most sure of the basic structure of our political life should also have been most prodigal of legislation. Two remarkable and complementary facts are that the amendments to our federal Constitution have been so few (only twelve in addition to the first ten amendments, or bill of rights) during the last century and a half, and that at the same time our legal experiments have been so numerous. For us it is enough to recommend a piece of legislation if a considerable number of people want it, if there is no loud opposition, and if there seems a reasonable chance that it might reduce some present evil. Our laws have been abundant and ephemeral as the flies of summer. Conservatism about our basic institutions, and the faith that they will be vindicated in the national experience, have made us less fearful of minor legislation.

Our mystic belief in the "preformed" national theory has thus restrained theoretical vagaries without preventing particular experiments. Without having ever intended it, we have thus stumbled on an evolutionary approach to institutions. Yet at the same time we have taken up a kind of social Freudianism; for the "preformation" concept of values implies belief that the childhood years of a nation's history are crucial for the formation of its character. More than that, we have given the national past a peculiarly normative significance. Small wonder that we should seem complacent, if we judge ourselves

by whether we are true to our own character. Our American past and
the theories of politics which it is thought to imply, have become the
yardstick against which national life is measured. This is the deeper
meaning of the criterion of "Americanism" which is so familiar in
the United States and sounds so strange to European ears.

II. VALUES GIVEN BY THE LANDSCAPE: THE LAND OF THE FREE

The notion of "givenness," as I have explained, has three aspects
which I shall discuss in this chapter. The first which I have been
dealing with until now was the axiom that our values were the gift of
our past, and actually of a particular period in the past. The second,
to which I shall now turn, is that our values and our theory are the
gift of the present: not of any particular men in the seventeenth and
eighteenth centuries, but of the peculiarly fortunate conditions of
life in America.

The first axiom is the one which I have just described and called
by the name of the "preformation" ideal. It is the notion that, in the
beginning and once and for all, the Founding Fathers of the nation
gave us a political theory, a scheme of values, and a philosophy of
government. As we have seen, it is an ideal, a static kind of "givenness"—a gift of orthodoxy, the gift of the past.

The second axiom is similar, in that it, too, is an excuse or a reason for not philosophizing. It is the notion that a scheme of values is
given, not by traditions, theories, books, and institutions, but by present experience. It is the notion that our theory of life is embodied in
our way of life and need not be separated from it, that our values are
given by our condition. If this second part of the idea of "givenness"
seems, in strict logic, contradictory to the first, from the point of
view of the individual believer it is actually complementary. For,
while the first axiom is ideal and static in its emphasis, the second is
practical and dynamic. "Preformation" means that the theory of
community was given, once and for all, in the beginning; the second
sense of "givenness" means that the theory of community is perpetually being given and ever anew.

Taken together with the idea of preformation, this second

"givenness" makes an amazingly comprehensive set of attitudes. The American is thus prepared to find in *all* experience—in his history and his geography, in his past and his present—proof for his conviction that he is equipped with a hierarchy of values, a political theory. Both axioms together encourage us to think that we need not invent a political theory because we already possess one. The idea of "givenness" as a whole is, then, both as idealistic as a prophet's vision and as hardheaded as common sense.

This second face of "givenness" is at once much simpler and much more vague than the concept of preformation. It is simply the notion that values are implicit in the American experience. The idea that the American landscape is a giver of values is, of course, old and familiar. It has long been believed that in America the community values would not have to be sought through books, traditions, the messianic vision of prophets, or the speculative schemes of philosophers but would somehow be the gift of the continent itself.

We Americans have always been much impressed by the simple fact that we are children of a brave New World. Even from the earliest settlements, but especially since the formative era of the late eighteenth and early nineteenth centuries, we have looked upon ourselves as the lucky beneficiaries of an especially happy environment. In the pamphlets which Puritans wrote in the seventeenth century to attract their brethren to New England, we read fantastic tales of the abundance of crops and game, the magic of the air and water; how life on the new continent cured consumption, gout, and all sorts of fevers; how the old became young, the young became vigorous, and barren women suddenly bore children. In the very same pamphlet we can read how the wilderness would toughen the effete and how the wealth of this unexploited paradise would enrich the impoverished.

The myth was no less alive two centuries later, when Paul Bunyan, the giant woodsman of the forest frontier (as James Stevens describes him),

> felt amazed beyond words that the simple fact of entering Real America and becoming a Real American could make him feel so exalted, so pure, so noble, so good. And an in-

domitable conquering spirit had come to him also. He now felt that he could whip his weight in wildcats, that he could pull the clouds out of the sky, or chew up stones, or tell the whole world anything.

"Since becoming a Real American," roared Paul Bunyan, "I can look any man straight in the eye and tell him to go to hell! If I could meet a man of my own size, I'd prove this instantly. We may find such a man and celebrate our naturalization in a Real American manner. We shall see. Yay, Babe!"

Then the two great Real Americans leaped over the Border. Freedom and Inspiration and Uplift were in the very air of this country, and Babe and Paul Bunyan got more noble feelings in every breath (*Paul Bunyan* [New York, 1948], pp. 27 ff.).

We have been told again and again, with the metaphorical precision of poetry, that the United States is the *land* of the free. Independence, equality, and liberty, we like to believe, are breathed in with our very air. No nation has been readier to identify its values with the peculiar conditions of its landscape: we believe in *American* equality, *American* liberty, *American* democracy, or, in sum, the *American* way of life.

Our belief in the mystical power of our land has in this roundabout way nourished an empirical point of view; and a naturalistic approach to values has thus, in the United States, been bound up with patriotism itself. What the Europeans have seen as the gift of the past, Americans have seen as the gift of the present. What the European thinks he must learn from books, museums, and churches, from his culture and its monuments, the American thinks he can get from contemporary life, from seizing peculiarly American opportunities.

It is surely no accident that the most influential, if not the only significant, general interpretation of our history has been that of Frederick Jackson Turner. He found the special virtues of our institutions and of our national character in the uniquely recurrent conditions of our frontier. Turner translated Paul Bunyan into the language of sociology:

> Behind institutions, behind constitutional forms and modifications, lie the vital forces that call these organs into life and shape them to meet changing conditions. . . . All peoples show development. . . . But in the case of the United States we have a different phenomenon. . . . This perennial rebirth, this fluidity of American life, this expansion westward with its new opportunities, its continuous touch with the simplicity of primitive society, furnish the forces dominating American character (pp. 2 ff.).
>
> The result is that to the frontier the American intellect owes its striking characteristics. That coarseness and strength combined with acuteness and inquisitiveness; that practical, inventive turn of mind, quick to find expedients; that masterful grasp of material things, lacking in the artistic but powerful to effect great ends; that restless, nervous energy; that dominant individualism, working for good and for evil, and withal that buoyancy and exuberance which comes with freedom—these are traits of the frontier, or traits called out elsewhere because of the existence of the frontier (*The Frontier in American History* [New York, 1920], p. 37).

These words—indeed, much of the work of Turner and his followers—are actually a theory to justify the absence of an American political theory.

How can we explain the origin, growth, and vitality of this idea of "givenness" in America? The most obvious and some of the most important explanations have escaped us for their very obviousness; to become aware of them it may be necessary to go to Europe, where some of us begin to discover America.

One fact which becomes increasingly difficult to communicate to the urban American, but which the automobile and our national parks have kept alive for some of us, is the remarkable grandeur of the American continent. Even for the early Puritan settlers the forest which hid savage arrows had a fascination. The magic of the land is a leitmotif throughout the eighteenth and nineteenth centuries. We hear it, for example, in Jefferson's ecstatic description of the confluence of the Potomac and the Shenandoah rivers; in Lewis and Clark's account of the far west; in the vivid pages of Francis Parkman's *Oregon Trail;* and in a thousand other places. It is echoed in the numberless travel-books and diaries of those men and women who left the comfortable and dingy metropolises of the Atlantic seaboard to explore the Rocky Mountains, the prairies, or the deserts. Their simple emotions should not be underestimated, nor should we interpret them with too much subtlety. It is misleading to associate too closely the appeal of virgin America with the bookish romanticism of European belles-lettres. The unspoiled grandeur of America helped men believe that here the Giver of values spoke to man more directly—in the language of experience rather than in that of books or monuments.

Our immigrant character has been an incentive toward this point of view. The United States has, of course, been peopled at widely distant times and for the most diverse reasons. Some came because they were Protestants, others because they were Catholics, still others because they were Jews; some because they were monarchists, others because they were opposed to monarchy. We have been too well aware of this diversity to try to seek our common values in our original cultures. It is true, as I shall explain in my fifth chapter, that we have developed a kind of generalized Christianity, which is probably what we mean by the "In God We Trust" on our coins. We have looked anxiously for some common faith. A few writers, like Louis Adamic, have even tried to make the motleyness itself a scheme of values: to make the patchwork seem the pattern. But the readiest solution, a necessary solution, perhaps the only possible solution for us, has been to assume, in the immigrant's own phrase, that ours is a "golden land," that values spring from our common ground. If American ideals are not in books or in the blood but in the air, then they are readily acquired; actually, it is almost impossible for an immigrant to avoid acquiring them. He is not required to learn a philosophy so much as to rid his lungs of the air of Europe.

The very commonness of American values has seemed their proof: they have come directly from the hand of God and from the soil of the continent. This attitude helps explain why the martyr (at least the *secular* martyr) has not been attractive to us. In the accurate words of our popular song, "The Best Things in Life Are Free." Men in America have had to struggle against nature, against wild Indians, high mountains, arid deserts, against space itself. But these struggles have seemed required to make the continent livable or comfortable, not to make our society good. In Europe, on the other hand, the liberal could not make the plant of liberty grow without first cutting out the weeds of tyranny; and he took that for his task. But the American has preened himself on his good sense in making *his* home where liberty is the natural growth. Voltaire declared, "Where liberty is not, there is my home." This was a fitting and thoroughly un-American reply to Franklin's "Where liberty dwells, there is my country."

The character of our national heroes bears witness to our belief in "givenness," our preference for the man who seizes his God-given opportunities over him who pursues a great private vision. Perhaps never before has there been such a thorough identification of normality and virtue. A "red-blooded" American must be a virtuous American; and nearly all our national heroes have been red-blooded, outdoor types who might have made the varsity team. Our ideal is at the opposite pole from that of a German Superman or an irredentist agitator in his garret. We admire not the monstrous but the normal, not the herald of a new age but the embodiment of his own. In the language of John Dewey, he is the well-adjusted man; in the language of Arthur Miller's salesman, Willy Loman, he is the man who is not merely liked but *well*-liked. Our national heroes have not been erratic geniuses like Michelangelo or Cromwell or Napoleon but rather men like Washington and Jackson and Lincoln, who possessed the commonplace virtues to an extraordinary degree.

III. THE CONTINUITY OF AMERICAN HISTORY

The third part of the idea of "givenness," as I have said, is actually a
kind of link between the two axioms which I have already described:
the notion that we have an ideal given in a particular period in the
past (what I have called the idea of "preformation") and the idea that
the theory of American life is always being given anew in the present,
that values are implicit in the American experience. The third aspect
to which I now turn helps us understand how we can at once appeal
to the past and yet be fervently unhistorical in our approach to it.

By this I mean the remarkable continuity or homogeneity of
American history. To grasp it, we must at the outset discard a European cliché about us, namely, that ours is a land without continuity
or tradition, while in Europe man feels close to his ancestors. The
truth of the matter is that anyone who goes to Europe nowadays
cannot fail to be impressed with the amazing, the unique, continuity
of American history and, in sharp contrast, the *dis*continuity of
European history.

This is true in several senses. In the first place, there is the obvious fact that the recent history of Europe has seen violent oscilla-
tions of regime. Each new regime has taken on itself a task of
historical amnesia: the fascists trying to deny their democratic past,
the democrats trying to deny their fascist past, etc. But there is a
subtler way in which the landscape and monuments which surround
the European tend to impress on him the various possibilities of life
in his place, while what the American sees confirms his sense of
"givenness," his belief in the normality, if not the inevitability, of the
particular institutions which he has evolved. "For the American
tourist," Aldous Huxley has shrewdly observed, "the greatest charm
of foreign travel is the very high ratio of European history to European geography. Conversely, for the European, who has come to
feel the oppressive weight of a doubtless splendid, but often fatal
past, the greatest charm of travel in the New World is the high ratio
of its geography to its history."

Let me explain. I have recently been abroad, where I spent the
better part of a year in Italy. My impressions there sharpened that

contrast which I have been describing between the American and the European image of the past. The first church I visited was the Capella Palatina in Palermo, where Christian mosaics of the twelfth century are surmounted by a ceiling of Moslem craftsmanship. Throughout Sicily one comes upon pagan temples on the foundations of which rose churches, in the Middle Ages transformed into mosques, later again to be used as Christian chapels.

The capitals of Europe are rich in evidence of the unpredictability of human history. Of all cities in the world, Rome is perhaps richest in such evidence: the retaining walls which early Romans built to protect the road up the Palatine are made of fragments stolen from Greek and North African temples; columns standing in the Forum bear witness not only to ancient Roman skill but also to the shattered schemes of the conquered peoples from whom they were taken. The fate which the Romans brought upon their predecessors was later, of course, visited upon Rome herself by the barbarians and Christians, who made the Forum into their stone-quarry. The Colosseum, where Christians and Jews were once slaughtered to amuse the mob, is now divided by partitions which later Christians erected to support the stage of their Passion Play. Its walls are pocked by holes from which barbarian and Christian soldiers extracted iron for their weapons in the Middle Ages; large segments were removed by popes to add splendor to their churches. The magnificent roads which Julius Caesar built for his legions are traveled by little automobiles which, with appropriate irony, borrow their name from "Mickey Mouse"—in Italian, "Topolino."

In Europe one need not be an archeologist or a philosopher to see that over the centuries many different kinds of life are possible in the same place and for the same people. Who can decide which, if any of these, is "normal" for Italy? It is hardly surprising, then, that the people of Europe have not found it easy to believe that their values are given by their landscape. They look to ideology to help them choose among alternatives.

In the United States, of course, we see no Colosseum, no Capella Palatina, no ancient roads. The effect of this simple fact on our aesthetic sense, though much talked of, is probably less signifi-

cant than on our sense of history and our approach to values. We see
very few monuments to the uncertainties, the motley possibilities, of
history or, for that matter, to the rise and fall of grand theories of
society. Our main public buildings were erected for much the same
purpose for which they are now being used. The Congress of the
United States is still housed in the first building expressly constructed for that purpose. Although the White House, like the Capitol, was gutted by fire during the War of 1812, it, too, was soon
rebuilt on the same spot and to a similar design; in 1952 another
restoration was completed. Our rural landscape, with a few scattered
exceptions—the decayed plantation mansions of the South, the
manor houses of upstate New York, and the missions of Florida and
California—teaches us very little of the fortunes of history. Even our
archeology is republican, designed to make the past contemporary;
you can spend a vacation at Colonial Williamsburg.

The impression which the American has as he looks about him is
one of the inevitability of the particular institutions, the particular
kind of society in which he lives. The kind of acceptance of institutions as proper to their time and place which tyrants have labored in
vain to produce has in the United States been the result of the accidents of history. The limitations of our history have perhaps confined our philosophical imagination; but they have at the same time
confirmed our sense of the continuity of our past and made the definitions of philosophers seem less urgent. We Americans are reared
with a feeling for the unity of our history and an unprecedented belief in the normality of our kind of life to our place on earth.

We have just been observing that our history has had a continuity: that is, that the same political institutions have persisted
throughout our whole national career and therefore have acquired a
certain appearance of normality and inevitableness. No less important is the converse of this fact, namely, that our history has *not* been
*dis*continuous, has not been punctuated by the kind of internal struggles which have marked the history of most of the countries of western Europe, and which have fed their awareness that society is
shaped by men. Two apparent exceptions to this observation are the
American Revolution and the Civil War, with which I shall deal in

later chapters. The important fact is what De Tocqueville observed a century ago, namely, that America somehow has reaped the fruits of the long democratic revolution in Europe "without having had the revolution itself." This was but another way of saying that the prize for which Europeans would have to shed blood would seem the free native birthright of Americans.

During these last one hundred and seventy-five years the history of the United States has thus had a unity and coherence unknown in Europe. Many factors—our geographical isolation, our special opportunities for expansion and exploitation within our own borders, and our remoteness from Europe—have, of course, contributed. Even our American Civil War, which shook us deeply and was one of the bloodiest wars anywhere in the century, can be understood with scant reference to the ideologies then sweeping Europe: to the intellectual background of 1848, of the Risorgimento, of the Paris Commune. It was not properly a counterpart of European struggles of the period, nor really an exception to the domestic continuity of our history.

But, whatever the causes, the winds of dogma and the gusts of revolution which during the last century and a half have blown violently over western Europe, making France, Italy, Germany, and now perhaps even England testing grounds for panaceas, have not ruffled our intellectual climate. The United States, with a kind of obstinate provincialism, has enjoyed relatively calm weather. While European politics became a kaleidoscope, political life in the United States has seemed to remain a window through which we can look at the life envisaged by our patriarchs. The hills and valleys of European history in the nineteenth century have had no real counterpart in the history of the United States. Because our road has been relatively smooth, we have easily believed that we have trod no historical road at all. We seem the direct beneficiaries of our climate, our soil, and our mineral wealth.

OUR CONSCIENCE-WRACKED
NATION

from CLEOPATRA'S NOSE, *1994*

EVERYBODY KNOWS THAT the founders of New England came
here for reasons of conscience. They aimed to "purify" Old
World institutions and set up a spiritually pure City upon a
Hill. But the European stereotype since the early nineteenth century
has depicted the United States as a nation of crass materialists. The
word "businessman" in its modern commercial sense, American in
origin, came into use around 1830. Alexis de Tocqueville, in the
most influential work ever published about the United States, observed that "the love of wealth is . . . to be traced, as either a principal
or accessory motive, at the bottom of all the Americans do; this gives
to all their passions a sort of family likeness." Travelers, from
Charles Dickens to Frances Trollope, documented the portrait of
the American philistine. This portrait has, of course, been reinforced
by Americans themselves, notoriously in Calvin Coolidge's quip that
"the chief business of the American people is business."

This complacent cliché has made it difficult for interested spectators abroad to understand the sources of some of the United
States' most troublesome domestic problems in the late twentieth
century. These do not come at all from American materialism, questions of cost-effectiveness, or the national deficit. "There is in most
Americans," the prescient Justice Louis Brandeis observed in 1953,
"some spark of idealism, which can be fanned into a flame. It takes

sometimes a divining rod to find what it is; but when found, and that means often, when disclosed to the owners, the results are often extraordinary."

Today we see how those sparks of idealism have been fanned into flame, in a startling renaissance of the New England conscience. In the United States, many of our most widely debated public issues are self-created. We are a people haunted by all past injustices and fears of future injustice. And against these evils we seem driven to find legislative panaceas.

Their robust conscience, the wits tell us, never prevented the early New Englanders from doing whatever they wanted to do. It just kept them from enjoying it. In later centuries the rise of liberal democratic government and majority rule, and the growth of a literate citizenry and a mass-circulation press produced a new arbiter for the conscience—a new voice for God. *Vox populi, vox dei.* And in the United States the Divine Conscience has long since been replaced by the Public Conscience, a force that increasingly haunts and dominates our lives.

Newsmen and politicians in the United States today are overwhelmed by issues of conscience. How can we devise laws, create watchdog commissions, or arouse public outrage to right ancient wrongs that violate our civic conscience? On one sample day (May 19, 1993), the front page of *The Washington Post* featured the following items: a proposed compromise on how to allow homosexuals to serve openly in the military; a young black woman chosen to serve as poet laureate; the first black lawyer with ties to the city nominated for U.S. district attorney; a task-force recommendation that colleges offer more teams and scholarships for women in athletics; and "Health Plan Threatened by Abortion Coverage." The front page of *The New York Times* for the same day featured an opinion poll showing that blacks back Mayor David Dinkins but whites do not, and Hispanics are divided; how the recent voting for school-board members showed people "profoundly roiled" by teaching about sexuality and multiculturalism; an award of $400,000 damages to a City University professor and chairman of the Black Studies Department for his having been demoted for anti-Semitic remarks (expressing satisfaction, the professor called this a victory for "African people"); an illustrated article on the difficulties suffered "When Disabled Students Enter Regular Classrooms."

The Cases of Conscience that exacerbate American political life give no signs of abating in the near future. And these issues of conscience are not imaginary. On the contrary, they are rooted deep in past injustices: blacks enslaved; homosexuals scorned and criminalized; women deprived of opportunities for self-fulfillment; American Indians driven from their lands; handicapped persons denied employment. We Americans today reach out to explore and exploit the frontiers of conscience much as nineteenth-century Americans explored and exploited the physical resources of our vast continent.

Americans have become champions not only of the victims of the gross and conspicuous historic injustices like slavery, but of the victims of countless hidden injustices, like those traditionally suffered by the mentally and physically handicapped. For example, recent laws have not only required ease of access to public buildings and the reconstruction of curbs and sidewalks and access to buses for those confined to wheelchairs, but have mandated employment opportunities. Champions of children's rights have awakened the public to cases of child abuse, and even opened paths to lawsuits by children against their parents. Prosecutions for long-past sexual abuses, real or imagined, are sometimes supported by child witnesses of doubtful reliability. Perhaps the bitterest and most divisive issue in domestic politics—which threatens to give religion a new and menacing role in our civic life—is the issue of abortion. Conscience-stricken citizens cast this issue too in terms of the violation of the "rights" of the unborn. Other Americans, outraged at violations of the purity of the environment, are organized to champion the rights of all animal species to avoid extinction. The survival of the spotted owl and the wolf have thus become substantial political issues. And law-review articles have actually been written on the "rights" of trees.

* * *

No one can guess what might be the next Cases of Conscience to stir Americans' public passions. Many thought that the passage of the omnibus Civil Rights Act of 1964 banning racial discrimination in voting, jobs, and public accommodations was the climax of the rights movement. But they underestimated the force and reach of the New England conscience in the twentieth century. The Civil Rights Act proved to be only one symptom of what has become an almost pathological hypersensitivity. Recently this protection has been expanded to include penumbral rights—perilously vague and difficult to define—such as the rights of women (and men) not to be "sexually harassed." Who would have predicted that our New World culture of spectacular material successes would offer a melodrama of the sensitive conscience.

This new American moralism, this renaissance of conscience, has not been without effect on our culture and our intellectual and aesthetic standards. Our vocabulary has been revised and enlarged, presumably to favor every one of the groups that have become wards of our newly sensitized conscience. The word "Negro," with a long and respectable history, reinforced in the titles of scholarly journals and work by champions of racial equality, became suddenly taboo. For a while "black" was demanded, but it was soon displaced by the hyphenated "Afro-American," or the now-preferred "African-American." Some of us who have believed the glory of our nation has been our ability to encompass all comers as Americans are shocked to see any of our fellow citizens demand to be known as nothing but hyphenated Americans. We should recall Theodore Roosevelt's shrewd warning in 1915 that "the one absolutely certain way of bringing this nation to ruin, of preventing all possibility of its continuing to be a nation at all, would be to permit it to become a tangle of squabbling nationalities." While we seem to have escaped many Old World ills—religious and linguistic wars, hereditary class distinctions, ideological politics—some citizens seem on the way to making us a Balkan America.

Anyone at his peril would use the outmoded descriptive terms. These are called signs of "bigotry" in a citizen or a newspaper, and are death to a politician. For women, too, one must be scrupulous, as Ms. has become preferred by many as a substitute for Mrs. or Miss. The nomenclature of our First Lady, once a matter of little journalistic concern, has become a minor public issue with the insistent designation of our new First Lady as Hillary Rodham Clinton. "Handicapped" or "otherwise endowed" has become a required euphemism for once-familiar words—blind, deaf, dumb—and the wholly taboo "cripple." The clearly descriptive "homosexual" has been pushed aside by "gay" (first used in this new sense about 1935), which has now lost its wondrous poetic uses, bolstered by the newly coined and polemical "homophobe." In the United States we no longer have the "aged" or "elderly" but only "senior citizens." It may surprise friends abroad to learn that in the United States we have no "ignorant" citizens, but only the "culturally deprived" or "disadvantaged." Nor are there "beggars" here anymore, but only the "homeless." American Indians are no longer Indians but "Native Americans"—to the implicit disparagement of all the rest of us native Americans who were born here. Outrage has been expressed by some citizens of Washington, D.C., at the continued use of "Redskins" as the name of the city's football team. Formerly "exceptional" children were the unusually bright. Now the word gives dignity to those who are exceptional because of their handicaps.

"Ableism" the Smith College Office of Student Affairs in 1990 defined as "oppression of the differently abled, by the temporarily able." And "Lookism" is the sin of "characterizing people by their physical appearance. The belief that appearance is an indicator of a person's value; the construction of a standard for beauty/attractiveness; and oppression through stereotypes and generalizations of both those who do not fit that standard and those who do." But of course we must beware of anything we say in our English language, which one enthusiastic feminist has labeled "Manglish"—"the English language as it is used by men in the perpetuation of male supremacy." To respect female sensitivities, must the once respectable university group called a "seminar" be rechristened an "ovular"? Short people are simply "vertically challenged." Spelling, too, must become more sensitive. I have been roundly reproached for referring to "mankind" or "humanity," and I have been told that "woman" must be respelled "womin" to avoid the offensive inclusion of the male referent.

The effects of our newly sensitized American conscience on our aesthetic and intellectual standards, while hard to measure, have become a sensitive subject in themselves. But surely they have been considerable. The Repatriation Office (established in 1991) of our National Museum of Natural History, one of our principal centers for the study of American Indian ethnography and anthropology, has dismantled its holdings of Native American skeletal remains and funerary or sacred objects, returning some two thousand sets of these to various groups. More than seven hundred sets of such remains were delivered to the native peoples of Larsen Bay, Alaska, where they were packaged and reinterred out of "respect" for their anonymous owners. The birthday of Martin Luther King, Jr., is now our only national holiday to honor a specified person, while the birthdays of Lincoln and Washington have been merged into a single eponymous "President's Day."

What Bertrand Russell once disparaged as "The Superior Virtue of the Underdog" has inevitably diluted our hypersensitive judgments of works of art and literature by all members of the once-victim groups. American schools and universities take it for granted that they can serve their large educational purpose only by relaxing standards to favor the once-disadvantaged. This practice, not always publicly admitted, is sometimes attacked, but only when it is institutionalized in the form of illegal "affirmative action" and quotas. In recent decades in the United States we have tacitly developed a sliding scale of standards to provide opportunities for those who for whatever reason have in the past been deprived of them. The perils for American culture come less from the application of varied standards than from the pretense that the standards are not being varied, or that there really are no standards anyway. The greatest peril is in the condescension and indignity to disadvantaged groups who are given the message that less should be expected of them, and that they need expect less of themselves.

This age of the hypertrophied conscience has created problems, too, for our traditional politics of majority rule. Instead, we see signs of national institutions similar to the notorious Polish constitution under which any national measure could be vetoed by a single prince. We are in danger of becoming a nation of "minorities" rather than majorities. And the definition of "minority" becomes increasingly vague and elusive. Women, though actually a majority of our population, have acquired the dignity and the claims of a "minority," while, for some reason or other, Jews seem to have lost that claim.

Our fortunately complex constitutional system, which makes it difficult to pass a law, gives ample opportunity for representatives of any of the conscience-benefited groups to prevent legislation they imagine to be to their disadvantage. President Clinton's first nominee for assistant attorney general for civil rights in the Department of Justice has actually suggested the possibility of "granting blacks a minority veto on issues affecting vital minority issues."

Ironically, in the conscientious society, as recent American history shows, the once-victim groups seek not community but "empowerment." And power knows no bounds. They demand compensation for past exclusion, not in the form of full and free admission to the competitive community, but in claims of empowerment to prevent their oppression in the future. The level playing field is not enough.

Yet the level playing field is precisely what America promised to refugees from the Old World. America meant the opportunity to start anew, to build new lives, far from ancestral cemeteries, from family landed estates, from feudal dues, from guild inhibitions. Far, too, from old boundary feuds and linguistic provincialism. But a conscience-wracked nation has no feel for the future. It is unwilling to take the chance that the future may not balance past accounts. It aims to ensure its wards, the disadvantaged, against failure. And can do this only by depriving them of the opportunity to take risks.

Yet ours has been a continent of uncertainties. Hope for the individual has come not only from community but from the willingness to chance competition, to forgo revenge, to give up both claims of ancestral privilege and of compensation for ancestral sufferings. Efforts to cast up the balance sheet of history would have made New World community impossible. American equality could not erase history and would not pretend to, but would only open gates to the future.

II

MODERN TIMES AND
PSEUDO-EVENTS

EXTRAVAGANT EXPECTATIONS

from THE IMAGE, *1962*

I N THIS BOOK I describe the world of our making, how we have used our wealth, our literacy, our technology, and our progress, to create the thicket of unreality which stands between us and the facts of life. I recount historical forces which have given us this unprecedented opportunity to deceive ourselves and to befog our experience.

Of course, America has provided the landscape and has given us the resources and the opportunity for this feat of national self-hypnosis. But each of us individually provides the market and the demand for the illusions which flood our experience.

We want and we believe these illusions because we suffer from extravagant expectations. We expect too much of the world. Our expectations are extravagant in the precise dictionary sense of the word—"going beyond the limits of reason or moderation." They are excessive.

When we pick up our newspaper at breakfast, we expect—we even demand—that it bring us momentous events since the night before. We turn on the car radio as we drive to work and expect "news" to have occurred since the morning newspaper went to press. Returning in the evening, we expect our house not only to shelter us, to keep us warm in winter and cool in summer, but to relax us, to dignify us, to encompass us with soft music and interesting hobbies, to be a playground, a theater, and a bar. We expect our two-week vacation to be romantic, exotic, cheap, and effortless. We expect a faraway atmosphere if we go to a nearby place; and we expect everything to be relaxing, sanitary, and Americanized if we go to a faraway place. We expect new heroes every season, a literary masterpiece every month, a dramatic spectacular every week, a rare sensation every night. We expect everybody to feel free to disagree, yet we expect everybody to be loyal, not to rock the boat or take the Fifth Amendment. We expect everybody to believe deeply in his religion, yet not to think less of others for not believing. We expect our nation to be strong and great and vast and varied and prepared for every challenge; yet we expect our "national purpose" to be clear and simple, something that gives direction to the lives of nearly two hundred million people and yet can be bought in a paperback at the corner drugstore for a dollar.

We expect anything and everything. We expect the contradictory and the impossible. We expect compact cars which are spacious; luxurious cars which are economical. We expect to be rich and charitable, powerful and merciful, active and reflective, kind and competitive. We expect to be inspired by mediocre appeals for "excellence," to be made literate by illiterate appeals for literacy. We expect to eat and stay thin, to be constantly on the move and ever more neighborly, to go to a "church of our choice" and yet feel its guiding power over us, to revere God and to be God.

Never have people been more the masters of their environment. Yet never has a people felt more deceived and disappointed. For never has a people expected so much more than the world could offer.

We are ruled by extravagant expectations:

1) *Of what the world holds.* Of how much news there is, how many heroes there are, how often masterpieces are made, how exotic the nearby can be, how familiar the exotic can become. Of the closeness of places and the farness of places.

2) *Of our power to shape the world.* Of our ability to create events when there are none, to make heroes when they don't exist, to

be somewhere else when we haven't left home. Of our ability to make art forms suit our convenience, to transform a novel into a movie and vice versa, to turn a symphony into mood-conditioning. To fabricate national purposes when we lack them, to pursue these purposes after we have fabricated them. To invent our standards and then to respect them as if they had been revealed or discovered.

By harboring, nourishing, and ever enlarging our extravagant expectations we create the demand for the illusions with which we deceive ourselves. And which we pay others to make to deceive us.

The making of the illusions which flood our experience has become the business of America, some of its most honest and most necessary and most respectable business. I am thinking not only of advertising and public relations and political rhetoric, but of all the activities which purport to inform and comfort and improve and educate and elevate us: the work of our best journalists, our most enterprising book publishers, our most energetic manufacturers and merchandisers, our most successful entertainers, our best guides to world travel, and our most influential leaders in foreign relations. Our every effort to satisfy our extravagant expectations simply makes them more extravagant and makes our illusions more attractive. The story of the making of our illusions—"the news behind the news"—has become the most appealing news of the world.

We tyrannize and frustrate ourselves by expecting more than the world can give us or than we can make of the world. We demand that everyone who talks to us, or writes for us, or takes pictures for us, or makes merchandise for us, should live in our world of extravagant expectations. We expect this even of the peoples of foreign countries. We have become so accustomed to our illusions that we mistake them for reality. We demand them. And we demand that there be always more of them, bigger and better and more vivid. They are the world of our making: the world of the image.

Nowadays everybody tells us that what we need is more belief, a stronger and deeper and more encompassing faith. A faith in America and in what we are doing. That may be true in the long run.

What we need first and now is to disillusion ourselves. What ails us most is not what we have done with America, but what we have substituted for America. We suffer primarily not from our vices or our weaknesses, but from our illusions. We are haunted, not by reality, but by those images we have put in place of reality.

To discover our illusions will not solve the problems of our world. But if we do not discover them, we will never discover our real problems. To dispel the ghosts which populate the world of our making will not give us the power to conquer the real enemies of the real world or to remake the real world. But it may help us discover that we cannot make the world in our image. It will liberate us and sharpen our vision. It will clear away the fog so we can face the world we share with all mankind.

A FLOOD OF PSEUDO-EVENTS

from THE IMAGE, *1962*

ADMIRING FRIEND:

"My, that's a beautiful baby you have there!"

MOTHER:

"Oh, that's nothing—you should see his photograph!"

T HE simplest of our extravagant expectations concerns the amount of novelty in the world. There was a time when the reader of an unexciting newspaper would remark, "How dull is the world today!" Nowadays he says, "What a dull newspaper!" When the first American newspaper, Benjamin Harris' *Publick Occurrences Both Forreign and Domestick*, appeared in Boston on September 25, 1690, it promised to furnish news regularly once a month. But, the editor explained, it might appear oftener "if any Glut of Occurrences happen." The responsibility for making news was entirely God's—or the Devil's. The newsman's task was only to give "an Account of such considerable things as have arrived unto our Notice."

Although the theology behind this way of looking at events soon dissolved, this view of the news lasted longer. "The skilled and faithful journalist," James Parton observed in 1866, "recording with exactness and power the thing that has come to pass, is Providence addressing men." The story is told of a Southern Baptist clergyman before the Civil War who used to say, when a newspaper was brought in the room, "Be kind enough to let me have it a few minutes, till I see how the Supreme Being is governing the world." Charles A. Dana, one of the great American editors of the nineteenth century, once defended his extensive reporting of crime in the

New York *Sun* by saying, "I have always felt that whatever the Divine Providence permitted to occur I was not too proud to report."

Of course, this is now a very old-fashioned way of thinking. Our current point of view is better expressed in the definition by Arthur MacEwen, whom William Randolph Hearst made his first editor of the San Francisco *Examiner*: "News is anything that makes a reader say, 'Gee whiz!' " Or, put more soberly, "News is whatever a good editor chooses to print."

We need not be theologians to see that we have shifted responsibility for making the world interesting from God to the newspaperman. We used to believe there were only so many "events" in the world. If there were not many intriguing or startling occurrences, it was no fault of the reporter. He could not be expected to report what did not exist.

Within the last hundred years, however, and especially in the twentieth century, all this has changed. We expect the papers to be full of news. If there is no news visible to the naked eye, or to the average citizen, we still expect it to be there for the enterprising newsman. The successful reporter is one who can find a story, even if there is no earthquake or assassination or civil war. If he cannot find a story, then he must make one—by the questions he asks of public figures, by the surprising human interest he unfolds from some commonplace event, or by "the news behind the news." If all this fails, then he must give us a "think piece"—an embroidering of well-known facts, or a speculation about startling things to come.

This change in our attitude toward "news" is not merely a basic fact about the history of American newspapers. It is a symptom of a revolutionary change in our attitude toward what happens in the world, how much of it is new, and surprising, and important. Toward how life can be enlivened, toward our power and the power of those who inform and educate and guide us, to provide synthetic happenings to make up for the lack of spontaneous events. Demanding more than the world can give us, we require that something be fabricated to make up for the world's deficiency. This is only one example of our demand for illusions.

Many historical forces help explain how we have come to our

present immoderate hopes. But there can be no doubt about what we now expect, nor that it is immoderate. Every American knows the anticipation with which he picks up his morning newspaper at breakfast or opens his evening paper before dinner, or listens to the newscasts every hour on the hour as he drives across country, or watches his favorite commentator on television interpret the events of the day. Many enterprising Americans are now at work to help us satisfy these expectations. Many might be put out of work if we should suddenly moderate our expectations. But it is we who keep them in business and demand that they fill our consciousness with novelties, that they play God for us.

* * *

The new kind of synthetic novelty which has flooded our experience I will call "pseudo-events." The common prefix "pseudo" comes from the Greek word meaning false, or intended to deceive. Before I recall the historical forces which have made these pseudo-events possible, have increased the supply of them and the demand for them, I will give a commonplace example.

The owners of a hotel, in an illustration offered by Edward L. Bernays in his pioneer *Crystallizing Public Opinion* (1923), consult a public relations counsel. They ask how to increase their hotel's prestige and so improve their business. In less sophisticated times, the answer might have been to hire a new chef, to improve the plumbing, to paint the rooms, or to install a crystal chandelier in the lobby. The public relations counsel's technique is more indirect. He proposes that the management stage a celebration of the hotel's thirtieth anniversary. A committee is formed, including a prominent banker, a leading society matron, a well-known lawyer, an influential preacher, and an "event" is planned (say a banquet) to call attention to the distinguished service the hotel has been rendering the community. The celebration is held, photographs are taken, the occasion is widely reported, and the object is accomplished. Now this occasion is a pseudo-event, and will illustrate all the essential features of pseudo-events.

This celebration, we can see at the outset, is somewhat—but

not entirely—misleading. Presumably the public relations counsel would not have been able to form his committee of prominent citizens if the hotel had not actually been rendering service to the community. On the other hand, if the hotel's services had been all that important, instigation by public relations counsel might not have been necessary. Once the celebration has been held, the celebration itself becomes evidence that the hotel really is a distinguished institution. The occasion actually gives the hotel the prestige to which it is pretending.

It is obvious, too, that the value of such a celebration to the owners depends on its being photographed and reported in newspapers, magazines, newsreels, on radio, and over television. It is the report that gives the event its force in the minds of potential customers. The power to make a reportable event is thus the power to make experience. One is reminded of Napoleon's apocryphal reply to his general, who objected that circumstances were unfavorable to a proposed campaign: "Bah, I make circumstances!" The modern public relations counsel—and he is, of course, only one of many twentieth-century creators of pseudo-events—has come close to fulfilling Napoleon's idle boast. "The counsel on public relations," Mr. Bernays explains, "not only knows what news value is, but knowing it, he is in a position to *make news happen*. He is a creator of events."

The intriguing feature of the modern situation, however, comes precisely from the fact that the modern news makers are not God. The news they make happen, the events they create, are somehow not quite real. There remains a tantalizing difference between man-made and God-made events.

A pseudo-event, then, is a happening that possesses the following characteristics:

(1) It is not spontaneous, but comes about because someone has planned, planted, or incited it. Typically, it is not a train wreck or an earthquake, but an interview.

(2) It is planted primarily (not always exclusively) for the immediate purpose of being reported or reproduced. Therefore, its occurrence is arranged for the convenience of the reporting or

reproducing media. Its success is measured by how widely it is reported. Time relations in it are commonly fictitious or factitious; the announcement is given out in advance "for future release" and written as if the event had occurred in the past. The question, "Is it real?" is less important than, "Is it newsworthy?"

(3) Its relation to the underlying reality of the situation is ambiguous. Its interest arises largely from this very ambiguity. Concerning a pseudo-event the question, "What does it mean?" has a new dimension. While the news interest in a train wreck is in *what* happened and in the real consequences, the interest in an interview is always, in a sense, in *whether* it really happened and in what might have been the motives. Did the statement really mean what it said? Without some of this ambiguity a pseudo-event cannot be very interesting.

(4) Usually it is intended to be a self-fulfilling prophecy. The hotel's thirtieth-anniversary celebration, by saying that the hotel is a distinguished institution, actually makes it one.

In the last half century a larger and larger proportion of our experience, of what we read and see and hear, has come to consist of pseudo-events. We expect more of them and we are given more of them. They flood our consciousness. Their multiplication has gone on in the United States at a faster rate than elsewhere. Even the rate of increase is increasing every day. This is true of the world of education, of consumption, and of personal relations. It is especially true of the world of public affairs which I describe in this chapter.

A full explanation of the origin and rise of pseudo-events would be nothing less than a history of modern America. For our present purposes it is enough to recall a few of the more revolutionary recent developments.

The great modern increase in the supply and the demand for news began in the early nineteenth century. Until then newspapers tended to fill out their columns with lackadaisical secondhand accounts or stale reprints of items first published elsewhere at home and abroad. The laws of plagiarism and of copyright were undeveloped. Most newspapers were little more than excuses for espousing a political position, for listing the arrival and departure of ships, for familiar essays and useful advice, or for commercial or legal announcements.

Less than a century and a half ago did newspapers begin to disseminate up-to-date reports of matters of public interest written by eyewitnesses or professional reporters near the scene. The telegraph was perfected and applied to news reporting in the 1830's and '40's. Two newspapermen, William M. Swain of the Philadelphia *Public Ledger* and Amos Kendall of Frankfort, Kentucky, were founders of the national telegraphic network. Polk's presidential message in 1846 was the first to be transmitted by wire. When the Associated Press was founded in 1848, news began to be a salable commodity. Then appeared the rotary press, which could print on a continuous sheet and on both sides of the paper at the same time. The New York *Tribune*'s high-speed press, installed in the 1870's, could turn out 18,000 papers per hour. The Civil War, and later the Spanish-American War, offered raw materials and incentive for vivid up-to-the-minute, on-the-spot reporting. The competitive daring of giants like James Gordon Bennett, Joseph Pulitzer, and William Randolph Hearst intensified the race for news and widened newspaper circulation.

These events were part of a great, but little-noticed, revolution—what I would call the Graphic Revolution. Man's ability to make, preserve, transmit, and disseminate precise images—images of print, of men and landscapes and events, of the voices of men and mobs—now grew at a fantastic pace. The increased speed of printing was itself revolutionary. Still more revolutionary were the new techniques for making direct images of nature. Photography was destined soon to give printed matter itself a secondary role. By a giant leap Americans crossed the gulf from the daguerreotype to color television in less than a century. Dry-plate photography came in 1873; Bell patented the telephone in 1876; the phonograph was invented in 1877; the roll film appeared in 1884; Eastman's Kodak No. 1 was produced in 1888; Edison's patent on the radio came in 1891; motion pictures came in and voice was first transmitted by radio around

1900; the first national political convention widely broadcast by radio was that of 1928; television became commercially important in 1941, and color television even more recently.

Verisimilitude took on a new meaning. Not only was it now possible to give the actual voice and gestures of Franklin Delano Roosevelt unprecedented reality and intimacy for a whole nation. Vivid image came to overshadow pale reality. Sound motion pictures in color led a whole generation of pioneering American movie-goers to think of Benjamin Disraeli as an earlier imitation of George Arliss, just as television has led a later generation of television watchers to see the Western cowboy as an inferior replica of John Wayne. The Grand Canyon itself became a disappointing reproduction of the Kodachrome original.

The new power to report and portray what had happened was a new temptation leading newsmen to make probable images or to prepare reports in advance of what was expected to happen. As so often, men came to mistake their power for their necessities. Readers and viewers would soon prefer the vividness of the account, the "candidness" of the photograph, to the spontaneity of what was recounted.

Then came round-the-clock media. The news gap soon became so narrow that in order to have additional "news" for each new edition or each new broadcast it was necessary to plan in advance the stages by which any available news would be unveiled. After the weekly and the daily came the "extras" and the numerous regular editions. The Philadelphia *Evening Bulletin* soon had seven editions a day. No rest for the newsman. With more space to fill, he had to fill it ever more quickly. In order to justify the numerous editions, it was increasingly necessary that the news constantly change or at least seem to change. With radio on the air continuously during waking hours, the reporters' problems became still more acute. News every hour on the hour, and sometimes on the half hour. Programs interrupted any time for special bulletins. How to avoid deadly repetition, the appearance that nothing was happening, that news gatherers were asleep, or that competitors were more alert? As the costs of printing and then of broadcasting increased, it became financially necessary to keep the presses always at work and the TV screen always busy. Pressures toward the making of pseudo-events became ever stronger. News gathering turned into news making.

The "interview" was a novel way of making news which had come in with the Graphic Revolution. Later it became elaborated into lengthy radio and television panels and quizzes of public figures, and the three-hour-long, rambling conversation programs. Although the interview technique might seem an obvious one—and in a primitive form was as old as Socrates—the use of the word in its modern journalistic sense is a relatively recent Americanism. The Boston *News-Letter*'s account (March 2, 1719) of the death of Blackbeard the Pirate had apparently been based on a kind of interview with a ship captain. One of the earliest interviews of the modern type—some writers call it the first—was by James Gordon Bennett, the flamboyant editor of the New York *Herald* (April 16, 1836), in connection with the Robinson-Jewett murder case. Ellen Jewett, inmate of a house of prostitution, had been found murdered by an ax. Richard P. Robinson, a young man about town, was accused of the crime. Bennett seized the occasion to pyramid sensational stories and so to build circulation for his *Herald*; before long he was having difficulty turning out enough copies daily to satisfy the demand. He exploited the story in every possible way, one of which was to plan and report an actual interview with Rosina Townsend, the madam who kept the house and whom he visited on her own premises.

Historians of journalism date the first full-fledged modern interview with a well-known public figure from July 13, 1859, when Horace Greeley interviewed Brigham Young in Salt Lake City, asking him questions on many matters of public interest, and then publishing the answers verbatim in his New York *Tribune* (August 20, 1859). The common use of the word "interview" in this modern American sense first came in about this time. Very early the institution acquired a reputation for being contrived. "The 'interview,'" *The Nation* complained (January 28, 1869), "as at present managed, is generally the joint product of some humbug of a hack politician and another humbug of a reporter." A few years later another magazine editor called the interview "the most perfect contrivance yet devised to make journalism an offence, a thing of ill savor in all decent nostrils." Many objected to the practice as an invasion of privacy. After the American example it was used in England and France, but in both those countries it made much slower headway.

Even before the invention of the interview, the news-making profession in America had attained a new dignity as well as a menacing power. It was in 1828 that Macaulay called the gallery where reporters sat in Parliament a "fourth estate of the realm." But Macaulay could not have imagined the prestige of journalists in the twentieth-century United States. They have long since made themselves the tribunes of the people. Their supposed detachment and lack of partisanship, their closeness to the sources of information, their articulateness, and their constant and direct access to the whole citizenry have made them also the counselors of the people. Foreign observers are now astonished by the almost constitutional—perhaps we should say supra-constitutional—powers of our Washington press corps.

Since the rise of the modern Presidential press conference, about 1933, capital correspondents have had the power regularly to question the President face-to-face, to embarrass him, to needle him, to force him into positions or into public refusal to take a position. A President may find it inconvenient to meet a group of dissident Senators or Congressmen; he seldom dares refuse the press. That refusal itself becomes news. It is only very recently, and as a result of increasing pressures by newsmen, that the phrase "No comment" has become a way of saying something important. The reputation of newsmen—who now of course include those working for radio, TV, and magazines—depends on their ability to ask hard questions, to put politicians on the spot; their very livelihood depends on the willing collaboration of public figures. Even before 1950 Washington had about 1,500 correspondents and about 3,000 government information officials prepared to serve them.

Not only the regular formal press conferences, but a score of other national programs—such as "Meet the Press" and "Face the Nation"—show the power of newsmen. In 1960 David Susskind's late-night conversation show, "Open End," commanded the presence of the Russian Premier for three hours. During the so-called "Great Debates" that year between the candidates in the Presidential campaign, it was newsmen who called the tune.

The live television broadcasting of the President's regular news conferences, which President Kennedy began in 1961, immediately after taking office, has somewhat changed their character. Newsmen are no longer so important as intermediaries who relay the President's statements. But the new occasion acquires a new interest as a dramatic performance. Citizens who from homes or offices have seen the President at his news conference are then even more interested to hear competing interpretations by skilled commentators. News commentators can add a new appeal as dramatic critics to their traditional role as interpreters of current history. Even in the new format it is still the newsmen who put the questions. They are still tribunes of the people. . . .

In the age of pseudo-events it is less the artificial simplification than the artificial complication of experience that confuses us. Whenever in the public mind a pseudo-event competes for attention with a spontaneous event in the same field, the pseudo-event will tend to dominate. What happens on television will overshadow what happens off television. Of course I am concerned here not with our private worlds but with our world of public affairs.

Here are some characteristics of pseudo-events which make them overshadow spontaneous events:

(1) Pseudo-events are more dramatic. A television debate between candidates can be planned to be more suspenseful (for example, by reserving questions which are then popped suddenly) than a casual encounter or consecutive formal speeches planned by each separately.

(2) Pseudo-events, being planned for dissemination, are easier to disseminate and to make vivid. Participants are selected for their newsworthy and dramatic interest.

(3) Pseudo-events can be repeated at will, and thus their impression can be re-enforced.

(4)   Pseudo-events cost money to create; hence somebody has an interest in disseminating, magnifying, advertising, and extolling them as events worth watching or worth believing. They are therefore advertised in advance, and rerun in order to get money's worth.

(5)   Pseudo-events, being planned for intelligibility, are more intelligible and hence more reassuring. Even if we cannot discuss intelligently the qualifications of the candidates or the complicated issues, we can at least judge the effectiveness of a television performance. How comforting to have some political matter we can grasp!

(6)   Pseudo-events are more sociable, more conversable, and more convenient to witness. Their occurrence is planned for our convenience. The Sunday newspaper appears when we have a lazy morning for it. Television programs appear when we are ready with our glass of beer. In the office the next morning, Jack Paar's (or any other star performer's) regular late-night show at the usual hour will overshadow in conversation a casual event that suddenly came up and had to find its way into the news.

(7)   Knowledge of pseudo-events—of what has been reported, or what has been staged, and how—becomes the test of being "informed." News magazines provide us regularly with quiz questions concerning not what has happened but concerning "names in the news"—what has been reported in the news magazines. Pseudo-events begin to provide that "common discourse" which some of my old-fashioned friends have hoped to find in the Great Books.

(8)   Finally, pseudo-events spawn other pseudo-events in geometric progression. They dominate our consciousness simply because there are more of them, and ever more.

By this new Gresham's law of American public life, counterfeit happenings tend to drive spontaneous happenings out of circulation. The rise in the power and prestige of the Presidency is due not only to the broadening powers of the office and the need for quick decisions, but also to the rise of centralized news gathering and broad-casting, and the increase of the Washington press corps. The President has an ever more ready, more frequent, and more centralized access to the world of pseudo-events. A similar explanation helps account for the rising prominence in recent years of the Congressional investigating committees. In many cases these committees have virtually no legislative impulse, and sometimes no intelligible legislative assignment. But they do have an almost unprecedented power, possessed now by no one else in the Federal government except the President, to make news. Newsmen support the committees because the committees feed the newsmen: they live together in happy symbiosis. The battle for power among Washington agencies becomes a contest to dominate the citizen's information of the government. This can most easily be done by fabricating pseudo-events.

THE DIRECT DEMOCRACY OF
PUBLIC RELATIONS:

Selling the President to the People

from America and the Image of Europe, *1960*

I N EUROPE the history-making political leaders have usually been
set apart from the crowd by qualities of the artist and the
prophet, but ours have generally been respectable spokesmen
for the respectable community. Compare, for example, the place of
Queen Elizabeth I, Cromwell, Robespierre, Napoleon, Bismarck,
Hitler, Garibaldi, Mussolini, Lenin, or Stalin in their national traditions with that of William Bradford, John Winthrop, Benjamin
Franklin, George Washington, Thomas Jefferson, Andrew Jackson,
and Abraham Lincoln in ours. The most remembered and most
adored European leaders have been erratic and charismatic, with at
least a touch of the daemonic. Claiming the inspiration of God, they
avow their desire to change the course of history. They are remembered as makers—not merely reflectors—of the spirit of their age.
By contrast ours have been simply "representative men," possessing
the commonplace virtues in extraordinary degree. Washington embodied the sober judgment and solid character of the Virginia
planter. Andrew Jackson was only one of many elevated by the rise of
the West. "This middle-class country," Emerson shrewdly remarked in his oration on Lincoln, "had got a middle-class president,
at last."

As the power of the President and of the Federal Government
increase, we should be troubled by whether the affairs of a great na-

tion can be conducted by no better than a "typical" American. Perhaps we can no longer rely on that remarkable Providence (first observed by an enemy of Lincoln who foresaw Lincoln's election but had faith the nation would survive him) which has helped our nation outlive the most insipid leaders. We cannot look cheerfully on further temptations to apotheosize the commonplace in the most powerful office in the land.

Yet a number of facts, so recent and so peripheral to the familiar topics of political history that they have hardly begun to enter our textbooks, actually add up to just this. They offer new temptations for our national political leader to be a passive spokesman for the Voice of the People. They make it easier and more necessary than ever before that any candidate for the Presidency should seem constantly to have his hand on the public pulse. And they make it easier than ever for Americans to confuse vigorous leadership with adept followership.

These new tendencies could be described as the rise of the Nationally Advertised President. Franklin Delano Roosevelt was our first. The attitude of the vast majority of the American people to him was as different from that of their grandfathers to the presidents of their day as our attitude to General Motors is different from that of our great-grandfathers to the village harness-maker. Like other "nationally advertised brands," F.D.R. could not, of course, have been successful if he had not had something to offer. But he might not have been able to sell himself to the American public—on such a scale, and for twice as many terms as any of his predecessors—without the aid of certain revolutionary changes in our system of public communication.

I.

During the nineteenth century the telegraph transformed American journalism. Until the 1830's—that is, until the coming of the telegraph—the reporting of political news in the United States was a bitterly partisan business. Newspapers were owned body and soul by one or another political party, and, generally speaking, lacked moderation, conscience, or decency. The practice of ignoring or misrepresenting the opposition's statements was pushed to a point unknown today even among the most partisan of our large daily papers. Not until the last years of the age of Jackson did news begin to be sold in the open market, and as it became a commodity its quality began to improve. And with the rise of the cheap newspaper—the "penny press" in those days—addressed to a vast audience, newspapers tended to become financially independent of political parties. The growing volume of advertising they carried further encouraged them to assert their political independence.

It was the telegraph, of course, that made possible the establishment of enterprises—the wire services—selling news to newspapers (the AP was founded in 1848), and these had a financial interest in seeing a crudely partisan press supplanted by an independent one. The wire services sold a nonpartisan product; very early they set a standard of impartial reporting that still distinguishes our press from that of most of the rest of the world.

Technical and economic developments made it possible to communicate news to more and more people more rapidly than ever before. The Fourdrinier machine for producing paper in a continuous strip instead of in sheets, and the Hoe presses, which by around 1900 could produce up to 144,000 sixteen-page newspapers per hour, acted as both cause and effect in making the news big business. By the turn of the century, major newspaper chains like Scripps's and Hearst's were going strong. The great rise in newspaper circulation set in soon after 1892; in that year there were only ten papers in four cities that had a circulation of over one hundred thousand; by 1914 there were over thirty of that size in a dozen cities. During this period, the average circulation of daily newspapers in the United States just about doubled. The combined circulation of daily newspapers in 1930 amounted to over forty-four million; by 1955 the figure was nearly fifty-five million.

To this growing business the government, and especially the federal government in Washington, offered the richest single source of raw material. At the beginning of this century there were less than two hundred Washington correspondents. The number increased sharply during the First World War, but even in 1929 the Washington press bureaus were only about a third their present size. By 1952 about fifteen hundred people in Washington made their living directly from collecting and reporting national news.

We sometimes forget that the Presidential press conference is an institution of very recent date. Only fifty years ago there were no regularly scheduled news conferences at the White House. From time to time, President Theodore Roosevelt, while being shaved, would allow Lincoln Steffens to ask him questions; and he was the one who first provided a special anteroom for White House correspondents. Under President Wilson, something like the present formal and regular White House press conferences first came into being. Although interrupted by the First World War, the institution was continued in one form or another by all presidents after him. The figure any one of these cut in newspapers all over the country depended very much on how he "handled himself" during these periodic interviews. F.D.R. was the first President to appoint a special press secretary, and the power of that office has steadily increased.

By the early twentieth century a continual, ever widening current of news was flowing from the White House. The news-gathering agencies themselves began to become self-appointed representatives of public opinion who put point-blank questions to the President, and from whom the President could learn what was troubling the public mind. Communication was now constant and two-way. No longer did the press await "statements" from the White House; it could prod the President when he was reticent, and focus attention on embarrassing questions. The corps of Washington correspondents became a more flexible, more regular, more direct, and at times more successful means than Congress itself of calling the President to public account.

* * *

The new continuity, informality, and immediacy of relations between people and President were furthered by the radio, which, with catastrophic suddenness, became a major factor in American political life during the twenties. The first Presidential election whose results were publicly broadcast was that of November 2, 1920: between five hundred and one thousand Americans were wearing earphones on that night to learn whether Harding or Cox had been elected. By 1922 about four hundred thousand radio sets were in use in the United States; by 1928 the number had increased more than twenty-fold to eight and a half million; in 1932 to eighteen million; by 1936 to thirty-three million; and by 1950 to well over eighty million. It was in the elections of 1924, however, that the radio began to acquire real political significance; in that year, for the first time, the proceedings of the two national party conventions were broadcast to the public. But not until 1928 did the major parties make extensive use of the radio in their campaigning, when for the first time millions of Americans heard the candidates' voices in their own homes. The inauguration of President Hoover, on March 4, 1929, was broadcast over a network of one hundred twenty stations.

These and other changes still to come in American political life were, of course, intimately connected with the rising American standard of living. For the ever accelerating need to cultivate the market to increase the wants of the people, and to attract them to specific products, was served by both press and radio. Advertising had begun to become big business by about the 1880's, but only in the last fifty years has its growth been spectacular. Until about 1890 most dailies still received more revenue from the sale of papers than from advertising; by 1914 advertising was providing many with two-thirds of their income, by 1929 with three-fourths. The bills that advertising clients received from radio stations amounted only to about five million dollars in 1927; the sum shot up to over one hundred and seven millions in 1936; by 1945 it was nearly four hundred and eighty millions; and in 1949 had increased by nearly another third, to the phenomenal figure of six hundred and thirty-seven millions. Advertising agencies in the United States, which handled a business of nearly six hundred million dollars in 1930, had an annual business in the neighborhood of a billion dollars about fifteen years later.

* * *

It is not surprising that the self-conscious and scientific study of public opinion, which was to become important in national political calculations by mid-century, had its roots in the efforts of advertisers to evaluate the reach of their advertising dollars. The first public opinion surveys were made by advertising managers to discover who was reading their copy. In 1919 there appeared the first survey department within an advertising agency, and the first independent surveying agency. It was not until 1935, however, that the representative sample method was used in public opinion surveys. In July of that year—in the middle of F.D.R.'s first administration—Elmo Roper published his first survey in *Fortune;* a few months later Dr. George Gallup began releasing his surveys as director of the American Institute of Public Opinion.

During this very period, a new philosophy and science of public opinion came into being. Walter Lippmann's *Public Opinion* (1922)—soon followed by his *Phantom Public* (1925)—advanced the important idea of "stereotypes" and explored some theoretical consequences of the new publicity. For the citizen was now becoming more and more like the customer. With the characteristic American directness, a new profession of "public relations" developed. The anti–big business sentiment of the 1880's and 1890's and the rise of muckraking had disposed big business men to offer high prices for skillful press-agentry. Ivy Lee, by paying some attention to the public interest and to the legitimate curiosity of newspaper reporters, helped put this new activity on a respectable (and profitable) footing. "This profession," observed Edward L. Bernays in the foreword to his *Crystallizing Public Opinion* (1923), "in a few years has developed from the status of circus agent stunts to . . . an important position in the conduct of the world's affairs."

By the time that Franklin Delano Roosevelt came into office on March 4, 1933, technological and institutional innovations had in many ways prepared the way for a transformation of the relation between President and people. Communications from the President to the reading or listening public, which formerly had been ceremonial, infrequent, and addressed to small audiences, could now be constant, spontaneous, and directed to all who could read or hear (sometimes whether they wished to or not). And now through the questions put to the President at his regular press conferences, and through the telegrams and mail received after his radio addresses or public state-

ments, he could sense the temper and gauge the drift of public opinion—he could find out what the sovereign people wanted. He could
even send up trial balloons to get some advance idea of public response to his future decisions. The President was no longer simply
dealing with the "people," but with "public opinion."

* * *

There is no denying that F.D.R. possessed a genius for using
these means of communication. Without them he could hardly have
developed that novel intimacy between people and President which
marked his administrations. In the little memorial miscellany published by Pocket Books on April 18, 1945 (less than a week after
F.D.R.'s death), we read in Carl Carmer's verse dialogue:

> Woman:
> . . . Come home with me
> If you would think of him. I never saw him—
> But I knew him. Can you have forgotten
> How, with his voice, he came into our house,
> The President of these United States,
> Calling us friends. . . .
> Do you remember how he came to us
> That day twelve years ago—a little more—
> And you were sitting by the radio
> (We had it on the kitchen table then)
> Your head down on your arms as if asleep.

For the first time in American history the voice of the President was
a voice from kitchen tables, from the counters of bars and lunchrooms, and the corners of living rooms.

F.D.R.'s relaxed and informal style, both in writing and speaking, enabled him to make the most of the new informal circumstances under which people heard him. That he was compelled by
his infirmity to sit while giving his radio talks only added to the informality. A whole world separates F.D.R.'s speeches from those of
his immediate predecessors—from the stilted rhetoric of the oratory

collected in such volumes as Calvin Coolidge's *Foundations of the Republic* (1926) or Herbert Hoover's *Addresses Upon the American Road* (1938). Earlier Presidential speeches had too often echoed the style and sentiments of commencement addresses; F.D.R. could say something informal and concrete even in such an unpromising State Paper as a "Mother's Day Proclamation."

Perhaps never before had there been so happy a coincidence of personal talent with technological opportunity as under his administrations. In the eight volumes of the *Public Papers and Addresses of Franklin D. Roosevelt,* which cover the era of the New Deal, we discover two new genres of political literature which were the means by which a new relationship between President and people was fashioned. The first genre was established in transcriptions of Presidential press conferences; the second, in F.D.R.'s radio talks, the "fireside chats." Both are distinguished by an engaging casualness and directness; but this is not all that makes them new genres in the literature of American politics. Here, for the first time among Presidential papers, we find an extensive body of public utterances that are unceremonial yet serious.

Only a year after F.D.R. assumed office, Theodore G. Joslin, who had handled press relations for President Hoover, observed that President Roosevelt had already come nearer than any of his predecessors "to meeting the expectations of the four hundred men and women who, in these times of stress, write half a million words a day to bring to our firesides news of developments at the seat of the Government." F.D.R. had already shown the camaraderie and the willingness to make news which made some correspondents (not always his political friends) call his administration a "new deal for the press." The unprecedented frequency of his press conferences established a continuity of relations with both correspondents and the reading public. During Hoover's administration there had been only sixty-six Presidential press conferences; but F.D.R. held three hundred thirty-seven press conferences during his first administration, and three hundred seventy-four during his second. Thus, while Hoover met the press on an average of less than once in every three weeks, Roosevelt would see them about five times in that same period. The record of his conferences shows how this frequency bred intimacy, informality, and a set of institutionalized procedures; before long the spirit of those press conferences became on both sides much like that of any other responsible deliberative body.

Similarly, the frequency with which the President went on the air effected a revolutionary change. Between March and October 1933, F.D.R. gave four "fireside chats." Through these, for the first time in American history, a President was able to appeal on short notice and in his own voice to the whole constituency. Neither the press conference nor the "fireside chat" was an occasion for *ex cathedra* pronouncements. On the contrary, they were designed to stimulate a more active "dialogue" between the people and the Chief Executive.

Perhaps the best index of the effect of F.D.R.'s radio talks was the volume of White House mail. In McKinley's time Presidential mail amounted to about a hundred letters a day, which were handled by a single clerk. Despite occasional flurries at inaugurations or crises, the daily flow remained small. Not until President Hoover's time did its volume increase significantly. Even then letters sometimes did not number more than a few hundred a day, and the system of handling them remained unchanged. Under F.D.R., however, Presidential mail acquired a new and unprecedented volume, as we learn from the reminiscences of Ira R. T. Smith, for many years chief Presidential mail clerk (*"Dear Mr. President . . .": The Story of Fifty Years in the White House Mail Room*):

> Mr. Roosevelt always showed a keen interest in the mail and kept close watch on its trend. Nothing pleased him more than to know that I had to build up a big staff and often had to work until midnight to keep up with a run of 5000 to 8000 letters a day, and on some occasions many more thousands. He received regular reports. . . . Whenever there was a decrease in the influx of letters we could expect to hear from him or one of his secretaries, who wanted to know what was the matter—was the President losing his grip on the public?

Before F.D.R. came to the White House, Mr. Smith had handled all the mail by himself. But when, in response to his First Inaugural Address, F.D.R. received over four hundred fifty thousand letters, it was plain that a new era had begun. During certain periods as many as fifty persons were required to open and sort the White House mail; before long an electric letter-opener was installed, and instead of the old practice of counting individual pieces of mail, Mr. Smith and his helpers began measuring stacked-up letters by the yard.

* * *

Also, a new self-consciousness governed F.D.R.'s communications to the public; the era of "public relations" had begun. It was not enough that the President (or someone else for him) should state what he really believed—one had to consider all the "angles." Andrew Jackson had had his Amos Kendall and his Frank Blair; and it had not been uncommon for Presidents to employ ghost writers and close personal advisers who, in some cases, were responsible for both style and content. But perhaps never before did a President depend so consistently and to such an extent in his literary product on the collaboration of advisers. Among F.D.R.'s speech-writers were men like Harry Hopkins, Robert Sherwood, Samuel Rosenman, Stanley High, Charles Michelson, Ernest Lindley, Sumner Welles, Raymond Moley, Rexford Tugwell, Archibald MacLeish, Tom Corcoran, Basil O'Connor, and Robert Jackson—and these are only a few. F.D.R.'s speeches, even the most important and those seemingly most personal, were as much a co-operative product as a piece of copy produced by a large advertising agency. The President's genius consisted very much in his ability to give calculated, prefabricated phrases an air of casualness. It was, of course, remarkable that his speeches retained any personal flavor at all. And it was significant that this collaborative literary activity was not kept secret. The public began to take it as much for granted that the utterances of a President should be a composite product as that an advertisement of the Ford Motor Company should not be written by Henry Ford.

II.

In the longer perspective of American history, these changes that F.D.R., aided by technology, brought about in the conduct of the Presidency may become permanent and take on the quality of mutations.

The Decline in the Periodicity of American Political Life. In the early years of the Republic, politics—or at least national politics—was a "sometime thing." Political interest would rise to fever pitch before national elections or in times of crisis, and tend to subside in between. The very vastness of the country reinforced this tendency to periodicity in American political life. And so our elections became notorious for their barbecue, holiday atmosphere: brief but hectic interruptions of the routine of life.

But the technological developments which I have described increased the President's opportunity, and eventually his duty, to make news. Now headlines could be produced at an hour's notice. To oblige the correspondents by making big stories frequently, and small stories constantly, became part of his job. In F.D.R.'s era, of course, the crises in economic life and international affairs were themselves rich raw material for the press. There had been crises and wars before, but never before had so large and steady a stream of announcements, information, "statements to the press," and description of "problems facing the country" poured from the headquarters of government. The innocent citizen now found no respite from this barrage of politics and government. Even over a beer at his favorite bar he was likely to hear the hourly news broadcast, or the very voice of his President.

The citizen was no longer expected to focus his attention only temporarily on a cluster of issues (conveniently dramatized by two rival personalities) at the time of national election. With the rise of the weekly news magazine (*Time* was founded in 1923, *Newsweek* in 1933), of news quizzes, news broadcasts, and radio forums, the citizen was given a new duty, that of being "well informed." The complex of alphabetical agencies, the intricate and remote problems of foreign policy, and the details of the legislative process came now, as never before, to burden his mind and plague his conscience. Whether or not the American citizen was consciously becoming more "political," he was surely finding it more and more difficult to escape politics. No longer was he granted the surcease of inter-election periods when his representatives were left to their own devices and he could turn to other things. Paradoxically, in spite of the great increase in population, the national government was becoming less and less republican, and more and more democratic; for elected officials were now in more constant touch with their constituencies.

Increased Communication Between the People and the President. The very agencies that the President was now using to communicate his views to the public were also employed to elicit the public's response. Letters to the President—and to Congressmen—became a special American version of the ancient right of petition. As communications to public officials multiplied, the temptations increased for the public official, and especially the President, to trim his sails to the shifting winds of opinion, which now sometimes blew with hurricane force into Washington offices. The weak representative or the demagogue would find it easier to be weak and yet to seem to be strong by following the majority view at every turn. Here was still another force to prevent the realization of Burke's ideal of the independent representative, and to make him a "mere" spokesman of popular views.

The Decline of Naïveté. The efflorescence of "public relations" techniques and of opinion polls increased the temptation for the President to rely on experts in dealing with the public. Even if Presidential utterances would still have the appearance of casualness, it would be a studied casualness, or one that the people would suspect of being studied. The President would scrutinize surveys of press opinions; he would employ (sometimes within the very agencies of government) specialists in "opinion research" to inform him of what the people liked or disliked. He would employ theatrical advisers to help him find his most appealing voice and posture before the television cameras. In these ways, the citizen was more and more assimilated to the customer; he had to be "approached," his responses had to be measured so that he could be given what he wanted, or thought he wanted.

The Inversion of Geographic and Political Distances. The new developments in communications made many of the oldest assumptions about the relations between geography and politics irrelevant. Jefferson and his "States Rights" disciples had started from the axiom that the citizen's knowledge and hence his capacity for an informed opinion were in inverse ratio to his geographic distance from the headquarters of decision. The closer he was to the scene, the more he would presumably know, and the more exact would be his knowledge. Thus the average citizen was expected to be best informed about the political affairs of his municipality, only a little less informed about those of his state, and considerably less informed about the affairs of the nation as a whole. The changes that reached their climax under F.D.R. not only exploded this assumption, they came close to making it the reverse of the truth. Both the multiplication of newscasts and the expansion of the profession of radio and television news-commentator have focused attention on national events—since these are sure to interest the largest number of listeners; and audience volume decides where money will be invested in communications. National affairs have become more and more a good thing for the commercial sponsors of newscasts. Inevitably, many of the ablest reporters, too, have been attracted to the national capital. The citizen, when he listens to the news from Washington, now has the benefit of sophisticated, well-informed, and competent interpreters who seldom have equals in the state capitals or on the local scene.

There thus has developed a new disparity between the quality and quantity of information about national as contrasted with state or local matters. By about 1940, largely owing to the press and the radio, the citizenry had already reached a point where it was better informed about national than about local issues. This reversal of a longstanding assumption, which was not just a result of the marked increase in federal activities under the New Deal, will require revision of accepted notions about federalism, and about the competence of the average citizen to participate in government.

*   *   *

We are already far enough from the age of F.D.R. to begin to see that the tendencies which I have just described were not ephemeral. American experience under F.D.R. created new expectations that continue to clamor for fulfillment. When we look on into the administrations of Truman and Eisenhower, we see that these expectations became institutionalized. F.D.R. had set a style that later Presidential candidates could only at their peril violate. President Truman's success and the defeat of Governor Dewey in the 1948 elections cannot be explained unless such novel factors are taken into account. The growth of television, and its frequent (and on the whole successful) use by President Eisenhower, only carry further the tendencies initiated in the age of F.D.R. While later Presidents might lack the vividness of F.D.R.'s personality, perhaps never again would any man attain the Presidency or discharge its duties satisfactorily without entering into an intimate and conscious relation with the whole public. This opens unprecedented opportunities for effective and enlightening leadership. But it also opens unprecedented temptations. For never before has it been so easy for a statesman to seem to lead millions while in reality tamely echoing their every shifting mood and inclination.

GRESHAM'S LAW:
KNOWLEDGE OR INFORMATION?

Remarks at the White House Conference on Library and Information Services, Washington, November 19, 1979

from THE REPUBLIC OF LETTERS, *1989*

AS THE LIBRARIAN OF CONGRESS I speak for a national fortress of knowledge. In other words, I speak for a library, and for libraries. Our relentless Jeffersonian quest tempts us to believe that all technologies (and perhaps, too, all ideas) are created equal. This favored axiom is only slightly clouded by another axiom, equally American. For we have a touching national belief in annual models. In our national lexicon, "newer" is a synonym for "better." The result is illustrated in the title—and I suspect, too, in the preoccupations—of this conference. Libraries (or as you say "library services") are here equated with "information services," which is perilously close to saying that knowledge can or should be equated with information.

In these remarks I would like to focus your attention on the distinction between knowledge and information, the importance of the distinction, and the dangers of failing to recognize it. You have a hint of my theme in the melodramatic difference today between the condition of our knowledge-institutions and our information-institutions. The last two decades have seen the spectacular growth of the information industry. We are exhilarated by this example of American ingenuity and enterprise—the frontier spirit in the late twentieth century. A magic computer technology now accomplishes the dreariest tasks in seconds, surpasses the accuracy of the human brain, controls production lines and refineries, arranges inventories, and retrieves records. All this makes us proud of the human imagination.

All this, too, I am glad to say, has produced a widening unpredicted world of profit and employment. The information industry, we are happy to note, is flourishing. It is a growth industry. It enjoys the accelerating momentum of technology and the full vitality of the marketplace. The information industries are a whole new world of business celebrity. The jargon of the stock exchange accurately describes theirs as "glamour" stocks. Their leaders hold the national spotlight, and with good reason. The President of the United States appoints the head of one of the greatest of these companies to be perhaps our most important ambassador—to the Soviet Union.

Meanwhile, what has become of our knowledge-institutions? They do not deal mainly in the storage and retrieval of information, nor in the instant flow of today's facts and figures which will be displaced by tomorrow's reports and bulletins. Rather, they deal in the enduring treasure of our whole human past. They include our colleges and our universities—and, of course, our libraries. While the information industry flourishes and seeks new avenues of growth, while people compete to buy into them, our knowledge-institutions go begging.

Knowledge-institutions do not pay the kind of dividends that are reflected on the stock market. They are sometimes called "philanthropic," which means that they profit nobody except everybody and their dividends go to the whole community. These knowledge-institutions—and especially our public libraries—ask charity, the community's small change, just to keep their heat and their lights on, and to keep their unrenovated doors open. We, the knowledge-institutions, are the poor relations. We anxiously solicit, and gratefully acknowledge, the crumbs. Today I would like to put into historical perspective the distinction between knowledge and information. For it is especially appropriate in this White House Conference that we should focus on the distinction.

In my lifetime we have moved from an Age of Publishing into

our Age of Broadcasting. In that Age of Publishing started by Guten-berg, printed materials (bearing the community's memory, wisdom, literary imagination, and knowledge) were, of course, widely dif-fused. The great vehicle was the book. Knowledge was thought to be cumulative. The new books did not displace the old. When today's books arrived people did not throw away yesterday's—as if they were newspapers or out-of-date information bulletins. On the contrary, the passing years gave a new vitality to the books of past centuries.

We too easily forget that the printed book, too, was a triumph of technology. The dead could now speak, not only to the select few who could afford a manuscript book but to thousands at home, in schools, and in libraries everywhere. The very words of Homer, Plato, Machiavelli, and Dickens now could reach everybody. Books became the carriers and the record—also the catalyst and the incen-tive—for most of the knowledge, the amusement, and the sacred vi-sions of the human race. The printed book has given all humanity its inexpensive, speedy, reliable vehicles across the centuries. Books have conquered time.

But the peculiar, magic vehicles of our age conquer space. The tube makes us constant eyewitnesses of riots in Iran, airplane wrecks in India, children starving in Cambodia, and guerrilla attacks in Rhodesia. Along, of course, with an everflowing current of enter-tainment programs. Yet the special commodity of our electronic Age of Broadcasting is *Information*—in all its amplitude, in all its formats.

While knowledge is orderly and cumulative, information is random and miscellaneous. We are flooded by messages from the instant-everywhere in excruciating profusion. In our ironic twentieth-century version of Gresham's law, information tends to drive know-ledge out of circulation. The oldest, the established, the cumulative, is displaced by the most recent, the most problematic. The latest in-formation on anything and everything is collected, diffused, re-ceived, stored, and retrieved before anyone can discover whether the facts have meaning.

A mountain-climbing syndrome rules us. Information is gath-ered simply because it is there. Electronic devices for diffusion, stor-age, and retrieval are used, simply because they too are there.

Otherwise, the investment would seem wasted! I am not complaining. On the contrary, I am charmed and amazed. For so much of human progress has come from people playing enthusiastically with their new technologic toys—with results that are astonishing, and often productive.

Whatever the motive, we see the knowledge industry being transformed, and even to some extent displaced, by an information industry. In the schoolroom, history tends to be displaced by current events. The resources of science and literature are overwhelmed and diluted by multiplying journals, by loose-leaf services, by preprints, and by information stored in computers, quickly and conveniently modified, and instantly retrievable.

To the ancient question, "What is truth?" we Americans now reply, "Sorry, I haven't seen the seven o'clock news!"

What does all this mean for the world of knowledge, which is also, of course, the world of libraries? It should be plainer than ever that our libraries are needed to keep civilization in perspective. The more electronic our society becomes, the more urgent it is that we have prosperous knowledge-institutions. Yet this urgency is less noted every year. If you consult the authoritative *Encyclopedia of the Social Sciences*, published in 1933, and look under "Libraries" you will be referred to "Public Libraries" where you find an extensive article. But if you consult its successor, the *International Encyclopedia of the Social Sciences*, published in 1968, and look for an entry for "Libraries" you will find no article. Instead there's a cross-reference which says "See under Information and Storage and Retrieval."

The fashionable chronologic myopia of our time tempts enthusiasts to forget the main and proper mission of our libraries. "Libraries have been selling the wrong product for years," one such faddist exclaims. "They have been emphasizing reading. The product that we have is information." But these are false messiahs. Of course, we must use computer technology and enlist the whole information industry. At the Library of Congress we have tried to be a leader in exploring its uses and in extending its applications. We will continue to do so.

In the long run, however, we will serve neither the information industry nor our civilization if we encourage extravagant or mis-placed expectations for the role of information or the devices which serve it up. We must never forget that our libraries are our fortresses of knowledge. If we allow these rich resources, still preserved mainly in books, to be displaced by the latest thing, by today's news and journals and preprints and loose-leaf services and telephone conver-sations and currently revised printouts, we will isolate the world of scholarship from the world of libraries. To avoid such dangers as these we have established in the Library of Congress a Center for the Book, to use old and find new ways to keep the book flourishing, to keep people reading books, and to enlist other media to promote reading. One such project, "Read More About It," with the enthusi-astic collaboration of CBS, the other night after the showing of "All Quiet on the Western Front" brought our suggested reading list to some thirty-one million viewers. We must and will do more of this.

If librarians cease to be scholars in order to become computer experts, scholars will cease to feel at home in our libraries. And then our whole citizenry will find that our libraries add little to their view of the world, but merely reinforce the pressures of the imperial instant-everywhere. To enlist scholars more actively and more inti-mately in the activities of the Library of Congress we are now setting up in the Library a Council of Scholars. They will help us discover the needs of the scholarly world and will help us provide an ongoing inventory of the state of our knowledge—and of our ignorance.

A great civilization needs many and varied resources. In our time our libraries have two paradoxical and sometimes conflicting roles. Of course we must be repositories of information. But somehow we must also remain places of refuge from the tidal waves of informa-tion—and misinformation. Our libraries must be conspicuously the treasuries of news that stays news.

The era of the Enlightenment, the later eighteenth century, the age of Franklin and Jefferson, the founding epoch of our nation, was an Age of Publishing. That age has left us a happy phrase. They said that people should read for *"Amusement and Instruction."* This was why they read the poetry of Dryden and Pope, the philosophy of Hume, the history of Gibbon, and the novels of Sterne and Fielding.

The two delights, "amusement" and "instruction," were inseparable. The book was the prototypical provider of both. A person who was "a-mused" (from Latin "muser," to idle or to pass the time) was engaged in a quite autonomous activity—set off by a catalyst, in the form of a book. In those days book publishing was an "amusement industry."

Today in an Age of Broadcasting "entertainment" tends to displace "amusement." While we once had to amuse ourselves, we now expect to *be* entertained. The program *is* the entertainment. The amusement is in *us*. But others can and must be our entertainers. Now, of course, there is a flourishing "entertainment industry." We generally do not consider book publishing to be part of it.

This is something to reflect on. It is another clue to our special need for libraries. The more omnipresent is the industry that tries to entertain us, the more we need libraries—where pleasure and amusement are found by the free and active spirit.

It is a cliché of our time that what this nation needs is an "informed citizenry." By which we mean a citizenry that is up on the latest information, that has not failed to read this week's newsmagazine, today's newspapers, or to watch the seven o'clock news (perhaps also the news at ten o'clock!)—always for more information, always to be better informed.

I wonder if that is what we need. I suggest, rather, that what we need—what any free country needs—is a *knowledgeable* citizenry. Information, like entertainment, is something someone else provides us. It really is a "service." We expect to be entertained, and also to be informed. *But we cannot be knowledged!* We must all acquire knowledge for ourselves. Knowledge comes from the free mind foraging in the rich pastures of the whole everywhere-past. It comes from finding order and meaning in the whole human experience. The autonomous reader, amusing and knowledging himself, is the be-all and end-all of our libraries.

THE RHETORIC OF DEMOCRACY

from DEMOCRACY AND ITS DISCONTENTS, *1969*

DVERTISING, OF COURSE, has been part of the mainstream of American civilization, although you might not know it if you read the most respectable surveys of American history. It has been one of the enticements to the settlement of this New World, it has been a producer of the peopling of the United States, and in its modern form, in its world-wide reach, it has been one of our most characteristic products.

Never was there a more outrageous or more unscrupulous or more ill-informed advertising campaign than that by which the promoters for the American colonies brought settlers here. Brochures published in England in the seventeenth century, some even earlier, were full of hopeful overstatements, half-truths, and downright lies, along with some facts which nowadays surely would be the basis for a restraining order from the Federal Trade Commission. Gold and silver, fountains of youth, plenty of fish, venison without limit, all these were promised, and of course some of them were found. It would be interesting to speculate on how long it might have taken to settle this continent if there had not been such promotion by enterprising advertisers. How has American civilization been shaped by the fact that there was a kind of natural selection here of those people who were willing to believe advertising?

Advertising has taken the lead in promising and exploiting the new. This was a new world, and one of the advertisements for it appears on the dollar bill on the Great Seal of the United States, which reads *NOVUS ORDO SECLORUM*, one of the most effective advertising slogans to come out of this country. "A new order of the centuries"—belief in novelty and in the desirability of opening novelty to everybody has been important in our lives throughout our history and especially in this century. Again and again advertising has been an agency for inducing Americans to try anything and everything—from the continent itself to a new brand of soap. As one of the more literate and poetic of the advertising copywriters, James Kenneth Frazier, a Cornell graduate, wrote in 1900 in "The Doctor's Lament":

> This lean M.D. is Dr. Brown
> Who fares but ill in Spotless Town.
> The town is so confounded clean,
> It is no wonder he is lean,
> He's lost all patients now, you know,
> Because they use *Sapolio.*

The same literary talent that once was used to retail Sapolio was later used to induce people to try the Edsel or the Mustang, to experiment with Lifebuoy or Body-All, to drink Pepsi-Cola or Royal Crown Cola, or to shave with a Trac II razor.

And as expansion and novelty have become essential to our economy, advertising has played an ever-larger role: in the settling of the continent, in the expansion of the economy, and in the building of an American standard of living. Advertising has expressed the optimism, the hyperbole, and the sense of community, the sense of reaching which has been so important a feature of our civilization.

* * *

Here I wish to explore the significance of advertising, not as a force in the economy or in shaping an American standard of living, but rather as a touchstone of the ways in which we Americans have learned about all sorts of things.

The problems of advertising are of course not peculiar to advertising, for they are just one aspect of the problems of democracy. They reflect the rise of what I have called Consumption Communities and Statistical Communities, and many of the special problems of advertising have arisen from our continuously energetic effort to give everybody everything.

If we consider democracy not just as a political system, but as a set of institutions which do aim to make everything available to everybody, it would not be an overstatement to describe advertising as the characteristic rhetoric of democracy. One of the tendencies of democracy, which Plato and other antidemocrats warned against a long time ago, was the danger that rhetoric would displace or at least overshadow epistemology; that is, *the temptation to allow the problem of persuasion to overshadow the problem of knowledge.* Democratic societies tend to become more concerned with what people believe than with what is true, to become more concerned with credibility than with truth. All these problems become accentuated in a large-scale democracy like ours, which possesses all the apparatus of modern industry. And the problems are accentuated still further by universal literacy, by instantaneous communication, and by the daily plague of words and images.

In the early days it was common for advertising men to define advertisements as a kind of news. The best admen, like the best journalists, were supposed to be those who were able to make their news the most interesting and readable. This was natural enough, since the verb to "advertise" originally meant, intransitively, to take note or to consider. For a person to "advertise" meant originally, in the fourteenth and fifteenth centuries, to reflect on something, to think about something. Then it came to mean, transitively, to call the attention of another to something, to give him notice, to notify, admonish, warn or inform in a formal or impressive manner. And then, by the sixteenth century, it came to mean: to give notice of anything, to make generally known. It was not until the late eighteenth century that the word "advertising" in English came to have a specifically "advertising" connotation as we might say today, and not until the late nineteenth century that it began to have a specifically commercial connotation. By 1879 someone was saying, "Don't advertise unless you have something worth advertising." But even into the present century, newspapers continue to call themselves by the title "Advertiser"—for example, the Boston *Daily Advertiser*, which was a newspaper of long tradition and one of the most dignified papers in Boston until William Randolph Hearst took it over in 1917. Newspapers carried "Advertiser" on their mastheads, not because they sold advertisements but because they brought news.

Now, the main role of advertising in American civilization came increasingly to be that of persuading and appealing rather than that of educating and informing. By 1921, for instance, one of the more popular textbooks, Blanchard's *Essentials of Advertising*, began: "Anything employed to influence people favorably is advertising. The mission of advertising is to persuade men and women to act in a way that will be of advantage to the advertiser." This development—in a country where a shared, a rising, and a democratized standard of living was the national pride and the national hallmark—meant that advertising had become the rhetoric of democracy.

* * *

What, then, were some of the main features of modern American advertising—if we consider it as a form of rhetoric? First, and perhaps most obvious, is *repetition*. It is hard for us to realize that the use of repetition in advertising is not an ancient device but a modern one, which actually did not come into common use in American journalism until just past the middle of the nineteenth century.

The development of what came to be called "iteration copy" was a result of a struggle by a courageous man of letters and advertising pioneer, Robert Bonner, who bought the old New York *Merchant's Ledger* in 1851 and turned it into a popular journal. He then had the temerity to try to change the ways of James Gordon Bennett, who of course was one of the most successful of the American newspaper pioneers, and who was both a sensationalist and at the same time an extremely stuffy man when it came to things that he did not consider to be news. Bonner was determined to use advertisements in Bennett's wide-circulating New York *Herald* to sell his own literary product, but he found it difficult to persuade Bennett to allow him to use any but agate type in his advertising. (Agate was the smallest type used by newspapers in that day, only barely legible to the naked eye.) Bennett would not allow advertisers to use larger type, nor would he allow them to use illustrations except stock cuts, because he thought it was undignified. He said, too, that to allow a variation in the format of ads would be undemocratic. He insisted that all advertisers use the same size type so that no one would be allowed to prevail over another simply by presenting his message in a larger, more clever, or more attention-getting form.

Finally Bonner managed to overcome Bennett's rigidity by leasing whole pages of the paper and using the tiny agate type to form larger letters across the top of the page. In this way he produced a message such as "Bring home the New York Ledger tonight." His were unimaginative messages, and when repeated all across the page they technically did not violate Bennett's agate rule. But they opened a new era and presaged a new freedom for advertisers in their use of the newspaper page. Iteration copy—the practice of presenting prosaic content in ingenious, repetitive form—became common, and nowadays of course is commonplace.

* * *

A second characteristic of American advertising which is not unrelated to this is the development of *an advertising style.* We have histories of most other kinds of style—including the style of many unread writers who are remembered today only because they have been forgotten—but we have very few accounts of the history of advertising style, which of course is one of the most important forms of our language and one of the most widely influential.

The development of advertising style was the convergence of several very respectable American traditions. One of these was the tradition of the "plain style," which the Puritans made so much of and which accounts for so much of the strength of the Puritan literature. The "plain style" was of course much influenced by the Bible and found its way into the rhetoric of American writers and speakers of great power like Abraham Lincoln. When advertising began to be self-conscious in the early years of this century, the pioneers urged copywriters not to be too clever, and especially not to be fancy. One of the pioneers of the advertising copywriters, John Powers, said, for example, "The commonplace is the proper level for writing in business; where the first virtue is plainness, 'fine writing' is not only intellectual, it is offensive." George P. Rowell, another advertising pioneer, said, "You must write your advertisement to catch damned fools—not college professors." He was a very tactful person. And he added, "And you'll catch just as many college professors as you will of any other sort." In the 1920's, when advertising was beginning to come into its own, Claude Hopkins, whose name is known to all in the trade, said, "Brilliant writing has no place in advertising. A unique style takes attention from the subject. Any apparent effort to sell creates corresponding resistance. . . . One should be natural and simple. His language should not be conspicuous. In fishing for buyers, as in fishing for bass, one should not reveal the hook." So there developed a characteristic advertising style in which plainness, the phrase that anyone could understand, was a distinguishing mark.

At the same time, the American advertising style drew on another, and what might seem an antithetic, tradition—the tradition of hyperbole and tall talk, the language of Davy Crockett and Mike Fink. While advertising could think of itself as 99.44 percent pure, it used the language of "Toronado" and "Cutlass." As I listen to the radio in Washington, I hear a celebration of heroic qualities which would make the characteristics of Mike Fink and Davy Crockett pale, only to discover at the end of the paean that what I have been hearing is a description of the Ford dealers in the District of Columbia neighborhood. And along with the folk tradition of hyperbole and tall talk comes the rhythm of folk music. We hear that Pepsi-Cola hits the spot, that it's for the young generation—and we hear other products celebrated in music which we cannot forget and sometimes don't want to remember.

There grew somehow out of all these contradictory tendencies—combining the commonsense language of the "plain style," and the fantasy language of "tall talk"—an advertising style. This characteristic way of talking about things was especially designed to reach and catch the millions. It created a whole new world of myth. A myth, the dictionary tells us, is a notion based more on tradition or convenience than on facts; it is a received idea. Myth is not just fantasy and not just fact but exists in a limbo, in the world of the "Will to Believe," which William James has written about so eloquently and so perceptively. This is the world of the neither true nor false— of the statement that 60 percent of the physicians who expressed a choice said that our brand of aspirin would be more effective in curing a simple headache than any other leading brand.

That kind of statement exists in a penumbra. I would call this the "advertising penumbra." It is not untrue, and yet, in its connotation it is not exactly true.

* * *

Now, there is still another characteristic of advertising so obvious that we are inclined perhaps to overlook it. I call that *ubiquity*. Advertising abhors a vacuum and we discover new vacuums every day. The parable, of course, is the story of the man who thought of putting the advertisement on the other side of the cigarette package. Until then, that was wasted space and a society which aims at a democratic standard of living, at extending the benefits of consumption and all sorts of things and services to everybody, must miss no chances to reach people. The highway billboard and other outdoor advertising, bus and streetcar and subway advertising, and skywriting, radio and TV commercials—all these are of course obvious evidence that advertising abhors a vacuum.

We might reverse the old mousetrap slogan and say that anyone who can devise another place to put another mousetrap to catch a consumer will find people beating a path to his door. "Avoiding advertising will become a little harder next January," *The Wall Street Journal* reported on May 17, 1973, "when a Studio City, California, company launches a venture called StoreVision. Its product is a system of billboards that move on a track across supermarket ceilings. Some 650 supermarkets so far are set to have the system." All of which helps us understand the observation attributed to a French man of letters during his recent visit to Times Square. "What a beautiful place, if only one could not read!" Everywhere is a place to be filled, as we discover in a recent *Publishers Weekly* description of one advertising program: "The $1.95 paperback edition of Dr. Thomas A. Harris' million-copy best seller, 'I'm O.K., You're O.K.' is in for full-scale promotion in July by its publisher, Avon Books. Plans range from bumper stickers to airplane streamers, from planes flying above Fire Island, the Hamptons and Malibu. In addition, the $100,000 promotion budget calls for 200,000 bookmarks, plus brochures, buttons, lipcards, floor and counter displays, and advertising in magazines and TV."

The ubiquity of advertising is of course just another effect of our uninhibited efforts to use all the media to get all sorts of information to everybody everywhere. Since the places to be filled are everywhere, the amount of advertising is not determined by the *needs* of advertising, but by the *opportunities* for advertising which become unlimited.

* * *

But the most effective advertising, in an energetic, novelty-ridden society like ours, tends to be "self-liquidating." To create a cliché you must offer something which everybody accepts. The most successful advertising therefore self-destructs because it becomes cliché. Examples of this are found in the tendency for copyrighted names of trademarks to enter the vernacular—for the proper names of products which have been made familiar by costly advertising to become common nouns, and so to apply to anybody's products. Kodak becomes a synonym for camera, Kleenex a synonym for facial tissue, when both begin with a small *k*, and Xerox (now, too, with a small *x*) is used to describe all processes of copying, and so on. These are prototypes of the problem. If you are successful enough, then you will defeat your purpose in the long run—by making the name and the message so familiar that people won't notice them, and then people will cease to distinguish your product from everybody else's.

In a sense, of course, as we will see, the whole of American civilization is an example. When this was a "new" world, if people succeeded in building a civilization here, the New World would survive and would reach the time—in our age—when it would cease to be new. And now we have the oldest written Constitution in use in the world. This is only a parable of which there are many more examples.

The advertising man who is successful in marketing any particular product, then—in our high-technology, well-to-do democratic society, which aims to get everything to everybody—is apt to be diluting the demand for his particular product in the very act of satisfying it. But luckily for him, he is at the very same time creating a fresh demand for his services as advertiser.

And as a consequence, there is yet another role which is assigned to American advertising. This is what I call "erasure." Insofar as advertising is competitive or innovation is widespread, erasure is required in order to persuade consumers that this year's model is superior to last year's. In fact, we consumers learn that we might be risking our lives if we go out on the highway with those very devices that were last year's lifesavers but without whatever special kind of brakes or wipers or seat belt is on this year's model. This is what I mean by "erasure"—and we see it on our advertising pages or our television screen every day. We read in *The New York Times* (May 20, 1973), for example, that "For the price of something small and ugly, you can drive something small and beautiful"—an advertisement for the Fiat 250 Spider. Or another, perhaps more subtle example is the advertisement for shirts under a picture of Oliver Drab: "Oliver Drab. A name to remember in fine designer shirts? No kidding. . . . Because you pay extra money for Oliver Drab. And for all the other superstars of the fashion world. Golden Vee [the name of the brand that is advertised] does not have a designer's label. But we do have designers. . . . By keeping their names *off* our label and simply saying Golden Vee, we can afford to sell our $7 to $12 shirts for just $7 to $12, which should make Golden Vee a name to remember. Golden Vee, you only pay for the shirt."

* * *

Having mentioned two special characteristics—the self-liquidating tendency and the need for erasure—which arise from the dynamism of the American economy, I would like to try to place advertising in a larger perspective. The special role of advertising in our life gives a clue to a pervasive oddity in American civilization. A leading feature of past cultures, as anthropologists have explained, is the tendency to distinguish between "high" culture and "low" culture—between the culture of the literate and the learned on the one hand and that of the populace on the other. In other words, between the language of literature and the language of the vernacular. Some of the most useful statements of this distinction have been made by social scientists at the University of Chicago—first by the late Robert Redfield in his several pioneering books on peasant society, and then by Milton Singer in his remarkable study of Indian civilization, *When a Great Tradition Modernizes* (1972). This distinction between the great tradition and the little tradition, between the high culture and the folk culture, has begun to become a commonplace of modern anthropology.

Some of the obvious features of advertising in modern America offer us an opportunity to note the significance or insignificance of that distinction for us. Elsewhere I have tried to point out some of the peculiarities of the American attitude toward the *high* culture. There is something distinctive about the place of thought in American life, which I think is not quite what it has been in certain Old World cultures.

But what about distinctive American attitudes to *popular* culture? What is our analogue to the folk culture of other peoples? Advertising gives us some clues—to a characteristically American democratic folk culture. Folk culture is a name for the culture which ordinary people everywhere lean on. It is not the writings of Dante and Chaucer and Shakespeare and Milton, the teachings of Machiavelli and Descartes, Locke or Marx. It is, rather, the pattern of slogans, local traditions, tales, songs, dances, and ditties. And of course holiday observances. Popular culture in other civilizations has been for the most part both an area of continuity with the past, a way in which people reach back into the past and out to their community, and at the same time an area of local variations. An area of individual and amateur expression in which a person has his own way of saying, or notes his mother's way of saying or singing, or his own way of dancing, his own view of folk wisdom and the cliché.

And here is an interesting point of contrast. In other societies outside the United States, it is the *high* culture that has generally been an area of centralized, organized control. In Western Europe, for example, universities and churches have tended to be closely allied to the government. The institutions of higher learning have had a relatively limited access to the people as a whole. This was inevitable, of course, in most parts of the world, because there were so few universities. In England, for example, there were only two universities until the early nineteenth century. And there was central control over the printed matter that was used in universities or in the liturgy. The government tended to be close to the high culture, and that was easy because the high culture itself was so centralized and because literacy was relatively limited.

In our society, however, we seem to have turned all of this around. Our high culture is one of the least centralized areas of our culture. And our universities express the atomistic, diffused, chaotic, and individualistic aspect of our life. We have in this country more than twenty-five hundred colleges and universities, institutions of so-called higher learning. We have a vast population in these institutions, somewhere over seven million students.

But when we turn to our popular culture, what do we find? We find that in our nation of Consumption Communities and emphasis on Gross National Product (GNP) and growth rates, advertising has become the heart of the folk culture and even its very prototype. And as we have seen, American advertising shows many characteristics of the folk culture of other societies: repetition, a plain style, hyperbole and tall talk, folk verse, and folk music. Folk culture, wherever it has flourished, has tended to thrive in a limbo between fact and fantasy, and of course, depending on the spoken word and the oral tradition, it spreads easily and tends to be ubiquitous. These are all familiar characteristics of folk culture and they are ways of describing our folk culture, but how do the expressions of our peculiar folk culture come to *us*?

They no longer sprout from the earth, from the village, from the farm, or even from the neighborhood or the city. They come to us primarily from enormous centralized self-consciously *creative* (an overused word, for the overuse of which advertising agencies are in no small part responsible) organizations. They come from advertising agencies, from networks of newspapers, radio, and television, from outdoor-advertising agencies, from the copywriters for ads in the largest-circulation magazines, and so on. These "creators" of folk culture—or pseudo-folk culture—aim at the widest intelligibility and charm and appeal.

But in the United States, we must recall, the advertising folk culture (like all advertising) is also confronted with the problems of self-liquidation and erasure. These are by-products of the expansive, energetic character of our economy. And they, too, distinguish American folk culture from folk cultures elsewhere.

Our folk culture is distinguished from others by being discontinuous, ephemeral, and self-destructive. Where does this leave the common citizen? All of us are qualified to answer.

In our society, then, those who cannot lean on the world of learning, on the high culture of the classics, on the elaborated wisdom of the books, have a new problem. The University of Chicago, for example, in the 1930's and 1940's was the center of a quest for a "common discourse." The champions of that quest, which became a kind of crusade, believed that such a discourse could be found through familiarity with the classics of great literature—and especially of Western European literature. I think they were misled; such works were not, nor are they apt to become, the common discourse of our society. Most people, even in a democracy, and a rich democracy like ours, live in a world of popular culture, our special kind of popular culture.

The characteristic folk culture of our society is a creature of advertising, and in a sense it *is* advertising. But advertising, our own popular culture, is harder to make into a source of continuity than the received wisdom and commonsense slogans and catchy songs of the vivid vernacular. The popular culture of advertising attenuates and is always dissolving before our very eyes. Among the charms, challenges, and tribulations of modern life, we must count this peculiar fluidity, this ephemeral character of that very kind of culture on which other peoples have been able to lean, the kind of culture to which they have looked for the continuity of their traditions, for their ties with the past and with the future.

We are perhaps the first people in history to have a centrally organized mass-produced folk culture. Our kind of popular culture is here today and gone tomorrow—or the day after tomorrow. Or whenever the next semiannual model appears. And insofar as folk culture becomes advertising, and advertising becomes centralized, it becomes a way of depriving people of their opportunities for individual and small-community expression. Our technology and our economy and our democratic ideals have all helped make that possible. Here we have a new test of the problem that is at least as old as Heraclitus—an everyday test of man's ability to find continuity in his experience. And here democratic man has a new opportunity to accommodate himself, if he can, to the unknown.

III

PREPARING FOR THE

UNEXPECTED

THE FERTILE VERGE

from HIDDEN HISTORY, *1987*

F OR THE SECRET alchemy of creativity, the mystery which opens the Book of Genesis, we are not ever likely to find a formula. But of the several kinds of creativity, the least secret, the most public, the most discussable is *social* creativity. While this subject is much vaster and more amorphous than creativity in Mark Twain, William James, Ernest Hemingway, Jackson Pollock, or Aaron Copland, it is more open to our scrutiny.

American creativity, I will suggest, has flourished on what I call the Fertile Verge.

A verge is a place of encounter between something and something else. America was a land of verges—all sorts of verges, between kinds of landscape or seascape, between stages of civilization, between ways of thought and ways of life. During our first centuries we experienced more different kinds of verges, and more extensive and more vivid verges, than any other great modern nation. The long Atlantic coast, where early colonial settlements flourished, was, of course, a verge between land and sea. Every movement inward into the continent was a verge between the advanced European civilization and the stone-age culture of the American Indians, between people and wilderness. The earliest flourishing of a new American civilization was in New England and in Virginia, where people enjoyed the commerce of the sea.

As cities became sprinkled around the continent, each was a new verge between the ways of the city and those of the countryside. As immigrants poured in from Ireland, Germany, and Italy, from Africa and Asia, each group created new verges between their imported ways and the imported ways of their neighbors and the new-grown ways of the New World. Each immigrant himself lived the verge encounter between another nation's ways of thinking, feeling, speaking, and living and the American ways.

In ancient, more settled nations, uniformity was idealized. The national pride of Englishman, Frenchman, German, or Italian was a pride in the special genius of his own kind. "Outside" influences might spice the culture, might spark renaissances, might stir it to fulfill itself in new ways. But the promise of the nation in the long run lay in the fulfillment of this one particular genius. The organic image was then apt. For the French aimed at the "flowering" of a pure French spirit. Grandeur and vitality came somehow from within, from purity, from a refusal to fulfill any other people's destiny.

The American situation was different. The creativity, the hope, of the nation was in its verges, in its new mixtures and new confusions. At least until the middle of the twentieth century, the United States remained rich in verges. The expansion of empires from the fifteenth through the nineteenth century did provide European nations with their remote verges—far-off colonies in Africa or Asia or America or Oceania. But for our United States, the verges were within, and were the most fertile part of us.

The brilliant historian Frederick Jackson Turner did us a great service by reminding us of "The Significance of the Frontier in American History" (1893). He directed historians' attention away from the genealogy-ridden, overworked chronicles of the Atlantic seacoast to the novelties of westward-moving peoples. Describing the frontier as "the hither edge of free land," he surveyed the characteristic American ways of thinking and governing, strewn across the continent as that frontier line moved toward the Pacific.

Turner also did us a disservice. For he overcast the whole American experience with what he called the Frontier experience, the special character of only one of our stages. He gave a new vividness and a new name to the whole drama. But he obscured the fact that the encounter of European civilization with a wilderness—what he called "the outer edge of the wave—the meeting point between savagery and civilization"—was only the First Act. Turner took his clue, of course, from the Census of 1890, which reported that in the newly populated American West there was no longer a "frontier line." Therefore, he said, the frontier habitat had disappeared.

While Turner thought he was describing the archaeology of American life, he was actually describing its physiology. His example dazzled and delighted historians desperately seeking a theme. Yet the kind of encounter of which Turner described one example had myriad counterparts. The creative American encounter was a much less local phenomenon than any physical frontier with Old World connotation of fortified borderlands, or nineteenth-century imperial overtones of the contrast between civilization and savagery. At the outer edge of the free mind American creative energies were continually refreshed.

On these verges—gifts of our geography, our history, our demography—we find three characteristic ways of thinking and feeling. First, there is our exaggerated *self-awareness*. On the verge we notice more poignantly who we are, how we are thinking, what we are doing. Second, there is a special *openness to novelty and change*. When we encounter something different, we become aware that things can be different, our appetite is whetted for novelty and its charms. Third, there is a strong *community-consciousness*. In the face of the different and the unfamiliar, we, the similars, lean on one another. We seek to reassure one another as we organize our new communities and new forms of community. These three tendencies are all both opportunities and temptations. They are sometimes complementary, sometimes contradictory. Creativity in our United States has been a harvest of these hypertrophied American attitudes stirred on the Fertile Verge. Here are a few of the countless Fertile Verges dramatized in our nation's history.

GEOGRAPHIC VERGES

The first English settlements in America called themselves plantations. We lose the flavor of their experience in the modern word "colony." Today we think of a colony as an outpost or a subordinated part of an empire.

The word "plantation" suggested something quite different. Francis Bacon's essay "Of Plantations" (1625) underlined the difference. "Planting of countries," he wrote, "is like planting of woods. For you must make account to lose almost twenty years' profit, and expect your recompense in the end. For the principal thing that hath been the destruction of most plantations hath been the base and hasty drawing of profit in the first years. It is true, speedy profit is not to be neglected, as far as it may stand with the good of the plantation, but no farther." A plantation, then, was a place of risk and of calculation. Its success required a sharpened self-awareness. You had to know what you were doing.

"If you plant where savages are," Bacon prescribed, "do not only entertain them with trifles and gingles [i.e. rattles], but use them justly and graciously, with sufficient guard nevertheless. And do not win their favour by helping them to invade their enemies. . . . Send oft of them over to the country that plants, that they may see a better condition than their own, and commend it when they return."

Two decades later, William Bradford called his classic chronicle a history *Of Plymouth Plantation* (1651) and his fellow planters were aware of a higher balance sheet. On the *Arbella*, John Winthrop made a familiar declaration of self-awareness for his community, who would be as a "City upon a Hill."

For the first time in modern history, large numbers of Europeans transplanted themselves to a place of mystery and emptiness. Of course, there were a few million of native Americans spread thinly. But it was the encounter with raw, uninhabited nature, with its unpredictable climate, its strange plants and animals, that sharpened their consciousness of where they were and what they were doing.

In the eighteenth century, American settlers came to be struck less by Divine Providence and more by the providential wealth and novelty of their new world. No longer could they follow the familiar routines of Old World agriculture. New crops—Indian corn (maize), tobacco, cotton, and others equally strange—offered new challenges, with a new need to become informed, to notice how and when to plant.

Natural History, as it was then called, flourished here. In 1743 Benjamin Franklin alerted his fellow Americans and enlisted their energies in what was to become the American Philosophical Society. He described as the special arena of their interests what might now be called the whole American "environment," which for quite other reasons still arrests our attention. The concerns shared by Franklin's group, announced in his circular letter, were all sorts of items "new-discovered" (plants, herbs, trees, roots; fossils, mines, minerals, quarries), "new methods," "new mechanical inventions," "new arts," and "new improvements" of every kind. Americans of lively mind became naturalists. Europeans eager to enlarge their catalogs of nature, disciples and ambassadors of Linnaeus, surveyed the strange American scene and explored the exotic American landscape. Peter Kalm and others came from Sweden, William Bartram set out from Philadelphia, and Haiti-born John James Audubon came, via France, to Kentucky and the fecund Mississippi Valley.

Not that Americans needed reminding, but the great European naturalists of the age still kept telling them that America was different. A delightful allegory of this inevitable American self-awareness was enacted one evening just outside Paris at the end of the American Revolution. For the American Peace Mission Benjamin Franklin was giving a dinner party at Passy, where half of those invited were French, the other half Americans. Among the French was the Abbé Raynal, a sprightly Jesuit-trained historian. Raynal steered the conversation to his theory, popular in France at the time, that all species of animals, including man, tended to degenerate and become smaller in the inhospitable American climate. Franklin, seeing how the guests were seated at the table (all the Americans on one side, and all the French on the other), proposed that they test the theory then and there. "Let both parties rise," he said, "and we will see on which side nature has degenerated." The Americans, including Franklin, who was not a tall man, towered over their French opposites—and it happened that the smallest of all was Raynal himself.

Even among our helpful French allies, Americans could not fail to be aware of countless still undiscovered consequences of being American. The City upon a Hill nourished cities in the wilderness. City-founding required an especially lively and informed awareness of what you were doing. In the Old World you were born into your city or onto the anciently settled countryside. Here, from the beginning, you had to help mark off where you and your children would be living. The colonial period was replete with town plans, still visible on the street maps of Savannah and Philadelphia, among many others. "Main Street" was a significant Americanism long before Sinclair Lewis gave it a sour connotation. Main Streets, so-called, bore witness all across the continent that *our* towns and cities were planned by self-aware Americans. The very first paid job undertaken by the Father of our Country, George Washington, was his assignment, at the age of sixteen, to work as assistant surveyor of a new town to be called Alexandria, just a few miles up the river from Mount Vernon.

When we think back on the situation of British North America at the time of the early settlements, it is quite conceivable that the cartographic ignorance and the vastness of the continent, its heart of darkness, the mountain ranges along both ocean coastlines, and the courses of the great rivers—all these might have impelled Americans to huddle along the seaboard. They might have clustered together in the first clearings to solidify, fortify, and populate areas already familiar. That was the settlement pattern of Africa, Australia, and elsewhere. It is not what happened here. Instead, the vastness, the mystery, the variety, the mountain and river and desert obstacles themselves became enticements. The center of population of the United States would be not far from midcontinent. Going West, where increasing numbers of Americans risked their lives and fortunes, meant willingness to face the unknown, to go out to the verge. The United States, then, became a civilization of more miscellaneous verges than we can count: river towns and prairie villages, mining camps and missions. Vitality of agriculture, commerce, industry, language, education, and folklore sparked where one place or people touched another.

American civilization grew by getting people out to the edges and by getting people and messages back and forth across the verges. This yen for the verges gave a newly dominating significance to technologies of transportation. American railroads, within only a few decades of their invention, were bringing thousands from Europe and the eastern United States out to the edge of the unknown. Much to the astonishment of Old World railroad experts, American railroads developed with no deliberate speed and reached beyond the reasonable needs of existing settlements.

In England, for example, railroads were solidly built, to run from London to Birmingham or Manchester or Edinburgh. In the United States, by contrast, the railroads seemed to run "from Nowhere-in-Particular to Nowhere-at-All." They went out to the verges and beyond. They were built hastily, sometimes flimsily—not so much to serve a population as to attract it, not so much to keep the wheels of old industries turning as to find new materials for new industries. And also to create new settlements to consume the products.

When the centers of growth were on the verges—in the Clevelands and Chicagos and Kansas Citys and Omahas and Denvers and Tulsas—the way to keep the whole nation vital was to keep it in touch with the outskirts. By the mid-nineteenth century, the United States had catapulted into primacy with the greatest railroad mileage in the world.

The same parable could be told of the American automobile, which also quickly outran the highways and the reasonable needs of existing settlements. By 1970 Americans were spending billions to send a few of their number as far into space as they could reach.

The desire to keep in touch and the momentum of technology gave a boost to communications. Once again Americans were tempted to exceed their existing needs. Thoreau, retreating to his New England pond when others were adventuring out to more distant verges, missed the point. "We are in great haste," Thoreau complained (in *Walden* in 1854) in one of his most-quoted jeremiads, "to construct a magnetic telegraph from Maine to Texas; but Maine and Texas, it may be, have nothing important to communicate." Thoreau's fellow Americans confidently assumed that two such different distant places as Maine and Texas would sooner or later have something to say to each other. Might not the telegraph encourage them to find out what that was? Every later advance in the technology of communication—the telephone, the radio, and now television—has flourished here before Americans knew what they should say over it. These too grew on the Fertile Verge of emptiness.

POLITICAL VERGES

Self-awareness breeds self-government and self-government breeds self-awareness. On board the *Mayflower*, even before arriving here, the Pilgrim Fathers noticed that if they were to have a government on landing, they would have to create it for themselves. The Mayflower Compact was dated November 11, 1620, and signed by forty-one passengers—all the heads of families, adult bachelors, and hired menservants. It was a declaration that they all intended to live under a rule of law and that they would shape a government for their special needs. Of course there had been so-called church compacts or church covenants often before, when a group of men and women decided to set up a new church. But now the *Mayflower* passengers extended their covenant to create a full civil government.

History and geography again and again sharpened Americans' awareness of the role that people played in shaping their own political institutions. The success of the American Revolution provided a vacuum which had to be filled by a new frame of government. The federal tradition, nurtured in the old "British" colonial system, required a nice awareness of the nuances of jurisdiction. Hypersensitized by the Revolution, Americans remained alert to the distinction between a constitution and mere legislation.

This drama of political self-awareness was reenacted all across the continent. Old empires had made the government of colonies simple problems of bureaucracy, of extending the jurisdiction of some colonial office. But the spread of self-governing states into the

American West was quite another matter. It required constitutional conventions and the making of new constitutions. Even in their transient communities of westward-moving wagon trains, Americans remained aware of the responsibilities of self-government. En route they took the trouble to frame constitutions for the government of their company during the transcontinental trek.

The multiplication of self-governing States, each with its bicameral legislature, multiplied legislation. Every law was a community's recognition of a problem, another sharpener of self-awareness. The United States was to proliferate legislatures and legislators, laws and legal decisions, without precedent in modern history.

Our nation had been born in the politics of verges. "These united [sic] States" came into being from the difficulty of defining the bounds between the authority of the government in London and the authority of the governments in each of the colonies. The verges between state governments and the national government, the main battleground in the Constitutional Convention of 1787, have remained foggy into our own time. There grew the great political and constitutional issues over which the nation fought the bloodiest war of the nineteenth century. On the verges between state and nation, the issues of interstate commerce, civil rights, revenue sharing, offshore oil, education, welfare, and taxing power dominated the nation's political, legislative, and judicial life into the twentieth century.

While these verges have been battlegrounds, they have also been arenas of experiment and of progress. Each State legislature, as Justice Oliver Wendell Holmes was fond of reminding us, was a laboratory. In the limbo between State and national powers appeared some of the most ingenious and controversial entities, including the Federal Reserve Board, the Federal Trade Commission, the Federal Communications Commission, the Federal Aviation Administration, and countless others.

Explicit and repeated public declarations of the extent and the boundaries of their government reinforced the American obsession with limiting government (rooted in bitter colonial experience) and had unexpected by-products. The public conscience of private citizens flourished on the verge. There appeared a characteristic American frontier for private and voluntary institutions and for mixed public and private institutions—in areas which in the Old World had been sharply defined by law and tradition and preempted by the state. This included higher education. (I spent twenty-five years on the faculty of the great University of Chicago, whose stationery said "Founded by John D. Rockefeller.") And museums. (There in Chicago my family and I enjoyed the Museum of Natural History, a benefaction of Marshall Field.) And libraries. (I exploited the research treasures of the library endowed by a certain Walter J. Newberry.) These are examples of private, voluntary beneficence without close counterpart in Western Europe.

TECHNOLOGICAL VERGES

As early as the mid-eighteenth century American technological verges bore fruit and stimulated the appetite for novelties. The so-called Kentucky rifle, earlier known here as the Pennsylvania rifle, was a good example. When Germans and German Swiss settled in western Pennsylvania, the German rifle, which had developed for Alpine uses, was still clumsy, heavy, and short-barreled. But here in America, hunting, Indian fighting, and skirmishes in the backwoods encouraged improvements. The Pennsylvania rifle became longer and more slender, with a smaller bore and using a ball weighing only about half the weight of that used in the German model. It was quicker to fire, became quicker to load, had less recoil, and offered more range and accuracy. By the time of the American Revolution this weapon, still practically unknown in England and found only among a few hunters in the mountain fastnesses of Europe, had become common in our backwoods. Americans became the best marksmen in the world. Revolutionary commanders encouraged troops to dress in the fringed buckskin of the backwoods to frighten their red-coated enemies. All this was possible because here on the edge, the Fertile Verge between expert and layman, German and Swiss gunsmiths could break traditional patterns.

And then American factories appeared in the wilderness. Just as with the rifle, the basic inventions and mechanized technology of the textile factory had been developed abroad, this time in England. But new things happened when they were brought here to the verge. After an adventurous young Englishman, Samuel Slater, managed to memorize the main features of the Arkwright cotton-spinning machinery and smuggled the secrets out of England to New England, a new era opened. Factories sprang up in the backwoods—on the New England rivers, in Waltham and Lowell—against a strange background of virgin countryside and tree-covered New England hills. Even Charles Dickens, who knew the English milltowns and who was not famous for his sympathy to anything American, could not restrain his enthusiasm in 1842 for these factories on the verges.

The most important American technological innovation of the early nineteenth century—the so-called System of Interchangeable Parts, which became known as the American System—also was a by-product of the verge. The scarcity of gunsmiths offered the opportunity, which Eli Whitney seized.

CULTURAL VERGES

This most familiar of American verges is expressed in countless clichés—a Nation of Nations, the Melting Pot, the Mixing Bowl, etc., etc. But the clichés must not dull us to the extraordinary nature of what happened here. In our unexpected mix of peoples, people discovered things about themselves and about others which they could not have known or noticed in their more homogeneous places of origin.

Of course there was nothing new in the mere juxtaposition of peoples of different histories and languages and traditions. What was novel here was not the to-be-expected ethnic islands but the everywhere-verges. A special American creativity would be found not *within* the enclaves but on the borders between them. Here the borders were omnipresent and with a few exceptions were more open than they had been anywhere else. Unpredictable cultural verges appeared on the prairies, in mining camps, in cities, in churches and schools. Everyone shared the jurisdiction of the same government. The Balanced Ticket proved that all were expected to take part.

Perhaps the least appreciated by-product of American self-awareness on the verges of our national life is our American language. Of the widespread modern languages no other has more effectively allowed a whole people, literati included, to be continually alerted to colloquial enrichment. For the French language the authoritative dictionary is that edited and revised by the Académie Française, an elite group of forty "immortals" who certify words by the usage of the best authors. What happens at the meetings of this legislature for the French language? One of the members, François Mauriac, explained quite simply, "We watch ourselves grow old." The *Oxford English Dictionary*, the counterpart of the dictionary of the Académie for the English language, is a monument of gargantuan scholarship. It too holds up as the mirror of linguistic propriety the published writings of the best authors.

But the spoken language is where the action is. And for our American language there is no single authoritative legislative source. H. L. Mencken's classic *American Language* is essentially an adventure story of what happened to respectable, virginal English when she encountered so many uncouth peoples in various places. The several standard unabridged dictionaries of our American language—Merriam-Webster, Random House—and the most widely used desk-dictionaries—American Heritage, New World, and others—are also distinctively different from those in French or English. Our American dictionaries hold up the mirror to our daily, ever-changing, colloquial usage. Others have tried to confine their sources to respectable literary matter. Our American lexicographers welcome the testimony of all speakers—gossips, athletes, reporters, businessmen, labor leaders, country-music singers, and all comers. Broken English is our true national dialect. When a New England Brahmin, proud of his *Mayflower* ancestry, objects to someone *kibitzing*, I hear what happens on the Fertile Verges of language.

Our dictionaries keep us promptly aware of how our fellow Americans are speaking, so we can understand them and ("hopefully," "at this point in time"!) imitate them. In our language, thanks to our lack of prestigious domineering academies and to the enterprise and alertness and docility of our own dictionary makers and our writers, we are unlike the members of Mauriac's French Academy. "*We* watch ourselves grow *young*."

GENERATIONAL VERGES

American circumstances created new verges between youth and age, between the generations. Self-government, as Thomas Jefferson again and again insisted, meant the sovereignty of the present generation. "We may consider each generation as a distinct nation," Jefferson wrote, "with a right, by the will of its majority, to bind themselves, but none to bind the succeeding generation, more than the inhabitants of another country." But every community includes relics of earlier generations, as well as scions of the next. Still, Jefferson expressed a characteristic American concern. Few other countries have been so preoccupied with the youthfulness of youth.

Immigration itself, for most of American history, deepened the sense of difference between the older and the younger generation, between parents and their children. While in long-settled countries the universal process was the parent instructing and acculturating the child, among millions of newly arrived immigrants in the United States the process was reversed. Parents spoke only German, Italian, Spanish, Polish, Yiddish, or Japanese. Their children, learning colloquial American English in the public schools, at home became instructors in the American language and in American ways.

Mary Antin's *Promised Land* (1912) is a classic account of how a little immigrant Jewish girl from Russia became an American and then taught her father how to speak and behave like an American. She reports her father's sentiments when he took her for her first day in the New York City public school:

> If education, culture, the higher life were shining things to be worshipped from afar, he had still a means left whereby he could draw one step nearer to them. He could send his children to school to learn all those things that he knew by fame to be desirable. The common school, at least, perhaps high school; for one or two, perhaps even college! His children should be students, should fill his house with books and intellectual company; and thus he would walk by proxy in the Elysian Fields of liberal learning.

Parents enjoyed their children's rapid rise. But the increasing gap between parent and child often produced heartaches. Today's American enthusiasm for youth may have roots in the peculiar American immigrant experience of children seeming wiser, or at least more acculturated, than their parents. All this, of course, was reinforced by speedy technological progress which bred admiration, or at least tolerance, for new models of everything, including new-model Americans.

*   *   *

In our own time, we see some perils in the traditional verges. The self-awareness, the City upon a Hill syndrome, threatens to become mere self-consciousness, conceit, or even self-flagellation. Old cultural verges threaten to become islands of ethnic or racial or pseudo-racial chauvinism. The appetite for novelty threatens to become the disease of Presentism, obsession with the recent and the present, when we displace history by social studies, classics by best-sellers, heroes by celebrities. Community consciousness, the concern of the *Mayflower* passengers for all their fellows, may become an obsession with the shifting currents of public opinion. The symptoms are demagoguery in politics, timid conformity in private life, and imitativeness in our businessmen, technicians, writers, artists, and architects.

The Fertile Verges of the next epoch of American life are bound to be somewhat different. American successes of the last two centuries have created unprecedented new verges. Perhaps these lie along the rim of creative dissatisfaction. Some living witnesses are our American institutions for teaching and learning, our American advertising industry, and our thriving enterprises of research and development.

Our institutions tell us that the Fertile Verges of our time are still on the outer bounds of the free mind. There is always more ignorance than knowledge, and on that boundary, which no Census can ever report closed, we find the verge which we must keep open, and which will always be fertile. We must be reminded not only of what we know, what we can do, but of what we do not know, what impossibilities still remain to be accomplished, or at least tried. Our task is to remain aware of these verges and to keep the borders open to a competitive world of new ideas, new products, new arts, new institutions. The frontier metaphor will no longer serve us. Surely we are not the last New World. The creativity of our nation will depend on our finding and exploring the verges between our new world and the next.

TWO KINDS OF REVOLUTIONS

from THE REPUBLIC OF TECHNOLOGY, *1987*

FOR ONLY A tiny fragment of human history has man been aware even that he had a history. During nearly all the years since man first developed writing and civilization began, he thought of himself and of his community in ways quite different from those familiar to us today. He tended to see the passage of time, not as a series of unique, irreversible moments of change, but rather as a recurrence of *familiar* moments. The cycle of the seasons— spring, summer, fall, winter, spring—was his most vivid, most intimate signal of passing time. When men sought other useful signposts in the cycle, at first they naturally chose the phases of the moon, because the reassuring regularity of the lunar cycle, being relatively short, was easily noted. It was some time before recognition of the solar cycle (a much more sophisticated notion), with its accompanying notion of a yearly cycle, became widespread.

And, in that age of cyclical time, before the discovery of history, the repetition of the familiar provided the framework for all the most significant and dramatic occasions in human experience. Religious rituals were re-creations or recapitulations of ancient original events, often the events which were supposed to have created the world. The spring was a time not only of new crops, but of a re-created earth. Just as the moon was reborn in every lunar cycle, so the year was reborn through the solar cycle.

Just as the sacred year always repeated the Creation, so every human marriage reproduced the hierogamy—the sacred union of heaven and earth. Every hero relived the career and recaptured the spirit of an earlier mythic prototype. A familiar surviving example of the age of cyclical time before the rise of historical consciousness is the Judaeo-Christian Sabbath. Our week has seven days, and by resting on the seventh day, we reenact the primordial gesture of the Lord God when on the seventh day of the Creation He "rested . . . from all his work which he had made" (Genesis 2:2).

The archaic man, as Mircea Eliade puts it, lived in a "continual present" where nothing is really new, because of his "refusal to accept himself as a historical being."

1

Perhaps the greatest of all historical revolutions was man's discovery—or his invention—of the idea of history. Obviously it did not occur in Western Europe on any particular day, in any particular year, or perhaps even in a particular century, but slowly and painfully. If we stop to think for a moment, we will begin to see how difficult it must have been for people whose whole world had consisted of a universe of seasons and cycles, of archetypes and resurrections, of myths relived, of heroes reincarnate, to think in a way so different.

This was nothing less than man's discovery of the new. Not of any particular sort of novelty, but of the very possibility of novelty. Men were moving from the relived-familiar, from the always-meaningful reenactment of the archetype, out into a world of unimagined, chaotic, and possibly treacherous novelty.

When did this first crucial revolution in human thought occur? In Western European civilization it seems to have come at the end of the Middle Ages, probably around the fourteenth century. The power of older ways of thinking, the dominance of cycles and rebirths, was revealed in the very name "Renaissance" (which actually did not come into use till the nineteenth century) for the age when novelty and man's power for breaking out of the cycles were discovered.

Symptoms of this new way of thinking (as Peter Burke has

chronicled in his *Renaissance Sense of the Past*) are found in the writings of Petrarch (1304–1374), who himself took an interest in history, in the changing fashions in coins, clothing, words, and laws; he saw the ruins of Rome not as the creation of mythic giants but as relics of a different age. Lorenzo Valla (c. 1407–1457) pioneered historical scholarship when he proved the so-called Donation of Constantine to be a forgery, and he also laid a basis for historical linguistics when (in *De elegantia linguae latinae*) he showed the relationship between the decline of the Roman Empire and the decline of Latin. Paintings by Piero della Francesca (c. 1420–1492) and by Andrea Mantegna (1431–1506) began to abandon the reckless anachronism of earlier artists and made new efforts at historical accuracy in armor and in costume. Roman law, which would continue to dominate continental Europe, ceased to be a suprahistorical, transcendental phenomenon. And other legal systems began to be seen as capable of change. In England, for example, where the common law was imagined to be the rules "to which the mind of man runneth not to the contrary," the fiction of antiquity began to dissolve, and by the seventeenth century innovation by legislation was thought to be possible. The Protestant Reformation, too, brought a new interest in historical sources and opened the way for a new kind of scrutiny of the past.

2

The awakening sense of history, which opened new worlds and unimagined worlds of the new, brought its own problems. Names had to be found, or made, for the particular novelties, or the kinds of novelty which history would bring. The new inquiring spirit, the newly quizzical mood for viewing the passing current of events, stirred scholars to look beneath the surface for latent causes and unconfessed motives. Early efforts to describe and explain historical change still leaned heavily on the old notion of cycles. A late version of this was offered in about 1635 in a rich baroque metaphor by Sir Thomas Browne:

> As though there were a Metempsychosis, and the soul of
> one man passed into another, opinions do find, after certain

revolutions, men and minds like those that first begat them
. . . men are lived over again, the world is now as it was in
ages past . . . because the glory of one state depends upon the
ruin of another, there is a revolution and vicissitude of their
greatness, and must obey the swing of that wheel, not moved
by intelligences [such as the souls that moved the planets]
but by the hand of God, whereby all estates arise to their
zenith and vertical parts according to their predestined periods. For the lives, not only of men, but of Commonwealths,
and of the whole world, run not upon a helix that still en-
largeth, but on a circle, where, according to their meridian,
they decline on obscurity, and fall under the horizon again.

But as the historical consciousness became more lively, the historical
imagination became both more sensitive and bolder. There were
more artists and scholars and lawyers and chroniclers who saw the
passage of time as history.

Several words which once had a specific physical denotation
began to be borrowed and given extended meanings, to describe
processes in history. By the early seventeenth century (as the *Oxford
English Dictionary* reveals), the word "revolution," which had described the movement of celestial bodies in an orbit or circular
course and which had also come to mean the time required to complete such a full circuit, had also come into use figuratively to denote
a great change or alteration in the position of affairs. In a century
shaken by "commotions" (as they were sometimes called) which
overthrew established governments and forcibly substituted new rulers, "revolution" came to mean what we still think of it as meaning
in the twentieth century.

At about the same time, the word "progress," which until then
had been used almost exclusively in the simple physical sense of an
onward movement in space, and then to describe the onward movement of a story or narrative, was put to new uses. Originally neither
of these senses was eulogistic. By the late seventeenth or early eighteenth century, however, "progress" had come commonly to mean
advancement to a higher stage, advancement to better and better
conditions, continuous improvement. That was the age of the En-

glish Enlightenment, which encompassed John Locke, Sir Isaac
Newton, Robert Boyle, David Hume, and Edward Gibbon. Hardly
surprising that it needed a name for progress! Similarly, by the mid-
nineteenth century, as a philologist explained in 1871, the word
"decadence" (derived from *de* + *cadere*, which meant to fall down)
"came into fashion, apparently to *denote* decline and *connote* a scientific and enlightened view of that decline on the part of the user."

The century after 1776 was not only a period of great revolutions, it was also a period of great historians. In England that century
produced the works of Edward Gibbon, Thomas Babington Macaulay, Henry Thomas Buckle, and W.E.H. Lecky; in the United States
it was the century of Francis Parkman, William Hickling Prescott,
George Bancroft, and Henry Adams. Western culture was energetically—even frantically—seeking a vocabulary to describe the new
world of novelty. Historians willingly grasped at metaphors, adapted
technical terms, stretched analogies, and extended the jargon of
other disciplines in their quest for handles on the historical processes.

Two giants came on this scene. And—partly from the desperate
need for a vocabulary, partly from their vigorous style, partly from
their own towering talents for generalizing—these two have dominated much of Western writing and thinking about history into our
own day. The first, of course, was Charles Darwin. In 1859 his *Origin of Species* offered with eloquent and persuasive rhetoric some
strikingly new ways of describing the history of plants and animals.
And he providentially satisfied the needs of man's new historical
consciousness, for unlike earlier biologists he offered a way of describing and explaining the continuous emergence of novelty. Darwin brought the whole animate world into the new realm of
historical consciousness. He showed that every living thing had a
history. The jargon that grew out of his work, or was grafted on to
his work—"evolution," "natural selection," "struggle for survival,"
"survival of the fittest," among other expressions—proved wonderfully attractive to historians of the human species.

There were many reasons why Darwin's vocabulary was attractive. But one of the most potent was the simplest. He provided a way

of talking about change, of making plausible the emergence of novelty in experience, and of showing how the sloughing off of the old inevitably produces the new.

In Europe the nineteenth century, like the seventeenth, was an age of "commotions." After the American Revolution of 1776 and the French Revolution of 1789, revolution was in the air. And the man who translated biology into sociology, who translated the origin of species into the origin of revolutions, was Karl Marx. He freely admitted his debt to Darwin. When the first English translation of the first volume of *Das Kapital* was about to appear, Marx wrote to Darwin asking permission to dedicate the volume to him. Darwin's surprising reply was that, while he was deeply honored, he preferred that Marx not dedicate the book to him, because his family would be disturbed to have dedicated to a Darwin a book that was so Godless!

Darwin and Marx together provided the vocabulary which has dominated the writing and thinking of historians—Marxist and anti-Marxist, Communist and anti-Communist—into our own time.

Since Marx, every sort of social change has been christened a revolution. So we have the Industrial Revolution, the "Sexual Revolution," and even the so-called "Paperback Revolution." The word "revolution" has become a shorthand to amplify or dignify any subject. Revolution has become the very prototype (I could even say the stereotype) of social change.

All this reminds us that mankind has generally been more successful in describing the persisting features of his experience—warfare, state, church, school, university, corporation, community, city, family—than in describing the processes of change. Just as man has found it far simpler, when he surveys the phenomena of nature, to describe or characterize the objects—land, sea, air, lakes, oceans, mountains, deserts, valleys, bays, islands—that surround him than to describe the modes of their alteration or their motion, just as man's knowledge of anatomy has preceded his understanding of physiology, so it has been with social process.

Political changes, including the overthrow of rulers, have tended to be both more conspicuous and speedier than technological changes. Those limited numbers of people who could read and write and who kept the records have tended to be attached to the rulers and hence most aware of the changing fortunes of princes and kings.

Rapid technological change—the sort of change that can be measured in decades and that occurs within the span of a lifetime—is a characteristic of modern times. There was really no need for a name for rapid technological change until after the wave of revolutions that shook Europe beginning in mid-seventeenth century and reaching down into this century. It is during this period, of course, that men have developed their historical consciousness. The writing of history, a task of the new social sciences, only recently has become a self-conscious profession. The Regius chairs of history at Oxford and Cambridge were not established till the eighteenth century. At Harvard, the McLean professorship of history was not established till 1838, and American history did not enter the picture till much later.

3

What is most significant, then, about technology in modern times (the eras of most of the widely advertised "revolutions") is not so much any particular change, but rather the dramatic and newly explosive phenomenon of change itself. And American history, more perhaps than that of any other modern nation, has been marked by changes in the human condition—by novel political arrangements, novel products, novel forms of manufacturing, distribution, and consumption, novel ways of transporting and communicating. To understand ourselves and our nation, then, we must grasp these processes of change and reflect on our peculiarly American ways of viewing these processes.

In certain obvious but crucial ways, the process of technological change differs from the process of political change. I will now briefly explore these differences and suggest some of the consequences of our temptation to overlook them.

First, then, their motives (the Why). People are moved to political revolutions by their grievances (real or imagined) and by their desire for a change. Stirred by disgust with old policies and old regimes, they are awakened by visions of redress, of reforms, or of utopia. "Prudence, indeed, will dictate," Jefferson wrote in the Declaration of Independence,

> that Governments long established should not be changed for light and transient causes; and accordingly all experience hath shewn, that mankind are more disposed to suffer, while evils are sufferable, than to right themselves by abolishing the forms to which they are accustomed. But when a long train of abuses and usurpations, pursuing invariably the same Object, evinces a design to reduce them under absolute Despotism, it is their right, it is their duty, to throw off such Government, and to provide new Guards for their future security. Such has been the patient sufferance of these Colonies; and such is now the necessity which constrains them to alter their former Systems of Government.

This was a characteristically frank and clear declaration which could be a preface to most political revolutions. The Glorious Revolution of 1689 had its Declaration of Rights, the French Revolution of 1789 had its Declaration of the Rights of Man, the revolutions of 1848 had their Communist Manifesto, among others, and so it goes. For our present purpose the particular content of such declarations is less significant than that they have existed and that the people who have initiated and controlled the far-reaching political changes think of declarations as somehow giving the Why of their revolution.

But, in this sense, the great technological changes do *not* have a *Why*. The telegraph was not invented because men felt aggrieved by the need to carry messages over roads, by hand and on horseback. The wireless did not appear because men would no longer tolerate the stringing of wires to carry their messages. Television was not produced because Americans would no longer suffer the indignity or the inconvenience of leaving their homes and going to a theater to see a motion picture, or to a stadium to see a ball game. All this is obvious, but some of its significance may have escaped us. In a word, it is no trivial matter that, although in retrospect we can always see

large social, economic, and geographic forces at work, still technological revolutions (by contrast with political revolutions) really have
no *Why*. While political revolutions tend to be conscious and purposeful, technological revolutions are quite otherwise.

Each political revolution has its *ancien régime*, and so inevitably
looks backward to what must be redressed and revised. Even if the
hopes are utopian, the blueprint for utopia is made from the raw
materials of the recent past. "Peace, Bread, and Land!" the slogan of
the Russian Revolution of 1917, succinctly proclaimed what Russian
peasants and workers had felt to be lacking. It was the obverse of
"War, Starvation, and Servitude," which was taken to be a description of the *ancien régime*.

But technological revolutions generally do not take their bearings by any *ancien régime*. They more often arise not from persistent
and resentful staring at the past, but from casual glimpses of what
might be in the future: not so much from the pangs of empty stom-
achs as from the light-hearted imagining of eating quick-frozen
strawberries in winter. True enough, political revolutions usually do
get out of hand, and so go beyond the motives of their makers. But
there usually is somebody trying to guide events to fulfill the motives
of the revolutionaries, and trying to prevent events from going
astray. Yet, by contrast even with the most reckless and ill-guided
political revolutions, technological revolutions are still more reckless.

An example comes from World War II. From one point of view,
the war in Europe was a kind of revolution, an international uprising
against the Nazis, which concluded in their overthrow and removal
from power. That movement had a specific objective and ran its
course: surrender by the Nazis, replacement of the Nazi regime by
another, "War Crimes" trials, et cetera. After that revolution took
place, a Germany was left which, from a political point of view, was
not radically different from pre-Nazi Germany. This was an intended result of the efforts of politicians inside and outside the country.

Now, contrast the course of what is sometimes called the Atomic
Revolution, which took place during these same years. The story of

the success in the United States in achieving controlled nuclear fission (which now is a well-documented chronicle) leaves no doubt that a dominant motive was the determination to develop a decisive weapon to defeat the Nazis. But the connection between Hitler and atomic fission was quite accidental. Atomic fission finally was a result of long uncoordinated efforts of scientists in many places—in Germany, Denmark, Italy, the United States, and elsewhere. And, in turn, the success in producing controlled nuclear fission and in designing a bomb spawned consequences which proved uncontrollable. Although efforts at international agreement to control the development, production, diffusion, and use of atomic weapons have not been entirely unsuccessful, the atom remains a vagrant force in the world.

The overwhelming and most conspicuous result, then, of this great advance in human technology—controlled atomic fission—was not a set of neat desired consequences. In fact, the Nazis had surrendered before the bomb was ready. Rather, as has been frequently observed, the atomic bomb was to produce vast, unpredictable, and terrifying consequences. It would give a new power to nations and level the power of nations in surprising ways. The Atomic Revolution has proved reckless, with extensive consequences and threats of consequences which make the recklessness of Hitler look like caution. Even when men think they have a *Why* for their technological revolution—as indeed Albert Einstein, Harold Urey, Leo Szilard, Enrico Fermi, and James Franck felt they had—they are deceived.

The tantalizing, exhilarating fact about great technological changes is the very fact that each such change (like the invention of controlled atomic fission) seems somehow to be a law unto itself, to have its own peculiar vagrancy. Each grand change brings into being a whole new world. But we cannot forecast what will be the rules of any particular new world until after that new world has been discovered. It can be full of all sorts of outlandish monsters; it can be ruled by a diabolic logic. Who, for example, could have predicted that the internal-combustion engine and the automobile would spawn a new world of installment buying, credit cards, franchises, and annual models—that it would revise the meaning of cities, and transform morality by instigating new institutions of no-fault reparations?

The course of political change is somehow roughly predictable, but not so in the world of technology. We discover to our horror that we are not so much masters as victims. All this is due, in part, to the wonderfully unpredictable course of human knowledge and human imagination. But it is also due (as the history of electricity, wireless communication, radio, electronics, and the transistor, among others, suggests) to all the undiscovered, still-unrevealed characteristics of the physical world. These will recreate our world and populate it with creatures we never imagined.

A second grand distinction concerns the How. It is not impossible to put together some helpful generalizations about how political revolutions are made. Some of the more familiar in modern times are those offered by Francis Bacon, Machiavelli, Montesquieu, Jefferson, John Adams, Marx, Lenin, and Mao Tse-tung. Political revolutions in modern times are the final result of long and careful planning toward specific ends, of countless clandestine meetings and numerous public rallies, of collaborative shaping toward a declared goal. Organized purposefulness, focus, clarity, and limitation of objectives—all these are crucial.

The general techniques for bringing about a political revolution—including propaganda, organization, the element of surprise, the enlistment of foreign allies, the seizure of centers of communication—have changed very little over the centuries, although of course the specific means by which these have been accomplished have changed conspicuously. John Adams, who knew a thing or two about how political revolutions were made, after the American Revolution remarked dourly on how little man had increased his knowledge of his own political processes. "In so general a refinement, or more properly a reformation of manners and improvement in science," Adams observed in 1786, "is it not unaccountable that the knowledge of the principles and construction of free governments, in which the happiness of life, and even the further progress of improvement in education and society, in knowledge and virtue, are so deeply interested, should have remained at a full stand for two or three thousand years?" And he ventured that the principles of political science "were as well understood at the time of the neighing of the horse of Darius as they are at this hour." He noted with some sadness that the ancient wisdom on these matters was still applicable.

Great changes in technology—in the very world of advancing scientific knowledge and enlarging technological grasp—paradoxically remain (as they have always been) mysterious and unpredictable. Much of the satisfaction of reading *political* history, and especially the history of political revolutions, comes from seeing men declare their large objectives, seeing them use more or less familiar techniques—and then witnessing them recognizably succeed or fail in their grand enterprise. These are the elements of frustrated ambitions and disappointed hopes, of epic and of high tragedy. But the stories of the great technological changes—even when we call them revolutions—are quite different. More often than not, it is hard to know whether an effort at technological innovation is tragedy, comedy, or bluster, whether it shows good luck or bad. How, for example, are we to assess the invention, elaboration, and universal diffusion of the airplane? Or of television?

While the patterns of political history remain in the familiar mode of Shakespeare's tragedies and historical plays (there are few changes of political regime that cannot be seen in the mold of Coriolanus, King Lear, Richard II, Richard III, Macbeth, or one of the others), technological history (despite some valiant and imaginative efforts of sociologists and historians) appears, by contrast, to have very little pattern. And much of the excitement in this story comes from the surprising coincidence, the inconceivable, and the trivial—from the boy Marconi playing with his toy, from the chance observation by a Madame Curie, from the lucky accident which befell Sir Alexander Fleming, and from myriad other occasions equally odd and unpredictable.

Even the mid-twentieth-century American Research and Development Laboratory—perhaps mankind's most highly organized, best-focused effort to promote technological change—is a place of fruitfully vagrant questing. "Research directing," explained Willis R. Whitney, the pioneer founder of the General Electric Laboratories, "is following the openings of acceptable new ideas. It is watching the growth of thought in the minds and hands of careful investigators. Even the lonely mental pioneer, being grub-staked, so to speak, advances so far into the generally unknown that a so-called director merely happily follows the new ways provided. All new paths both multiply and divide as they proceed." A modern research laboratory, then, as Irving Langmuir observed, is not so much a place where men fulfill assignments as a place where men exercise "the art of profiting from unexpected occurrences." Of course, the most adept managers of political revolutions—the Sam Adamses, the Robespierres, and the Lenins—have had to know how to profit by the unexpected, but always to help them reach a prefixed destination.

The brilliant technological innovator, on the other hand, is always in search of his destination. He is on the lookout for new questions. While he hopes to find new solutions he remains alert to discover that what he thought were solutions were really new problems. Political revolutions are made by men who urge known remedies for known evils, technological revolutions by men finding unexpected answers to unimagined questions. While political change starts from problems, technological change starts from the search for problems. And, as our most adventuring scientists and technologists provide us with solutions, our society is faced with ways of preventing the newly discovered uses of the solutions (for example, the new uses of inflammable synthetics for bedclothing, nightgowns and dresses, of cellophane for packaging, of gasoline combustion for vehicles, of plastics for "disposable" containers) from themselves becoming new problems.

Of course, there are some conspicuous examples—the building of the first atomic bomb or the effort to land a man on the moon—where the purpose is specific, and where the organization resembles that of political enterprises. But here too there are special characteristics: the sense of momentum, the movement which comes from the size of the enterprise, the quantity of the investment, and the unpredictability of knowledge.

If we look back, then, on the great political revolutions and the great technological revolutions (both of which are clues to the range of mankind's capacities and possibilities) we see a striking contrast. Political revolutions, generally speaking, have revealed man's organized purposefulness, his social conscience, his sense of justice—the aggressive, assertive side of his nature. Technological change, invention, and innovation have tended, rather, to reveal his play instinct, his desire and his ability to go where he has never gone, to do what he has never done. The one shows his willingness to sacrifice in order to fulfill his plans, the other his willingness to sacrifice in order to pursue his quest. Many of the peculiar successes and special problems of our time come from our efforts to assimilate these two kinds of activities. We have tried to make government more experimental and at the same time to make technological change more purposive, more focused, more planned than ever before.

These two kinds of change—political and technological—differ not only in their Why and their How, but also in their What of It? By this I mean the special character of their consequences. Political revolutions tend, with certain obvious exceptions, to be *displacive*. The Weimar Republic displaced the regime of Imperial Germany; the Nazis displaced the Weimar Republic; and after World War II, a new republic displaced the Nazis. Normally this is what we mean by a political revolution. Moreover, to a surprising extent, political revolutions are *reversible*. In the political world, you *can* go home again. It is possible, and even common, for a new regime to go back to the ideas and institutions of an earlier regime. Many so-called revolutions are really the revivals of *anciens régimes*. The familiar phenomenon of the counter-revolution is the effort to reverse the course of change. And it is even arguable that counter-revolutions generally tend to be more successful than revolutions. The reactionary, whose objective is always more recognizable and easier to describe, thus is more apt to be successful than the revolutionary. It is the possibility of such reversals that has lent credibility to the largely fallacious pendulum theory of history, which is popularized in our day under such terms as "backlash."

Technological changes, however, thrive in a different sort of world. Momentous technological changes commonly are neither

displacive nor reversible. Technological innovations, instead of displacing earlier devices, actually tend to create new roles for the devices which they might at first seem to displace. When the telephone
was introduced in the later nineteenth century, some people assumed that it would make the postman obsolete (few dared predict
that the United States Post Office might become decrepit before it
was fully mature); similarly when wireless and then radio appeared,
some wise people thought that these would spell the end of the telephone; when television came in, many were the voices lamenting the
death of radio; and we still hear Cassandras solemnly telling us that
television is the death of the book. But in our own time we have had
an opportunity to observe how and why such forecasts are ill
founded. We have seen television (together with the automobile)
provide new roles for the radio, and most recently we have seen how
both have created new roles (or led to the new flourishing of older
roles) for the newspaper press. And, of course, all these have created
newly urgent roles for the book.

A hallmark of the great technological changes is that they tend
not to be reversible. I have a New England friend who has not yet
installed a telephone because, he says, he is waiting until it is perfected. And a few of my scholarly friends (some of them, believe it or
not, eminent students, writers, and pundits about American civilization) still stubbornly refuse for even less plausible reasons to have a
television set in the house. Who, having had a telephone, now does
without one, or having once installed a TV set, no longer has one?
There is no technological counterpart for the political restoration or
the counter-revolution. Of course there are changes in style, and the
antique, the obsolete, and the camp have a perennial charm. There
will always, I hope, be some individuals, devotees of "voluntary simplicity," who go in search of their own Waldens. But their quixotry
simply reminds us that the march of modernity is ruthless and can
never retreat. In France, for example, the century following the Revolution of 1789 was an oscillation of revolutions and *anciens régimes*;
aristocrats were decapitated, parties were voted out of power, old
ideologies were abandoned. But during the same years the trend of
technological change was unmistakable and irreversible. Unlike the

French Revolution, the Industrial Revolution—despite an occasional William Morris—produced no powerful counter-revolution.

Finally, there remains a crucial difference between our ability to imagine future political revolutions and to imagine future technological revolutions. This is perhaps the most important, if least observed, distinction between the political and the technological worlds. Our failure to note this distinction I describe as the "Gamut Fallacy." "Gamut," an English word rooted in the Greek "gamma" for the lowest note in an old musical scale, means the complete range of anything. When we think, for example, of the future of our political life and our governmental forms, we can have in mind substantially the whole range of possibilities. It is this, of course, which authenticates the traditional wisdom of political theory. It illustrates what we might call "John Adams' Law" (to which I have already referred), namely, that political wisdom does not substantially progress. No wonder the astronomical analogy of "revolving" (the primary meaning of "revolution") was so tempting!

But the history of technology, again, is quite another story. We cannot envisage, or even imagine, the range of alternatives from which future technological history will be made. One of the wisest (and, surprisingly enough, one of the most cautious) of our prophets in this area is Arthur C. Clarke, the author of *2001* and other speculations. Clarke provides us with a valuable rule-of-thumb for assessing prophecies of the future of man. In his *Profiles of the Future* (after offering some instructive examples of prophecies by experts who proved beyond doubt that the atom could not be split, that supersonic transportation was physically impossible, that man could never escape from the earth's gravitational field and could certainly never reach the moon), he offers us "Arthur Clarke's Law": "When a distinguished but elderly scientist states that something is possible, he is almost certainly right. When he states that something is impossible, he is very probably wrong."

This is Clarke's way of warning us against what I have called the "Gamut Fallacy"—the mistaken notion that we can envisage all possibilities. If *any*thing is possible, then we really cannot know what is possible, simply because we cannot imagine *every*thing. Where, as in

the political world, we make the possibilities ourselves, the limitations of the human imagination are reflected in the limitations of
actual possibilities themselves. But the physical world is not of our
making, and hence its full range of possibilities is beyond our imagining.

4

What are the consequences of these peculiarities of our thinking for
how we can or do—or perhaps should—think about our problems
today? Even in this later twentieth century, when much of mankind
has begun to acquire historical consciousness, we are still plagued by
the ancient problem of how to come to terms with change. The same
old problem—of how to name what we so imperfectly understand,
how to describe the limits of our knowledge while those very limits
disqualify us from the task—still befuddles us.

Much of mankind, as we have seen, has tended to reason from
the political and social to the technical, and has drawn its analogies
in that direction. Faced from time immemorial with the ultimately
insoluble problems of man in society, most of mankind has tended to
assume that other kinds of problems might be equally insoluble. The
wise prophets of the great religions have found various ways to say
that, on this earth, there is no solution to the human condition. In
our Western society, the parable of man's personal and social problem is the Fall of Man. "Original Sin" is another way of saying that
perfection must be sought in another world, perhaps with the aid of a
savior. We have been taught that in human society there are only
more or less *in*soluble problems, and ultimately no solutions. The
problem of politics, then, is essentially the problem of man coming
to terms with his *problems*.

But our problem in the United States—and, generally speaking,
the central problem of technology—is how to come to terms with
solutions. Our misplaced hopes, our frustrations, and many of our irritations with one another and with other nations come from our
unwillingness to believe in the "insoluble" problem, an unwillingness rooted in our New World belief in solutions. Inevitably, then,

we overestimate the role of purpose in human change; we overvalue the power of wealth and the power of power.

One way of explaining, historically, how we have been tempted into this adventurous but perilous way of thinking is that we Americans have tended to take the technological problem—the soluble problem—as the prototype of the problems of our nation, and then, too, of all mankind. Among the novelties of American experience, none have been more striking than our innovations in technology, in standard of living, in the machinery of everyday life. And, as I have suggested, one of the obvious characteristics of a problem in technology is that it may really be soluble. Do you seek a way to split the atom and produce a controlled chain reaction? You have found it. That problem is solved! And so it has been with many problems, large and small, in our whole world of technology. Do you want an adhesive that will not require moistening to hold the flaps of envelopes? Do you want a highway surface that will not crack under given variations in temperature? Do you want a pen that will write under water? Do you want a camera that will produce an image in twenty seconds? Or, perhaps, do you want it in full color? We can provide you all these things. These are specific problems with specific solutions.

Taking this kind of problem as our prototype, we have too readily assumed that all other problems may be like them. While much of the rest of mankind has reasoned from the political and social to the technological (and therefore, often prematurely, drawn mistaken and discouraging conclusions), we have drawn our analogies in the other direction. By reasoning from the technological to the political and the social, we have been seduced into our own kind of mistaken, if prematurely encouraging, conclusions. It may be within our power to provide a new kind of grain and so cure starvation in some particular place. But it may not be in our power to cure injustice anywhere, even in our own country, much less in distant places.

Without being arrogant, or playing God, who alone has all solutions, we may still perhaps learn how to come to terms with our problems. We must learn, at the same time, to accept John Adams' Law (that political wisdom does not significantly progress, that the problems of society, the problems of justice and government, are not now much more soluble than they ever were, and hence the wisdom of the social past is never obsolete) while we also accept Arthur Clarke's Law (that all technological problems are substantially soluble, that "anything that is theoretically possible will be achieved in practice, no matter what the technical difficulties, if it is desired greatly enough," and hence the technological past is always becoming obsolete).

We must be willing to believe both that politics is the Art of the Possible and that technology is the Art of the Impossible. Then we must embrace and cultivate both arts. Our unprecedented American achievements both in politics and in technology therefore pose us a test, and test us with a tension, unlike that posed to any people before us in history. Never before has a people been so tempted (and with such good reason) to believe that anything is *technologically* possible. And a consequence has been that perhaps no people before us has found it so difficult to continue unabashed in search of the prudent limits of the politically possible. In this American limbo—in this new world of hope and of terror—we have a rare opportunity to profit from man's recent discovery that he has a history.

THE AGE OF NEGATIVE
DISCOVERY

from CLEOPATRA'S NOSE, *1994*

WHEN ALBERT EINSTEIN was asked about forty years ago how the West had come to the idea of scientific discovery, he gave a simple answer. "Development of Western Science," he explained, "is based on two great achievements, the invention of the formal logical system (in Euclidean geometry) by the Greek philosophers, and the discovery of the possibility to find out causal relationship by systematic experiment (Renaissance). In my opinion one has not to be astonished that the Chinese sages have not made these steps. The astonishing thing is that these discoveries were made at all." Einstein was surely correct in seeing scientific discovery as an institution of Western culture. His characteristically simple explanation, however, does not take account of the remarkable transformations of the venture of discovery in this century.

The works of discovery in every age shape—and shake up—the thinking of the whole literate community. And this effect has multiplied with the rise of democracy and of literacy. The familiar example, of course, is how the works of Copernicus (1473–1543) and his followers disturbed Western culture with the realization that the earth was no longer the center. More recent examples are the impact of Darwinian biology and Freudian psychology. Nowadays, the space sciences, arcane and specialized though they have become, continue to have a profound and wide influence on the whole community's thinking.

We in the lay community continue to reach for the meanings of scientific discoveries that are beyond our layman's understanding. We enjoy having our imagination titillated. How otherwise can we account for one of the most remarkable publishing phenomena of recent times? Stephen Hawking's short but difficult *Brief History of Time: From the Big Bang to Black Holes* (1988) has entered the *Guinness Book of World Records* for the longest period (four years) of any book on the British best-seller list, and with a sale of some five million copies. We have seen the wide and enduring popular interest in the readable tales of Jules Verne and H. G. Wells, in the charming personality of ET and his tribe, in the science fiction of Isaac Asimov and Arthur Clarke, and even in older serious works like those of James Jeans and Arthur Eddington, and in the current writings of Herbert Friedman.

Nowadays public interest in discovery is greater than ever. But the role of the discoverer in the space sciences has been transformed, with novel consequences for the thinking of laymen like me.

* * *

For the modern realm of discovery in the space sciences our prototypes should not be the familiar heroes of the so-called Great Age of Discovery—Leif Eriksson, Columbus, Cortés, Magellan, Drake. Our proper prototype, instead, is the prosaic, less romanticized Captain James Cook (1728–1779). He has not had his due in the annals of discovery. This may be a common fate of negative discoverers. Of them, Captain Cook was perhaps the greatest. You will recall that he earned his place in the chronicles of seafaring by proving that the fabled Great Southern Continent did not exist. That fabled land was supposed to reach up from the Antarctic toward Southeast Asia, making the Indian Ocean a lake. We are inclined to forget or underestimate the difficulty of negative discovery. For it is far easier to encounter some new island or even an unexpected new continent than to prove that some long-admired fixture of the imagination does not exist. To put a new land, a new passageway on the map one needed only to go there, and happily surprise the world with a new presence.

But to prove a negative, even if the logicians had not insisted that it was theoretically impossible, is an exhausting enterprise. It demands the exploring and discarding of all imaginable possibilities. Negative discovery is also much less welcome than an act of simple affirmative discovery. People don't like to have their imaginations unfurnished. The legendary Great South Land, which Cook erased from the map, had been a promising field of empire, with natural wealth of incalculable value. It remained so, as long as it was never found.

To prove that the Great South Land did *not* exist was not only an unwelcome disillusion, it required one of the most terrifying sea voyages in history. Leaving England in July 1772, Captain Cook did not return till July 1775. With two newly built Whitby colliers, the *Resolution* (462 tons) and the *Adventure* (340 tons), he came down around the Cape of Good Hope, reached 71°10′ South, traversed the whole southernmost rim of the Pacific in the Antarctic regions, then into the Atlantic toward the Cape of Good Hope and back up to England. This was no voyage through any becalmed Sargasso Sea, but one teetering on the edge of Antarctic ice, overshadowed and threatened by crackling and crumbling iceberg-alps.

Captain Cook's instructions took account of both possibilities— that the continent did or did not exist. If he found any part of it he had orders from the Admiralty to survey it, claim it for Britain, and distribute medals to the natives. Officers and crew were to observe strict secrecy about the voyage, and all logs and journals were to be confiscated after the ship's return. In this, one of the greatest, and surely one of the longest, discovery voyages in history, Cook sailed more than seventy thousand miles. Never before had there been so long a voyage with one focused inquiring purpose. Not to plant a new colony, not to seek an Eldorado, nor find gold or silver or precious gems, nor capture slaves. Cook had made his earlier voyage to Tahiti—also a brilliant feat of navigation—for astronomical observations of the transit of Venus, on June 3, 1769. Now his grand success with the *Resolution* and the *Adventure* was resounding testimony to the courage of the modern skeptical spirit. The Antarctic was dangerously different from the Arctic, of which Europeans had had some glimpses. The uncharted Antarctic, scenes of perpetual mountainous ice beyond the belief of temperate Europe, was a happy hunting ground for extravagant *a priori* speculation. And Cook's voyage itself would spark the ominous allegory of Coleridge's "Rime of the Ancient Mariner."

To scotch those ancient legends and speculations required a kind of discovering courage and passion that would characterize our modern age of negative discovery. This passion and courage and the sophisticated purpose of Cook, his crew, his expert naturalists and skilled astronomers were brilliantly summarized in the homely wisdom of Josh Billings (1818–1885): "It ain't what a man don't know as makes him a fool, but what he does know as ain't so."

There was a shining symbolism in Cook's whole career. Self-educated, as a young man he turned down an opportunity to command a ship, and chose instead to widen his knowledge of the sea as a volunteer able seaman in the British navy. Rapidly promoted, he became a master, and surveyed the St. Lawrence River before the fall of Quebec. He showed a practical man's experimental spirit in his sympathy for the newly improved Harrison and Kendall chronometers and was one of the first to prove the chronometer's utility as a navigational instrument. Incidentally he was ready to learn new ways of dealing with the scurvy, the curse of long voyages in his time, and astonished contemporaries by bringing back his *Resolution*, after his three-year voyage, without losing a single man to the disease. He fought the scurvy by enforcing cleanliness on board and trying new diets of orange, lemon, and their juices along with sauerkraut, onions, and grasses encountered en route. It was precisely this practical sense, this imaginative openness to new techniques, that would distinguish the great negative discoverers in the following centuries.

* * *

The history of Western science confirms the aphorism that the great menace to progress is not ignorance but the illusion of knowledge. I will now suggest why I see Captain Cook as the prototypical modern discovery hero. The negative discoverer is the historic dissolver of illusions. Perhaps we could call ours an age of negative discovery.

This feature of the realms of discovery in our age is conspicuous in the results of recent efforts to describe the universe. Marc Davis, Professor of Astronomy and Physics at the University of California, Berkeley, has provided us with a convenient summary. Here are the six main products of the progress of cosmology over the last four hundred years:

The Earth is *not* the center of the Universe.
The Sun is *not* the center of the Universe.
Our galaxy is *not* the center of the Universe.
Our type of matter is *not* the dominant constituent of the
    Universe (dark matter predominates instead).
Our Universe (seen and unseen) is *not* the only Universe.
Our physics is *not* the only physics. There might exist separate
    universes with completely different physics.

My poetic wife, Ruth, has eloquently suggested that this may make ours the Age of Gordian *Nots*.

In addition to these modern notions about space, there is also an equally modern view of time. On our distinctly modern menu of alternatives the experts offer us at least three different cosmological models:

Steady-state theory: The Universe is of infinite age; matter is
    continuously created at all times.
The Big Bang: The Universe is of finite age; matter and energy
    are conserved as the Universe expands.
Eternally inflating Big Bang: Our Universe has a finite age.
    The creation of all matter-energy in our Universe occurred
    at the end of the inflationary phase, when the incredible
    energy density of the false vacuum converted to ordinary
    matter and radiation.

All three possibilities are signposts to terra incognita. These propositions taken together provide what Professor Davis calls the Modern Creation Myth. This he deftly compresses into the notion that "the entire Universe we observe, and unimaginably far beyond, was created out of a single tiny vacuum fluctuation having zero energy content at an incredibly early time. . . . our entire Universe was quite literally created out of nothing." And Davis, in the modern spirit, instead of pursuing the heavy theological implications, concludes with Alan Guth's unforgettable suggestion that "the Universe is the ultimate free lunch."

How have we come to this vast and tantalizing expansion of terra incognita, to include the whole universe and our place in it? Professor Davis himself has succinctly described the triumphs of modern Western science as experiments in cosmology. These, I will suggest, are not simply the fruitful work of bold individual scientists. They are a by-product of large cultural and institutional changes of the last century, of processes that are accelerating and are likely to continue to accelerate. Put quite simply, they are a consequence of the application of developed technology to the processes of scientific discovery and the rise of the mechanized observer. The momentous consequence, which increases the scope and the realms of negative discovery, is a changed relation of data to meaning. Before the age of the mechanized observer, there was a tendency for meaning to outrun data. The modern tendency is quite the contrary, as we see data outrun meaning.

It is of course no accident that the heavens, where man had no direct personal experience, was the realm of the gods. Fertile in myth and legend, that unexplored realm was supposed to be rich in meaning for life on earth. Until the nineteenth century the data of space outside the earth were filtered through the interests and capacities of the human observer. The telescope and the microscope have, to be sure, extended, broadened, and deepened our human faculties of vision. But these are only tools, extensions of the human bodily senses. A machine is something else—a device that can be activated by forces outside the human body, bringing data not accessible to the unmechanized human body. The crucial new element is that the discoverer is no longer simply confronted by nature, by the data accessible to the person. Man creates machines, and the machines create data. Here are infinitely expanding new realms to be explored. Every new observing machine adds a new revelation of negative discovery, opening hitherto unrecognized areas of ignorance.

Some distinctive features of this modern realm of discovery were vividly revealed in the progress of *Voyager 2*, one of the most impressive and successful recent efforts to reach out beyond the solar system. The perceptive science reporter Stephen S. Hall has given us his eyewitness account of what happened at 9:00 P.M. on the evening of August 19, 1989, as the technology team, a dozen "postmodern helmsmen," gathered on the second floor of Building 264 of NASA's Jet Propulsion Laboratory in the San Gabriel foothills of Pasadena, California. *Voyager 2*, already twelve years into its journey, had so far accomplished its assignment perfectly in flying by Jupiter, Saturn, and Uranus. Within just five days it would, as Hall observed, "brush the treetops of Neptune and hurtle past Triton." The staff had met to agree on the radio adjustment of the rudder of the craft (2.7 billion miles away) to ensure its reaching the appointed target.

A map of the solar system on the wall showed where Neptune, traveling at 12,000 miles per hour around the sun, and *Voyager 2*, traveling at about 61,000 miles per hour, were to meet for the planned observation by the spacecraft. Beside it on the wall, a sign read, WE DO PRECISION GUESSWORK. While this familiar chart of the solar system was visible, the navigational chart of *Voyager 2* remained out of sight inside the computers, continually revising as the voyage progressed. The JPL computers indicated that *Voyager 2* would reach within one light-year of Sirius, the Dog Star, in the year A.D. 359,000. Meanwhile, the achievements of *Voyager 2* were sensational. On the morning of August 25, 1989, it provided images of Triton. *Voyager 2* had traveled some 4,429,508,700 miles during twelve years, and was now being remotely guided to its intended target. It arrived five minutes ahead of the schedule that had been made years before, and 0.6 seconds later than its last advertised time. Its scientific product was some five trillion bits of data.

* * *

The road to this universe of the mechanized observer, of *Pioneers 10* and *11* and *Voyagers 1* and *2*, had been opened years before by the application of photography to astronomy. The mechanization of the telescope had made it possible to focus on the desired object, and to enhance the human eye by exposing photographic plates for hours, building up images of faint objects and their spectra. By 1949 the Hale Telescope, the American astronomers' Big Eye, was being activated by a mere one-twelfth-horsepower motor to follow the stars.

No longer was the patience and devotion of astronomers tested by their willingness to keep their eyes glued to the telescope while they sat at high altitudes in the cold night after night in electrically heated suits. Of course, that patience had paid off in the works of intrepid astronomers like Milton Humason, Edwin Hubble's collaborator, who spent some twenty-eight years recording the spectral patterns of far-off galaxies to measure red shift. Gathering that data required that Humason first find and fix on a faint nebulosity among the stars, then center the image on the narrow slit of his spectrograph and hold it there throughout the night. The plate would be kept from irrelevant daylight and then the tedious observation would be repeated on following nights. It was just such data for the momentous new knowledge of red shift and of the nature and number of galaxies for Hubble's constant that exploded our view of the universe.

Only a century ago, in 1889, the precocious George Ellery Hale's new spectroheliograph opened the sun to new modes of exploration with new data, and with a technique applicable across the heavens. Improvements by Robert H. McMath revealed unexpected new realms of solar spicules. This was only one of a series of openings to new realms of our ignorance, which Herbert Friedman, a pioneer in rocket astronomy, properly labels the Invisible Universe. While the visible universe has limits, the Invisible Universe is, of course, limitless—and with it, too, countless new realms of negative discovery—ever outward to radio astronomy, the infrared, the ultraviolet, X-ray astronomy, to gamma rays, to the baffling neutrinos and endless new realms still unnamed.

In this age of negative discovery, of the mechanized observer, of machine-created data and ever newer kinds of data, we must note a new kind of momentum. Familiar enough is the momentum of knowledge, the ancient and perilous self-catalyzing quest for more knowledge, embodied in the parable of the apple and expulsion from the Garden of Eden. But the machine also has a momentum of its own.

The momentum of the technology of the mechanized observer is vividly illustrated in the Report of the National Research Council (from its Astronomy and Astrophysics Survey Committee in 1991) with a program and priorities for "The Decade of Discovery in the 1990's." The report calls for continued support for the great observatories and increased support for individual research grants. But the bulk of its recommendations, a prelude to its description of "Science Opportunities," gives priority to the "ground-based infrastructure" and calls for four "instrumental programs."

At the top of this list is the Space Infrared Telescope Facility (SIRTF), which would be "almost a thousand times more sensitive than earth-based telescopes operating in the infrared. Advanced arrays of infrared detectors would give SIRTF the ability to map complex areas and measure spectra a million times faster than any other space-borne infrared telescope." These would be based on the "technical heritage" of two successful Explorer missions. Closely following, to "draw on a decade of progress in the technology of building large mirrors," comes the proposal that "an infrared-optimized 8-m U.S. telescope operating on Mauna Kea, Hawaii, would provide a unique and powerful instrument for studying the origin, structure, and evolution of planets, stars, and galaxies." And then the "Millimeter Array (MMA) . . . of telescopes operating at millimeter wavelength, would provide high-spatial and high-spatial-resolution images of star-forming regions and distant star-burst galaxies," which "would bring new classes of objects into clear view for the first time." But this is only the beginning of the list, followed by six "Moderate Programs," nine "Illustrative Small Programs," and nine space-based initiatives. All these come to an estimated cost for the decade of $3 billion 23 million.

The momentum of discovery-technology is further accelerated by two innovative techniques—adaptive optics and interferometry, "which promises spatial resolution better than a thousandth of an arc second by linking the outputs of widely separated telescopes." All this would be an extension to the spectacular Very Large Array, already in being. And there is the suggestion of improved instruments to detect neutrinos and "dark matter" (still so cryptic that it must be left in quotation marks). The momentum startles us with the final suggestion that "the chief advantage of the moon as a site for space astronomy is that it provides a large, solid foundation on which to build widely separated structures such as interferometers." Is this a promise to transform the whole solar system into an attractive novel base for interferometers focused on the universe?

* * *

For most of Western history interpretation has far outrun data. And there was an overwhelming and universal human temptation to ignore or discount data that menaced familiar and appealing interpretations. A well-known example is the reluctance of theologically oriented scientists in Galileo's day (1610) to accept the fact of sunspots, which his telescope had newly revealed. Some of the most respected men of learning refused to look through a device so diabolical that it purported to contradict Aristotle's appealing notion of the sun as the embodiment of unspotted fire, and even hint at imperfections in God's handiwork. The eminent Aristotelian scholar Caesar Cremonini said he would not waste his time looking through Galileo's contraption just to see what "no one but Galileo has seen . . . and besides, looking through those spectacles gives me a headache." Some even solaced themselves by saying that while Galileo's device might represent the facts here on earth, where it could be verified by experience, "in the sky it deceives us as some fixed stars are seen double." Father Clavius, professor of mathematics at the Collegio Romano, laughed at Galileo's four satellites of Jupiter, and said he could produce the same result if allowed a little time to build the images into some glasses. Galileo himself, wary of allowing novel facts to contradict familiar meanings, reported that after seeing an object magnified in his telescope he would again and again go up to the object to see that he had not been deceived.

So long as the aids to discovery were mere tools, extension of the bodily faculties, their products might be surprising or even shocking but were not unimaginable or unintelligible. The revisions of Ptolemaic into Copernican astronomy took centuries to secure acceptance, but the debate, even to the layman, was still intelligible. At worst the problems arose from what seemed the violations of common sense—such as the discovering that in fact heavy objects fell no more speedily than light objects, or the troubling suggestion that the solid, apparently static earth on which we stand is in fact in constant rotating motion. This became Galileo's own legendary dramatic affirmation of his discovery, when he reputedly stamped his foot, saying, "Anyway, it moves" *(Eppure, si muove!)*.

But the development of the machinery of discovery of course allowed observations of which the unmechanized human body was incapable. The new data then extended and was limited only by the capacity of the machines—photography, spectrography, rocket astronomy, radio astronomy, and their successors. No longer bounded by the imagination of an observer fixing his telescope, the mechanized observer has been gathering whatever the proliferating machinery of discovery can report or record. A clue to the endless novelty of realms of discovery is the ever-enlarging vocabulary of discovery, with which even our best desk dictionaries can hardly keep pace. Every report of the progress of discovery must carry its own glossary of new terms and acronyms. Even the brief "Decade of Discovery" report of the National Research Council that I have mentioned carries a glossary of ten pages. Each new term is an omen of newly discovered areas of our ignorance. A familiar example is how Robert N. McMath's device for making time-lapse movies of the sun in hydrogen light gave us our first vision of spicules, with a new vision of the sun and hosts of new questions about the photosphere and chromosphere and the corona of the sun, all to be enriched and amplified in due course by the later data of X rays and the ultraviolet captured by rocket astronomy.

The momentum of invention and of proliferating technology accumulates data at a rate and in forms prescribed by the machines themselves. The ever-accelerating data provide hosts of answers to questions not yet asked. This challenges the discoverer with an ever-expanding task. No longer does he simply seek answers to conventional questions, nor demand that meager facts provide comforting cosmic meanings. Instead he tantalizes himself by making machines that pose new questions in uncharted oceans of expanding data. If a machine exists, or can be devised, it must be enlisted to produce data.

We are not worried—perhaps not as much as we should be—that our twentieth-century Galileos are deceiving us by the data of machines. Instead we applaud all askers of unimagined questions, every reacher to negative discovery.

The mechanized observer would, of course, be vastly more productive of data than the human observer. Electronic imaging proved some two hundred times more sensitive than the photographic plates of the 1940s exposed to Hale's telescope. New uses of the silicon chip improved telescopes by a factor of 10 and silicon "pixels" yielded digitally readable data with a dynamic range of 1 million compared with a range of some 10 to 100 in a photographic emulsion. By 1978 the Charge Coupled Device (CCD) once again enormously multiplied the astronomer's research data. A single astronomical image made by a CCD required about 0.5 megabyte (= about a half-million characters). One night of CCD observation would fill seventy-five floppy disks for storage, which led to the use of magnetic tapes by the thousands. And the laser disk (each one of which can store one thousand megabytes of information), while of course not solving problems of meaning, made it easier for astronomers to enrich (or burden) themselves with more convenient modes of storing the daily accelerating volume of data. Thus, the word "astronomical" has taken on a metaphorical meaning more vivid and more daunting than ever before.

*   *   *

Perhaps as a layman I am not sufficiently grateful for the new treasures of data that the modern technology of discovery has brought into being. Every new byte is another chip of raw material for some scientist's improved description of what the universe really is, some new speculation of how it came into being, and how it may end. But even the most arcane scientific notions, however garbled, penetrate somehow to conscientious literate laymen, among whom I count myself. If we cannot grasp the meanings of Einstein's theories of special and general relativity, or the implications of quantum mechanics, we still can have some general impression of how and where modern discoverers are pointing.

Some obvious characteristics of the modern realms of discovery are perhaps more striking and affecting to a layman than to the scientist who lives among them. While space scientists and cosmologists may not yet have succeeded in producing a satisfactory Grand Unified Theory (GUT), they have, at least in the eye of the lay spectator, actually produced a universe of Grand Unified Data—expanding at an ever-accelerating rate. As never before, space scientists have brought all the cosmic questions together—questions of the very small and the very large, questions of first-time beginnings and final ends, the relations of present phenomena to the whole past and the whole future. They have turned astronomy into a historical science, and made physics into cosmology. And with what effect on us, the lay community?

The familiar troubled voice of John Donne (1572?–1631) eloquently complained, in 1611, that the new Copernican notions were "creeping into every man's mind" and "may very well be true."

> And new Philosophy calls all in doubt,
> The Element of fire is quite put out;
> The Sun is lost, and th'earth, and no man's
>   wit
> Can well direct him where to looke for it.
> And freely men confesse that this world's
>   spent,
> When in the Planets, and the Firmament
> They seek so many new; then see that this
> Is crumbled out againe to his Atomies.
> 'Tis all in peeces, all coherence gone;
> All just supply, and all Relation. . . .
> And in these Constellations then arise
> New starres, and old doe vanish from our
>   eyes . . .

If the mere displacing of the earth from the center of the solar system was so disturbing to the thoughtful layman then, what must be the consequence in our time of the discovery that our whole solar system, our whole Milky Way, our whole galaxy, our whole universe is only a negligible peripheral one of countless billions? John Donne was troubled that the old answers were no longer true. But modern science has long since inoculated us against the permanence of all answers.

Perhaps we are no longer merely *Homo sapiens* but rather *Homo ludens*—at play in the fields of the stars. Perhaps we have learned to luxuriate—as Stephen Hawking's little book suggests—in the expanding universe of expanding questions. Perhaps the modern realm of discovery is no longer a realm of answers but only of questions, which we are beginning to feel at home in and enjoy. Perhaps our modern discoverer is not a discoverer at all but rather a quester, in an age of negative discovery, where achievements are measured not in the finality of answers, but in the fertility of questions. So let us enjoy the quest together. As Claude Bernard (1813–1878), the great French physiologist, observed, "Art is I; Science is We."

And we may express our common challenge in an age of negative discovery in familiar words far less elegant than those of John Donne,

> As I was going up the stair
> I met a man who wasn't there.
> He wasn't there again today.
> I wish, I wish, he'd go away.

But he won't go away, and not only that. The little man who isn't there, the little question we never imagined, will be the constant enticing companion of our common quest.

LAND OF THE UNEXPECTED

from CLEOPATRA'S NOSE, *1994*

W ITH A EUROPE in disarray, in a century plagued by two murderous world wars, by genocides without precedent—the German Nazi massacre of six million and the Stalin-Soviet massacre of thirty million—how can I speak hopefully about the American future?

One answer is very personal. I was raised and went to public school in the 1920s in Tulsa, Oklahoma, which then called itself the Oil Capital of the World, but could perhaps have been called the Optimism Capital of the World. Only ten years before my family came to Oklahoma, the Indian Territory had been admitted to the Union as the forty-sixth state. The city thrived on "booster" pride, and before I graduated from Central High School it boasted two daily newspapers, three skyscrapers, houses designed by Frank Lloyd Wright, and a public school system superintended by the former U.S. commissioner of education. The Kiwanis, Rotary, and Chamber of Commerce competed furiously in projects of civic improvement. For our high school English classes we memorized and declaimed patriotic orations—from Patrick Henry's "Give Me Liberty or Give Me Death" and Lincoln's Gettysburg Address to Henry Grady's "New South" and Émile Zola's "Plea for Dreyfus." We wrote speeches on the virtues of the federal constitution for a national contest that held its finals before the Supreme Court in Washington. Of course there were dark shadows—such as the relentless racial segregation, the brutal race riots of the 1920s, and the Ku Klux Klan. But these were not visible or prominent in my life. The city burgeoned, proudly built a grand new railroad depot, a university, and an elegant public library and city hall—and soon it was embellished by art museums of national rank.

My father was one of the most enthusiastic boosters and the growing city seemed to justify his extravagant optimism. I came to sympathize with that American-frontier newspaperman who was attacked for reporting as facts the mythic marvels of his upstart pioneer village, including its still-unbuilt impressive hotel and prosperous Main Street. In America, he said, it was not fair to object to the rosy reports of community boosters simply because they had "not yet gone through the formality of taking place." I suppose I have never been cured of my distinctively American Oklahoma optimism, bred in the bone and confirmed by the real history of Tulsa.

Another answer is in American history. The exhilarating features of our history and culture have in the past been captured in the idea of American Exceptionalism. This is a long word for a simple idea—the traditional belief that the United States is a very special place, unique in crucial ways. It is symbolized in our national capitol in Washington, which proclaims our European heritage in the elegant classical motifs of its dome. But the dome is held together by a triumph of pioneer technology, a hidden cast-iron frame, which in its making provided the needed employment for American workers. American Exceptionalism is a name too for a cosmopolitan, optimist, and humanist view of history—that the modern world, while profiting from the European inheritance, need not be imprisoned in Old World molds, nor limited by the ancient raw materials of community. And therefore that the future of the United States and of the people who came here need not be governed by the same expectations or plagued by the same problems that had afflicted people elsewhere.

How have we lost sight of this beacon? We have been seduced by the rise of our country as a "superpower." For power is quantitative, but the uniqueness of the United States is not merely quantitative. We have suffered, too, from the consequences of our freedom. Totalitarian societies exaggerate their virtues. But free societies like ours somehow seize the temptation to exaggerate their vices. The negativism of our press and television reporting are of course the best evidence of our freedom to scrutinize ourselves. Far better this than the chauvinism of self-righteousness, which has been the death of totalitarian empires in our time.

While nations of the Old World have enjoyed their legendary heroes shrouded in historic mists, our nation was founded in the bright light of history. They have embroidered glowing myths of Romulus and Remus, Joan of Arc, Saint Louis, and Richard the Lionhearted. But our founders—our John Smith, William Bradford, John Winthrop, Benjamin Franklin, George Washington, and Thomas Jefferson—are vividly and conspicuously human. So they remind us, to our benefit, of the human origin of all institutions. But our founders become ready targets for journalistic history. We see Jefferson depicted as a philanderer and Lincoln degraded from the Great Emancipator to a small-town lawyer. So, too, the achievements of recent presidents are over-shadowed by docudramas of bedroom peccadilloes.

The founders of our nation were well aware of the uniqueness of their situation and sought inspiration in the uncanny novelties of America—past, present, and future. Even before the American Revolution, Benjamin Franklin organized an American Philosophical Society in Philadelphia, to explore the unpredicted promise of this unknown continent. In his Circular Letter of 1743 Franklin sketched their open-ended concerns: "All new-discovered Plants, Herbs, Trees, Roots . . . New Methods of Curing or Preventing Diseases. All new-discovered Fossils . . . New and useful Improvements in any Branch of Mathematicks; New Discoveries in Chemistry . . . New Mechanical Inventions for Saving labour . . . All new Arts, Trades, Manufactures, &c . . . New Methods of Improving the Breed of useful Animals . . . New Improvements in Planting, Gardening, Clearing Land, &c . . ." Thomas Jefferson himself, president of the society and its inspired leader (1796–1815), believed that here at last the happiness of the human species might advance "to an indefinite, although not to an infinite degree."

We must never forget that while to the Old World we were the

Unexpected Land, we have ever since been the Land of the Unexpected. The main features of the culture of our United States are just what the wise men of Europe, looking at their own past, could not have conjured up. A short list of the American surprises includes what we have done here with four basic elements of culture—religion, language, law, and wealth.

Take religion as a starter. By the time of the European settlement of North America the history of the rising nations of Western Europe had been punctuated by torture and massacre in the name of religion. There was the notorious Spanish Inquisition of the fifteenth century, in France the bloody Massacre of St. Bartholomew (1572), and in Germany during the very years of the Puritan settlements in New England the Thirty Years' War (1618–48), which spread into a general conflict between Protestant and Catholic Europe. In that war alone some 10 percent of the German population was slaughtered in the name of religious orthodoxy. This seemed not to augur well for a nation like ours, whose Pilgrims were obsessed by religion and had fled England to fulfill their passionate dream. Their religious faith gave them courage to brave the ocean crossing, the hardships of an unknown land, and the risks of hostile natives, despite their lonely remoteness from ancestral homes.

Who could have predicted that the United States, unlike the nations from which our people came, would never suffer a religious war? That the Protestants and Catholics who had tortured and massacred each other in Europe would establish peaceful neighboring communities from New England to Maryland and Virginia? That Jews would here find asylum from ghettos and pogroms? And that, though the United States would remain conspicuously a nation of churchgoers, the separation of Church and State would become a cornerstone of civic life? Or that public school principals in the twentieth century would be challenged by how to promote a holiday spirit without seeming to favor or neglect Christmas, Hanukkah, or Kwanza?

In Europe, languages had made nations. Spanish, Portuguese, English, French, German, and Italian had produced their own literature even before there was a Spain, a Portugal, an England, a France, a Germany, or an Italy. But the United States would be the first great modern nation without its own language. Our country has been uniquely created by people willing and able to borrow a language. Oddly enough, the English language has thus helped make us a congenitally multicultural nation, since most Americans have not come from the land of Shakespeare. So we have learned here that people do not lose their civic dignity by speaking the language of a new community. The English language has been invigorated and Americanized by countless importations of words from German, Italian, French, Spanish, Yiddish, and American Indian tongues, among others. With the surprising result that without a national language unique to the United States, our community has developed a language wonderfully expressive of the vitality and variety of our people. Perhaps we should really call Broken English our distinctive American language, for it bears the mark of our immigrant history.

Nowadays we can be puzzled at the spectacle of peoples from Russia to South Africa contending over how, whether, and when to adopt a "constitution." They seem to have the odd notion that a "constitution" can be created instantly by vote of a legislature or by a popular election. All this offers a sharp contrast to our Anglo-American experience. The tradition of a fundamental law—a "constitution"—that we inherited from England reached back to at least the thirteenth century. The by-product of a nation's whole history, the unwritten English constitution was a pillar of government and of the people's rights. No one could have foreseen that such a tradition would find a transatlantic written reincarnation in the deliberations of fifty-five colonials meeting in Independence Hall in Philadelphia in 1787. So our United States was created by a constitution. With another surprising result—that our parvenu nation at the end of the twentieth century now lives by the most venerable (and probably most venerated) written constitution in the world. And that the Constitution would survive by its very power to be amended (with difficulty).

Yet who could have predicted that a nation whose birth certificate bore the declaration that "all men are created equal" should have been one of the last to abolish slavery? In 1772 Lord Mansfield in the famous Somerset's Case held that any slave would become free on landing in England. Then slavery was abolished in the British Empire in 1834. Still, three decades passed before Lincoln's Emancipation Proclamation of 1863 freed slaves in the Southern secessionist states, followed by the Thirteenth Amendment (1865) to the Constitution outlawing slavery in all the United States. The slave trade survived only in certain Muslim states and in parts of Africa.

On the other side, we must note that our only civil war was fought in a struggle to free a subject people. For this, too, it is hard to find a precedent. And a legacy of the history of slavery in the United States has been the equally unprecedented phenomenon of a conscience-wracked nation. Which has led us to create a host of novel institutions—"equal opportunity" laws, "affirmative action," among others—in our strenuous effort to compensate for past injustices.

We should not be surprised that Russians are obsessively suspicious of foreigners coming to their country—after their long domination by the Mongols, their invasion by Napoleon and his forces of "liberation" who burned Moscow, and by the Germans in World War II who left twenty million casualties. No wonder they see the foreigner as the invader or the agent of invaders. We have been luckily free of this stereotype in the United States and instead have inherited the vision of other newcomers refracted in the experience of our own recent immigrant ancestors. "Strangers are welcome," Benjamin Franklin explained in his *Information to Those Who Would Remove to America* (1782), "because there is room enough for them all, and therefore the old inhabitants are not jealous of them." This has been the mainstream of our history—welcoming the newcomer as worker, customer, community builder, fellow-citizen-in-the-making. The uniquely American notion of a nation of nations was never more vivid than today.

We are told that the United States is a *rich* nation. But what really distinguishes us is less our wealth than our radically novel way of measuring a society's material well-being. "Wealth," which was at the center of English mercantilist thinking before the American Revolution, was a static notion. The wealth of the world, measured primarily in gold and silver treasure, was supposed to be a fixed quantity—a pie that could be sliced one way or another. But the size of the pie could not be substantially increased. A bigger slice for Great Britain meant a smaller slice for France or Spain or somebody else, and one nation's gain was another's loss. Our New World changed that way of thinking. People have come here not for wealth but for a better "way of life." America bred a vaguer and more expansive view of the material world, and blurred the boundary between the material and the spiritual. All this was reinforced by the spectacular progress of our technology, exploiting the resources of a rich, little-known, and sparsely populated continent.

The American Revolution, then, was among other things a struggle between the time-honored idea of Wealth and a New World idea of Standard of Living. This characteristically American idea appears to have entered our language only at the beginning of this century. It could hardly have been conceived in an Old World burdened with the legacy of feudal "rights," landed aristocracies, royal courts, sacrosanct guild monopolies, and ancestral cemeteries. Wealth is what someone possesses, but a Standard of Living is what people share. Wealth can be secretly hoarded, but a Standard of Living can only be publicly enjoyed. For it is the level of goods, housing, services, health, comfort, and education agreed to be appropriate.

All these remarkable transformations of the culture of the Older World add up to American Exceptionalism. This is quite the opposite of Isolationism—"the Dracula of American foreign policy." "We shall nobly save or meanly lose the last, best hope of earth" was Lincoln's way, in the heat of our Civil War, of declaring the nation's unique mission to the world. More recently we have heard apologies for such expressions of belief in American uniqueness, as if it were somehow provincial or chauvinist. But our ex-colonial nation in this postcolonial age would do well to see what the prescient French man of letters André Malraux observed on his visit to President Kennedy in the White House in 1962, which is still true. "The United States is today the country that assumes the destiny of man. . . . For the first time a country has become the world's leader without achieving this through conquest, and it is strange to think that for thousands of years one single country has found power while seeking only justice." And, he might have added, "while seeking community." We must see the unique power of the United States, then, not as the power of power, but as the power of example. Another name for history.

The depressing spectacle today of a Europe at war with itself has offered us a melodrama of those same ghosts of ethnic, racial, and religious hate that generations of immigrants have come to America to escape. Now more than ever we must inoculate ourselves against these latent perils. Luckily, the states of our federal union are not ethnic, racial, or religious enclaves. Luckily, we have remained a wonderfully mobile people. There is no better antidote to these perils than a frank and vivid recognition of the uniqueness of our history—of the special opportunities offered us. Nor could there be a greater folly than refusing to enjoy the happy accidents of our history.

The uniqueness that Jefferson and Lincoln claimed for us, we must remember, was for the sake of all mankind. Our Declaration of Independence takes its clue from "the course of human events." The Great Seal of the United States on our dollar bill still proclaims *NOVUS ORDO SECLORUM*—a new order of the centuries. When before had people put so much faith in the unexpected?

MY FATHER,
LAWYER SAM BOORSTIN

from CLEOPATRA'S NOSE, *1994*

I NEVER KNEW anyone quite like my father, but then I never really knew my father, either. He was a man without a single vice, but with a hundred foibles. He was a "devoted" husband in a miserably unhappy marriage. He was embarrassingly proud of me and advertised my small academic triumphs by stopping fellow Tulsans on the street to show them newspaper clippings, and he thermofaxed my letters home to give to passing acquaintances. Yet he never once praised me to my face. When I won my Rhodes Scholarship to go from Harvard to Oxford, he had no comment, but noted that a neighbor boy had been given a scholarship to send him from Tulsa Central High to the University of Oklahoma. My mother was one of the world's best cooks, not in the gourmet category, but in the Russian Jewish style, spending endless hours in the kitchen to make her cheesecake or her blintzes just right. Then when my father came to dinner from his office (always later than expected) he seldom failed to say that he "would just as soon eat a bale of hay. . . . Man should eat to live, and not live to eat."

Still, there was never any doubt that my mother ruled the roost, and her tribal feelings confined the family's social life. For most of our years in Tulsa we lived in a duplex apartment, with my mother's sister Kate and her husband and daughter living below. My mother's only friend was this sister, but my father was everybody's friend and spent his spare hours in the lobby of the Tulsa Hotel, and later the Mayo Hotel, chatting with acquaintances or strangers or simply reading the newspaper and hoping to be interrupted by a strange or friendly voice. My mother was suspicious of anyone who was not a blood relation (including especially her brothers' wives), while my father's suspicions (with some reason) fell especially on the blood relations themselves.

Except for two or three occasions when we entertained at dinner a local merchant who was my father's prize client, I cannot remember a single occasion when we had nonfamily guests in our house or were in another Tulsa home. Everything about our life—including our coming to Tulsa—seemed dominated by my mother's family. I never understood how two people so ill suited to each other could ever have married. But the story of how my father and mother first met was supposed to explain it. And behind that was the story of the last years of my father's independence, back in Atlanta.

My father always spoke with a warm and soft Georgia accent. His father was one of the many Jews who emigrated from the Russian pale in the late 1880s to escape pogroms, military service, and persecution. This Benjamin Boorstin came on his own and for some reason, never explained, settled in Monroe, Georgia. His brother came about the same time. But the immigration officers spelled his brother's name Boorstein, and so he remained. The two brothers had stores on opposite sides of the street in Monroe, where their differences of name were constant reminders of their recent arrival. Benjamin Boorstin sent for his wife, who came over with their infant, Sam. My father went to school in Monroe. While working in a general store in his spare time he managed to collect the premium tags attached to the little bags of cigarette tobacco he was selling. He sent off a stack of these tags and received one of the primitive plate cameras.

This camera changed his life, for he used it to earn his way through college. Arriving in Athens, Georgia, the site of the state university, he quickly found his way into the office of the president. He showed the president his photographs of the cracked walls and peeling ceilings of the university classrooms. These pictures, and more like them, he said, would persuade the state legislature to grant appropriations for repairs and for new university buildings. With that he applied for the novel job of university photographer and got it on the spot. Then he worked his way through by helping the president with his campaign for larger appropriations and by taking class pictures.

In those days law was an undergraduate subject. When Sam Boorstin received his LL.B. degree he was still under twenty-one, and when he appeared before the judge to be admitted to the bar, it was objected that he was under age. He won his first case when he persuaded the judge to admit him anyway, and so became the youngest member of the Georgia bar. In Atlanta he began practice as junior member of one of the most prestigious old law firms. He spent his spare time joining every fraternal organization that would let him in. These included the Elks, the Odd Fellows, the Red Men, and the Masons. I still have the fine Hamilton gold watch with the Masonic emblem engraved on the back that was given to him when he became the youngest Worshipful Master in the United States. He kept his hand in as a beginner in Georgia Democratic politics, which became easier when Governor John Marshall Slaton engaged him as his private secretary. One of Sam Boorstin's qualifications—in addition to personal charm and an outgoing manner—was his elegant handwriting. He had acquired a beautifully rotund and flourishing hand by attending a penmanship school. His flamboyant signature was one of the first mannerisms that I tried to imitate—without any success.

*　　*　　*

He might have had a career in Georgia politics, even though he was a Jew. But unpleasant events surrounding the infamous Leo Frank case intervened and made this impossible. In 1913 the innocent pencil manufacturer Leo Frank was railroaded on a charge of raping and murdering one of his employees in a turbulent trial that roused the ugliest passions of racism and anti-Semitism that Georgia had ever seen. The case became a newspaper sensation. My father, though still one of the most junior members of the bar, lent a local hand to the defense, as aide to several eminent imported Eastern lawyers, including the distinguished Louis Marshall. When, to no one's surprise, Frank was convicted, my father had the bitter assignment of carrying that word to Frank's wife. In 1915, after his death sentence was reduced to life imprisonment by the courageous Governor Slaton, Frank was seized and lynched by a raging mob, who had the shamelessness to have their photographs taken standing proudly beside the dangling body of the innocent Frank.

There followed in Atlanta one of the worst pogroms ever known in an American city, an unpleasant reminder of the Russia from which the Boorstin-Boorstein brothers had fled. My mother's brothers then owned a men's clothing store in Atlanta, whose store windows, like those of other Jewish merchants, were smashed in the aftermath of the Frank case. The prospects were not good for a young Jewish lawyer interested in politics.

Meanwhile, in 1912, my father had married my mother under legendary circumstances. She had come down from New York City to visit her brothers in Atlanta. The handsome and promising Sam Boorstin began courting the attractive Dora Olsan from the "East." The society section of the *Atlanta Constitution* carried a picture of the pretty visitor with the story of a dinner held at the hotel in her honor. Governor Slaton was present, and at the end of the dinner he arose, offered a toast, and said, "Sam Boorstin, if you don't marry that beautiful girl, I'll see that you're disbarred." Sam married Dora.

The Frank case impelled my mother's three brothers—along with my father and the husband of her sister—to leave Atlanta. They went to Tulsa (then still pronounced Tulsy), Oklahoma, a frontier town in what only nine years before had still been Indian Territory, set aside for the so-called Five Civilized Tribes. In 1916 Tulsa had few paved streets and fewer paved sidewalks. My three uncles opened a bank, and the husbands of the two sisters tagged along, with Kate's husband joining the bank. My father opened a law office, slightly separating himself from the family, and he soon became one of Tulsa's most energetic boosters.

After settling in Tulsa—which my mother despised (and never stopped despising)—my father never really took a vacation. He made a few business trips and once came to England to visit me when I was at Oxford. But he thought Tulsa was a good enough year-round place. My mother (usually with her sister) left town at the first crack of summer heat, usually to go to Atlantic City or some other resort.

* * *

It is still hard for me to understand—much less explain—my father's love affair with Tulsa. He thought, or at least said, it was the greatest place on earth. In fact, Tulsa was a frontier village translated into the architecture and folkways of the 1920s. With endless prairies stretching around, there was no good reason for skyscrapers. Still, Tulsa built the Philtower, the Philcade, and the Exchange National Bank Building, all of which cast their twenty-two-story shadows across the barren plain.

As for culture, there wasn't much. Only a Carnegie library, the annual visit of the Metropolitan Opera Company—heavily sponsored by the best ladies' "ready-to-wear" clothing stores—and Kendall College, a Baptist missionary school to which none of the wealthy local citizens sent their sons and daughters.

My father joined in the manic optimism for the future of Tulsa, which soon called itself the Oil Capital of the World. Oil was mother's milk to all of us raised in Tulsa. And the gambling spirit infected my uncles, who played for, and won and lost, fortunes in oil. Would their next well be a "gusher" or a "dry hole"? Was it possible to open a new "oil field" on this or that farmer's land? This was the adult jargon most familiar to me.

While my father was a booster for Tulsa, he never became an oil gambler. Instead he became a species of lawyer now nearly obsolete. He was a lone "general practitioner." He never had a partner (my mother would not have tolerated it), but through his office came a stream of young lawyers just out of law school whom he trained in the old apprentice style. They adored him, but found him difficult to work for. Many of them became district attorneys and judges, or they founded prosperous law firms that far outshone his own. He had his own way—his very own way—of doing everything. This included the way you use an index, the way you hold a pen, the way you talk to clients. Each of these apprentices stayed for a few years and then went on—much wiser in the law and how to practice it, but relieved at not being told how to do everything. I personally suffered more than once from my father's insistence on doing things his way. After I had been shaving for many years my father still insisted on my running the razor against the grain of my facial hair, as "the only way to get a close shave." His golf lessons, offered in a warm spirit of paternal helpfulness, made me hate the game, and I've never gone near a golf course since.

* * *

My father would have been happy to see a SAMUEL A. BOORSTIN AND SON shingle outside his office, and to that end he really hoped I would go to the University of Oklahoma. My mother's insistence that "only the best" was good enough and that I must "go East" to Harvard helped save me from all that.

Still, my father's law practice was exemplary for those who believe that the law is a public-service profession. The big money was in oil, and he had a share of corporate oil practice. But what he enjoyed most, and talked about most, was his "general" practice. This was more like the work of a village curate than of a city lawyer. He was especially proud of the occasion when he saved a hapless girl from disaster. He prevailed on her mother not to seek annulment of a quickie marriage until several months had passed—and so ensure the legitimacy and the financial provision for the baby he wisely suspected was on the way. This despite the mother's and the girl's protests that "nothing had happened." There were countless occasions when he prevailed on irate husbands and wives not to go for a divorce. And there was the time when he helped secure the acquittal of one of his clients on a murder charge for shooting a rival merchant on Main Street.

As a prominent Democrat he was naturally the best general counsel for the *Tulsa Tribune*, an outspoken, right-wing Republican daily. He defended the *Tribune* against numerous libel suits, and despite their sometimes provocative postures, he never lost a case for them.

He never got rich in the practice, but he had one profitable piece of good luck. A representative of Amtorg (the Soviet oil combine), who had come to Tulsa to improve his knowledge of oil-well technology, was run over by a truck and had to spend weeks in a local hospital. My father took his case and won one of the largest personal-injury verdicts on record in Tulsa at that time. The damages awarded were in the neighborhood of seventy-five thousand dollars. This was by far my father's biggest case—which somehow gave me a warm feeling for the Soviet Union. But from a family point of view there was a price to pay. I don't think my father ever told my mother how much of a fee he had received in this case. But I do remember my mother's frequent question: "Whatever happened to all the Kapalushnikov money?"

My father's law office was a piece of Americana. The place of honor went to a pen-and-ink drawing of a mythical judge representing the Majesty of the Law—which my father had had me trace from a picture that impressed him—and a photograph of the justices of the hallowed Supreme Court of the United States. On the walls and under the glass on his desk were mottoes, uplifting aphorisms, and lines of verse. The most poignant message (and now the most obsolete) in those days of breach-of-promise suits was the framed commandment: "Do Right and Fear No Man; Don't Write and Fear No Woman." There were some Edgar Guest poems and Kipling's "If—" in an ornate version printed by Elbert Hubbard's press. And then: "When the One Great Scorer comes to write against your name—He writes—not that you won or lost—but how you played the game." His favorite modern literature was Elbert Hubbard's "A Message to Garcia."

My father still seems to me to have been the most unmercenary man in the world. He took cases because he thought he could somehow help someone. He never pressed for his fees and took cases without thinking whether the client could ever pay him—which of course infuriated my mother. He also loved to give gifts, and never worried about the cost. There was a particular kind of loose-leaf address book bound in leather that he thought (and insisted) everyone should use. If a celebrity came to lecture at Town Hall, afterward he would send him one of these books and try to begin a correspon-

dence. Each address book must have cost over ten dollars and they
added up. He treasured the letters of acknowledgment he received
from the celebrities, which he pasted in a book and showed to visitors to his office.

His law practice required a good deal of reading—in the extensive law library that he maintained in his office. He invited other
lawyers—especially the young ones just beginning—to use freely
this library, which must have been one of the best and most up-to-
date law libraries in town. His nonlegal reading was myopically
focused. If he found a book that he really liked he would give it biblical status. One particular biography of Judah P. Benjamin—the first
professing Jew elected to the U.S. Senate (1852–61), who held high
office in the Confederate States of America and at the end of the war
emigrated to England, where he prospered as a barrister—caught his
fancy. He never failed to refer to it whenever any question of history
or literature arose, and pressed me to read and reread it.

He was an early champion of gummed and printed name stickers
and Scotch tape, which he affixed to everything—books, golf clubs,
hats, tennis rackets. He could never understand why I preferred the
pristine book. This was only one expression of his love of gadgets,
his booster faith in the newest way to do anything, including laxa-
tives and the latest electronic belts and exercise machines to cure all
ills. As an optimist he was a ready victim for visiting book salesmen
and their multivolume subscription sets, often in "simulated
leather." I remember particularly the unbroken (and mostly un-
opened) sets behind the glass doors of our living-room bookcase,
which included the *Works of Theodore Roosevelt, The World's Great
Orations, Beacon Lights of History*, and the speeches and writings of
the notorious atheist Robert G. Ingersoll.

My father's enthusiasm for Robert G. Ingersoll did not interfere
in the least with his public stance as a Jew. We were members of all
three Jewish synagogues—the Orthodox on the impecunious North
Side and the Orthodox and Reform synagogues on the prosperous
South Side. My father was active in the Anti-Defamation League
and in various interfaith activities. But I can never remember his
presence at a religious service. Very different from my paternal

grandfather was my mother's father, who lived with us for many years and was scrupulously Orthodox. Jacob Olsan went to shul every day, did no work on Saturdays, and was the reason for our maintaining a kosher kitchen with a separate set of dishes for Passover. The status of Jews in Tulsa was curious. Tulsa was a headquarters of the Ku Klux Klan, which was responsible for burning down the Negro sections of town in one of the worst race riots of the 1920s. The Klan had no patience for Tulsa Jews, but the Jews somehow paid little attention to their gibes. My father and his Jewish friends looked down condescendingly on them and their like as a bunch of "yokels."

* * *

I don't know how much life in Tulsa had to do with it. But just as my father was totally without vice—he never smoked, drank, or to my knowledge womanized—so he was an irritatingly tolerant man in his opinions. I could never get him to express an adverse or uncharitable judgment on anyone—including the Klan bigots and the rising Nazis. He always tried to make allowances for why people did what they did. He was a living example of how immigrant, mobile, westward-moving Americans wore off the edges of their convictions—how the West saved some people from bigotry but provided a fallow ground for bigots. I will never forget his contagious enthusiasm for the novelties of American life, and for the undocumented halcyon future.

THE AMATEUR SPIRIT

from LIVING PHILOSOPHIES, *ED. CLIFTON FADIMAN, 1989*

A RTISTS AND WRITERS, I believe, have a special role, creating new questions for which they offer experimental answers. We are tested, enriched, and fulfilled by the varieties of experience. And as the years pass there are increasing advantages to being a questioner. Answers can trouble us by their inconsistency, but there is no such problem with questions. I am not obliged to hang on to earlier answers, and there can be no discord—only growth—between then and now. Learning, I have found, is a way of becoming inconsistent with my past self. I believe in vocation, a calling for reasons we do not understand to do whatever we discover we can do.

I have observed that the world has suffered far less from ignorance than from pretensions to knowledge. It is not skeptics or explorers but fanatics and ideologues who menace decency and progress. No agnostic ever burned anyone at the stake or tortured a pagan, a heretic, or an unbeliever.

If our knowledge is, as I believe, only an island in an infinite sea of ignorance, how can we in our short lifetime find satisfaction in exploring our little island? How can we persuade ourselves to be exhilarated by our meager knowledge and yet not be discouraged by the ocean vistas?

There may be ways to accommodate ourselves to our ignorance while enjoying our common exploring. What might they be?

In history. Since it is my vocation to be a historian I am tested every day. For history is a world of dark continents. Any historian worth his salt knows that the unknown past—enlarging every moment—will always be incomparably vaster than what we know or think we know. And current events become widening currents of ignorance. So every day I work at finding a sensible soul-satisfying compromise with the unknown. What are the terms of my everyday treaty? How much am I allowed to know or can I expect to know? How can I avoid being or seeming a charlatan by pretending to offer too much?

My first refuge is honesty. I am on solid ground so long as I do not pretend to offer the only or the final explanation for anything—the voyages of "discovery," the settlement of America, the American Revolution, the works of any artist or writer. I am a charlatan when I say anything about the past that excludes the probability of our always learning more, or when I stop listening to new voices.

Another refuge is to exploit and enjoy the little that we really seem to know. This means luxuriating in the cosmic significance of trivia. What do we learn from the appalling increase of packaging in our country? What can we learn from the fact that the "public" theaters in Elizabethan England offered open-air afternoon performances, while we go to the movies in encapsulated darkness, or are newly segregated by our personal TV sets and VCRs? While their problem, even in their candle-lit indoor "private" theaters, was to find enough light, ours is to create enough darkness. What a wonderful iridescence there is in any fact! So we must love facts indiscriminately without professional or conventional snobbery, and be grateful for them all. We express our gratitude by finding surprising meanings.

When we make our history into literature—with the genius of a Shakespeare, a Parkman, a Joyce—we find refuge from the discouragement of the vast ocean. Making our history into literature becomes a way of confessing the limits of our knowledge, of expressing our hope to find some meaning in experience, and of playing on the frontiers.

In institutions and in politics. For me institutions have been welcome symbols of my quest for community, the vehicles of our immortality. And, luckily, I have been given the opportunity to share in
the life of great institutions—the University of Chicago, the Smithsonian Institution, the Library of Congress (and the Congress). Such
institutions have a wonderful power to change by surviving and to
survive by changing.

I see democracy, government by amateurs, as a way of confessing
the limits of our knowledge. The amateur is not afraid to do something for the first time. With our amendable constitutional congressional government we avoid the tyranny of anybody's pretense to
know all the right answers. And so we need not suffer the paralysis of
indecision because we don't know it all.

In religion. Being born a Jew makes it easier to be a questioner.
For the Jewish God remains a mystery whose very name we cannot
confidently utter. And being a Jew in a Christian society makes me
wary of easy respectable answers to the deepest questions of theology and morals. It also makes me wary of those who would mold
Judaism itself into an imprisoning chauvinism or orthodoxy.

Probably no one of us has the True Religion. But all of us together—if we are allowed to be free—are discovering ways of con-
versing about the great mysteries. The pretense to know all the
answers to the deepest mysteries is, of course, the grossest fraud.
And any people who declare a Jihad, a holy war on "unbelievers"—
those who do not share their believers' pretended omniscience—are
enemies of thinking men and women and of civilization. I see religion as only a way of asking unanswerable questions, of sharing the
joy of a community of quest, and solacing one another in our ignorance.

In science. I see science, too, as only a search for temporarily an-
swerable questions. Therefore I find the history of science especially
chastening and adventurous. No dogmas have been more confidently asserted than those of the scientists—from Aristotle to Ptolemy to Copernicus to Newton. Yet no dogmas are more suddenly or
more unexpectedly upset. The courage to imagine the otherwise is
our greatest resource, adding color and suspense to all our life. The

courage to believe is easy, with lots of respectable company, but I admire more the courage to doubt.

In literature and the arts. The menace here is in the academies, the pretentious self-appointed custodians of prestige and respectability. Balzac was never elected to the Académie Francaise. Posterity and the free public are our authentic Académie. Dickens was quite right when he declared that "the people have set literature free"—from the arrogance of patrons of which the professions are the latest and the most assertive.

In love and the family. I believe in commitment, another name for love, which can only be for reasons we do not understand. Yet our love for our children commits us to duties we can never properly discharge. How can we guide our children if we know how crudely we have governed our own future? Still, we cannot help feeling a duty to share with our children our convictions and suspicions about the future. We feel we have not done our duty if we have not insisted that they avoid some simple mistakes we have seen ourselves or others making. But we feel we are imposing on them (who will know the future better than we do) the limits of our own experience. This I find an unanswerable question. What is enough—but not too much—advice to give our children? And isn't it a comfort to know there is little chance they will follow it?

The amateur spirit. My own experience has made me wary of the institutions, the ways, the attitudes of all professionals. With the good fortune to be permitted to be a historian without conventional credentials, I have delighted in pursuing history for the love of it. This amateur spirit has guided my thinking and writing. Of course we need devices to economize our intellectual sallies, and the professions can somehow serve us in this way. But the rewards and the refreshments of thought and the arts come from the courage to try something, all sorts of things, for the first time. These first-time adventures are the spice of life. An enamored amateur need not be a genius to stay out of the ruts he has never been trained in.

All this is because I share Einstein's belief that there is nothing more beautiful than the mystery of things. The world would be a desert if we knew all the answers—yet each of us has the desiccating power to make the world less interesting by our pretensions to know.

In our age we are menaced by the cost-effective syndrome, which is the more menacing because it masquerades as prudence. It is a way of promoting the extinction of cultural species. The best things in life are free! Love, knowledge, art, music, literature, community, have no bottom line. I worry when I see the leaders of our great cultural institutions—universities, publishing houses, museums, libraries—measuring out our hopes and possibilities in the homogenized hash of cash. With the momentum of technology these assassins of the bottom line can impoverish our lives by removing from our daily experience countless passenger pigeons and whooping cranes that once enriched our view. How will this stunt the experience of my grandchildren?

I am, then, a short-term pessimist but a long-term optimist. If our mission is an endless search, how can we fail? In the short run, institutions and professions and even language keep us in the discouraging ruts. But in the long run the ruts wear away and adventuring amateurs reward us by a wonderful vagrancy into the unexpected.

BOOKS BY DANIEL J. BOORSTIN

Following is a list of books by Daniel J. Boorstin with the original publisher and date of publication, followed by the publisher of the paperback. Many have been translated. Altogether, books by Boorstin have been translated into some twenty-five languages.

The Mysterious Science of the Law, Harvard University Press, 1941; University of Chicago Press paperback.

The Lost World of Thomas Jefferson, Henry Holt & Co., 1948; University of Chicago Press paperback.

The Genius of American Politics, University of Chicago Press, 1953; University of Chicago Press paperback.

The Americans: The Colonial Experience, Random House, 1958; Vintage paperback (Random House).

The Americans: The National Experience, Random House, 1965; Vintage paperback (Random House).

The Americans: The Democratic Experience, Random House, 1973; Vintage paperback (Random House).

America and the Image of Europe, Meridian Books, 1960.

The Image, or What Happened to the American Dream, Atheneum, 1962.

The Image, a Guide to Pseudo-Events in America, Harper & Row, 1964; Vintage paperback (Random House).

The Landmark History of the American People: From Plymouth to Appomattox, Random House, 1968.

The Landmark History of the American People: From Appomattox to the Moon, Random House, 1970.

The Decline of Radicalism: Reflections on America Today, Random House, 1969; Vintage paperback (Random House).

The Sociology of the Absurd, or, The Application of Professor X, Simon & Schuster, 1970; Touchstone paperback (Simon & Schuster).

Democracy and Its Discontents: Reflections on Everyday America, Random House, 1969; Vintage paperback (Random House).

The Exploring Spirit: America and the World, Then and Now, Random House, 1976, Vintage paperback (Random House).

The Republic of Technology: Reflections on Our Future Community, Harper & Row, 1978; Colophon paperback.

A History of the United States, with Brooks M. Kelley, Ginn & Company, 1981; Prentice Hall, 1996.

The Discoverers, Random House, 1983; Vintage paperback (Random House), 1985.

Hidden History, Harper & Row, 1987; Vintage paperback (Random House).

The Republic of Letters, Library of Congress, 1989.

The Creators, Random House, 1992; Vintage paperback (Random House).

Cleopatra's Nose: Essays on the Unexpected, Random House, 1994; Vintage paperback (Random House).